MASS

MERCHANDISING

Revolution & Evolution

MASS MERCHA

MERCHA

REVOLUTION

...NDISING

EVOLUTION

ROBERT DREW-BEAR

Fairchild Publications, Inc., New York

PHOTO CREDITS: Associated Arts, p. 199; ATP Bilderdienst, p. 365; Fabian Bachrach, pps. 51, 87, 171, 194, 230, 308, 329; Beake-Huntington, Inc. p. 54; Blackstone-Shelburne N.Y., p. 465; Conway Studios Corp., pps. 63, 65, 190, 208; Myron Ehrenberg Scope Assos., pps. 445, 446; Bill Mitchell Photography, p. 2; Pressedienst Diamant Foto, pps. 366, 367.

To my wife, Lotte

Contents

PREFACE   *11*

INTRODUCTION   *13*

SECTION 1
Mass Merchandising's Cast of Characters

I   *Beginnings*   *23*

Piggly-Wiggly
King Cullen
Big Bear
A & P
Cut Rate Drug Co.
N.Y. Lace Store
Second floor Catalog Stores
Farmer's Markets
Filene's Bargain Basements

II   *The Pioneers*   *38*

The Mill Outlet Phase
Rockdale Stores (William Palestine)
J. M. Field's
King's Department Stores, Inc. (Aaron Goldberg)
Arlan's Department Stores, Inc. (Warren Eisenberg)
Coatsfield Shoppers World
Ann and Hope Factory Outlet (Martin Chase)
Kermell Bargain Center (Selwyn Lemchen)
Mammoth Mart, Inc. (Max Coffman)
Alden's Shoppers World (Alvin D. Star)
Yankee Stores, Inc. (Joseph Megdell)
Bargain Barns (Bernard, Mark, Robert & Lewis Goodman)

7

Lechmere Sales Company (Abraham Cohen)
Caldor, Inc. (Carl Bennett)
Vornado, Inc. (Herbert & Sidney Hubschman)
E. J. Korvette (Eugene Ferkauf, Murray Beilensen & Ray Treiger)
Spartans Industries Inc. (Charles Bassine)
Atlantic Thrift Centers (Sidney Mittleman)

III *"Promotional Department Stores"* 154
S. Klein Department Stores, Inc.
Alexander's Department Stores
Ohrbach's

IV *Traditional Stores Move Into Discounting* 169
Zayre Corporation (Bell Shop . . . Nugent Stores)
Mangel Stores Corp. (Shoppers Fair)
Hartfield Stores Inc. (Zody's)
Interstate Dept. Stores (White Front & Topps)
L. S. Ayres & Co. (Ayr-Way Stores)
Allied Stores Corporation (Almart Stores)
J. C. Penney Co. (Treasure Island Stores)

V *Enter, The Variety Stores* 206
M. H. Fishman Co., Inc. (Centers & Masons, Fishmans)
Neisner Brothers, Inc. (Big N)
S. S. Kresge Company (K Mart, Jupiter)
F. W. Woolworth Co. (Woolco Division)

VI *Food Makes Its Discount Move* 235
Grand Union (Grand Way Division)
Stop and Shop (Bradlee's Division)
Jewel Companies (Turnstyle Discount Stores)

VII *Closed Door Approach* 251
Parkview-G.E.M., Inc.
FED MART
National Bellas Hess, Inc.

VIII *Leased Departments* 272
Unishops (Men's & Boys' Wear)
Lee Venture Corporation (Apparel)

8

Table of Contents

Bernard Abrams Associates (Domestics)
American Toy Wholesale Corporation
Carter Overton (Drug Departments)
Morse Shoe, Inc.
Gilbert Shoe Company
United Overton Corporation (Hardwares, Housewares)
Hardlines Incorporated (Housewares)
The Ward Company (Appliances)
Forest City Distributors, Inc. (Stationery)

IX   *Discounting With a Difference*   *344*
The Gibson Products Company
The Worldwide PX

X   *Mass Merchandising Abroad*   *352*
Canada   – Allied Towers Marts, Toronto
             La Salle Stores
             Ed Mirvish's
Mexico   – Arrango Brothers
             Viana y Cia S.A.
Germany – Quelle Market
Belgium – Super Bazars, S.A.
Russia
England
Sweden – Wessel's Stormaknad
Japan
Switzerland – Federation of Migros Cooperatives

SECTION 2
Major Problem Areas in Mass Merchandising

XI   *Mass Merchandising Casualties*   *373*
Towers Marts International
Grayson-Robinson Stores, Inc.
Marrud, Inc.
John's Bargain Stores
Credit Ratings of Mass Merchandisers
Confessions of a Shoplifter

XII   *Do Foods Belong in Discount Stores?*   *392*

XIII *Central Warehousing vs. Drop Shipping* *403*

XIV *Personnel Problems of Discount Stores* *411*
Training Programs Analyzed (Ben Rosenthal, Dex Personnel)
Payroll-Profit Relationship: Peak Productivity from
    Your Employees (Robert Kenzar, Zayre Corp.)
Creative Excitement Draws Talent (Robert Pure, Zayre Corp.)
Management's View of Personnel Problems (Meshulam
    Riklis, McCrory Corporation)

XV *Union Activity in Mass Merchandising* *423*

XVI *EDP for Store Systems* *442*
Capturing Information at the Point of Sale
EDP Use by Zayre Corporation
Bizmatic Data Control Centers
Payroll Management

XVII *Resident Buyers for Mass Merchandising* *463*

XVIII *The Advertising Trap* *469*
Bo Bernstein Advertising Agency

SECTION 3
Mass Merchandising: Revolution & Evolution

XIX *Summary and Conclusions* *475*
Contribution of Mass Merchandising to the Economy – the
    Views of Sen. William Proxmire of Wisconsin
The Mass Merchandising Foundation

APPENDIX *482*

KEY STIPULATIONS IN TYPICAL LEASE *488*

BIBLIOGRAPHY *491*

INDEX *495*

Preface
How this Book Came to be Written

As assistant professor of marketing at the University of Massachusetts, I had chaired, since 1958, an organizing committee for annual retailing conferences sponsored by the University's School of Business Administration. In April, 1961, the University sponsored the first conference ever held on the management of Open and Closed-Door Self-Service Discount Department Stores. This conference attracted international attention and we were deluged with telephone calls from people who wanted to come. Inquiries came from California, Montreal, Toronto, France and Belgium.

Listening to the lively panel discussions, I was deeply impressed by the dedication and imagination of this new breed of retailer and by the tremendous growth potential of a totally new pattern of retailing based on suburban locations, self-service, central checkouts and shopping carts. Typical of the new retailer were what Gerald B. Tallman and Bruce Blomstrom called "Soft Goods Supermarkets"[1] in which men's, women's, and children's apparel were sold using food supermarket techniques. As editor and publisher of the proceedings of this and following conferences I gained some knowledge of recent developments in the history of mass merchandising.

In 1964, I decided to undertake what then appeared to be an almost impossible task. It was the setting up of a Pilot Research Program on the merchandising operations of self-service promotional department stores. The problem was to get enough companies to submit their confidential figures to the University so as to have a representative and valid sample of operators. Under the chairmanship of Abe L. Marks, now president of Hartfield Stores, Inc., an industry research committee was set up and provided very valuable assistance in getting enough companies to cooperate. The School of Business continued this annual study until 1967 when it was transferred to Cornell

[1] "Soft Goods Join the Retail Revolution," *Harvard Business Review*, Sept.-Oct. 1960. Article by G. B. Tallman and Bruce Blomstrom.

University in order to take advantage of the experience of Dr. Earl Brown who has done a series of annual operating studies for the food industry.

Having had a very stimulating and active association with many of the leaders in the mass-merchandising industry, I thought it would be a useful service to write a book about the recent revolutionary developments in this field. My good friend, Professor Malcolm McNair of Harvard, was kind enough to read some of my manuscript and encouraged me by saying that he thought that such a book would fill a gap in the literature of retailing.

SCOPE OF THIS BOOK.

After touching briefly on some historical aspects of mass merchandising, this book deals with representative companies according to the background from which they entered low-margin retailing. The policies of any single company were greatly influenced by the kind of traditional operation in which it had been previously proficient. According to whether they had been operators of army and navy surplus stores, women's specialty stores, variety, food, junior, or department stores – each came to mass merchandising differently. At the start, they almost invariably relied heavily on lessees who provided the capital needed for inventory and fixtures as well as the personnel and know-how for a wide range of departments. Typical operations of major leased departments are illustrated with sample companies. There is also a section on European and Canadian developments in mass merchandising.

The latter part of the book deals with certain aspects of trade union activities in mass merchandising and with major operating problems and techniques. It includes a section on failures and how they came about. The final chapter contains the author's summary and conclusions. In the Appendix are some samples of leased department contracts.

I am indebted to the officers of numerous companies who were generous in giving me interviews. Special thanks is due for the encouragement of Bud and Dan Kessler, founders of Unishops, of Max Coffman, president of Mammoth Marts, and of Sol Lebow, president of the former Hardlines Distributors.

Introduction

Most great merchandising innovations result from the responses by businessmen to changing social and economic events. Towards the end of the nineteenth and the beginning of the twentieth centuries, the department store fulfilled the merchandise needs of our increasingly urban populations. With the advent of the automobile, people in surrounding areas could more readily make their way into the central cities. A rapid rise in newspaper circulation combined with improvements in transportation made the chain store possible with its more efficient techniques and massive buying power. In the depression of the 1930's, the need to make every cent go as far as possible created the trailer-truck-serviced farmer's markets and the pine-board supermarkets such as the "Big Bears".

The increased use of the automobile necessitated the building of a vast network of good roads around our major metropolitan areas, providing easy access to the suburbs. With the "explosion to the suburbs" came the widespread establishment of shopping centers and branch stores of downtown establishments. Following World War II, manufacturing plants turned their attention to the consumer market; increased production absorbed the great majority of capable employees. Many downtown department stores occupied massive multi-storied buildings built more to impress rather than to provide the customer with low-cost service. Downtown property taxes were high. Maintenance expense of older buildings with their elevators and escalators was a steadily mounting problem. Low wages in retailing made the large department stores inviting targets for union activity. Retailers, unable to match the high wages paid by factories, were plagued with irresponsible and incompetent personnel. They were unable to increase distribution sufficiently to match the increased production of consumer goods. The ensuing back-up of goods opened the way for retailing innovations.

In the early fifties, operators of both small and large chains of specialty stores, junior department stores, and variety stores found their sales volume shrinking as a result of increasing competition from new types of retail operations. To meet these pressures many department stores decided to

13

curtail the extra services which the shopper had come to expect. Customers were asked to pay for credit and delivery; yet the reduction in expenses was not sufficient to provide a noticeable reduction in markup.

Until the 1950's, mass merchandising, with few exceptions, had been the exclusive domain of chain stores in the drug, variety, junior department store, specialty store, and food fields. With the expanding middle-income group came a new mass market based on a mounting wave of customer wants. The solution came in the form of "discount stores." The term had an unpleasant connotation, having been applied to questionable second-floor and back-room operations, where customers bought nationally-branded items at a sizeable deduction from list price. It also connoted cut-rate drug stores which did not always carry merchandise of the best quality. Although the term started as one of ill-repute, it became more and more respectable as it began to be applied to bountifully-stocked promotional, self-service department stores located in suburban areas with bright neon lights, plenty of parking space, evening opening, shopping carts, and an exciting bargain atmosphere. To the general public, the word "discount" gradually came to have a more magic quality. Nevertheless, the more conservative of the new operators strictly avoided using the term in their promotions, feeling that the word was associated with "cheapness" or fraudulency. The term came to be applied to New England mill and factory outlets in small cities and to "closed door" stores, which required a membership card from customers. As "discount" stores matured and financing became available, they were able to avoid the sale of seconds, or cheap importations, and "distress" merchandise; yet, the name "discount store" stuck.

A characteristic of the new retailing picture is confusion between the traditional lines of demarcation separating types of retailers. During and after World War II, shortages brought about a marked increase in "scrambled" merchandising. Drug stores, unable to get their regular merchandise, diversified into such fields as small appliances, food, luggage, and toys. Supermarkets began to carry clothing, kitchenware, hardware, cosmetics, and drug items. Department stores opened gourmet shops, liquor departments, and a variety of service departments. With self-service discount department stores came "one-stop" shopping, including both food and general merchandise.

Judging from the extraordinary consumer acceptance of discount stores, as evidenced by constantly increasing sales, the customer apparently favors this form of retail distribution. The appeal is not just price; convenience of parking and shopping hours are major factors. Unfortunately the U.S. Bureau of the Census, unlike Canada's Dominion Bureau, does not separate "discount" department stores from "traditional" department stores, so only trade source figures on discount store sales are available. Undoubtedly, the severe competition from discount stores forced the management of orthodox

Introduction

specialty, variety, and department stores to reappraise their operations with the aim of decreasing their expenses and increasing their efficiency. Those with available capital and competent management started their own discount stores, witness Kresge's K Marts, Woolworth's Woolco, Allied Store's Almarts and Penney's Treasure Island Stores. Somewhat later, even Federated Department Stores, Inc., the country's largest department store chain, formed a discount store division in June, 1967.

In 1962, the debacle came for incompetent discount store operators. Those without a genuine knowledge of merchandising or who had over-extended their capitalization by unwise expansion, went to the wall. The operators who survived grew phenomenally; the most successful carry a broad range of general merchandise in constant demand and have attained a high level of merchandising efficiency using well-defined operating formats, and sophisticated computer-controls.

As for the future, discount operators claim that there are many untapped markets which are "understored" as far as discount stores are concerned. They feel a constantly growing population creates new opportunities.

Discount Merchandiser, in its issues of June, 1966 (p. 52) and July, 1967 (p. 19) estimates that in 1965 and 1966 discounters had the following sales record in certain classes of merchandise.

MERCHANDISE LINE	DISCOUNT STORE % SHARE OF TOTAL		TOTAL RETAIL $ VOLUME IN BILLIONS	
	1965	*1966*	*1965*	*1966*
Garden Supplies	42.9	40.7	.6	.7
Camera and Photographic	35.5	37.1	.6	.7
Children's and Infants'	33.9	37.8	3.0	3.0
Millinery	32.0	30.0	.2	.2
Linens and Domestics	24.5	16.0	2.0	3.6
Sporting Goods	21.3	21.9	2.1	2.3
Toys	19.7	21.6	2.3	2.5
Auto Accessories	16.9	21.7	3.4	3.3
Men's and Boys' Wear	14.7	14.3	7.4	8.8
Paints	12.9	13.0	1.2	1.4
Records	12.9	14.0	1.0	1.0
Drugs and Toiletries	12.4	13.0	4.6	5·2
Women's Wear	11.4	9.3	11.3	16.0
Shoes	10.2	9.8	4.5	5.2
Housewares	8.2	16.5	7.4	4.3
Major Appliances	7.8	7.7	6.4	7.0
Furniture and Floor Coverings	7.6	7.0	5.9	7.0
Stationery and Greeting Cards	7.5	8.6	1.4	1.4
Jewelry and Watches	6.3	8.4	2.4	2.1
Hardware	6.1	14.9	2.7	2.9
Traffic Appliances	6.0	7.0	3.5	3.7
Books and Magazines	16.4	16.7	.8	.9

15

In women's wear, the discount volume came basically from staple merchandise. By 1968-9, leading discounters were "tooling up" to sell more of the higher-priced lines of ready-to-wear.

The entrepreneurs responsible for the development of self-service promotional discount department stores take pride in the fact that they have been eminently successful in the development of a new system of distribution which, it is claimed, helped to achieve the full production and full employment objectives of the U.S. economy. Conventional stores, it is said, were not capable of handling and distributing to the consuming public the enormous output of our plants.

Discounting has created millions of new jobs not only in stores but also in manufacturing, transportation, advertising and wholesaling. Federal, state and local governments have also benefitted from increased taxes. In 1965, according to the annual survey (June, 1966 issue) of *Discount Merchandiser* magazine, discount store sales reached a peak of $13.2 billion in sales which was 9.8 per cent of major retail sales including food. *Discount Merchandiser*'s July, 1967 issue gives $15,011,094,000 as total discount store sales for 1966 – an increase of 14.1 per cent.

But the figures for 1968 as reported in the June, 1969 issue of *Discount Merchandiser* demonstrate the impact that the discount store has had on the American economy. The magazine reports: "Although supermarkets and other grocery stores lead in total sales over all other retailers, the discounters are in first place with respect to general merchandise stores. The total retail sales for the major outlets listed came to $175.9 billion or 6.7 per cent higher than in 1967. By contrast, discount store sales rose 17.2 per cent in the same year. Total discount store volume for 1968 was $19.4 billion, or 11.04 per cent of total general merchandise outlets. Totals for department stores were $15.3 billion, or 8.7 per cent.

Samuel Flanel, a vice president of the National Retail Merchants Association and manager of its controller's congress, was asked what he thought of the *Discount Merchandiser* figures. He said they are, "Open to serious question and could be fallacious in view of the fact that the criteria are so ill defined." Flanel was a member of the Retail Trade Committee which acted in an advisory capacity to the U.S. Census Bureau in 1963. At that time, according to Flanel, the Bureau was seriously considering reporting the statistics of "discount" stores separately. However, the only definition of a true discount store which was considered anywhere near accurate was that which described a closed-door discount store. The Bureau, in view of definition difficulties, decided not to differentiate between discount stores and "orthodox" or "traditional" department stores. In 1968 the Bureau listed sales for the "General Merchandise Group" as $54,493,000; department store sales (excluding mail-order sales) were given as $33,323,000. Presumably this figure includes the sales of discount department stores. The matter becomes more complicated when it is considered that discount stores often have extensive food departments. Many of them also operate gasoline stations and sell automotive supplies.

The *Discount Merchandiser* defines a discount store as: a departmentalized retail establishment utilizing many self service techniques to sell hard goods, health and beauty aids, apparel and other soft goods, and other general merchandise. It operates at uniquely low margins. It has a maximum annual volume of $500,000 and is at least 10,000 square feet in size.

At the November, 1961 Discount Seminar held in New York City by the NRMA, there were some amusing exchanges between discounters and traditional merchants. Stephen Masters, whose firm was later to go bankrupt, called orthodox department store heads "executive paper shufflers," and said that they charged "fat cat" prices for services used by only a few. Richard Tumpowsky, who then operated the soon-to-become bankrupt American Dixie Shops chain of leased departments in discount stores, called the department store and its traditional lessees snobbish and non-aggressive advising them to "wake up and look around." NRMA's then president, Alfred C. Thompson, was moved to retaliate by reminding "these retail kids" that they "have a lot to learn" from the traditional department store which has every intention of staying in business. "We hope you will be around for a while," he said, "and we hope some of you will survive for the brand new world of retailing and will move forward – so far forward that you will understand the social and moral obligations of a traditional old-line department store." (*Stores*, December, 1961, p. 18.)

Although in the past the heaviest emphasis of discount store advertising has been price, there are many of today's operators who feel that the time has come to de-emphasize price and to stress instead value and standards. This is especially evident in soft lines. Many customers are still unconvinced that quality and style in apparel can be bought in discount stores at lower prices than those of conventional department stores.

Said Sol Cantor, president of Interstate Department Stores, in an address before the London, England, financial community in July, 1966, "We know, for example, that the vaunted department store leadership in fashion merchandising is largely an apparition. Fashion knowledge is becoming universal, and women want to enrich their lives with fashion, but not become enslaved to it. They want to be better dressed, but they want to spend less time on it. This greater independence means that many women will be less inclined to stand in awe of the store labels. Thus, ready-to-wear and other soft lines should be susceptible to increased penetration. . . . According to our research, the families which five years ago had an income of $7,000, and now have an income of $12,000, often encounter increased pressures on their budgets. Their dollars are tagged before they even receive

17

them, and there is still a great receptivity to bargain values. . . . The United States is witnessing an increased acceptance of the concept of directed social change. Because of higher minimum wages, the anti-poverty program, higher social security payments, and non-discriminatory employment practices, many Americans are now coming into our market for the first time.

"You may have read of the recent suggestion by an assistant attorney general that the United States Government consider regular publication of reports on the quality of all types of consumer products. This is not a new suggestion: The concept of Federal 'grade labelling' has been promoted since the 1930's. But never before has there been such widespread and continuing vigor to the so-called 'consumer protection' movement. The effects of the increased level of general education plus this vast new consumer movement are beginning to show in the nature of our laws, in the curricula of our schools, and in the very content of the manufacturer's advertising. The American consumer rapidly is becoming a 'product sophisticate.' It is the growing number of these 'product sophisticates' which leads me to believe so strongly in the future of true discounting. Our job is to convince the customer that we can continue to give her that same proportional value, even in the better quality, higher-priced merchandise she will seek as her family's income rises."

What are the major economic factors responsible for these new trends in retailing?

1. According to U.S. Department of Commerce statistics, the 1968 income group of $5,000 to $10,000 comprised 40.4 million families compared with only 12.5 million in 1950, an extraordinary increase. Incomes of over $10,000 were earned by 34.4 million families in 1968, as opposed to only 2.8 million in 1950.

The 1964 Federal tax cut brought about an annual increased purchasing power to the average family of four of about $1,200. More families have two or more paychecks today, since working wives (average age, 41) now represent one of every four married women. Personal income in the nation was over $585 billion in 1968, which may be interpreted as potential retail sales of $25 billion a month. Furthermore, the U.S. population is increasing at an average annual rate of 2.8 million. Thus we see a change in the income pattern with a greater concentration of buying power in the middle income group. Higher taxes have cut down the purchasing power of many in the professional class. An additional factor calling for a higher standard of living is the marked increase in the number of high school graduates, which more than doubled between 1940 and 1968.

2. During the decade from 1940 to 1950, prices were creeping up, owing to the prevalence of a sellers' market. Although personal incomes rose faster than prices during this period, consumers were generally annoyed with the constant increase in prices. However, in the early 1950's production overtook

consumption; merchandise shortages had become surpluses, especially in the hardgoods field. Thus nationally advertised brands of appliances became available to discount stores.

Why are self-service promotional department stores popular?

1. The 10 a.m. to 10 p.m. and Sunday opening hours of these new and aggressive stores made it possible for the working man and his family to shop together in the evening. They felt at home in their informal clothes matching the informality of the new retail outlets. Furthermore, there was plenty of parking space.

2. The widespread use of shopping carts carried with it the supermarket-buying psychology of abundantly filled shelves and ease of purchase, as well as the do-it-yourself idea. The man of the house found the automotive and hardware departments of these new stores of major interest because of his car and home repair activities. As worker-productivity increased, more leisure time became available for do-it-yourself activities.

3. The fact that unorthodox discount stores were frequently able to carry nationally advertised brands inspired faith and buying confidence in the other merchandise they carried. Many manufacturers were finding it difficult to dispose of their output through the traditional retail channels. They were secretly intrigued by, and sympathetic to, these "illegitimate" retailing upstarts, who demonstrated a remarkable ability to move vast quantities of merchandise.

4. Application in 45 states of resale price maintenance ("fair trade" laws) permitted the fixing of minimum retail prices on specified branded goods; yet, these laws left many loopholes for evasion. Although the American Fair Trade Council in 1953 claimed that 78.6 per cent of 12,000 housewives "selected at random" from telephone directories favored fair trade, the public in its purchasing voted differently. The public seemed to consider the laws an attempt to bottle up price competition at a time when it was sorely needed.

5. The rapidity with which new products were introduced placed pressure on the distributors to make the older models available to discount stores. Further, the setting by the manufacturer of a "regular" or "suggested" retail price afforded a standard against which the discounter could match his lower price. In addition, the margins given to the conventional retailer were more liberal than the rendered services warranted. The manufacturer had gradually assumed more and more of the retail functions, including advertising, storage, repair, maintenance and warranty. This margin left plenty of room for customer discounts.

6. Suburban branch stores of conventional department stores were too often elaborate structures duplicating the downtown image with a range and price of merchandise assortments aimed predominantly at the middle to upper-middle income market. The downtown store's bargain basement was

not maintained in the branch. Thus, these branches abandoned the rapidly-growing suburban market of lower-middle to low income customers.

In the late 1950's, the new "unorthodox" retailers had erected buildings designed to meet their merchandising needs. These stores ranged in size from 35,000 to over 100,000 square feet. Fixtures, cash registers and checkout counters were remodelled according to their specifications. They now began to stress balanced inventories and better merchandise assortments, as opposed to limited quantities of seconds and distress merchandise. There was more diversification into both food and soft goods. Private-brand merchandise began to be substituted for the hard-to-get national brands.

As for the future, it appears that the retail giants, Kresge, Woolworth, and J. C. Penney, will continue to expand their discount domains giving serious competition to well-entrenched chains such as Zayres, Kings, and Interstate department stores. The Woolco and Penney stores, although they have the chief characteristics of discount stores such as central checkouts, suburban locations, self-service, and shopping carts, are not considered discount stores by their parent companies. Woolworth calls its Woolco units "popularly-priced promotional department stores " Penney calls its Treasure Island stores "experimental stores." These stores are impressively large (180,000 square feet) and have built into them all the expertise and know-how of this extremely capable merchandiser. The pattern for these "experimental stores" has now been set; their future expansion backed by huge cash reserves, may be on a scale which will dwarf the efforts of competitors.

SECTION 1

Mass Merchandising's Cast of Characters

I

The Beginnings

Mass Merchandising and Low-Margin Retailing Concepts

In Southern California large food markets had evolved "self-service" as a partial solution to the problem of getting help during World War I. Woven baskets were used to carry merchandise in these so-called grocery "coliseums." In San Francisco in 1923 the Crystal Palace opened in a large steel frame building erected by Rousseau and Rousseau on the site of a circus ground and baseball diamond. The Palace had 68,000 square feet of selling area, parking for 4,350 cars, and one-hour free parking. Although food concessions accounted for 87 per cent of the sales, additional lessees were established in drugs, tobacco, liquor (the Volstead Act was repealed in 1934), barber shop, beauty parlor, jewelry store and hat cleaning. The management had absolute control over the kind and quality of merchandise sold. Advertising was on a 50–50 basis and concessionaires' prices were to be no higher than prevailing prices. Records set in this store as reported in the January, 1937 issue of *Supermarket Merchandising* follow: 51,000 pounds of sugar in one hour; 200 tons of lemons in one year; 5 carloads of eggs monthly; 250 tons of oranges annually; and 300 tons of apples in one year. The Crystal Palace finally sold out to the owners of The Emporium, San Francisco's largest department store.

23

Piggly Wiggly Stores

An early retailer with new ideas was Clarence Saunders who, in 1916, started his "Piggly Wiggly" stores in Memphis, Tennessee, ending with 2,660 stores and $180 million in sales. He had a turnstile for both entering and leaving customers, who selected their own merchandise and paid cash at a checkout. Far ahead of his time he invented the "Keedozle" stores in 1945. The customer served herself by merely turning a key causing an item in a case of merchandise to drop onto a moving conveyor belt. Technical problems of maintenance and operation proved too costly and the project was abandoned.

The Shopping Cart

Credit for the invention of the shopping cart is given to Ellis D. Turnham, an employee of the J. Weingarten grocery store in Houston. In the early twenties he took a toy express wagon, removed the handle and fastened a shopping basket on the wagon. The front wheels were made stationery, and the customer pulled the cart by the basket handle. That his idea was slow in being accepted is shown by a January, 1937 *Supermarket Merchandising* advertisement featuring, "GLIDERS WITH REMOVABLE BASKETS WHICH NEST IN EACH OTHER – PATENT APPLIED FOR." This ad was inserted by the Wire Form Co., Jersey City, N.J.

Michael Cullen

The retailing somnolence of the late twenties and early thirties was rudely shattered by a distribution atom bomb with the 1930 "King Cullen" opening, and the 1932 "Big Bear" opening. In 1930 Michael Cullen worked at the Cincinnati Kroger Grocery Co. Convinced that he could operate a grocery store much more profitably than his employer, he put his ideas into an historic letter which he sent to Kroger's vice president. Some excerpts from his letter follow:

"This is the kind of cut-rate chain of wholesale direct-to-the-public that I want to operate: I want to sell 300 items at cost, 200 at 5 per cent above cost, 300 at 15 per cent above cost, and 300 at 20 per cent above cost. I want to gross 9 per cent . . . and make a net profit of $2\frac{1}{2}$ per cent . . . when I come out with a two-page ad and advertise 300 items at cost and 200 items at practically cost . . . the public . . . would break my front doors down to get in. It would be a riot . . . I would convince the public that I could save them from one to three dollars on their grocery bill . . . when the great crowd . . . came to buy those low-priced and 5 per cent items, I would have them surrounded with 15 per cent, 20 per cent and, in some cases, 25 per cent items . . . I could afford to sell them a can of milk at cost if I could sell a can of peas and make 2 cents, and so on . . . The fruit and vegetable department . . . would be a gold mine. This department alone may make a profit of 7 per cent due to the tremendous turnover . . . It would not surprise me if we could net 5 per cent in the meat department."

He was turned down. Undaunted, he persuaded Harry Soloff, vice president of Sweet Life Foods Corp., to become a partner. On August 30, 1930, he started his first store in Jamaica, N.Y. By 1935 he had fifteen large units and was doing more business than could be done by a hundred neighborhood stores. Typical of his promotional approach is his advertisement in the Flushing, L.I., *Journal* of Nov. 23, 1931: "COME IN YOUR LINCOLN, COME IN YOUR FORD, COME WITH THE BABY CARRIAGE. COME WITH ANY OLD THING BUT COME, COME, COME! FRI. 9 P.M., SAT. 10 P.M."

The Big Bears

Robert M. Otis and Roy O. Dawson, in early 1932, persuaded the American House Grocers Co. to join them in leasing a vacant Durant Auto plant in Elizabeth, N.J., with 50,000 square feet on the ground floor. They established a Big Bear store in a huge circus-like emporium with food at the hub and with eleven other specialty departments including auto accessories, paints, radios, hardware, drugs and a lunch and soda fountain. Only 30 per cent of the space was devoted to food. The merchandise was set up on tables and customers were provided with market baskets. Meat, fruit and vegetables were concessions. There was a free parking lot across the road. They advertised national brands at ridiculous prices and brought in customers within a 50 mile radius. Concessionaires paid 5.13 per cent on gross sales. Food sales were 56 per cent of the total sales. With an investment of about $10,000, the venture in one year earned for its three promoters $166,507 on total sales of $3,874,279. Traditional chains and independents were furious in their condemnation of these upstarts and forced the New Jersey papers not to accept Big Bear ads. They had to resort to distribution of four-page broadsides to every household within ten miles of the store.

Another excellent example of a forerunner of modern concepts of low-margin retailing was another Big Bear in Somerville, Mass., opened by Arthur H. Smith in May, 1933, in a rented five-floor building. Each floor had 32,000 square feet. Operating only the food market himself, Smith eventually leased out tobacco, flowers and plants, wallpaper and paint, shoes, cleaning, shoe repair, auto supplies, a lunch and soda fountain, wines and liquors, refrigerators, radios, men's furnishings, patent medicines, linoleum and floor coverings and a delicatessen, dairy, meat and fish, a barber shop and a beauty parlor. In 1937, he negotiated for leased men's and women's clothing and jewelry. He had parking space for 3,605 cars and yearly sales of $2,500,000. More than half of his sales were from concessions other than food. His markup on groceries was $12\frac{1}{2}$ per cent.

At first no wholesale house would cooperate with him; brokers and jobbers refused to sell. He had to buy his merchandise in New York. Denied advertising space by the local newspapers, he distributed 75,000 circulars weekly within a five-mile radius. Despite all opposition he sold a carload of 48,000 cans of Campbell's soup in five days and 24,000 one-pound cans of Maxwell House coffee in two days.

An Early Low-Margin Chain—The Great Atlantic and Pacific Stores

The first Atlantic and Pacific store was established by George F. Gilman and John A. Hartford in 1859, at 31 Vesey Street in New York. The front was painted in vermillion red and gold. Strings of red, white and blue gas-lighted globes decorated the windows. Inside were tea bins painted red and gold and cashiers' cages designed as brilliantly-colored Chinese pagodas. Live green parrots were displayed on stands. An added customer attraction was a brass band which played throughout the day and evening on Saturdays. Public attention was solicited by a team of eight dapple-gray horses pulling tremendous weights throughout the city. A prize of $20,000 was offered to anyone who could guess the combined weight of team and wagon.

At that time tea was sold in New York through brokerage houses and retailed for $1.00 a pound. Hartford and Gilman figured that if they bought direct from Japan and China, they could eliminate brokerage, cartage, storage and waste. High volume at a low profit was the key. In 1912, the company operated 400 stores which extended credit and delivery services. Large numbers of horses and wagons had to be maintained. John Hartford noted the success of one of the early cash-and-carry stores operated in New Jersey by Henry Cole. He decided to open "Economy Stores," staffed by one man, and designed for cash-and-carry with the lowest possible profit but with a very high volume. These stores were so successful that all regular A & P stores were closed in favor of the Economy types. From 1912 to 1915 Economy Stores opened at the average rate of one every three days; eventually there were 1,000. Sales volume in 1916 amounted to $75 million.

26

Cash-and-Carry Stores

The beginnings of many of today's low-margin promotional department stores or "discounters" and of many legitimate department stores was in the early twenties before, during and after World War I, when numerous "cash-and-carry" stores opened. Among these were the Pawtuxet Mills and Presco Mills in Rhode Island. Most were started by small businessmen who wanted to make a living in retailing instead of working at a "regular" job. Many did not survive. One that did survive is the "Factory Outlet" store, founded in 1910 by the Samuels brothers in Providence, R.I. The brothers, former jobbers of men's clothing, were newcomers to Providence. At first, Providence newspapers refused to take their advertising. The Samuels then hired a brass band, put it on a horse-drawn wagon and with it distributed circulars all over the city announcing that the Providence *Journal* would not take their advertising because they were selling for less that the "traditional" merchants. The Outlet, as it is known today, is the biggest department store in Rhode Island.

Cut-Rate Drug Stores

About 1938 there appeared a wave of mass merchandising in the form of many cut-rate drug stores. Fair trade, at this time, was not enforced; prime locations were available, leases were easily signed, and you could get in and out of business very quickly. The Carroll Cut-Rate Drug Company was a pioneer, with headquarters in New Haven, Connecticut. The Allan Cut-Rate Drug Company swept the East Coast. The Sun-Ray Drug Company dominated the Philadelphia area; the Thrifty Drug Company still survives on the West Coast. These were pine-board operations that sold national brands below regular prices. As the price war grew in intensity, many of the weaker operators fell by the wayside. The traditional drug stores were so badly hurt that they combined to enforce fair trade.

The New York Lace Store

The "New York Lace Store" was a cash-and-carry store started right after World War I and destined to become one of the earliest of the "discount-type" specialty stores. It was operated in downtown Pawtucket, R.I., by the Zwetchkenbaum family and carried laces, linens and remnants. Joe Zwetchkenbaum added dresses and women's apparel when he saw that home sewing, or going to the dressmaker, was going out and that ready-to-wear apparel was coming in. He died while comparatively young. His brother Edward and brother-in-law Morris Kaplan took over the operation. It rapidly grew to be directly competitive with any women's and children's ready-to-wear specialty store of its type in Rhode Island. The company did not open budget or charge accounts as so many others did but continued for many years on a cash basis. In 1934 they acquired the services of the Bo Bernstein Advertising Agency, and with Bo's advice they were extremely successful in projecting the following image: "Thrifty Fashionable New York Lace Store Where All You Can Buy Is Fashion – Fashion At A Price And Fashion As Fashion."

The Anderson Little Company

In 1936, Anderson Little, manufacturer of men's clothing, ran into a serious problem as a result of the cancellation, by a customer, of a large order. The banker who had financed the manufacturing operation suggested that Little try selling the merchandise right in his own factory in Fall River, Mass. This venture was successful and was the start of Anderson Little's activities as a direct-to-the-customer men's clothing manufacturer. Ray Anderson, the guiding genius of the firm, decided he would never be caught again in a similar situation. Up to that time they had been making private label men's wear for the major national chains and for big department stores such as R. H. Macy, Jordan Marsh, Filene's and the Fintex Stores. They opened additional stores in Providence, R.I., and New Bedford, Mass. All stores were in out-of-the-way factory buildings. The Bo Bernstein Advertising Agency was engaged in 1941 by the Anderson Little Company. Bernstein advised them not to go into downtown locations which would ruin their "factory-to-you" image. He also was very emphatic in insisting they be open *every* night. At that time they were one of the few companies which stayed open every night 'til nine. Since they sold largely to men, the bulk of their business was done at night. Customers did not have to guess if they were open only on Thursday nights or some other night. Slowly the automobile was taking over all transportation, and from the start parking became a very important consideration with Anderson Little. The company was a pioneer in the low-margin field. Then you could buy an Anderson Little suit for $19.95; a Howard or a Bond suit cost $21.95. They were leaders both in the open-every-night idea and in providing abundant parking space.

Second-Floor Catalog Stores

A certain type of discount store, the second-floor catalog operation, flourished in New York City in the 1930's. The extraordinary ramifications of these unorthodox companies is shown by the following excerpts from an article

The Beginnings

by Earl Lifshey in the December 20, 1937 issue of *Retailing* (Home Furnishings Edition).

"The extent to which a species of retail outlets goes far beyond the mere practice of price cutting . . . is little short of amazing. Name practically anything from a radio or razor to an automobile or aluminium ware; if you go to the right place, you can buy it 'wholesale' or nearly so. Furniture? Almost everything . . . Rugs? Some of the best known names . . . Lamps, radios, refrigerators? Of course, easy! . . . Maybe it's something in sporting goods, watches, jewelry or cameras? Clothing, millinery, electrical appliances? How about accommodations for the weekend in Atlantic City or New York City, in a first class hotel–at a big discount of course? Something in one of the town's hot spot night clubs . . . or an exclusive restaurant, perhaps? Possibly treatments in a beauty parlor? . . . And, oh yes, before it's overlooked, should you require a daily diaper service for the baby, 'They can get it for you wholesale.' "

Lifshey gives the following list of major second-floor operations active in New York City in 1937: F. V. Franklin, 507 Fifth Avenue; Employees Trading Co., 65 Nassau Street; Benco Sales Co., 21 Maiden Lane; Rose Distributors, General Motors Building; Modern Supply Co., 221 Fulton Street; T. S. Alling, 7 Dey Street and Hartford, Conn.; W. F. Batterham Co., 170 Broadway; Baitinger Electric Co., 95 Chambers Street; Employees Association, 32 Broadway; Murray's Distributors, 72 Cortland Street and 126 East 16th Street; Disco, N.Y., Inc., 16 John Street; Drake Distributing Co., 80 Nassau Street; Erb Electric, 15 East 40th Street; C. T. Morrison Co., 10 East 41st Street; LeCount and Co., Inc., 9 Maiden Lane; Furniture Industries of America, 39 East 29th Street; Bennett Brothers, Inc., 485 Fifth Avenue and 175 Broadway; L. and C. Mayers Co., Inc., 385 Madison Avenue, 545 Fifth Avenue, 170 Broadway and with branches in Philadelphia, Albany, Buffalo and Hartford; Keystone Organization, Inc., 1886 Broadway, 139 Hillside Avenue, Jamaica; Yale Organization, 5 West 61st Street; Oscar F. Friedman, 489 Fifth Avenue; Community Home Furnishings, Inc., 198 Broadway; Davega-City Radio, Inc. (School and Contract Department), 831 Broadway; Furniture Shoppers Bureau, 51 East 42nd Street; Morgan and Dornich, 30 Irving Place and 200 Varick Street.

This is only a partial list. A complete list, said Lifshey, if it were possible to compile, would fill a lot of space. Some idea of how this practice has developed is gleaned from a statement made to Mr. Lifshey by Roscoe Rau, executive vice president of the National Retail Furniture Association, when he estimated a retail "leak" of half a billion dollars' sales a year nationally.

Lifshey talked to operators of the firms listed above and reached the following conclusions: " . . . Some common aspects seem to apply to pretty nearly all of them. They all carry some inventory although very often they will remark, 'We haven't that mixer in stock just now but we will have it here by tomorrow.' A good deal of the volume comes from relations with purchasing agents of large corporations who send employees to the discount house with an introductory card. Few of them will sell you without some sort of introduction or other; in some houses this is meticulously observed, in others it is just a ruse or pretense exercised for the psychological effect it will have on the shopper. A great deal of the merchandise is listed in their catalogs or bulletins – and some of their catalogs are quite elaborate – at prices from which they offer enticing discounts, sometimes as high as 50 per cent . . . Products on which list prices prevail are practically always available at cuts that are in many instances substantial."

Lifshey interviewed Paul Silken, head of the Employees Association Discount Department Store at 32 Broadway, Manhattan. His store was located on the upper floor of a modern office building near the heart of the New York financial district. It consisted of a combination showroom and offices, roomy, but not large; a wall fixture and a few tables were filled with appliances, cameras, golf balls, soda syphons, etc.; a few major appliances were also on display. Said Silken to Lifshey, "From the way some people talk and from some of the stories one reads, you might think this discount selling was all something new. I've been in it for about 18 years. Is that what some of the critics would call a 'fly-by-night' setup?"

Answering Lifshey's question as to how he managed to offer the consumer discounts as high as 40 per cent and still stay in business, Silken said, "Because we have found that a markup of 15 to 22 per cent is adequate to give us a legitimate profit. If we can operate on such a basis so as to pass savings of that kind to our customers why shouldn't we do it? Of course, if it becomes illegal for us to sell something below the established prices set by the manufacturer we will be guided accordingly. But we won't cross that bridge until we come to it." Economies pointed out were the low upstairs rental and the lack of frills and fixtures. Assortments are not large and bad debts few since most sales are on a cash basis.

In its circular, the Employee Association states: "Experts are employed by us for the handling of such articles as furniture, rugs, automobiles, refrigeration, radios, jewelry, electrical appliances and many other articles a partial list of which appears on this sheet. Our experts are well trained in their professions. They know the best wholesale houses and they know the right price you should pay. Best of all there is no charge for this service . . . . Every article you buy is a standard advertised brand with a 100 per cent guarantee."

Lifshey asked if discount houses did not have to resort to "bootlegging" through small suburban dealers since it was commonly thought that discounters could not get merchandise through regular channels. Silken's answer was, "Absolutely not. We buy 95 per cent of our requirements through regular distributor outlets. We have no trouble. Of course, occasionally a distributor may be out of an item or we may not do business with the wholesaler of a certain item and then have to pick it up somewhere to accommodate a customer. But that is the exception rather than the rule. I cannot say as to all the statements concerning some discount houses attributed to jobbers and manufacturers; all I know is that they are glad to get our business."

Lifshey found a veritable nest of discount stores on Maiden Lane, one of New York's jewelry centers. A Maiden Lane store executive told Lifshey that the jewelry center had moved uptown to 47th and 48th streets and that the discount houses had moved in. He said that silverware, watches and jewelry, especially the first two, were among the earliest products on which growing distribution of a well-established brand name prompted the establishment of list prices. List prices for cameras, automobiles, appliances, radios and other goods came long after. Being items of a relatively high unit sale, there was a natural desire on the part of consumers to get them at a lower price and a temptation to silverware dealers to offer some sort of a discount.

Two of the biggest discount houses, L. and C. Mayers Co., and Bennett Brothers, Inc., began in the jewelry business many years ago. Wrote Lifshey: "Their handsome, inch-thick catalogs offer not only jewelry and silverware but almost everything else in the way of home furnishings including furniture and rugs. . . . Their catalogs are issued to the purchasing agent or employees' shopping agent of several thousand large industrial firms in all parts of the country. The employees of these firms are privileged to buy goods thus listed at a very substantial discount from their catalog list prices. This may be done by mail or over the counter – but in the latter case the customer must come with a purchase order or other identification. The companies also do a considerable business in the sale of goods for prizes and premiums as well as serve in a wholesale capacity to a number of dealers."

The catalogs of both discount firms offer a straight 50 per cent discount from most of the catalog list prices shown with certain special exceptions that are noted in each. This is made possible by weighting the regularly established retail prices to some degree to compensate for such a discount. The Mayers catalog notes: "Why we use list prices: Because they enable our dealers to sell as well as to buy from this catalog. Dealers can show this catalog to their customers and take orders from it without revealing their costs. List prices enable us to quote one uniform discount – they are not retail prices."

Lawrence Mayers of the L. and C. Mayers Company explained to Lifshey: "Most of our business is done with industrials. No one can walk in off the street and buy anything in our places. They must have an order from the purchasing agent or a card of identification. And as to hurting the business of retail establishments, less than 15 per cent of our business is done on branded merchandise. One of the biggest portions of our business is in diamonds. We import our own. We have been in business for 25 years and we still do a considerable business selling to dealers. Much of it is furnishing prizes for sales contests which we help organize for many firms."

According to George H. Jungen, vice president of the Baitinger Electric Company, a big catalog house, the practice of giving discounts on electrical appliances started many years ago. He told Lifshey: "Electricity was first used in factories and office buildings before being introduced into the home. Electrical appliances, such as they were at the time, could not be purchased by interested consumers from dealers simply because there were few or no such dealers around. . . . When a person wanted to get an electrical appliance, it was . . . the purchasing agent to whom such orders were entrusted. The supply firms extended a courtesy discount. It is still the custom."

Retailers hurt by such practices point out that not only the employees of one of these large concerns such as big oil and insurance companies get the advantage of "wholesale" buying, but their families and friends as well. Many of the discount houses arrange to take over the entire task of "serving" the purchasing requirements of large firms of this kind who find it more expedient to do this rather than attempt to cater to such demands through their own purchasing department. Since some form of identification was necessary, the signed "courtesy card" came into being. In many instances its value is only psychological. But sometimes the customer is required to sign a registration book and the signature must compare.

Commenting on his investigation, Lifshey wrote: "Lest anyone be laboring under an impression that these discount dealers and similar agencies are prone to assume an apologetic attitude for the manner in which they conduct their business or violating what are generally looked on as 'Fair Trade' practices, let him dismiss any such ideas. Many of these firms have been in business many years; they have large followings of customers and they are proud rather than apologetic." E. S. Wallace of the 15 year old William F. Batterham Company, told Lifshey, "I suppose you might call this growing interest on the part of the public in firms of this kind something of a 'buyers strike' against ordinary retail outlets. People want their money's worth as well as the much talked about 'service' and we give it to them here."

Davega's[1] maintain a school and contract department with headquarters at the 831 Broadway store managed by T. H. Isaacs. The department outfits the various teams of schools and colleges as well as large industrial firms at special prices in group lots. If a member of one of those teams wanted to get something for himself from Davega's, he would find a special price available to him. In addition to members of a team, students could take advantage of the low prices. Employees of large industrial firms on the Davega list could also purchase there.

[1]Davega's has since gone out of business.

32

The Beginnings

Davega had a branch in the Madison Cooperative Association, Inc., the co-op of the Metropolitan Life Insurance Company. "Make it clear," Lifshey was told, "that the Metropolitan Life Insurance Company has nothing whatever to do with us officially; this is run by the employees for the employees." Madison serves 15,000 employees of the insurance company. The manager was certain that retail merchants were not deprived of much business since, he explained, Metropolitan employees come from so widely scattered an area and their purchases are so thinly distributed that they are "practically insignificant." He commented, "If the retail merchants got a legitimate and not an excessive markup on their goods there wouldn't be any co-ops or discount buying. The cost of distribution is excessive." One reason given for the co-op's low markup (about 25 per cent) is that it paid no rent, light, or heat bills and that it did not advertise.

Life insurance companies, with their thousands of employees, afforded one of the most fertile fields among the so-called "industrials" for the discount houses. Lifshey cites as an example the Prudential Insurance Company in Newark which had its Prudential Insurance Company Athletic Association (P.I.C.A.A.) issue to members (employees of the company) a little booklet entitled "P.I.C.A.A. Discount List." In it were about twenty pages of names and addresses of firms in all sorts of businesses and lists of discounts or other special concessions extended to employees. Items listed included almost everything from batteries and tires to surgical belts and trusses.

Perhaps the oldest of the discount houses uncovered in Lifshey's investigation is the Keystone Organization of which John B. Kepner was president. The concern occupied a large showroom and upper floor with a total of 20,000 square feet in the heart of the New York City automobile district. The bulk of its volume was done in automobiles. In addition it handled a long list of appliances and equipment ranging from airplanes to washing machines. In its prospectus were 4,700 units of stock. Yet very little merchandise, except cars, was on display. A Keystone booklet entitled, "Why a Discount?", explains: ". . . Keystone makes more money in a given period of time by reason of these lower prices made possible by 'mass distribution'. . . . Much has been heard about mass production but very little has been said about mass distribution. . . . Keystone affects mass distribution . . . by the elimination of waste in energy – no lost motion . . . Keystone employs no soliciting salesmen – every customer is a potential salesman." Included in the customers listed by Keystone were Abraham and Straus, Gimbels, Hearn's, Macy's and Wanamaker's. Excessive price cutting displeased manufacturers of branded appliances and the Hoover Company filed suit against Keystone for cutting prices on Hoover vacuum cleaners violating the New York Feld-Crawford Resale Price Maintenance Law.

The New York City Better Business Bureau made a survey in 1937 to determine the extent to which industrial concerns were encouraging their employees to circumvent normal retail channels since it appeared that such practices seriously interfered with established methods of distribution. The views from a representative cross section of 106 large firms was summarized in *Retailing* as follows: "The replies plainly indicate that too many large concerns are unintentionally or unconsciously baiting the hooks of an element in trade which is not only contributing nothing to distribution but laying the groundwork for undermining it. The problem seems more serious than many imagine. It will require a rude awakening to bring about this realization. . . . The Better Business Bureau is particularly interested in the elements which may constitute misrepresentation on the part of those dealers who claim to sell at 'wholesale' or at prices substantially below prevailing retail prices. Our experience indicates that proof of such misrepresentation is difficult to obtain."

Farmer's Markets

Country auctions have been commonplace for years and out of them evolved "Farmer's Markets," said to be the forerunners of today's mass merchandisers. One of the earliest on record is in Upper Bucks County, Pennsylvania, started in 1932 by Stanley Rotenberger in his father's dairy barn. Local farmers who grew more vegetables than they needed and did their own butchering, rented stalls in the barn. From year to year, the variety of merchandise carried gradually increased. It started with home-made quilts, rug weaving, lace, embroidery and baked goods, and ended with "one stop shopping" for everything imaginable.

These markets are generally open Friday from 6 p.m. to midnight and on Saturday from noon to midnight. The Quakertown Farmer's Market occupies about 160 acres of land, and has parking space for 8,000 cars. On a summer weekend, from April through October, there may be as many as 75,000 customers who stroll through an immense building containing an impressive, intriguing variety of stalls, booths and stores. The market loudspeaker informs everyone within hearing, "you can buy everything you eat, wear or use."

There are more than 225 firms offering not only goods but also services you would never expect to find in rural surroundings: You can have a tooth pulled, eyeglasses fitted or get expert advice on what stocks or bonds to buy. The customer is looking for bargains and there are many. It may take considerable time and shoe leather, but it is fun. There is excitement in the air; the combination of novel displays, bright lights and the frequent loudspeaker announcements of bargains creates a circus atmosphere.

Merchants of all kinds are attracted by the low overhead and the fact that, given good weather, they can increase their normal stock turnover many times, and even with lower prices, turn a good profit. There are the husky, barrel-chested operators of trailer trucks who haul potatoes, watermelons, cantaloupes and tomatoes from Southern states. Loads may run to twenty tons per truck, an indication of the volume of business that may be done in an intensive eighteen-hour selling period. As the growing season progresses, the hauls get shorter. This two-day selling period is very acceptable to part-time merchants, such as the second-hand bookseller who can spend the rest of the week going to sales and hunting out more of the kinds of books he knows his market customer wants.

Additional excitement is afforded by the chants and cries of auctioneers who during the early part of the week assemble a miscellaneous assortment of "distress" merchandise: goods purchased from overstocked or bankrupt sellers, factories which have overproduced or fire sales. The housewife can do all her shopping in an immense supermarket. For the man, every kind of hardware and building supply is available. Clothing, lampshades, furniture of all kinds – almost anything you need may be found in this huge market. The best time to shop is said to be between ten and eleven o'clock on a Saturday night when merchants are closing out their stocks at cut prices.

Robert Woldow, now president of the Quakertown Sales Co., which owns the business, embarked on an extensive rebuilding program in 1963. Tile floors, new lighting and air conditioning for the 110,000 square-foot brick and concrete building have been added. Woldow claims to have assembled the best group of non-food discount merchandisers obtainable. The non-foods division is now called the Q-Mart. Sales in 1962 were $7 million, with customers coming from a 25-mile trading area. The company advertises extensively in the Allentown and Bethlehem daily newspapers, although these towns are 20 miles distant.

Filene's
Automatic Bargain Basement

This is a unique mass-merchandising operation which out-discounts discount stores and which no one has copied successfully.

William Filene, a tailor who emigrated from Germany, opened a tiny store in Boston, on Washington Street, in 1849. The store lasted only a short time. Undaunted he successfully opened two stores in Lynn, Mass., one specializing in women's wear and the other in boys' and men's wear. He opened a third store in Bath, Me. In 1881 Filene sold his Lynn and Bath stores and started a Boston store at 10 Winter Street. It was 24-feet square and described as one of the most modern stores of the day with a genuine white marble floor. The company prospered and in 1890, Mr. Filene expanded his business by leasing a five-story building at 445-447 Washington Street. The space was believed to be the greatest in Boston devoted exclusively to women's ready-to-wear and accessories. With the opening of the new store, William Filene retired and turned the store over to his two sons, Edward and Lincoln, launching one of the most famous brother partnerships in retailing. Edward became president and Lincoln was in charge of personnel, and for years both brothers did the buying. Today Filene's is the world's largest specialty store.

In 1909, Filene's Automatic Bargain Basement, one of the store's most famous innovations, was inaugurated. This came as a result of a study by Edward A. Filene and his associates of methods to lower distribution costs. Under this system, basement goods are automatically reduced 25 per cent after twelve selling days, another 25 per cent if still unsold at the end of eighteen selling days and a third 25 per cent if goods remain after twenty-four selling days. Items still on hand after thirty days are given away to organized Boston charities. By 1912 the annual sales volume of the store had grown to $4,500,000, and it moved to its present site at the corner of Washington and Summer Streets.

Filene's Basement, a space through which 75,000 people walk on an average Saturday and where 150,000 once jammed in a single day, has annual sales of over $30 million. Instances are on record of 17,000 pairs of shoes selling in one day; 1,000 fur coats sold in one day; more than 500,000 pieces of infants' wear sold annually; 21,000 pairs of women's silk stockings sold in one day; nine mink coats, averaging $1,000 each, sold for cash in 30 minutes; 400 big English-type baby coaches sold in a few hours; and 4,600 men's suits and coats sold in $8\frac{1}{2}$ hours.

MERCHANDISE HANDLED

Filene's Automatic Bargain Basement acts as a clearing house for leading Fifth Avenue New York stores; for top designers, and importers; and for the most exclusive specialty shops. Basement buyers make as small a purchase as a single mink coat and as large a purchase as complete going-out-of-business stock, with over $300,000,000 worth of clothing and accessories.

For almost forty years, Filene's Basement has been selling seconds – not shabby or worn merchandise – but seconds with wearing quality that can be guaranteed; every piece must give satisfaction. The price tag attached to the garment is marked "second" or "irregular," and today they are probably the largest outlet in the world for this type of merchandise, distributing millions of dollars worth annually. Vast quantities of merchandise are bought and sold on a simple basis; it must be dependable quality and it must be priced below regular prices. Over 5 million pieces of one article from one maker alone have been sold there underpriced because of slightly irregular quality. Several leading brands of women's silk stocking "irregulars" are usually on sale. Frequently featured are seconds from four of the country's leading men's shirt makers, a dozen or more noted shoe brands as well as other nationally-known branded merchandise.

Some of the best known manufacturers have disposed of their surplus lots and seconds through Filene's Basement for more than 20 years without a scrap of written agreement. National advertisers and proprietors of widely-advertised brands are against allowing their brand names to appear in a special price advertisement. Yet the Basement has, from time to time, given its customers the opportunity to purchase nationally-known brands at bargain prices with or without the use of the name. Hundreds of these manufacturers find Filene's Basement a handy outlet for their excess accumulations. Merchandise varies from needles to mink coats, from nationally-known brands to unbranded merchandise which must be of dependable quality and sold at less than regular prices.

Buying is on a self-service basis with a minimum of sales help. Clerks are too busy ringing up sales to help customers, and most shoppers prefer it that way. Although huge quantities of ladies' clothes are sold, there are no dressing rooms. The whole basement, it is said, is a public dressing room!

The Pioneers

The Mill Outlet Phase of Discounting

Among the earliest discount operations were those which started as mill outlets. An excellent example is that of the Ethan Ames Factory (Monarch Mills) outlet in New Bedford, Mass.; by 1950 it had become the first of the Arlan's chain.

The extraordinary success of this company inspired imitation and in the early 1950's many mill operations got underway. Among these were Ann and Hope in Cumberland, R.I. (1953); Atlantic Mills in New Bedford, Mass. (1955); Coatsfield Shoppers' World, Pawtucket, R.I. (1955); J. M. Field's, Salem, Mass. (1957); Mammoth Mart, Framingham, Mass. (1956); Murray Candib's store (later King's Department Stores), Springfield, Mass. (1949); Aaron Cohen's store, Brockton, Mass. (1955); Rockdale Stores, Turners Falls, Mass. (1953); Kermell Bargain Center, Fall River, Mass. (1955).

In these early stores turnover was extremely fast enabling the operators, in many instances, to sell their merchandise before the 30 day due-date of their supplier's bills. In effect, then, they were being financed by the capital of their suppliers. These "kids in retailing" as they were called by then

38

NRAM president, Alfred C. Thompson, encountered the animosity of established "traditional" or "orthodox" merchants who goaded their suppliers not to sell to discount operators and brought pressure on newspapers not to take their advertising. This only served to harden the resolve of these hardy entrepreneurs who still managed to get merchandise through devious channels. Threats to bring suit brought the newspapers to heel.

The image of these early mill stores was one of low price, convenient shopping hours, plenty of parking and a carnival buying atmosphere. Customers were from the low and middle income groups. Merchandise was seldom presented in full variety or depth and often included seconds, irregulars, distress merchandise and other one-shot deals. With a markup approximating 20 per cent, prices were really low and there was something to interest every member of the family. Having very little capital and being expert in only one line of merchandise, most of the pioneers relied heavily on leased departments. Only in this way could they achieve a department store look. Lessees provided their own inventory, fixtures, personnel and paid a percentage of sales for the use of the space they occupied. These early lessees deserve a great deal of credit for the part they played in building up companies – many of which later became giant operators.

Rockdale Stores
Filene's Bargain Basement of the Countryside

It has been said that most discount stores are almost identical. If you were blindfolded and set down in the middle of one, it would be hard to tell whether you were in a Zayre's, a Bradlee's, a Topps, or an Arlan's. Not so with Rockdale Stores. This is an operation with individuality and a very special image. It is not to be confused with any other. The company is the creation of William Palestine. With his brothers, Herbert and Lester, he had in 1945 started what is now Arlan's discount store chain in the factory store of the Ethan Ames clothing factory in New Bedford, Mass.

A true New England pioneer, William Palestine decided in 1953 to leave the New Bedford operation and to start his own store in an old mill in Turner's Falls, Mass. Asked why, he said: "Our company owned an unused factory in Turner's Falls and I knew the area. I always liked the Turner's Falls-Greenfield area very much. It is one of the most beautiful spots in New England and I decided that that was the place where I would like to live and bring up my family which includes three daughters. I started with very little money and at first leased the hardgoods, jewelry, toys, sporting goods, cosmetics, and automotive departments. Sales for our first year were about $200,000. We gradually bought out our lessees. Today, after 14 years of operation, we lease only two departments: cosmetics to the Carter Overton Company, and shoes to the Ideal Shoe Company. Carter is an excellent promotional operator, and I admit that I personally could not do as good a job as they do.

"We painted the outside of the factory white, spruced up the parking lot which holds 500 cars, and put in some pipe racks and home-made wooden racks and tables to hold merchandise. No ceilings were installed, but we did put in rows of fluorescent lights. The building has a total of 100,000 square feet on three floors. We used 50,000 feet for warehouse space on the top floor and the remaining 50,000 feet (on two floors) for selling. The second floor is entered from a ramp since the ground is high enough on that side of the building. Inside there is a staircase from the first to the second floor. Shopping carts are in use but cannot be moved from floor to floor. There are check-outs at the exits of both floors.

"As a pioneer we had some tough going at first. Local retailers thought that a discount store in Turner's Falls was the very worst thing that could happen to them. The newspaper, at the instigation of local merchants, would not take our advertisements. It was only after we threatened to bring suit that it relented. The Chamber of Commerce, although it accepted our check for dues, would not give us membership. We still don't belong. Further, we were socially ostracized by the leading merchants, who to this day will not speak to us. They won't even give employment to local people who have worked for us! They do not seem to realize that if they want to maintain a healthy retailing community they need a strong operator like us; our presence here draws a great deal of traffic into the region. With the excellent highways all about us, people have many shopping choices open to them. There is no longer any such thing as 'country' in the real sense. We have found that if we offer excellent values and maintain a strong promotion, we draw people from far beyond what would be considered normal."

On the difference between suburban and rural discount store operations, Palestine commented, "We have made ourselves specialists in serving the rural type of customer who in many respects is quite different from the suburban dweller. We sell more basic merchandise. Rural people want a little better grade of merchandise, although they are not as style conscious as suburbanites. When you deal with a limited number of people, as we do, you must develop a certain loyalty so that the same customers will come back again, and again, and again. Unless your customer is handled properly you court failure. You must have the right kind of merchandise. We are very strong in domestics. About 60 per cent to 65 per cent of our sales are in soft goods and about 35 per cent is in hard goods. We do not carry major

A very early pioneer (1945). The Ethan Ames Mill store, New Bedford, Mass.

appliances, furniture, television, or bedding. We do have small radios and traffic appliances. Our biggest ticket items are lawn mowers and traffic appliances. We stay away from 'dressy' dresses in women's apparel. We avoid fashion. But we carry housedresses for older women. We are also very strong in women's sportswear, including sweaters, skirts, slacks, blouses, since we have found a continuing demand for these categories. We compete with department stores in women's sportswear. For men we carry a full line of men's furnishings, including jackets but not suits; we are extremely strong in work clothes. We find most men in our area may buy clothing only once in several years. Categories in which we have depth and variety are toys and children's wear. Housewares and hardware are in strong demand here and we carry a wide variety and assortment. Plans are on foot to carry more building supplies and do-it-yourself materials. Cameras and photographic supplies are not normally carried. We do not give credit, but the bank credit card plan is spreading rapidly and we may get into that.

"Actually, we will sell anything if our buying price is such that we can give our customers exceptional value. We have promotions on a regular and consistent basis. This is something that our small size enables us to do. We have specials on items such as Arrow or Van Heusen shirts. We get brand name specials that would not be offered to metropolitan stores. Next

41

William Palestine, president, Rockdale Stores.

week, we are having a special on Excello shirts. We may have a McGregor sport shirt at one-third the normal cost. For women we may have a top label in sportswear which sells in town for $30 compared to our price of $9 or $10. We give them variety. One week, we may come out with a matched skirt and sweater special, the next with a fabulous raincoat buy or a big blouse deal.

"We are about to offer Simonize Wax at a way-off price. I just bought 2,000 cases of jams and jellies with which we can undersell supermarkets by about 40 per cent. This morning we had Del Monte Alaskan King Crab for 67 cents and Bumble Bee Chunk Tuna at 24 cents a can instead of a normal price of about 37 cents. A big company couldn't possibly do this.

"There are two things involved in our operation: one is getting the merchandise to Turner's Falls and the other is processing it. By processing I mean dividing it among my four stores and deciding which store gets which promotion. This in itself is an art. I just bought a big jag of polished cotton Lee pants, the stay-pressed cottons. Normally they sell for $6.95; I can sell them for $2.95 if I want to. A major factor in this business is the kind of deals we are able to get in better quality merchandise. In order to know what merchandise to stock, I keep in close contact with our customers. I am in the store every day and many of my customers are personal friends. I keep probing to see what they want. What was good last year may not be good this year."

Two years after he started the Turner's Falls store, Palestine opened another Rockdale Store, in an old mill, in Leominster. He bought another old mill in Lebanon, New Hampshire, and started a store there in 1961. A fourth Rockdale mill store was started in 1965 in a leased factory in Bellow's Falls, Vermont. All stores are open daily from 10 a.m. to 10 p.m. Total volume of the privately-owned chain approximates $7 million, with an average of $1¾ million from each store. "We feel that we have been moderately successful," said Palestine. "Our four units give us enough volume to buy well, and yet we are small enough to retain mobility so that we can make good buys and be in and out of the market much more actively than the major chains. In this way we maintain a healthy volume. In addition to our Turner's Falls warehouse we use part of the Lebanon mill for warehousing. Instead of a weak chain, we are a strong independent."

Asked if he did all the buying, Palestine said, "No. I handle special deals; we have a staff of seven buyers and a merchandise manager. We have a total of about 300 full-time employees, most of whom are middle-aged housewives. We find they are very stable employees and tend to have excellent relations with customers. We have the normal fringe benefits, including retirement plans and vacations with pay. Our employee relations are excellent. If a person shows any ability or capacity to handle a better job than he or she now holds, he is in line for promotion."

For his advertising, William Palestine uses eight newspapers which cover the area in which he operates. He said, "We advertise regularly twice a week with a full page on Wednesdays and a quarter page on Fridays. We buy lineage on a yearly basis. Circulation of these papers varies from 4,000 to 15,000. In the Greenfield-Turner's Falls area, it is 13,000. Cost for a full-page ad in the Greenfield paper is $100. With this advertising policy, unlike a major chain, we are extremely flexible. With our four stores we can create eight different ads every week. I do not believe very strongly in circulars, although we occasionally put one out as a sort of institutional gesture. In the long run the values we present week in and week out are our best advertisements and a much healthier way of doing business."

Asked how he went about choosing rural locations for his stores, Palestine said, "In most of these areas where we have stores, there were no statistics available. We had to find out by ourselves what the draw was. We got some help from radio stations, newspapers, and some chambers of commerce. In our new locations, we did not encounter the animosity that we met when we first started – people had become familiar with the discount store concept."

43

As for the future, Palestine commented: "We have developed customer loyalty to such an extent in these small communities that in my opinion it would be extremely difficult for any chain to come in and take away our trade. The Mammoth Mart store which opened recently near Greenfield has not affected our sales. We do not want to expand any more because we would lose our greatest weapon – flexibility."

J. M. Field's–a Division of Food Fair

THE ENTERPRISE STORES – A JUNIOR DEPARTMENT STORE CHAIN WHICH STARTED J. M. FIELDS

Itself a pioneer in discounting with its J. M. Field's Stores, the Enterprise Company played an important role in the early discounting picture by serving as a training ground for executives who became dissatisfied with the vacillating policies of management and left to start their own discount stores. The experience of the founders and chief executives of King's, Mammoth Mart, and Topps was gained in Enterprise Stores.

In 1951, Enterprise was a chain of thirty-three junior department stores with some fifty years experience. Capitalized at over $3 million, it had stores throughout New England and in New York state. At the beginning of the discount boom in the late fifties they were at the height of their expansion having opened ten traditional stores in the course of three years. This move proved unwise since downtown locations began to sour with volume at a standstill. W. T. Grant, a giant variety store, was trading up and becoming a new competitor to the junior department store field. To make matters worse, the new discount stores, wherever encountered, were giving Enterprise serious price competition. When Ann and Hope opened in Cumberland, R.I., Enterprise stores in Pawtucket and Providence suffered a loss in sales of between 20 and 25 per cent. Management was confronted with two choices: either they could go into the discount field or they could continue on their present collision course with W. T. Grant.

Ownership of Enterprise was divided among three families, the Beckerman, Glass, and Feldman families. Among them were strong differences of opinion concerning the desired store image. Theirs, they reasoned, was a legitimate business in which they had been brought up and which they had known all their lives. Discounting rated low on the retailing ladder and tended to be on the "illegitimate" side. Nevertheless, security was at stake. Opening costs of the new stores, lease-hold improvements, mortgage payments and long-term notes had to be met.

Not fully convinced that discounting was the answer, management

44

decided in 1951 to experiment with their Lawrence, Mass., store which was in a mill. They tried putting in promotional goods but found difficulty in getting used to the low mark-up. Milton Annis, merchandising manager at the time, said, "Management could not get used to operating that way – it was a constant battle to get the right approach. We never did get off the ground in Lawrence because there was indecision and no one would take the bull by the horns and say 'This is it – for better or for worse.' One day it was a promotional store; the next it was a seconds store. We would go on one tack for about three months and then not have the courage to follow it through. Frankly, I think the thing that triggered Enterprise into going into discounting was the fact that several of their key personnel left and started their own discount stores."

One of their top buyers, Selwyn Lempchen, left to start his own low-margin operation. Three more top echelon personnel left to start their own discount stores: Aaron Cohen opened a store in a shoe-factory basement in Brockton, Mass. in 1955; Murray Candib started his store in 1949 in an old Indian Motorcycle factory in Springfield, Mass.; and Bill Kenney also left to go into discounting. They had all had years of experience in retailing, both at Enterprise and in "legitimate" department stores. At Enterprise they were working on a bonus plan which, because of declining sales, provided no incentive. Further, they had the highly stimulating challenge of owning their own businesses. Another former Enterprise employee who became an independent operator was Max Coffman, who started his Mammoth Mart chain in an old foundry in Framingham, Mass.

Although younger members on the Enterprise management team were enthusiastic about entering discounting, there was considerable opposition from older members. Frank Beckerman, who was then Enterprise controller, said: "I went to visit Ann and Hope Mill Outlet in Cumberland, R.I., and was singularly unimpressed. I knew the business they were doing, but I couldn't understand it. In my opinion a basic principle in running a store is to have balanced stocks for customers so that they will find what they want. The discount principle – at least in the beginning – was based on a discount price; people walked in with a basket and picked up something as they saw it, on impulse. The store did not have to carry a complete line. On the basis of my experience, I was convinced that what we needed was better sales help. I had found that if you took a bad department and put a good girl in, the department immediately picked up. I thought we needed more sales help, but not discounting. In 1955 we opened our first discount-type store in Pequot Mills in Salem, Mass. Although we did a good business, I was still unimpressed. The whole thing went against my nature. Although my investment remained in the business, in 1958 I decided to become inactive and made up my mind to concentrate on getting my C.P.A. in accounting."

The Salem store, under the name of J. M. Field's, had higher sales volume in its first year than their number one junior department store, so they knew they were on the right track. Yet there were many problems. Gradually, thirty of the junior department stores were discontinued by selling out, subletting, or closing them when the leases ran out. They found that stores in in-town locations just could not exist. "Then," said Annis, "We decided against more mills. We were going to have a store tailor-made to our specifications. We started looking for land in suburban areas and found a developer in Manchester, N.H., who was willing to build a 45,000-foot store for us. We later developed our prototype J. M. Field stores in Medford and Natick, Mass. These were built exactly alike, having 60,000 square feet, and a parking ratio of three square feet of parking space to one square foot of selling space. We think we were pioneers in establishing the prototype building for discount stores. Our arrangement of checkouts, stockroom space, parking and even fixtures set the standard for the industry. We were the first to use coupon books for money. We were open before Zayre.

"Management, fully convinced they were on the right track, caught the disease of very rapid expansion. We had vastly more experience and a much better credit rating than did most of the unsophisticated opportunists who were our competitors. In our haste to get started we never took the time to set up proper inventory controls. This may work when you are a small chain but as we soon found out, when you are expanding you must have good inventory control. We were practically the only discounter to start out with almost no leased departments; we thought we would make more money. Actually we were wrong because we could have gotten know-how by leasing departments unfamiliar to us. There was still some vacillation among management on just what merchandise to carry. Some wanted automotive supplies such as tires; others didn't. A snackbar was turned down. By 1959 our twelve discount stores were doing a bigger volume than the junior department stores were before we closed them. Actually we were expanding beyond our capital means. Our management found it difficult to adjust to a fast-moving discount operation with different markets, resources and dating.

"As a total company we were making money, but with our expansion program and our closing program, we were not gathering enough cash flow to take care of both. We had either to get more capital or associate ourselves with a stronger financial situation. There was a plan to go public, but it was just the wrong time. We had either to merge or sell. By 1961 our sales were in the neighbourhood of $60 million from thirty-five stores when we decided to merge with Food Fair. To Food Fair this was exciting and new since their sales had been dropping, and they were looking for a shot in the arm. Hy Glass and Ted Feldman stayed with them."

At that time the food industry was just getting into discounting. Grand-way had made the jump, but they were still struggling with unfamiliar problems in the non-food area. Food Fair policy was not to mix foods and non-foods as had Grandway. Yet a completely new set of problems arose. The technique of food merchandising is not always compatible with non-food merchandising. Food Fair was unionized, and J. M. Field's was non-union. It was agreed that, in those areas where Food Fair had a union contract, the J. M. Field stores would also be unionized; those which were free-standing, and not associated with food, would remain non-union.

Annis commented on the situation, "In those early days there was much pirating of personnel causing tremendous turnover. Acquisition by Food Fair slowed down this turnover because it gave us a more powerful financial position. We were able to get a better caliber of personnel. At the time of the takeover, I was vice-president in charge of retailing, and I kept this job until I left Food Fair in May, 1965. The problems were largely concerned with merchandising methods, store layout, and site selection. They started experimenting and new problems arose. Twenty additional discount stores were opened, and we couldn't develop people fast enough to man them. Corporate-wise, the chain has shown an improvement and an operational profit. But I have yet to see a strong operation taken over by a food chain gain in strength as quickly as one taken over by a parent company, such as Zayre, which understood the business."

King's Department Stores, Inc.

INTERVIEW WITH AARON GOLDBERG
(Vice President in Charge of Sales Promotion and Merchandising)

When did you start in the retailing business?

"In 1922."

When did you come to King's?

"It was in 1956. At that time we had five stores, Brockton, Springfield, Lowell, Manchester, and West Palm Beach. We were then in the process of opening the Hartford store. This was the sixth store. Since then we've opened thirty-six stores."

What was your previous background?

"Before coming to King's I was with Enterprise stores in Boston for twelve or thirteen years. They ran a chain of junior department stores. I worked primarily as a buyer in the home furnishings division. Prior to that I was with Interstate Department Stores as manager of their Springfield store. Before that, the greater portion of my retail experience was with R. H. White and C. F. Hovey Company in Boston."

About when did you get to Interstate?

"Twenty odd years ago. I got into discounting very early and one of the assets that I had to draw upon was the fact that my retail experience had been

47

Ollie Cohen, chairman of the board, King's Department Stores, Inc.

Murray Candib, president, King's Department Stores, Inc.

48

quite varied. When I worked in R. H. White's it was a Federated department store. C. F. Hovey was an Allied store. Earlier I had worked in a specialty shop, so my experience was quite diversified."

How old were you when you started in retailing?

"Seventeen years old – when I finished high school."

What high school did you go to?

"Boston English High."

You had discounting experience with Enterprise for how many years?

"I think we were operating for about two years. I was a buyer."

What were some of the problems of the early days?

"In the early days we had several problems. The first was to get merchandise. We had no credit rating. Many manufacturers and credit bureaus refused credit when our financial statement showed that we were working with the manufacturer's money. Actually that was what we were doing."

This was at Enterprise?

"No, Enterprise had plenty of money. This was at King's. We had a continuous problem of making sure that when our bills came due we had enough money to pay them. We always managed to do this even if we had to run a special sale to get the money. Although our capitalization was nowhere near adequate to cover the volume of business we were doing, we always had a reputation in the market for paying our bills on time. The other problem was opposition from the conventional-type merchants, who looked upon us as the worst thing that could happen to them. As a result we did have problems in buying certain lines of merchandise that had historically received most of their volume from department stores."

Such as?

"This applied particularly to ready-to-wear and style merchandise, particularly the ready-to-wear brand lines which we are still having trouble getting. But even some of the manufacturers of unbranded lines were reluctant to sell to us because they were afraid of jeopardizing their department store business.

"Today, many manufacturers find that their volume with discount stores far exceeds the volume they did in the old days with the conventional-type stores; so they are very happy to sell to us.

"The background of most of us at King's is that we all worked together at the Enterprise stores. When I joined Enterprise, I went to work in the Cambridge store when Aaron Cohen was the manager. Later Murray Candib joined us at that store as an assistant or section manager. We worked together at Enterprise stores for ten to twelve years. We knew each others' qualifications and character. With Bill Kenney and me, Mr. Cohen and Mr. Candib were able to create a team with whose capabilities and experience they were thoroughly familiar. I think this is one of the reasons why King's has had the success that we have had. We started off all thinking the same, knowing

49

pretty well what the other fellow thought, and working together as a close team.

"In my opinion the junior department store chain operation is probably the closest to being a training school for the discount field. It had the same type of merchandise as far as price lines and assortments, and the methods of operation were rather similar.

"My real knowledge of the discount field came when I joined King's and saw how Mr. Cohen and Mr. Candib were operating versus the method that we used at J. M. Field's."

What was the difference?

"The big difference was that we worked on a much lower markup and were more concerned about promotion, sales and turnover. This was a matter of necessity. We had to pay our bills.

"At J. M. Field's, they had plenty of credit and were perhaps lax. They minimized the importance of turnover and promotion."

How did you choose the merchandise? Did you carry limited lines but in depth?

"We carried limited price lines, but in depth. We have always made it a practice at King's to carry a wide variety in each range. For example, in most of the cities that we are in, we would probably have the largest assortment in any store of women's fancy blouses at $2.58 or 2.68. These would normally sell for $2.98. We would not have the largest assortment of women's blouses at $3.98, $5.98 or higher prices."

How about sizes?

"On sizes it is always our program and method of operation to carry those sizes in demand, even in the women's and extra sizes. We find that the conventional cuttings of most manufacturers are not exactly to our liking. When this exists we size our orders to our needs. We try to eliminate as many fringe items, fringe sizes, and colors as possible. When we do have something that moves slowly, it's usually through an error in buying or anticipation. We don't go on the department store theory that to have a department you have to carry everything. We carry those items that have a reasonably fast turnover. The basic rule of retailing should be to carry only merchandise that the preponderance of customers want to buy."

In those early days you leased a great deal, didn't you? Was it in order to be a department store?

"No, our original policy remains unchanged; to operate with a minimum of leased departments. Such departments as shoes, millinery, health and beauty aids, jewelry, cameras and in a few instances sporting goods and automotive, were leased in the beginning because they required warehousing or sales personnel. Since then King's has taken over the operation of the health and beauty aids, sporting goods and automotive departments. We were fortunate that King's early stores had excellent sales volumes and low

Aaron G. Goldberg, vice president and general merchandise manager,
King's Department Stores, Inc.

operating expenses which combined with high stock turns generated a cash flow that compensated for an initial low capital investment. We have never knowingly passed a due date on an invoice. Each new store was opened on the profits of those preceding it. King's has never made any long-term borrowings."

Where was King's first store?

"The original store was opened in 1949 by Mr. Candib in Springfield, Mass., in an old Indian Motorcycle Factory.

"Mr. Cohen opened his first store in 1955 in Brockton, Mass., in the basement of a shoe factory. When he outgrew that store, which was 11,000 or 12,000 square feet, he moved into the old bus barn of the Eastern Mass. Railway in Brockton. He bought that building a few years later. Now it is owned by the trustees."

What is your present policy in regard to real estate. Do you lease, primarily, or can you make any money on the real estate?

"No, the company does not own property. We feel that we can make a greater profit in our retail operation.

"The thing that was fascinating in the early days of discounting was that we were making our own rules as we went along. There were no historical methods of operation. As we progressed we developed policies and created our own system and methods of operation. This was the fascinating part of the early days. There were no books to read. Past experience was of very little value. You had to look at everything with a new approach."

How does buying for a discount store differ from buying for a junior department store? You did both.

"The first qualification is that merchandise bought for a self-service discount store must be merchandise that can be readily sold by itself without any sales person. Secondly, I would say that it requires a greater degree of accuracy in buying for a self-service discount store because you don't have the services of a sales person to push something that might not be so desirable, but that with a little extra pushing might be sold. Here the merchandise has to stand on its own merits."

Don't you feel that recent developments in packaging have been tremendously helpful?

"Packaging has been one of the biggest improvements in merchandising in general. However, I think that there is still a long way to go. Manufacturers still forget that the purpose of packaging and the printed matter on the packaging is to inform the consumer. Many times manufacturers neglect to feature the most important factors of the particular piece of merchandise being offered for sale. They also fail to take into consideration the shape of the package, which may not lend itself to being stacked on a table."

In a sense, then, you have educated the manufacturers selling to the discount industry concerning the importance of packaging and labeling.

"We both learned together. In the early days of course, we couldn't go to a manufacturer and tell him that we wanted a certain item made a certain way or packaged a certain way. We weren't large enough. Today, we find that most manufacturers are very happy to accept packaging suggestions which will sell more of their merchandise."

Do you work through buying offices in New York at all?

"Yes, we now have our own buying office in New York where we purchase all ready-to-wear, children's, men's, and boys' clothes for the entire chain. Home furnishings are purchased out of the main office. Prior to that we used the Jack Hartblay office for buying ready-to-wear and children's clothing. This was the buying office used by Mr. Candib and Mr. Cohen when they started out."

Do you ever do any group buying?

"No, we do all our buying on our own."

Do you use the same sources for your merchandise as do the traditional junior department stores?

"In a lot of cases we do. What we like to do is to buy exactly the same merchandise that the better department stores carry in our various cities. One of the apprehensions of our customers is that our merchandise may not be of good quality because it is low in price. I think we are convincing them that we do sell a regular $1 item for 82, 84, or 86 cents and that we do sell a $2 item for $1.58 or $1.68."

When you say a $2 item do you mean suggested retail?

"No I mean that these are the prices that this merchandise, either exactly the same or of comparable quality, would be selling for in the conventional-type stores. Our average prices are 15 per cent to 25 per cent off conventional prices."

Haven't the manufacturers ceased suggesting prices?

"They still suggest prices, but of course the Federal Trade Commission has eliminated all 'fake' list prices. In pre-discount store days, department stores or conventional-type retailers would get full price for toys. Since the advent of discount stores, most departmental stores have been forced to discount their toys also. I'd say that we would sell a typical $5 item for $3.97 or in that vicinity. Some of the conventional stores have also come down on certain items to the same price. Most department stores pay about $22.50 a dozen for women's tailored blouses and get $2.98 on each. We would sell it for $2.58 but our markup would be better than 20 per cent."

Do you feel that the small retailer is on the way out as a result of discount operations?

"I have always felt that there was room for all types of retailers if they know their business and are willing to work at it. One won't do without the other. There is no reason why the intelligently-operated small specialty shop should not only continue in business, but also prosper and grow. Not everyone wants to go to a discount store; not everyone wants to serve herself. Some people want an experienced person behind the counter to whom they can talk and from whom they can get advice. There is no reason in the world why the independent merchant shouldn't succeed."

How long are your store leases?

"They generally run about 20 years."

Suppose industry moves away and a location goes sour, aren't you stuck with that building?

"Yes, we are."

Has that ever happened?

"Every retailer has some stores that he wishes he didn't have, but I think that is part of the mix."

What do you do with them?

"By giving problem stores special promotional programs and personal attention, we have been able to solve their problems with a fair degree of satisfaction so far."

Why don't you settle down and stop opening stores? Wouldn't it be easier

William F. Kenney, executive vice president
and general manager, King's Department Stores, Inc.

to consolidate your operation and make it more effective?

"We took a breather two years ago when we opened only a few stores. Like any organization, you either grow or go backwards. We now have built up a home organization that can handle, I would say, twenty to twenty-five more stores with a very minor addition to our cost."

Do you have IBM equipment?

"We have IBM in certain of our ready-to-wear and men's wear classifications. We are continually adding to the group of merchandise on IBM. We are far away from having a major part of our business on IBM."

What, would you say, are your major problems today?

"I would say our major problem is in communication; in conveying in detail to all our managers and personnel the program that we have lined up for our method of operation. The program does vary from time to time but the basic principles always apply. To have everyone thinking the same way on certain specific details is a very difficult matter."

54

Do you have a training manual?

"We are now in the process of creating one. We do most of our training at our monthly store managers' meetings where views are exchanged and our thinking is expanded and enlarged on as much as possible."

Do you get your store managers from all over the country and bring them together for these meetings?

"Yes. Our last two-day meeting was held in Boston at Kenmore Square.

"The store manager plays an extremely important part in our setup. He must show initiative and enterprise. We lean heavily on our store managers. We expect them to be merchants. For example, we may set up an advertisement on a coat as fast as we can get delivery because five, six, or seven store managers sent in re-orders. They've got a dozen coats: one sold six in a weekend, another sold eight. We then buy it across the board for all the stores. We don't have to wait one week before the computer report comes in.

"It has to be done right or we don't do it."

Do you pay these store managers on the basis of achievement?

"We pay them a flat salary and a bonus."

Is the bonus on sales?

"No. It is not always feasible to base the bonus on sales because there may be complications. If a man maintained his sales he still might have done a better job than a man who went ahead on sales, because the former might have had difficult competitive circumstances in his area. We found that it was practically impossible to come up with a formula that would work right across the board."

Do you have any retirement plan?

" We are working on one."

How about fringe benefits?

"We give the same benefits and pay scale, and sometimes even more, than the going retail rate in the towns that we are in. In the old days, I could tell you how much money we owed, and what we were doing in each town. I don't know any more."

Do you consider food important?

"We have never considered food as an important part of our business. In fact we've always said that if we weren't good enough merchants to attract customers without depending on food, then we probably didn't belong in the retail business. We do have food in our Stamford store. It is a concession. That is in the old Yale and Town building where we had space that we couldn't utilize."

Is it your policy to build new stores or do you try to get stores already built and rent them?

"Basically our policy is to have stores built for us on locations that we think are desirable, but we are also interested in, and will entertain at any

55

time, an offer of acquisition of existing stores if we feel the deal is beneficial to us."

I understand that your success is very largely the result of very expert location. Do you have a real estate department?

"We now have a real estate department which we formed this past year. Previous to that Mr. Kenney was handling all the real estate. Before any location is accepted it must be approved by the executive board."

Are you having difficulty finding locations?

"No, strange as it may seem, there are still plenty of areas open for stores. Of course the retail business is growing as our population increases and prosperity continues. The average working person now has more money. Where there was room for only one or two discount stores, there now seems to be room for another. This may not have been the case four or five years ago. In addition, and there is no question about this, every year more people are finding it to their advantage to rely on discount stores for making a fair percentage of their total purchases. We feel that if we run our business properly there is no reason why we can't count upon having more people shop with us as time goes on."

How about the competitive impact of Woolco and K Mart?

"Most of us who are successful in the discount department store business have sufficient capital to take care of almost any circumstances in the foreseeable future."

What, in your opinion, was the reason for the failure of Towers Marts?

"I never considered Towers as being in the discount field. The president, Sam Rosenstein, was more in the real estate business. That was one hundred per cent concession idea that started out the same way as GEM. This was doomed to failure since each concession wants to grab off as much profit as it can today. He is not too concerned about tomorrow because he doesn't know what is going to happen tomorrow. You can't build a business by trying to get the maximum price and trying to overcharge if you can get away with it. This actually is what happens in one hundred per cent of major per cent concession operation. If Rosenstein used a qualified retail merchandising organization to supervise the various concessions, perhaps he would have lasted a little longer."

How about your policy of going way out to Colorado and so on? Isn't that a little bit overextended?

"At the time we originally went out to Denver it was our idea to open up a division in that area. Now we feel that it would be much more beneficial to us to be concentrated along the Eastern portion of the country rather than extending that far geographically."

But, for the time being, you are still keeping your Denver store?

"Yes, we are."

Are your stores now accepted in shopping centers?

56

The Pioneers

"In the early days most variety chains refused us as fellow tenants in shopping centers. Today, I believe, the situation is completely reversed. Most variety chains want to go into shopping centers where we are and now we are the ones that are calling the tune. I believe they have found that they are much better off in a shopping center with a discounter because the discounter takes the shopping center out of just being a local center, with a drawing power of maybe a mile or two, and creates a shopping center that will draw from twenty to thirty miles. They are getting more business because of the much wider draw, even though they must limit the merchandise that they carry when they are a neighbor of a discount store. The same also applies to food stores."

Are you going into credit?

"We are experimenting with credit in our Brockton and Newton stores. We sell the script coupon books for $25 or $50, and the customer pays us so much a week. In our four Buffalo stores we have credit through the local banks and at the present time I would say that it is still in the experimental stage. It does not appear to have increased our business to any great degree."

Do you think there is any danger of your becoming more of a traditional operator as you trade up and increase your services, your fixture expenses, etc?

"Basically we are discount stores and we should do nothing that in any way causes us, by increasing our expenses, to increase our retail prices. We also feel that customers like our way of doing business."

How about trading up?

"We are carrying better merchandise because we find that our customers have indicated that they are willing to buy better merchandise. The only limitation we have on higher prices is that because we are self-service, the merchandise by itself must indicate quality and value."

Don't you deliver in the stores where you sell major appliances?

"Yes, we deliver, but we don't run these departments ourselves. They are concessions."

Is this concession more for traffic building and customer convenience than for profit?

"Both.

"Cameras, radio, television and major appliances are service departments. Where we have a department of that nature, we feel we are much better off giving it to a good operator. At least we know exactly how much money we are taking in on this kind of a deal. A good operator in a service department, because he is working as a specialist in that limited area, generally can operate more efficiently than a chain operation can."

Do you have any difficulty getting adequate personnel?

"We are looking for additional personnel for our buying organization. We want people who have worked in a successful discount operation. My

57

theory is that at least they have lived with a successful operation, and if they were successful there they could fit into our organization and continue to be successful. They would digest some of our program and maybe eventually we could digest some of theirs. King's would benefit by it. We took our men's and boys' wear merchandise manager from Arlans; our men's wear buyer from Alexanders'; our boys' wear buyer from Korvette. The latter had also been with Bamberger's and Macy's."

Do you have any buying problems?

"It depends greatly on the type of merchandise. For style merchandise we try to buy as close to the selling period as we can because it changes so fast these days that we don't know what the style is going to be. We find that we not only have drastic style changes in women's fashions but also colors come in and go out fast. This applies to girls' and children's ready-to-wear and even to sheets and towels. A dark maroon can be a strong color one season and next season, all of a sudden, it switches to yellow. This also takes place in men's shirts. Pink shirts came in for a while and then yellow came in. We had a period in one area when big checker-board shirts were very strong. You get colors now even in sheets. In the old days if you had white sheets, you were in business; nowadays in addition to white, you have to stock colors, stripes, prints and florals. It is necessary to be liquid at all times so that you can bend the way the wind is blowing."

Do you find that manufacturers cooperate by taking back merchandise?

"We do not ask manufacturers to take back merchandise. We are willing to pay for our own mistakes and all we expect from them is to ship us the merchandise according to our purchase order specifications."

Do you have problems with late deliveries?

"Occasionally we have problems but nothing serious. We run into it occasionally on import merchandise. This past year we ran into it on muslin sheets when the Government stepped in and bought a lot of sheets for the military."

Who are your major resources?

"This is the first year that we are going to compute the total dollars that we do with each of our resources. Before we haven't had the accounting to tell us."

Do you sell Prestone as a loss leader?

"If necessary. We don't do it intentionally – only to meet competition."

What is your philosophy about sales promotion?

"We now have four major sales a year. We believe first that if we run too many sales we holler 'wolf' too often and customers either won't believe us or won't be impressed. Secondly, if they are real sales we think it will affect our markup by too great a degree if we have too many. Thirdly, if we run too many real sales, why should customers come in on regular days? We are very careful not to over-promote. This calls for the right mix; and

58

here is where we differ with a lot of our competitors. When we do run a sale, and there are four a year: one in spring for Easter; one in the early summer; one for back-to-school; and one for the beginning of the fall season; we think that in most cases we get a much greater response than most of our competitors, particularly those who adopt the practice of having a sale every month or even more often. We have found that some of our competitors put out beautiful ads and beautiful circulars. But when you check their stores, they don't have the merchandise. This we never do. All our stores are in the newspapers every week.

"If there is a sale, it is what we consider a minor sale; for example, in January we advertise some domestics at lower than usual prices. We had a cosmetics sale at prices lower than our usual prices. But these aren't what we consider major sales. In our advertising, we never use superlative terms or anything of a sensational nature and we practically never use comparative prices. We never use list prices."

If you drop-ship, how can you have enough backup of merchandise for a sale?

"One of our problems is that when we run a major sale, we tend to jam up our stock rooms. We start receiving merchandise for a sale in the stores about two months in advance. We also make it a point never to run bulky items on a sale, those that would take a lot of space and not contribute too much in dollars. For example, we never run a bed pillow in one of our major sales, because if you gave a store $1,000 worth of pillows, it is enough to fill up a stockroom. That is one of our ways of minimizing the necessity for big stock room space."

Do you ever do cost accounting on profitability by item?

"No. We don't think it is worth the money. We just take the department as a whole."

What kinds of research do you think is necessary in the mass merchandising field?

"Probably the most important research would be to determine the best way of displaying different types of merchandise and getting customer reactions; to learn what changes in sales result by taking the same merchandise and displaying it in different ways. Color and packaging should be studied. We want displays that sell more merchandise.

"We want fixtures that will sell just as much merchandise as we are now selling, but ones that will eliminate stock work. This is very important. For example, suppose men's work pants are stacked up. One customer could pull that pile apart and it would take a stock boy three or four hours to straighten it out. In the course of a year we may spend more in labor to straighten out this counter of work pants than we take in from sales. We haven't figured out how much stock work it really takes. We know our approximate sales on work pants, but we may be losing our shirts on this one counter because of

59

the amount of stock work involved. This is one very important area that needs research. Fixtures are needed that would eliminate or considerably reduce the stock work. Another area needing study is ticketing. Switching of tickets by customers can be a serious problem."

Don't you have pins that bend so that you can't easily pull them out?

"A sharp person at the checkout register will catch most switched tickets. Replaced pins can be seen if watched for."

Have you had any trouble with the Federal Trade Commission?

"Yes."

When was that?

"This past year, on cases that went back two or three years. We were charged with failure to comply with the fur-labelling laws. These laws spell out that if you have a garment which has a fur part worth $7 or more wholesale, then you must give the customer a receipt specifying the nature of the fur, the country of origin, the way it is dyed, and the part of the animal it comes from. You must keep a copy of that receipt on file for three years, even though the manufacturer's label attached to the coat has all this information. The garments that we sell with fur attached to the amount of $7 wholesale amount to 1/100th of 1 per cent of our total business."

Have you ever been involved in fair trade problems?

"We sold 'fair-traded' merchandise off-price until we got an order to cease."

What items were involved?

"It generally happens in cosmetics. Incidentally, DuPont is going off fair-trade with auto accessories."

Did the manufacturer sue and make you pay damages?

"No, we never paid any fine. Once we agree to stop, we stop. We prefer to stop before we get a court injunction because then, if we do it again through error, we aren't subject to contempt of court. If we think the manufacturer is serious we stop."

Have you noticed any changes in customer shopping habits? Aren't people with higher incomes getting fed up with waiting in checkout lines, carrying things to their car, etc.?

"I think that it is now the smart thing for the sophisticated person to shop at discount stores. When we first started, Mrs. Jones might have been a little embarrassed if her neighbor saw her buying something at a discount store. The exact opposite is now true. The sophisticated person and the smart person, regardless of income, patronize discount stores, not necessarily for all types of merchandise that the discount store handles, but in various departments. The person of the highest income level can shop in any of our cosmetic departments and pay minimum prices for her cold tablets, vitamin pills, toothpaste, facial tissues or toothbrushes. A person of the highest income level could do a fair degree of shopping in our housewares department, where we carry General Electric irons, or Toastmaster toasters, or Universal percolators, or Sunbeam frying pans, or Ecko kitchenware. Our sporting goods department attracts upper income people with Spaulding golf equipment and tents up to $100 or $150, power lawn mowers, Black & Decker power tools, and Stanley tools. In our paint department we carry Sherman-Williams, Glidden, or DuPont paint."

What kind of research do you do in your stores?

"For example, to refine our mailing on major sales, we are now analyzing our refunds and lay-aways in certain stores to see where our customers live. When we send out 100,000 circulars we want to do it where we are getting our regular customers. In addition, we survey customers and ask what newspapers they read."

Do you feel that businessmen and universities should work more closely together?

"Yes. I find that talks to college groups are a tremendous help to a person who has lived in the business for a long time and who has a pretty good command of the situation. In assembling your thoughts before addressing a group, you sometimes consider aspects that you never thought of before. If you are talking to the right group, you might wind up with some new ideas yourself. No one knows it all. The fellow who thinks he knows it all is in trouble. Just getting the reactions from a group of young people is of benefit to anyone in the retail business."

There is one thing about discounting that always impressed me and that is that you fellows give your lifeblood just so that the customer gets something cheaper. You neglect your homes and your families. You get married to the business and the average person doesn't like that idea.

"That was done only in the early days and is no longer necessary. Anyone who is doing that today hasn't grown with the business. We don't expect any regular employee to work more than eight hours a day. When he works additional hours he gets time off to compensate for it.

"As for executives: if you interview any major executive in any business you will find that he works ten to twelve hours a day, and in addition takes home work at night or over the weekend. There are no time limits to an executive's job. You are either working or thinking. You still have time to enjoy yourself. The days when it took all my waking hours are gone."

But you probably enjoyed it at the time.

" I did enjoy it and for a young man or young woman, retailing presents a greater opportunity than do most industries. They may not start off as high as in a technical job, but in ten years they would very likely find themselves much further ahead in retailing as far as income goes. Salaries of $25,000, $30,000, or $40,000 are not uncommon for some of the better jobs in the discount field, and as time goes on this will increase."

What is your specialty?

"I am in charge of merchandising and sales promotions. Anything that pertains to merchandising is my job."

The Evolution of the Ethan Ames Factory into Arlan's Department Stores, Inc.

Starting in 1945, as a 5,000 square-foot factory retail sales room for seconds, Arlan's is today a national chain with sales of over $200 million. Their stores are in the Northern tier of the country, going as far West as Denver, and to Portland, Me. on the East Coast. They go South to Louisville, and to Roanoke, Va., and to Durham, N.C. So far as the author can ascertain, Arlan's was the first "self-service discount department store" to be established in New England and possibly the first in the United States.

The Ethan Ames Company, in New Bedford, Mass., manufactured boys' clothing and in 1945 was operated by the Palestine family. There were three brothers active in the business. When Bill and Herbert came back from the war in 1945, Herbert was put in charge of the factory store, which carried goods they manufactured and some items purchased elsewhere. At the start, 5,000 square feet was assigned for retail sales. Gradually, general merchandise of all kinds was added. In 1947, Edward Zwetchkenbaum, operator of the New York Lace Store, leased the women's wear department, and the Bo Bernstein Advertising Agency was engaged to help with sales promotion. The sales area now occupied a total of 20,000 square feet on the ground floor of the factory. At first they were open only three nights a week, but it was soon found profitable to stay open six nights a week.

Instead of "Ethan Ames Store," the name was changed to Mammoth Mills and later to "Arlan's", the name of Lester Palestine's daughter, which was a combination of the names of Arthur and Allen, Lester's first and second sons. At the suggestion of Bo Bernstein, the Al Glassman Floor Covering Company became a lessee, and the Elkins and Perlman Shoe Company leased the shoe department. The business was so successful that by 1950 it occupied not only the 40,000 square feet on the ground floor, but an additional 40,000 feet on the second floor. Furniture and major appliances were added and sales were running between $2 million and $3 million annually. No other stores were started until 1955, when the Palestines opened two additional stores, one in Fall River and one in Lawrence, Mass., under the name of "Arlan's". The original Arlan's was really

Herbert Palestine, chairman of the board,
Arlan's Department Stores, Inc.

created by Lester and Bill Palestine. The Palestines now felt they were able to operate the ladies' apparel department themselves and bought out Zwetchkenbaum's remaining lease for approximately $75,000. Zwetchkenbaum then opened his own discount store, Coatsfield Shoppers World Center in a Pawtucket, R.I. mill building.

Bill Palestine, in 1953, decided to open his own discount store in Turner's Falls, Mass. Herbert and Lester Palestine, with Hyman Feinstein, then took over Arlan's with Herbert as president. By 1956, the news of Arlan's great success had spread, and many individuals started what were called "discount stores." Some of them were short-lived opportunist operations. Others, like King's, Mammoth Mart, and Zayre's, became powerful chains. The Palestine family decided to form the nucleus of a national chain. They had wanted to have a store in a big Midwestern metropolitan area. In 1957, Arlan's started a store in an old warehouse in suburban Detroit with 40,000 square feet and

63

lots of parking space. It was an immediate success. In 1958, they opened another store in Detroit. In that year, the combined volume of these stores was $3 million. Today, their first Detroit store has been enlarged to 100,000 square feet, and Detroit is one of their major markets.

In 1959 Arlan's opened a store in an old building in Louisville. By 1960 the company had seven stores, all in old buildings. In this year, their financial strength was such that for the first time they were able to have new stores built. Four stores were opened in new buildings, one each in Cincinnati, Grand Rapids, Mich., Rochester, N.Y., and Roanoke. It was the first year that the company opened more than two stores. In 1961 five more stores were opened, bringing it to a total of 16; total sales exceeded $40 million, and the company "went public". Shares opened at $18. There were in 1968 2.7 million shares outstanding, and the stock has never gone lower than its original price. It went up to $70 before the 2.5 for one split, and in 1966 it sold for about $22. In 1962, in an extremely ambitious program, the chain opened twenty stores, more than doubling its size. Central general and buying offices were moved from New Bedford to New York.

In 1966, in an extremely ambitious program, twenty additional stores were opened, a total of 87. Some of these new stores are in small cities, such as Mason City and Clinton, Iowa. Others will be put in big cities, such as Toledo and Denver, where Arlan's are already established. Store size varies from 60,000 to 125,000 square feet. By the end of 1968, the firm was operating 90 stores with 14 more planned for 1969. In addition, Arlan's has opened two in a new line of Play World Stores, both in Connecticut.

INTERVIEW WITH WARREN EISENBERG, PRESIDENT ARLAN'S

How long have you been in retailing?

"I started out in 1947 so I have spent 19 years in retailing. I graduated from New Bedford High School when I was 16 and had no idea what I wanted to do. I was not financially able to go to college so I decided to seek employment. I really got into this business by accident. I went to a very large boys' clothing manufacturing company in New Bedford, Monarch Clothing Company, to see what kind of job opportunities were available. I walked through the wrong door into a room with some boys' clothing and I found that it was the Monarch Clothing Company retail sales room, used to sell their own overproduction and seconds. I bumped into a man by the name of Herbert Palestine, who was managing the store. His brothers, Lester and Bill, were running the factory. Herbert and I got to talking and he decided he needed a stock boy and hired me that day. So I never got to the factory and that was the start of my association with Mr. Palestine. Today he is chairman of the board. That was the beginning of Arlan's,

Warren Eisenberg, president,
Arlan's Department Stores, Inc.

and that was the beginning of my career with them. At that time it wasn't called Arlan's because it was only a factory sales room.

"In early 1948 the Palestines realized that they were doing so well in the retailing business selling their own merchandise, that they decided to bring in a few other lines and expand the store a little. They had about 5,000 square feet at the time. After this first expansion they put in a few woolens and a few cosmetics. They then changed the name to Arlan's, the name came from Lester Palestine's daughter, Arlan. The store just kept growing from that point on. We kept adding more and more merchandise as our volume warranted and the store just kept getting bigger and bigger until finally – it took us about three years – we ended up in that same building occupying two whole floors, 40,000 square feet on each floor. That was the first store. There was parking and the location lent itself nicely to retailing. We opened no other stores until 1955."

Did you have leased departments?

"We ran everything ourselves except shoes and women's wear. We leased that until the early '50's when we took those over. By 1954 we were running all departments. At the beginning it was exclusively boys' wear. We did make mistakes as we were all new at retailing. I eventually went from stockboy to take over the domestics department as domestics manager and buyer. In the early '50's I took charge of all the non-apparel departments, hardlines, and domestics merchandise manager."

Were you established before Marty Chase?

"I saw his operation and it was just about the same time. We weren't too far away from him."

How long had this factory been in existence?

"It was started by Mr. Palestine's father about 40 years ago. When the retailing business got so large, it was the tail wagging the dog and at that point they discontinued their manufacturing operation."

What were your sales in your first full year of full operation?

"Between $2 and $3 million and that was in the early '50's."

Did you have food?

"No, no food or major appliances at first, but by the early '50's we added furniture and major appliances when we expanded to 80,000 square feet."

When did you get the idea of having other stores?

"We went along until 1955 without opening another store. In 1955 we opened two other stores, one in Fall River, and one in Lawrence. We stayed with those three stores until 1957. In 1957 we took a very big step. We moved all the way out to Detroit and at that time the Palestines were eagerly anticipating getting into a big metropolis. They felt that New England was merely a starting point so we moved to Detroit. Today Detroit is one of our major cities. Herbert Palestine felt that if we were ever going to become really big we would have to learn how to operate a store far away. This was a good time to learn because it wasn't competitive then and we could afford mistakes. We had no warehouse. He found an old building in Detroit with only 40,000 square feet but in a good location. Actually it was an old warehouse. We had parking and it was a nice building set in a suburb but with good access. We are still operating that store. It is on one floor but we have added on to it so that today it is 100,000 square feet."

What is your real estate thinking, to buy property or to lease it?

"Up until very recently we always leased property. We are at the point today where we own our own stores wherever it is practical. We own stores in Lancaster and Pottstown, Pa. We own six or seven of our Louisville stores. In the beginning we weren't financially able to own a building. Today we are able to get excellent financing."

What did you do for personnel?

"We had been building it right along. Our principals always had a lot

Arlan's department store, Colorado Springs, Colo.

Interior view of Arlan's, Colorado Springs, Colo.

67

of foresight. They recognized that if they were going to become big, they would need an organization to do so and we kept expanding our organization. We built a very good one because most of our early people are still with us today. Whenever possible we promoted from within. I am a good example of promoting from within!"

Do you have a training program?

"We unfortunately do not have a formal training program as such, but we do on-the-job-training through assistant managers and assistant buyers. We don't have a full personnel department."

What departments do you operate today?

"Today our stores operate about 85 per cent of the business as they did in the early 1950's. The only departments that we lease are shoes, millinery, jewelry, and the luncheonette."

Who is your shoe lessee?

"Morse Shoe and Melville Shoe. Morse is in most of our stores and Melville is in a small part of our chain. We feel that Melville does a good job and in certain geographical areas we pick him instead of Morse. We like having more than one concessionnaire. It makes it a little more competitive and we are able to analyze it better. This sort of thing isn't customary but our expansion program of 20 new stores a year is so great that we are able to give each lessee sufficient stores to grow with us."

Who leases the other departments?

"The Schimmel Company leases millinery. We have several different lessees in jewelry."

How many stores do you have now?

"Now we have 57. [90 as of Jan., 1969.]

"If we like a development location and we are unable to buy the property, we take the location anyway. The most important thing, as far as we are concerned, is the right location. Of secondary importance is whether we own it or not. If we have a good opportunity to buy, we are able to get all the money we need."

How about your warehousing situation?

"We do not warehouse; everything is drop-shipped. We have never believed in warehousing and have always felt that it was an added cost that we just did not want to incur except for highly specialized items. We use a service in New York, the Gilbert Company, a warehouse concern which distributes ladies' dresses and coats for us. They get the merchandise, mark it, and ship it out to our stores. But this is very specialized. They are distributors and truckers and perform this service for many retailers. All of the ladies' coats and dresses come out of the New York market anyway, so they are delivered to their warehouse. Our buyers are able to see the merchandise before it goes out.

"All our buying is centralized here in New York."

68

The Pioneers

How do you train your store managers and give them initiative?

"We have district managers out in the field and each one has a staff of coordinators who specialize in a certain department. All store managers are on a profit-sharing program whereby they participate in the profits of their own store."

What kind of a profit-sharing – is it a percent of sales?

"We give the manager a statement every month telling what his sales were, his markdowns, what his errors – right down to the bottom line profit. At the end of the year he gets a percentage of that profit."

How do you fit in this central administration expense in order to compute profits?

"The bigger stores pay more for their share of the central overhead. We have built a very simple formula that the men are very pleased with and it gives them a good chance to earn and show improvement over the years."

What if a man is doing an excellent job and despite all his efforts, industry is moving away?

"When that happens, and we feel that a man is doing a good job, we move him to a better store. That is the advantage of opening so many stores. There are always opportunities for men to move into better stores."

Are you interested in college graduates?

"Yes, we are interested in college graduates, but we would start them in stores where they would have to work themselves up. We have taken bright young fellows and turned them into store managers in just about a year."

What is the average earning for the store manager?

"Our average range would be about $15,000 a year. Of course, in a company that is expanding as rapidly as ours, every eight or nine new stores require a district manager so store managers can still move up to over $20,000."

What is your average markup?

"It has crept up to where it is now in the high 20's."

What is your present volume of sales?

"1968 sales were $336.9 million, including leased departments. Sales of owned departments came to $290.2 million."

Do you use computers?

"We have had computers for quite some time and we are just installing the new IBM 360, which will be delivered in the early fall. We are presently using an Indianapolis-Honeywell computer. We use the two-pass system and have been in it for the past two years. It works out fine. We use it on most of our style merchandise and soft goods. We don't use punched tickets."

What is your personnel setup?

"We have 37 buyers. Each division is headed by a merchandise manager who supervises the buyers. Then there are two general merchandise managers, one for soft goods and one for hard goods. Over them are other executives.

69

We have a vice president in charge of real estate, a treasurer, the executive vice president, a president, and the chairman of the board Herbert Palestine). He is good at anything and is the man who built the company. He now spends most of his time on fiscal policy as well as in the real estate area. Mr. Naylor, who served as president before me, and I, handle merchandising and store operations."

Who makes the decisions on locations?

"We have a real estate vice president, Leonard Cohen. He and Mr. Palestine make all the final real estate decisions."

Who owns the controlling stock?

"Mr. Palestine is the largest stockholder with about 10 per cent."

Do you have any stock-sharing with employees?

"The key executives participate in a stock-option plan."

How about unions, are your stores unionized?

"Some are and some are not."

How do you feel about the unions?

"Well, we have had no major union problems. What happens is that when we go into a city, each store becomes a separate entity. The union, of course, attempts to organize every store. The employees vote. In some stores the unions are successful and in some they are not. We never had a major strike in the company and no real trouble."

What are your employee benefits?

"We have a pension plan for all our employees which provides life insurance and retirement after 65 and it is wholly paid for by the company."

The only disadvantage of unions then is inflexibility?

"Where there are no unions, you can deal directly with the employee rather than going to a grievance committee. We find we can have a closer association with our employees without the unions."

How do you account for the phenomenal financial success of Arlan's?

"I think one of the greatest assets we had was that we were not conventional retailers who were going into discounting. Because we did not know retailing we did a lot of things that conventional retailers never would have dared to do. We used unconventional, unorthodox methods because we didn't know any better; they were successful. Frankly I think that, for everybody in this company, from the chairman on down, this was a brand new career. It was a brand new field for all of us and we learned from our mistakes in building what we felt was what the customers wanted. Our greatest advantage was that we didn't have to unlearn anything. Now we can't afford to make any mistakes, but we avoid them by experience. We are also big enough so we can afford a few mistakes. We have been in this business for over 19 years and we have learned a lot. Mr. Palestine believes in the importance of good organization and we have very little personnel turnover. A tremendous number of people have been with us almost from the beginning. They form the nucleus of the organization.

"There are many reasons for this. I think that we all recognize the future in the company. We have all been able to grow with the company. We have all done well and we feel a sense of pride, I suppose, in the company. We have all built something here and I think it is very unusual for a company to come from nowhere and become a national chain doing over $336 million in volume. We all worked and built this thing together. Mr. Palestine is certainly a remarkable man."

How far do you spread across the country?

"We have tried to stay in the northern tier of the country. We go as far west as Denver, and to Portland on the east coast. We go as far south as Louisville, Kentucky, and Roanoke, Virginia. However, in 1966 we opened two stores in North Carolina; one in Durham and one in Raleigh. Because we are centrally merchandised, we like to stay in one climatic belt."

How many employees do you have in an average store?

"We have about 100 employees. The key man is the store manager. The other employees we recruit locally, but we always send out an experienced store manager and assistant manager."

How about your buying policies, what agencies do you use?

"We don't use any buying offices, since we're right in New York."

Can you give me a few of the specialties?

"We have a buyer who buys nothing but ladies' skirts and ladies' co-ordinates; we have a ladies' sportswear buyer, a ladies' sweater buyer, and a specialist in bathing suits; we have a separate buyer for dresses and one for coats. When you get into hard lines you don't require as fine a break-down, because you are not buying as frequently. We have one buyer who buys all our toys, one who buys all our hardware, and another for house-wares. We have four different buyers in home furnishings. We run only four major appliance departments in Detroit, and we have a merchandise manager who works right out of the city for us to merchandise those four stores. We don't have furniture."

Are you finding it necessary to trade up?

"Definitely. We have been trading up substantially in the last few years, not only because the buyer today has become more affluent, but also because our buildings today are so much nicer that we can sell better goods. We have traded up buildings, fixturing, and our merchandise."

Is this going to mean a higher markup?

"No, because as the cost of doing business goes up, it affects the department stores even more than it affects us. Let us say that the department store's payroll averages 16 per cent, and an average payroll for a discounter is 8 per cent. If payroll goes up 10 per cent, ours goes up .8 per cent. But his goes up 1.6 per cent, so he is in more trouble than we are. If a department store carried an item at $1.98 and we sold it for $1, we now sell it for $2 but they have moved it up to $2.98. I don't think there is any danger of us becoming a department store."

71

Do you have acoustical ceilings?

"Yes, but we have not added on services, credit, or deliveries. We avoid them. Our major appliance department in Detroit is handled by an outside agency and we have nothing to do with it. If anything is to be sold on time we put it through a finance company and they handle it. The customer pays around a 6 per cent carrying charge."

Do you consolidate the work of your department managers so they may cover several departments?

"Yes, it depends on the size of the store and the volume. It can vary from three per store up to eight. One might handle all of ladies'; another girls'; another, would handle boys' and men's; another, home furnishings; one would handle cosmetics, records, candy, and stationery; another would be in housewares, gifts, and small appliances; and another would be in hardlines. We are able to use women very effectively in most of the softlines. The reason for this is that if you pay a man $125 a week, either he is very bright and you have got to move him up because you can't keep him very long as a department manager, or he isn't too bright and you don't want to keep him as a department manager. If you can get a very competent, capable woman, who you start paying over $100 a week, she will want to stay with you and can handle the job very well if she is a bright girl."

Do you get out in the field very often?

"I try to get out in the field every third week or so. I aim to visit every store at least once a year. I attend most openings and feel that it is very important that someone from the New York office be out in the stores to see what is going on."

What do you do when you go to these stores?

"The most important thing is to try to talk to the store people and try to get their ideas as to what has happened, and what the problems are, and also to see first hand what our merchandise people are doing, how the merchandise looks, how the stores look, and how we can improve them. Just as important is to constantly check the competition to see what they are doing in the field. You have to know what is going on so you can keep improving."

How about services?

"Until recently we had no services of any kind, but we have just opened our first auto service center."

What were some of the early problems that you had?

"In the early stages, the conventional retailers in town would try to tell the suppliers they could not sell to us, that they'd have to choose between them and us. There are still companies today who don't want their merchandise in discount stores. That is, they don't mind you having the merchandise, but they won't let you cut prices. We stay away from fair-traded items. We prefer items that we can sell at our own prices and in many cases we are even putting in our private brands."

What brands have you got of your own?

"We use the Arlan's name on many items, such as cosmetics, men's and boys' underwear and work clothes, sheets, pillow cases, and bedding items. We are going more and more into the Arlan's label. This is a way of getting good quality merchandise and avoiding fair trade. We are very particular about specifications on the quality of the items. We feel that if people are happy with the item they will come back to Arlan's to buy that item again."

In your pioneer days how did you establish a credit rating?

"We used the Monarch Clothing Company as credit so we had no real financial problem in getting merchandise. The problem when we first started was not in getting merchandise. There were many desirable locations that we wanted that we could not get because people would not build for us. We were not as strong financially as an A & P or Sears. Today we have no trouble. The banks were reluctant to go with us at first."

Have you ever had trouble getting into shopping centers?

"We have much greater acceptance in shopping centers today since many developers feel that a discounter is an asset because he brings in so much traffic."

Have you had any experiences where competition has come in where you just had to pull out?

"Well, we have had many competitors open against us, and every time a competitor opens, no matter how good or bad he is, he usually affects your volume. For the first year you drop some volume, but if you keep fighting, the population catches up. You keep improving and adding new departments and you can overcome this drop in volume.

"In only one instance did we ever close a store. One of our original stores, back in 1955, was in Lawrence. That store was a very peculiar three-story building and we were on the second and third floors. As soon as the competition began to open new buildings in the town it didn't make sense for us to stay there."

Coatsfield Shoppers World

Founded in 1952 by Edward Zwetchkenbaum in a Pawtucket, R.I., mill, Coatsfield Shoppers World is reputed to be the first of the discount-type stores to use shopping carts and the first to set up a row of checkout counters near the exit rather than to have department checkouts. In the pioneer Arlan store there were department checkout registers, and the merchandise was wrapped there as in a traditional department store. Another very impoitant innovation was the installation of a meat department. The butcher operation was subsidized by Zwetchkenbaum with the idea of building traffic for general merchandise.

Edward Zwetchkenbaum died in 1964, and now the New York Lace Store, Coatsfield Shoppers World, and the Warwick Shoppers' World are being operated by his son, Joseph Allen Zwetchkenbaum.

Ann and Hope Factory Outlet

INTERVIEW WITH MARTIN CHASE, FOUNDER OF ANN AND HOPE FACTORY OUTLET

One of the most dynamic and colorful pioneers of low-margin, self-service, cash-and-carry retailing was Marty Chase, who at the age of 20 became a store manager for Fintex, one of the originators of the one-price ($23.50) men's clothing store chains. The Providence Fintex store was discontinued in 1929, and Chase became store manager of a Howard Chase store in Providence. He later decided to go into business for himself. In 1938 he rented a first floor loft in a jewelry factory building on Eddy Street in South Providence. At that time "credit clothing" had just started. It allowed customers to buy with a small down payment and weekly installments. Since Chase could not afford to give credit, he decided to give such exceptional values to his customers that the average retail store would not be able to compete. His method was to run his business not on a percentage of total sales markup, but on a unit markup basis. If a suit cost him $15 he would take a markup of only $2.50 and sell it for $17.50. Expenses were cut to the bone. Merchandise was displayed on pipe racks and, in the beginning, not even alterations were given. Chase says, "I had to have salesmen and give service because I had to make sure my customer would pick a model and size that he could easily get altered. Otherwise it would cost him more to have the suit altered than he saved by buying from me. I called the place 'Marty's Clothing Mart.'

"At first the manufacturers were so dubious about this new kind of operation that they were afraid to sell to me. They said: 'You've got to go broke. How can you open a store in the outskirts of town in a manufacturing building and sell clothing?' Nevertheless I persevered, and the business turned out to be a tremendous success. My clothing mart was the forerunner of Robert Hall's. Between 1938 and 1944 I made more than $75,000 from this operation. In 1944, during the war, the clothing business declined because so many men were in the service and even young men were not

Martin Chase, discount store pioneer and founder,
the Ann and Hope Mill Supply Outlet,
Cumberland, R.I.

buying suits. I decided to close up and look for another business. I found a factory in Norwich, Conn., which made tinsel and corsage ribbons used by florists. I paid $75,000 in cash for it and ran the factory until 1953. I began to get tired of driving 55 miles between Providence and Norwich every day and decided to look for a factory in Providence. In 1945 I bought, for $307,000, the Ann and Hope Mill building located near Providence in Lonsdale. At 4 per cent interest, we paid $21,500 a year. The last payment was made in 1965. It was formerly the Lonsdale Textile Mills and had 550,000 square feet. We moved our ribbon manufacturing operation into Ann and Hope and it used 35,000 square feet. I rented the rest of the space to small manufacturers of various kinds. We spent about $25,000 in renovation and by the end of 1946, I had 34 tenants who employed about 1,800 people with a total payroll of around $6 million.

"In 1953 my brother and I decided to semi-retire and liquidate the ribbon business since we could not compete with a new synthetic ribbon. I wanted to find a business for my son."

Arlan's store in New Bedford was known to Marty. One day he said to

75

his friend, Bo Bernstein, "Bo, if they can do it, why can't I?" Bo said, "There is absolutely no reason why you can't do it. How many people are working in and around your place?" Marty said, "About 3,000." Bernstein continued, "Put the merchandise in but do absolutely no advertising whatsoever. Let the word seep out gradually but be God damn sure that you're letting people steal it!"

Marty says, "We had a lot of ribbon left over from our ribbon factory operation. Some of it was faded – some of it was good. I told my son that he should bring this ribbon to a room on the third floor of the mill and sell it to the tenants and their employees. About that time I had bought a defunct greeting card company, the National Printing Co. in Thompsonville and Rockville, Conn., one of the largest printing companies in the world. Since we were in the process of liquidating this company, I had about 100 million greeting cards which we put on sale with the ribbon. We were selling 10-cent rolls of ribbon for a quarter a dozen. Although people had to walk up two long flights to reach us (mill buildings have 18-foot ceilings), they were so excited with the buys that they asked, 'Can we bring our friends?' Some friends of mine manufactured ladies' cotton print housedresses in Fall River. When I told them what had happened, one said, 'I'll put in a hundred dozen dresses. If you don't sell them, we'll take them back.'

"We put in some plain pipe racks, filled them with $2.98 housedresses which we sold for $2.19. The customers grabbed them so fast that even the manufacturer was surprised. At the end of the month we had made $5,000. I said, 'This is terrific! Let's see if we can't find a space downstairs.' There was a room in the cellar, formerly used by a manufacturer of the kind of twine used in tying corned beef. It was filthy. When you make this twine, the lint goes all over; it looked like dirty snow and it was all over the ceiling and everywhere. I took my son there and said, 'This is where you are going to open your store.' He said, 'What, down here in the cellar! You're crazy!' Although people only had to walk down ten steps to get to it, it looked like a dungeon. I said, 'We'll paint this up and it will look terrific. We'll put in lights and a new floor. I'm going to Florida for three weeks. You go ahead and get this done.'

"When I got back nothing had been done so I had it cleaned up and painted. There was a space of about 30,000 square feet, and we put approximately $10,000 worth of goods into the whole business. A plastic garment bag manufacturer in our building gave us a load of seconds which we sold at a ridiculous price. We had no help at all. I brought in my bookkeeper, who handled the building accounts for me, and put her desk near the entrance. If people came we let them roam around, and when they were through, she would go over and take the money. We had no cash register, but used a cash box and a spindle. We wrote the items down on some old manufacturing billheads, added the prices up, and put the paper on a spindle. We added a little men's and boys' wear, some women's wear, and odds and ends. We opened up April 1, 1954, and the first week we did $1,100 which I thought was very good. The second week we did $1,300; the third, $1,500; the fourth, $1,700; and the fifth, $1,900. The sixth week was Mother's Day week and it was our big week. We did $3,450.

"I'll never forget that Sunday. I was sitting at my desk and my son said to me, 'Dad, do you think we will ever do $3,450 again?' I said, 'Look, some day you'll do a million dollars a year, if you stick by our policy to sell everything less than our competitors. Buy at as low a price as you can, but always put only a 20 per cent markup on it because absolutely nobody can compete with you at 20 per cent. You have no overhead here and you can make a lot of money.' The thing spread so fast that before 1954 was over, we had $2 million in sales. We needed more space, so I started to put my tenants out and even paid them to move elsewhere. Today we occupy 475,000 square feet. We constantly added merchandise including domestics, hardware, automotive supplies, jewelry, toys, housewares, etc."

Ann and Hope established a food market in their store in 1959 with the idea of making it a one-stop shopping center. Food has always been considered a number one traffic builder in such a center. Chase says: "A good discount store generates large traffic into its food department, just as much as the food department generates traffic into the general merchandise departments. We would no more think of our stores without dresses than we would think of them without food. However, the food department must be a true discount food market and not merely a transplant of a conventional branch of a supermarket chain. You must show your customer that he

Ann and Hope, architect's design, Warwick, R.I.

will save by buying food regularly at your store. We first thought that we must locate the food market within our store so that food shoppers used the same checkouts as the non-food shoppers. Our thinking has since changed since customers did not want to put meat on top of a $40 dress or coat. Today, at our Cumberland store, the food market is in the same building, but there is no connection between the food and the non-food departments. Both have completely separate checkouts. This is the case in our recent 140,000 square foot Warwick, R.I., store[1] where we hold their food carriages for them in the lobby while they shop the general merchandise side of the store. In Warwick we have a corridor fifty feet wide and seventy-five feet long to separate the food market and the general merchandise departments. The partitions are glass to make the customer feel that he is in the same store. Further, the food division has its own entrance from the parking lot."

When the same checkout counters are used for both food and general merchandise, a considerable slowdown in the overall checking-out process results, especially during heavy food shopping hours. A large quantity of small items of food amounting to $30 obviously takes considerably longer to check out than a $30 coat. The customer buying only the coat becomes impatient waiting behind the food customer and sometimes objects out loud. On the other hand, customers who are checking out with food seem to be conditioned to waiting patiently while the preceding customer's food orders are being processed. It was also found that many customers who buy general merchandise during the same shopping trip usually prefer to shop for the general merchandise first, place it in their cars, and then buy food and perishables.

When Marty Chase was operating his own food department his main idea was to bring the customer in whether he made money or not. He says, "When we opened our Warwick store we decided to let the real experts go in if we could make a deal with them to operate the way we wanted them to. We picked Sidney Rabb of Stop & Shop over three of the largest food chains in the country. The first year we opened we did over $5 million in that one store. Everything must be discounted. Our man goes through the store twice a week; if he sees anything that is not discounted, they pull it off the shelves or mark it down."

The only other leased department in the two Chase stores is shoes, and that is operated by his brother-in-law, Sidney Flanzbaum, who formerly ran "John the Shoeman" and various other shoe stores which he sold out to the Butler Shoe Company of Atlanta. He is now president of the Butler division which leases shoe departments. Regarding lessees Marty says, "I don't believe in leased departments as a way of doing business. We much prefer to operate all our own departments since we feel we can give better values and maintain our image by running our own departments."

[1] Built in 1962 on 24 acres of land at a cost of about $1,800,000.

The Pioneers

The image projected by Ann and Hope is that of a store in which the average or less-than-average income person or family can save money and at the same time get good quality. Store fixtures are plain but functionally adequate; fancy decor is absent but the fluorescent lighting is excellent. Merchandise of every variety is piled high, most departments stock impressive assortments and depth. There are occasional "loss leaders," such as Prestone antifreeze which is sometimes sold below cost. On this point, Marty says, "It doesn't mean much even if we sell below cost – take ten cars of Prestone; say there's 6 gallons to a case and 600 cases to a car; ten cars would be 36,000 gallons. Including the cost of delivery, it may cost $1.52 and you sell it for $1.49. You lose 3 cents. Now 36,000 times 3 cents is $1,080 – not even the cost of a page of advertising in our local paper. If such a sale is going to bring the customers in, it's cheap advertising. I do not regard it as 'bait,' because we discount everything we sell."

Ann and Hope is one of the few stores of its type to operate a pharmacy where prescriptions can be made up. Asked why he wanted a pharmacy, Marty said, "It is common knowledge that the prices for prescription drugs are very high. I felt that I could apply my low-margin merchandising theory to prescription drugs and still make a profit. I knew there would be a great market for prescriptions at a discount, especially among less affluent people, old people on pensions, and the chronically ill. The dispensing of prescriptions is a highly professional undertaking and we hire only the best professional pharmacists at the current wage scale or higher. We do an exceedingly large prescription business at big discounts and we make a fair profit. At the same time we feel we are giving a real service to the community by lowering the cost of prescriptions to customers who can least afford them. We run our pharmacies on the highest ethical level."

Martin Chase, like any good discounter, has always been actively opposed to fair trade and has even taken a case to the Supreme Court of Rhode Island in an effort to prove that it was unconstitutional. Asked how this came about, he said, "It involved the Timex watch which we've been buying direct and selling for the last eight or nine years. Suddenly the manufacturer decided that we would have to maintain the price. He said, 'You sell it at the fair trade price or you won't get it.' We were selling it at 25 per cent to 30 per cent off the list price.

"In another case, we bought an automotive additive from one of the largest manufacturers in the country. His regular distributor sold it to us for 45 cents, and we sold it for 65 cents while the fair trade price was $1.25. We thought that we were doing O.K. when we marked it more than we normally do, because we knew if we marked it for less, they would jump on us. They took us to court on that. We happened to win the case because we proved that they had not enforced their fair trade price fairly and properly. At the $1.25 price, the average merchant is going to push that item. Under competition, both the manufacturer and the distributor make their fair profit even if the retailer sells at 65 cents. They keep the price at $1.25. Is that fair trade? Is that quality stabilization? There are 27 or 28 states that don't have fair trade which, in my opinion, is no more than a price-fixing proposition. The manufacturer is merely guaranteeing a high profit to the retailer so that his product will be pushed by the retailer at the expense of the customer."

Many operators of low-margin stores feel that in hiring buyers, the best prospects are individuals who have not worked in a "traditional" store but who have bought merchandise for other low-margin operators. On this point Chase says: "Conventional operators have maybe four or five buyers, each buying different items for a single department. We wanted a buyer who knew his entire buying department; the men's buyer should know all of the men's and boys' departments; a women's buyer should know all of the women's department; a dress buyer should know all dresses and coats. We look for buyers who are not order-takers; who don't just go to a vendor and say 'give me so many sizes of this.' We want individuals with initiative. Our store manager, assistant managers, department heads and other middle management people have been developed from our ranks. We strive to attract people who have potential for growth and who can absorb training. Our policy is to promote from within wherever possible.

"Each Monday night, when they leave for the market, our buyers know everything they sold the past week in fashion merchandise; every item, every size, every dress. We have a double-ticket system, and these tickets are collected every morning and sorted out. They're coded and taken off every day by the checkout girls. The next day they're sorted and re-coded. We know every size that's sold of this particular dress, or that particular coat or children's item. We also know the amount of cash taken in each day in each department from the departmental keys in our registers."

Asked whether inventory control presented a problem, Marty said, "Our biggest problem is that we run out of merchandise (especially hardgoods) so fast, that no matter how much or how fast we buy it we still run out. Control is not easy with tools, hardware, sporting goods, and merchandise of that sort. We work on the basis that whatever's on the floor is sold. We don't count whatever we have in our Warwick warehouse. Our warehoused goods are hand inventoried on a regular basis so our buyers get enough information. They must go to Warwick at least once or twice a week and check their stock by actually seeing what's there. With fashion items, they know from our ticket stubs what each store sells before they go to New York each week. We are associated with three buying offices, including Biddle, and we also deal with specialized buying offices in wearing apparel, hardware, and automotive goods. However, we depend primarily on our own buyers."

In regard to employee incentives, Chase says, "We have a profit-sharing plan based on a percentage of our profits that is put into the fund. This plan is for everybody who works here. The actual dollars put into each employee's account depends on the amount of money he earns. If he makes $5,000, it may amount to 10 per cent of his salary or $500. The plan is ten years old now, and there is over $1 million in the fund since it accumulates. You have to be in the plan a minimum number of years to get 100 per cent when you leave. If you leave before this minimum time, you get a stated percentage of your interest in the fund according to a formula."

In their relations with the community, Ann and Hope management has an excellent record. It contributes liberally to all the large organized charities, to local drives, churches, and service organizations. Marty says, "My religion is to give. I feel that whatever you give is in some way eventually returned to you. We believe in helping people who need help and often anonymously cooperate with local police and service organizations to help individuals who are in serious trouble."

A universal problem with all low-margin, self-service retailers is shoplifting. Chase has had his share and says, "The law in Rhode Island is so lax that even if we prosecuted every case, as we do, it is hard to stop shoplifting. We have quite a few male and female detectives in both stores and in the course of a year we catch about two a week. Some weeks we get ten. We catch between 125 to 200 in each store per year. We once caught three professionals from New Jersey. The judge fined them $5 plus costs and told them not to come back to Rhode Island. If we are going to cure shoplifting, we must make our laws stronger. The kids in school talk about it; you're 'chicken' if you don't shoplift."

In general, both Ann and Hope and Warwick stores operate on a cash-and-carry basis. However, a customer can buy $100 worth of goods and pay $5 down to finance it. He has five months to pay it off. Comments Chase, "We made a deal with a finance company for a 5 per cent addon. The customer would pay $21 for five months consisting of $20 on the principle and $1 interest. That is extremely low. If he wanted ten months, he'd pay an $8\frac{1}{2}$ per cent addon which is 85 cents a month. We can't go into credit unless we charge for it. Credit costs a lot of money, more than we make in our net markup, so we must sell goods strictly on a cash basis. On the deal with the finance company, we get the money the next day. Their charge is nothing compared to what I'd have to charge if we handled the credit ourselves. If a man goes into a conventional store and pays cash, he subsidizes those who pay on credit."

Asked whether he would be interested in hiring college graduates, Marty said, "We certainly are interested in those who have dedicated themselves to retailing as a career. They have to be willing to start at the bottom to learn this business. They have got to love the business and sacrifice all the time and effort necessary to learn it. A boy with education can simply learn that much faster if he puts his mind to it and if he really wants to do it."

81

Kermell Bargain Center
A Pioneer Discounter

INTERVIEW WITH SELWYN LEMCHEN, FOUNDER OF KER-
MELL BARGAIN CENTER AND GENERAL MERCHANDISE
MANAGER, TOPPS DEPARTMENT STORES

How long have you been in retailing?

"I went to Memorial High School in Boston and to Boston University for two years. After coming out of the service in 1941 I went into the shoe business with my father who ran the shoe concession in the Enterprise specialty chain store. I was with Enterprise until 1955 and eventually I merchandised the ladies' sportwear and girls' departments."

What started you off in discounting?

"There was considerable talk at the time Marty Chase opened his store in Lonsdale. Everyone was talking about it and even the people at Enterprise decided it was something we should see. When I went out to see Marty's store it was very busy with a lot of traffic. Yet it was probably the worst location that anyone could pick for a retail store. His merchandise was probably as bad as I could find in any retail store. The people were buying it because it was priced very low. The things that were not bad merchandise still sold at good prices. I felt that if someone knew this business and had courage enough to open a mill that looked like this and kept expenses down to a minimum, he could really do a good job. Then I went looking on my own time for a mill to open up in. I found one in Fall River, rented it, resigned my job, and that was really the start. I think that Marty's started it all. I went down to Marty's several times and became friendly with him."

Did he tell you where to buy your merchandise?

"No, he didn't. He asked me where to buy his merchandise because I was the pro, not him. In fact, he wanted to hire me, but he told me he couldn't afford me at the time and I doubt if he could have. So the seed was really planted by Marty's operation. I opened my own store in Fall River in April, 1955."

What was your store called?

"Kermell Bargain Center. It was a 45,000-foot store on the outskirts of Fall River. We operated everything ourselves except shoes. This included jewelry, appliances, paints and wall paper, drugs, toys, and sporting goods. We didn't have millinery and hardware."

How did you capitalize the business?

"It was probably the most under-capitalized business in the entire retail history. I had an original capitalization of $30,000, and did $3 million the first year, including concessions. I had accumulated quite a bit of money while with Enterprise. Since I received a good salary, I had saved this $30,000."

Did you then think of expanding or going public?

"No, in those days you didn't think of going public. It was a long time before anyone thought of going public in the discount business."

You must have had all the trials and tribulations of fair trade as well as the animosity of local merchants.

"I was then probably as unpopular as any merchant could have been. There was tremendous pressure, especially in the drug field, to get fair trade enforced against us. We fought it to the hilt and settled it on the courthouse steps. We were able to maintain our low markup in many cases, even though there were all kinds of law suits. Of course we realized they didn't mean anything. Gillette sued me for $100,000 damages but it didn't worry me because Gillette couldn't prove it anyway. I wasn't too concerned. Dun and Bradstreet used to get concerned but it never bothered us much. We didn't particularly care about Dun and Bradstreet ratings since we were paying our bills."

You had 60 days to pay, didn't you?

"No. We were operating on normal 30-day terms. In the early days of discounting it was unbelievable the way we turned our stocks."

What happened after the first year?

"I opened a second store in Lancaster, Pa., in 1956. It was an old skating rink in the middle of a park and had a lot of parking space, but it wasn't paved. It was on the grass, but the people didn't seem to mind. This store had only 20,000 feet and we did about $1.3 million the second year we were in business. Then I opened a soft goods concession in a successful retail shoe operation in Holmesdale, Pa. There was a man up there who had a shoe factory and he used this Holmesdale outlet to dispose of returned shoes. He sold them at excellent values to the consumer. This store ran at an amazing rate for a town of only 6,000 people. We were doing close to $1 million a year between shoes and softgoods. The place probably had no more than 15,000 or 16,000 feet. We did more business in August than in December because it was a resort area and the population jumped to 60,000 in the summer.

"Around the same time, in 1957, I also opened a store in another old factory building in Chester, Pa., in an area of about 18,000 feet. Our annual sales were about $1 million."

How many stores did you have when you decided to give up your own operation?

"I owned four stores at this stage of the game: Kermell in Fall River, Maple Grove Bargain Center in Lancaster, Shoppers World in Chester, and Husco Factory Outlet in Holmesdale. Three were my own stores and in the fourth I was a concessionaire.

"At some point I got into the Topps thing with Frank Beckerman and Ted Schwartz. Mr. Beckerman and I were old friends and we were buyers together in Enterprise many years ago. Frank and Ted Schwartz were operating two Topps stores and wanted to expand. I became a financial partner with them but continued to run my own stores separately. In addition to being treasurer of Topps, I merchandised their ladies' and children's wear; Mr. Beckerman merchandised the men's and boys' wear. In 1960 we sold Topps to Interstate. We came along with the sale. Mr. Beckerman resigned after finishing his contract and he is now very active in real estate."

How is Interstate organized?

"It's a public company listed on the New York Exchange and Robert Riesner is president. They were primarily department store operators but were experimenting with four discount stores of their own when they took us over. When we joined Interstate we took over the management of all their discount stores. They bought us because they wanted our knowledge and organization."

How many stores did you have when they bought you?

"Together we sold them ten stores. I only sold them two of my stores, Lancaster and Fall River. The other two I disposed of elsewhere a year later. The one in Holmesdale is still in business.

"In the early days of this business everyone knew each other and we were good friends and helped each other. Ollie (Aaron) Cohen opened up his store in Brockton the week after I opened mine. He came down and helped me with my opening and I helped him with his. Even people like Zayre's came to visit our stores and we showed them what we were doing. We kept no secrets because in those days we didn't foresee that we would eventually be giants competing with each other. We were thinking in terms of one store in one town."

Which of the Feldbergs came?

"The young boys, Stanley and Sumner, came. When I first started I was in the same office with Murray Candib and Ollie Cohen. Stanley is now president of Zayre Inc., and Sumner is Treasurer."

How many stores does Interstate now have?

"There are 21 White Front Stores on the West Coast between the Los Angeles and San Francisco areas; we have 43 Topps stores; and 34 conventional department stores."[1]

What percentage of your volume is generated by the discount division?

"About 80 per cent."

Do you warehouse at all?

"We distribute through a central distribution point ready-to-wear and some sportswear. We have our own warehouses. Right now we are exploring and studying extensively the advantages of central distribution. We may

[1]At the end of 1968, the firm operated 94 discount stores and 31 conventional stores. In November, 1966, the company acquired Children's Supermart chain, Washington, D.C. and the seven-store Children's Bargain-Town chain in March, 1969.

have to have regional warehouses because we're spread around. Now we do warehouse on the West Coast, but our business there is a little different. Out there we are probably the number one sellers of brand appliances in the entire country. We warehouse these appliances and ship from a central warehouse."

Do you have any preference as to free-standing locations or shopping centers?

"We find both good."

Do you have a real estate department?

"Yes. We decide where we want to go and then seek out locations. Brokers seek out the locations and it is then cleared with our real estate department."

Do you have a research department?

"No. We use outside people for the research I mentioned before."

Do you think it would be a good idea to start a research department?

"It's a point, but we haven't gotten to that stage yet. The only research we do is in testing the quality of goods. We do that in conjunction with the testing labs and have somebody here who is responsible for it."

Do you have a training program?

"We have a manager training program."

Are you interested in college graduates?

"Yes, of course. We start trainees either in a receiving room or a department, and then move them around from one department to another so that they get acquainted with the entire store. A good man who is alert, wants to learn, and is willing to work can become a manager in three years. Store managers in the biggest stores can earn as much as $40,000."

Where did you buy in these early days?

"Our original buying office was Jack Hartblay. His office has been recently taken over by King's and it is now their exclusive office. He was one of the first buying offices to go after servicing discounters. I was one of his first customers with Harry Garf from Worcester, who was also one of the pioneers. Harry had a discount store in Worcester (United Factory Outlet) before I had mine in Fall River."

How do you feel about the trend in trading up?

"Well, we're going through the most affluent times that this country has seen and you must keep pace with the consumer. The consumer wants better goods today, and she wants to buy them in better surroundings. You must trade up to take advantage of today's customers. They have more dollars to spend than they ever had before. They have great security. They are not worried about their jobs so they are spending their money."

Max Coffman, Founder of Mammoth Mart, Inc.

In a sense, the story of Max Coffman might be considered old-fashioned – something in the mold of the old Horatio Alger stories. And in that sense the label is accurate. Max Coffman has spent his entire life in retailing, starting with after-school jobs while he was still a young boy obtaining an education. However, his story is also a modern story in that the results of his achievements reflect the accumulation and application of modern merchandising techniques acquired over the years.

The roster of Max Coffman's early employers runs the gamut from small, conventional junior department stores through the predecessors of today's supermarkets, through conventional types of individually-owned retail stores. His first association was with the Enterprise chain of junior department stores in 1929. He stayed four years with the Enterprise chain and became a store manager. His next employment was with a company which became the Food Fair chain, a pioneer in the concept of consumer self-service. He stayed with this organization for three years, specializing in merchandising and operations. He then joined the Stop & Shop chain, specializing in new store locations.

As with many another young man with entrepreneural instincts, he decided to go into business for himself. By 1941, with a capital of about $1,000, he opened up an army and navy store in Quincy, Mass., near the Bethlehem Steel shipyards. Since there was no Government surplus merchandise available then, he carried work clothes, caps, overalls, and some workmen's footwear. As Government surplus clothing became available the opportunities for this type of merchandise appeared more attractive, and by 1948, Coffman was operating six stores in the Boston area.

In his merchandising career, Max Coffman had been exposed to the entire range of retail operations, from site selection, new store openings, operations, and merchandising. He had seen the virtue of mass distribution, including the attractiveness of operating high-volume, low-margin types of business. As he operated his more or less conventional retail stores in the Boston area, the urge to embark on the high-volume sale of soft goods in a self-service type of operation became more and more compelling.

In 1956 Max Coffman made his move. He leased an old foundry building in Framingham, Mass., at a nominal rate (50 cents a square foot for about 51,000 square feet) and prepared for business. He black-topped the parking lot, built a ramp through the old receiving door so that it became an entrance for customers, had a local carpenter put together tables and checkout counters, and bought some secondhand cash registers and shopping carts.

86

Max Coffman, pioneer discounter and founder,
Mammoth Mart, Inc.

His total available capital at that time was about $20,000. With it he bought all the goods he possibly could. Initially he operated the men's and women's clothing and sporting goods departments, and leased out shoes, hard lines, domestics, and cosmetics.

This first Mammoth Mart Discount Store was opened in March, 1956, in a very heavy snowfall. As a matter of fact, even the large searchlights were buried by the storm. Nevertheless, the buying public came to the store opening and a new era was born for Max Coffman and Mammoth Mart.

The basic lessons learned in that first forerunner of today's discount department store enabled Max Coffman to open a second unit. The army and navy stores were closed up (the return on capital in discount department stores was so much greater than that in the retail stores), and Mammoth Mart began its campaign of opening new stores. Today Max Coffman looks back on those early years with nostalgia and affection. He remembers that

87

many of the people with whom he was associated in those early years are still associated with Mammoth Mart; and Max Coffman particularly emphasizes people. For example, his first lessee in domestics is still with Mammoth Mart. Max Coffman now says that while Mammoth Mart never made much money on lessees, they were invaluable to the company in that they provided what was needed to make a total store. (At the very least, they contributed to overhead.)

In 1969 Mammoth Mart is a 27-unit chain, recognized as one of the fastest growing discount department store chains in its operating area. However, the chain's initial growth was rather carefully contained. Coffman recognized the dangers of over-expanding, or moving too rapidly, and as he says, "I wanted to get a good solid foundation established first." From its first unit in 1956, it took three years for a second unit to be established in Bangor, Me. The third unit, in Lewiston, Me., joined a year later; in 1961 two units were opened; in 1962, two more; in 1963 three units were opened; one was opened in 1964; two in 1965, and in 1966 six units were opened. One of these six was a replacement for the first Framingham unit which had been opened in an old foundry.

The record of growth reflects considerable attention to detail. Basically, Mammoth Mart has refrained from opening warehouses. As a result, all of its merchandising is drop-shipped to each store, and this policy was made possible by planning each additional unit within a radius of approximately 50 miles from another Mammoth Mart store. Today, with 27 units in operation, the firm will have added seven new units to the chain, bringing the total to 34 stores. Three are located in North Carolina; one in Maryland; two in Maine and one in Vermont.

Mammoth Mart has always felt that the needs of its customers must be recognized and met. Therefore, despite an initial inclination not to carry fair-traded items, a variety of fair-traded merchandise is handled by Mammoth Mart today. However, as much as is possible, the chain attempts to limit such items to 5 per cent of any one particular department. One of the chain's greatest successes has been in shoes. Because of the availability of outstanding talent in shoe buying and merchandising, Mammoth Mart is one of the few chains that runs its own shoe department. Like other merchandise, shoes are drop-shipped to each of the Mammoth Mart stores. The chain started out as a soft goods purveyor and today soft goods are still the most important items in the store. While Mammoth Mart does not carry a full line of major appliances, it does carry television, small home appliances and cameras.

Another area of close corporate control relates to new locations. Mammoth Mart runs its own real estate department and is constantly on the lookout for new, attractive locations. Generally sites are brought to the chairman's attention by real estate developers. With the exception of the

88

An early Mammoth Mart in Lewiston, Maine.

Bangor unit, all of the stores are in shopping center complexes. In terms of the future, Mammoth Mart sees no difficulty in expanding, believing that good merchandising centers are an ever-present need as the economy of the country develops. Mammoth Mart stores range in size from 42,000 feet to the 88,000 square-foot Brockton store; the largest does well over $4 million annually, and on the average each store does about $2.5 million.

The Mammoth units have in common an attractive appearance. All stores are meticulously planned with acoustical ceilings, air conditioning, excellent lighting, attractive tile floors, and convenient, good-looking fixtures. They are, in fact, designed for the customer's convenience. For example, rest room facilities are provided in the front of the store, an aspect frequently and gratefully noted by the customers.

From an operating standpoint, some consistent policies have aided each unit to become well-established in its operating area. For example, store managers are very important. They are considered "key" personnel and they

89

contribute regularly in merchandise selection and in other areas of store operation. Buying for all stores is centralized in Brockton. This provides substantial purchasing economies and enables the chain to control inventories quite effectively. Mammoth Mart has recently taken over operation of jewelry departments which were previously leased, and all leased departments now contribute less than 20 per cent to over-all volume. There is a basic policy of promoting from within; all regional supervisors have come up through the ranks. In some cases Mammoth Mart has its own branded items. In nylon stockings, for example, Princess Anne is the private label. More and more fashion merchandise has been emphasized. The chain carries some of the finest labels in men's casual clothing; shoes have become a fashion item.

From a financial standpoint, the firm's future looks good. Record earnings were realized in fiscal 1968. For the year ending February 1, 1969, total sales were $66.9 million, compared with $53.1 million for the previous year. Net earnings for fiscal 1968 were $1.9 million as opposed to $1.5 million for the previous year. In addition, Mammoth's board of directors voted in April, 1969 to split the firm's stock two-for-one.

Alden's Shoppers World
A subsidiary of Gamble-Skogmo, Inc.

(THE FOLLOWING INFORMATION WAS OBTAINED FROM ALVIN D. STAR WHEN THE AUTHOR VISITED HIM IN HIS OFFICE AT THE UNIVERSITY OF CHICAGO.)

The original Shoppers World was started in Chicago in March, 1956. It was the first discount store in that city and was opened by two young men, Alvin D. Star and Jerome Spier. Both had gained several years of experience as buyers for William Filene's Specialty store in Boston. After expanding to six stores they sold out to Alden's, a Chicago mail order house. The chain is now known as Alden's Shoppers World and in 1965 it took in sales of $45 million.

Alvin Star graduated from Harvard College in 1949. He went into Filene's as a trainee, becoming an assistant buyer and then a buyer of linens and domestics. His friend Jerome Spier was a sportswear buyer at Filene's. Their first idea was to start a chain of specialty stores selling ladies' sportswear. In July, 1955, however, they visited Ann and Hope Factory Outlet in Cumberland, Rhode Island and decided to change their plans. Star describes his visit:

"Filene's was closed, it being the Fourth of July holiday, and it was very, very hot. Jerry and I drove to Cumberland and here was this mill with no air conditioning but jampacked with people. Somehow it had a tremendous attraction. People were buying soft goods like mad at checkout counters. We were just amazed! We looked at each other, and both of us knew right then and there that this was the kind of operation we wanted. It appealed to us on economic grounds since here was a way to lower the costs of distribution by eliminating sales people and cutting overhead. Certainly this new approach had fantastic popular appeal. We talked about it on the way back and were very excited. We immediately drew up profit and loss statements and tried to figure out how much capital we would need. We then started to look around Boston for a location. At the time we were convinced that we had to have an old mill since this seemed almost the essence of the operation. All those we found had rotting floors and ceilings.

"We got some money together from our families and friends—we borrowed from all over. Just about that time my brother came in from Chicago where we had a small family clothing store. I talked to him about Ann and Hope, and we took a trip down to see it. My brother was at once convinced that this would be an excellent operation. Although Jerry and I had already started negotiations with some Boston landlords, we finally agreed that if we could find a good location in Chicago, we would go there. My brother was convinced that Chicago would be economically better than Boston. By October 1, 1955 we found a location at Milwaukee, Foster and Central Avenues in Chicago. It was to become our first store. The building was only partially finished with three walls and a roof, but no store front. The landlord was persuaded to put up $25,000, and Jerry, my brother, and I put up an additional $25,000. We resigned from Filene's effective January 1, 1956, and during that month we went to New York to buy our initial stock. We were able to get credit through various agencies.

"Our store fixtures were minimal, consisting largely of tables and cash registers. Our initial stock was delivered in February, and it arrived when the building was still uncompleted. It was a big mess but we managed to mark the merchandise in time for our opening on March 8, 1956—almost nine months after our visit to Ann and Hope, about the time it takes to have a baby! We ran an opening-day promotion in city newspapers. Sales were far beyond our expectations. Although we only had 12,000 square feet, we had phenomenal sales per square foot and did almost a million dollars in sales the first year. We had some problems with the landlord, who was our partner, but through our options we were able to buy him out.

"We started off without any leased departments. In several departments, including hardware, we used jobbers who set us up with complete lines of merchandise. Our strength, however, was in soft lines where Jerry had experience. My brother bought the ladies' and men's wear, and I became the children's wear buyer, although I had had no experience in this field. We all enlarged our knowledge of merchandising very quickly. Our inexperience in many product lines did not seem to hurt us at that point because the operation was immediately successful. We had a rule that limited markup to 25 per cent with very rare exceptions. As the first store of this type in Chicago, we had the same sort of experience as Marty Chase had when he started. Later it was necessary to get professional buyers for each department. At first, inventory control was no problem since we turned our stocks so fast; we were usually short of stock. Our vendors capitalized our business for us in those days. Perhaps our undercapitalization was a blessing in disguise! We were constantly underestimating our ability to sell merchandise. We sold only traffic appliances and all sales were strictly cash. At the start we didn't even have shoes; later we brought in a leased shoe department, our only leased department. At first the lessee was a local store operator, but he could not adjust to discounting. When we had several stores, we leased shoe departments to Morse and later on to Miles.

"The first year of operation we worked extremely long hours to keep costs down. We worked seven days a week and fourteen hours a day. The store was open twelve hours a day, and we arrived an hour early to straighten out the stock. When one of us went to New York, the other had to be at the store for thirteen hours plus whatever time it took to close up the place and set the burglar alarm. Hiring cash register operators and stock clerks was not difficult, since, during the early years of the war, we were in a recession, jobs were scarce and there were always a large number of housewives who were willing to work part-time hours convenient to us. In fact we were able to get some very high caliber personnel in this way. For evening work it was possible, under proper supervision, to utilize high school girls and boys. A strong store manager could get a lot of work out of these people, whereas with a weak store manager, they soon got out of control.

"Getting good store managers or buyers was extremely difficult. As a price-cutter or discounter, we were granted a very low status on the retail ladder. Anybody working with an established store, or even without a job, wanted to go into another established store. They were fully convinced that if they worked for a discounter their future career would be contaminated for ever after. This made it very difficult to recruit people with retailing experience and was a constant harrassment during the first few years of operation. Although we did get some good people, the problem was never solved satisfactorily. We would have interview after interview with people from retailing backgrounds, and then they would go elsewhere even though they earned less pay.

The Pioneers

"We had no problems getting the Chicago newspapers to take our advertisements. Frankly, in the beginning things were so hectic that we almost felt that we did not have to do any advertising. It was hard for us to tell what we would have in stock and almost impossible to plan item advertising. We did much better by using institutional advertisements stressing our large assortments and pricing. At the end of the seasons we always used institutional clearance ads rather than resorting to long lists of clearance items. In those days we also used radio a lot. We did not use circulars. In the first years of this store we drew customers from very long distances. It was nothing to find checks from suburbs such as Arlington Heights, fifteen miles away.

"Fair trade was somewhat of a headache, and we had several harrassment lawsuits. It was customary for discounters in those early days to bootleg branded merchandise, and we did much of that. We had very carefully chosen an innocuous corporate name, Gateway Corporation, which did not give the connotation of a discount operation. Vendors gave us merchandise not suspecting that we were discounters. They only found out when our competitors screamed in anguish! In the early days we bootlegged through certain independent retailers who were not in direct competition with us and who were not interested in saving the price reputation of other established retailers who were in competition with us. We paid them the usual fee of 10 per cent. Many retailers were very happy to make a 10 per cent profit on open branded lines for very little effort. The merchandise came from their overstocks. In some cases, we had them buy merchandise for us after selecting styles, sizes and colors for them.

"When we bootlegged, we went to the best brands: Playtex bras and girdles, Maidenform bras and Oshkosh work clothes. We did very well with these lines. We sold enormous quantities of bootlegged toys like most discounters did in those early days. Anything sold through a wholesaler was very difficult for a manufacturer to control, and in most cases the manufacturers did not want to know about it. However, in areas where there was direct selling from the manufacturer to the retailer, the retailer usually wanted to protect his franchise.

"In the early days we relied on wholesalers a good deal more than we did later on. Our second store had a second floor which we had to take with the store and a basement. We used both the basement and the first floor for selling and converted the second floor into offices. We also had space for a small warehouse which enabled us to buy certain merchandise in minimum trade shipment lots which were too large for one store, but which could be divided between two stores. We tried to minimize shipment from one store to another because it was costly. We did not use central warehousing but tried to make each store big enough to handle direct shipments. At times this was feasible. Then there were times when we wished that we had a warehouse for certain lines. In toys and drugs we were limited by warehousing,

93

so we had to work closely with wholesalers on limited amounts. In the drug field some wholesalers would not sell to us because it impaired their relationship with the independent druggists, their primary customers. Nevertheless, there were always some who would sell to us so we did not have much difficulty getting merchandise.

"We opened up a second store in 1956 on the West Side in Cicero, a suburb. In 1958 we opened a store in Melrose Park, a far west suburb, the first specifically built for us. The following year we took over a former farmer's market in Highland, Indiana, south of Hammond. This was our first large-scale venture. We remodeled the entire store which had close to 60,000 square feet. This was an extremely profitable store. In 1960 we opened two more stores, one in the northwest area of the city and one in the southwest. Although we were making a good deal of money, it simply was not enough for expanding the business. When the second and third stores were opened, we sold stock to friends, relatives, and suppliers. It became increasingly difficult to keep our various interests straight. We had a separate corporation for each store plus an overall management corporation called Shoppers World Company. Finally, in 1959 we merged all the corporations. Actually the merger was a recapitalization and a simplification of our capital structure so that ownership was in one shell.

"In 1961, when we had six stores, Alden's became interested in our operation and we decided to merge with them on an exchange of stock basis. For the three of us who had founded the company it was quite profitable. In my case it financed my studies at the University of Chicago for a Ph.D. degree, making it possible for me to teach, something I have always wanted to do."

Yankee Stores

INTERVIEW WITH JOSEPH MEGDELL, PRESIDENT OF YANKEE STORES, INC., FLINT, MICHIGAN

What has been your experience in retailing?

" I was a shoe salesman in Detroit from 1935 to 1943. From 1943 to 1946, I was in the Army where I attained the high rank of Private First Class in the 85th Division. I saw action in the Infantry in Italy during that period."

When did you open your first store?

"My present associate, Wilbert Roberts, and I opened our first store in Flint, Michigan on April 1, 1948. It was opened as a surplus store under the name U.S. Surplus Sales. The store was only 20 by 100 feet in size and was located in an old building on the fringe of the downtown area. Our inventory consisted of 99 per cent Army surplus gadgets. The only non-surplus items we carried were men's socks and Cannon towels and wash cloths. If I remember correctly, we started with 100 dozen of each of these items."

How much capital did you have?

"Our capital was meager. We started with approximately $6,000 borrowed from relatives. It seems that many discounters claim to be the first in the field of discounting and mass merchandising. I am not certain whether we were first, but I definitely know that we were among the earliest. Because our financial position would not permit the hiring of sales personnel, we mass-displayed our inventory on tables that we built ourselves and we operated on a self-service basis. Customers paid for their purchases at the front checkout register. Because practically everything we sold was Army surplus, we immediately established a low price image."

Was Army surplus hard to come by?

"There were such large quantities of Army surplus available at that time that we soon purchased more than we could carry in one 2,000 square-foot store. We opened our second store in Saginaw, Michigan on August 1, 1948; and the third store in Lansing, Michigan on September 1, 1948. From the beginning of our retail careers we faced the problems inherent in the operation of a chain. We had to devise systems and controls to meet the various problems with which we were confronted. By sheer accident, we started our retail chain using the format that many of the retailing giants such as K Mart, Woolworth, Interstate and others spent many years of research to develop. We soon began to realize that if we were to stay in the retail business, Army surplus was not an adequate inventory. Our customers were looking for other items: tools, automotive accessories, work clothing, etc. We found it necessary to expand our lines."

Did you discontinue selling Army surplus?

"Salesmen began calling on us and we started to place orders for various types of merchandise. We discovered that manufacturers were not eager to ship to Army surplus stores on open account. We realized that Army surplus stores were a retailing fad and that the availability of Army surplus merchandise could not last indefinitely. If we were to have any longevity in the field of retailing, we had to change our name from U.S. Surplus Sales to a name that would be easy to remember. This name had to be one that could be economically promoted without the necessity of spending thousands of dollars on advertising promotion. I selected the name 'Yankee Stores,' and in November, 1949 we began to advertise under that name. Our stores all got off to a good start, and by using steady advertising, we attracted many customers who enjoyed browsing through our stores."

How many stores do you have?

"We continued to open small stores in small Michigan cities. In keeping with the national trend to larger stores, we closed all of our original small stores. Now we operate twenty-six Yankee Department stores, all in Michigan. As of January, 1969, our total store area was 1,703,300 square feet. Our total sales volume for the year ending January, 1969 was $87.8 million. By the end of 1969, we will have added four new units, bringing our total operating number up to 30. In April, 1965, we merged with Borman Food Stores, Inc., of Detroit.

Have you developed any theories on how to operate a discount store?

"As far as theories on how a discount store should be operated, there is no new theory that I can advance. There is really nothing new in retailing. Stores have to be well stocked, well maintained, and there must be enough sales personnel available to help the customer serve himself. A strong steady advertising program must be maintained. Yankee uses all advertising media: newspapers, television, radio, and approximately twice a year we run a direct mail program. It is imperative to develop customer confidence in your store and in the merchandise you carry."

Bargain Barns

INTERVIEW WITH BERNARD GOODMAN, PRESIDENT, HARDGOODS DIVISION, BARGAIN BARNS, DAYTON, OHIO (An example of a family owned regional chain of discount stores)

When did you start in discount retailing?

"In 1958 my brothers and I mortgaged our homes, borrowed $30,000 and bought out a store called Bargain Barns. It was a converted 6,500 square-foot dance hall and was started by Charles Killingsworth in 1953. Today we have seven stores of which six are in Dayton and one in Springfield, Ohio, 23 miles to the east of Dayton. We are also building a new store in Centerville, Ohio. The company is privately owned and has total sales of approximately $9 million. We are open from 9 a.m. to 9 p.m. seven days a week."

Do you lease out any departments?

"We operate all departments with the exception of toys, drugs, shoes, furniture and paint. My brother Bob heads up our soft goods department; brother Mark is responsible for operations including personnel and real estate; brother Lewis, an attorney, takes care of legal matters and finance."

You were pioneer discounters in this area.

"Yes we were pioneers and, to my knowledge, the first to go into the central checkout system. We contacted the National Cash Register Company here and two of their men worked with us for a year designing a cash register for central checkout."

Do you plan to expand?

"We have a lot to conquer in metropolitan Dayton before we go elsewhere. We have the advantage of being able to cover all of our six Dayton stores with one newspaper. On Thursdays we run a two-page ad for the weekend; on Sundays we have some 'door buster' type ads for what we call 12-hour specials for Sundays only."

Do you use buying services in New York?

"Yes, we have two buying offices in New York. We use Merchants Buying Syndicate and Atlas Buying Service: Atlas is primarily for soft goods and MBS for hard goods. We work closely with them; we participate quite extensively in private brand operations and we go along on group buying. We feel that if we are going to be a part of an office, we must participate; otherwise, that office isn't going to be very strong."

Are Dayton department stores open on Sunday?

"No, just the discount stores. According to figures just released by National Cash Register, the 15- to 20-mile Dayton trading area has more discount stores per capita than any trading area in the United States."

What percentage of your sales do you do on Sunday?

"When we first started, it might have been as much as 50 per cent of the total week's volume. While it is still a substantial day, it's down to about 22 per cent."

What is your volume of business on Sunday morning?

"Sunday morning is very quiet. We have staggered shifts and give Sundays off to the people who go to church. On Sunday morning we have a chance to get the store freshened up after Saturday's hectic business. You need those hours."

How do you rate with Dun and Bradstreet?

"We don't issue any financial statements except to some of our big suppliers who send us hundreds of thousands of dollars worth of merchandise. There are personal reasons why we don't issue the statement through D. & B. We sit down with our suppliers and work closely with them. They know all about us from mother and dad on down. To give out a financial statement for one company without having the full pattern tied in sometimes confuses things. Some of the reports they have sent out after we have sat down with them have been ridiculous. Consequently, we will just wait a while longer before we apply for a rating."

From how many miles do you draw your customers?

"As far as 100 miles. Our town is very progressive. We are the home of National Cash Register, employer of 20,000, and of Wright Patterson Air Force Base, employing 18,000 people. General Motors' total employment must be around 30,000. We enjoy the highest weekly industrial payroll in the state of Ohio and it has been that way for years. The average check is around $120 per week and the next highest Ohio average is $102. We also have a large university with about 10,000 students."

What is your policy on promotion? Do you promote from within?

97

"Yes, we promote practically 100 per cent from within. We have only one store manager who was brought in from the outside. All of our buyers have had limited experience because my brothers, Mark, Bob, and myself, wanted to run this business our way. We didn't want to bring in any high-faluting merchandising managers who may have good ideas and are smart men, but who might not know the discount business. We learned it from the shoestrings up."

INTERVIEW WITH MARK GOODMAN

What is your position in the company?

"I am president of the Giant Value Distributing Company. GVDC operates the business. It runs the stores and the warehouse. Giant Value is the operating and real estate company handling all personnel and labor relations and finances.

"We just purchased over fifty of the most modern cash registers from NCR. They are equipped with optical fonts. We also purchased a class 400 optical font which reads into a 315 computer. When this installation is completed, we will be able to know at the end of each day how much auto-motive oil we sold, for example, or how many spark plugs, or any given commodity. We have programmed the categories which we feel are the most important so that we know exactly what area of our business is giving us the greatest yield."

Do you sell antifreeze at a loss?

" Yes, it is a form of advertising; we discount it very greatly. Union Carbide told us that we are their largest distributor in this part of the country. We would rather not sell at a loss but some of our competitors do, and we must fall in line. We must meet, and we do meet, every price on like and identical items. By like and identical I mean that if we had a 2 × 2 broadcloth Pima Arrow shirt in our stock at one price, and the lowest price in town was a lower price, then it would be necessary for us to meet that price. We don't want to create a merchandising problem in the area. We prefer to meet prices rather than undercut anybody because we feel that is fair and equitable."

What per cent of your volume is hard goods?

"At the close of our fiscal year we had 60 per cent hard goods and 40 per cent soft goods. In another year or so we will probably reverse that and be about 50–50 or 60–40 with soft goods taking the dominance because we know that the soft goods area is more exciting, more challenging, more attractive and more dramatic."

How many employees do you have?

"We have 250 to 300 employees, depending upon the season. A lot are part-time workers, and although we operate from 9 to 9, we have a 40-hour

98

week. We hire part-time people to cover us over peak periods. We must do that to operate economically and maintain our competitive position.

"We don't have services, we don't have charges and we don't have deliveries. To get business away from the traditional stores, we must have the finest merchandise at the lowest possible price."

INTERVIEW WITH ROBERT GOODMAN

What kind of men's wear do you carry?

"We go into the men's furnishings field very extensively in shirts, ties, pants, socks, and the whole furnishings field except suits. We do a very big job in men's work."

How far do you go in fashion merchandise in women's dresses?

"Price ranges go up to $19.95. I purchased these higher priced goods while I was in Florida. There is a tremendous market in women's and children's fashions in Florida. The manufacturers were in Florida, and while I was there the Florida Fashion Council met at the Lido Hotel. I bought women's knitted suits. Where we normally go to a $2.95 retail, I bought things to sell at $4.95. We traded way up. We will sell these things at a discount.

"We are building a store in Centerville; we are going to carpet the floor and provide extra space for better merchandise."

Are you going to have an acoustical ceiling?

"No, acoustical ceilings cost between $25,000 and $50,000 to put in. We feel that we would rather give tremendous values. Women will still shop in nice clean surroundings, but they don't have to be the finest there are."

Do you think you are going to be able to keep up with style changes?

"We think we can do that by broadening our buying staff, with Atlas' (buying office) help. We get daily bulletins on fashions. As we expand we will have somebody who will just concentrate on women's fashions in ready-to-wear. Our fashion problems are really only in Dayton."

What kind of terms do you get on soft goods?

"We try, in purchasing soft goods, to work all prices down to a net-sixty basis. At times there are terms of 2/10 EOM. But if they ship on the 18th of the month you end up with only 18 days to pay for the goods. If they ship the 20th or the 25th of the month, we take sixty days from the date of shipment. A lot of manufacturers will make out the invoice date and not ship the goods until eight or nine days later. If we find that a man is taking ten to twelve days between the date of invoicing and the date that the bill of lading shows, we call this to his attention and take an additional five to seven days to pay. If it happens to be somebody that's factored, we send a letter to the factor. In that way everybody is notified exactly of what is happening. We don't do anything with terms unless we send written confirmation of everything we are doing and why."

99

INTERVIEW WITH LEWIS GOODMAN

"My domain is primarily the handling of all leases and contracts. I handle all the financing, not only of the buildings, but also of retail operations. We own all our own buildings. Each one is set up as a separate corporation, a limited partnership, or a general partnership. Then we lease it to an operating company. This operating company holds the leases on all of our stores. They in turn lease out to the subtenants. Among those subtenants are our own departments including our R & R Distributing Company and Dixie Enterprises. Thus we have broken down the tax structure to the best possible tax advantage for our particular company. We have to keep in mind that our business is owned by three brothers and a sister, so there is no attribution between brothers and sisters. In this way we avoid the surtax penalty of a corporation that has common stock holders such as a husband and wife. In our setup we pay the minimum amount of federal income tax on our profits."

Have you had any trouble with fair trade?

"We have never gotten into a fair trade problem *per se*. Right now there is one company that we are planning to sue because they refused to sell to us. This is the Levi Strauss Company. They refused to sell to us on the grounds that they have so many dealers set up in Dayton that they don't want any more dealers here. This will be a suit under the Robinson-Patman Act. They make blue jeans and they are the outstanding company in this product area in the United States. I think they have to sell to us. If we can prove that our credit standing is such that it meets their requirements or the requirements of other people we are buying from, I don't feel that they can refuse to sell to us."

What are some of the pitfalls of leases?

"The biggest pitfall in a lease is not having enough escape clauses in case the leased department is not a good operator. The second biggest pitfall is not putting enough controls on the leased department regarding what it can do with returns, its relations to employees and whether or not we have the right to fire one of its employees. We want to be sure that they maintain coverage on the floor in their leased department so that customers are always taken care of. On return policy we feel it is very important that we have unrestricted rights to grant a refund, make an exchange, or do anything that we want to do with the customer. The customer doesn't know you have a leased department. As far as they are concerned it is all one store. You can't let a leased department have anything in its lease that might affect the overall operation.

"Advertising is another area where you can get yourself into trouble with a leased department. Proper controls must be set up in the lease so that they have to go along with promotions; they must advertise so many inches every week."

100

How can you tell how many inches?

"Let us say that we feel that they should do $1,000,000 worth of business, and we want them to spend 3 per cent or $30,000. So instead of saying 3 per cent of gross volume, we set it up at a minimum of $30,000 worth of advertising in a 12-month period. This guarantees us the advertising that we feel this department should do."

What is your opinion as to the future of your leased departments?

"We don't feel that we would ever want to get into the shoe business, the drug business, or the furniture business. The toy and paint business we might be willing to take over ourselves. We feel that those three departments should be operated by specialists. Eventually we expect to operate around 83 or 84 per cent of the volume and maybe 16 or 17 per cent will be operated by leased departments. That is the only way we can be competitive."

Do you feel that your policy of owning your own real estate is good even though it is contrary to the policy of most discount operators?

"I think that you have to realize that most discount operators don't own their own real estate because they can't afford to. In the beginning of discounting they didn't have the money to get into it so they had to lease. We own every piece of equipment in our stores outright. This is unusual. Most discounters lease their equipment. All this has come about because of limited operating capital. If you want to look at it from a realistic viewpoint as to whether you should own your own real estate or not, regardless of capitalization, I would agree and say that you should not own your real estate. We look at it and say, 'We don't own the real estate as a discounter. We own the real estate as an investment with our other real estate investments.' This has been our theory. We feel that we own very good real estate, get a good return on it, and we can control our own rentals this way. Our stores are probably paying an average of 22 cents a square foot less rental than the average discounter.

"When we built our south Dixie store, we bought a piece of land with the thought of putting up a discount house on it. Now we had a little piece left over in the corner of the property that we couldn't use for anything. But a national restaurant chain came to us and wanted it because of the location; they felt that they could do a terrific job. A piece of land that meant nothing to us when we bought it became worth about $60,000 in the lease transaction. It made the land that we bought down there cost next to nothing.

"In this city everybody knows us. That makes it a tighter operation. Now if we were in other states, or at other ends of the country, real estate becomes a problem. We have never gone out of Dayton for our money. We have gotten all our real estate and operating money from local banks and building and loan associations."

What do you think of this name "Bargain Barn"? It seems that this doesn't fit.

"I can only say that this is something that we talked and talked and talked about. We spent hundreds of thousands of dollars trying to build up the name when we first started. Now we say to ourselves, 'Should we change the name?' We feel that we probably will; when we do, it is going to be on a gradual basis. We will change the name to XYZ Bargain Barns. As the years go by we will increase the size of XYZ and decrease the size of the name 'Bargain Barn,' until we get something the way we want it."

What does it cost you to finance an average store?

"A 60,000 square-foot store equipped with fixtures and merchandise and ready to open up would have a minimum of three-quarters of a million dollars in it, and that doesn't include the cost of the land. With the parking area you need, the amount of space to build a 60,000 square-foot store, the bricks, fixtures, and inventory, you can easily invest $700,000 to $1,000,000."

The Lechmere Sales Company

Abraham Cohen, founder of Lechmere Sales, was born in Rouna, a city near Warsaw, Poland. As a youth he worked for three years without pay as an apprentice harness-maker and became a master in this craft. In 1909, at the age of 19, he arrived in this country as an immigrant on the steamship *Martha Washington* penniless, but determined to succeed. He went to night school to learn English and during the day he worked at his trade.

In 1913, with a capital of less than $100, he set up his own harness-making shop at 222 Cambridge Street in Boston. At that time expert saddle and harness-makers were scarce, and Cohen very soon established himself as an expert craftsman. (One of his European innovations was a "doughnut" made of leather which, when fastened to a horse's leg, prevented hoof-inflicted injuries.) He bought his leather from the Massachusetts Whip and Saddlery Company, then a flourishing Boston concern. By 1914, he had saved enough money to pay his wife's passage from Poland. In 1916 he became a citizen. Said Cohen, "After my wife arrived, I never saved money. Instead I reinvested earnings in new merchandise."

With the coming of Henry Ford's horseless carriage, Mr. Cohen was astute enough to see that it would not be very long before the demand for saddles and harnesses would decline. He, therefore, added tires and automotive supplies to his stock and moved his establishment to 4 Cambridge Street, Cambridge, Mass. Meanwhile, his four children Maurice, Philip, Norman, and Nan, in due course, were indoctrinated into the family business which in 1930 became the Lechmere Tire and Sales Company. The company rolled along at a steady, if not spectacular, rate until World War II when Cohen's sons went into the armed services. With gas rationing and the conservation of rubber, the fate of the tire business became precarious, but Cohen persevered. At that time an important decision was made: to enter the major appliance business. Maurice, Philip, and Norman returned from the service and once more became active in the business. They made personal calls to the purchasing offices of large factories, office buildings, and other big employment centers in the Boston and Cambridge areas to inform purchasing agents and employees that Lechmere would give off-list prices on appliances. These selling tactics proved so successful that in a few years more space was needed. An old three-story building was remodeled and expanded. Six years after starting in the appliance business, Lechmere was doing a volume in excess of $2 million. By 1956, volume reached $5.5 million; in 1957, it was $9 million; in 1959, $11.25 million; in 1960, $13.5 million; and in 1965, $33 million. The company is privately owned.

Today the president of Lechmere is Maurice M. Cohen; Abraham Cohen, now 73 years old, is treasurer; Norman D. Cohen is vice-president and sales manager; Philip W. Cohen is vice-president and merchandise manager. Daughter Nan Weinstein is office manager. The Boston Lechmere store has approximately 160,000 square feet and ample parking space, except at Christmas and on special sales days when parking space is hard to find. On November 1, 1965 the company opened a 180,000 square-foot unit in Dedham, Mass., in what was formerly a GEM store. With an appliance background, the company at present carries almost no softgoods, except for ski and golf clothing which supplements a large sporting goods department. In addition to very large major and minor appliance departments, Lechmere has expanded into a variety of merchandise including full in depth assortments of toys, lamps, office furniture, and fine jewelry. In the latter department, items, including diamonds, are carried ranging from $10 to $10,000. There is a "diamond room" where expert sales advice is available.

There are no lessees – all departments are company-owned and operated. Lechmere remains non-union and employs from 1,000 to 1,500 depending on the season of the year. Employee fringe benefits include Blue Cross, Blue Shield. Employee training programs are conducted by manufacturers' representatives at the store for five hours a week on a twelve week basis. Most departments are run on a customer self-selection basis with sales help available if needed. In the radio department, a wide selection of radios and radio clocks are connected and may be turned on by the customer thus facilitating self-selection. Thirty, sixty, and ninety-day charge accounts are offered, as well as revolving credit including ABC (Automatic Budget Credit) and extended contract terms. Lechmere specializes in brand names and claims to be the largest dealer in New England in the following brands: Zenith, Hoover, R.C.A., and Maytag. In 1959 the company achieved the distinction of being made brand-name retailer of the year; in 1965 it was runner-up. Further acclaim came with the choice of a Lechmere advertisement by the

National Appliance Retail Dealers Association as the best advertisement of the year.

Sixty-five per cent of Lechmere advertising is in newspapers, 25 per cent in radio and television, and 10 per cent in direct mail. Charge account customers receive notices of special "super" sales. Cooperative advertising is used with manufacturers paying from 25 per cent to 75 per cent of the cost. Lechmere is one of the biggest users of advertising space in Boston.

The Company is active in community affairs and in 1965 Maurice M. Cohen was elected president of the Boston Chamber of Commerce for a one-year term. Abraham Cohen continues to be active in the store. If he loses his job, he claims, he could still earn $500 a week making saddles for Sears Roebuck!

Caldor Inc. – Discounter Par Excellence

Carl Bennett, founder of Caldor (the name "Caldor" is a combination of Bennett's first name and that of his wife Dorothy), attended the School of Business Administration at New York University for one year after which he became a wholesale liquor salesman. Following a tour of duty in the armed services, he got married and decided to go into business for himself. He was not a complete novice in retailing since his family operated a grocery store in Greenwich, Conn.

He decided to start a discount operation. His capital consisted of $10,000 in savings and with this he opened his first unit in November, 1951 at 70 Westchester Avenue, Port Chester, N.Y. The store consisted of a second-floor show room with an area of about 2,500 square feet. Merchandise carried was luggage, traffic appliances, toys, jewelry, silverware, and luggage. This was a true discount operation similar to that of Eugene Ferkauf who started Korvette in New York with a second-floor operation carrying the same kind of merchandise. Referral cards were given to key purchasing agents and to employees of big companies in the Port Chester area indicating that substantial discounts from list prices on branded merchandise could be obtained. First year sales were about $500,000. In 1953 the business was moved to the first floor. It was not until 1960 that a second store was opened in Greenwich-Riverside, Conn. In January, 1961 the company was incorporated under the laws of the state of Delaware and since then ten more stores have opened in New York, Connecticut, and Massachusetts. Sites of Caldor stores are leased and are usually along or near highways in medium to high income areas. Most stores form part of a regional shopping center with a food store as a neighbor. Stores are open Monday through Friday from 9:30 a.m. to 10 p.m. Saturday closing hours vary with the seasons.

Caldor supplies its units from a central warehouse which until recently was located in Stamford, Conn. In 1965 the central warehouse and executive

CALDOR
Eleven Year Financial Summary

	NUMBER STORES	NET SALES	EARNINGS BEFORE TAXES	NET EARNINGS
1958	1	$1,218,247	$53,044	$30,863
1959	2	2,912,755	94,316	55,564
1960	2	3,633,530	178,956	96,082
1961	3	6,549,858	378,687	196,225
1962	4	9,361,501	382,755	205,895
1963	6	15,504,268	562,486	329,627
1964	8	35,620,773	1,901,061	1,066,309
1965	9	48,884,347	2,837,547	1,595,455
1966	12	69,738,148	2,045,117	1,159,267
1967	13	80,274,113	3,183,394	1,738,394
1968	13	84,187,001	4,974,448	2,385,448

offices were moved to leased facilities in Norwalk, Conn. in an area strategically located with direct access to the main line of the New Haven Railroad.

Of all discount retailers, Caldor claims to have the most courteous, well-trained employees. An attempt is made to staff all stores with qualified local people from each community. Company policy is to fill all vacancies from the ranks with as few exceptions as possible. Commenting on this policy, Bennett said, "Our vice-president, Frederick Teitel, started as a department manager in 1958 when the Norwalk store was opened. Herman Effren, now personnel manager, started in 1961 as a department manager in major appliances. The second employee hired when we first started the business is now assistant vice-president in charge of hardgoods. Nicholas Benedict, the third employee hired is still with us as a buyer. Altogether we have 2,000 employees." In 1958 the RCIA (Retail Clerks International Association) had a campaign to organize all the retail stores in Port Chester. Caldor happened to be on the list. It was just before Christmas and rather than run the risk of a crippling labor dispute, management decided to let the union organize its store.

President Carl Bennett attributes the success of his company to his ability to surround himself with capable, hardworking people. The emphasis is on "youth plus experience" in management. The management team's average age is forty-two and its average experience is nine years. A high

105

Carl Bennett, president, Caldor, Inc.

degree of control over costs and inventories is maintained since no store is more than three hours driving time from the central office and warehouse. At Caldor's the position of buyer is on a higher level than that of the store manager. All buyers work in the stores two or three nights a week to keep abreast of customer acceptance and taste. This policy and the fact that everyone from department managers on up is on a stock option plan is a unique feature with Caldor and one duplicated by few retailers. A central buying and merchandising staff operates out of company headquarters in Norwalk. The buying function is shared with department managers of each store on a fifty-fifty basis.

The system has worked well for Caldor; in the period from 1957 to 1968, sales rose from $1 million to $84 million. The company went public in 1961. It has compiled a growth record, both in sales volume and in earnings, which is almost unparalleled in the history of retailing. Caldor prefers to retain its earnings for further expansion and therefore it has not been paying dividends.

106

The Pioneers

A policy of "methodical aggressiveness" and careful control has enabled the company to avoid financial pitfalls, the nemesis of companies that expand too rapidly (such as Maxam's and Towers Marts). Slow expansion on a solid base with stores near enough to permit one-day visits by top executives has enabled the company to grow quickly and at the same time avoid too thin a spread of both its capital and human resources. The company plans to expand the outer perimeter of its service area. It will continue to build stores within its present perimeter and expand and improve existing stores. During the next five years three or more new store openings a year are contemplated. Caldor is also interested in the possible acquisition of other chains or individual discount stores in its area of operation.

Said Bennett, "Our major problem at the moment is getting adequate personnel for our stores – people problems. Ten years ago we had money problems; today we have no problem getting all the money we want since we are well established and enjoy a good reputation on Wall Street. This year (1968), our total sales volume reached $84.1 million and next year our sales should go up to $90 million. Our problem is to get good people whom we can train. We opened a new store in Framingham on April 10, 1967 after training men in our Stamford and Norwalk stores to take it over. I feel sure that our Framingham (Mass.) store is going to be a tremendous operation. It is on a site next to Jordan Marsh and Filene's called the "golden mile." Our store will be next to Sears so we will have good, clean competition. (They are also very near our Stamford store.) There is also a Zayre store close by but that is a completely different kind of operation from ours. We may eventually open two or three more stores in the Framingham-Natick area."

In regard to store layout and decor, Caldor sees itself as one step higher than the ordinary discount store; actually it is comparable to a chain of "traditional" department stores because of its wide range and assortment of merchandise, its excellent fixtures, its high acoustical ceilings and the general unhurried atmosphere. The customer is invariably impressed by wide aisles, decorative lighting, and the attractive and orderly manner in which the merchandise is presented. Wood paneling enhances the appearance of the walls and columns. In each section departments are separated by walls of a different color. Some departments even have carpets. The overall impression is one of brightness and airiness with an underlying emphasis toward sophistication. Of the company's 13 stores, seven have furniture departments ranging from 9,000 to 15,000 square feet; three have tire, battery, and automotive accessory departments. The latter are free-standing units under company operation.

As for its merchandise, Caldor aims at a quality image and purchases no seconds, irregulars, secondary brand specials, factory rejects, or low grade imports. More than one price line is featured in each category. Quality

107

national brands are stressed, but in addition there are many quality soft goods bearing a Caldor label. Until 1958 Caldor had been primarily a hardlines operator doing the majority of its business at night. But in 1960 and 1961 it started an increasingly aggressive women's apparel program. Caldor does not use a buying office to obtain its soft goods but relies on its seven buyers who frequent the New York market. In the beginning, when Caldor was known only for its hardgoods, company buyers had no difficulty buying nationally-branded soft goods which they could sell at a low markup. Turnover on soft goods averaged ten to twelve (against only eight in hardgoods) and maintained markup was higher, ranging from 25 per cent to 28 per cent. Complaints of "orthodox" retailers on Caldor's low markup policy sometimes causes manufacturers of nationally-branded apparel items to refuse to sell merchandise to the company. If they do sell, it will be the identical merchandise but under a different brand name. A manufacturer can hardly refuse a tempting order which may amount to 8,000 dozen men's shirts, or 600 dozen of a basic style. Nevertheless the pressures from large department stores or chains on suppliers to not sell to Caldor continue. As a result Caldor buyers are alert to find new and sometimes better resources.

Apparel accounts for about 30 per cent of Caldor sales with a total volume in fiscal 1968 (ending January, 1969) of over $84 million. Selling women's apparel, the company has found, is more profitable than selling hardgoods. Management feels that the relative volume of apparel should eventually total about 40 per cent of total sales. Thus Caldor has blazed a trail for other discounters. Most of them, however, are not in a position to follow Caldor's lead since they do not have the middle and upper income image of exclusivity so carefully and successfully fostered by Carl Bennett. Without question, Caldor's continuing expansion into the apparel field is a distinct threat to competing "traditional" specialty and department stores. Since 1964 Caldor policy has been to emphasize "couture" fashion. Bennett has attracted capable buyers from such stores as Alexander's Department Stores, E. J. Korvette, Arlan's and J. W. May's. Of its total apparel sales, private label merchandise represents about 40 per cent. Caldor registered private labels include Marc Mitchell for men; Marc Mitchell, Jr. for boys; and Robin Cheryl for girls. In sporting goods it is Bruce Kenny. To publicize its new fashion look, Caldor holds annual fashion shows in country clubs or restaurants near the stores. In December, 1966 a 90-minute fashion show was presented to the Norwalk chapter of the National Secretaries Association. The audience consisted of 370 women before whom ten models showed sixty items. Gifts of perfume, hosiery, and candy were contributed by the suppliers. Said Bennett, "They gave us a tremendous reception; it is very exciting for us and something new in our type of operation."

For the most part, apparel deliveries are drop-shipped direct from the

New York market by a shipping consolidator. Each store does its own marking. Speaking of his suppliers, Bennett commented, "We have very cordial relations with our vendors, many of whom have been with us from the beginning. If we get in a tight spot we can always count on their help, and if one of them is in trouble, we will always help them out. We feel that it is more important to establish cooperative relations with vendors than to always work on the basis of price competition. As a general rule, most manufacturers will sell to us except in branded lines of soft goods such as Arrow Shirts. We are gradually picking up more and more name-brand merchandise since we carry a higher quality of ready-to-wear than do most other discount stores."

Caldor's new Framingham store was completed in 1967 and is competing with Sears Roebuck, Jordan Marsh, and Filene's. The two latter stores are in the same shopping center. It remains to be seen what share of this lucrative market Caldor will obtain. Store plans call for a women's department of 11,403 square feet; girls' wear, 3,120; men's wear, 5,500; boys' wear, 2,880; layette and infants' wear, 1,800; shoes, 2,888. Vice-president Fred Teitel plans a separate shop approach with a junior shop, a mod shop, a maternity shop and a "children's world."

Carl Bennett lays great stress on inventory control through the use of electronic data processing. Caldor stores have optical font registers providing punched tapes which are collected by store managers at the end of each day and sent to the Norwalk headquarters. The tapes are fed into an optical scanner which reads the tapes electronically and relays the information to a computer which sorts and produces a sales analysis and a buyer's report.

To assist the merchandise manager and the buyers are three supervisors and a district manager. Supervisors visit the stores twice a week to see how goods are selling and if display is adequate; on Saturdays they meet with the buyers who report on market conditions, new plans for promotions, etc. Supervisors are equal in rank and salary to buyers; the district manager is on the same footing as a merchandise manager. Buyers customarily visit the stores on Fridays and Saturdays. Ladies' opinions on what goes on in Caldor stores and suggestions for improvement, are obtained from the wives of executives who each month are asked to send in a written report listing their observations. Hard work and a 100 per cent dedication to Caldor is stimulated by employee stock options, bonus arrangements, and the policy of promotion from within.

A unique feature of Caldor, not found in most discount stores, is its furniture mart. In some Caldor stores, the mart is in the main store, in others, it is in an adjacent building. The image created is that of a solid, neighborhood type of furniture dealer carrying a full selection of home furnishings including all types of furniture and floor covering. Brand names for case goods include

Kroehler, Broyhill, Lane, Stanley and Nelson; for bedding: Blue Cross, U.S. Koyon and Englander; for floor coverings: Maslan, Sweet Water and Cabin Craft.

In its advertising the company operates on the "do-it-yourself" principle. Advertising for all stores is handled centrally with the exception of the Northampton, Mass. store which is allowed some autonomy in regard to local advertising. The biggest advertising appropriation goes to newspapers; in 1964, it was $460,000. Radio advertising amounted to $341,700. Television is coming into greater use on the local level. John Nightingale, director of Caldor's new TBA Auto Service Centers, credits much of his business to word-of-mouth advertising from satisfied customers. Caldor's merchandising philosophy calls for courtesy and service coupled with a range and selection of merchandise comparable to the conventional department store but at lower prices.

Though primarily a cash-and-carry operation, the company offers many services beyond those of the typical discount store. Bank and finance company credit on a non-recourse basis is available to finance sales of major appliances. Limited charge accounts are maintained for business, non-profit, and state institutions. Another accommodation to Caldor customers is a "rain-check" policy covering all advertised sale merchandise. If an out-of-stock situation should arise during a sale period, the customer is guaranteed the advertised product at the sale price as soon as the stock is replenished. Coupled with this "rain-check" policy is the refund which will be granted on merchandise purchased ten days prior to a sale of that specific item. The company also offers ten-day unquestioned money-back guarantees on its merchandise. Home delivery of furniture and major appliances are offered to Caldor's customers at no additional expense. To service its major appliances, including R.C.A., Whirlpool, Westinghouse, General Electric and Norge brands, Caldor contracts with a factory-authorized appliance, radio, or television service organization in its trading areas. To assure customer shopping ease, all entrances and exits are equipped with electric doors; rest rooms are adjacent to the main entrance, and a public telephone is placed next to the courtesy desk for the use of shoppers.

Says Bennett, "I want to grow with planned supervision; to me, the peace of mind in knowing that we have control and know where we are going is of major importance. Actually, we only have two policies in our company; one is 'No relatives in the business.' If someone who works for me is good, he is rewarded not because he is a cousin or nephew but because he is good. Our other policy is that all bills must be discounted. This is something about which I am very fussy and, as a result, we have a triple A credit rating with Dun and Bradstreet. I am fanatical about this. We anticipate as much as possible whenever we can get extra discounts by doing so. In today's tight money market, it is a wonderful position to be in!"

OUTLETS OF CALDOR, INC.[1]

LOCATION	TYPE OF STORE	SIZE (SQ.FT.)	OPENING DATE
Port Chester, N.Y.	downtown	9,600	April, 1955
Greenwich-Riverside, Conn.	shopping center	40,000	April, 1960
Danbury-Brookfield, Conn.	shopping center	50,000	Nov., 1961
Danbury-Brookfield, Conn.	furniture mart	15,000	Oct., 1965
Peekskill, N.Y.	shopping center	50,000	Oct., 1962
Peekskill, N.Y.	furniture mart	15,000	Spring, 1966
Hamden, Conn.	shopping center	62,800	Nov., 1962
Hamden, Conn.	furniture mart	12,000	June, 1965
Norwalk, Conn.	shopping center	60,000	Oct., 1963
Norwalk, Conn.	furniture mart	9,000	July, 1964
Waterbury, Conn.	shopping center	70,200	April, 1964
Mt. Kisco-Bedford, N.Y.	shopping center	50,000	Oct., 1964
Mt. Kisco-Bedford, N.Y.	furniture mart	15,000	Dec., 1965
Stamford, Conn.	downtown	120,000	Nov., 1965
Kingston, N.Y.	shopping center	90,000	March, 1966
Manchester, Conn.	shopping center	90,000	June, 1966
Northampton, Mass.	shopping center	90,000	March, 1966
Framingham, Mass.	shopping center	100,000	May, 1967

Vornado, Inc.

In 1944 Herbert Hubschman and his brother, Sidney, operated a diner near a large R.C.A. plant in Harrison, N.J. Through their contacts with R.C.A. merchandising personnel, they began to sell, on the side, radios and appliances at less than manufacturers' list prices. When merchandise was hard to get after World War II, the word got around to "see those two guys from Harrison." The name "Two Guys" stuck. The profits from this off-list operation proved so good that the brothers decided to build a small store next to their diner. With their own hands, in 1947, they built a twenty by forty-foot cinder-block structure, without a show window but with a large electric sign. Business boomed. The appliance industry was expanding at a tremendous rate and the market had not become saturated. Initial success enabled the Hubschmans to build a number of identical one-story cinder block structures, each with 8,000 to 10,000 square feet of selling space. Most of them were constructed by Hubschman employees on weekends and in their spare time at a cost said to approximate $2 a square foot. Each store required a minimum initial investment of about $65,000. By 1951 and 1952 Hubschman stores were located on virtually every highway leading out of New York City to the West, highways among the most heavily travelled in the entire

[1]Four new units scheduled for Fall, 1969 opening; three in Conn., and one in N.Y.

country. The brothers sought minimum twelve-acre sites and were willing to pay $1,000 an acre provided the land was within one mile of a resident population of 15,000 to 18,000 families. The central idea was to cater to the home owner, the gardener, the do-it-yourselfer, and the car owner.

Herbert was the buyer, controller, advertising and personnel manager. Sidney was the store supervisor and warehouseman who took charge of buildings and equipment. Stores were open seventy hours a week including Sundays. The brothers were on the job seven days a week. Herbert was a daring and imaginative buyer known for fantastic off-season buys in carload quantities especially on seasonal items such as fans, anti-freeze, shovels, Christmas tree ornaments, summer furniture, garden supplies and toys. He was also an expert in close-out sales. His advertising stressed price and he never took less than a full page. He died in September, 1964 after succeeding beyond his wildest dreams. His imaginative approach to merchandising was shown in his decision to operate nine buses as mobile showrooms selling white goods, TV and air conditioners in the Woodbridge, N.J. area.

In 1949 the brothers acquired control of a business originally chartered in 1936 and known as Windsor-Fifth Avenue, Inc. It consisted of a small Fifth Avenue store and single-story unit located in Harrison, New Jersey. Recognizing that retailing was passing through a revolutionary transition that called for revised techniques and merchandising skills, the Hubschmans immediately instituted a new policy based on the rapid turnover of brand name appliances at a low markup. Housewares were added to their line in 1950 and the following year saw the establishment of a third leased outlet in Woodbridge. During 1952 and 1953 eight more units were added. The additional units were located in former factories and mills and bore the name "Two Guys From Harrison." It was not until 1954 that the semblance of today's departmentalized stores came into being with the opening of three 20,000 square-foot units in Watchung, Totowa, and Woodbridge, New Jersey. A thirty-eight acre chicken farm, said to have been bought for $50,000, is now the site of the 187,000 square-foot Totowa store. This store marked the turning point into big store merchandising with better fixtures, fireproof structures and solid construction. In 1959 Two Guys merged with the O. A. Sutton Co., Wichita manufacturer of fans and air conditioners. Vornado was taken as the new corporate name of the merged firms. As a result, the Hubschmans obtained $1 million additional working capital and the Vornado trade name for its private label appliances.

Vornado's superior rate of profitability is due to a combination of many factors, among the most important of these is the heavy concentration of most of its stores within a relatively compact geographic area (New Jersey, Eastern Pennsylvania, Baltimore, Virginia and Massachusetts). The main advantage of this concentration is the economies which result from the ability

112

to utilize centralized warehousing and control systems which keep handling costs down and merchandise availability for each store up. As of January 31, 1965 Vornado's warehouses at Port Newark and Garfield, N.J. (for general merchandise and appliances) and Hanover, N.J. (where apparel is inventoried) represented a combined total of a million square feet of warehouse space. A 186,000 square-foot addition to the Hanover facility has been made. All Vornado stores are a maximum of eight hours trucking time away from the warehouses and are served on a daily basis by the company's own trailer fleet, consisting of a fifteen-man motor pool with 50 tractors and 145 trailers. Operated around the clock, Vornado's warehousing operation also allows the company to make bulk purchases, thereby eliminating the profit which would accrue to wholesalers. It also enables the company to take advantage of specially-priced buying opportunities on merchandise to be offered for sale in later periods.

Because the company either owns, or has options to purchase nearly all of the property on which its stores are located, rentals, as a percentage of sales, tend to be lower than for most other retailers. As most of its property purchase options are not adjusted for possible appreciation in value over their twenty to twenty-five year lives, it is expected that the company will ultimately be able to purchase these properties at prices considerably below their future prevailing value. Experience with the Totowa store is indicative of the manner in which real estate values increase when the company opens a store. Its traffic attracts other merchants, who, in turn, create an enhancement of property values. In 1964 $2 million was borrowed against the Totowa property and its total value was placed at $3.7 million.

Vornado's most common financial approach to properties is, in effect, a sale-leaseback plan with an option to purchase for a nominal payment after the original cost of the property has been amortized. This generally involves a third party corporation which purchases the property through an insurance company loan secured by the property itself, and a long-term lease from Vornado providing for a rental fee sufficient to pay both interest and gradual amortization of the loan. When the loan has been retired Vornado purchases the property in return for a token payment. This method permits the company to finance the purchase of properties through insurance loans without increasing its long-term debt. At the same time it enables the company to list as expenses its purchase of properties as funds are paid out, rather than depreciating them and recouping a capital expenditure over an extended future period.

By January 31, 1965 the company's then 23 stores averaged close to 140,000 square feet and most were generating sales between $8 million and $12 million annually; the largest stores averaged up to $16 million. They drew customers from a ten to fifteen mile radius.

Most of the operating departments are headed by long-time employees, trained by the Hubschmans, who have grown with their jobs. Mickey Tamburri is in charge of construction and has been with the company since 1947. He and his men evaluate sites; operate pre-contract borings to determine building methods; design a building in their own drafting department; and actively specify, purchase, and even install much of the equipment. Said merchandising vice president Don Gomes, "We have always maintained that we can bring in a store ourselves from 20 to 30 per cent cheaper than we could if we had used outside help—from the purchase of the land to the completion of the store structure. As a result, we can recoup all our costs in the sale price and obtain a lease with repurchase operations. Another advantage is that we can move very quickly from the time we purchase the land to the time the building is finished. Our own architects always have a store on their drawing boards that is flexible enough to conform to a given plot."

In addition to being responsible for merchandising, Don Gomes is in charge of a seventy-five man advertising department which gets out and prints a hundred or more ads every week plus a twenty-four page tabloid. The do-it-yourself spirit, in the tradition of Herbert Hubschman is shown by the company's operation of: 1) their own layout and mechanical art staff; 2) their own offset negative and plate facilities; 3) their own graphic arts department, producing stats, veloxes, and surprints; 4) their own mat roller, producing some 600 mats a week; 5) their own silk screening facilities; 6) their own offset sign printing facilities; 7) up to date mailing list of 1.5 million names filed by postal carrier route. The company does its own sign making, velox, and touch up. Their costs per sign are close to three cents compared to the 28 cents they formerly paid an outside service. Further, great flexibility is achieved by getting the cards organized at the point of sale in record time.

Vornado has its own printing presses for newspaper preprints and circulars. They estimate that they save 60 per cent to 90 per cent in printing costs. Deadlines can be shortened and the fixed cost is spread over a greater number of stores. The advertising department presently runs some 17 million lines of advertising per year in more than fifty newspapers. Vornado is the first retailer to print more than fifty circulars a year. The company handles its own addressing, sorting, tying, bundling, and mailing, all geared to the carrier route and thus gaining the ability to manoeuver and sharpen timing. They can put together inserts and send them to 1.5 million people in five states. Says Don Gomes, "We can have our merchandising meetings on Tuesdays, go to press Tuesday night, and still get the insert into the newspaper or the mailer into the home in time for the following week's program. Specials on food items can be advertised within hours after the buyer has made his purchase."

The Hubschman brothers surrounded themselves with a group of highly skilled executives. Among them was Frederick Zissu who played a significant role in the company's transition from a relatively small retailer to the second largest discount operation in the country. Zissu, who was named vice president in 1956, is an attorney and corporate executive with a Wall Street background. He conceived and executed the original merger pooling the interests of the Hubschmans into the corporate image of Two Guys. In 1958 he worked with Bache and Company in floating the first public issue of the company's stock. Under his direction the firm was admitted first to the American Stock Exchange and later to the New York Stock Exchange. Zissu was the prime mover in putting together the Vornado deal in 1959. He is now chairman of the board.

In 1959, with company earnings at close to $2 million on sales of $80 million, the company bought the O.A. Sutton Company in Wichita, manufacturer of Vornado fans and air conditioners. This merger gave Two Guys a new corporate name and a nationally-known brand name. In addition, it obtained $1 million in additional working capital as well as a $9 million tax loss carry forward.

In the mid-fifties, lacking capital and know-how for multi-department operations, Herbert Hubschman leased apparel, photographic equipment and auto accessory departments. By 1959, 46.7 per cent of total sales were from lessees. Since 1959, however, company policy has been to absorb lessee operations preferably with the operators continuing to run their own departments. Today, less than 6 per cent of total sales come from leased departments Several former lessees are now major executives in the company. Most of them are listed as assistant vice presidents. Said Don Gomes, "They chose to ride the crest of the wave with us and their rewards have been excellent. An outstanding example is our president who, until two years ago, was himself a lessee and owner of the Jaunty Dress Shops which we acquired with him. Don't forget that we put a tremendous load on these people as we expanded. Some lessees were fairly limited on just how far they could reach into their pocketbooks and come up with the dollars to keep pace. So you could say, to a degree, that they welcomed this kind of change." Vornado is by no means a "one-man company." President Murray Siegal is considered one of the top operational men in retail discounting, while real estate and labor relations vice president Leo Zwiebach and Don Gomes, merchandising vice president, are highly respected for their site selection and merchandising abilities. In addition, there are twenty-one assistant vice presidents, all of whom have had extensive experience with the company.

By 1966 there were twenty-three Vornado stores: sixteen in New Jersey; three in Pennsylvania; two in Maryland; and one each in New York and Virginia.

Employees then totalled over 6,500 depending on the season. Present sales mix was then estimated to be as follows: appliances 20 per cent; clothing and apparel 21 per cent, food 26 per cent; miscellaneous merchandise such as jewelry, luggage, phonograph records, drugs, and liquor 33 per cent. About 8 per cent of volume is derived from the wholesaling of goods to others, goods manufactured by outside sources to the company's specifications. These are primarily in the Vornado line of appliances consisting of approximately 55 items and accounting for 25 per cent of the appliances sold by the company. Management tries to keep the markup average under 23 per cent, as compared to about 35 per cent for most discount stores. Merchandise carrying the highest markup are soft goods and private brand appliances.

Despite initial difficulties encountered in its supermarket operations, the company has solved its food problem with the establishment of a central warehouse. In 1966, sixteen of the twenty-three Vornado stores included company-owned supermarkets ranging in size from 22,000 to 31,000 feet. A 31,000-foot supermarket was added to the Camden County Plaza Shopping Center store in Cherry Hill, N.J. Future policy calls for company-operated supermarkets at new locations which can be served out of a central warehouse. In cases where this is not feasible, space will be leased to independent chains. It is estimated that regional grocery volume of $40 million to $50 million is necessary to justify the construction of a new warehouse which implies a need for twelve to fifteen units within any new region that the company may ultimately enter. The strong central warehouse concept has been with the company from the beginning.

A teletype system protects in-stock positions and has the advantage of being able to store information from stores even when the office is closed and then play it out on request the next morning. Said vice-president Gomes, "Every morning we get a complete report on the previous day's business via the direct line we have to all our stores. It's tabulated and set up by our bookkeeping and accounting department. Every single night we have a register tape reading, department-by-department. A report of this, by dollar volume and by store, is ready the following morning. Outs or low counts on special sale goods are teletyped to the warehouse and truck deliveries are scheduled to meet ad deadlines. The company has long been an advocate of electronic data processing and has recently installed the versatile Honeywell H200 equipment which gives analysis of sales by categories and other operating statistics.

In 1966 eight new units were added including stores in Springfield, Mass., Baltimore, Md., and Rochester, N.Y. In 1967 came Two Guy's first major metropolitan downtown store – a traditional department store conversion – in Newark, N.J., and a store in the Buffalo suburb of Cheektowaga, N.Y. A further 1967 expansion came by merger with Los Angeles-based Food Giant Markets (Unimart). This company operated sixty-nine supermarkets, six liquor stores and fourteen discount stores on the West Coast with total 1966 sales of about $120 million.

However, the Unimart discount stores did not live up to company expectations and these units will all be phased out by the end of 1969. Aside from the four Unimart units still in operation, Vornado now operates 42 Two Guys stores; 66 Food Giant Supermarkets; 21 Builders Emporium hard goods stores and 241 Foster's Freeze Franchised Drive-Ins. Total net sales, including leased departments, for the fiscal year ending January 26, 1969, were $788.7 million.

OPERATING RESULTS

YEAR TO AUGUST 31	NET SALES*	NET INCOME*	EARNINGS PER SHARE
1954	$12,139	$325	$.27
1955	17,903	591	.50
1956	28,265	556	.47
1957	38,029	815	.69
1958	60,573	953	.80
1959	76,054	1,048	.89
1960	99,142	1,747	1.48
1961	105,094	3,053	2.44
1962	115,124	3,501	2.67
1963	154,425	4,130	3.15
YEAR TO JANUARY 31			
1963	154,425	4,130	1.26
1964	518,758	8,946	1.63
1965	586,903	11,888	2.16
1966	679,909	11,818	2.07
1967	724,013	10,450	1.83
1968	788,789	10,491	1.76

E. J. Korvette

In Sept. 1966, Korvette became a division of Spartans Industries, Inc. (Sales were $60 million in 1955; $180 million in 1961 and $800 million in 1965. Stores grew from seven major stores and four smaller units in 1958 to forty major stores and sixty-three supermarkets in 1966. Combined sales of Spartans Industries in 1968 were $930.4 million. In February, 1968, Eugene Ferkauf retired from Spartans and Korvette's.)

In 1948 Eugene Ferkauf started his first store in Manhattan, one flight up at 6 East 46th Street and staffed by Ferkauf and Murray Beilenson, now secretary of the company. (The nature of this operation and the types of

Eugene Ferkauf, founder of E. J. Korvette,
a division of Spartans Industries, Inc.

merchandise handled are described by Murray Beilenson in the interview which follows this section.) In February, 1951, the store moved to a street-level unit at 12 East 46th Street. In December, 1961 an additional 4,000 square-foot unit was opened on the second floor of 12 East 46th Street.

In December, 1954 Korvette opened a 90,000 square-foot store in West-bury, Long Island, with 60,000 square feet of selling space. Forty per cent of the goods on hand consisted of linens, domestics and men's, women's and children's wear. One of the biggest sellers was a $4.60 dress. Every ten days to two weeks, 2,500 of these dresses were sold, a turnover of about twenty-five times a year. At the time, the low-margin revolution in style goods selling was barely getting underway, but Korvette was in the lead.

The company went public in 1955 with the issue of 2,220,000 shares. At $10 each, they were quickly snapped up and raised in the neighbourhood of $2 million. Thirty-four fair-trade lawsuits were pending against the company at the time; nevertheless its policy of cutting fair-traded prices received a legal boost in 1956 when a New York court threw out a suit brought by the Parker Pen Company when it was shown that Parker was not making a reasonable attempt to enforce its fair-trade program.

The Korvette theory is that it is easier to put one more store in a metropolitan area where three or four other stores already exist. This facilitates greater efficiency and less expense in advertising, management, warehousing, servicing, and, most important of all, customer acceptance. This is true only until the stores begin competing with each other. The volume that comes off the top from one store into another comes off at the top of a very high profit margin, but it goes into the new store at a low profit margin. The company must constantly ask itself, "If we don't take it away from ourselves, will somebody else take it away?... Given stores on the North, South, and West side of a metropolitan area, are we better off to put a store in the Northeast and Southeast or should we let someone else do it?"

By 1966, in addition to ten stores in the New York metropolitan area, the company had five stores in metropolitan Philadelphia, and four in the Baltimore–Washington area. Between 1963 and 1965 five large stores were opened in metropolitan Chicago, three major stores in Detroit, and two large stores in St. Louis.

In volume of goods sold, Korvette is one of the fastest growing companies in the history of retailing. In 1966, as a direct result of what appears to have been poor planning, the company encountered severe control problems. Management was still centralized in New York, but buyers and supervisory staff found it increasingly impossible to cope with the vast flow of merchandise despite valiant efforts. Dissatisfaction and disenchantment resulted. Sufficiently careful, thorough forethought and planning apparently was not allowed.

Fortune magazine of February, 1966 stated: "All things considered, it is surprising that Korvette brought off its expansion as well as it did, even in the Midwest. The constant addition of stores from 1961 to 1965 put enormous pressures on management. Executives trying to do their jobs were confronted with the impossible proposition of being in two- or more-places at once. To run the existing operations, and simultaneously to manage a growth that was new in this or any other company's experience, turned out to be a highly difficult undertaking. Buyers who were busy filling the needs of the old stores found themselves obliged to plan and provide for the needs of the new ones as well. Section and department supervisors had to be moved quickly into jobs as store managers; senior salespeople, in turn, were pushed up to take over the management of the many departments—over sixty in a single store.

"Korvette had neither the central machinery nor a clear enough line of management responsibility to control such confusing conditions. Geographical dispersion obviously makes personal control from headquarters unfeasible as well as undesirable. But the company apparently was slow in giving responsibility to its managers in the provinces; many of them still do not have the senior status normally given by more mature organizations."

When Korvette went into food in 1962 to create more customer traffic, it soon found itself in additional difficulties as a result of inexperience. Korvette supermarkets were without warehousing; limited storage space in the stores had to be used for food. This made close control very difficult, if not impossible, resulting in a low turnover. Further complicating the situation was the prevailing food price war both in the East and in the Detroit and Chicago areas. Losses arising from the food operation were estimated to be about $2 million in 1964. Pre-tax profit margins dropped from 4 per cent in 1961 to 2.4 per cent in 1965. Korvette stock slipped from its peak of 50 in 1965 to 13 in January, 1966.

To solve this problem Eugene Ferkauf turned to Hilliard J. Coan, then president of Hill's Supermarkets, Inc., an extremely well-managed and highly successful food store chain on Long Island. Coan was widely experienced in food and the company had a 330,000 square-foot warehouse in Long Island with the capacity to service both Korvette and Hill's markets. A merger was arranged resulting in Korvette food division's annual volume exceeding $200 million. Nevertheless, competitive price-cutting remained a serious problem; the Chicago and Detroit food operations were leased to local operators.

When the operations were concentrated in the New York–Philadelphia area, it was possible for Eugene Ferkauf to exercise considerable personal supervision. But with forty stores and sixty-three supermarkets in widely-spread locations, this became impossible. Despite these problems, non-food sales from 1961 to 1965 grew from about $170 million to approximately $500 million; pre-tax profits almost doubled from $9 million to $17 million.

Another serious problem plagued the company in its leased furniture department, for nine years operated by the H. L. Klion Company. Apparently undercapitalized, this lessee expanded so rapidly in 1963 that control became increasingly shaky and resulted in serious management and inventory problems. Non-deliveries, due to strikes, caused customers to cancel furniture orders amounting to approximately $2 million. They were unaware that the furniture department was a leased operation, and Korvette's reputation took a severe beating. This difficult situation eventually forced Korvette into taking over the Klion Company and underwriting very heavy losses.

In 1966 Hilliard J. Coan became president and under his leadership executive duties were clarified and work loads made more equitable. Additional experienced buying personnel were hired, and the company made arrangements to install data processing, previously handled at outside electronic data processing centers. A new warehouse to serve as a distribution

120

center was built in northern New Jersey. Consolidation of existing stores is the present policy with only three new stores opened in 1966 (Pelham, N.Y.; Baltimore, Maryland; and Woodbridge, N.J.). Four more were built in 1967. Earnings in fiscal 1969 are expected to be very much improved. (See page 136 for earnings figure.) The company has added many new departments in its new stores and gone more extensively into credit. In addition to the furniture department, Korvette now owns the formerly leased carpet department. A line of credit has been established with banks and insurance companies, and in 1966 the outstanding debt exceeded $35 million with $5\frac{3}{8}$ per cent interest paid to the Prudential and Massachusetts Insurance Companies.

Rather than being classified as a "discount store," the company prefers to be known as a "promotional department store." "But when it comes to pricing," according to Korvette executive William Wilensky, "we are a discount house."

The arrangements whereby E. J. Korvette became a Division of Spartans Industries, Inc. will be found in the section entitled, "Spartans Industries, Inc.," page 136.

INTERVIEW WITH MURRAY BEILENSON, SECRETARY OF E. J. KORVETTE AND MERCHANDISING MANAGER OF TRAFFIC APPLIANCES AND HOUSEWARES

How many years have you been in retailing?

"Eighteen years, all with Korvette. I started with Mr. Ferkauf, who was a young man of 27 at the inception of the business in 1948. We were selling traffic appliances, luggage, fountain pens, and photography equipment. The first store was one flight up in a building at 6 East 46th Street. At that time we had a showroom and gave a discount of approximately a third off on everything. We contacted purchasing agents who were responsible for buying for large organizations, such as the Girl Scouts, or companies such as the Texas Company. We invited them to come to look at the various items. They would go back with our catalog to their people and say, 'you can buy this and this,' and recommend they come in to see us. We started off trying to get a key person in three companies to recommend us, but it spread like wildfire, and soon we didn't have to go to these various companies. You had to have one of our cards to buy, but we gave two to everyone who came in."

You must have had tremendous complaints from the traditional department stores who usually sold this merchandise?

"There were a lot of items that were fair-traded and many that were not fair-traded. This wasn't anything new. People had discounted and sold below a set list price for many many years. We were unique in that we offered a straight one-third off to the public. I would say that basically the concept of the company was to get people into the store, no matter what price we got

Murray Beilenson, secretary and general merchandise manager,
E. J. Korvette Division, Spartans Industries, Inc.

for the merchandise. If you have volume, even with a low margin, you are going to make a profit. This was one of the concepts of our business from its inception.

"We were very fortunate, I believe, through Mr. Ferkauf, being in the Grand Central area; he was very familiar with the railroad people, and they had an association, if I recollect correctly, whose members patronized our store. It was a sort of railroad association: people working for the city out of Grand Central. When we opened up, these people just flocked to the place and they found such tremendous values that they figured, 'why go elsewhere'?"

What was Eugene Ferkauf's background before he started Korvette?

"He had a few stores called Rex Luggage. One was right up in the Grand Central tower."

What were your duties?

"I did everything. I ordered, I sold, and I received. The first year it was a two-man operation, and after that most of the boys who are with us today joined our operation. I would say that everyone who joined us in the second year is still with us. George Yemen is senior vice president in charge of labor relations. Joseph Blumenberg, the treasurer of the company, is also a director.

Bill Wilensky is in charge of real estate. Mel Freeden is vice president in charge of store operations.

"After our first success we opened a store downstairs at 12 East 46th Street and called it J. G. Murray. When we opened up at 166 Mamaroneck Avenue, White Plains, N.Y., we called it E.A. Melt and Company. For a while we used different names for corporate reasons."

What were your greatest assets in the early days?

"I think that number one is the love of our people for merchandising instead of just buying and selling, and number two the honesty of the people in putting in a full day's work and then some. The biggest drawback today, in my opinion, is that you don't find enough people who enjoy the business."

What was Mr. Ferkauf's specialty?

"He commands a lot of respect because he is right in there doing. His is an overall talent. I think it is just getting people together. He has terrific talent as far as locations and timing are concerned, which are very important. He has gone into locations that people said were no good, and these turned out to be the start of our company, actually. The best example is when we went into Westbury, L.I. Mr. Ferkauf picked a location and at that time everybody thought he was picking out a cow pasture. It was in an area not far from Roosevelt Field where Macy's was contemplating building a shopping center. Macy's had their location and were thinking about building; Korvette was up a year before they even started putting up their building. We just created a tremendous name for ourselves because of our liberal policies and the merchandising ability that we acquired over the years in the other stores. We also loved our business. We had drive. The Westbury store was the turning point for the company. We didn't lease any departments there."

How did you finance it?

"Over the years we had made money on all our stores, and we had good relations with the banks. We didn't go public until 1965."

Can you tell me something about your expansion?

"At one point, for a period of two or three years, a new store opened on the average of every six weeks. Something like twenty-five stores opened in a period of about three years. This was phenomenal considering the small base we had. We had nine stores, and then suddenly there were twenty-five."

How did you get the personnel?

"We were fortunate in being able to entice people to come into the company to man the various departments. With a minimum training program we trained a good number of people in the Korvette way to take over the departments in the stores that existed. We then could move out the regular department managers from the existing stores into the new stores."

What is your field now?

"When we started in Westbury, I stopped managing one of the smaller stores and set up the hardgoods buying office. As we grew, everything else grew, and we started picking specialists. Today I merchandise only two departments which is enough since we are responsible for 45 stores plus the 40 new stores projected through 1973. We are kept quite busy."

Who invented the name "Korvette"?

"We get dozens of letters and calls every year asking how the name originated. For some strange reason the theory has gotten around that E. J. Korvette stands for Jewish Korean Veterans. Obviously this couldn't be accurate because Korvette started up in 1948 and the Korean War came later. The E stands for Eugene, the founder's first name, the J stands for Joseph Blumenberg, his friend, who is presently the treasurer of the company, and 'Korvette' was the name of a Canadian subchaser in the first world war that was spelled with a C but was changed to a K. And that is how E. J. Korvette was created as a name."

Doesn't Korvette have a sort of schizophrenic image, because here you are a promotional department store and yet in Long Island you sell paintings at $26,000 to $30,000, a high income group idea? You are also selling fashion merchandise which is intended solely for the upper income group.

"It is not schizophrenia so much as it is flexibility. Remember we are on 5th Avenue, only two or three blocks from some of the most fashionable stores in the world. If you stand on 5th Avenue and watch the taxis stop and watch the customers walk in with Bonwit Teller, Lord and Taylor, or Henri Bendel bags, you begin to understand that it isn't schizophrenia; it's the fact that everybody loves a bargain. We have Cadillacs that pull up to the store, and women get out and they enjoy, as everybody enjoys, being able to buy something a little bit cheaper than they normally would. We have some of the most famous people come in to our stores. No matter how wealthy you are, there is still a tendency to enjoy getting a bargain on a branded item when you know the list price; it is understandable that there is no stigma attached to buying it cheaper."

Where is the art gallery?

"It is at Douglaston, on Long Island, about 35 minutes from the Midtown Tunnel. You can buy anything from $10 up to $40, $45, to $50,000. We try to offer something for everybody. The gallery is open from noon to 9 p.m. We had space that originally was intended for a restaurant. But then we decided instead to put in an art gallery, and the response was tremendous."

What sort of art has Mr. Ferkauf collected?

"He has everything; Chagalls, Picassos, Miros."

In locating stores do you stick to metropolitan districts where you already have a foothold?

"We have our stores surrounding metropolitan areas here in the East, and if there are gaps we go in to take advantage of the savings that come with already established advertising. If we were to go to California, Miami, or up to New England, for example, it would mean the start of a whole new operation."

What is your theory about warehousing?

"We are about to build our own warehouse, somewhere in New Jersey, which will be our first move in this direction."

What have you done for warehousing previously?

"During a season such as Christmas we rent warehouse space temporarily."

What are your plans for the 34th Street building in New York City?

"The building was bought by our subsidiary, Arlens Properties. Now we are operating an eight-floor department store on the site where the Saks 34th Street store was. The problems that Saks confronted won't confront us. They were part of Gimbels, and Gimbels was across the street. In the profession it is pretty well known that the Gimbels people threw all of their haymakers, all of their merchandising quality into this store. They abandoned the Saks store because it was a specialty store. After a while they realized that they could not ride both horses at the same time so they abandoned the store. It is our feeling that this traffic location is one of the best in the whole country. It may even be the best in the whole world."

Have you gone into computers yet?

"We have had data processing for a long time. Our data processing cards were sent out to four or five different processing specialists. Under our new setup we are planning to operate the data processing completely on our own. We may farm out a little bit, but we will have our own data processing on inventory control. We are now working with the giant computer companies to set up a system."

Have you developed your own brands at all?

"Our soft lines have developed many brands, and we sell vitamins and drugs under our name. We have household items, detergents and air fresheners, under the Spring name. We have hand tools under Craft King. We have a Korvette line of tennis racquets, baseball gloves, and golf balls. Korvair is a major appliance line with refrigerators, washing machines, and dryers. Leonard Korvair was the name. Leonard, of course, being American Motors Company."

Are you big enough so you can control manufacturers?

"I would say in certain lines we do. I believe in the Nelson lines we control them. Even in our Spring line some of these companies find we are their major customer. If we were to drop the line I think they would go under. I think a lot of brand merchandise distributors fall into the same category. With our tremendous volume we are a major factor to them. We have a heavy responsibility to these people. We are one of the best companies that General Electric has for traffic appliances. We are also Polaroid's best customer."

Did you have any fair-trade problems?

125

"We have managed to do pretty well without fair-traded merchandise. We may have sold some in the beginning, but when they started cracking down, we decided that this wasn't the only way to make a living. There were other secondary major companies and I think we made a few of those secondary, major brand companies into big companies. We have encouraged anti-monopolists by supporting these small companies."

Are there some companies that gave you special consideration in the past?

"I think of people like Westinghouse who went along with selling us merchandise. Today they are considered one of the low boys on the totem pole. We are still sort of indebted to them so we carry whatever we can from them, if it is good merchandise. We don't carry their entire line. Since they have the atomic submarine contract, they have neglected the retail end of their business. In my particular line of traffic appliances, their management has changed hands many times, and they haven't yet been able to get the right people. They are not a G.E., and will never be a G.E., because they haven't got the kind of thinkers and planners that General Electric has. We owe them a debt because in the days of fair trade, they weren't fair-traders, and we were able to get appliances. And Westinghouse is certainly as good a name as anything you would want."

Did other companies abandon fair trade because of your volume?

"I believe, and again this is my own belief, General Electric went off fair trade because of people like ourselves. The proof of the pudding is that they can live with us. We are doing a tremendous volume. There is a need for this mass selling. Yet there was one appliance company, Dominion, which we helped to build, and then they went on fair trade and wouldn't sell to us.

"Gimbels and Macy's helped us fight fair trade on appliances. I think that period of our history was one of the greatest. Korvette stores flourished in the price war. People came running to us because we were selling Sunbeam mixers just a little bit cheaper than competitors."

Do you believe in institutionalizing advertising?

"We only do it for a store opening. In the recent water crisis we ran one institutional ad in the New York *Times*."

What media do you use?

"Almost all media. We are very happy with newspapers, but we have gone into TV recently; we are on radio, and we have circulars. We spend more for promotions than for regular advertising. We have something that the traditional store doesn't have – the best advertising in the world – and that is word-of-mouth. The traditional store must advertise. You don't get word-of-mouth advertising for some of these 5th Avenue stores. People who are smart buyers come here. We had an ad Sunday in the New York *Times*, a two-piece woman's suit. A smart buyer can believe our low price, but not if he saw it in a regular department store ad. People tell each other, 'I got a G.E. radio or an RCA television $10 cheaper.' "

126

What were you doing before you met Gene Ferkauf?

"I went to New York University and worked in my dad's store. My dad had a stationery and luncheonette business. I loved people and I used to do the buying for it as a kid. The war, for five years, interrupted my stay at NYU. I ran warehouses for the Army in France and England. I was in the quartermaster corps. I got my love for what I am doing now partially from what I was doing then."

Do you have an organizational chart for executives?

"The company considers that some phases of its operation fall in the realm of corporate administration which the public really could misinterpret. It represents no particular contribution to understanding of the company."

Where is your greatest competition, would you say?

"Let me give you one example of what goes on. In Brooklyn we have a store on Fulton Avenue right across the street from Abraham & Straus. They compete with us, and they try to price the way we do. If you go in there and say that Korvette is cheaper, they will meet our price. But up the block on Bridge Street there is a guy who runs an appliance store whom I have known for years. I walked in there and asked him how he competes with us. He said Korvette is the greatest thing in the world for him. In the first place they bring in traffic. In the second place people come to him and say, 'I have been at Korvette to price this appliance. Can you beat it?' He would accept a nickle less, or anything less, to get the sale. Korvette made this retailer. I was amazed. I thought we were going to put him out of business. A good small merchant would be able to benefit from an operation like ours. I think we do more good for them than bad."

Do you have a research department?

"Yes. We have a department which has been researching consumers, products, and competitive pricing. We have also brought in a new person whose job it is to research store locations."

E. J. Korvette, Division of Spartans Industries

INTERVIEW WITH RAY TREIGER, KORVETTE STORE LOCATION CONSULTANT

How long have you been in retailing?

"For fourteen years; I've been with Korvette only four months. I was formerly with Larry Smith and Co., a consultant for department stores and land developers in connection with shopping centers, etc. I got started with them in 1951 and was with them until four months ago. They have offices all around the country. I went to the University of Washington in Seattle and got my Bachelor's degree there. I work for Korvette on their store locations."

What is your theory as to how to chose locations?

"There are no hard and fast rules. Korvette, of course, is in absolutely free-standing locations. We are also in shopping centers other than our own. The most outstanding example is The King of Prussia Shopping Center in Pennsylvania which, I believe, was the first four-department shopping center in America. This center started out with E. J. Korvette and J. C. Penney, and about a year ago John Wanamaker opened up its branch as an integrated part of the center; under construction is Gimbels which will be the fourth. The King of Prussia center is a totally integrated regional shopping center.

"Locations depend on the trade area, the nature of the population, and the drawing power. What Korvette might do in a city like New York where we've got a degree of dominance and market share is one thing; in some other city it could be a totally different thing."

Do you prefer shopping center locations?

"From my standpoint the shopping center will provide a degree of long range stability for a real estate location that is not going to be subject to as much competitive whittling away as would a free-standing location. However, Korvette is more flexible than Sears, Penney's or Ward's. I think it is interesting that Sears and Ward's, who previously always had locations on their own, have now by and large adopted a shopping center policy. For many years we have made studies and found that wherever a conventional department store had been located in a business district, even before shopping centers came out, apparel and other specialty retailers were located on the business district block across the street, ready to funnel off their traffic. By and large you would never find much specialty retailing in a Sears' location.

"It seems to me that it hasn't been until the last three or four years that they have adopted a fashion merchandising concept. I've often thought that a small retailer would have a better chance of living off traffic next to an Allied or a Macy than he would next to a Sears. I think that historical experience proves this. I don't know how sales have been for the kind of chain stores that are in shopping centers with Sears as opposed to Macy's. We are flexible enough to go either way. Where we are on our own, however, we do like to have with us, as a minimum, a supermarket, a cleaning store, a variety store, etc. This provides the one-stop convenience to the woman shopper."

What are the most important considerations in locating branch stores?

"From the standpoint of advertising coverage, management, warehousing, servicing, and most important, customer acceptance, it's easier to put in another branch where three or four branches already exist, than it is to put a single new store in a new city. But that only holds true up to a point;

The Pioneers

I have in mind such things as transfer implications from existing stores. Volume that comes off the top from one store into another comes off at a very high profit margin and goes into the new stores at a low margin. The thing that we always have to ask ourselves is if we don't take it away from ourself will somebody else take it away? In other words, given a store on the North side of a city, and on the South side and West side, are we better off to put a store in the Northeast and Southeast and in the Northwest and Southwest or are those locations susceptible to somebody else doing it. That's the kind of analysis that is more difficult to make."

What statistical references do you use?

"We use the Census of Business, and *Sales Management Magazine*. This magazine provides other more recent information and takes into account things that weren't in existence at the time of the 1963 Census of Business. We consider the population and its characteristics. We also use area studies; most important is a detailed study of competition of all kinds – both present and projected. Discussions with land owners and developers indicate what is going on in an area."

How do you find out that composition of the population?

"We use the Census, which is as accurate as anything is. In many cities you have planning associations which keep abreast of population changes in the various segments of the city.

"Locations are always being developed which obviously means that that location is not going to be available tomorrow. The population of this country is growing at the rate of 3 million a year, and to satisfy that you need 55 million to 60 million feet of retailing a year just to keep pace with growth plus replacement for outmoded and obsolete facilities. There's hardly going to be a time, at least in the urban parts of the country, where the market for new stores will have disappeared. As growth continues there are always good locations developing. I believe in the concept whereby merchants make a location rather than locations making merchants. In any particular city of the country I think that the number one store that can dig a location that might not be as good as the number two or three store has, can do more business in the same size branch even in a secondary location. The intersection of two main highways can be occupied by a shopping center that has the number two department store in that city in it, and yet, if the number one store came along at a different location, it will still do more business because it is the number one store."

Do you rely on developers to find locations?

"There have been three different developers that have done a number of recent Korvette projects for us; we are now dealing with different developers in different parts of the country. Part of our new store locations come from people who write in or whom we meet and who are developing some area. It may be through a relationship with another department store which

129

invites our co-tenancy in a center. We may decide on our own where we want to be. After scouting the area pretty closely, we finally get somebody in whom we have confidence and ask them if they want to develop a center for us in that area."

Don't you sometimes get more offers than you can finance?

"We know how many stores we can absorb in any year well in advance and we direct our site development program toward that number of stores, plus a few, because some fall by the wayside as you go.

"Within the past several years our stores have been quite narrowly defined between 150,000 and 210,000 square feet. There is one new three-story store in Baltimore recently completed but by and large, they are two-story stores. We haven't standardized our architecture. Of course, when we are by ourselves in a Korvette city, we have all the flexibility that we want. If we were in a shopping center we would have to tailor our requirements somewhat to the needs of the developer, recognizing that he has to develop a traffic flow for the small stores to get the benefit of the traffic. We are attempting to develop a concept of stores of about 150,000 square feet and another concept for stores of 200,000 square feet. There are certain basic concepts which we have developed. In 1966 we opened a store in Pelham, New York, and a store in Baltimore. In addition to those two facilities, we opened another store in Woodbridge, New Jersey, around Christmas, 1966. At the present time, we have 45 units.

"We're looking right now at stores and markets that will be opening in 1969 and 1970. Generally speaking, there is a minimum of two to three years lead time between shaking hands with the property owner on a site and the day that the ribbon is cut at the store door. The research and the making of the deal has to occur before the shaking of hands. The development of the lease form takes considerable time. Our lawyers get together on such things as assignment, bankruptcy, subordination, condemnation, etc.

"There must be a liaison between the land owner and ourselves. Financing must be provided during construction of the store. Our real estate department deals with the plans for the store and supervises construction. The layout, as far as the site plan is concerned, is our baby and the layout of the store is based on merchandise considerations. There's a mass of detail work from the time that the deal is made until the store opens. But we can't say, 'well, we've got our three stores for next year and therefore we won't have anything to do because we'll be out of business in 1968.' If we're not going to be in on a certain market somebody else is going to be there. We've got to be ready to take a look at anything because you never know which one might be a 100 per cent location."

Where are your market areas?

"Our market areas are more limited than a Macy's, a Penney's, or a Sears Roebuck; all of our cities are within a one day trip from New York."

What do you think about the future of downtown locations?

"In the large metropolitan areas, I don't think that our company is interested in downtown locations. On the other hand, I think that in some smaller cities (small but yet large enough to support department store merchandise), where downtown re-development is taking place, it is conceivable that there are communities where no single suburban location could adequately tap the whole market as well as a downtown location. If we wanted to hit that market the only place to hit it might be from a downtown store. (I'm talking about an area where the metropolitan area supports the downtown location.) I don't think a downtown location is worth a damn, no matter how much parking a town or private capital creates, unless the planning of the central district is done on a broad basis and not just directed to the single store location. I'm talking about such things as malls.

"Malls aren't that essential. Too many times it is a panacea that so many smaller communities are seeking. I just don't think that it is worth thinking about except where it is done as a part of a broad program. I'm talking about a highway program, an arterial program leading from all segments of the metropolitan area into downtown. I'm talking about such things as a ring road separating through traffic and keeping it out of the downtown. People that are not going downtown for shopping and that don't want to go downtown just make a mess of the area for the retailers. If these two things are available, plus downtown parking and an adequate system of public transit, then a good plan can be developed whether it's a mall, underground parking, or on-top parking. Downtown then makes sense. Rochester, for example, developed a midtown plaza which is a fine illustration of that; there is a belt system going around it, a radial system leading into it and plenty of parking downtown, and it has a very good public transit system. Everything together made it possible for McCourteys and Farmans to develop the midtown plaza. They certainly couldn't have done it without those elements coming in first."

Do you plan to expand in the Midwest or Far West?

"We are in Chicago, St. Louis, and Detroit. St. Louis is the farthest West. I think that we may go out to the West Coast someday, but I don't think that it will happen within the next two or three years. I think that we may attack the big market in the geographic confines of the St. Louis, Washington, D.C., Detroit, and Chicago quadrants before we go to the West Coast."

Do you have warehouses?

"We have some warehousing in our various cities, and we also drop-ship to our stores."

Do you get into predictions of sales volume on the basis of population studies and the fact that statistics show that an average family spends, say, $300 for clothing?

131

"I haven't done it as yet for any Korvette locations. The consultant firm that I was with is in the business of estimating volumes and I've always thought that we've had a pretty good record in coming quite close to it. For stores that have a predetermined market acceptance, that is, if a store does 30 per cent of the department store business in the sections of the metropolitan area where it does have stores, then by and large it knows that it should be able to do about 30 per cent in the new section that it's going into. Some sections might do a little better or worse.

"Given the end of a census decade, it becomes very difficult to guess population in a section of a metropolitan area. In 1962, for example, when you're away from the time of the census by only a year and a half, a projection based on the 1950 to 1960 rates might have been o.k. But by 1966 you're kind of out of date by using the '50–'60 census. On that basis you're in trouble unless there's a good planning group in that city."

Do you get much help from Chambers of Commerce?

"The Chamber of Commerce information on the whole is usually too broad."

How do you go about determining what the competition is in a given location.

"The measurement would be by visual observation, approximate square feet, and determining who it is. A store in a given community would have a reputation for better productivity than C or D. One might be doing $60, the other $40 per square foot. It's an estimate that you have to make."

What are your most successful locations?

"There's no type of location that is more successful than the other. Our downtown units in New York are outstanding and our suburban units in New York and in other large cities are also outstanding.

"We have five stores in the metropolitan Philadelphia area – one of which is over in New Jersey. We've got close to a million feet of retailing there."

Ferkauf: The Man and The Myth[1]

Eugene Ferkauf is probably the object of more idolatry, bitterness, and mysticism than any merchant in American history. The youthful boss and founder of E. J. Korvette has achieved fame without inviting it. Despite its current problems, the growth and present position of E. J. Korvette, Inc., is an accomplishment unmatched in the history of retailing. It is also some-

[1] Excerpts from an article by Richard Rosenthal in *Women's Wear Daily,'* December 23, 1965. (Three years after this article was written, Eugene Ferkauf left Spartans Industries to develop his own boutique chain.)

132

thing of a tribute to Ferkauf that the abundance of hatred and reverence with which he is regarded cannot be explained in terms of his power and success.

"Ferkauf," said a former Korvette executive, "is the luckiest retailer alive. He personifies the American genius for making idiots of millionaires, and millionaires of idiots. He runs Korvette as if it were a high school fraternity. If you are a friend, you can get away with anything, even incompetence. But it's almost impossible to be a friend unless you were with him before the 10th store. If you came later, it doesn't matter how strong or loyal you are."

But another former associate still worships him. "Eugene," he said, "is the greatest merchant, and maybe the greatest American, living."

A more balanced view comes from another who has been close to Ferkauf for years. "No one knows Eugene," he said. "There will be no Boswell to write about him. Only Estelle (Mrs. Ferkauf) is close enough, and she's not going to talk."

Although Eugene Ferkauf is a familiar, energetic figure in many markets, and in each of Korvette's 39 stores, he has long been remote.

Years after Korvette repulsed the lions in New York's retail arena, he was virtually unknown. For many years, his identity as Korvette's leader was only suspected. No photo or interview of him was published until *Women's Wear Daily* did so in 1956. To this day, the list of big retail names who have not met him is imposing. Ferkauf's desire for obscurity has led one investor to have his signature analyzed by a graphologist. Another reportedly paid a psychiatrist to observe Ferkauf during the recent stockholders meeting, at which the Korvette boss sat mute.

However, despite the mystery and passion, something of a pattern emerges. Whether Eugene Ferkauf is being damned or praised, he is invariably described as uncertain and supersensitive. Also, there is virtually no questioning his intense devotion to E. J. Korvette, or the fact that he is its boss.

"The one thing that stands out about Eugene," said a man who has been close to him for years, "is his uncertainty."

Another aspect of Ferkauf is given by a man close to the scene. "Gene will listen. He won't put anyone down for having strong views, and you can argue with him, really. But you better not look like you're becoming a star. Gene doesn't want to be a star himself. So no one else should star."

Although Ferkauf has never shown much liking for "yes-men," associates often have a strong feeling they have offended him without knowing why. Some say that he is just moody, others that he must feel an unwarranted degree of personal commitment from those closest to him.

"If he believes he has this devotion," says a former Korvette man, "he might just very casually decide he should help make you a millionaire."

Though some Ferkauf detractors say his determined informality is itself a pretense, Eugene Ferkauf seems never to have considered making a big deal of himself. Throughout his business life, he has chosen to be as remote and anonymous as possible. He gives money generously, but avoids charity functions. He helped hang pictures for the excellent art gallery in the Douglaston store, and then reportedly disappeared into an office as people arrived for the gallery's press preview. Neither did he appear at the reception marking the new quarters for Yeshiva University's Ferkauf School of Social Work.

No one close to him believes Ferkauf's lack of an office and secretary, or his casual dress are phony or have become any the less genuine for being partly abandoned. Contempt for formaility is consistent with Ferkauf's shyness and thinking. For one important aspect of the Korvette story, often overlooked in the excitement engendered by the store's policies, growth, and success, is Ferkauf's conviction that conventional retailing had lost touch with the public and became cluttered with pomp and red tape.

To Ferkhauf, retailing is people, not physics. Instinct is worth more than science, devotion and hard work more than organization. It is all too easy for critics to forget that Ferkauf's ideas built a $720 million company revolutionized merchandising, and profoundly altered the policies of conventional retailers. Also many of Korvette's best moves such as the opening of Korvette 5th Ave., were ordained by Ferkauf, in the face of "professional advice."

Ferkauf does not want his life cluttered. He lives like a wealthy man, but hardly like the multi-millionaire he is. His personal tastes are straightforward. He enjoys Puccini, Leon Uris, Irving Stone, Richard Tucker, and Italian food. He watches his weight. Apparently to his own surprise, he found he likes Italian movies. He is said to have a genuine feeling for good music. He wants to know more about art, and has reportedly bought two recent Picassos, but unlike Nathan Ohrbach and George Farkas, he is not likely to sponsor promising young painters.

Unlike most other retailers, Eugene Ferkauf does not have a reputation for ruthlessness or indifference to people. He is often responsive to the young man struggling on his own, and he loves listening to ideas. But people who have known him for a long time feel that he cares mainly about his family and business.

Korvette's moves to the Midwest have not dampened Ferkauf's determination to be home every night. "He will fly at night from St. Louis to New York to be home," said an associate, "and then he will fly back to St. Louis or to Chicago the next morning. The hardest thing for him when he goes to Europe is not getting home nights."

Without being able to define it, Ferkauf's associates are convinced that Estelle Ferkauf has been important to Korvette as well as to her husband.

"Gene is the boss of the family," said a former associate, "and Estelle is a big help in the business. I wouldn't be surprised to see her selling at the opening of the next store, keeping her eyes and ears open. I know she's done it."

"He has little time for a social life," said a former intimate. "Like a lot of retailers he's friendly with a supplier or two, but he watches that. He's also close to Charles Bassine, head of Spartans Industries. But Ferkauf is careful not to get too close to many people he works with, or against, or buys from."

Ferkauf's desire for obscurity also influences his philanthropies. He and/or the E. J. Korvette Foundation give generously to such worthy name brand causes as the United Jewish Appeal. But Ferkauf's heart is obviously in the welfare of his synagogue, Israel, Yeshiva University, and a number of other causes which do not demand his exposure. Most of his charity is for medical purposes. An example: The E. J. Korvette Foundation has pledged at least $24,000 to a children's hospital in Minneapolis, in honor of the late Jerry Gamble, an executive of Gamble-Skogmo.

Ferkauf's philanthropies are not all sectarian. Another philanthropy, the Korvette Medical Foundation, has also donated substantial funds to a Columbia University program which aims to improve the health of natives of North Brazil. And Ferkauf made a large donation to Lincoln Center.

Everything about Korvette, its achievements and its problems, are an extension of Eugene Ferkauf's personality. The store's incredible growth from $55 million to $750 million within 10 years, its restless atmosphere, its willingness to shift policies abruptly, its disdain for organization and formality, its supersensitivity to publicity, are all Ferkauf.

The trading up has been the most radical departure from the policies which made Korvette. Markup rose from less than 8 per cent in 1950 to some 33 per cent in 1965. Soon after going public it became bad form, and inaccurate, to call Korvette a discounter. Actually, Korvette became more a massive basement store, operating on a base of standard markup with a promotional message of loss leaders and an increasing proportion of soft goods (now about 45 per cent) in the merchandise mix. Approximately 90 per cent of soft goods is in clothing.

Following Korvette's merger, Eugene Ferkauf is now a director of Spartans Industries, Inc., and is a member of the Executive Committee. Charles C. Bassine is chairman of the board of directors. Brooklyn born and 57 years old, he is determined to restore Korvette (now a division of Spartans) to its original vigor. Without doubt, under the Ferkauf regime, administration got out of hand. Major emphasis of the new Bassine policy is to be on every type of control in the broadest sense. This will include merchandise, costs, markup, markdowns, shrinkage and expense. There will be no more unrecorded markdowns. No major change in the customary Korvette merchandise mix is expected although the 34th street New York store will put more emphasis on fashion lines, since more space will be available than in other Korvette stores.

Korvette is trading up but this does not mean that they are trying to take customers from Saks Fifth Avenue. According to Bassine, it means that as the customer indicates her preference for a better dress, you must have such a dress in stock. The initiative must be taken by the customer, not the store.

Prior to the merger with Spartans Industries, Eugene and Estelle Ferkauf owned more than 26 per cent of Korvette's stock, some 1.12 million shares. Ferkauf's major problem had been where and when to exert his authority. He wanted to be the idea man and let the others operate but the buck ended at whatever desk, counter or corridor he happened to be. Reportedly he now shares an office, officially, if rarely in person, with another Korvette executive. And as he has grudgingly done at other vital moments in Korvette's development, he is working with a magazine (*Fortune*) on a Korvette-Ferkauf story.

Eugene Ferkauf is not likely to fret that much of Wall Street's reverence has turned to scorn, or that oracle Malcolm McNair, professor emeritus of retailing at the Harvard Business School, has delisted him as one of six great merchants in American history.

Like many a postwar millionaire, Ferkauf is not in awe of the financial community or of academic personages.

Spartans Industries, Inc.

Retailing history was made in September, 1966 with the merger of Spartans Industries with E. J. Korvette. A consolidated statement of operations and retained earnings taken from Spartans' Annual Report for 1967, for the fiscal years ending July 31, 1966 and July 30, 1967 is shown below.

CONSOLIDATED STATEMENT OF OPERATIONS AND RETAINED EARNINGS

	FISCAL YEAR ENDED	
	July 30, 1967	*July* 31, 1966
Net sales	$1,152,307,112	$1,075,657,959
Finance and service charge income	5,514,007	3,554,963
Income from licensed and leased departments	7,260,441	6,173,322
Anticipation and interest income	940,410	1,361,650
Other income	1,261,797	1,103,128
TOTAL	$1,167,283,767	$1,087,851,022

Cost of sales and expenses (exclusive of items listed below:		
Cost of sales, including buying and certain occupancy expenses	$ 885,623,395	$ 839,743,695
Advertising, selling and general and administrative expenses	197,879,250	171,192,224
Rent	33,279,166	29,198,089
Depreciation and amortization (Note C)	10,124,378	8,601,770
Maintenance and repairs	3,998,163	4,199,355
Taxes other than federal income taxes	17,010,189	16,013,887
Interest	9,103,041	6,366,518
TOTAL	$1,157,017,582	$1,075,315,538
Earnings before income taxes	$ 10,266,185	$ 12,535,484
Federal income tax (Notes C and J (2))	$ 3,113,000	$ 4,517,605
Hong Kong tax	47,616	29,589
TOTAL	$ 3,160,616	$ 4,547,194
NET EARNINGS (Note D)	$ 7,105,569	$ 7,988,290
Retained earnings—beginning of year	61,615,704	54,983,144
TOTAL	$ 68,721,273	$ 62,971,434
Dividends paid:		
4 per cent preferred stock	$ 80,156	$ 80,070
Class A stock ($.40 a share in 1967 and $.32½ a share in 1966)	1,701,707	1,275,660
TOTAL	$ 1,781,863	$ 1,355,730
RETAINED EARNINGS—END OF YEAR (NOTES F, G and H) (TO BALANCE SHEET)	$ 66,939,410	$ 61,615,704
Net earnings per share	$.75	$.84

(NOTE C) – DEPRECIATION AND AMORTIZATION – INVESTMENT CREDIT:

Depreciation for federal income tax purposes is computed at accelerated rates permitted by the Internal Revenue Code; for financial accounting purposes, the straight line method of depreciation is used. The attached statement of operations reflects a charge to earnings of 50 per cent of the excess of the depreciation and amortization reported on income tax returns over the

137

amount reflected on the financial statements; the estimated amount of income taxes thus deferred ($724,000 in 1967 and $748,000 in 1966) is included in "deferred income taxes."

Investment credits are reflected in net earnings to the extent utilized against income tax liabilities. Earnings for the fiscal years ended July 30, 1967 and July 31, 1966 were thus increased by $720,000 and $656,000 respectively.

(NOTE J 2) – INCOME TAXES:

The provision for federal income tax for the fiscal years ended July 30, 1967 and July 31, 1966 have been reduced by approximately $500,000 and $33,000 respectively, as a result of the utilization of prior years' net operating loss and investment credit carryforwards of certain subsidiaries.

(NOTE D) – INVESTMENT IN STOCK OF ALEXANDER'S AND REALTY AFFILIATE:

In 1961 Spartans acquired approximately 38 per cent of the outstanding stock of Alexander's Department Stores, Inc., and Retail Realty, Inc., an affiliate which owns several real estate properties occupied by Alexander's. The cost (for financial accounting purposes) to Spartans of this acquisition aggregated $9,834,436 comprising a cash expenditure of $6,482,436 and the issuance of 251,400 shares of common stock valued at $3,352,000. . . . No portion of Alexander's earnings is included in the attached consolidated statement of operations and retained earnings.

(NOTE F) – REVOLVING CREDIT AGREEMENT WITH BANKS:

Under the terms of a revolving credit agreement effective September 25, 1966, a group of banks agreed to make loans to Spartans from time to time to April 30, 1968; the aggregate amount of such loans outstanding at any one time is not to exceed $80,000,000. Each loan made under this agreement is repayable 90 days after the date of the loan (but not after April 30, 1968) with interest at the rate of $\frac{1}{4}$ of 1 per cent above prime interest rates; however, the interest rate can not be less than $5\frac{3}{4}$ per cent or more than $6\frac{1}{2}$ per cent a year. The banks are entitled to a commitment fee computed at the rate of $\frac{1}{2}$ of 1 per cent a year on the unused amount of the total commitment. The revolving credit agreement contains provisions concerning minimum amounts of working capital, maximum amounts of debt and guarantees and restrictions against making certain leases, loans and investments. The agreement also contains dividend restrictions which are similar to those provided in the note agreement with the Prudential Insurance Company of America (Note G).

138

(NOTE G) – NOTES PAYABLE:

Notes payable at July 30, 1967 are summarized as follows:

Prudential Insurance Company of America	$54,000,000
(Due in the 1980's with options and provisions)	
Massachusetts Mutual Life Insurance Company	3,325,000
(5¾ per cent annual installments of $175,000, balance of $525,000 due on August 15, 1983)	
Massachusetts Mutual	1,870,000
(5½ per cent monthly installments of $52,083 through July 8, 1973)	
Massachusetts Mutual and three banks (notes payable)	8,986,667
(Payable in installments aggregating $980,000 a year)	

The agreement with Prudential further provides that Spartans is restricted from paying any dividends or redeeming any shares of its stock or any of the 5 per cent convertible subordinated debentures if the total of such dividends and redemptions exceeds 60 per cent of consolidated net earnings, as defined, from August 2, 1965; the amount available for dividends and redemptions at July 30, 1967 was approximately $5,100,000 . . .

(NOTE H) – 5 PER CENT CONVERTIBLE SUBORDINATED DEBENTURES:

The debentures were issued, pursuant to an indenture dated January 28, 1966, in connection with the acquisition of Atlantic Thrift Centers, Inc. . . . .

Spartans manufactures and distributes a diversified line of apparel and hosiery in basic styles throughout the United States in over 15,000 retail stores including nationally known chains, department stores and specialty shops. The company, organized in 1959, grew out of a manufacturing business started in 1936.

In 1960, under the chairmanship of Charles Bassine, the company entered retailing and opened five experimental discount stores, four of which were in Dallas, Austin, Fort Worth and San Antonio, Texas. One was in Oklahoma City. Management wanted to find out if a savings could be effected by eliminating the wholesaler, so far as garments were concerned. Bassine said that these stores were engaged in "automated low cost selling." Spartan-made apparel and other soft goods accounted for about 60 per cent of their merchandise; drugs, toys, jewelry, and a luncheonette were leased. Sales in 1960 were $32.7 million and earnings $1.23 per share.

Spartans' entry into retailing brought no major complaints from wholesale customers. Discount stores had become important Spartans' customers and just two of them accounted for a total of $10 million of business annually.

Charles C. Bassine, chairman of the board,
Spartans Industries, Inc.

Bassine rented his store fixtures and kept his working capital requirements at a minimum. Expansion was extremely rapid and return on invested capital enormous. By 1963 there were 42 Spartan Department Stores and a chain of 11 Crank Drug Stores[1] which had merged with Spartans. In 1963, a loss of $1,789,000 was sustained from sales of $116,532,000. However, a spectacular comeback was made in 1964.

In 1965, Spartans doubled its manufacturing capacity with new plants in Kentucky, Tennessee and Louisiana; sales reached $161,000,000 with an after-tax profit of $2,922,000. The Atlantic Thrift chain of 46 stores was merged with Spartans in 1966 so that, in addition to the Crank Drug Store Division, the company then operated 96 stores.

By 1967, Spartans had established itself as the leading American buyer of promotional soft goods from the Far East, with annual purchases estimated to be near $30 million in the Hong Kong market alone. In Taiwan, according

[1]In Sept., 1967 and March, 1968 respectively, Spartans Ind., sold at a profit, substantially all the assets and business of its Crank Drug Division and its Hills-Korvette Supermarket Division, for cash.

to J. W. Cohn, in the January 4, 1967 issue of *Women's Wear Daily*, Spartans obtained the exclusive rights to the output of a men's shirt factory in the Export Processing Zone. The factory is owned and operated by General Garment Manufactury, Ltd., a subsidiary of General Garment Co., Hong Kong, which is Chinese-owned. Spartans obtained exclusive right to the factory's output for six months beginning in January, 1967. The Taiwan branch also produces goods for Alexander's. Spartans currently sends designs from the United States and fabrics from Japan to the Taiwan factory.

Spartans' products consist principally of basic style men's, women's, and children's apparel in the popular price field ranging from $1.00 to $5.95. The following categories of clothing are included: women's, juniors' and girls' – sportswear (principally coordinates including blouses, skirts and pants), shirts, dresses, blouses, pajamas, nightgowns, dusters and house-dresses; men's and boys' sport and dress shirts, pyjamas and pants. During the twelve months ended January 29, 1966, Spartans produced approximately 75,000,000 units of apparel. In units, women's, juniors' and girls' apparel accounted for approximately 60 per cent and men's and boys' for approximately 40 per cent of total production.

Approximately 70 per cent of Spartans' total dollar volume of apparel is sold under its trademarks and brand names, while the remaining 30 per cent bears customers' labels and tradenames. Substantially all of Spartans' sales are handled by its own salaried sales organization of approximately 45 people, none of whom is employed on a commission basis. Most of the goods produced are sold directly to retailers. A minor portion is sold to wholesalers, principally for export. Spartans sells its products to approximately 8,000 retail accounts. Except for Spartans' own retail division, no customer accounted for more than 7 per cent of the gross apparel sales of Spartans during its last fiscal year. Long-term commitments for the sale of its products are avoided.

The company claims that its customers are so diverse and its garments are so styled, made of such fabrics and such variety, that there are no substantial seasonal variations in the volume of its manufacturing operations. Its products, which are mass produced at low unit cost and relatively unaffected by style changes, are comprised principally of clothing considered basic to most wardrobes. Its plants are so equipped and the nature of the apparel is such, as to permit a ready interchange of manufacturing facilities for the production of the different kinds of merchandise. Moreover, the production schedules make year-round utilization of plant facilities possible.

A substantial portion of Spartans' production is against existing purchase orders, yet inventories of finished goods are maintained to furnish prompt deliveries of "spot" orders. Approximately 90 per cent of Spartans' manufacturing volume is accounted for by apparel made in its own plants in the United States; the balance is made in foreign plants operated by

141

others. Both woven goods and knit fabrics are made of cotton, wool, synthetics and blends of such fibers. All finished piece goods used by Spartans are purchased domestically. Approximately 8,500 persons are employed in the manufacturing operations.

MARO INDUSTRIES

Maro Industries, Inc. was organized in 1961 and grew out of a business originally founded in 1912. All of its outstanding stock was purchased by Spartans in April, 1966. Maro and its subsidiaries are engaged in the manufacture, import and sale of diversified lines of moderately priced men's, women's and children's apparel, principally hosiery, shirts, sweaters and other related items of sportswear. Approximately 63 per cent of Maro's sales currently consist of hosiery, of which approximately 40 per cent is marketed under various tradenames under license agreements. These include "B.V.D.," "Oleg Cassini," "Sea n' Ski" and "Walt Disney." Men's sportswear, sold principally under the names "Bud Berman" and "Bermont", and women's apparel have accounted for an increasing percentage of Maro's business. Approximately 60 per cent of Maro's manufactured products are made in its own plants; the balance is manufactured under its supervision by independent contractors. Maro has approximately 800 employees.

Maro owns warehouses in South Carolina and California, having an aggregate of 119,000 square feet. Its manufacturing facilities and certain warehousing space are in leased premises in North Carolina, California and New Hampshire and have an aggregate of 264,000 square feet.

E. J. Korvette

E. J. KORVETTE WAS ABSORBED BY THE CORPORATE STRUCTURE OF SPARTANS INDUSTRIES, INC.

"It has been the experience of Korvette that it realizes, in a particular fiscal year, its greatest quarterly volume and pre-tax earnings in its second quarter, i.e., the 13 weeks ended on the Sunday nearest January 31 each year. It has also been its experience in recent years that it realizes its lowest volume and usually a loss in its third quarter, i.e., the 13 weeks ended on the Sunday nearest April 30 in each year . . . although net sales for the 26 weeks ended January 30, 1966, were $431,940,000, an increase of $46,857,000 over net sales for the comparable period ended January 31, 1965, earnings before federal income taxes declined from $16,634,000 in the 1965 period to $13,877,000 for the 1966 period. Although net sales for the 39 weeks ending May 1, 1966 were $604,580,000, an increase of $63,820,000 over the comparable

39 week period ended May 2, 1965, earnings before federal income taxes declined from $15,510,000 for the 39 weeks ended May 2, 1965 to $9,425,000 for the comparable period ended May 1, 1966. The decline ... in earnings before federal income taxes was caused principally by substantial losses experienced in Korvette's furniture division ... and by a decline in the profits realized by the other Korvette divisions." (From the Proxy Statement dated July 27, 1966.)

Korvette currently operates 45 promotional department stores ranging from 70,000 to 225,000 square feet, and 59 food supermarkets of from 10,000 to 36,000 square feet, in the metropolitan areas of New York, Philadelphia, Harrisburg, Hartford, Baltimore, Chicago, Detroit, Washington, and St. Louis. Furniture-carpet centers are operated by Korvette, generally in a separate building of from 20,000 to 38,000 square feet, at 35 of the department store locations, and carpet departments are included at two others. Tire stores are operated by an unaffiliated corporation, under the Korvette name, at a number of the locations with Korvette receiving royalty income based on sales. Fourteen of the food supermarkets, operated under the name "Hill's-Korvette," are located adjacent to Korvette department stores or in the same shopping centers, while the remaining 45 supermarkets are operated under the tradename at other locations in the New York metropolitan area. [As indicated, this division was sold for cash in 1968.]

All of Korvette's stores, offices, warehouses and other distribution facilities are leased. The leases of the department stores and related supermarkets provide for initial terms ranging from 21 to 30 years and, with the exception of the Hartford store, grant Korvette options to renew for one to four additional terms of from 5 to 20 years each. The leases of the separate supermarkets provide (except for two month-to-month leases) for initial terms of from 10 to 25 years and a majority grant the lessee options to renew for one or more additional terms of from 5 to 25 years. The initial terms of the furniture-carpet centers vary from 15 to 25 years.

It is Korvette's policy to offer quality merchandise at prices which are, for the most part, designed to be lower than the prices at which comparable merchandise is sold by conventional department stores. The profitability of such sales depends upon Korvette's ability to sell large volumes of merchandise, to effect more frequent turnovers of inventories, and to effect reductions in the cost of goods sold through centralized merchandising policies and procedures, centralized purchasing of merchandise in substantial quantities, the distribution of advertising costs over a substantial number of stores and other operating economies.

Sales in the department stores are on both a cash-and-carry and a credit basis. Deliveries are made on request at the customer's expense. Retail installment and revolving charge account sales are estimated by Korvette to be 19 per cent of its total department store, furniture and carpet sales

143

volume, and are processed by arrangements with unaffiliated corporations which have obligated themselves to purchase customers' installment credit contracts and revolving charge account sales invoices. A portion of Korvette installment credit contracts and revolving charge account sales are currently serviced by a wholly-owned Korvette subsidiary.

The supermarkets operated by Korvette are self-service, cash-and-carry units handling foods and non-food items normally found in such stores. Many products are sold under regional brand and private labels. Korvette is a member of a supermarket cooperative organization through which many of the food products are purchased.

Most of the meats, produce and dairy products sold are initially received and processed at Korvette's warehouse. Many of the supermarkets formerly gave trading stamps but, since September, 1965, the practice has been discontinued. Supermarket operations are conducted from centralized office, warehouse, processing and shipping facilities in Brentwood, New York and aggregate approximately 334,500 square feet. Since September, 1964 Korvette subleased to unaffiliated supermarket organizations 14 supermarkets formerly operated by it at department store sites located outside of the Connecticut-New York-New Jersey area. Six supermarkets in the Washington-Baltimore-and Cheltenham (Pa.) areas were subleased in May and June, 1966.

Korvette has approximately 15,000 full-time and 9,800 part-time employees. Collective bargaining agreements with various locals of Retail Clerks International Association (A.F.L.-C.I.O.) and, to a minor extent, other unions, cover most of its non-exempt employees. With the exception of a work stoppage of 9 business days at 13 of the New York metropolitan area department stores and the New York City offices in the spring of 1965, labor relations have been satisfactory. Korvette has in effect a variety of employee benefit programs including stock option plans, a Deferred Profit-Sharing Plan, Retirement Plan and Incentive Compensation Plan.

FEDERAL TRADE COMMISSION CONSENT ORDER AGREEMENT

In connection with the merger of Spartans and Korvette and pursuant to a Consent Order Agreement, the Federal Trade Commission issued an Order with the following principal provisions:

(1) Spartans is to divest itself of its investment in the stock of Alexander's and its affiliate, Retail Realty, by September 25, 1969 or, under certain conditions, by September 25, 1971.

(2) Spartans is to divest itself by September 25, 1971 of the Spartans-Atlantic self-service department stores.

The divestitures in (1) and (2) above may be effected by a sale in a public offering, by a sale to a buyer approved by the Federal Trade Commission or by a distribution to the shareholders of Spartans. Spartans' Board of Directors has tentatively determined that the Spartans-Atlantic division should be disposed of as a single enterprise in a public offering of the stock in a new corporation into which these stores will be transferred. Sales for the division were approximately $215,000,000 for the fiscal year ended July 30, 1967.

In September, 1967, Spartans sold substantially all the assets and the business of its Crank Drug Division for approximately $4,200,000 payable $3,200,000 in cash and the balance in four equal annual installments commencing October 1, 1968 with interest at 6 per cent a year.

REMUNERATION OF DIRECTORS AND OFFICERS
(Those receiving over $30,000)

The following table sets forth information regarding the amounts to be paid or accrued by Korvette and its subsidiaries for the fiscal year ending July 31, 1966, and by Spartans and its subsidiaries during the fiscal year ended January 29, 1966, to each person who is to be a director or officer of the Surviving Corporation. It is expected that this compensation will remain unchanged for the fiscal year beginning August 1, 1966. (Summarized from Proxy Statement of July 27, 1966.)

Name of Individual	Corporation	Capacity	Aggregate Direct Remuneration
Charles C. Bassine	Spartans	Chairman of the Board	$90,000
Eugene Ferkauf	Korvette	Chairman, Executive Cttee.	58,369
Murray Sussman	Spartans	President	60,000
Samuel Weissman	Spartans	Vice-President, Treasurer	52,000
Edward Katz	Spartans	Vice-President	55,000
Raymond Blank	Korvette	Officer of Subsidiary	37,752
Melvin Friedman	Korvette	Senior Vice-President – Store Operations	34,824
17 Officers and Directors as a Group			475,262

Spartans' Report to Stockholders for 1966 states that the limitation on acquiring specific types of retail and manufacturing enterprises will not prevent growth. Management will concentrate on increasing the retail activities of both Korvette and Spartans, as well as the manufacturing business. The Atlantic Mills Division will be made stronger. The limitations of goods stated in percentages of store requirements that Spartans' factories may furnish the Korvette and Spartan-Atlantic Divisions should have no adverse effect on the business, since the present percentages of hosiery and apparel furnished are less than the stated restrictions; furthermore these restrictions do not apply to new products. Since it has always been the company's intention to maintain its position as a leading supplier of soft goods, management has limited the amount of apparel that its stores may obtain from company plants. These limitations, self-imposed as a matter of good business, have been more restrictive than those of the Federal Trade Commission order.

Brooklyn-born Charles Bassine is determined to restore Korvette's original vigor. His first step has been to initiate every type of control including merchandise, costs, markup, markdowns, shrinkage and finance. In regard to the Klion leased furniture operation which Korvette took over when it was on the verge of bankruptcy, Bassine explained that delivery delays had caused the backup of inventory with resulting financial problems. In an interview with J. W. Cohn published in the *Women's Wear Daily*, January 4th, 1967, Bassine stated that he was deeply aware of his responsibility saying, "I want dignity and responsibility. I am responsible for 40,000 employees and their destiny."

CERTIFICATE OF INCORPORATION OF THE SURVIVING CORPORATION (STATE OF DELAWARE)

The purposes for which the Corporation is to be formed are:

"To purchase or otherwise acquire, manufacture, produce, invest in, store, transport, own, service, repair, sell at wholesale or retail, distribute, exchange, assign, transfer or otherwise dispose of, or in any way trade or deal in and with any and all kinds of goods, wares, merchandise, manufactured articles, raw materials, metals, animal and plant products, substances and other articles or personal property of every kind and description, and generally to conduct a mercantile business and such other business or businesses, including those of factors, traders, importers and exporters, as may be incidental or advantageous thereto.

"To purchase, lease, or otherwise acquire lands and interests in lands of every kind and description and wheresoever situated; to purchase, lease or otherwise acquire, and to construct, build and erect, maintain, equip, alter and repair buildings, structures, works and improvements of all kinds in and on any lands, for any use or purpose; to own, hold, use, improve, develop, operate, administer, let, lease, mortgage, sell, convey, exchange and transfer, or otherwise dispose of such property or any part thereof.

"To acquire by purchase, exchange or otherwise all or any part of, or any interest in, the properties, assets, business and good-will of any one or more persons, firms, associations, corporations, or syndicates engaged in any business which this corporation is authorized to carry on; to pay for the same in cash, property, or its own or other securities; to hold, operate, reorganize, liquidate, sell, or in any manner dispose of the whole or any part thereof; and in connection therewith to assume or otherwise provide for any and all

146

liabilities, obligations or contracts of such persons, firms, associations, corporations or syndicates, including, but not by way of limitation, the assumption or discharge or liens or encumbrances upon the properties, assets, business or good-will so acquired; and to conduct in any lawful manner the whole or any part of any business thus acquired, provided that such business is one of the nature authorized to be carried on by the Corporation.

"To acquire by purchase, subscription or otherwise, and to own, hold for investment or otherwise, and to sell, assign, transfer, mortgage, pledge, exchange or otherwise dispose of and generally deal in and with shares of stock, bonds, debentures, notes, scrip, warrants, securities, evidence of indebtedness, contracts or obligations of any corporation or corporations, association or associations, domestic or foreign, or of any firm or individual, or of the United States, or any state, territory or dependency of the United States, or any foreign country or any municipality or local authority within or without the United States, and also to issue in exchange therefor stocks, bonds, or other securities or evidences of indebtedness, of the Corporation; and while the owner or holder of any such property, to receive, collect and dispose of the interest, dividends and income on or from such property, and possess and exercise in respect thereto, all of the rights, powers and privileges of ownership, including all voting powers thereon.

"To acquire, organize, assemble, develop, build up and operate constructing, producing, selling, servicing, supplying, transporting, distributing, and operating and other organizations and systems and to hire, sell, lease, exchange, turn over, deliver and dispose of such organizations, in whole or in part, as going organizations and systems or otherwise; to organize or promote or facilitate the organization of subsidiary companies; and to enter into and perform contracts, agreements and undertakings of any kind in connection with any or all of the foregoing purposes.

"To aid in any manner any person, entity, partnership, association, trust, corporation, syndicate, government or subdivision or agency or instrumentality thereof, domestic or foreign, any securities of which are held by or for the Corporation, directly or indirectly, or in which or in the welfare of which the Corporation may have any interest, and to do any acts designed to protect, preserve, improve or enhance the value of any property at any time, held or controlled by the Corporation or in which it may be at any time interested directly or indirectly, or through other corporations or otherwise, including but without limitation of the generality of the foregoing, the making of loans, advances or subsidies, the execution of guarantees and the incurring of any debts, obligations or liabilities, contingent or otherwise, in connection with the underwriting, issuance, sale, distribution, purchase, exchange, or modification of any securities or other property in which the Corporation has an interest.

"To acquire, purchase, hold, own, use, sell, exchange, apply for,

147

control, assign, lease, dipose of, deal in, discover, improve, work upon and grant licenses to use patents, patent rights, copyrights, inventions, improvements, processes, trademarks and trade names, relating to or useful in connection with any business of the corporation.

"To borrow money, contract debts and to issue bonds, promissory notes, bills of exchange, debentures and other obligations and evidences of indebtedness, whether secured by mortgage, pledge or otherwise, or unsecured, for money borrowed or in payment for property purchased or acquired or for any other lawful object; to mortgage or pledge all or any part of its properties, rights, interests and franchises, including any or all shares of stock, bonds, debentures, notes, scrip or other obligations or evidences of indebtedness at any time owned by the Corporation.

"To purchase or otherwise acquire shares of its own stock (so far as may be permitted by law) and its bonds, debentures, notes, scrip or other securities or other evidence of indebtedness and to cancel, hold, sell or reissue the same to such persons, firms, corporations and associations and upon such terms and conditions as the Board of Directors in its discretion may determine.

"To conduct its business through one or more stores, offices or branches within or without the state of New York.

"To enter into, make and perform contracts of every kind and description with any person, firm, association or corporation, municipality, body politic, country, territory, state, government or colony or dependency thereof, necessary, incidental or convenient to the effectuation of any of the purposes of the Corporation.

"To do all and everything necessary and proper for the accomplishment of the objects enumerated in this Certificate of Incorporation or necessary or incidental to the protection and benefit of the Corporation, and in general to carry on any lawful business necessary or incidental to the attainment of the objects set forth in this Certificate of Incorporation or any amendment hereof, and to do any or all of the things hereinbefore set forth to the same extent as natural persons might or could do, as principal, agent, contractor or otherwise, and either alone or, to the extent permitted by law, in conjunction with any other persons, firms, associations, trust estate or corporations.

"The foregoing clauses shall be construed as objects, purposes and powers, and it is hereby expressly provided that the foregoing enumeration of specific powers shall not be held to limit or restrict in any manner the powers of this Corporation."

Atlantic Thrift Centers
(Formerly Atlantic Mills)

NOW A PART OF SPARTAN DEPARTMENT STORES, A
DIVISION OF SPARTANS INDUSTRIES.

An outgrowth of the Virginia Dare chain of women's apparel stores, Atlantic
Thrift became one of the fastest-growing and most successful retail operations
in the history of mass merchandising. It was started by the Virginia Dare
Company, a chain of approximately thirty women's apparel stores with total
sales in 1954 of $5.7 million. In 1955, under the presidency of Ralph
Applebaum, the company opened the first of its "mill" units, the Fairhaven
Mills Bargain Center in New Bedford, Mass. It was a pioneer store of its type
and carried a full line of women's apparel. All non-apparel departments were
leased. Three more units were added in 1956 under the name "Atlantic Mills."
A fourth unit was leased in Grand Rapids, Mich. and a fifth in Detroit. In
1957, a Knoxville, Tenn. unit opened.

The company continued to operate its twenty-eight Virginia Dare stores
using sophisticated IBM inventory control equipment and automated warehouse facilities. With its entry into discounting, sales increased rapidly. By
July, 1957 sales reached $17.3 million with after tax profits of $493,000. This
compares with 1956 sales of $10.4 million and net profits of $116,435.

Additional units opened in Jacksonville, Milwaukee, Providence,
Minneapolis and Youngstown. The 1958 net sales reached $22.6 million, with
after tax profits of $610,028. Just before the sharp stock market decline in
1962, Virginia Dare increased its total capital to $10,193,462, and its working
capital rose from $4,585,382 to $7,476,991. This was accomplished by the
successful sale, on January 30, 1962, of 100,000 shares of common stock and
negotiation of a $2 million five-year term loan. In six months sales rose to
$60.8 million with after tax profits of $1.1 million. Two leased departments,
domestics and infants' and snack bars, were bought out. An agreement was
made with Kelly Springfield Tire Company to operate automotive service
centers in selected stores on a long-term basis. A new, high-speed IBM1401
computer was installed in the accounting department.

In 1963, under the presidency of Sidney Mittleman, and board chairman
William I. Nathan, the company's rapid expansion continued. A massive
advertising program heralded the sensational opening of eight stores on a
single day in the greater Philadelphia area, one of the largest single day
expansion moves in discounting history. All of these stores were former
Bargain City units, re-modeled and re-fixtured by Atlantic Thrift. By July
sales soared to $69.7 million with after tax income at $561,808.

Record sales of $93 million were registered in 1964 with after tax profits

149

Fairhaven Mills Bargain Center, New Bedford, Mass.
First unit of Atlantic Thrift Centers (1955).

of $1.8 million. The company's training program expanded with regular seminars held in the New York office for supervisors and store managers. Five more stores were opened: a fourth store in Detroit; a third store in Milwaukee; and second stores in both Wichita and Cleveland. Exclusive of leased departments, 1965 sales were $93.6 million with after tax profits at $1.8 million. A research program was launched, leading to a program to upgrade stores, modernize fixtures, and eliminate unprofitable items. Middle-price lines were strengthened and higher-price merchandise added. To help implement this program, Sidney Mittleman put together a new executive team. Harold Gottfried was elected executive vice-president; Philip Albert, Harold Fein, and Cecil Morgan were elected vice presidents in charge of merchandising. Max Bierman was appointed to the new post of advertising director. Each merchandising vice president had his own direct responsibility and chain of command.

In January, 1966, with sales at an all-time high of $135 million, the directors and stockholders decided that the long-term interests of the company would be best served by a merger with Spartans Industries, Inc. Existing management was retained; Sidney Mittleman acted as president of the Spartan stores and the Atlantic Thrift Stores. Harold Gottfried, executive vice president, backs up Mittleman. Both chains retain their names, but operate as a single Spartan-Atlantic division of Spartans Industries. Stores with the names of Spartan, Atlantic Thrift Centers, and Spartan-Atlantic operate in 27 states.

The June 3, 1967 New York *Times* reported that Spartans Industries

150

planned to sell the ninety-seven Spartan-Atlantic discount department stores to King's Department Stores, Inc. for $30 million in cash and $20 million in notes. This deal did not go through and Spartans is preparing to spin off its store division as a separate entity by means of a public issue. A new president for the Spartan-Atlantic chain is being sought to succeed Sidney Mittleman.

According to the *New York Times* of August 15, 1967, the company will realize about $13 million in cash and securities from the completed or proposed sales of several of its properties. Included is an agreement to sell its Hills-Korvette supermarkets which have annual sales of about $225 million, to H. C. Bohack. Sale of the thirteen-store Crank Drug-Store division to the Katz Drug Company of Kansas City was completed. Spartans reported a loss in the third quarter, ending April 30, 1967, of $3.1 million compared to a loss last year in the same period of $1.4 million. Sales dipped from $241.9 million to $241.8 million in the latter quarter.

A Graphic Review

VIRGINIA DARE STORES CORPORATION – ATLANTIC THRIFT CENTERS

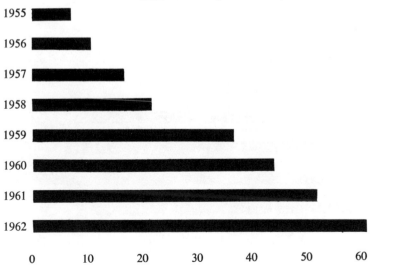

SALES VOLUME (IN MILLIONS)

| 1955 | 1956 | 1957 | 1958 | 1959 | 1960 | 1961 | 1962 |

0   10   20   30   40   50   60   70

MASS MERCHANDISING

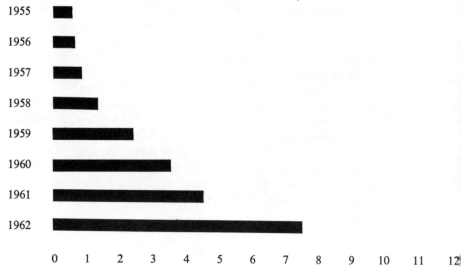

WORKING CAPITAL (IN MILLIONS)

1955
1956
1957
1958
1959
1960
1961
1962

0 1 2 3 4 5 6 7 8 9 10 11 12

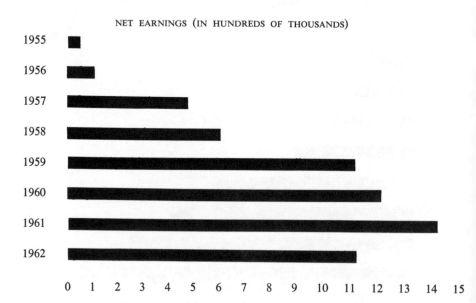

NET EARNINGS (IN HUNDREDS OF THOUSANDS)

1955
1956
1957
1958
1959
1960
1961
1962

0 1 2 3 4 5 6 7 8 9 10 11 12 13 14 15

152

The Pioneers

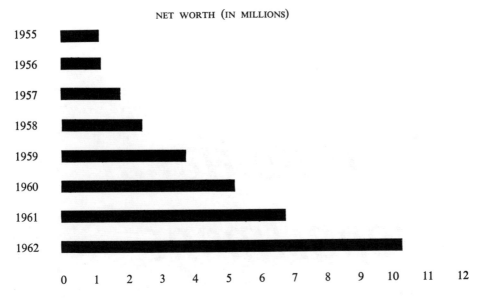

NET WORTH (IN MILLIONS)

III

"Promotional Department Stores"

With a few exceptions during the past fifteen years, the orthodox department store has shown less dynamic growth than any other basic type of retailing institution. Large percentages of total volume in most categories of merchandise have been lost to the newer and more aggressive forms of retailing. Active interest on the part of many large downtown traditional department stores has been too little and too late in catering to the new masses with self-selection, self-service, evening openings, parking, and the establishment of effective suburban branch stores. They have been slow in carrying and promoting full lines of wanted merchandise such as toys, automotive and garden supplies. Their merchandising of appliances and radios has been a dull routine without imagination.

Despite these shortcomings, the downtown department store is still a senior citizen among mass retailers. For example, Federated Department Stores, had total 1968 sales of $1,813,771,463. Concentrated in the hands of a few powerful organizations, such as Federated and Allied Stores are world-famous names including Macy's, Gimbels, Wanamaker, Sak's Fifth Avenue, Abraham and Straus, Filene's, Nieman-Marcus, Bullock's, and

154

many others. Such stores are still the nation's most highly respected leaders in fashion and high fashion clothing. Some discount chains such as Caldor and the Korvette division of Spartans Industries are making a determined effort to undermine this fashion leadership but, so far, with no noticeable success.

Not to be classed with the orthodox department stores are a number of promotional department stores whose merchandising and promotional policies are not only similar but in many instances even antedate those of discount stores. Examples of such stores in New York are S. Klein, Ohrbach's, and Alexander's.

When Samuel Klein opened his first women's and children's clothing store on Union Square in New York in 1906, he established policies which were basic to early mass merchants. He kept expenses to a minimum by using plain pipe racks, self-service, and almost no sales help. His cardinal rule was rapid turnover at a low margin. The company was incorporated in 1944 and by 1965 was operating ten full-line department stores in New York, Philadelphia, and Washington, D.C. In 1965 it was acquired by the McCrory Corporation. Sales that year were $195,970,427. The twelve existing S. Klein stores are now being re-vitalized under the new management.

One of the country's most successful retailers, Alexander's has probably developed to its fullest potential the underselling concept based on low markup and rapid turnover. Established by George Farkas in 1928, Alexander's is essentially a ready-to-wear department store; it does not carry furniture, carpeting, or refrigerators, nevertheless hardgoods account for 15 per cent of its total sales which in 1968 exceeded $259 million.

Nathan Ohrbach, in 1923, opened his first store in New York on 14th Street in direct competition with S. Klein. Although he started as an aggressive advertiser of odd lots of low-priced clothing, he gradually achieved a national reputation as one of the very few merchant pioneers who had mastered the formula for selling high quality, high-fashion merchandise on a self-selection, self-service, cut-rate basis. Nathan Ohrbach is credited as being the originator of many of the techniques used by today's mass-merchandisers to increase turnover and cut costs. In 1965 the four-store chain had a volume of $80 million and in that year it was sold to the Brenninkmeyer family who are continuing basic Ohrbach policies.

S. Klein Department Stores, Inc.
Pioneer Mass Merchandiser

Samuel Klein opened his first store on Union Square in New York in 1906. He specialized in retailing women's and children's dresses and coats, furs, and millinery. Klein devoted himself to selling clothes as cheaply,

Samuel Klein, founder, S. Klein Department Stores.

quickly, and in as large a volume, in a limited space, as humanly possible. He accomplished his aim by using the simplest sort of pipe-rack fixtures, hiring almost no sales help, doing no advertising except by word-of-mouth, and keeping operating costs at a minimum. This store was a highly successful pioneer in low-overhead, low-markup, self-service, rapid-turnover mass merchandising.

The company was incorporated in New York in April, 1944 and in 1946 a new management came in. It retained some of the old policies but introduced an intensive advertising program. It also added many new departments to diversify and broaden the sales range of the store. These included men's wear, shoes, accessories, jewelry, luggage, and sporting, nursery, and gardening equipment.

Expansion has been slow and careful: a second store was opened in 1949 in Newark, N.J.; a third store opened in 1955 in Hempstead, L.I.; and a fourth store was opened in 1959 in Westchester County, N.Y. By 1965,

156

the company was operating ten full-line department stores and had expanded its operations to metropolitan Philadelphia and to Washington, D.C. Total selling space is now over 3 million square feet. Credit is available in all stores with the General Electric Credit Corporation handling charge accounts in the Woodbridge, Greenbelt, Philadelphia, and Alexandria stores. Approximately 5 per cent of the company's sales are made on a credit basis and leased departments account for about 16 per cent of net sales. All the existing stores are held under leases for the most part based on percentages of gross annual sales on the premises. Most recent leases provide for a fixed annual rental. Lease expiration dates range from 1984 for the Newark store to 1995 for the Alexandria store. A 150,000 square-foot warehouse was completed for the company in Plainfield, N.J. in 1961 under a sale leaseback arrangement. A major portion of all store fixtures are leased.

In June, 1964 an issue of $5\frac{3}{4}$ per cent convertible debentures was successfully marketed with resulting proceeds of $3,325,000. For the fiscal year ending July 31, 1965, sales were $195,970,427 with a loss of $251,237, as compared with fiscal 1964 sales of $172,181,798 and a loss of $8,869. In August 1965 the directors approved a proposal by the McCrory Corporation whereby S. Klein stockholders received, for each share of common stock, an $8 – 15-year McCrory sinking fund debenture bearing 5 per cent interest, plus a warrant, expiring in 1976, for the purchase of one share of McCrory common stock for $20. S. Klein is now a subsidiary of the McCrory Corporation, headed by Meshulam Riklis.

Samuel Neaman, president and chief operating officer of the McCrory Corporation, was elected chairman of the board and chief executive officer of S. Klein Stores, Inc. in September, 1965. He appointed Duffy Lewis director of merchandising in January, 1966 and later President.

Indicative of the vigorous rebirth of S. Klein in New York City was the opening of a new four-level, 170,000 square-foot unit in Flushing, L.I. in February, 1967. Built at a cost of $6 million, the store features a windowless facade of stone, porcelain, enamel, and aluminium. There is indoor parking for 300 cars. The store carries a full line of fashions, home furnishings, and major appliances. The addition of this unit brings the total number of S. Klein stores to thirteen. Neaman conceives the Queens store as a test site for a new brand of discounting techniques, in a brighter, more attractive shopping atmosphere, with fewer bargain counters and provisions for service where and when it is needed. Pricing policies, however, will remain promotional.

It is expected that the new unit will be followed by more stores in New York City. No new S. Klein stores have been built in metropolitan New York since 1906 because the Klein estate, prior to a recent settlement, had stipulated that a percentage of the sales of any new S. Klein store opened in the metropolitan area be turned over to the estate. The purpose of the stipulation was to protect the 14th Street store. The estate owns the 14th

157

Street building and received an annual rental of $300,000 and 2 per cent of all sales volume over $12 million. A new arrangement stipulates that the estate will receive a minimum annual rental for the 14th Street property of $700,000 plus 2 per cent of all volume over $32 million. The per cent of sales of any new S. Klein stores opened in the metropolitan area was reduced to a fraction of 1 per cent. The 14th Street store will be completely modernized.

Alexander's Department Stores

George Farkas, chairman of the board of Alexander's, was born in Paterson, N.J. in 1902. Asked about his retailing experience, he said, "Even before I entered my teens, I worked in my father's specialty shop after school. At the age of sixteen, upon the death of my father, Alexander Farkas, I took over the operation of the family's two small women's specialty stores. About ten years later, in 1928, I founded the present chain and then named the company after my father. I am married to Ruth Lewis Farkas, a sociologist and former faculty member of New York University. We have four sons."

Alexander's has grown from one small ladies' ready-to-wear store at 152nd Street and Third Avenue in the Bronx to one of the largest privately-owned companies in the United States. In thirty-eight years Farkas transformed a small, 1,500 square-foot shop with annual sales of $200,000 to a privately-owned chain of seven super-stores located throughout the New York metropolitan area, with a total annual volume of over $200 million.

Since its inception, the original store at Third Avenue in the Bronx has been enlarged thirty times; from the original 1,500 square feet to about 160,000 square feet. Its dollar volume is about $17.5 million, or eighty-seven times greater than the first year's sales. The Fordham Road store in the Bronx was opened in 1933 and enlarged to ten times its original size – to 302,000 square feet. It claims the enviable distinction of annually registering the highest sales dollar volume per square foot of any department store in the country. The 160,000 square-foot White Plains store, built in 1956, was the first department store in the country to use automation to a great extent. It has a six-level garage. The three level, 240,000 square-foot Rego Park unit, opened in 1959, has been enlarged by 170,000 square feet – giving the store a total area of 410,000 square feet.

The 370,000 square-foot Paramus, N.J. store, opened in March, 1962, is the second largest, next to the more recently opened Manhattan unit. Its main floor is over one city block wide and three city blocks long, making it the largest main floor of any store in the nation. Striking out in other ways as a unique store, its interior is adorned with murals and sculpture, and it is completely mechanized behind the scenes, with monorail and conveyor belts

158

George Farkas, founder and chairman of the board,
Alexander's Department Stores.

to expedite moving merchandise. Its most famous feature is what is said to be the world's largest mural, painted by Stefan Knapp of England. A huge abstract painting costing over $250,000, the mural adorns the exterior wall facing Route 4. It consists of 280 panels, each one eight feet high and four feet wide, extends the length of one city block, and reaches a height of five floors. Mr. Knapp developed a special process of fusing glass to steel to make the mural suitable for exterior architecture.

Opened in August, 1962 the 200,000 square-foot Milford, Conn. unit marked the company's first step outside the New York metropolitan area. Company policy is to own rather than lease; six of its seven units are owned.

One of the most successful retailing companies in the nation, Alexander's stands midway between the traditional department store and the discount house; its purpose is to combine the best of both. Its low prices compete with pipe rack operations, but it endeavors to match the tasteful decor and

159

high fashion aura of conventional department stores. Alexander's is probably the foremost exponent of the underselling concept, based on low markup and high turnover and elimination of costly peripheral services such as charge accounts, delivery, and direct mail. Essentially it is a ready-to-wear department store with minor emphasis on hardgoods. While best known for high-fashion-at-low-prices available in variety and depth, Alexander's wide range of merchandise is designed to meet the various needs of the entire family, making it a household word in the New York metropolitan area.

In recent years, the company has won recognition for its large collections of merchandise gathered from all parts of the world and offered to the New York shopper at prices sometimes below those found in the lands of origin. Alexander's is particularly known for its departments featuring imported fine ready-to-wear beaded and knit dresses, suits, handbags, boutique items, exotic plants and gift ware. Among its specialized departments are boutiques, gourmet shops, pharmacies, garden centers, and art galleries. The hardgoods division accounts for approximately 15 per cent of total sales. The company does not carry furniture, carpeting, refrigerators, or other large-sized appliances.

Alexander's was the first department store in the United States to go into the car rental field. Its subsidiary, Alexander's Rent-A-Car, is the third largest rental agency in the New York area, with more than 2,000 vehicles in operation. In keeping with the traditional Alexander's policy of offering high value at low prices, the rent-a-car division rates on daily and long term leases are well below the current charges in the area. Alexander's Travel Service, the company's second fully-owned subsidiary, opened in October, 1965. Initially the travel bureau is based in three of the chain's seven units: Fordham Road, in the Bronx; Rego Park, in Queens; and the Manhattan flagship unit. It offers package plans with the rent-a-car divisions, including ski weekends. The company also offers packages to Florida, the Bahamas, and several foreign countries.

A capable management team, directing an expert buying staff, is continuing the fresh and unfettered Alexander's approach to retailing. The company is now under the leadership of 36-year-old Alexander Farkas who after active experience at all levels of the organization has been president for the past five years and his two brothers Robin and Bruce. Robin, 32 years of age, is treasurer and head of the car rental and travel divisions; Bruce 27 years of age, is the company's secretary. George Farkas' fourth son Jonathan, 18, is now in high school and planning an active retailing career with the company.

A broad three-year expansion program calls for two new units in Brooklyn and Yonkers and a major addition to the store in Rego Park, Queens. The chain will mark its entrance into the Brooklyn area with a 300,000 square-foot store to be constructed on a twenty-acre site at Avenue U and Flatbush Avenue. Alexander's and Macy's are co-developing the center which will include a 300,000 square-foot Macy store. Originally scheduled for opening fall, 1967, the unit would have been the first department store in New York City to feature a marina, selling nautical equipment and enabling boating enthusiasts to sail directly to the store and dock their craft while shopping. To accommodate "land lovers," a parking field would have been available. Also planned was a complete garden center. But plans for the unit were scrapped.

The Yonkers unit, built at Central Avenue and the Cross County Shopping Center, is about 300,000 square feet. It includes a multi-level parking garage and opened in 1968.

A 150,000 square-foot addition to the three-level, 240,000 square-foot Rego Park store, on Queens Boulevard and 63rd Road, in Queens, has just been completed; it brings this unit's total square footage to 390,000. Opened in 1959, the store boasts one of the city's largest department store parking areas. A 300,000 square-foot store opened in Valley Stream, L.I. in the late summer of 1967. A second Manhattan facility is planned for 1971.

Alexander's has a very active and extensive community relations program functioning in its Manhattan, Rego Park, Paramus, and Milford stores. Among its most successful activities are: yoga classes, bridge courses, investment seminars, how-to-ski lessons, bowling, fishing clinics, gardening and flower-arranging lectures, and spring-cleaning and photography fairs; all are a part of the company's annual programming. In addition, there are courses in art appreciation and career planning for women. These courses are sponsored with the cooperation of New York University. A speech course is taught by Dorothy Sarnoff, Broadway and concert star. Cooking classes and golf lessons are now being planned.

Alexander's has distinguished itself in the field of community service with its special holiday shopping day held on a Sunday morning each December exclusively for the aged and disabled patients of non-profit homes and hospitals in the greater New York area. This event has attracted national attention. Alexander's support of the Youth Symphony Orchestra of New York, made up of talented young people between the ages of twelve and twenty, has enabled this group to give a number of concerts at Carnegie Hall. These performances are held free of charge for youngsters from settlement houses, community centers, and schools throughout greater New York, many of whom have never before been exposed to serious music.

Answering a question as to company policy on personnel training, George Farkas said: "We offer a comprehensive personnel training program, but I strongly favor on-the-job training, which comprises about 90 per cent of the program. The formal training sessions are designed to give employees the necessary concepts and tools for their jobs, and to motivate and sustain interest in the company. All executives and junior executives are given a

161

three-day general orientation at the flagship store in Manhattan, and then they proceed to their respective stores where they receive eight weekly sessions of instruction by specialists in various areas. Following this, training is given when an employee is ready for promotion. These sessions vary depending upon the job level of the individual. Non-executive personnel also have a training program. This consists of general orientation and sales training classes. In addition, classes in grooming, fashion and product information, protection and safety, are held periodically."

In regard to the use of EDP, Farkas said, "Prior to the advent of the computer age, Alexander's pioneered in utilizing sales information for merchandising purposes. We are one of the first to make use of print-punched tickets. Our program was further accelerated when we installed computer equipment in 1961. We were the first store to use a highspeed reader with direct input to the computer which enabled us to cope with our expansion program."

Asked whether Alexander's warehoused or drop-shipped its merchandise, Farkas, said "Most of our receiving is decentralized and each unit has its own receiving and marking sections. Copies of orders are received from the buyers, and the merchandise is processed accordingly. In the main, we drop-ship. In addition, we use our own warehouses to receive advanced domestic shipments, thus giving us the ability to buy advantageously and to provide our customers with the lowest possible prices. Imports involve a substantial warehouse program. This merchandise is received centrally and stored. It is then distributed to various stores based on merchandising requests."

Alexander's flagship unit, the most expensive department store to be constructed in the history of retailing, is a nine-level, 486,000 square-foot structure, which opened August 30, 1965, on Lexington Avenue and 58th Street. Costing well over $20,000,000 in land, construction, equipment, and interior design, the upper East Side store has an impressive list of "firsts." It is the largest department store built in Manhattan in over forty years and the first windowless department store built in New York City; the first to offer on-site parking for over 200 automobiles; the first to provide off-street unloading of merchandise; and the first to install a unique floodlight system on the store's marble facade each night, which makes the new Alexander's a New York City landmark. The 58th Street store also marks Alexander's entrance into the downtown area and, at the same time, into one of the most fashionable shopping districts of the world. An underground passageway links the store with the 58th Street station of the IRT subway. Oriented to Lexington Avenue and 58th Street, the windowless building, of contemporary monumental design, is constructed predominantly of white marble, precast concrete, and black aluminium. The facade has been designed for street-level show windows in the form of "stage set" display cases. These are located

Alexander's department store at Lexington Avenue
and 59th Street, New York City.

on 58th Street, and 59th Street, and on the Lexington Avenue frontage. Combined sales for 1968 for all eight units were in excess of $259 million.

Prior to his 65th birthday celebration held in Paris on January 30, 1967, George Farkas said in a New York *Times* interview,[1] "My life is so tied up with this company that I can't seem to find anywhere else the glamour I find in retailing. In retailing you never grow old – you suddenly disappear – and you're never missed. Your colleagues are just too busy moving forward to spend any time worrying about your passage from the scene. You don't dedicate yourself to the glory of having been at the top, but for the joy of living it every day." Commenting that his real estate interests had been very profitable, he said, "But that only represents money and money can be a very empty thing – money does not give you an identification with something alive and moving . . . I am so excited by every phase of the business – the merchandising, the competitive battle, the entrepreneurial challenge – that every day I have to decide what to give up. I hope that all those conventional

[1]New York *Times*, February 1, 1967, page 1. Article by Isadore Barmash.

stores that are trying to dry up our sources of supply never stop. What they don't realize is that by attempting to pressure their suppliers into not selling to us at all, they are making us try harder so that we have become keen and sharp."

Alexander's fiscal year ends in July and 1967 sales are expected to total $212 to $215 million. In the next ten years the company plans to expand to other major centers by acquiring suitable store chains. George Farkas said that although he would prefer to keep the company privately held, he would not hesitate to go public if a suitable opportunity arose. Such an occasion might be a merger with a successful, publicly held company. At this time, Spartans Industries, the parent company of E. J. Korvette, owns 42 per cent of Alexander's stock. Asked if his company planned to buy back this stock, Farkas said, "No. We would much rather use our funds for expansion."

It was announced in the New York *Times* of Sept. 15, 1967 that Alexander's had reached an agreement with Spartans Industries, Inc., which holds a 38 per cent interest in Alexander's, whereby the way will be paved for a public offering of 50 per cent of the 240,000 shares held by Spartans. Price per share is expected to range between $60 and $70 per share. Based on this offering price, Spartans will receive approximately $14.4 million, or almost 50 per cent more than its E. J. Korvette division paid for it six years ago. The Federal Trade Commission has ruled that Spartans must divest itself of its holdings in Alexander's by September, 1969.

Ohrbach's

A pioneer in offering self-service and self-selection in quality women's wear, Nathan Ohrbach was born in Vienna in 1885 and came to this country as a child. At 14, he started in retailing with a job sweeping out a wholesale coat and suit store operated by J. M. Tobias. After working for several years as salesman and buyer for wholesale and retail firms, he and a partner, Max Wiesen, opened a store in 1923 on 14th Street in New York, with an investment of $62,500 each. Three years later the partners had a disagreement on policy, and Ohrbach decided to buy out his partner. Wiesen, however, would not sell; Ohrbach leased another store nearby and advertised that he was opening a business of his own. Wiesen gave in and agreed to accept $500,000 for his share of the business.

At the start the store stocked only staples; coats and suits sold on a cut-rate, self-service, cash-and-carry basis. The infant Ohrbach's faced the remorseless price competition of merchants such as Samuel Klein just across Union Square. Klein was the originator of many mass-merchandising

164

Nathan M. Ohrbach, founder and chairman of
the board (retired), Ohrbach's.

techniques designed to increase turnover and cut costs. Ohrbach's gradually
abandoned its image as an aggressive advertiser of odd lots of low-priced
clothing and began "trading up." Over the years it has added an ever-
increasing variety of quality and even high fashion items, some of which it
originates. In retailing history, Ohrbach's was a pioneer in extending the
principles of self-service, as well as self-selection to the field of quality
women's wear. Nathan Ohrbach was a man of strong convictions; once he
decided on store policy, he did not waver. He decided to keep his prices from
15 per cent to 20 per cent below those of his competitors, but to carry quality
and high fashion merchandise. A large percentage of garments carried are
from nationally-known designers, whose labels have been ripped out. A
minimum sales force was hired and told not to bother customers but to

165

The J. W. Mays Company – a promotional department store in New York City – borrows the "boutique" lure of traditional department stores.

The J. W. Mays Company tones up its image with a "Gourmet" department formerly associated only with traditional department stores.

answer questions when asked. All sales were for cash only and there were no alteration or delivery services. The interior of the store was kept as plain as possible, but enticing feminine clothing filled every square foot of selling space. There were no sales and little advertising.

Ohrbach's clientele is extremely varied, ranging from bargain-hunting salesgirls, housewives, models from fashion agencies, wealthy matrons, top movie stars, and even titled nobility. Herbert Brean, in his January 26, 1953, *Life* story on Ohrbach's relates the famous tale of one genteel lady caught in an Ohrbach crush and pushed squarely into another woman. "Oh, I do beg your pardon," she fluttered delicately, "I simply could not help myself." The bumped lady regarded her with acute aversion, observing, "If you are so goddam polite, why aren't you shopping at Altman's?"

Ohrbach's sends its buyers to Paris, Rome, and London several times a year to buy originals by top couturiers. These are shown to Seventh Avenue manufacturers, who are commissioned to make relatively inexpensive copies in two weeks. This makes it possible for women of low and moderate incomes to find very good reproductions of late fashion models at prices suited to their taste. An original may sell for $1,000, but at Ohrbach's a copy sells for $99.50. With competition on its neck and knowing its copies will be copied, Ohrbach's might even commission $57.50 versions, and eventually a modified copy might be commissioned for as low as $27.00. Ohrbach may buy $150,000 worth of a single model of a suit at one time. It is reputed to turn over its stock as much as 15 times a year, in contrast to that of six or seven for the average department store. Everything must sell within two weeks. If an item does not sell there is a series of scheduled price reductions designed to move unsold merchandise not later than a month after purchase. Ohrbach does not believe in sales, but women shoppers know that when they visit the store, there is a good chance of their finding a Paris original in the last stages of markdown.

One of the obsessions of Nathan Ohrbach was his refusal to have any store promotions, such as Mother's Day Sales. "Promotion," he says, "is like taking dope. You use one dose of it, and you have to have another, and another, and then another. A store advertises a sale of shoes, that originally retailed at $24.50, for only $14.95. Actually, they are telling the customer: 'We thought we could get you to pay $24.50 for these things and you wouldn't. So now we are trying to get you to buy them for $14.95'".

Ohrbach's chain of four promotional department stores was doing an approximate annual volume of $80 million in 1965 with stores in New York, Newark, Westbury, L.I., and Los Angeles. Since Nathan Ohrbach is an octogenarian, and since his son Jerry was not interested in continuing the business, the chain was sold in 1965 to the Brenninkmeyers, a Dutch merchant family. Elmar Brenninkmeyer is now Ohrbach's president and is assisted by three young cousins, Anthony, John, and Derick. For a time Nathan

Ohrbach was retained as a consultant; he is now retired. The Brenninkmeyers are old and well-established continental merchants known for keen business acumen, who run their European mass-merchandising enterprises with strict rules, a strong hand, and a sharp eye for profit. They picked the Ohrbach business because the one-track Ohrbach policy, "fashion at a price," appealed to them. Nathan Ohrbach was the originator of this policy and has promoted it from the start. Through the years it has proved itself sound and more important, profitable.

The Brenninkmeyer financial strength brings excellent expansion possibilities for the company. Because of limited capital the company's expansion to date has been only moderate. Nevertheless, Nathan Ohrbach always believed in hiring the very best administrators. One of these is Sydney Gittler who is known throughout the trade as a leading expert in the merchandising of coats and suits. Gittler has now been made a vice president, since coats and suits have always been Ohrbach's trump card. He has continued the line-for-line copy-Paris dress program and has even expanded it, since imports are highly favored by the Brenninkmeyers with their many European contacts. Imported fabrics are now used on some of the Paris originals which sell as high as $250. A new VIP shop, stressing better grade fashion but still at a price, is an innovation, but it is an expansion rather than a departure from the Ohrbach formula. Ohrbach's biggest competition comes from Macy's and Gimbels and from the many New York specialty stores, such as Franklin Simon.

Proof that Ohrbach's is still one of New York's chief attractions is evidenced by the following excerpt from an article in the New York *Times* of March 17, 1967, by Enid Nemy. "Ohrbach's cup of joy overflowed yesterday, and the brew was potent. For there, on the roped-off fifth floor, sitting on a spindly gold chair (one of 24 fitted with red velvet seat cushions) sat the Duchess of Windsor. She was awaiting the start of the store's spring show of European couture copies given for an invited list of celebrities. The public show was held later in the afternoon.

"And there, also in a front-row seat (but not one of the prestigious ones along the side of the runway), perched on a garden-variety folding chair was Mrs. Nikolai Fedorenko, whose husband is the Ambassador of the Soviet Union to the United Nations.

"The Duchess, who was recognized in a relay of whispers, posed a small problem for the audience estimated at 2,500 persons. They were obliged to balance delicately the lure of Windsor-watching against a fashion line-up, that included eleven designs by Saint Laurent, six by Cardin, four from Chanel, and five from Givenchy."

IV

Traditional Stores Move Into Discounting

By the late 1950's, traditional specialty store chains, junior department stores, variety chains, and some department stores found that they were losing sales to discount stores. Furthermore, downtown locations were decaying with the explosion to the suburbs. This was the case with the Bell, Nugent chain of 77 women's wear specialty shops operated by the Feldberg family of Boston. "If we wanted to stay in business," said president Stanley Feldberg, "we had to go into discounting." The first full-sized unit of Feldberg's Zayre chain opened in 1957 in Medford, Mass. Great care went into the concept, building, and design of this store. It became the prototype for those one-story, fluorescent-lighted, suburban discount stores of today.

Enterprise Stores, a chain of traditional junior department stores, was hard hit by discount competition in Rhode Island. Management decided to close its ailing stores and begin a discount operation with its J. M. Field stores. Diana Stores, a chain of women's and children's specialty shops, made a drastic change in its operation in 1959 when for $1.6 million it took over the R. H. Miller Company with its 12 discount stores. In 1961 it picked up two other discount chains: Great Eastern Mills and Gulf Mart. Moreover,

169

Diana began to operate leased departments in women's and children's wear in other discount chains. As a result Diana became primarily a discount operation with only 30 per cent of its sales (in 1965) from its specialty shops.

The Virginia Dare chain of 30 women's apparel stores opened its first "mill" unit, the Fairhaven Mills Bargain Center, in New Bedford, Mass. in 1955. Four more units were added in 1956 and it became the Atlantic Mills (Atlantic Thrift) chain. Interstate Department Stores operated 46 conventional department stores until 1958 when it bought a two-store White Front discount chain in Los Angeles. Today almost 90 per cent of the company's sales come from discount stores. The New York Waist House (Mangel's) ran 120 women's specialty stores; in 1956 they went into discounting and now have 42 discount stores (Shopper's Fairs), in addition to their 92 specialty stores.

The Hartfield chain of 47 women's and children's specialty stores entered the discount field in 1960 and by 1969 it had 14 Zody's stores in its discount division.

The L. S. Ayres Corporation, traditional department store operators, started its Ayr-Way discount division in 1961; in 1969 it had 11 Ayr-Way stores in Indiana.

Allied Stores, with 102 traditional department stores and $1.16 billion in sales, entered discounting in 1961 and now has nine Almart stores.

Cincinnati-based Federated department stores, the country's largest department store chain with 1968 sales of $1.4 billion, has created a discount division and opened an 116,000 square-foot prototype store in May, 1968 in suburban Columbus, Ohio. Emphasis is on casual wear; neither furniture nor appliances is sold. Space has been provided for a 20,000 square-foot supermarket.

The J. C. Penney Company operates more than 1,880 stores with annual sales of over $3.3 billion. With the acquisition of the General Merchandise Corporation in 1962, Penney entered discounting. It now has four 100,000 square-foot Treasure Island stores encircling Milwaukee. Three 180,000 square-foot Treasure Islands opened recently in the greater Atlanta area. Although these new stores have central checkouts and shopping carts, Penney management prefers them to be known as "experimental stores," rather than as discount stores. In view of the extraordinary and successful expansion of K Mart and Woolco, it seems entirely possible that there may be many more Treasure Islands in the Penney future.

Zayre Corp.

INTERVIEW WITH STANLEY FELDBERG, PRESIDENT

When did your family start in the retailing business?

"My father, Max Feldberg, and my uncle, Morris, started a jobbing

170

Stanley H. Feldberg, president, Zayre Corporation.

business in 1919 known as 'The New England Trading Company.' This company sold hosiery and men's and women's underwear to traditional department stores and to specialty stores. They bought their merchandise from mills and from other wholesalers. In 1929 they started Bell Hosiery Shops. In the early thirties the lines of merchandise were expanded. First they added lingerie, then corsetry and undergarments of that nature such as bras, girdles, panties, etc. The name of the stores then changed to Bell Shops. Sportswear, blouses, and ready-to-wear merchandise were added later in the thirties. By 1936 and 1937 they were directly in competition with chain stores such as Lerner's, Diana Stores and Three Sisters. By 1944 they had become a popularly-priced specialty chain selling a full line of ladies' apparel with 27 stores in New England.

171

"Immediately after the war in 1946, the company purchased a similar-type chain whose headquarters were in New York City with stores in New York state, Pennsylvania, New Jersey and Delaware. These extended as far South as Washington, D.C., as far West as Erie, Penn., as far North as Niagara Falls and Buffalo, New York. This chain was known as Nugents. It represented a doubling of volume and a doubling of the physical number of stores. Obviously it was a good move in the sense that the operations were contiguous geographically to those we already had, and therefore afforded us transportation and supervision – not necessarily economies – but certainly the ability to handle these functions in a logical fashion. We did not have to jump to Chicago or to the Middle West. We could just extend our lines in a natural movement."

As a wholesaler you were accustomed to buy direct from manufacturers. When you became retailers I presume you continued to buy direct?

"Yes. The nature of that business was changing too. If you go back into the twenties and before, there were large mills, especially hosiery mills and underwear mills, who preferred to work with jobbers and wholesalers, thus having fewer accounts than they would selling directly to retailers where the vast numbers of accounts would have been impractical to handle. This situation changed through a gradual evolution. As the retailers increased the size of their operations, the mills decided that their best interests lay in having a much closer relationship with their ultimate customers, namely the retailers. Thus the jobber's place in the distribution scheme became less and less important."

What was your warehouse situation in those early days?

"The warehousing space that we used as a jobber was now used as a supply and distribution depot for the retail stores. Of course, the Nugent stores had their own warehouses in New York City."

What influenced the decision to go into the discount field? Were you suffering from the competition of the early discounters?

"No, it was not competition but management saw the handwriting on the wall. There were warning signs of a leveling-off or actual diminution in volume as early as 1951 and 1952. We had gone through a period of postwar boom buying. We had experienced the physical expansion of our chain in terms of additional units: larger and more important stores in better communities. We wanted to lift ourselves from what we considered 'marginal' stores – the third, fourth, or fifth guy on the totem pole in terms of customer patronage. We wanted to be the store the customer would visit first. To accomplish this we began to build larger stores with more sophisticated furniture and fixtures including wall-to-wall carpeting. We tried to set ourselves up in some major cities where we had already had considerable success in the past."

Did this policy result in increased profitability?

172

Traditional Stores Move Into Discounting

"As early as 1952 we saw that in some of these newer stores, and in some of the older stores, the volumes were leveling off and in some cases going down rather sharply."

Could you mention any specific competition which caused this?

"Actually, it was not a matter of competition. It was really the beginning of the population explosion to the suburbs with a resulting decay of downtown as a shopping center. It was difficult to get people to come downtown. Even if they did get downtown with their cars, parking was either very inconvenient or non-existent. In those days we used to talk to the chambers of commerce in various cities, point out to them what was happening, and urge them to follow the examples of two cities which had successfully stemmed the tide by taking steps to provide adequate downtown parking. In both our Quincy and Malden stores the volume had not dropped because the chambers in these towns made them alive and vibrant by creating a downtown shopping center. They had the sagacity to provide big parking lots. Actually, Quincy started to do this in the forties. These are two prime examples of cities which were somewhat insulated from this flight of population to the outskirts.

"In other Massachusetts cities the volumes of our downtown stores were drying up pretty rapidly. At the same time, suburban shopping centers were being created. In some cases they were community centers, in others regional, strip, or neighborhood. Of whatever type, these centers were beginning to serve the need of the suburban consumer. They gave her the convenience of easy parking, night shopping hours, and easy access without the necessity of taking a trip downtown.

"To top it all off, we saw the advent of the discount department store oriented to soft goods merchandising in 1954 and 1955. (I am not talking of the hardgoods variety of discounters, such as Sol Polk or Lechmere.) These were soft goods merchants like us. We saw vast numbers of customers going through these discount stores and loading up shopping baskets with no salesgirls in view.

"Our top management spent a great deal of time visiting the pioneers in Rhode Island – so much time that the help must have thought we were fellow employees. We came away convinced that if we wanted to stay in retailing, we were going to have to shift our business considerably."

In what year was this?

"1955. We saw that this was going to be the new type of distribution and that it might parallel the growth of the food supermarket chains which had their earliest beginnings in the thirties. These also were in car barns and old mill properties. Such makeshift establishments were soon outgrown and made it necessary to erect new buildings with all the accoutrements of a good physical plant including better parking lots than those we had seen in Rhode Island. They were the kind you saw in the food supermarkets of those days. We reasoned that if this was so, and that if this type of distribution would have a parallel growth to the food mart business, then we might be well advised as an organization to skip the car barn and mill outlet development phase and build stores designed for our purpose from the ground up. We did. We were the first organization, certainly in this area, and as far as we know the first company in the country, that built a store designed from the ground up for this type of retailing."

Could you give me a little more detail on this building phase of your operation?

"At the time prospects looked bleak for the Bell Shop-Nugent stores, so we determined to do something about it. If we had done nothing the chances are high that we would no longer be in business."

What was your volume at this time and approximately how many stores did you have?

"We had 77 Bell Shop-Nugent stores throughout the northeastern part of the country and were doing between $15 million and $16 million. We developed in late 1955 what we called a two-pronged plan, the Z plan and the Y plan. The Z plan was designed to try and answer our questions regarding downtown locations. We felt that if we could take those stores, or some stores, and run them on a discount self-service basis, perhaps we could stem the tide of volume diminution, make up some of that slack, and salvage some of those real estate problems and difficult store situations. The other plan was to create larger physical plants and to embrace as many of the merchandise categories that one finds in a department store as we possibily could. We thought that the best method would probably be to use the technique of leased departments because at that time we were only experienced in merchandising ladies' and children's departments. To begin with, we did not feel that we had either the talent or the capital to invest in merchandising organizations, or to finance the inventory necessary to operate departments other than ladies' and children's.

"Having once developed a plan like this, you can say, 'Well, I am going to open up a store here, I am going to open up a store there, and I am going to do this and that in a very logical way.' The problem is that real estate opportunity does not always present itself in the logical, geographical scheme of things as one would like. The first opportunity, the very first opportunity we had, was a piece of ground in Hyannis, Mass. In the scheme of things, it was a very unlikely place to get started in the discount business. But we knew Hyannis fairly well because we had a Bell shop there, and we had done reasonably well with the Bell shop on a twelve-month basis, not just on a summer colony basis. Stop & Shop offered to build a store for us down there since they had acquired some property on Main Street and were opening a food store. They wanted some tenants and this seemed like a good opportunity. Our store in Hyannis at that time was 5,000 square feet. In addition to the ladies' and children's wear, we put in leased shoe and men's wear departments.

174

"This center, which is actually still there in Hyannis, opened in June of 1956, close to ten years ago. It was successful almost from the word go. We subsequently enlarged that store to 7,500 feet and finally to 10,000 feet. In 1962 we opened a 45,000 square-foot store right behind this one on another piece of ground that we were able to acquire. We then opened up the back of the old store so that both stores faced one another, and we operated the 45,000-foot store plus the 10,000-foot annex store. We had discovered that although Hyannis was successful, the costs of operating it in terms of management and supporting management were almost the same in that small store as they would be in a big 50,000 or 60,000-foot store. We could not hire someone of lesser caliber or lesser ability to be the manager or assistant manager. It is true that he would have a lesser number of hands underneath them because the number of hands was always conditioned to how much volume you were going to be doing. The management of the store, and its allied problems, were just as intense, probably more intense, than in the larger store, a type of store we got a crack at in September of 1956.

"A real estate opportunity came to our attention in a Roslindale development. Roslindale is a part of Boston; the development was on the American Legion Highway. In retrospect this seems the most unlikely of locations for a discount store. Today, if someone gave us that location to look at, it is doubtful that we would be smart enough to say 'That's a good location. We are going to put a store there.' Why? Because the American Legion Highway is only two miles long and goes from no place to no place. It's just a complete nonentity in terms of roads. It's a wide road, four lanes, and a median strip with crossovers, but it goes from Blue Hill Avenue on one end to Cummins Highway at the other end. Cummins Highway itself is a very short highway and only goes from Mattapan Square to Roslindale Square. We're sitting in the middle of the American Legion Highway, not even on a corner. On all sides of us are cemeteries, and a mental institution is on the corner of the American Legion Highway and Morton Street. The developer had already put in an A & P store and had some additional land. We made a deal with him. The important point is that he was smart enough and lucky enough to be able to finance the development.

"In those days you couldn't finance a discount store. If we wanted to go to the Prudential or any other big insurance company to put up a Bell shop, we could have gotten financing very easily even though we looked at the business and said, 'this is ridiculous because the Bell shops are on the way out.' The insurance companies were betting on the wrong horse. No amount of persuasion could convince them in those days. At any rate the original plans for that store called for 20,000 feet. Management saw that this was not going to be enough and changed it to 30,000; ultimately we grabbed off another piece of available land and we finally opened up with 39,000 square feet. The grand opening was in September, 1956. We really knew

175

nothing about this kind of business. Nevertheless we had augmented our own merchandising know-how with leased departments in men's wear, domestics and infants, housewares and hardwares, shoes, millinery, and toys. We did not have appliances, sporting goods, or photography. The only department that we ourselves operated was ladies' and children's wear. Some of these lessees are now acquisitions of ours; others are still operating as our leased departments. We have been faithful, and they have been faithful. We think we have the best operators in the field. We have helped each other prosper.

"Our experience in our Roslindale store from September through Christmas was most exciting and enjoyable. I recall the Saturday before Christmas. (After all, it was our first big store.) Our offices and distribution center were on Commonwealth Avenue; practically everyone in the office including the company officers came out to the store to help. Everybody was there that Saturday. We had a tremendous day and remember, this was only ten years ago. We took in $39,000 that Saturday. That taste indicated to us the way to go as fast as we could. At the end of the second year we made the store much larger by adding 17,000 square feet, making it 56,000 feet."
Where did you get operating capital?

"Well, let's see what was really required. Nothing for bricks and mortar because we were on lease; relatively nothing for inventory because we were operating only ladies' and children's departments. We worked the store very closely, set up the normal thirty-day trade terms, and operated a chain of 77 other stores. So it was not that much of an impact on the business from an inventory point of view. We really needed no additional money. We were turning our inventory in the store faster than we had to pay for it. We were actually generating dollars to help out elsewhere. Furniture and fixtures were a problem, and we had to finance that ourselves at the beginning. But in the second year, my father worked out a scheme, and we were able to do our financing for fixtures, both in the past and in the future, by bank loans. This has become Zayre Leasing, a wholly-owned subsidiary.

"From the earliest beginnings relatively little capital was needed. We probably could have paced our expansion a lot faster if we weren't hindered by the ability to get development of new properties; that is, to get landlords to develop properties for us."
Were you able to find competent personnel to man the new stores?

"At that time we had a large and talented man-power pool of home office staff, trained in the 77 Bell Shop-Nugent stores. All received a great deal of encouragement and training from the first generation of the family and were exposed to all phases of retailing, including warehouse operations, chain management, and buying. We, as managing officers, still had plenty of time to develop the stores themselves. Any member of our top management could get a whale of a lot more out of a store if given nothing else to do but operate

176

that store. This is one of the reasons why those first few stores developed as rapidly as they did from a volume and profit point of view. After two or three years, we never saw the same kind of rapid increase in volume and profitability as we did in the first four or five stores. No doubt the advent of competition had something to do with it.

"My father and uncle gave us a tremendous amount of encouragement. The youngest man in this organization today is my father. His office is right next door to mine. He is still as aggressive as they come and forward thinking, never satisfied with our accomplishments, and sure that we can increase our operations both in size and efficiency.

"In January, 1956, Stanley Feldberg was relieved of all of his responsibilities with Bell Shop-Nugents; these were picked up by others. Mr. Feldberg concentrated on Zayre; the layout of the new stores, the purchase of fixtures, negotiations with the leased department operators, and the hiring of help."
What agreements did you have with lessees?

"No one knew then what the actual costs of operating a store would be. Therefore, the leased department rents were based on figures which management thought would cover all expenses. Later we re-evaluated our operating expenses and came up with a more realistic figure. We charged so much of the store management costs such as cashiering, back office help, etc., on a pro-rata basis. If the leased department was doing 10 per cent of the store's business, then we took 10 per cent of these charges and made them allocable to the leased department. In addition, we added occupancy costs since we knew it cost us so much per square foot for rent, light, heat, and occupancy costs in general. Advertising expense too was allocated on the basis of volume. Rents were considerably lower than they are today because nobody really knew just what the right charge was, so you struck off a figure you thought would take care of your expenses and throw off a little profit.

"Experience later on indicated two things: one, the leased department operator was making more money than the store operator. This is still true today from a percentage of sales point of view. Second, when we examined our costs carefully, they were higher than we had anticipated."
Did you have any difficulty in buying the merchandise you wanted and did you encounter any opposition from "traditional" department stores?

"The difficulties of this nature were very minor. First of all, we were not Tom, Dick, or Harry just starting out. We had a business that already had a good credit standing. In merchandising and resource circles we were known as the New England Trading Company. They did not know what stores we operated since all transactions were with the New England Trading Company. This company had a fine reputation, a fine credit standing, and bought a lot of merchandise. We were buying more merchandise than ever so when some complaints came from traditional department stores, the manufacturer listened very politely and said, 'Well, these people buy in such large quantities,

177

as much as $100,000 worth of goods at a time, and this represents too much volume to me. I am going to do business with them and that's it. You either like my merchandise or forget about it.' So we had very, very little trouble."
How about problems with Fair Trade?

"Yes, there were some with health and beauty aids. The Massachusetts Fair Trade Laws were tighter on these items than elsewhere. As a matter of fact, we did not really mark down fair-traded items. We never tilted windmills in Massachusetts. You may recall that others tried to circumvent it with discount stamps. We never got involved in that. If we could not discount the item, we kept it at the regular price. Signs were made saying that we were unable to discount the item because it was fair-traded."
How was your expansion financed?

"When we embarked on an expansion program outside of New England, the Zayre Corporation became the parent company and acquired all of the capital stock of the other companies. The net worth of the combined companies at that time was $2.5 million. We changed the fiscal close of Zayre from July 31st to January 31st. In that next six months' period we earned a half million dollars net, so we then raised the net worth to $3 million.

"In the spring of 1961, we arranged for a $1.5 million long-term loan from State Mutual in Worcester. At the same time, State Mutual bought 10,000 shares of Zayre common stock. We were told at the time that we should consider this to be quite a feather in our cap because, although insurance companies and banks like to have options on the stock, it is rare that they will put up cash immediately at the outset. Secondly, the price that they paid for it without any really hard negotiation was two-and-a-half times book value as per our statement of July 31, 1960. We got $45 a share for the 10,000 shares, a total of $450,000.

"We take advantage of favorable market conditions to raise the capital we feel we will need, so that when we do have need of the money we have already stockpiled it. We never really hit a financial crisis such as Towers and a lot of other people did.

"Our corporate financial picture was sound and we had the backing of some fine institutions. In all our areas of operation it has always been our policy to try to line ourselves up with what we thought were the number one institutions. We get a benefit locally because when a local bank is talking and says, 'We have the Zayre account,' the word spreads around and you take on a different image in the city. We have deliberately pursued that policy. We may have been lucky in having achieved it."
How are the Bell Shops-Nugent stores working out today?

"At the present time we are still operating forty-six stores in that chain. A new corner has been turned. Three years ago we were able to bring in a new merchandising staff of buyers for the Bell Shops-Nugents Division. This staff is entirely separate from the Zayre operation. Since they have no other

178

responsibility but the Bell Shops-Nugent stores, they make them work. Previously, the buyer was buying lingerie for both Zayre and the Bell Shops-Nugents chain. Obviously he was tempted to play the winner, namely the Zayre stores from which he gets ten, fifteen or twenty times the volume in a given store. Thus the poor Bell Shops got the short end of the stick. Today, instead of buying merchandise similar to that which we carry in Zayre's, they buy clothing more suited to the Bell Shops' image of a ladies' specialty store. They have introduced several higher-priced lines than we have at Zayre's and discontinued the lower-priced merchandise. It has become an entirely different operation. One of these stores is located in a Chicopee (Mass.) shopping center where we have a Zayre store right next to it. We did precisely the same thing in our shopping center in South Hadley, Mass. The surprising thing is that they are doing very, very well right next door to the discount store."

What types of merchandise do you carry in the Bell Shops-Nugent stores?

"We are dealing in sportswear that ranges upward from where the Zayre store stops, a different kind of merchandise entirely. There are merchandise categories similar to Zayre's, but not similar price lines."

Rather than operate two stores, would it not be better to carry higher-priced lines in Zayre's? Do you cater to a different income group in each store?

"I really don't know."

Getting back to operations, what is your thinking in regard to the functions of store managers? How do you retain their active interest?

"We have very much dreaded the possibility of becoming a chain of mechanics as we grow larger. We would not like to see store management trained in a way similar to that used by variety chains in the past. In this system, there was a counter form laid out in detail in advance. This takes away some of the manager's initiative, and a store is, or ought to be, most successful when it reflects the abilities of the store manager on the local scene. So far as our managers are concerned, my feeling is that we should do our best to give them every opportunity to improve their know-how and to encourage the use of any initiative with which they may be endowed. We are not certain that we always deliver the right merchandise at the right price at the right time to each store. We cannot send out directives saying, 'Reserve counter number 11 for item such-and-such that you will receive shortly.' We don't actually know when the store does get the merchandise. It may be a week or two weeks. When it finally does arrive, the store room may be jammed up with a big load of toys making it impossible to unpack the shipment, thus adding to the delay. The store manager must exercise merchandising initiative as far as the store display is concerned. The central buying office does take into consideration the tastes of individual sections of the country, and the manager can seek additional goods if he feels that the tastes of his customers warrant it.

179

"Many of our stores run individual level promotions such as Crazy Days, Circus Days, Old-Fashioned Bargain Days, etc. We have established a schedule of semi-annual seminars in which all our managers are brought to Boston for four or five days. During that time we show them what merchandise we have purchased for them and also give them suggestions on how to display and merchandise the goods. An extremely important aspect of these seminars is the exchange of ideas between the managers themselves and the managers and home office management. We learn to recognize their problems more quickly, and in turn they recognize ours."

As you rapidly grow larger is there not danger that the home office may fall behind in keeping up the paper work for a rapidly-increasing volume?

"One thing that this company always had was plenty of home office overhead. This goes way, way back. In other words, even when we were Bell Shops-Nugents we had more overhead and more people than we really needed. In 1949 we were in the never-never land of being so small that we could run things ourselves with a very tight organization. We had more than enough trained and experienced personnel to get Zayre rolling. As we continued to grow we kept pace by adding home office personnel. Zayre has tried, at all times, to keep ahead of its personnel needs. In addition, Zayre has been on top of the developments in EDP and was one of the first retail chains to use punchtape registers on the store level in conjunction with its data-processing equipment. We recognized that human hands were not going to be able to take care of the paper work and that is why we moved into the kind of IBM equipment we now have."

Do you think the time will come when you will have to stop expanding because of a shortage of good locations?

"Never. Management feels that we can go on expanding indefinitely."

But how about the competition for good locations today?

"There is competition. But what happens is that we go back to those areas where we already have a stake. This is our prime objective today. We have 25 stores throughout Mass., and two distribution centers. Boston has a population of about 2.7 million. Pittsburgh and Cleveland are relatively the same size. We have only three stores in Cleveland and three in Pittsburgh. All six stores happen to be extremely good stores. What is the right number of stores for these cities? Obviously more than three."

But how about competition?

"Right, but you have to consider competition in Boston too. Nobody is afraid to come and open up stores in Boston; the same is true in Pittsburgh and Cleveland. Undoubtedly there is competition; nevertheless we are looking principally to increase our stake in places where we already have a foothold. Among the advantages is the ability to cut down the advertising expense per store. Someone taking a cold look at a new city might say, 'Why do you want to go there and face the competition?' You look at it and say, 'Yes, but the numbers are such and such and what is nature of the competition? I think I'm a better merchant than the other guy.' Otherwise you would not be in business. Unless you have that kind of confidence, then you're doing things wrong to begin with. 'Why can't I come into this city and build a better mousetrap and merchandise it better than the competition?' As a matter of fact, there are two large metropolitan areas in which we are giving that kind of consideration this very day. If we decide to go ahead in these areas we may be successful; but then again maybe we won't. Initially we may have difficulty, but I have a theory that ultimately any reasonable metropolitan location is going to be sound."

I assume you are counting on the population increase?

"That is exactly the point, since the numbers are working in our favor, assuming that the economy is sound."

How do you get the right kind of people to run your stores? Does the presumed difference between discount and "traditional" retailing make it necessary to hire a special type of individual?

"In my opinion there is really no difference between regular retailing and so-called discount retailing. There is no special secret or magic formula; it's nothing but good, hard, dogged work and common sense when you come right down to it. Sure our distribution system may be somewhat different. We're self-service. But the department store today is so much more self-service and self-selection than it was twenty years ago that the difference is now rather small between what we are doing and what a department store is doing."

INTERVIEW WITH SUMNER FELDBERG, TREASURER, ZAYRE CORP.

How did you get into retailing?

"Basically, I recognized during my schooling days that I would be entering the family business started by my father and uncle. My cousin Stanley and I both planned, on completion of our schooling, to enter the family business. I attended Harvard College, class of 1945. This period of school was interrupted by war service and I got back to college in time to get my degree in 1947."

What did you major in as an undergraduate?

"American government. I then went on to the Harvard Graduate School of Business Administration and got my M.B.A. degree, with a major in retailing, in 1949. I was elected to Phi Beta Kappa and graduated with distinction at the business school. I then joined the family concern, a chain of women's apparel stores. We applied ourselves with a good deal of vigor to trying to make this business grow and prosper. The women's apparel popular-priced chain stores at that time was a very mature form of retailing with a great deal of competition. In subsequent years after Stanley and I came into the company in 1949, I would say we virtually doubled the business to almost 75 per cent over what it was in 1949, but it was hard work. It was a field of highly developed retail people with plenty of competition. This was Main Street retailing.

"We became aware in the mid-'50's of the advent of the so-called discount store. We saw it here in New England. Discounting started in three forms. In New England it was the mill type of outlet – mills were available – with an orientation towards apparel. In New York it very often started with the upstairs type of store selling appliances at a discount. On the West Coast it very often started with food as the point of entry. We observed it rather carefully because basically these people were selling apparel which was our livelihood. We came to the conclusion that the method of selling merchandise was sound. By developing high volume you were able to radically reduce certain costs of your distribution cycle, such costs being not only personnel by use of self-service, but also reduced percentages such as markdown and rent. For that reason we became convinced that this was sound development, not unlike what had happened in the food business in the '30's, and that this format of retailing, self-service retailing of general merchandise, was here to stay. We also became convinced that the mill outlet stage was only a temporary thing as was the so-called 'big bear' stage in food discounting. Therefore, we decided that we would go in with new stores."

What part did you play in this decision?

"The family company moved as a unit. The way it worked was that each of us was performing certain functions in the business at the time. I, myself, in the years since 1949 spent a lot of time in the merchandise area having originally been a merchandise buyer in foundations and then I increasingly took on responsibilities for merchandising not only ladies' small wear, but children's wear. I became store operations manager of the chain, then Bell and Nugents stores. When the firm decided to go into discounting we decided to take one member of the family and excuse him from other duties for the Bell Shops and Nugents chain, and ask him to focus on the new stores. Therefore, Mr. Stanley was relieved of other duties and asked to operate the two new Zayre stores that we were creating; other members of the family were asked to continue whatever their other responsibilities were to the entire chain.

"Our approach was to make the Zayre stores successful and then go down the line of creating more Zayre stores as rapidly as we possibly could and as quickly as our finances would pe mit. Starting as a small firm with limited financing, we made the decision that all our resources would be best applied to this new Zayre operation. Nevertheless, the bulk of our operations were still in the specialty chains; a tremendous effort was made to maintain those

182

specialty stores at as high a degree of excellence as was possible. We were not giving them new stores because all of the new-store money was going to Zayre; but we tried to maintain as well as we could what we had.

"Our policy was to discontinue those specialty stores losing money but to keep operating the good ones. It took us perhaps four or five years before our Zayre volume equalled our Bell Shop volume. In the meantime, for economy, virtually every operating executive, without exception, certainly in the merchandise end, was expected to provide management and merchandise for both chains. Our buyers and merchandise managers were oriented to serve the requirements of both chains. Therefore my responsibilities, which at that time were largely merchandise, and those of my buyers, were to provide the best merchandise in the proper fashion for both chains.

"Once Zayre became so large that it generated volume several times the apparel specialty stores volume. We found that our buyers were perhaps not fulfilling their obligations to the small system. At that point we recommended to management the creation of a separate staff for Bell Shops.

"In the period as the Zayre operations grew larger, my responsibilities tended to focus around what I call everything inside. I was responsible for merchandise and control, whereas Stanley was responsible for everything outside, that is, store operations and real estate. That was basically the way we split responsibilities. My background was in merchandising. Therefore, in the years that succeeded, it was largely my responsibility to hire the merchandise managers, motivate them, and to do the hiring and firing of buyers. In addition, I took over the responsibility for finances and for the control division and though I have had the title of treasurer from the beginning, I come more out of the merchandise larder. The needs of finances in this business were so very large, that a great deal of my time and effort in the years from 1960 to say 1963 were devoted to control and finance. At the same time, I maintained a very heavy interest in merchandising and I was the guide to whom the merchandise managers reported.

"More recently, within the past year-and-a half, I have relaxed my interest in merchandising somewhat through the appointment of Mr. Burton S. Stern as senior vice-president and general merchandise manager. Today I spend less time in merchandise. In this particular firm, each member of the family has always carried operating responsibilities. In the conduct of those responsibilities he is fulfilling them the same as any other operating executive. In addition, and wearing a different hat, he is a member of a family ownership in which he participates as a major stockholder in the company. This was done before we were a public company. In 1962 we became a public company and the family can still exercise management by participation on the board of directors."

What, in your estimation, is the difference between buying for a discount operation and a traditional department store?

Sumner L. Feldberg, senior vice president
and treasurer, Zayre Corporation.

"We try to buy merchandise which will have a tendency to sell itself on its own. Obviously there are types of merchandise that require salesmanship. For example, we consider photography a service department because there the technical aspects of the product are such that we try to provide sales persons' help. On the other hand, when you go to a department like children's wear, we expect that the merchandise we carry will largely sell from self-service fixtures. Other aspects of the shift are largely in terms of dealing with merchandise on a fairly fast turnover. When selling in a self-service discount store you are trying to grope for that type of merchandise that will sell very freely and repetitively and in large volume. Your requirements increase pretty rapidly; you are confronted with logistics problems in having an adequate supply of desirable merchandise. In our constant growth, we found that we had to project our requirements further and further ahead, so that as we grew in discounting, we were committing our dollars and buying our

184

commitments weeks and months ahead of the time that we did it in our apparel chain. We entered the discount field with a background in apparel and we were more fashion-oriented and more oriented towards women's apparel than others who entered the discount field. The process of committing yourself earlier and earlier as your dollar requirements get larger is as true in fashion as it is in non-fashion."

How do you feel about merchandising additional services?

"We have taken a relatively conservative viewpoint on service departments. They are rather difficult to operate on a chain-wide basis and we in Zayre are largely oriented along a chain principle. Almost everything we have done from the beginning has been based upon a conviction that this business is, over the long run, not so much a discount business as it is a new form of chain store operation.

"Service businesses are about as good as the people who are running them on the local scene. Therefore they do not lend themselves to chain operation as effectively as other departments. We do have some service departments and we will continue to add them where we feel that they can be profitably executed. However, we do not probe as far with service departments as many independent individual operators do."

Zayre's 50th store which opened in August 1963 in Portsmouth, Va.
In 1969, Zayre had more than 150 stores.

185

Are you increasing the fashion aspect of your business?

"There is fashion in all merchandise – in sheets and in dresses. Everything that we carry has fashion in it. There is fashion in the appliance department. It is only a matter of degree. No department succeeds unless the merchant responsible for it is playing up the fashion within his retailing area or industry. He will be a very poor buyer and merchant if he is not pursuing fashion – the fad of the moment."

What are some of your operating problems today?

"One of our major operating problems at the moment is to build and increase middle management on the executive level of the business. We are growing very rapidly because we have very aggressive management and because we are located in a business where there is a tremendous growth potential. Therefore, much of the talent that we need is produced from within; but we are growing at a more rapid rate than breeding your own talent permits. As a result, we are forced to go to the outside to add talent.

"Large numbers of people are needed to fulfill our growing requirements for managers and assistant managers. At the same time there are increasing numbers of positions to be filled at the buyership level; more buyers, more merchandise managers. There are a great many positions that we must fill with competent people in the control and accounting areas as well. As the chain emerges as a bigger and bigger unit, you get specific staff functions that become very important in terms of control of payroll, store operation, taxes, insurance, and fine specialties of that sort.

"Another problem that we are dealing with at the moment is the nature of the control which will permit continued excellence running this large group of stores. We are already a good deal more sophisticated than most in this field and at the moment we are wrestling with further steps that will in the next two, three, and four years further sophisticate the type of decisions that will have to be made in our business – decisions that have to do with merchandise replenishment decision-making."

Will you open 15 to 20 stores a year for the next few years?

"It would appear that we will."

Aren't good locations getting difficult to find?

"We are finding more desirable locations in which we would like to locate stores than we have the ability to open."

Do real estate companies come to you with these offerings?

"Yes. Increasingly we go out and look for locations. We are trying to develop our real estate department to not only receive the offerings of developers who come in, but also to aggressively go out and search for locations in areas where we want to enlarge our franchise."

186

Mangel Stores Corp. and Shoppers Fair

SOL MANGEL, PRESIDENT

Who started your conventional stores?

"Well, it was an accident. I had a brother-in-law who was a manufacturer and he was stuck with over production of black satin blouses. His wife said that there was only one thing for him to do and that was to open a little store in downtown, New York. He took her advice and opened a store on 7th street on the East Side. He made it a one-price store. This was a special attraction since they didn't have one-price in those days. We had only one price: 98 cents! That started the specialty blouse business in the United States. The name of this factory was Guzy Bros. and this was in 1898. We then opened some stores called the New York Waist House. When we went into the discount field we had about 120 of these stores. Now we're down to 92. We had no alternative but to go into discounting unless we wanted to go out of business."

What made you go into discounting?

"With the growth of outlying shopping centers, business moved away from downtown. We heard about discounting and visited a couple of stores. It was only a question of buying the same merchandise, selling it for less, and giving as little service as possible. But you needed parking. We did this in 1956 and now have 42 discount stores in addition to our 92 conventional women's fashion specialty stores. Our discount stores are called Shoppers Fair and the specialty stores are known as Mangel Stores. We're contracting in our conventional stores but expanding our discount operations. There are still a few cities where our downtown stores are good. When leases run out and the economics are not in our favor we close the location. This applies to both kinds of stores." As of 1969, we had 150 stores and leased departments.

Where are your discount stores?

"They are in the eastern half of the U.S., but for the most part in the Middle West. We have many of them in the Michigan, Indiana and Ohio areas. We went out there instead of the East because we wanted industrial cities. The discount store is only good when you have a large enough population to draw from.

"The type of individual who works in factories is likely to go to the discount store."

Do you warehouse centrally or do you drop-ship?

"We do both. We lease shoes, drugs, millinery and jewelry. The average size of our store is 60,000 to 80,000 feet."

Are you invited to put stores in shopping centers?

"Sometimes they like us because we attract traffic. For the most part, in

187

the past, we've taken free-standing stores, but what happens is that before long other stores join us. We don't refuse to join shopping centers."

Do you like to own or to lease?

"If we had enough money we'd own all of our stores. We do own some."

What is your volume?

"For both types of stores our volume was $100 million in 1965. Including our leased departments, 1969 volume was $122 million."

Do your buyers buy for both your discount and conventional stores?

"We have the same buyers in soft goods but different buyers for hard goods. Our specialty stores don't necessarily carry better merchandise. We compete against ourselves in some cities with both a specialty store and a discount store."

Do you have your own brands?

"We've gone into building up our own brands. We hook up with a manufacturer who we know will make deliveries on staple goods and we'll pick out a name or they'll give us a name and that's what we carry. It'll be a nationally-branded item but with our brand – our own trademark. We do this in men's wear, lingerie, and staple merchandise that's well made and that we're not ashamed to sell to anybody. We don't care what the other fellow sells."

What advertising media do you use?

"We go into circulars mainly and we do a lot of newspaper advertising, too. I'd say it's about 50–50."

What's your policy on training personnel? Do you promote from within?

"We'd like to if we had the right people, but all the stores are stealing our people. We do a certain amount of training but we have no training program as such."

Do you feel well equipped to face future competition?

"The competition hasn't got any better know-how than we have. There is no big difference in buyers. We change them and they change them. We've been in the soft goods business for many years; many of them are just starting out. We have gone into electronic data processing, IBM 21401 computers. We use them for everything, including well over a hundred stores on credit."

Are you trading up?

"No. We may sell a $2 or $3 shirt but it's not a $5 or $6 shirt. By the time we reach $5, the best shirts will be $8, so we're not really trading up .'

188

Hartfield Stores Inc.:/Zody's Discount Department Stores

The Hartfield chain of 54 women's and children's specialty stores was founded in 1929 by Leo Hartfield. In 1960 the company decided to enter the discount field. The principals, Leo Hartfield and Milton Gutterman, made extensive tours of discount stores nationally with special attention to those discounters who had entered discounting with an apparel specialty store background such as theirs. The first Zody's was opened in Garden Grove, Calif. Major emphasis was placed on women's and children's departments.

In 1965 Abe L. Marks, a CPA and formally a partner in Clarence Raines and Co., was made president. (He is a founder and president of the Mass Merchandising Research Foundation.) A new policy was instituted whereby all departments other than women's and children's apparel were leased out to well-known national lessees: linens and domestics with the Bernard Abrams Company; toys and sporting goods with American Toy. Abe Marks said, "Our aim is to meet the shopper's widest possible family needs. Few discounters make real money down the line department by department. Our own experience is that we make most money by operating the departments we know best. To operate our other departments, we have chosen the strongest possible group of associated merchants operating nationally in the mass merchandising field."

As a result of this policy, Zody's maintains a strong apparel image and competes successfully in the Los Angeles area with such stores as Bullock's, Sears, Lerner's, Penney's, as well as with its own Hartfield stores. Zody's ranks high in sales of women's coats and dresses priced at $16.95 and under, and in lingerie. It is very competitive in attire for teenage boys and girls and in infants wear for up to five year olds.

Many of the old, established retail companies who entered the discount field have gradually phased out their original specialty stores to concentrate on more profitable and faster growing mass merchandising units. With Zody's, however, the 47 sizeable Hartfield specialty apparel stores continue to play an important role in the total picture. These stores, under the direction of Milton Gutterman, are located in suburban areas and shopping centers in seven states, including Hawaii, with the major concentration in California. Hartfield contributes substantially to the success of Zody's fashion operation. "Our very large fashion departments are the keys to Zody's traffic pulling power," observed board chairman Leo Hartfield. "They give our stores a fashion image which makes us distinctive from other West Coast discount stores, which derive for the most part from food and hard goods origins."

The older Zody stores have been re-fixtured and Abe Marks envisions an expansion to 15 or more units in the next few years. The new Zody's are

189

Abe L. Marks, president, Hartfield Stores, Inc.;
also president of the Mass Merchandising Research Foundation.

in the 100,000 square-foot class. Company policy is to concentrate in the Southern California market.

Sales for the fiscal year ending February 3, 1968 were $105,699,994 (leased department sales: $24,600,436). Net earnings were $1,088,306, compared to $312,398 for the previous year. New stores are being opened in Huntington Beach, Anaheim, and Buena Park, California.

Interstate Department Stores – White Front and Topps

Prior to 1958, Interstate was a well-established merchandiser with forty-six stores in the conventional department store field. Said Sol Cantor, president:

"Back in 1957 and 1958, we acquired a two-store discount chain – White Front in Los Angeles – that did $20 million a year in volume. Today we operate two major discount networks, White Front on the West Coast and the Topps chain, as well as conventional department stores elsewhere in the nation. With more than one hundred stores at the end of 1968, our sales passed the half-billion dollar mark to $641,069,000; a sizeable increase over fiscal 1965. More than eighty-five per cent of our sales and our earnings come from discounting.

"At Interstate we are very proud of our White Front division head-quartered in California. With the opening of our new store in Downey, we now have twenty-two White Front units. By October, 1966 White Front did an annual volume of $250 million. In sales per square foot, these units have been running at $131 against a national average of $67 for discount retailers. Their traffic is better than one million Californians per week. White Front is second in refrigerator and washing machine sales in California and actually outsells Sears in television sets.

"None of our conventional department stores are located on the West Coast. We have closed down or sold off the marginal operations and our existing conventional stores are doing well. For example, at our Latham store near Albany, New York, sales were up 12.5 per cent this year in spite of a new Macy's that opened a half-mile away. In addition to their contribution of sales and earnings, our conventional stores gave us experience and background with both merchandise and personnel. We will probably expand White Front into more western states, as well as into more California communities as long as we can do it profitably. Three years ago, when we first started moving north in California, one of my friends in the financial community asked, 'Your sales per store in the Los Angeles area are the highest of any discounter in the country. Can you keep it up in the North?' Well, today the volume and profitability of, say, our stores in south San Francisco, Sunnyvale, and San Jose are as good as our stores in Southern California. In Covina, for example, one of the most saturated areas in the United States, we opened a store that is running about 20 per cent ahead of plans. I can cite a number of similar case histories: Lansing and Kalamazoo, Mich., and Fairfield, Conn., where we have thrived despite heavy competition.

"In expanding today we are even more selective in the sites we seek. We took our major risks several years ago when we opened twenty-one stores in one year. In 1967 we opened ten to twelve new stores. As for growth by acquisition, we are regularly approached to take over existing operations. We look into these offers but up to this time we are happier about the kind of sales we can build through our own expansion. We believe that discount sales will continue at a minimum $2 billion a year growth rate. Our own plans back that faith. This year (1969) Interstate will open several new stores.

191

Sol Cantor, president, Interstate Department Stores, Inc.

"How are we going to finance this expansion? Fortunately, we accomplished a major financing prior to the present tight-money market. Thus, with these funds, plus retained earnings and depreciation, we will have adequate money available to cover our foreseeable expansion plans and the upgrading of existing stores. This year for example, after the provision for dividends, we have available from retained earnings and depreciation over $11 million in cash. We believe the potential for sheer geographical expansion of discount retailing is enormous.

"There has been a certain status symbol in making a purchase at a department store. Particularly in soft lines, 'status symbol' labels enable the department store to take a higher mark-up, even though we have the same item at a lower price. However, as the consumer gains increased confidence in her own judgment, she will begin looking for the same tangible values in soft lines as she has been able to get in hard lines from us. Thus, ready-to-wear

192

and other soft lines should be susceptible to increased penetration. We have taken firm steps at Interstate to move aggressively into these new product areas. For example, when we purchased the White Front chain in 1959, it was a hardgoods specialist. While we have vastly increased White Front's sales, we have also changed the product mix so that today only about 65 per cent of White Front sales are in hard lines. Within that, only 25 per cent is in big ticket items. Similarly, our Topps division originally was strongly oriented to soft wares. Today we are balancing Topps' assortment by steadily adding housewares, toys, sporting goods, and other hardlines so that today we have a 50–50 mixture.

"One of the most significant steps in developing new product markets is our specification buying program – especially in soft lines. Now, we are directing what we want made, rather than going to the market and taking what is offered. We are taking active steps to accelerate our specification merchandising in the soft lines area. We are working directly from the mill level to the final package to create a product which will meet our exact specifications. The results are encouraging. We are by no means abandoning our traditional lure of name-brand merchandise at discount prices. Well over half of our business is in this well-known, nationally-advertised merchandise. For example, we are General Electric's largest West Coast customer for its branded appliances. We are Admiral's largest retail customer in the world."

Asked what he thought about EDP, Cantor said, "There are three key ways that computerization will enable us to make significant savings and increase our earning power. These are accounting data processing, headquarters-directed merchandise control, and increased sales. The first of these areas, accounting data processing is already in effect. We are now routinely working with computerized data in traditional accounting, such as the company's payroll, accounts payable, etc. The second area, headquarters-directed merchandising control, is almost completely in effect. Within the next six to eight months, we will be able to tell the current inventory for each of the fifty thousand items in our stores. 'Exception reports' furnished to our buyers and merchandise managers will enable them to tell which are best sellers and which are 'dogs' that should be eliminated. All our discount stores have their registers equipped for this program so that the computer will print out an automatic reorder whenever the inventory of a basic staple falls below a predetermined level. The third area of benefit from computerization, increased sales, is one that is presently least appreciated. Computerized inventory control will free our local store managers for more creative and effective merchandising in their communities. Today a very high percentage of every department manager's and every store manager's time is concerned with inventory taking and control. Our computerization program alone will generate substantial net savings in each store.

"Most discount chains try to run a store with a manager and three

193

Selwyn Lemchen, vice president, Interstate Department Stores, Inc.;
general merchandise manager, Topps Division.

department managers, four executives in all. We use nine executives per store because that is what it now takes to keep up inventory freshness and to run a clean, attractive store. Despite the higher payroll costs, we operate on lower margins, with faster turnover, and a higher return-on-investment. We place emphasis on our group managers who supervise stores in a geographical area. We have given broad discretion to produce profits within policy guidelines set by headquarters. There is a two-way flow of information: the group managers visit headquarters every two weeks to participate in decisions on merchandise planning, store operations, payroll reviews, etc. Most of our executives have been developed by us. For example, the director of stores for the Topps division joined us as a store trainee in 1953. A graduate economist, he had been program coordinator of the United Nations International Children's Emergency Fund in New York. He was elected a corporate vice-president this spring. His career is not only a tribute to his own ability, but an illustration of the opportunity for talented people in discount retailing.

"We are placing at the disposal of these younger executives every sophisticated management tool available. The real objective is to direct all the creative energy that these new tools can release. The key to our success will be adherence to the basic principle which called the discounting industry into being, the principle of offering the best possible quality merchandise at lower markups and higher turnover. We believe the next five to ten years will prove even more stimulating for the discount industry than the past decade. We are confident that the American economy will expand and will provide more opportunity for our growth. It has taken thirty-eight years for Interstate to reach $500 million in sales; we believe it will take only another five years or so to add the next half billion dollars in volume."

Answering the question, "What has been the investment record since Interstate made its major move into the discount field?" Cantor said, "As a result of two stock splits and regular stock dividends paid at the end of each year, one hundred shares of Interstate stock purchased in 1958 would have increased to 791 shares in 1966. In 1958, those one hundred shares had a market value of $2,325. At the end of 1965, the equivalent 791 shares had a market value of about $28,872. In addition to the rise in market value, those one hundred shares would have earned more than $1,445 in cash

White Front, Interstate Department Store, Downey, Calif.

dividends. Over the seven-year period, this would have averaged 8.7 per cent yield per year. Our net earnings have grown over 1,200 per cent in eight years – from $600,000, or 29 cents a share, in 1958, to earnings in 1968 of $10.9 million, or $2.27 a share, on a vastly increased number of shares. An earnings' range of $2.80 to $3 a share is a reasonable target for 1969. From 1958 to 1965, our rate of earnings-to-sales rose consistently from 1 per cent to 1.8 per cent. Our ultimate target is 2 per cent. In the same period our working capital climbed from $1.36 million to $39.3 million. And the stockholders' equity rose from $15.6 million in 1958 to $49.2 million last year. We feel our shareholders have been well-rewarded thus far for their faith in Interstate.

"Now, how do we see the future of this innovative venture in retailing? We believe that discount sales will continue at a minimum two-billion-dollar-a-year growth rate. Our own expansion plans back that faith. In 1966 Interstate opened ten new stores. We have announced that we are in negotiation for a desirable property in downtown San Francisco where we will open our largest unit. However, the criterion cannot be 'growth for the sake of growth'; it must be 'growth for the sake of profit.' We constantly tell our people, 'Profits alone will give us all we want. Recognition, money, more job satisfaction, and the only job security that counts, that which stems from giving the investors a superior return on their investment.' Pressures on profit are increasing. Not only is there more competition, but many costs of business, especially payroll, are rising. However, let's be frank. Increasing competition and rising wage scales have always been components of a dynamic economy. The hallmark of competent management is the ability to recognize and meet these challenges to growth. Never before has management had so many tools with which to meet these challenges. Alert executives can supplement their own experience, imagination, and energy with vast systems of instantaneous communication, with electronic data processing, and with sophisticated marketing research."

On January 23, 1967, it was announced in the New York *Times* that Interstate had acquired the four-store Children's Supermarket, Inc., Washington, D.C. In an interview with Isadore Barmash of the *Times*, president Sol Cantor said the discount store has been responsible "for making toy selling a 12-month-a-year operation. . . . Interstate plans to open a new division of large, free-standing discount stores, each about 25,000 square feet, patterned after Children's Supermarket. . . . Department stores have not been as aggressive as discount stores in selling toys year-round because toys have not produced as high a profit for them as they would like." Mr. Cantor asserted that his stores have an initial markup of 26 per cent and 27 per cent on toys and a gross margin of 23 per cent to 24 per cent which was considerably less than that of department stores. "Toys lock up the loyalty of customers from their early youth and also bring the parents in," he said. "Toys have met every

196

test in our operations producing a good profit margin on sales and return on investment. . . . In 1968, we aggressively moved in a grand plan to open a series of toy discount stores. We could well, for example, open 25,000 square-foot stores near or adjacent to our White Front stores in California where each has a 15-acre site."

Children's Supermarts, has stores of about 25,000 square feet and sales of about $160 per square foot of selling space. Cantor said that this was the best in the toy business. The toy sections in Interstate's own discount stores range from 2,800 to 3,200 square feet and, according to Cantor, yield in excess of $100 per square foot. Quoting *Times* reporter Barmash, "Retail toy sales have grown from $1.8 billion in 1961 to an estimated $2.6 billion last year. In 1965, when retail (toy) sales totalled $2.4 billion, discounters did 19.4 per cent of total sales, department stores 10.6 per cent, mail order operations, 9.3 per cent, and toy stores, 9 per cent. The remaining approximate 30 per cent was accounted for by a diverse group of retail establishments."

Asked how he was able to sell merchandise at substantially lower prices than traditional retailers, Cantor said, "The answer is at the very heart of discounting. First of all, our stores are especially designed for self-service, mass merchandising. Last year, conventional department store real estate costs were $15 to $25 a square foot; ours ran $3 a square foot.

"While our stores have varying physical characteristics (some are medium-sized and some are large) they are all clean, orderly, and inviting. They are designed to be attractive but functional, because we believe our customers desire superior merchandise values and friendly service far more than elegance in appointments and decorations. But the store's total image must be comfortable to all income levels even to those above the mass market. Second, our customers are primarily interested in only those basic services that do not work against the most economical distribution of merchandise. These include lay-away plans, check-cashing privileges, clean restroom facilities, telephone availability, parking privileges, and thoughtful assistance when needed. We believe in providing mass-desired consumer services without the penalty of higher prices to non-users of these services. Third, and the principal factor, is the increased efficiency of the discounter in comparison with conventional merchants.

"According to the trade association of the department stores, last year their average gross margin was 36.9 per cent of sales, ours was 23.2 per cent. Their payroll costs were 17.1 per cent of sales; discounting payroll costs were 9.4 per cent. Their cumulative markdown was 6 per cent; ours, 3.1 per cent. Their returns were 8.3 per cent; ours, despite a more liberal return policy, were only 4 per cent. In summary, their net operating costs were 29.8 per cent of sales; ours were only 19.8 per cent. Interestingly, our promotional pressure slightly exceeds theirs. Discount stores spent 2.7 per cent of sales for advertising to their 2.6 per cent. Our cumulative markup was only 26.6 per cent, compared to a conventional department store average of 40 per cent. That means that when we both bought a quality item for 60 cents, they probably sold it for $1; we probably sold it for 82 cents.

"The essence of our business is simple. By turning over inventory six to eight times a year instead of the conventional three to four times a year, we have been able to increase our earnings despite the lower gross margins. The success of this policy is reflected in our return-on-investment which is in the range of 20 to 30 per cent."

In April, 1967, the company re-opened its Watts store in Los Angeles. This store was razed during the Watts riots of 1965. The first original unit under the White Front name, it was opened in 1929 and was the nucleus of a three-store group purchased by Interstate in 1959. The new 35,000 square-foot Watts store is expected to do about $6 million in annual sales and will carry TV, major and small appliances, hardware, housewares, men's, women's, and children's wear, jewelry, and packaged foods. It will also have a pharmacy.

L. S. Ayres & Co. – Ayr-Way Stores

Ayr-Way Stores is a wholly-owned subsidiary of L. S. Ayres and Company, an Indiana corporation with sales of $137.7 million for the fiscal year ending January 29, 1968. The parent company was founded in 1872 by the grandfather of Lyman S. Ayres who today is chairman of the board. The company operates a fine quality traditional department store in Indianapolis with branches in Lafayette and Fort Wayne. There are 2,794 employees.

Ayr-Way was organized in 1961 as the self-service, low margin division of the parent company. It operates under the leadership of David P. Williams, president, and Rupert A. Miller, executive vice president. Both have had long merchandising records with L. S. Ayres and Williams is vice-chairman of the parent company. The first Ayr-Way was located in northeast suburban Indianapolis. Announced in April, 1961, the store opened in October. Ayr-Way has grown at the rate of one or two new units per year with a steady expansion of sales volume as units are added and as each attracts customers from its market. L. S. Ayres, in the company's 1965 annual report states: "Only four and one-half years old, Ayr-Way Stores, Inc. has justified our confidence in this form of self-service, low-margin retailing."

In 1966 there were four stores ringing metropolitan Indianapolis, another in Richmond, and one in Evansville. Expansion is planned on a continuous basis. As desirable sites become available the company intends to expand its operation throughout major metropolitan markets in Indiana.

Self-service nylon counter at the Ayr-Way discount division
of the L. S. Ayres' in Indianapolis, Ind.

Real estate policy is to construct buildings to company specifications on sites selected by management. These buildings are then sold and leased back. The company is highly selective in choosing store locations and will consider only prime locations preferably as part of a shopping center. Future stores have been announced in Anderson, South Bend, and an additional store in Evansville. Others are in the planning stage.

Ayr-Way operates all departments except four food departments and two snack bars. Merchandise lines consist of ladies' apparel and accessories with some sportswear, and a complete line of children's wear. Except for suits, a complete line is carried in men's wear, including separate jackets and slacks. In home furnishings Ayr-Way carries housewares, lamps, draperies, rugs, TV, and major appliances. Unfinished and dinette furniture is stocked but there are no case goods or upholstered pieces. There is a full line of sporting goods, toys, cameras, books, hardware, paint, tires, and auto accessories. There is also a strong garden shop in all stores.

All sales promotion for Ayr-Way is directed and produced in Indianapolis for newspapers, radio, TV and circulars. Separate programs are established for each market area.

199

Transit card advertisement featuring price appeal of the
ten-store Ayr-Way discount division.

Ayr-Way has its own personnel supervisor and operates with clearly-defined personnel policies. Regular merit reviews are used to evaluate performance and to select and develop employees with promotional abilities. There is a formal training program for new employees and a trainee program for individuals who demonstrate executive ability.

From the start, data processing has been used for sales analysis and inventory control. NCR Salestronic Registers are standard throughout and tapes are sent to a service bureau in Indianapolis for processing. Payrolls and unit control reports are prepared on data-processing equipment by the parent organization. The great majority of goods is received at a central service building where it is marked and distributed to the stores. Only a few bulk items are sold from sample and certain seasonal merchandise is warehoused.

L. S. Ayres and Company stock is traded over-the-counter. In 1968 working capital and common shareholders' equity exceeded $64 million.

200

Allied Stores Corp. – Almart Stores

Allied stores is an aggregate of 114 centrally-owned traditional department stores. Each store is individually operated as an autonomous concern but under central guidance. Included in the group are two stores in metropolitan New York, Stern Brothers and Gertz in Long Island. A resident buying office is maintained in New York City. In 1965 the Federal Trade Commission ruled that for the next ten years Allied Stores must obtain FTC approval before acquiring a department store in any metropolitan area in which the chain is already operating a store. Sales of Allied in 1968 were $1,168,309,000.

In April 1961 Allied Stores' president, Theodore Schlesinger, announced the company was forming a new discount-type store division under the name of Almart Stores. The new division is headed by Seymour Ainbinder, formerly an executive at S. Klein's in Newark, N.J. Locations of the new stores would be in areas where the company is not represented. By the spring of 1964 three large one-story Almart stores were in operation, each averaging about 120,000 square feet. Two units are near Wilmington, Del., one of which is on the much-travelled Kirkwood Highway. A new Delaware unit, opened in 1966, is in the Concord enclosed shopping mall adjacent to Route 202, the second most heavily travelled route in the state. It employs 400 people in about 54 separate departments, a large Colonial style restaurant, as well as an imposing, raspberry-colored beauty salon. Cash registers produce punched tape which is mailed to the home office for inventory-control purposes.

The merchandise carried in the Almart stores includes women's suits ranging up to $150, bedspreads in the $55 to $65 range, and high-quality, high-priced men's wear. This kind of merchandise is not found in most "discount" stores. Following is an excerpt from an interview between Ron Schneiderman and Seymour Ainbinder, reported in the March 17, 1966 issue of *Women's Wear Daily*. "Mr. Ainbinder does not use the word 'discount' in conversation. [He said] 'It connotes something . . . well not cheap, but we're carrying some pretty nice merchandise in our stores. Did you get a chance to see the jewelry counter? Our selection of diamonds is as good as any around here.' "

Almart Stores functions as an autonomous organization within Allied Stores Corporation. Total Almart sales are not available from the company's annual report. There has been a constant increase in sales and profits and Allied management considers this operation a success. By the end of the sixties, it is rumored, there will be at least ten more Almarts.

J. C. Penney Co. – Treasure Island Stores

James Cash Penney, now 93 (1969), started the first Penney store 70 years ago in Kemmerer, Wyo. Today there are more than 1,880 Penney stores from Anchorage, Alaska to San Diego, California, with sales of more than $3.3 billion a year. J. C. Penney holds 258,018 shares of Penney stock worth over $19 million. Until recently 96 per cent of Penney's merchandise was in soft-goods sold for cash in small towns. In 1957 William M. Batten undertook a two-year study of the company and recommended policy changes. Top management was impressed and in 1958 Batten was promoted from vice-president to president and given a free hand in implementing his recommendations. Penney expanded into hard goods, added auto centers, and moved into the cities and suburbs. Many small stores were remodelled or relocated. New stores average three times the space of stores opened five years ago and their multi-floors, escalators, and restaurants are comparable to Filene's in Boston. Goods are also sold by catalog. In 1964 Batten was made chairman of the board. In 1968 earnings were $109 million after taxes. Expansion is financed from cash reserves.

Penney acquired its Treasure Island operation in 1962 when it bought a catalog firm, General Merchandise Corporation. By 1966 the company had four identical 100,000 square-foot Treasure Island stores roughly north, south, west, and northwest of Milwaukee. There are 1,000 shopping carts in each store. An officer of the company claims they are not discount stores, "Most discount stores are dirty, filthy, and cheap with pipe racks, etc. We want to build very attractive buildings with twelve-foot aisles and better than normal lighting with less expensive fixtures than department stores, but more exciting and good looking, and with an assortment so complete that the average person will find what he needs. We have well-maintained, broad assortments, nice decor, and our floors are waxed every week." Penney calls its new stores, "experimental stores." The Treasure Island units started with their main strength in soft goods. Soon were added hard goods and house-wares as well as tire, battery, and accessory departments. The company runs soft goods and housewares. Leased departments are: supermarkets, operated by Hinky-Dinkey; health and beauty aids by Thrift Drug Company of Pittsburgh (who have 145 departments); cameras, sporting goods, and toys are leased to Gateway Sporting Goods Company; paint and hardware to Glidden; tires, batteries, and accessories to Ameron. Lessees must adhere to Penney advertising policy which prohibits price advertising and leans heavily on institutional type ads. For example a Treasure Island ad would say: "We have 21 brands of toothpaste – more than any store in Milwaukee,"

Traditional Stores Move Into Discounting

James Cash Penney, founder, J. C. Penney Company.

without mentioning prices. Treasure Island rarely runs sales and runs no comparative pricing. Its only sales are of sheets, held twice a year. In addition to the Treasure Island stores, there are twelve regular Penney stores in Milwaukee; when there are sales, sheets have to be priced the same at both stores. The advertising budget is based on a 30 per cent expenditure for radio and TV, and 70 per cent for newspapers. According to Penney philosophy, "Advertising is a trap. We believe in earning every dollar!"

In Penney's new-look stores there are 450 desks where catalog orders may be taken either directly from shoppers or by telephone. Penney's catalog exceeds 1,000 pages and has over 65,000 items. In 1965 catalog orders amounted to over $700 million. The company has built, in Bay Shore, L.I., its largest "new-look" store which has three floors, a restaurant, a beauty salon, and a 20-bay auto center that dispenses Penney gasoline and the company's tires under the Penney brand, "Foremost." In its women's apparel, Penney has traded up and is now using such stylish designers as Mary Quant of London and Mitzou of Madrid to create its dresses. Penney has its own label for soft goods sold in Treasure Island stores. It is the Wells Family of Fashion: James Wells and Susan Wells for adults, Jim and Sue for teenagers, Jimmy and Susie for toddlers, and Wells Royal for miscellaneous items.

Penney made a survey of its customers and discovered that 24 per cent of them have college degrees as opposed to the 10.5 per cent average; 60 per cent of Penney customers have an average income of $8,217. Sales of its Treasure Island stores are estimated to average $8 million per store. Customers can buy $150 coats, cameras for $300, guns for $250, and rings for $2,500. As sales promotion manager George W. Gish, Jr., said, "We want sophistication in everything but price. For example, we carry a women's coat with a Jean Harlow look. This is one of our hottest coats, a double-breasted wool-type with a big fox collar. Filene's sells it for $125, and J. C. Penney sells the same coat for $84. Sears sells it for $85. Most chain store men do not understand fashion. Discount store chains do not understand fashion. We try to find four or five silhouettes acceptable to women for a given period. When it comes to towels, sheets, blankets, and shoes, we know all there is to know. We are developing a New York staff of fashion specialists. Store managers can recommend but the final decision is centralized. We have a teletype to each store through which we can make known advertising plans, mark downs, etc.

"In regard to locations, we are in shopping centers but we believe in free-standing units and have the highest paid store managers in the business."

In 1965, Penney moved into its gleaming, new 45-floor New York building at 1301 Avenue of the Americas. There Penney's occupies 800,000 square feet using 31 floors. New services include an entire floor devoted to merchandise testing rooms. Twelve floors are devoted to merchandise displays enabling Penney's buying staff of 360 to evaluate full lines of goods. A centralized receiving department is on the concourse level and fashion goods can be shipped out to any of the stores within one hour after the receipt of the order. There is a laboratory in which Penney designs its own testing equipment. A miniature radio and TV station generates its own signals and is used to test radios and television sets. On the 36th floor is the data-processing center where the latest equipment speeds a constant flow of information to and from stores and suppliers. Punched tapes relay orders directly to a supplier's own equipment.

In April, 1967, Penney announced that it will open three 180,000 square-foot self-service stores in the greater Atlanta area. They are one-stop shopping centers with an inside supermarket at each location. Customer service departments will include a beauty salon, dry cleaner, optical shop, photo studio, small appliance repair shop, and pharmacy. The stores will

A unique "speedramp" solves the problem of getting shopping carts from floor
to floor at the Boston Store, Milwaukee, Wis. The carts lock to the moving ramp
and cannot "run away".

carry the customary lines of department store merchandise. Treasure Island
stores have distinctive inverted "V" rooflines. The Atlanta stores are free-
standing and have parking lots for 1,200 to 1,500 cars. In conjunction with
each store there is a 20,000 square-foot auto service center with twelve
gasoline pumps, sixteen auto service bays, and a diagnostic lane for electronic
testing. Architects for the new stores are Jordan Miller and George Waltz of
Milwaukee. Penney's has just realized its aim to reach sales of $3 billion.

205

Enter, The Variety Stores

Until 1959, the M. H. Fishman Company operated a chain of 5 cent and 10 cent variety stores. In 1957 the company converted one of its downtown stores into a discount store. Today the company still operates 26 variety stores but 80 per cent of its profits come from 24 discount stores.

In 1961 Neisner Brothers, a national chain of 172 variety stores, decided to go into discounting with the purchase of Myrtle Mills in Unionville, Conn. By the end of August, 1969, 27 Big N promotional department stores had been opened.

Frank Williams, then president of S. S. Kresge, in 1957 appointed Harry B. Cunningham to make a study of discount stores on a national basis. In 1961, it was officially decided to enter mass merchandising with the K Mart discount store division. Although a latecomer to the field, Kresge is now the nation's biggest mass merchandiser with (in 1969) 273 full-line K Marts and 116 Jupiter stores (converted variety stores), in addition to 593 traditional variety stores. Additional K Marts are planned for 1970. Sales in 1968 reached $1.7 billion.

F. W. Woolworth, the world's largest variety chain with 1968 sales of $1.9 billion, opened its first Woolco Department Store in 1962. Vice-president L. F. Davis, Woolco division manager, says his stores are not discount stores but "mass-selling promotional department stores." On January 1, 1969, 92 large (115,000 to 118,000 square feet) Woolco stores were in operation. Shopping center locations are preferred and the merchandising approach is, in many respects, similar to that of traditional department stores with heavy emphasis on quality merchandise and trained personnel. Thirty new Woolcos are planned for 1969.

M. H. Fishman Co., Inc. – Centers and Mason's, Fishman

Founded by M. H. Fishman in 1917 with a 25-foot wide dime store in Rutland, Vermont, the company now operates a chain of 54 discount department stores and variety stores in 11 eastern states and doing business under the names Fishman, Mason's, and Centers. The company was incorporated in 1927 as the M. H. Fishman Company, Inc., operators of 5 cent to $1 stores. Until 1959, Fishman had been a prosaic variety store chain with an unglamorous past and an uncertain future. In 1959 the company opened one discount department store under the name of Mason's. "Our traditional stores," said M. L. Polk, president, "were all making money, but I felt we were in a most difficult position for future growth. The variety store historically was limited to pins and needles, buttons and bows, and even though we had expanded into almost every line that department stores carry, including even appliances, the old stores were not really profitable in terms of the amount of time and manpower that went into them. Also, the American downtown had declined drastically and was getting competition from suburban centers that sprang up along new expressways, with none of the downtown traffic and parking problems.

"Actually, the original variety store concept of mass-merchandising at the lowest possible cost was similar to the new discount operations. Both were built on the same techniques. What we did was to capitalize on our long experience in moving a great variety of retail items at low cost." Polk's first venture into larger discounting stores was a cautious one. "At that time," he explained, "it was a gamble. Nobody yet knew enough about discount stores. We wanted to be conservative." In 1957 Fishman's converted one of its old downtown dime stores into a Centers store, a cross between a dime store and a discount department store. A year later management was ready to try a larger discount store but still not ready to operate all departments.

207

M. H. Fishman, founder, M. H. Fishman Co., Inc.

About 30 per cent of the departments were leased by concessionaires in shoes, housewares, health and beauty aids, photographic supplies, jewelry, home furnishings, and snack bars and soda fountains. Today the company operates all departments except shoes. Said Polk, "Shoes are a unique problem in retailing. We tried running our own shoe departments, but have gone back to leasing them." Stores were planned and opened at a relatively slow rate and it took until 1964 for the full impact of these stores to be realized in sales and earnings. In this year sales showed a jump of 16.7 per cent and earnings advanced 140.5 per cent. 1965 showed a sales advance comparable to that of 1964 with profits up 20 per cent and sales of $38 million, while 1968 sales were $55.6 million.

While the company was always profitable, it had never been able to generate substantial growth through the variety stores. The decision was made to enter the department store field by establishing Mason's, and to close down variety stores which were not profitable or change their inventories and reopen them as Center Stores, a discount chain. At the end of 1968, there were 26 Fishman stores in operation, located in Maine, New Hampshire,

New Jersey, New York, Vermont, and Virginia. The chain of 24 Mason's stores is located in Alabama, Ohio, Pennsylvania, and Virginia. In 1965 a new Mason's was opened in Asheville, N.C. Recently, new stores were opened in New York, North Carolina and Tennessee.

"Years ago," says Polk, "if a store did a business of $150,000 or $200,000, we thought it was a good little store, and if its lease ran out, we tried to renew it. We still do not have any unprofitable dime stores – but we are no longer interested in volume of that size." Today, Fishman's makes 80 per cent of its profits in discount stores, "but," says Polk, "we still have not left the variety store business." The company still has 26 variety stores including its first one in Rutland, Vt. "What has happened," says Polk, "is that we are moving department store merchandise in discount stores with techniques we originated in variety stores. We now (January, 1969) have four Centers Stores and 24 Mason's."

Fishman's tends to locate its new stores in towns that nobody in Wall Street has ever heard of; but there was nothing obscure about the company's annual report for 1964 which showed the results of its conversion. Sales were up from $27.8 million to $32.5 million, and earnings up from $383,670 to $922,553. Fishman rents its new stores from real estate developers who finance their construction. Company investment is confined to fixtures and inventory.

By what he calls a "very, very careful policing" of all opening costs except advertising, Polk reports that new units show a profit "within months after opening." Data processing is done with a Honeywell 120 installation. Personnel training is on an informal basis. As a discounter, Polk looks with horror on what he calls the "luxuries" of conventional department store operations: home delivery, expensive fixtures, and displays. Polk gets around fair trade laws by selling Fishman-labelled products (mainly house cleaning and health care items) whose price tags do not have to make a contribution to the advertising cost that went into establishing the same products as famous brands. Polk considers fair trade unbusinesslike.

"There is no longer any economic reason," he says, "for the existence of small specialty stores such as hardware, sporting goods, and apparel shops. The only limits to what can be sold in discount stores are space and imagination." M. L. Polk plans to limit Fishman's moves in this market to "leap frog" jumps rather than a long hop to the West Coast but he sees no reason why Fishman will not eventually become a national chain.

CAPITALIZATION AND FINANCES

Long term debt: $1,082,334. Common stock: 1,003,620 shares ($1 par). Management owns approximately 40 per cent of the common stock outstanding. At December 31, 1968, current assets were $13,624,380 and current liabilities $3,972,294. Sales for 1968 were $55,675,018.

Neisner Brothers, Inc. – Big N

Abraham H. and Joseph M. Neisner opened their first 5 cent to $1 variety store in Rochester, N.Y. in 1911. By 1961 they had 177 units, each with an average volume of over $400,000. Today Neisner Brothers is a national chain of department and junior department stores, operating over 190 stores in 17 states with concentrations in the Northeast, Middle West, Texas, and Florida. Greatest expansion is currently in Florida and New York. The company has approximately 6,500 employees and annual net sales are in excess of $100 million. The company is today headed by Fred Neisner, son of Joseph Neisner, who is chairman of the board, and by Melvin B. Neisner, son of the other founder, who is president.

In 1968, the company continued to remodel and expand existing outlets. This was done in Florida, Illinois, Massachusetts, New York and Texas. In 1968, the firm phased out 12 units. Current plans call for the opening of at least five Big N units a year, with three to five planned for Rochester by 1972 and one for Arcade, New York. Currently, 35 per cent of the merchandise requirements are supplied directly to stores. The company has a fleet of leased trucks, and delivery service is maintained from the distribution center to practically all stores, including Florida and Texas units. The distribution center stocks 15,000 to 18,000 items. It is expected, after the center is enlarged, that 70 per cent of all merchandise sold will be shipped from the distribution center to the stores. Only 30 per cent will be drop-shipped by vendors.

The company embarked on a credit program early in 1961. It has grown to cover 61 junior department stores in New York, New Jersey, Pennsylvania, Massachusetts, Ohio, Connecticut, and Texas, as well as all of the Big N Department Stores. The credit program is divided into two types of accounts: a revolving charge account, and a contract account for higher priced merchandise. Recently the company took on additional credit facilities in Chicago and Detroit, joining other retailers establishing credit directly with local banks. This method of credit has been most successful and stimulates business.

In 1961 the company entered the discount field with the purchase of Myrtle Mills, a 130,000 square feet unit in Unionville, Conn. Soon after, several leases were signed for Big N stores varying in size from 45,000 to 70,000 square feet. During the last half of 1966, the program was accelerated with the opening of two new department stores, bringing the total number of Big N's to 27, as of January, 1968.

The company continues on annual accelerated expansion programs. In 1966 nine junior department stores and two Big N stores were opened. In 1970, the company plans to open several more junior department stores and at least three Big N stores. Many existing successful junior department stores

Fred Neisner, chairman of the board,
Neisner Brothers, Inc.

are being expanded by as much as 50 per cent which should also add to the company's sales picture.

The company is extending its private brands, Andrew Lewis, Andy Lewis, Anita Lewis, Baby Lewis, and Lewis Family Brand. Neisner buying policies are described as follows: "We welcome new sources of supply, which means that we welcome new salesmen. If the new salesman has a staple line, he may have to visit us several times before he obtains an order, if our old source of supply is satisfactory. There are suppliers' names on our books which have been there ever since our first small store was opened. But if the man with a staple line has a better value, which may mean a lower price or a better product at the same price, he may walk out with an order from his very first call.

"Even though he obtains no order, the salesman should continue to call. Suppliers change. They have strikes, fires, or serious production delays.

211

M. B. Neisner, president, Neisner Brothers, Inc.

They may discontinue the items we buy, go out of business, or allow quality to deteriorate so that we are forced to change suppliers. If the salesman of a competitive line has been calling regularly, we are likely to turn to him when it is necessary to make a change. With specialty items (items we call 'hot') such as new products, novelties, and style goods, a salesman visiting us for the first time stands a better chance of getting an order than the new salesman of a staple line. We welcome salesmen selling items which have only a local or regional appeal. Sometimes a salesman will visit us and tell us frankly that his merchandise is in demand only in one or two cities or in a certain locality. We are glad to have these locally popular items although it simplifies our work to stock items which can be sold in all our stores."

The home office does the buying, plans the merchandising, and lays down the policies. Yet, no matter how efficient the headquarters may be, Neisner's top management feels that the district manager, working with the individual manager of a store unit, can either make or break his store. Some executives assert that the unit or store manager is responsible for 60 per cent of the store's success.

Store managers, under the direction of the district manager, are trained to follow well-tested routines. For all major tasks there are carefully prepared instructions; but the headquarters staff looks to the individual managers for many suggestions, new ideas, and for facts and policy recommendations to fit local conditions. Managers can, and are expected to, control expense; they can authorize markdowns on slow-moving merchandise. Each manager works on a budget, and if his inventory becomes too high, he is penalized because he has no budget to cover seasonal needs. For example, if he has too many bathing suits he may not have the budget to buy school supplies. This reduces sales and profits and penalizes the manager himself in his bonus arrangement. Being out of merchandise is considered one of the cardinal sins of retailing.

One of the basic policies of the company is to train, train, train. New men in the organization begin as stockmen. For them there is a 32-page book called "The Stockroom," which contains explicit instructions about receiving shipments, handling invoices, putting stock away, storing seasonal merchandise, installing store fixtures, handling returns and transfers, and many other daily problems of the stockroom. Stockmen, after they have served a reasonable time, are eligible for promotion to section manager where they have charge of a section of the store. In this job their knowledge of stock becomes valuable; as floormen, they learn management. The next step is to become an assistant manager – then a store manager. There is a special program for training assistant managers. Starting at the bottom, it normally takes three to four years to become a store manager.

Food service has always played an important part in the overall volume and profit picture. In 1961 there were 120 restaurant and fountain operations in the 177 Neisner stores in 19 states. Food operations are made to pay by menu simplification, mass production, and high volume selling. All menu items are numbered. Each food serving location has a manager and an assistant and there are five district supervisors who constantly check standards and practices. Carry-out business is heavily promoted with special menus and stand-up counters for fast food take-out. Food store managers are answerable to the store manager.

Neisner's feels that it must remodel several stores each year, otherwise there would come a time when the entire chain would be obsolete in equipment, arrangement, and appearance. There is a perpetual program of store remodeling, interior rearrangement, and painting. To stay abreast of the latest developments in store design and equipment, Neisner's has a department of full-time engineers, draftsmen, designers, and lay-out men who prepare plans for new stores and for remodeling old stores. When Neisner Brothers leases a property, careful surveys and studies are made to determine the best use of every available square foot of floor space.

213

In the operation of a chain of stores there is a natural tendency to turn store managers into bookkeepers and report-makers. Yet it is plain that the store manager has more important duties. Neisner policy is to do much of the necessary record keeping, accounting, figuring, and statistical work at headquarters. This relieves the store manager of every bit of paper work which can possibly be done at headquarters. The store manager is asked to put down only the bare necessities in the way of original records. Consolidation, recapitulation, analysis, and interpretation are done at Rochester. There is a constant effort to leave the store managers free to attend to merchandising, personnel, and promotion work, rather than remain tied to a desk handling paper work.

Stores are stocked by a staff of fourteen buyers working out of Rochester. Buying personnel are maintained in New York on a permanent basis to maintain contact with the markets. The services of a style buying office are retained to supplement company fashion buyers' purchases, insuring a fresh flow of new style goods. Reports are also received on world fashion markets of Italy, Spain, and France.

Supporting the Neisner stores is a Univac solid state computer in the Rochester general offices. This computer, with its 36,000 memory characters, is programmed to analyze daily the items carried at the distribution center. For administrative purposes, Neisner Junior Department Stores are divided into six districts: Buffalo, Chicago, Detroit, Florida, Texas, and the eastern district. Administration of the Big N stores is at Rochester.

The junior department stores lease very few departments; in Big N stores, leased departments are shoes, women's apparel, paint, hardware, and electric appliances, about 25 per cent of each store's departments.

All stores are leased and the only properties owned are the general offices in Rochester. Store location for the past few years and for the immediate future is pointed in the direction of shopping centers in small towns. The administration feels that the new store expansion program should be in towns of 10,000 to 50,000 with a retail population draw of three to four times that number. This is true both for junior department stores and Big N stores. In the latter type of store, the company is confining its expansion to within 300 miles of Rochester. Junior department stores have been mostly in the states of Florida and New York during the past few years. However, Neisner's is also considering small towns in Illinois, Michigan, and Ohio as well.

Said Fred Neisner, "We make a careful survey of the area, getting as much information as is available on existing retail sales, the road pattern to the particular site, and the proximity of the site to the so-called existing downtown of the small city. Of course we are much interested in the future growth of an area, and whether the city fathers are trying to promote the town with an idea towards getting new industry to come."

214

S. S. Kresge Company – K Mart and Jupiter

SEBASTIAN SPERING KRESGE

Sebastian Spering Kresge, founder of S. S. Kresge, was born in 1867. He was the son of Sebastian and Catherine Kunkle Kresge, both of Swiss ancestry. They operated a farm near Scranton, Penn., and their son first attended rural schools, known then as Fairview Academy and the Eastman Business College at Poughkeepsie, N.Y. As a boy, Kresge worked part-time as a deliveryman and clerk in a Scranton grocery store, and this is where he got his first taste of merchandising. While working in a hardware store in 1889, he noticed the serious problems arising from the too liberal granting of credit. As a result of this experience Mr. Kresge later insisted on only cash dealings in his own stores. He became a traveling salesman for W. B. Bertels Sons and Co., selling hardware and tinware in New England and in the north central states. One of his customers was Frank Woolworth, who had founded his dime stores in 1875. Woolworth then had 19 stores. He gave Kresge an order for 19 gross of saucepans, one gross for each store. It was a cash transaction made on a centralized basis, and Kresge was immediately impressed with the tremendous potential of the chain-store business.

In 1897, after he had saved $8,000 from his earnings as a salesman, Kresge joined with John G. McCrory in the opening of 5 and 10 cent stores in Memphis and Detroit. Within two years, Kresge became manager and then sole owner of the Detroit store. In 1900, with his brother-in-law, Charles J. Wilson, Kresge organized the Kresge & Wilson Company to open and operate dime stores in other cities. By 1907 he bought out Wilson's shares and changed the company name to S. S. Kresge. He was operating stores in Detroit, Port Huron, Toledo, Pittsburgh, Cleveland, Columbus, Indianapolis, and Chicago. In 1912, when the company went public with a capitalization of $7 million, there were 85 stores. In 1925, when Kresge gave up the presidency, there were 385 stores and the stock was selling at close to $900 per share. When inflation set in after World War I, there was a serious shortage of items that could be profitably sold for a dime or under. To overcome this problem, Kresge added the green front store to his Red Front line of dime stores and proclaimed items for sale at 25 cents to $1. After World War II, the company expanded into the discount and variety store business.

S. S. Kresge was an ardent prohibitionist, staunchly opposed to the use of nicotine. Personally parsimonious, it is related that he lined his shoes with paper when the soles got thin and that his suits were threadbare by the

215

Harry B. Cunningham, president and general manager,
K Mart and Jupiter Stores Division,
S. S. Kresge Company.

time he discarded them. Nevertheless Kresge was extremely generous in rewarding his associates and employees. In 1925, when he retired as president, 13 of his management team had become millionaires. He was a pioneer in giving his employees sick leave, paid holidays, profit-sharing bonuses, and pensions on retirement. He also was a generous philanthropist through the Kresge Foundation, which he set up in 1924, "to help human progress through benefactions of whatever name or nature." In 1968 the net worth of his foundation was more than $175 million, with grants totalling in excess of $70 million.

In the early years of the company, Kresge was very active in visiting all his stores and in selecting sites for new ones. He insisted on knowing every store manager as well as his family. He made it a point to shake hands with his clerks at each visit. One of the chief reasons for his success was his ability to pick competent employees and to inspire them with loyalty.

216

S. S. Kresge's K Marts[1]

In the course of six years S. S. Kresge has converted itself from a conventional variety store operation into a dynamic discount chain. In three years the company achieved a 60 per cent sales gain; a 100 per cent profit gain, and a 150 per cent gain in stock values. It is one of the world's most successful merchandisers in its dramatic achievement of upgrading its soft goods counters into modern "fashion centers." In 1968 sales reached $1.7 billion with about 273 full-line discount stores and 116 Jupiter Stores (five in Canada) in operation, in addition to approximately 593 variety stores (89 in Canada). As a variety chain it took sixty years to build half the volume it built in five years with its discount chain. Sales in 1968 were $1,731,533,000.

In the first two years of its discount operation, Kresge added $80 million in sales and, in the amazingly short period of three years, became the biggest operator of discount stores in the nation. In 1955 the chain had 673 variety stores in 26 Midwestern and Northeastern states with sales of $354 million. It was a blue chip company with a solid reputation of Midwestern conservatism and with dollar reserves of $19 million. In 1957, Frank Williams, then president, picked one of his most able young executives, Harry B. Cunningham, to find out what discounting was all about. Freed from all other responsibilities, he spent from 1957 to 1959 studying competition all over the country. Traveling more than 200,000 air-miles, he paid particular attention to the discount houses. Between 1955 and 1961 Kresge's volume gains were slowing and earnings had slipped from .0374 to .0204 on the sales dollar. Cunningham thought that the company was overstored and was competing with itself in the shopping centers. Meanwhile, discount stores were cutting deeper every day into sales, despite the fact that Kresge sales had increased from $418.9 million in 1960 to $432.8 million in 1961. However, profits in these two years dropped from .0260 on the dollar to .0204. More important, the return on before tax investments for Korvette in 1961 was 37.9 per cent as opposed to 9 per cent for Kresge.

Variety store managers were measuring their efficiency not on how many dollars they produced but on how high their mark-up percentages were. Another principle stressed by discounters was return on investment. With a high volume and fast turnover they were frequently able to run their business on their supplier's money. Evidencing a policy about-face, the value of Kresge's inventory in 1961 was $70 million and its accounts payable were $18 million; but two years later inventory value was $87 million, accounts payable were $34 million. In other words, the manufacturers were now carrying a large part of the inventory burden.

[1]Much of this material is a summary of an article on S. S. Kresge, "Kresge Restructured" in *Chain Store Age*, December, 1965, p. 48.

217

In May, 1959 Cunningham was made president and chairman of the executive committee. To build a foundation for the expansion he saw ahead, he appointed Gene Sturges as vice-president of personnel with the immediate job of launching a nation-wide recruiting program and setting up a comprehensive training program. John Hearst was made vice-president in charge of real estate. The drastic change in management is shown by the fact that by the fall of 1961, there was not a single operating vice-president, regional manager, assistant regional manager, or regional merchandise manager who was not new on the job. Nevertheless they were all insiders who had proven themselves in the Kresge business.

To stem downward trends, the company accelerated the discontinuance of as many deteriorating locations as possible. By 1963, 202 stores had closed. As of today there are only about 125 conventional Kresge units left. In 1957 the chain operated in twenty-six states; today it is in forty-five. To salvage some of the weak variety stores with long leases, a bantam discount store was created under the name of "Jupiter." There are now 116 Jupiter stores.

In March, 1961 the official decision was made to move into discounting. Vice-president Lloyd Yohe (now general manager of the Discount Division) was relieved of his variety store duties and told to make a study of major discounters throughout the United States. On his return he set up guidelines for the discount operation including salaries, operating ratios, productivity, layout, etc. In October of 1961 Cunningham told his real estate department that he wanted signed leases for no less than sixty stores, since forty K Marts would be opened in 1963. To man the stores, Gene Sturges was assigned the job of working out a man-power formula. One of the big questions was whether or not the existing Kresge buyers would be competent to buy for the new discount operation. The decision had been made to run the K Marts, not as a separate division of the company, but as a Kresge operation. The buyers were emphatic in declaring that their new duties would not interfere with buying for the variety stores and were eager to get into the new project. Management decided that they were capable of buying, not only for the variety stores, but for both the K Marts and the Jupiter stores too.

In the beginning, cameras, sporting goods, jewelry, and men's and boys' furnishings were leased. By the end of 1962 eighteen discount stores were in operation; four were bantam K Marts ranging from 25,000 to 30,000 square feet in size. Operating changes included better assortments of merchandise to generate a higher volume; many store functions were eliminated and turned over to the regional and headquarters offices; cash pick-ups were increased.

The fascinating aspect of the operation is that its three different store types are integrated at all levels. The advertising manager works on a Kresge advertisement along with one for a K Mart and one for a Jupiter store. Major activities, however, flow from the K Marts. The merchandising successes of one type of store are effectively applied to the other types. To handle the

218

increased and steadily increasing volume, the Kresge buying staff has been increased by 35 per cent since 1963. Eight merchandising specialists tour the stores, five for K Marts and three for Kresge.

The immensely increased volume of merchandise has made it necessary to enlarge the Fort Wayne, Ind. warehouse from 670,000 square feet to 840,000 square feet.

One of the results of the new venture is a vastly increased enthusiasm on the part of the rank and file personnel who now see many excellent opportunities to get into the big money: Jupiter store managers aspire to be K Mart managers. Gene Sturges set up a training program designed to train a minimum of 100 assistant managers for promotion to store managers. Over 400 new men were hired after recruiting teams visited over 100 colleges. Management considered the drive for new manpower to be equally as important as the drive to open new stores. In January, 1965, 38 per cent of Kresge trainees were college graduates, and 64 per cent had at least two years of college. Emphasis is put on programmed training and systematic personnel reviews. All male personnel are kept under the personnel division until they become managers, and until one year after they get their first store. Thus the personnel department is responsible in seeing that they make good.

The company offers more and bigger jobs for alert young men than ever before. In 1959 Kresge employed about 38,000; by the end of 1965 the figure was over 42,000. Personnel increase now averages about 5,000 a year. Sales personnel go through an eight-week programmed course with reviews and on-the-job training to eventually become department heads. There is also a four-month indoctrination program with a store manager who is glad to have him because he is "free," that is, he is paid by the home office. A premium is put on back-up experience at the store level. Each store is required to appoint a personnel supervisor whose duty it is to hire and train new department heads who will be self-motivated men. In 1964, 25 per cent of all Kresge store managers earned from $13 to $18,000, and 25 per cent earned $18,000 or more.

In locating new stores the Kresge real estate department has largely freed itself from the restrictions of shopping center developers by searching out K Mart sites itself. Operations have been streamlined so that from the time foundations are poured, it takes about six months to put up a K Mart. In 1958 K Marts existed only on blueprints in the Detroit office; by the end of 1962 there were 18 K Marts in operation. Fifty-three were in existence at the end of 1963 and 88 by the end of 1964. At this writing the chain is operating 273 K Marts in 45 states, Canada, and Puerto Rico. By 1969, the company expects to be operating 250 K Marts, comprising more than 20 million square feet of selling space that will blanket nearly every state in the union. Each year the stores have grown bigger; three years ago the average size of a single unit was 70,000 square feet. 1966 K Marts each averaged 94,000 square feet.

219

In the years ahead there will be stores in the 120,000 to 130,000 square feet class. Present plans are to build about 35 stores a year.

Kresge first concentrated its stores in midwestern areas, where it already had wide acceptance; its home base, Detroit, rapidly became a K Mart stronghold and today there are over 700,000 square feet of K Marts ringing the city. The policy was to establish more stores in metropolitan areas where they already had a foothold. Pittsburgh, for example, has seven K Marts with plans for two more. One of the reasons for the remarkable rapidity of K Mart's growth was the decision to avoid delays by establishing free-standing stores instead of tying up with existing shopping centers. Kresge variety stores are still of extreme importance in the operations, and produce a good share of its profits; but very few new units are being planned. Those that are being built are in the 30,000 to 40,000 square-feet class with a full range of merchandise incorporating the latest developments in this special field.

To salvage 16 of its old-line variety stores which had long leases and were either in the red, or becoming marginal producers, Kresge converted them into "Jupiter" stores. The idea behind this new type of store was to carry only a limited line of merchandise in the greatest demand at discounted prices. It was found that the increased traffic made it possible to move items such as price-maintained men's underwear with extreme speed, whereas the same line barely moved as a variety store item. Jupiter stores serve as testing grounds for merchandise such as folding slippers and mohair sweaters, both of which proved excellent items for K Mart promotions. Since 1963, other variety chains have copied this type of store. Woolworth has its Woolco, Grant's, its Diskay, Newberry's, its New-Way, and McCrory's, its Bargain Buy. Health and beauty aids are the number one traffic pullers at Jupiter stores.

Kresge has its own label, K 6, in a cartouche featured in its ready-to-wear department. In their variety stores they no longer carry eleven sizes of toothpaste and every color of thread. Avoided are slow movers with a stock turnover of less than four or five per year unless they are accommodation items. Despite lower gross margins, many of the variety stores are making 20 per cent sales increases and handsome profit gains. K Marts now do 40 per cent of the company's sales in drygoods, compared to 50 per cent for the variety stores. Many of the lines that are doing very well in K Marts are those which were best items on the variety store lists. These include piece-goods, curtains, drapes, and hardware assortments. Conversely, Kresge is admittedly borrowing ideas and learning from its growing K Mart family about such areas as new fixturing, different types of gondolas, new up-graded items, and fewer but better assortments.

In regard to food, Kresge policy from the beginning has been to make food a part of their over-all package. The average size of their food units is 20,000 square feet. In July, 1965 there were 96 K Marts with food units, most of which were operated by lessees. Kresge itself was operating five units experimentally.

In contrast to its old-line variety store days, Kresge is now a big user of newspaper and circular advertising, spending about 59 per cent of its budget on K Mart promotions. The 1966 ad budget was $22 million. Much more advertising stress is now put on ready-to-wear with an increase of about 15 per cent in this area over the amount in 1959. Ready-to-wear apparel is an important trade-up category in the company's operation with a concentration of 30 per cent of total merchandise in K Mart lines and 50 per cent in its variety stores. Kresge likes to use the "big buy" approach; for example, ivy plants normally priced at 29 cents will sell for 9 cents on a three-day promotion. Item promotions in all three divisions under the control of the Detroit office get top priority; 98 per cent of the advertising goes into newspapers. A budget of $100,000 to $200,000 per city is not uncommon. Advertising programs are forwarded to the stores two months in advance so that managers can plan for them and order merchandise. Items with high sale volume and traffic production are favored. The store manager has the option of lowering the recommended advertised price; however, he is not permitted to raise it.

There are some cities in which all three kinds of stores operate: Kresge variety stores, K Marts, and Jupiter stores. Although their advertising is separate, the advertisements do not hide the fact that they are associated with the parent-Kresge. Total K Mart credit volume ranges up to 15 per cent and is growing in importance. The company has the largest checkout credit operation in the world. The customer is charged a fee of 1.5 per cent on the unpaid balance; there is no charge if the bill is paid within 30 days of purchase. Big ticket items such as color television sets are financed by banks and commercial credit companies.

Professional service has boosted K Mart sales in high-priced and intricate cameras and photographic supplies. Each camera department is headed by an expert backed up by a regional traveling field specialist whose job is to keep the expert up to date on new developments. Management believes that top know-how is needed to sell cameras priced from $100 up. Items in this price range now account for 25 per cent of their camera business. The three types of stores exchange their merchandising successes. If an item takes off in a Kresge variety store, it will very likely move by the ton in a K Mart. Variety and Jupiter stores are today selling one line of $1.98 women's cotton and dacron blouses at the rate of several thousand dozen a year.

Research plays an important part in Kresge management. They know, for example, that 5 per cent of present sales come from cameras, 4 per cent from candy, 7 per cent from toys, and more than 10 per cent from health and beauty aids. Leased electronic departments are now being tested in six stores and lumber supplies in two stores. Furniture departments are also

221

under test in five units. In 1964 president Cunningham appointed four vice-presidents as a research committee to draw up a list of proposed research projects as an aid to charting the future course of the Company. Research areas include merchandise reorder systems, sales forecasting, and consumer-buying habits. Of high priority today is research and salary control and the development of a more efficient reorder system which will automatically activate store orders on the basis of past history. Warehouse location is another important research area since trade discounts depend on buying carload lots, which must be warehoused.

How the Future of Retailing looks to S. S. Kresge[1]
W. EUGENE STURGES, VICE PRESIDENT, S. S. KRESGE, INC.

I want to talk primarily about the retail revolution in general merchandising. The symbol of the revolution today is the self-service discount department store. Now, several years ago a number of discounters opened in back-alley locations. Sometimes inferior goods were sold, sometimes sharp practices were employed; often there was little concern for employees and an utter lack of good customer relations. Many of us here and many of our wives would not wish to be seen shopping in that type of discount store. But this type of discount store brought something more into retailing – a concept that had been lost for a number of years – the economics of plenty – a willingness to slash the unit profit and to rely on volume and turnover to produce a satisfactory store profit. It brought into general retailing mass-merchandising techniques not unlike the mass-production techniques of our industries.

The discount department store is the latest significant factor in retail business, but it was preceded by other significant changes back at the turn of the century. Many of these changes can be seen in the development of the Kresge Company – from the door-to-door selling of Sebastian S. Kresge in the late 19th century, to the K-Mart department stores of today. (Incidentally, Mr. Kresge was 99 years young on July 31, 1969. He is still very much interested in retailing and he is chairman of the board of directors.)

Certainly, in general retailing no single type of business has had a greater impact on retailing than the 5 and 10 cent stores when they were introduced by Frank Woolworth and followed by other pioneer merchants in the late 19th century. Masses of merchandise were piled on open counters. Prices were dramatically low. In the Kresge Company, our magic slogan for

[1]Talk at the University of Massachusetts, April, 1964, Conference on Mass Merchandising.

years was "nothing over 10 cents." Merchandise could be touched and inspected. New merchandise – household wares, notions – was available, and with heavy turnover stocks were fresh and, despite low markups, business prospered. In that era, if a visitor wanted to find the center of Main Street, U.S.A., he would only have to follow the traffic to the cluster of dime stores with their characteristic red background signs and elaborate window displays.

The next development was the establishment of the 25 cent to $1 stores in the clothing and soft line merchandise field. In the Kresge Company, a new division was created – the green-front stores, to compliment the familiar Kresge red-front dime stores.

My personal start in the Kresge Company's training program was in December 1925, in our so-called green-front 25 cent to $1 store division. The store was located in Kansas City and did an annual volume in excess of $2 million. The manager had come up through the ranks. He never reached the high school level of education, but he was a natural merchant. He had the knack of keeping in tune with the customer's needs and had the guts to buy huge quantities of demand items. I remember our first trial order of ladies' felt houseslippers in October of my first year. We had never carried this item before. We received three cases of 36 to a case. They sold out in two days. Our reorder was for 1,500 cases for the holiday season. They cost 80 cents a pair and we sold them for $1 – a 20 per cent markup. Men's pigskin gloves cost us $11 per dozen, but we were a store with a $1 selling value limit and that was our selling price for the gloves. The gross profit on these gloves was less than 9 per cent. However, he wanted them as a sales leader. He did not worry about the profit on such an item. During the season, we sold several thousand dozens. There were hundreds of other items selected by this manager as sales leaders. We made a normal profit out of an abnormal sales volume. The greater the volume the lower our expense percentage dropped. Our total gross profit percentage was 5 per cent lower than that in our dime stores, but the operating expense percentage was comparably lower too. We did not have the label; but we were a downtown discounter at that time. In these stores, we sold merchandise in the 25 cent to $1 range – nothing above $1. At their peak of popularity the Kresge Company had 195 of these stores located in cities near our dime stores. In the 1920's, the future looked most promising for this type of store.

When the depression of the 1930's hit the United States, the department stores began opening "bargain basements" in an effort to stimulate volume. This new revolution in retailing made many of our dollar stores unprofitable and as a result our firm is operating only two such units today. Where physically possible, we combined these stores with our dime stores in order to get the advantage of the variety stores' traffic, and thus was born Kresge's variety department stores.

The next major change in general retailing did not occur until after the

223

war when, spurred by suburban real-estate developments, there arose the first wave of shopping centers. Now, this idea was not completely new. G. C. Nichols, a Kansas City realtor, conceived of such a project a number of years before. Kresge's opened the first variety store in America's first suburban shopping center, Country Club Plaza, Kansas City, Mo., on January 5, 1929. This new variety store was different. It was a combination of the 5 and 10 cent and the 25 cent to $1 stores. This was a successful center, but the depression and World War II delayed the second opening until a generation later. The change was inevitable. Free and ample parking was offered in place of traffic-congested downtown. Shopping once again became available close to home as in the small-town and smaller cities of yesterday, and with this change came a far greater emphasis on self-service and check-out operation.

Kresge's was one of the first variety chains to experiment with this type of self-service, check-out operation, and under the leadership of Harry B. Cunningham, our president today, who was then manager of our Sales Department, we were one of two variety chains to adopt this program extensively. From a concentrated start in 1953 under his leadership, we have 706 check-out operations in the United States, Canada, and Puerto Rico. Now, this decision did not come easy and there were many merchants, both within and without the company, who predicted dire results for the company who gave up counter service and abandoned their customers. We had the example of the supermarkets in the food business, and we had the experience, shared with all of you, that in the general merchandise field very little merchandise is sold - a great majority of it is purchased. Self-service has become an outstanding success, but it could not have been in the absence of the power of advertising to pre-sell the goods on our counter, and were it not for the tremendous gains in packaging and in display. Self-service is not merely a way of cutting the cost of selling, but even more importantly it is a way of accelerating the distribution of merchandise.

We have all had this experience. You are standing at the counter in a department store, with only a couple of items to purchase. There are six or seven people at the counter, all waiting in various stages of frustration. Behind the counter are two salesgirls, a little irked by the incessant demands of the customer, "Can't they see we're busy?" In any case, behind the counter there is a display of Gillette Stainless Steel Blades. Now, you do not have to be sold on the merits of Gillette Stainless Steel Blades versus Gillette Blue Blades or Gillette Blue Blades versus Gillette Thin Blades. You have seen the football games and the fights on television. You have heard everything that can be said about Gillette Stainless Steel Blades, and besides, you know that Mickey Mantle uses Gillette Stainless Steel Blades. You are sold, but there you are, flashing a dollar bill and perhaps a smile to charm the salesgirl into establishing some sort of a priority rating in your right to purchase. At this point we may have some time to wait and you have plenty of time to think, and you may think dark thoughts.

The Gillette factory is a model of efficiency. In goes steel, plastic, paper, and out comes razor blades, packaged and loaded in freight car lots, mass production, mass transportation, millions for advertising, and millions for display. In the meantime, there you stand, still waving that dollar bill, and there is that beautiful display of Gillette Stainless Steel Blades – and in between is one counter, one salesgirl (she is downright hostile now, because she thinks you are inconsiderate). Here she comes. "No, I am sorry, sir; I am not the salesgirl, I am the supervisor. But if you will wait a moment, I will get someone to help you."

Gentlemen, this simple illustration of a customer trying to buy an advertised product proves one thing: Something has broken down in our distribution system. It is not really help that is needed – we only wish to remove the obstacles to the customer's purchase of merchandise. Self-service is a device permitting more goods to move more rapidly, permitting customers to browse as desired, and freeing salespeople to give help where help is needed. I heard about a Britisher who visited the United States and was talking about the trend of self-service in non-food stores. "Why, in England, the Queen herself will come into a store to shop," he said. "How could we expect the Queen to serve herself?" "Well," said the American, "the first thing the British merchant has got to decide is how many Queens he has got."

Following the success of the shopping centers, the discount department store made its entrance but a few years ago. Its growth has been remarkable, a good deal more remarkable than the average layman realizes. The sales of discount department stores throughout the United States today (1964) is well over \$6 billion annually. By comparison, this is well beyond the total sales of all the variety stores. The beginning and growth of the discount department store is often compared with the emergence of the food supermarkets. Their secret of success from their inception was selling more goods at a better price – cutting package costs – cutting dollars out of all store costs and passing this savings on to the customer. The food supermarkets were successful in creating the merchandising image that they were selling groceries in retail quantities at wholesale prices. This merchandising principle caught fire.

When we take a close look at the new self-service discount department store system today, we find the supermarket "formula of success" has been copied:

1. The stores are big enough to be overpowering.
2. They pile the merchandise high and sign it at discount prices.
3. They hold down the selling cost by letting the customer do the work.
   (*a*) The serve-yourself-and-save idea has been sold to the customer.
   (*b*) Customers are convinced, and they do, in fact, have a price advantage when they shop in these outlets.

225

4. A carnival atmosphere exists in a well-operated store. There is excitement in the air.

5. Parking is free, and there is plenty of it; and the store is open at all hours to accommodate family shopping.

After extensive research, the Kresge management became convinced that the discount department store had a large and growing part to play in the retail economy. The term discount has already lost some of its magic, but the retail development referred to is here to stay and grow. We were convinced that such a business was right down our alley and we are presently (1969) operating 273 K-Mart discount department stores. The first one was opened just four years and two months ago. Kresge managers who have proven managerial ability were selected to manage these new K-Marts – a check reveals their ages average 46, and their business experience with our company averages 25 years. We have experienced management!

These new K-Mart stores offer all the economies that mass merchandising can produce, plus nothing but first quality merchandise that is guaranteed, plus the 65 year-old Kresge reputation of having automatic charge privileges at K-Mart stores. We have found that our K-Mart customers are from all income groups; but we know the bulk of our volume must come from the middle and lower income levels simply because there are more of these people, and they are better K-Mart customers. These folks shop as families, particularly in the evening. K-Mart attempts to maintain the kind of informal atmosphere that makes the male head of the family feel comfortable shopping with his wife and his kids in his work clothes or casual clothes after dinner. You seldom see a blue collar worker shopping with his family in a regional shopping center; but you will find him in K-Mart. When father is along, unit sales are always higher.

We have enormous respect for the astuteness of the American shopper. She is far more sophisticated than many merchants believe. Certainly, she is impressed by store image; but she is much more impressed by brand image and value image. The store that does the best job of controlling overhead will be in the best position to earn her continued loyalty, regardless of her income level. An article in *Fortune* put it this way: "Consumers who want a new car, a boat, a trip to Paris, and a college education for their children are likely to go out of their way to save 20 per cent on the children's underwear."

There are many entrants into the discount department store field and the competition is expected to be intense, but we have some "plus" factors which we feel will assure for us an important place in this segment of the retail economy:

1. Seasoned and strong top-management team, flexible in their thinking and ready to adopt any progressive change, one that is not bogged down with so-called red tape which might normally be a handicap to some 65-year-old corporation.

2. A financially strong corporation.

3. A tradition of integrity.

4. Eleven years of profitable experience with self-service, check-out operations.

5. A definite program of store security.

6. An established waste control pattern of operation.

7. Available supervision.

8. Experienced merchandising, buying, shipping, and modern accounting departments already functioning smoothly.

9. An aggressive sales and advertising department.

10. Manpower-proven training methods in use.

What effect has the discount store had on retailing generally, and what permanent effect may be expected? The primary effect is obvious to all. The conventional pricing structure has been altered in every retail store that in any way competes with a discounter and dual price markings may be seen in everything from refrigerators to records, to toothpaste.

From the viewpoint of a retailer who has been on the outside looking in, I might explain that a principle effect of the discounter was to make it difficult for some retailers to make money unless they are willing to change their operating programs and arrive at a lower cost-to-sell. From the viewpoint of the consumer and from the viewpoint of the country, I would have to say that the direct and indirect result of this innovation will improve the efficiency of the entire United States retail distribution system, make more things available to more people, leading to increased production and growth-rate of the United States economy.

The potential market for discount department stores cannot be known at this time; but it will certainly be substantially more than has been achieved to date. In today's competition for the consumer's dollar, every general merchant is emphasizing his unique characteristic and advantages from the variety store, to the specialty shop, to the conventional department store. The efficiency of all of these will adjust and prosper to meet the needs and desires of the American consumer.

What about the future of retailing? It is great! There is a new baby customer born in these United States every seven seconds. By 1975 that "old stork" will have built our population to 230 million. By 1975 our population of those over 65 will have increased in number to equal 29 new cities as large as Washington, D.C. Right now, it is estimated that the United States population of those under age 25 represents 59 per cent of our total population. The retailer who finds a way to serve large numbers of people is assured of a bright future.

The most important change that has happened in America since I worked in a grocery store as a boy is that the standard of living today is unmatched in history. Monday, I was in New York. With a stroll down Fifth Avenue, it is not unusual to see opera glasses in the show windows at $169 and up, necklaces and diamond rings at $500 to $16,000, party dresses at $450, umbrellas at $37.50, pipes at $25, cigars at $1 each, and many other expensive items for sale at very high prices – that sell! You can go to Florida and see yachts at anchor costing $197,000 and many times you see the owner sitting there with a cold drink in his hand and find he flew from New York or from Texas in a private plane for the weekend. You can find a $5,000 sports car in your neighbor's garage and if you do not have a color television you have not arrived! Personal consumption expenditures in 1953 were $323 billion. Ten years later, 1963, it had jumped to $373 billion . . . a 60 per cent increase.

Today's standard of living has an important helper. It is described by two words: Selling and Advertising – when pronounced together, they sound like – Distribution.

To stay in business, retailers must have what the people want, and we must serve busy America fast. Fantastic stores with fast systems for service will grow in popularity. The future is great. As retailers, however, we will find that it pays every now and then to slow down a little and ask ourselves, "Who is the boss?" Some may think that the boss is the man who sits behind a big desk directing the operation of the company. However, if we happen to be the man behind the desk and we want the retail formula for success to work, we will teach our employees the facts of life: that the real boss is the customer. She is the one who bosses the boss and if he pays heed to her needs his business firm will be assured of a bright future.

Our topic today: "How does the future of retailing look to us." As we face the future, we are not afraid of this revolution in retailing. We are most inclined to be thankful to the original discount department stores, regardless of where they may have started in business – thankful to them for making us apply, in a bigger way, those principles of merchandising on which our business was originally founded. From the beginning our Kresge stores were built to serve the masses . . . we worked on the theory that low-income people need low prices and that rich people love low prices.

Working on this formula, we anticipate opening many additional K-Marts as the future unfolds. These stores will offer all the economies that mass-merchandising can produce, plus first-quality merchandise that is guaranteed, plus friendly service where needed; and we expect to extend Kresge's tradition of integrity. We face the future in retailing enthusiastically.

F. W. Woolworth Company–Woolco Division

The F. W. Woolworth Co., the fourth largest retailer in America, with 1968 sales over $1.9 billion, has been in the retail business for 89 years. It is the world's largest variety chain with over 2,400 stores in the United States, Alaska, Hawaii, Puerto Rico, Mexico, and Canada, and over 100 in West Germany. In addition to the variety stores, the company operates Harvest House Restaurants in the United States and Canada and over 870 Kinney Shoe Stores in the United States and Canada that include leased shoe departments. The F. W. Woolworth Co. Ltd. of England operates over 1,100 variety stores in the British Isles and West Indies and has opened its first 3 Woolco Department Stores there. Recently the first Woolworth store to open in Spain was announced. On January 1, 1967, 52 large Woolco Department stores were in operation in the United States and Canada with more to come.

Frank Winfield Woolworth opened his first 5 and 10 cent store in Lancaster, Penn., in 1879. Woolworth Stores grew through the years to the complete variety store of today. Recognizing the changing trend in retailing, the management of the F. W. Woolworth Co., under the direction of Robert C. Kirkwood, chairman of the board, decided to move into the department store field. The first Woolco department store opened in Columbus, Ohio in June, 1962. L. F. Davis, vice-president of the F. W. Woolworth Co. and general manager of the Woolco Department Stores division since its inception in 1962, defines these stores as "mass-selling, promotional department stores." They are designed to satisfy the modern shopper's appetite for color television, air conditioners, power lawn mowers, electric can openers, high fashion dresses, diamond rings, golf carts plus a wide assortment of everything for the home.

Woolco has had an advantage in being able to tap the resources of the parent company by utilizing the financial resources and the experience of its executives in all phases of the operation. Three stores in the United States and four in Canada were opened in 1962. These operations were carefully evaluated and in 1963, three more were opened; in 1964, six more. By the end of 1965, 27 had opened. By November 30, 1966, the 52nd Woolco Department Store opened. Proceeding at this pace, Woolco had the opportunity to study and restudy its operation and concept. It ignored the tremendous pressures to develop more quickly in order to make the type of store they wanted a reality. More than 30 new Woolco Department Stores are scheduled to open in 1969.

Economic and real estate surveys are made for each possible site. All Woolco department stores are in or immediately adjacent to shopping centers; no Woolco stores are free-standing. Woolco prefers the stability of a shopping center location even though lengthier negotiations with a developer are necessary.

Nationally-advertised department store merchandise is carried: wearing apparel for the entire family, hardware and household accessories, home appliances, and all major appliances including color and black-and-white television sets, radios, refrigerators and freezers, air conditioners, phonographic equipment, toys, sporting goods, pets, and pet supplies. Service

229

Robert C. Kirkwood, chairman of the board,
F. W. Woolworth Co.

features include an in-the-store optometrist, a pharmacy, a Red Grille Restaurant, automotive service, complete credit facilities with time payments, revolving credit, and lay-away services. Credit services are operated and supported by Woolco. It is their feeling that credit enhances traffic. It is absolutely essential to major appliance, high-priced clothing, expensive camera, and jewelry sales.

In the United States and Canada most Woolco stores are in the 115,000 to 180,000 square-foot range. They are a one-story sales floor operation with wide aisles and distinct signing, all of which aids customer traffic flow and shopping convenience.

Certain departments in Woolco stores are leased to well-established and

L. F. Davis, vice president, F. W. Woolworth Co.;
general manager, Woolco Division.

substantial firms. However, the same licensee does not necessarily operate a particular department in all stores.

Woolco uses a department store approach in its advertising. Each store has an advertising manager who is under the direction of the general manager of a store. Woolco's aim is to present an image of quality merchandise at competitive prices, customer service first, complete assortments of merchandise at all times, satisfaction guaranteed, convenient and fair credit service, and fashions for the entire family. Most of the advertising is in newspapers, although radio is utilized extensively. Television advertising is limited.

Woolco's personnel is set up along department store lines. There is a general manager, assistant general manager, division managers, a credit manager, an advertising manager, and major department managers, and some leased department managers in each store. All of the managers are

231

supervised by the general manager and are responsible to him. Under them are full organizations for the various departments. Woolco draws on the vast manpower resources of the Woolworth Co. and from the department store field.

There is a strict department sales structure throughout the store. There is a centralized record keeping system and detailed department sales reports are turned out periodically.

A recent brochure, "Woolco Department Stores – A New Fashion In Modern Retailing," was sent to all stockholders of the F. W. Woolworth Co. An excerpt follows:

"Keeping pace with the rapid progress of today, the Woolco Department Stores Division continues to be a fast growing, although new member of the Woolworth family. Since the opening of the first store on June 6, 1962, in Columbus, Ohio, Woolco has grown to a group of 52 large, modern department stores in cities throughout the United States and Canada with more scheduled to open each year. We invite you to visit one of these stores and acquaint yourself with the up-to-the-minute retailing methods which have contributed to the success of stores designed to serve the needs of the particular community where they are located. You'll find a full line of department store quality merchandise, including nationally famous brands, at competitive prices, in all Woolco Department Stores."

The 1968 stockholder's report showed that consolidated net income of the F. W. Woolworth Company declined to $65,739,270 in fiscal 1966 from the revised net of $70,050,121 in 1965. This decrease in profit was caused primarily by a decline in earnings of the British Woolworth company.

A typical Woolco store – architect's drawing.

Woolco Department Stores Now Open[1]

1962

Brantford, Ontario
Columbus, Ohio (2)
Hamilton, Ontario
Richmond, Virginia
Sudbury, Ontario
Windsor, Ontario

1963

Gretna (New Orleans), Louisiana
Tempe (Phoenix), Arizona
Westminster (Denver), Colorado

1964

Calgary, Alberta
Corpus Christi, Texas
Memphis, Tennessee
Phoenix, Arizona
Sydney River, Nova Scotia
Victoria, British Columbia

1965

Aurora (Denver), Colorado
Columbus, Mississippi
Columbus, Ohio
Las Vegas, Nevada
Louisville, Kentucky
Memphis, Tennessee
Regina, Saskatchewan
Sault Ste. Marie, Ontario
Shreveport, Louisiana
Sioux City, Iowa
Wisconsin Rapids, Wisconsin

1966

Agincourt (Toronto), Ontario
Brossard (Montreal), Quebec
Calgary, Alberta
Dallas, Texas
DeKalb, Illinois
East Brunswick, New Jersey
Edmonton, Alberta
Fort Lauderdale, Florida
Frederick, Maryland
Granby, Quebec
Hamilton, Ohio
Kinston, North Carolina
London, Ontario
Louisville, Kentucky
Nashville, Tennessee
Pleasantville, New Jersey
Roanoke, Virginia
Rock Forest, Quebec
San Antonio, Texas
Springfield, Illinois
Sumter, South Carolina
Terre Haute, Indiana
Transcona (Winnipeg), Manitoba
Tulsa, Oklahoma
West Palm Beach, Florida

1967

Amarillo, Texas
Bowling Green, Kentucky
Charlotte, North Carolina
Charlottesville, Virginia
Edmonton, Alberta

Grand Rapids, Michigan
Kingston, Ontario
Kitchener, Ontario
Mesquite (Dallas), Texas
Montgomery, Alabama
Natchez, Mississippi
North Vancouver, British Columbia
St. John's, Newfoundland
Temple, Texas
Tuscaloosa, Alabama

1968
Atlanta, Georgia (2)
Bradenton, Florida
Charlotte, North Carolina (2)
Claymont (Wilmington), Delaware
Cornwall, Ontario

Dover, Delaware
Enid, Oklahoma
Flint, Michigan
Harlingen, Texas
Houston, Texas (2)
Laval (Montreal), Quebec
Lethbridge, Alberta
Memphis, Tennessee
Metairie (New Orleans), Louisiana
Muscle Shoals, Alabama
Nashua, New Hampshire
Norfolk, Virginia
Port Arthur, Texas
Saint John, New Brunswick
St. Petersburg, Florida
San Antonio, Texas
Windsor, Ontario

[1]Fifty-six Woolco stores are scheduled to open in 1969–70.

234

VI

Food Makes Its Discount Move

The principles on which the pine board supermarkets of the early 1930's were founded, namely high volume at a low margin, cash and carry, and self-service, were precisely those of the early discounters. Both had their origins in old mills and garages. It is not surprising, therefore, that supermarket operators were strongly tempted to enter discounting. Many were already carrying many non-food items. In fact the sales of general merchandise in food stores rose from $200 million in 1950 to approximately $1 billion in 1960.

The earliest of the giant food chains to take the plunge was Grand Union. In 1956 it opened in Keansburg, N.J. its first combined general merchandise and food store under the name Grandway. A 20,000 square-foot supermarket was enlarged to 40,000 square feet and, in addition to food, an extensive line of general merchandise was installed. It comprised some 15,000 items including major and traffic appliances, sporting goods, hardware, giftware, cameras, and some soft goods. As was to be expected at the start,

235

there was a painful lack of managerial know-how. Inventory control got out of hand and some departments operated at a loss. Conflicts constantly arose in regard to policies relating to advertising, sales, merchandising and customer service. Selling a full line of general merchandise was quite different from selling meat and potatoes. The Grand Way division of the Grand Union Company learned the hard way; however, these early growing pains were soon overcome and by 1961 there were 20 Grand Ways most of them in the 60,000 to 100,000 square-foot class. The company in 1968 operated more than 537 supermarkets and under its Grand Way division are 31 discount stores. Total sales in 1968 were more than one billion dollars.

Another of the nation's largest food retailers, Stop & Shop, discovered in the late 50's that discount stores made excellent neighbors. A Connecticut chain of six discount stores called Bradlee's ran into financial difficulty in 1961 and was acquired by Stop & Shop in a stock transaction. Benefitting from Grand Way's experience, Stop & Shop management moved slowly and to avoid controversy, made its Bradlee's division completely autonomous. By 1968 there were 39 Bradlee's stores and combined sales of the company, including over 135 supermarkets, was over $556 million with net earnings of $7,885,965.

The Jewel Companies, formerly Jewel Tea, operate internationally over 630 stores, including 368 supermarkets, 151 drug stores, ten discount stores, and a wholesale division. In 1962 it acquired the Turnstyle discount chain of four stores in the Boston area. Since then six more Turnstyle stores have been added. Total Jewel sales for fiscal 1968 were $1,244,000,000.

The Grand Union Company – Grand Way Division

The Grand Union Company has been in business since 1872. Primarily a food retailing organization, it now operates more than five hundred supermarkets. In recent years, the company has played an increasingly important role in the field of general merchandise retailing through its Grand Way Department Store division. This division now includes 31 outlets distributed as follows: six in Connecticut; eight in Florida; four in New Jersey; ten in New York; one in Vermont; and two in Pennsylvania.

Grand Union's total sales of $1.017 billion in fiscal 1968 ranked the company ninth among the nation's food retailers and 21st on *Fortune's* list of the 50 largest firms. In 1966 the company's sales totalled more than $800 million of which approximately $175 million were Grand Way sales.

First of the nation's major food chains to go into general merchandise

236

on a large scale, Grand Union added over 671,000 square feet of department store space in 1967, increasing its general merchandise shopping facilities by 50 per cent to a total of more than 2 million square feet. Beyond this, the company expects to annually open an average of six to eight Grand Way department stores ranging from 60,000 to 100,000 square feet.

The first Grand Way opened in June, 1956 as a 40,000 square-foot supermarket. This was doubled in size and an extensive general merchandise line was added including major and traffic appliances, sporting goods, hardware, giftwares, and some soft goods. Most supermarkets had long ago discarded the concept of selling food only and were stocking toiletries, housewares, stationery, magazines, health and beauty aids, and other inedibles. Non-food sales in supermarkets zoomed from $200 million in 1950 to $2 billion by 1960. The company's commitment to general merchandise retailing on a large scale was made under the presidency of Lansing P. Shield. It has been continued under Thomas C. Butler who succeeded him as president and chief executive officer in 1960.

From its beginnings as a one stop supermarket operation (with the stores known as Grand Way Savings Centers) through a discount merchandising phase, Grand Ways have emerged as full-fledged promotional department stores.

Joseph L. Eckhouse, formerly executive vice-president of the Grand Union Company, and a director, was put in charge of the Grand Way Department Store Division in 1962. Before his death in January, 1967, Eckhouse in a speech to stockholders, outlined the evolution of the Grand Way operation:

"Changes in the kind of merchandise Grand Way sells have been taking place at a rapid rate in response to customer interest in better goods. Merchandise has been carefully traded up to embrace higher price lines particularly in *fashion* merchandise. Grand Way now sends buyers abroad to find interesting new merchandise in various international markets. Many new departments are selling items of merchandise to Grand Way customers for the first time. Men's suits and coats are now sold at several Grand Way stores. Yarns, fabrics, and piece goods for the woman who sews are now available at Grand Way. Decorator items, gift wares, and artificial flowers are significantly expanded departments. Pet shops are planned for most stores; smoke shops, luxury candies and nuts and international gourmet foods represent classes of merchandise newly available in our stores."

Eckhouse said that in keeping with customer preference for better merchandise, Grand Way has introduced a selection of famous national brands to its merchandise assortments especially in ready-to-wear and cosmetics. At the same time the company is marketing a growing range of quality products under its own label. Customers can open charge accounts in all new Grand Ways.

In addition to offering better merchandise, said Eckhouse, "We are trading up our shopping climate in terms of both exterior architecture and interior decor." Of special interest is Grand Way's first 100,000 square-foot two-level store opened in November, 1966 in East Paterson, N.J. in a mall adjacent to the parent company's general headquarters. Grand Way is giving favorable consideration to building other such non-food department stores in heavily populated areas where two floors are a must because land is scarce. The company is convinced that such stores in densely populated areas and offering easy parking will be able to generate a high level of sales.

The work done by Eckhouse is now being carried on by George W. Darby, divisional executive vice-president in charge of Grand Way. The key Grand Union executives are Thomas C. Butler, chairman and chief executive officer, and Charles G. Rodman, president.

INTERVIEW WITH CHARLES MILLER, SALES PROMOTION DIRECTOR, GRAND WAY DIVISION

When did you come to Grand Way?

"In 1958. Before that I represented the advertising department of the New York *Post* to Metropolitan New York department stores."

Do the new Grand Way stores always carry food as well as general merchandise?

"When conditions warrant, we install general merchandise without food; we are getting away from the concept of food as a necessity in all locations. The parent company has been expanding its food store operations at the same time as new Grand Ways are being opened. Our acquisition of the Stevens chain of supermarkets in Florida has added substantially to our food operation."

Don't you have warehousing and buying problems in handling both food and general merchandise?

"This has been a problem and we are still working on it. The Grand Way advertising, merchandising, and operating group report to an executive head who is exclusively concerned with general merchandise. These departments constitute the major expenses in the general merchandise area so in these areas we pay for what we use. We are still dependent on Grand Union for certain staff functions with accounting being one since they have the manpower, skill, and computers. We don't use their warehouses since we have our own. We prefer to call them distribution centers since we do not intend to tie up capital by storing merchandise in warehouses."

Do you have any leased departments?

"We lease millinery, shoes, beauty salons."

With a background in food didn't management have problems when it took on soft goods?

238

Food Makes Its Discount Move

"We tried and at first did not do very well at it."

Why didn't you lease all non-food departments at the start?

"That did occur to the company and our former president, Mr. Shield, may have been in conversation with the Master's people with that concept in mind but it was not done. When it came to stocking those early Grand Ways the major consideration was not ready-to-wear but pots and pans and convenience items such as toiletries and nylons. By 1962 it became clear that we were on the right track and by 1963 things were rolling more smoothly. These were very decisive years for us."

Personnel must have been a problem?

"It was. In the early years personnel was drawn from a melange of variety stores, chain stores, department stores, and a few buying offices. In the beginning Mr. Shield carried the chief responsibility. Despite his vigorous efforts, at his death, Grand Way still had many merchandising problems. The company then decided to hire Joseph L. Eckhouse, one of the top general merchandise retailers in the country. He had been with Lerners, Gimbels, Bloomingdales and Macy and was formerly the executive head of Gimbels in New York. As a matter of public record, on assuming management at Grand Way he was paid a very substantial sum, $100,000 odd, and an attractive stock option. As vice-president of Grand Union and executive head of Grand Way, his leadership was most effective and significantly changed the course of Grand Way development.

Have you developed your own brands?

"Yes. We use some variant of the word Grand Way, sometimes it is simply Grand Way brand, sometimes it is Grand brand, or with men's wear, Mr. Grand. There is also Miss Grand. The company which makes our men's shirts with the Mr. Grand label makes more men's shirts than any other manufacturer of men's shirts in the world. It makes only private brands including J. C. Penney's Penncrest brand shirts. Nearly all of our foods have a Grand Union brand."

What is your major problem as of now?

"I think our overwhelming number one problem is the logistics of merchandising – the maintenance of a good solid flow of goods appropriate to the demand on a day-in and day-out basis. This applies particularly to staples since our ready-to-wear merchandise is being fairly successfully controlled by IBM computer techniques. We are making inventory control progress at a very rapid rate."

239

Stop & Shop's – Bradlee's Division A Giant Food Chain that went into Discounting

The company that was to become Stop & Shop started in 1915 with 27 neighborhood shops called Economy Grocery Stores. Clerks waited on the customers. In 1935 their first self-service Foodmart on Memorial Drive in Cambridge, Mass. opened. By 1945 there were 442 stores and in 1946, Stop & Shop became the official name for the business. Under the adroit leadership of Sidney A. Rabb and Irving W. Rabb, sales have reached new heights every year and there has been a tremendous program of building and expansion. An ultra-modern bakery opened in Boston in 1948 in addition to a grocery distribution center in Readville, Mass. In 1960 the company established a milk-processing facility and a quality control laboratory. The Tedeschi Supermarket division and the Bradlee's Self-Service Promotional Department Store chain were added in 1961. For the 52 weeks ending January 28, 1967 sales totalled more than $566 million and net earnings $7,885,965.

How did Stop & Shop get into discounting? The company has a very active real estate department which develops locations. Much of the company's real estate is owned. Management noticed the very rapid expansion of discount stores. It was quickly discovered that a discount store made an excellent neighbor for a Stop & Shop. Such stores were not readily financed; so Stop & Shop was often asked to endorse a lease. The company went looking for discount stores and became neighbors of J. M. Fields and Zayres. In Connecticut they had as neighbors six discount stores under the name of Bradlee's. These stores were founded by Morris and Edward Kouzon and Isadore Berson who also operated a children's specialty store chain called Youth Centres in Hartford and Springfield. All departments were leased except the children's. Stop & Shop had some arrangements with them about future sites but in 1961 Bradlee's ran into some financial trouble and in May, 1961, a deal was consummated whereby the 6 stores were bought in exchange for Stop & Shop stock.

For the first six months after the takeover, management let Berson run the stores and they just looked at it in an effort to decide on operating policies. By the end of 1961 it was definitely decided that the business should be given a good push; that it was a profitable opportunity. Policy planners said that this was a different business from the food business and should be autonomous. For annual report purposes the company avoids the word discount and calls its new stores "convenience department stores!"

Jack Solomon was called in to manage the new chain. Solomon is a Yale graduate who went through Filene's training program and stayed with

240

them as a buyer from 1938 to 1955. In the latter year he came to Stop & Shop as vice-president for sales in charge of non-food items which lent themselves to supermarkets. Several problems had to be overcome. Stop & Shop was unionized so the union organized Bradlee's. The presence of the union makes Bradlee's a little less flexible than its competitors and there are some limits on productivity but this is not significant as Stop & Shop has always operated with a union.

Bradlee's sales increased rapidly and management decided to open more stores. In 1965 a new store was opened in Fall River, Mass. adjacent to a Stop & Shop. Also in that year the company bought three Orbit Stores located in Dorchester and Lynn, Mass. and in Groton, Conn. Also acquired were three Family Circle Stores in Keyport, Eatontown, and Laurelton, N.J. New stores were opened in Dorchester and Dennisport, Mass. Six other new units were under construction in 1967. There are new Bradlee's in New Britain and Orange, Conn. and in Brockton, Mass. Underway is a project for four new stores in the Hartford area. The West Hartford store will be opened as an experiment. It will cater to an upper income group in this area and will carry different and higher caliber merchandise. Chief competitor will be Lord and Taylor.

In 1968 there were 46 Bradlee's stores which are now making an important contribution to company sales and earnings. Even brighter prospects are ahead. The sales of both Stop & Shop and Bradlee's are combined so that separate figures for the latter company are not available.

All Bradlee's stores are serviced through a central distribution center in Braintree, Mass. Conditions in the previous center on E Street in Boston had become unbearably crowded. The new 250,000 square-foot complex was occupied in the summer of 1966. The building is ultra-modern with brightly colored desks, a large cafeteria, and the latest in materials-handling equipment. This includes a fully automatic underfloor conveyor, a power and free monorail, a conveyor and pipe-type slide to carry goods from the delivery dock to the hanging rails in the mezzanine. There is also closed-circuit television and a paper-veyer. Cartons are dropped off a moving overhead conveyor into proper department working areas; hanging gondolas expedite the marking and sorting of goods, and fork lift trucks operate both up and down and in and out. Over one million pieces of merchandise are handled each week. Every shipment is spot checked for quality control.

EDP is used extensively in both the Stop & Shop and the Bradlee's operations. Equipment includes an IBM 360, an IBM 1401, and NCR equipment. Another IBM 360 is on order. Data processing for Bradlee's is used to transmit detailed items and classification information from stores to headquarters. All the present Bradlee's stores are integrated into the system which contributes significantly to decisions on buying, warehousing, and inventory controls. Cash registers with punched tape are in all stores. The cashier punches in the amount of the sale and then makes a "second pass" by punching in coded details about the merchandise which she finds on the sales tickets. The tape is then shipped to headquarters where a tape reader and computer make a detailed list of all items sold including style, color, vendor, price, etc. These lists are given to buyers every Monday morning for aid in making buying decisions.

The trend in Bradlee's stores is towards better designed fixturing plus a continuous effort to improve fixtures and interior decoration. Store size is relatively constant at 60,000 to 80,000 square feet. Merchandise carried is similar to other stores of its type except that major appliances, bedding, or furniture is not usually stocked. All merchandise is of first quality and no seconds are sold. The image projected is that of a well-ordered, well-lighted store which is more beautiful than most discount stores. There is a courteous and pleasant atmosphere. Most Bradlee's stores offer both layaway and bank credit financing.

The majority of the company's advertising is done in newspapers; contracts are made with local newspapers on a yearly basis for maximum economy. Direct mail is also extensively used. Advertisements cover the entire chain and are not tailored to specific areas. Point of purchase signs are considered of great promotional importance.

Stop & Shop employs 13,229 full time employees; to keep them informed it puts out an excellent monthly magazine called "Contact." Stop & Shop management places unprecedented emphasis on selection and training of people. College recruiting is felt to be a necessity. A new corporate committee, the executive manpower board, has been established specifically to identify high-potential employees for their rapidly-expanding organization. Members of this nine-man team are responsible for screening candidates for an accelerated training program. There are additional formal training programs for office employees, store managers, department managers, and store employees. Scholarships and tuition refunds are available to those wishing to further their education. Wherever possible, promotion is from within the organization.

The Jewel Companies Turnstyle Discount Stores (Formerly The Jewel Tea Company)

The Jewel Tea business was a door-to-door business founded by Frank Vernon Skiff in 1899 with a horse and wagon and $700. His brother-in-law,

Frank P. Ross, joined him in 1901 and originated a technique that is still fundamental in the route operation – giving premiums to housewives after they have bought enough goods to earn them. Sometimes a salesman disappeared or a company went out of business after a housewife had bought enough groceries to earn her premium. Ross, therefore, gave his premiums in advance. The company entered the retail store field in 1932 when it bought for $1 million 81 grocery stores. Seventy-seven of these had been Canada-based Loblaw "Grocerterias."

In 1968 the company operated 368 supermarkets concentrated in the Chicago metropolitan market area; 31 Eisner super markets in central Illinois and western Indiana; 48 Star supermarkets centered in the Boston area; 77 Osco drug stores, 50 per cent of which are adjacent to or included in Jewel food stores; 10 Turnstyle self-service department stores averaging about 100,000 square feet, including a food store, and carrying 60,000 odd general merchandise items; 82 Brigham's ice cream sandwich shops in Star's operating area (introduction of these into the Chicago area is pending). In addition, Jewel operates 1,902 home service routes in 44 states. The company is also in the wholesale grocery business through the Eisner operation whose warehouse began serving other markets in 1963. Jewel also has significant interests in international marketing. For $3.1 million it acquired 36 per cent control of Supermarches, G.B., which operates 53 supermarkets in the Antwerp and Brussels areas of Belgium and has total sales in excess of $30 million. It also acquired an 18.75 per cent equity interest in another Belgian company, Super Bazars, which operates ten self-service department stores each with a Supermarches supermarket. With an investment of about $430,000 the company acquired 49 per cent of the stock of Societa Italo Americana Supermarkets; an Italian food manufacturer and restaurant operation holds the remaining 51 per cent. The company has 12 supermarkets in Milan and its vicinity. Jewel has recently expanded its family of affiliates through a merger with Montana based Buttrey Foods which operates 31 supermarkets, most of them in Montana. Buttrey's newest units are called "superstores"; half of the floor space of each is devoted to general merchandise. Buttrey's 1965 sales were $54 million.

Total Jewel Companies sales for 1968 were $1,016,655,000 with before-tax earnings of $37,876,000. The company's organizational philosophy was expressed at an executive meeting in February, 1966: "Jewel is now an association of companies whose basic function is to be of service to the consumer in a variety of ways. These are autonomous companies associated under one corporation, but operating quite independently in their own market areas. Retailing is a regional – and as a matter of fact, a neighborhood – business. So Jewel is an association rather than a line operation." George L. Clements, board chairman, maintains that his headquarters serves primarily as a "management consulting organization to strong operating companies. The key," he said, "is local autonomy. The decision-making organizations can be local on a regional basis or local on a neighborhood basis. But it's the local autonomy – as opposed to the centrally-directed chain organization – that brings back the entrepreneur spirit. This is the spirit of the individual merchant which I think we must have in our business if we are going to grow."

President Donald S. Perkins said, "The great operating challenge of any multi-store operator is to make certain that each operating unit is run primarily as a special service for the customers in its own neighborhood, and only secondarily as one more link in the chain. This we think is terribly important. We don't want to be described as a chain of stores. We operate a lot of individual, local stores under the Jewel name in Chicago; a lot of individual, local stores under the Star name in Boston; and a lot of individual, local stores under a meaningful name wherever we operate." A good example of this policy is seen in the use of trading stamps. Jewel does not offer stamps in Chicago; the Eisner super markets have stamps; the Star supermarkets changed from one stamp plan to another and the decision was made by John Mugar, Star president.

Jewel's adherence to the policy of giving each of its component companies free rein is also illustrated in the buying function. For example, Jewel is a major merchant of toys throughout its route division. It also retails toys in the food stores, in the Osco drug units, and in the Turnstyle department stores. When a manufacturers' toy show is held, Jewel has a cadre of highly experienced toy buyers who devote about nine or ten weeks to a thorough evaluation of the items and trends. However, they do not buy the toys for Star or Osco or Turnstyle. They narrow down the broad assortments of all manufacturers to a group of items that they know would interest the various retailing groups affiliated with Jewel. Then Jewel holds its own toy show and the representatives of the various Jewel retailing units make their individual selections. In some product areas a general merchandise central service would not be effective. The fashion requirements for the route catalog are so different from those of Turnstyle that separate buying groups must be used.

Regional variations in consumer taste dictate that each of the operating units should, under most circumstances, have separate food buying organizations. For example, there are marked differences in grocery brand preferences between Boston and Chicago. Jewel and Eisner fill most of their produce needs in California and Arizona; Star draws mostly from Florida.

Although operating divisions are autonomous, Jewel management sets certain policies. One of these is that each division must project its financial budget for three years. Thus if 20 new food stores are budgeted for 1970, it is obvious that locations must be found in 1969 and financing must be planned ahead.

The Osco Drug chain of 77 stores are really "drug-variety" stores and carry a wide range of drugs and other merchandise. Prescription filling is emphasized in providing a full service of drug and related products. Other merchandise lines include housewares, small appliances, hardware, toys, cameras, garden tools, lawn mowers, and auto supplies. These stores offer a friendly atmosphere in the community and rely on low retail markups, high turnover, and self-service to provide low prices for customers and above average profits. The store manager exercises wide discretionary authority and judgment in merchandising his store to satisfy local demands. He and his assistants derive a substantial part of their cash compensation from the profits of their own store. Some Osco stores have been incorporated with Jewel food stores and share a large store building, known as a neighborhood center, with common checkouts, entrances, and exits. Osco drug-variety stores operate in the main business sections of medium-sized cities such as Elgin, Joliet, Rockford and Waukegan on the far reaches of the Chicago metropolitan area. The Osco central buying offices in the Merchandise Mart Building in Chicago makes available, as ordered by each store manager, the merchandise lines required to please customers in each locality.

In February, 1962 Jewel acquired the Turnstyle Operating Corporation on a pooling-of-interests basis through the exchange of 60,727 shares of Jewel common stock for all of the shares of Turnstyle. This organization supplemented the Jewel-Osco experience in self-service merchandising, extending it to men's, women's, and children's apparel, and to other soft lines and cosmetics. Turnstyle operated four self-service department stores in the Boston area ranging in size from 45,000 to 70,000 square feet. All of them were modern stores, built during 1957 to 1962. Since this acquisition, the company has established six more Turnstyle stores including a 110,000 square-foot Turnstyle Family Center in Racine, Wis. This center is operated under a general manager, who uses the existing Jewel Food Store buying organization for supermarket items; the Osco organization for drugs, variety, and traffic hard lines; and the Turnstyle organization for soft lines. Shoes and millinery are the only leased departments. The Center incorporates an extensive line of clothing and other soft goods: auto accessories, hardware, small appliances, sporting goods, and a wide assortment of drug and variety items as well as a complete Jewel supermarket. There is a year-round toy department.

In 1957 the Eisner family's interest in the Eisner Food Store chain was merged with Jewel. The 31 Eisner Food Stores and their thirty-nine affiliated franchise outlets are unusual in the supermarket industry inasmuch as they serve the major metropolitan cities of central Illinois and Indiana, as well as numerous rural towns and villages. The original forty-three Eisner stores have been consolidated into 31 modern supermarkets serving the six larger downstate cities with multiple stores in each, and nine other smaller cities with single stores in each. Eisner is now franchising independent store owners as Eisner affiliate stores in small communities which are served from the Eisner distribution center in Champaign, Ill. In 1965 an institutional food supply operation to serve restaurants, schools, etc., was introduced in the Eisner Division.

In 1964 about 20 per cent or $150 million of Jewel's sales were in the general merchandise area compared with 6 per cent in 1959. The company first entered the general merchandise field through the expansion of the lines offered by the home service routes, including the addition of a catalog home shopping service. Home service customers shop in their homes from a selection of approximately 300 food and related products and more than 2,600 general merchandise items. The 1965 fall and winter 144-page catalog devoted much space to women's fashions – the fastest growing catalog department. Supplementary catalogs for outdoor activities and for Christmas selling are also issued. Over 4,000 men and women serve Jewel customers in 42 states and the District of Columbia. The states with most routes are California with 295, Illinois with 130, Michigan with 129, North Carolina with 149, Pennsylvania with 223, and Ohio with 146. Merchandise is shipped from the Jewel warehouse in Barrington, Ill. to 507 routes in 8 states. Under a new cooperative franchise plan, an operator is paid on the basis of the profit he produces on his route after deducting expenses such as customer turnover, bad debts, and breakage. Higher compensation of route operators under this plan resulted in a reduction of expenses controllable at the route level and has attracted higher caliber operators.

The Jewel Companies are strongly "people oriented." The company's human resources have been developed over the years as a result of deliberately sharing responsibilities, financial rewards, and inner satisfactions of progress with everyone in the company. Jewel people at every level receive a share of the profits they produce for the company. Their achievements bring greater profits, which, in turn, generate a better return for the individual responsible and for the investors. President Perkins said, "This sharing of a business has helped us preserve the spirit and dedication of each individual as a partner in our business, in addition to providing the future and the security that most readily come from belonging to a progressive and publicly-owned enterprise. We have a Jewel-wide management dedication to the development of people at all levels of each operating company and for all functions of corporate management."

Scholarship programs provide an important contribution in recruiting personnel. Scholarships are given to part-time high school boys and girls with the requirement that they be available for employment at Jewel for at least ten weeks each summer between school years, but no strings are attached for their services after graduation. There are 25 annual scholarships all of which are for four years. Ten provide a maximum award of $6,000 and 15 a maximum of $2,000 each. Winners may choose any course of study at any accredited college or university. High school seniors employed by Jewel for an average of at least 15 hours per week during the senior high school year are eligible. About 600 part-timers apply each year for the scholarships. The final choice is by a committee of educators not employed by Jewel. About 20 per cent of scholarship winners to date have joined Jewel after graduation. The scholarship program is a big talking point with store managers who continuously keep in contact with high schools to obtain part-time workers. One of the first scholarship winners has degrees from Michigan Law School and Harvard's Graduate School of Business; he has joined Jewel's real estate department.

The company has also gained excellent results from its participation in college cooperative programs. Students each year work full-time for six months and attend school for the other six months. The cooperative system enables boys to begin their college educations and their careers at the same time. In 1966, thirty-six students were in this program at Western Michigan. A related junior college program includes ten students at the Loop Junior College and six at Wilson Junior College. Jewel recognizes that programs such as these can yield valuable management talent potential and at the same time eliminate that awkward stage that occurs when individuals with considerable academic training still lack adequate store-level experience.

Jewel's desire to bring in youngsters as part-time apprentice meat cutters has met with meat union opposition. Expansion of the store business requires more meat cutters and this area of the business has been particularly unattractive to young men. Jewel says that the union's concern over displacement of full-time people is not warranted.

Sponsorship is an important word with Jewel and signifies the company's system of keeping in close touch with its young talent on a continuous basis. Looking at the company's organization chart, president Perkins said, "If there's anybody there that isn't sponsoring several people, he doesn't deserve to be on the chart." When a young man is in a training or development program, he and his sponsor get together every month or six weeks so that the trainee feels he has a friend who is interested in him and in his progress in the company. "The Achilles' heel of the chain in its competition with the independent store owner is the motivation of ownership," says president Perkins. Jewel aims to overcome this weakness by providing the same incentive of earnings based on achievement that keeps the independent hard at work. It is recognized that payments related to earned profits, provided as immediately as possible, can be highly meaningful. Each operating unit in the company is regarded as a profit center. Every effort is made to enable the individuals whose effort produces the profit to share in the fruit of their labor.

Route operators, until recently, received a commission of 12.5 per cent of their collections. When this payment schedule was reviewed in terms of profit incentive, it was recognized that the operator could not control the price and margin of merchandise, but was fully responsible in expense areas such as bad debts, the added cost of replacing customers he lost, and related factors. Elements under his control were added up, averaged, and added to the 12.5 per cent commission; rounded off, it comes to 20 per cent. In a new route profit formula it was presented as a 20 per cent gross margin. Operators were given the incentive of receiving whatever they had not "wasted" in the difference between the basic 12.5 per cent commission and the 20 per cent gross margin, with a potential of most of the entire difference. This procedure provided considerable added income and reduced annual turnover from 66 per cent to 45 per cent in the ranks of operators.

CONTROL SYSTEM

Jewel operates a huge Barrington, Ill. distribution center. Every three minutes, eight hours a day, and five days a week, a complete weekly merchandise order destined for one of 751 home delivery route operators is loaded into a district dray truck. The average order includes 170 different stems selected from a warehouse inventory of more than 3,500 regularly stocked product lines. To prevent paperwork pileup and to maintain accounting control, an IBM 1440 data processing system is used. Since its installation in 1963, the number of route territories has grown by 59 per cent, from 450 to 751. The system improves service to the route operator through faster and more accurate order assembly. At the same time, packaging has been improved. The system also simplifies location and control of merchandise in the warehouse providing a more reliable basis for projecting inventory reorder needs. The entire route billing process is faster while control over related accounting functions is increased.

Prior to the use of the computer, order pick lists simply listed available items and quantities in product sequence. There was no attempt to arrange stock for easy assembly in the warehouse. The computer prints the itemized pick invoices, allows proper discounts for items on special sale, accumulates and prints a weekly list of quantities and discounts by items, and accumulates and prints total shipment lists within various sales program categories. It takes only 16 minutes for an incoming order to go from key punch to 100 per cent verification and printing, with two orders being printed every minute. The system integrates warehousing, inventory control, order filling, and accounts receivable control. A salesman makes out a "tally and load sheet" containing the name, address, and order of each customer. This tally sheet is sent to the central warehouse. IBM cards are then punched for every item ordered to show that item's page and line on the tally sheet, the total quantity to be shipped, and the route number. These punch cards then go into the system's card reader three times. In the first pass all cards are arranged according to the eleven divisions of goods stored in the warehouse. In the second pass the computer gets the item number, item description, unit retail price, unit bonus credits (for salesmen), sales discounts, and the item weight and cube from the master disc record of all inventory items. These items are automatically extended by quantity ordered. Thus a very complete and accurate invoice is produced.

Totals are then made on the invoice and part of the printed form goes out with the shipment, the first part of phase three. During this phase the master disc record of inventory is automatically up dated. Jewel's computerized system provides inventory control, fast order filling, and warehouse storage efficiency. The process also produces an accounts receivable record on punch cards.

The Jewel retirement plan is called "Jewel Retirement Estates" and operates through a trust fund built up through employee and company contributions. The company annually contributes 15 per cent of profits before taxes through interest and dividends resulting from investment of the fund. This is the prospect of JRE benefits as presented to prospective employees: "If you are employed at age 25, you are eligible for JRE at 27. If you contribute 6 per cent of your income to retirement at age 60, and if your income averages only $134 per week for this time, and the corporation profits are no more than they have been for the past five years, you would have $151,000 for retirement." Retirement is automatic at 65.

Finance committee chairman Franklin J. Lunding sums up the philosophy of the company: "Each one of our executives is asked to consider that he works as the first assistant to the next person in line below him. He begins by developing an understanding with himself that he does not run the business, but assists those who do. He tries to forget that he is boss and remember that any prestige he might have comes from what he can accomplish for others rather than as the symbol of his office. Each executive is charged, not so much with the directing and supervising of people, but with offering and giving assistance to those who look to him for leadership. The practical effect of this first-assistant philosophy is to turn the organization chart upside down. Each executive should feel that his job is to help the next man up the line on the upside-down chart."

Lunding maintains that with the right kind of encouragement, and a sufficiently broad and deep understanding of top management's plans and problems, many men who seem only "average" can share much more of the executive load than they are being asked to carry. If enabled, they can relieve their superiors of much pressure, and at the same time develop within themselves a sense of responsibility and of individual worth and dignity; to most men this is the highest form of compensation. In the end, of course, the leader of the organization must make the important final decisions. But he will make them better and with a more certain touch if he calls to his aid the thinking and advice of those who will be affected by the policies he adopts.

Sharing the company's problems is a practice which benefits everybody.

Jewel differs from most multi-store operators in the extent to which it invests and develops real estate. This is primarily the result of the 1957 development of its affiliated real estate corporation plan for ownership and financing of retail store properties. Under this plan, after a store location is found and the owner of the property agrees to sell at the company's price, Jewel purchases the land and constructs the store building and parking facilities. It then creates a real estate corporation to which the property is sold for the full amount of Jewel's investment in land and improvements. A net lease is executed between Jewel and the real estate corporation, which then borrows the funds needed to pay the purchase price to Jewel.

Thus, the development of these properties has been a very important factor in providing facilities for the various operating departments of Jewel and its subsidiaries. Also, where more land has been available that was needed for their own facilities, the company has developed small shopping centers with outside tenants helping to carry the cost of the project and providing additional merchandising strength to the location. In its real estate operations three primary objectives are uppermost: 1) Avoid large investments of equity capital in retail store locations. 2) Preserve long-term property values, created largely through Jewel's rent payments. 3) Maintain flexibility to discontinue operations if a store should become unprofitable.

Closed-Door
Discount
Approach

The state of California is the chief stronghold for the closed-door type of store which got its start during the depression of the 1930's. They developed as resale price maintenance grew, since they could cut prices with impunity. When fair trade became a negligible factor, they opened their doors. An early closed-door operation is FEDCO (Federal Employees Distributing Company), which is unique in that it is a true square-foot store rented for $75 a month. By 1961 it had five stores in Southern California. At first, members served without pay. Today their stores are staffed with professionals. Nevertheless they are still owned and operated by members. Most of the closed-door discount chains operating today started in the late 1950's or early 1960's.

The now defunct National Association of Consumer Organization (NACO) was the trade association of these membership department stores, most of which are on the West Coast. In 1961 NACO had 16 members operating 36 stores with total aggregate sales of over $400 million.

Ordinarily, closed-door membership stores are open only to state, Federal, or municipal government employees, and not to the general public. Employees of a company with government contracts would be eligible. A membership fee, usually $2, is charged either on a one-time or an annual

251

basis. Advertising is limited to a monthly illustrated bulletin or catalog mailed only to members. The basic idea is to establish a mutual trust between customers and store management with the cultivation of the atmosphere of an exclusive club of discriminating buyers. College scholarships are donated and administered by a committee on which customers serve. An active employee interest in community activities is encouraged.

A distinctive feature of these stores and one that often leads to serious management problems is that almost all departments are leased, usually on a short-term basis. Lessees must comply with strict management rules, agree to meet all price competition, and to maintain a full range of appropriate merchandise categories. It is obvious that to avoid conflict with absentee lessee management, the manager of a closed-door store must possess diplomatic qualities of the highest order. Some locations have proven inhospitable to the membership idea and in these areas closed doors have been opened.

The biggest operator of closed-door stores is G.E.M. (Government Employees Mutual). The company started in 1957 in Denver. In 1966 it had 33 stores with sales of $262,923,600. G.E.M. in June, 1966 merged with Parkview Drugs, Inc., becoming PARKVIEW-GEM.

FED-MART was organized in 1954 in Los Angeles. A former employee of the pioneer FEDCO company became general manager. In 1962 a pilot program was started with the purpose of franchising smaller stores under the name of FED-MART FRANCHISE. The company, in 1963, decided to become an open-door operation. There were 38 full-line FED-MARTS in 1968. Total sales for fiscal 1968 were $135,574,601 and net earnings, $1,798,923.

National Bellas Hess, with headquarters in North Kansas City, operates both open and closed-door discount stores. Its first G.E.X. (Government Employees Exchange), was started in 1957 in Oklahoma City. Strictly enforced closed-door policies are followed in G.E.X. stores. The open-door division consists of Bellas Hess Superstores, the first of which was started in Sioux City, Iowa in 1963. Aggregate sales in 1968 were $205,865,528 and net income $1,113,823.

Parkview-Gem, Inc.
(Operator of closed-door discount stores)

GEM (Government Employee Mutual), the biggest operator of closed-door discount houses, started in Denver in 1957 and now operates 38 stores with total 1968 sales of $328,976,560.

Closed-Door Discount Approach

In June, 1966 GEM International, Inc., was combined with Parkview Drugs, Inc., operator of leased departments in GEM stores. The new company is now known as Parkview-Gem, Inc. In 1962 Parkview operated a drug store chain in the Kansas City area and gradually bui.t up leased drug departments in discount stores. It also operates such departments as cosmetics, candy, tobacco, books, greeting cards, stationery, school and office supplies, pet supplies, housewares, sundries, specialties, toys, and groceries. In 1966 it was operating 54 leased departments, 34 of which were in GEM stores, seven in GEX, two in Dixiemart, five in GES, four in Bellas-Hess Superstores, two in Corondolet, and two in Medallion.

As of July 31, 1968, according to the annual report, the combined Parkview-GEM firm had current assets of $34,479,621, including $4,530,173 in cash and equivalent. Current assets were 2.0 times current liabilities of $17,432,348. Total stockholder's equity of the combined companies equalled $23,586,705. The long-term debt of $5,289,487 included $858,000 of Parkview Drugs, Inc., 5.5 per cent convertible subordinated debentures due June 1, 1977, and $3,750,000 of GEM International 5.75 per cent subordinated convertible debentures due May 1, 1979, both of which are convertible into the company's common stock. During the year of 1966, $139,000 of Parkview's 5.5 per cent debentures have been converted into 11,120 shares of common stock.

In a true closed-door discount store, buying is restricted to card-holding members. Cards are shown both at the entrance and at the cash register. However, members may bring guests and buy for them. Four to six months prior to the opening of a membership store a team of "recruiters" goes into the market area. A survey is made of civil service employees and those of federal, state, county, or municipal governments. The employees of companies having government contracts are also included, as well as members of the armed forces and government-supported colleges or universities. Employment lists are assembled and announcements and invitations are mailed. In addition to direct contacts with firms and their in-plant journals, newspaper advertisements are used with invitation-to-join coupons. Top recruiters obtain permission to appear at plants to discuss with employees the advantages of membership. For GEM stores, the aim is to obtain about 35,000 members during the first four months of operation. This number will grow with repeated mailings until, after about a year, it reaches 70,000 to 100,000. The fee for membership may be either a single payment of a nominal sum such as $2 or it may stipulate an annual membership renewal fee of $1 in addition to the initial payment.

Thus the store ends up with a list of customers and potential customers whose characteristics in terms of income, employment, and buying needs are known. The merchandise carried is geared precisely to the wants of this group and its availability is made known by direct mail. Newspaper advertising is cut down to a very small sum. Membership seems to carry a strong psychological appeal since people like the feel of exclusivity. Each GEM store publishes a monthly journal of 16 to 30 pages which is mailed to all members. Merchandise is advertised, but in addition there are new items and editorial material bearing on the reader's buying interests. For example, the pros and cons of fair trade are explained. Stores having full supermarkets now find it necessary to mail bi-monthly journals. The cost of printing and mailing is partially defrayed by manufacturers and distributors in the form of cooperative advertising. With these mailings GEM management feels that they can build up a steady buying habit rather than sporadic day-to-day advertising. There is a special mailer at Christmas. Parties for members are held on holidays, and the journal may contain social notes with pictures of newlyweds, babies, or of members who win special honors. Another approach is to create a membership board or council to pass on membership requirements and to advise GEM management on how to adjust complaints. This council also originates and runs social functions, and administers the charity and scholarship funds for the children of members.

In addition to reduced expenditures for advertising, other advantages cited by closed-door operators are: reduced theft as a result of built-in customer loyalty; far less expensive locations; and a smaller capital outlay for top management. GEM store buildings are usually put up by developers and inventories are supplied by licencees. Another closed-door operation, GEX (Government Employees Exchange), is a wholly owned subsidiary of National Bellas Hess. GEX stores are large and gross from $8 million to $12 million a store.

Prior to the merger with Parkview Drugs all departments in GEM stores were customarily leased with the exception of gasoline stations which are company operated. The licencee fee varied from 2 per cent to 10 per cent depending on the type of merchandise. Lessees who pay the higher fees are jewelry and fashion; the appliance department would pay perhaps 6 per cent. Parkview-GEM now operates its own soft-goods department. Licencee agreements with GEM have a 30 to 60 day cancellation clause. Every licencee must agree to offer the lowest possible prices every day on every item and must maintain depth, breadth, and continuity of merchandise. If comparison shoppers find an item in a competitor's store which is priced lower than a similar item in a given department, the licencee must lower his price to that of the competitor. Suggestions on improving operations are given to lessees by a research team consisting of the general manager, executive controller, executive credit manager, director of public relations, the store manager, and assistant store manager. There is a sharing of information contained in previous records of operations in other GEM stores and the advice of veteran licencees is given. Emphasis is put on the partnership theory instead of "order giving." Department employees are rated as to capability, efficiency, and conscientiousness. GEM top management stresses the point that they are not

254

just landlords, but are also merchants who try to obtain top caliber lessees. Such lessees have a fair degree of independence but must use methods in agreement with GEM overall policy. The company insists that it does its best to help its licencees do a better job. Each licencee buys his own stock and fixtures and hires his own personnel; therefore corporate investment is minimal. This is not the case with GEX which retains ownership of its buildings and sites and also operates women's and children's wear departments. Credit costs are born by the licencee in whose department the purchase is made. Appliance licencees must offer service with purchases.

Lessees of food departments can be large, capable chains such as Kroger in St. Louis or Stop & Shop in Boston. They can also be local independents who are willing to become lessees. Another method is for the company to run the food department themselves, but this requires know-how. A food market is very desirable because of the traffic it provides. GEM tells its food operators that their prices must be six to seven per cent under those of conventional supermarkets. This is achieved by not giving stamps and by limiting the sizes and brands to those which move fast and create a large volume. The efficiency of "traystack" is used to save time and labor. Food differs in the licencee agreement. Instead of a 30 or 60 day cancellation clause, there is a 16-month or longer guarantee. The charge levied by the principal is designed to cover rental, utilities, and advertising. The responsibility of GEM or GEX management is to bring in traffic. In most closed-door operations each department has its own cash register. There is no waiting in line at check out counters.

The merchandise carried in closed-door discount stores is similar to that carried by many conventional department stores. A number of these companies are developing their own private brands. There is a GEM brand of gasoline, oil, batteries, ice cream, hosiery and many other items. GEM anti-freeze is made by Prestone. Although the label does not indicate this, the company has permission from Union Carbide to display it with a sign saying, "Made for GEM by the manufacturers of Prestone." Vitamins formerly sold under the NACO (National Association of Consumer Organizations) label now have a GEM label. GEM has a merchandising division in New York City to standardize and improve the character of its company-operated soft goods departments which include children's, women's, and men's departments. Through centralized purchasing, the merchandising division has been able to develop and coordinate an exclusive private-brand program which enables members to purchase the products of brand name manufacturers under the GEM label at lower costs. Lessees may also use this service.

The big problem in operating a closed-door discount store is that with leased departments you are dealing with absentee management which frequently makes it very difficult to get the kind of follow-through you need.

255

The wage scale for lessee personnel may not be high enough to attract capable people. Both the leased department and the operator have to make a profit and yet work on a very low margin. Unless volume is assured, trouble arises. GEM, for example, has no maximum or minimum lessee fees but a straight percentage of sales. If sales are low, income drops. Constant pressure must be put on leased departments to perform effectively. The majority of the original closed-door stores have now opened their doors; however, GEM, with the exception of its Detroit stores, has remained firm in keeping its doors closed. Regardless of whether doors are open or closed, any store that is operated almost entirely on a lessee basis has serious problems of organization and control. It is not easy to find qualified lessees who will price properly, give value, and maintain the store image on a consistent basis. Another area of potential conflict is advertising. The store manager has complete control and allocates space to the various departments. Departments must turn in their items to him for approval. He can either select them or turn them down as unsuited for insertion in the monthly journal.

Fed-Mart

Fed-Mart is a San Diego-based regional chain, with operations in California, Arizona, New Mexico, and Texas. It started in 1954 as a closed-door operation, but has opened its doors and also gone into franchising. Sales for fiscal 1968 (ending August 31) were $135,574,601 and net earnings were $1,798,923.

In 1954, E. L. Bertrand, Mandell Weiss, Leo Freedman, and Sol Price organized a company similar to that of Fed-Co, Los Angeles. A former employee of Fed-Co was hired as general manager of the new organization which opened in December, 1954 in a San Diego warehouse. Starting capital was $50,000; the initial departments included jewelry, housewares, major appliances, men's apparel, and furniture. The only concessionaires were men's apparel operated by Seven Seas Clothiers and furniture by Herbert Haimsohn. The original format, both in corporation and pricing arrangements, was quite similar to Fed-Co. Fed-Co, however, is a non-profit corporation owned by its members and operated through directors who, in effect, perpetuate themselves in office through the use of proxies. Fed-Mart, on the other hand, started as a private-profit corporation and became a publicly-held corporation in 1959.

Until 1963 the company concentrated on developing large, 75,000 to 100,000 square-foot stores on a closed-door basis. Management then decided to abandon the closed-door policy. A company statement explaining this change follows: "It became apparent that there was no logical reason for selecting the members eligible to use the facilities on the basis of Federal

FEDCO (Federal Employees Distributing Company), a "closed-door" discount store in Los Angeles, Calif. (Note the pharmacy.)

employment alone. Gradually it became the policy of Fed-Mart to make membership available to those groups of personnel who, because of the nature of their work, had already been screened carefully for honesty and intelligence, and who were employed in such industries, either public or private, that lend themselves to stability rather than to the ups and down of the economic cycle. These industries attracted people who were more interested in long-term employment, who planned their lives on an orderly basis, who are better than average credit risks; who generally fit into one broad economic stratum, and who are generally inquisitive and intelligent enough to seek out merchandising values without the necessity of hard-hitting salesmen or extensive advertising. They are the type who would more normally be 'home-owners', with somewhat similar wants. Therefore, gradually, the membership eligibility was expanded first to city, county, and state employees, then to selected groups, such as telephone and telegraph people, gas and electric people, hospital personnel, and ultimately to bank employees, and later, in very selected cases, to other groups. This policy led to the present company-wide, open-door operation.

Very early in the life of Fed-Mart, it became apparent that the conventional merchants of the community were going to exert as much political and police pressure against the operation as was possible. On the first day of Fed-Mart's operation, a bedding inspector cited it to show cause why it should not be denied a license to sell pillows, etc. It became apparent that this action was provoked by the downtown competitors. A list of questions was presented to Fed-Mart which went far beyond anything that could have any bearing on bedding or pillows. Some questions involved what bank the corporation dealt with, the identity of the owner of the property, and the identity of the stockholders. Fed-Mart was made extremely conscious of the fact that everything it did would be examined by its competition, by legislative authority, by police authority, by manufacturers, and by the FTC. All of this was designed to "catch" the organization so that it could be shown up to its members and to the public as something somehow sinister, or illegal, or dishonest. Management then decided that Fed-Mart would never do anything that in the slightest smacked of misrepresentation or sharp dealing. As a result, Fed-Mart anticipated the FTC regulations on tire advertising by a full two years. It has consistently gone beyond the FTC regulations on using comparative prices in ads. Fed-Mart claims to be the first company to cut and destroy non-recappable carcasses in the presence of the customer.

It was determined that close-outs, discontinued models, obsolete merchandise, and substandard merchandise were not items that Fed-Mart should carry. The company now handles only top grade gasoline, tires, ice cream, coffee, etc. In a sense, the conventional competitors can be thanked for having pushed Fed-Mart into an ideal type of merchandising operation.

When Fed-Mart opened it followed the same formula of many similar operations by adding five per cent to the posted price of any article in the store. This had always seemed a deception, and when the second Fed-Mart store opened in Phoenix the practice was discontinued. About one year thereafter, the FTC began serious and intense investigations of all establishments like Fed-Mart. One of the first things the FTC lit upon was the five per cent add-on. The FTC investigated Fed-Mart, Gov-Mart, and Fed-Co. thoroughly. Fed-Mart received a notice stating that there was no evidence of any violations of FTC regulations.

CONCESSIONAIRES

It was obvious to management that there would be a direct conflict between store policy and concessionaire policy insofar as value, misrepresentations, exchanges, employee attitudes, etc., were concerned. It was determined very early to take over concessions. This situation had been anticipated because all concessionaire agreements were originally drawn with a 24-hour cancellation clause.

The first concessions taken over were men's clothing and furniture. Management was concerned with the development of a merchandising approach that would give members a reason to come to Fed-Mart more frequently. It was therefore decided to add a service station to the San Diego

258

Eager customers wait for the grand opening of CMA (Consumers' Mart of America), a closed-door discount store in Oaklawn, Ill.

store. It was not put in for profit, but as a traffic-getter. It used only one grade of low-priced, good quality, gasoline. Fed-Mart claims to be the first discount store in its area to have a service station; the first with a nursery; and the first to get into hardware and building materials.

In February, 1962 the company told stockholders: "For some time we have been actively searching for means whereby we could better utilize our purchasing power and spread costs over a broader base . . . We have begun a pilot program for franchising smaller stores under the name of Fed-Mart Franchise. This is a new concept in the discount field and seeks to apply to this field certain techniques of operation in smaller communities which have proven highly successful with some conventional chain operations."

Two months later the first Fed-Mart Franchise, a 15,000 square-footer, opened its doors in Chula Vista, Calif. Forty per cent of its selling area was devoted to food with the remaining 60 per cent in apparel, domestics, soft goods, housewares, and other household items. The concept was to move into small communities with a population of from 12,000 to 35,000 with very little risk and no serious problems. The potential territory for franchises could then be widened to include fringe areas of metropolitan cities. The financial arrangements, reported in the January, 1965 *Discount Merchandiser* are as follows: The store operator puts up a sum somewhere between $15,000 and $25,000. Fed-Mart will then supply approximately $150,000-worth of inventory and fixtures. For its services Fed-Mart realizes a 6 per cent interest on its loan to the franchisee, plus 3 per cent on taxable sales and 1.5 per cent on non-taxable gross, an average of 2.6 per cent. When Fed-Mart lends the typical franchisee the re-conversion money, it takes a lease on the physical plant from the operator, then leases the store back to him. A clause in the contract permits the parent company to take over the complete operation in any 30-day period.

Each owner is primed for his task via a training program and can draw up to a certain amount of profit until Fed-Mart is repaid its original costs. Most of the older franchise store operators reportedly draw up to $7,500 a year. Stores are largely restricted to staples and fast turnover merchandise; but if they are willing to settle for a 10 per cent profit on major appliances, they can carry this category. For stores that do not have the space, there are plans to supply catalogs featuring furniture and appliances. The franchisee buys from the company's central buying offices, using a master list. "Through Fed-Mart's central warehousing, buying power, advertising, and merchandising," the company explains, "it is possible to place the franchisee in the best competitive position in his area." Some of the company's future franchise locations might be the starting point for shopping center developments on land it either owns or in land in which it has a part interest. The sixth franchise unit in Tucson has 30,000 square feet. Unit number seven, formerly known as the CMC stores, combines both supermarket and general merchandise departments under its 45,000 square-foot roof in Escondido, California.

In 1968, Fed-Mart stores were located as follows: California, 17 units; Arizona, 7 units; New Mexico, one unit; Texas, 13 units. Net current assets for 1968 were $9,433,936 with a long-term debt of $9,097,855. Stockholders' equity in 1968 rose to $11,932,389, compared to $7,542,849 for fiscal 1967. Net earnings after taxes for 1968 were $1,798,923.

"In contrast to big stores, which need $600,000 volume a month to break even," says Sol Price, "a franchised unit of 10,000 to 20,000 square feet brings its owner and Fed-Mart a monthly profit of $60,000. In fact, this represents a better return on investment than the big stores . . . The most exciting aspect of our retailing picture is the franchised store." The company is continually seeking new franchise locations. On land purchased in Brownsville, Pasadena, Las Cruces, and Lancaster, franchise-type store buildings were erected and opened in 1966. Fed-Mart has always owned the land and buildings where it operates; the real estate division of the company has traditionally played a major role in expansion.

Merchandise carried in the larger Fed-Marts includes: white goods, television, radio, phonographs, traffic appliances, furniture, housewares, groceries, fresh meat, health and beauty aids, sundries, prescription drugs, women's wear, men's wear, children's wear, sporting goods, camera and jewelry, automotive accessories, gasoline, infants' furnishings, hardware, nursery, building materials, toys, records, shoes, patio furniture, liquor, and notions. One of the most significant product areas is Fed-Mart brand merchandise. There are currently over 300 "FM" branded products ranging from milk and toothpaste to paint and gasoline. As stated in the 1965 annual report: ". . . we have encouraged our buyers to continually explore sources for FM Brand products which meet the following requirements:

1. Does the product have sufficient volume to warrant the expense of labeling, warehousing, and committing for large quantities?

2. Can we be certain that the FM Brand will be at least as high in quality as the leading national brand?

3. Can the FM Brand afford our customers a substantial saving?

4. Will it improve our profit margin?

"The following are typical examples . . . About three years ago we purchased our own tire molds and contracted with one of the largest tire manufacturers in the country to make an FM brand tire, equal in quality to their top tire. We have had outstanding success with this tire. We sell it at retail for slightly less than the wholesale cost to the manufacturer's conventional dealers. This cost is approximately half the price of a similar tire with the manufacturer's brand on it. We have done the same thing with motor oils which we retail for less than half the going national brand price. FM vitamins and aspirin, the composition and quality of which are federally regulated, are sold by Fed-Mart for as much as 75 per cent less than nationally advertised brands. Ladies' hosiery, men's underwear, soaps and detergents, dry milk, margarine, paints, automobile batteries, oil filters, beer and distilled spirits, razor blades, mouthwash, toothpaste, toothbrushes, toilet tissue, facial tissue, gasoline, golf balls, watches, bread, jams, jellies, and coffee are just some of the other FM brands producing similar benefits to the company and to its customers.

"Many companies which have entered the area of private labels fall short of receiving the full benefits which are derived by Fed-Mart. For the most part they attempt to turn too much of the savings to profits. Also, they devote a disproportionate share of time and money promoting vast selections of national brands. In many other instances they are not sufficiently careful about the quality of their private brand. We feel that we are entitled to a great margin when we develop an FM brand product; but we never attempt to take the drama out of the retail price to the customer. It is our opinion that the FM brand, priced dramatically low and of good quality, perpetuates the customer's loyalty and carries it over to other products and services in the store. The search for additional FM brand products continues. We are looking forward to major and traffic electric appliances which will be marketed under the FM brand. We will shortly have a spark plug equal in

261

quality to the top spark plug in the country, which will sell for as much as 60 per cent less than the advertised prices of national brands. We are constantly exploring the potential of any product which, in our opinion, has too high a combined advertising, distribution, and packaging cost. We have already created FM brand products numbering in the hundreds and, almost without exception, they have proved their merit."

Until 1961 each Fed-Mart store ordered and received merchandise individually. Management reasoned that to simplify the operations at the store level and to help standardize the Fed-Mart operation, a central warehouse was necessary. Therefore, a 375,000 square-foot warehouse was built in Anaheim, Calif. The company also has a warehouse in Houston to serve the Western division. In some grocery products and a few miscellaneous areas, it is still necessary for stores to make direct purchases.

In 1965 Fed-Mart decided to liquidate all non-merchandising investments and activities. The company's wholly-owned subsidiary, Jaffe and Martin Construction, Inc., was sold. It disposed of 200,000 shares of the First Financial Life Insurance Company, formerly Fed-Mart Life Insurance Company.

In 1968 Fed-Mart had 2,250 regular employees; in the peak season it employs an additional 500 part-timers. Employees have life insurance coverage, medical and hospital benefits, sick pay, vacation, holiday, and overtime pay. There is also a profit-sharing plan, whereby eligible employees will receive up to a 5 per cent bonus each month in Fed-Mart common stock. The company expects to continue its ambitious expansion program during 1969 and 1970.

National Bellas Hess, Inc. (Operators of both closed and open door discount stores)

From bankruptcy in 1932, the sales of National Bellas Hess in 1968 reached an all time high of $205,865,528, including licensed departments in the G-E-X and Superstore operations. This represents a 12 per cent increase over 1967. Earnings, after taxes, were $1,113,823. How the company came into being follows.

Early in 1883, S. G. Rosenbaum, age 15, went from Raleigh, N.C., to New York City to seek his fortune. He found employment in a lace and embroidery house as a messenger, at a salary of $3 per week. Rosenbaum's father, with the rest of the family, followed him to New York and established a small shop at 21 Wooster Street, where he manufactured women's cloaks. In the spring of 1888, Rosenbaum, Jr., then 19 years old, conceived the idea of making women's cloaks to order from measurements sent by mail. His father consented to invest some of his savings to give the specialty mail-order plan a trial.

Styles were secured and printed in a few thousand catalogs. In October, 1888 the first order was received. Until then selling made-to-measure cloaks by mail had never been done. Rosenbaum was a pathfinder with his firm, which became the National Cloak and Suit Company. The business grew and flourished and helped to pave the way for mail order retailing. In 1918 the company opened a plant in Kansas City; in 1927 it merged with the Bellas Hess Company, which had originated in New York City some years before. Thus, the National Bellas Hess was born.

In the 1929 stock market crash, the merged company's working capital was more than $7 million. Over $4 million of that amount was lost in 1930. Liquidation proceedings were begun in 1932. Some of the important assets were sold to a corporation formed by a group of ex-National Bellas Hess Company executives. They were George Marks, I. R. Dickson, Carl Berry, Samuel Cutler, and A. E. Dawson. This group had the active and financial help of William Becker, owner of Becker Studios, New York City, and Herman Benjamin, attorney. Sixteen people put in a payless seven months working on the reorganization plan. Without money, financial statement, or credit rating, the management purchased $543,000 worth of goods and $180,000 worth of printing paper and art work and reorganized the company as National Bellas Hess, Inc. in 1932.

The company began to flourish as a mail order firm during the late 30's. Today, under the presidency of Lawrence H. Gabrini, National Bellas Hess, Inc., with headquarters in New York City, Kansas City, and Hato Rey, Puerto Rico, is serving millions of families in the United States and abroad, with mail order, retail, and insurance service. It maintains 52 catalog order stores, and mails catalogs to all 50 states, United States possessions, and a number of foreign countries. The retail division currently operates 13 retail stores (membership and open door) in the U.S. Seventeen retail stores are maintained in Puerto Rico. The company also operates two insurance divisions, the Heart of America Life Insurance Company, with headquarters in Kansas City, and the National Bellas Hess Life Insurance Company of Puerto Rico.

MEMBERSHIP RETAILING

A need for serving military personnel, government employees, and the like, was keenly felt at the end of World War II. Pioneers in the membership retail field recognized that the nation-wide rising standard of living, brought about by increased salaries, was not affecting, to any great degree, military and government personnel with fixed incomes. Membership store operators sought to cater to this middle income group who had become accustomed to commissaries, PX stores, and the like.

THE ORIGIN OF G-E-X (Government Employees Exchange)

The success achieved by membership discount operators and the prospect of their future growth prompted National Bellas Hess officials to consider entering the area in 1957. A plan was formulated for an initial chain of five stores under the name G-E-X (Government Employees Exchange). Original licencees were Medco (jewelry), Recco (records), Gateway (sporting goods), and Parkview (drugs). Oklahoma City was chosen as the site for the first G-E-X- store, as officials felt the area lent itself to the membership form of retailing. Land was acquired on a lease basis for the erection of a 60,000 square-foot store. As a first venture, it was felt the store should begin on a somewhat conservative scale; additions and remodeling could come at a later date when the store had become established. Shortly after the Oklahoma City store was in operation, the land and building were purchased.

BASIC PRINCIPLES AND POLICIES

With the inception of G-E-X came the establishment of basic principles and policies as stated in the employee's Guidebook:

1. WE WILL NOT KNOWINGLY ISSUE A MEMBERSHIP CARD TO ANYONE WHO DOES NOT QUALIFY FOR MEMBERSHIP UNDER OUR RULES AND REGULATIONS.

G-E-X does not deviate from this policy. Other membership operations have fallen by the wayside by "opening up" their membership eligibility and "stretching" eligible groups to include home owners, utility workers, and others. G-E-X recognizes that such a change in fundamental policy is harmful to a membership operation; established members and potential new members are therefore not misled by an operation which stresses exclusiveness, and then allows almost anyone to enter its locked door. By remaining loyal to its eligibility pledge, G-E-X has continued to grow and to maintain the confidence of its members.

2. WE WILL NOT SELL MERCHANDISE TO ANYONE WHO DOES NOT PRESENT A MEMBERSHIP CARD OR PURCHASE PASS AT TIME OF PURCHASE.

While this might seem unnecessary, since the membership card is shown at the door for admittance, G-E-X feels that it is but a second opportunity to safeguard the exclusive shopping privileges of its members.

3. WE WILL AT ALL TIMES ENDEAVOR TO OFFER OUR MEMBERS THE BEST QUALITY MERCHANDISE AT THE LOWEST POSSIBLE PRICES IN THE CITY.

Perhaps the most important of G-E-X policies, the concept of offering famous brand names at recognized savings has been instrumental in G-E-X's growth and success. How G-E-X can make good its claim of quality merchandise at lower prices is best explained in a brief analysis of G-E-X's internal operation:

A. Eliminating costly advertising expenses.
B. Offering a clean, modern, attractive store with no costly frills or window displays.
C. Operating in a low-rent district (away from shopping centers and downtown areas).
D. Volume buying. (10 G-E-X closed-door stores, 3 open-door operations, and nationally prominent licencees, combine their vast buying power and marketing knowledge to reduce costs.)

G-E-X relies on high volume to generate high profit, a concept which we again stress is basic and fundamental to success in low-margin retailing.

4. WE GUARANTEE THE MEMBERS SATISFACTION WITH OUR MERCHANDISE, OR WE WILL WILLINGLY EXCHANGE IT OR REFUND THE PURCHASE PRICE. THE MEMBER IS THE SOLE JUDGE, AND WE RESPECT HIS HONEST AND SINCERE JUDGMENT IN THE MATTER.

To quote from the G-E-X Employee Manual, "In other words, we mean the Member is always right, and what the member wants, he gets. Employees in their every action must demonstrate their willingness, without question, to make exchanges and refunds."

5. THE PATRONS OF G-E-X ARE MEMBERS, NOT JUST CUSTOMERS, AND WE WILL ENDEAVOR AT ALL TIMES TO MAKE CERTAIN THAT EACH AND EVERY MEMBER RECEIVES THE HIGHEST TYPE OF SERVICE AND COURTESY.

A great deal of emphasis is placed on this principle. It is not considered an idle boast: it is a promise. Headquarters maintains a sales training director, whose duties and responsibilities are in the area of obtaining maximum sales, customer service, and efficiency through our sales personnel at store level, as well as training and developing personnel to uphold our creed.

GROWTH PATTERN OF G-E-X

The original G-E-X store in Oklahoma City was successful from its inception. Additional G E X stores, now increased to 100,000 square feet, opened in Atlanta (July, 1960), Norfolk (September, 1960), Albany (September, 1961), and Camden, N.J. (October, 1961). The 125,000 square-foot stores later opened in Hampton, Va. (August, 1962), Buffalo, N.Y. (September, 1962), Milwaukee (September, 1962), Charleston, S.C. (October, 1962), and New Orleans (August, 1963).

Eligible shoppers pay a fee for the privilege of shopping in a G-E-X store; therefore, it is imperative that G-E-X offer its members the finest name brand merchandise at the lowest possible prices and provide "extras" common to the department store, but not found in the discount operation.

G-E-X offers over 90,000 items in more than 50 departments. Unique services include a gasoline station, prescription pharmacy, laundry and dry cleaning, a beauty salon, barber shop, portrait studio, and insurance and optical departments.

Striving for an "image" different from that of most discount stores, G-E-X effects a complete department store image by offering families virtually all their wants and needs under one roof, amid pleasant surroundings, with an emphasis on cleanliness and high standards of merchandising and display.

THE CREDIT OPERATION

With the opening of its initial store in Oklahoma City in 1959, G-E-X obtained a licencee for its credit operation; on opening the Atlanta G-E-X store in 1960, the company organized its own credit department. Today, with its credit staff housed in its Kansas City headquarters, the retail division of National Bellas Hess does close to 40 per cent of its sales through credit. Credit facilities rank high in the list of services available to G-E-X members and Superstore customers. Revolving charge and time payment plans are offered under its credit program, "Budget-Aid," with a period of up to 36 months to pay for major purchases.

THE ADDITION OF FOOD DEPARTMENTS

It was not until the opening of the Albany G-E-X store (1961) that serious consideration was given to the profit and traffic building possibilities of a food operation.

G-E-X experimented with food in their Atlanta and Albany stores in the fall of 1961. A small department was added consisting mainly of dry groceries, without fresh meats. Immediate success prompted plans for full-size supermarkets in the Milwaukee, Buffalo, and Hampton operations, which were at that time on the drawing board. Supermarkets became an important part of the overall operation as the newer stores were expanded to a total of 125,000 square feet. The initial operation in Oklahoma City was expanded from 60,000 to 80,000 square feet to include a grocery supermarket.

THE OPEN DOOR OPERATION (BELLAS HESS SUPERSTORES)

The success of its G-E-X operations prompted management to consider expansion into the open-door field. The company was experienced in licencee-

266

operated ventures, and its licencees shared its desire to grow and expand. It seemed reasonable to open in markets with a highly concentrated farm and industrial population. Sioux City, Iowa was selected as the first site for an open door operation (March, 1963) because the area did not have a low-margin retailing operation. Sioux City also offered a highly concentrated farm and industrial market. Mobile, Ala. was selected as the second site for a Bellas Hess Superstore (May, 1963), for essentially the same reasons as the Sioux City selection. Mobile offered a large industrial population to provide the needed traffic.

Superstores were patterned after the G-E-X operations; merchandising, service, principles, and policies remained the same. The only marked difference was in the approach to advertising and promotion. While the membership operation lends itself to circulating monthly publications to members, the open-door stores must rely almost exclusively on conventional newspaper advertising, along with some radio and television advertising.

With the exception of Oklahoma City, the first six G-E-X stores were initiated by the outright purchase of land and construction by National Bellas Hess. For the G-E-X store in Buffalo, the company purchased land and arranged for lease-back agreements. In March, 1966 an existing store of 120,000 square feet was acquired in Montgomery, Ala. It was transformed into an up-dated Superstore by a roster of competent licencees, effective advertising programs, and a solid base of credit-eligible customers prior to opening. The store continues to operate as a profit maker today. The future possibility of acquiring such existing units, for adaptation to G-E-X merchandising, is eagerly anticipated.

G-E-X LICENCEES

Among the factors which have added to G-E-X's success is the relationship it enjoys with licencees. (The term "licencees" is based on "lessees" for, while various departments are leased, agreements for such arrangements are made through a licencee; therefore, the term "licencee.")

G-E-X considers its licencees as "partners" in all endeavors and the feeling is mutual. It is emphasized by the respect shown G-E-X management and the willingness, based on years of mutual trust and confidence, to work hand in hand to maintain G-E-X policy. G-E-X and Superstore licencees include Medco (jewelry), Gateway Sporting Goods, Berland Shoes of St. Louis (a division of Genesco), and Unishops (men's and boys' wear).

Contrary to the growing trend of retailers to take over their licencees, National Bellas Hess has expressed no intention of changing its method of operation.

NBH considers its licencees as "pros," and while checks and balances are provided through license agreements, licencees have demonstrated to

267

G-E-X management that they are the true veterans in this business. The company relies heavily on their experience and ability to do the best possible merchandising job in all NBH stores.

HEADQUARTERS – THE HOME OFFICE STAFF

The retail division of National Bellas Hess headquarters is in North Kansas City. It is headed by Lawrence M. Hatfield, executive vice-president and general manager. Assisting Hatfield is a group of eight staff members. It is a general practice to advance members of the organization to a staff position after a successful tour-of-duty as a store manager. While each staff member has specific duties and responsibilities, all work together in a mutual exchange of ideas and talents.

MEMBER RELATIONS

With the advent of membership retailing there emerged a new expression, "member relations," which refers to the personal contact activities designed to inform all potential members about G-E-X. Planned programs and events create and maintain the intimate image of a "Government Employees Store." Members are the "life blood" of G-E-X, and it is the responsibility of "member relations" to obtain these members. Its approach is a soft-sell; one geared to government employees individually, or in groups, both on the job and in club or association meetings. This continuing "member relations" effort is unique with G-E-X. Each store has a full time member relations director; there are regional member relations supervisors and an overall member relations manager. The annual budget for this activity is in excess of $250,000.

A long list of programs and events, designed to help G-E-X take part in community affairs include:

A. A scholarship awards program, which gives in excess of $28,000 annually in scholarship grants to deserving sons and daughters of members.

B. The annual public service achievement awards program, to honor an outstanding federal, state, county, and city employee, from each G-E-X store area.

C. The in-store luncheon program, which invites groups to use G-E-X facilities for luncheon and dinner meetings as guests of G-E-X.

D. Annual bowling tournaments in which G-E-X joins local bowling establishments in the awarding of valuable cash prizes.

E. The recent addition of a "community room" in those G-E-X stores undergoing remodeling. Eligible groups are invited to use the room's facilities for meetings, lectures, displays, etc.

Proof of the value of member relations activities is the tremendous membership growth. A members' advisory council composed of prominent residents is selected for each store. The council works closely with membership and store management in administering the college scholarship fund. It also plays a vital role in overall coordination between members and management.

RECRUITMENT AND TRAINING OF PERSONNEL

National Bellas Hess makes a conscientious effort to search out and hire personnel with experience and background in the department store, chain store, or low-margin retailing field who can be trained to assume the responsibility of store management and other positions at store level. New personnel are hired as either store manager trainees or as assistant store manager trainees. Each trainee is assigned to a seasoned store manager. The formal training program lasts up to six months. Careful attention is given to the full development of the trainee in every phase of the operation. The home office staff makes periodic checks into the progress of the individual. All store managers in the chain have been promoted from within the organization via the training program. Personnel policy also considers individuals in lower echelons of responsibility as candidates for the training and development program. NBH recognizes that recruiting and training of new personnel is vital to its growth and progress.

THE G-E-X STORE AND SUPERSTORE MANAGER

Store managers work within the framework of budgeted expenses that are mutually planned and approved by the store manager and NBH. He provides leadership, direction, and guidance to licencees in all phases of merchandising. Merchandising policies are spelled out in the license agreement and operating manual and cover such matters as average mark-up, item and classification presentation, depth and assortments of stock, pricing policies, inventory control, advertising, and standards for presentation and display of merchandise.

ADVERTISING AND PROMOTIONS

In the first five years of its operation, G-E-X employed an advertising agency to handle printed material and promotions. As the chain grew, it became necessary for the retail division to create its own advertising and promotion division. A store manager with talent in the area of publicity and promotions was appointed to head up the advertising office with a staff of fourteen talented people. Advertising for all G-E-X membership stores is presented through a monthly bulletin-catalog sent via mail. The company experimented with newspaper advertising for its G-E-X stores. Although coverage was only geared to a portion of the circulation, in some instances, it was highly successful. During the past year, the company has pursued a limited program of newspaper advertising for the G-E-X operation. In most instances it has been semi-institutional in character, designed to stimulate additional membership, traffic, and volume.

Advertising for the Bellas Hess Superstores is prepared at the local level, since it has proven more convenient for an in-store staff to work directly with hometown newspapers. In this manner, the flexibility necessary for taking advantage of local conditions is achieved. Guidance, advance preparation, and planning is provided by the Kansas City staff to maintain continuity in presentation and image. Company policy dictates integrity as the basic ingredient of all advertising material prepared by the Kansas City staff. All forms of advertising (newspaper, radio, television, catalog) must withstand the closest scrutiny of the FTC, the Better Business Bureau, and most important, the members and customers of G-E-X and Superstores.

A NEW LOOK AND A NEW APPROACH

The changing retail scene indicates that today's shopper is more sophisticated. She demands maximum quality, service, and convenience.

Through study and analysis, G-E-X management came to realize that in-store decor was playing a more important part in the success of a low-margin retail operation. It concluded that it needed a modern, imaginative approach to color, design, fixtures, merchandise displays, and arrangements. In the spring of 1965, more than a quarter of a million dollars was invested in the modernization of the Oklahoma City operation. Its new look is indicative of future G-E-X and Superstore operations. Other stores are scheduled for similar modernization in the near future.

MAINTAINING A CONSTANT AWARENESS

G-E-X has taken a firm stand on Quality Stabilization and Fair Competition laws by stressing its belief that "price fixing" is contrary to offering the American Public the finest merchandise at the lowest possible prices. G.E.X believes that pricing is primarily for the benefit of the customer. Thus, it has used its influence, at both state and national levels, to discourage the passage of any laws which might hinder genuine savings to members, customers, and the general buying public. Management is concerned with becoming a part of those communities where NBH stores are located. Membership in the Chamber of Commerce and other civic organizations, and an interest and active participation in various civic affairs is a tradition with the company.

CURRENT EXPANSION

A second Atlanta G-E-X store opened in the spring of 1967 to serve eligible members in the North Atlanta area. At the same time, a G-E-X store opened in Huntsville, Ala., a city where eligible members are engaged primarily in missile and space project work. Recently, a new Bella Hess Superstore opened in Albuquerque, New Mexico. These three stores are approximately 125,000 square feet in size.

NBH is now considering sites for stores in the Midwest and South. The company feels that these areas lend themselves best to its low-margin retail concept.

VIII

Leased

Departments

Without the help of lessees, pioneer discounters would not have succeeded. Lessees provided the working capital, inventory, fixtures, personnel, and know-how for their special departments. In return for the use of his selling space, the principal received a rental based on a percentage of sales ranging from 2 per cent to 10 per cent, depending on the merchandise carried. Without the very considerable help of lessees, a store could not become a "department store" with a full range of merchandise. If the owner made a profit of even 1 per cent on his leased departments, he was satisfied. The leased departments attracted more customers; and they brought in the "owned" departments. However, as his business grew and additional stores were added, the lessee was required to grow with him. Some lessees, unable to provide either the capital or the personnel for rapid expansion, were dropped.

After opening ten stores, management may have built up a substantial backlog of working capital; the company is no longer a struggling pioneer with limited know-how about operations other than its specialty. Store management reviews its lessee relationship and tries to push for a better bargain. There ensues a kind of cat and mouse game: each party tries to make the best possible deal. Management tries to get the highest rental

272

possible without tipping over the applecart, that is, without forcing its lessee to raise prices and ruin the store's discount image. When lessee prices creep up, the store manager has to say, "Hey, your prices are too high. Your stocks are not so good. Give me a special for next Tuesday!" Disputes may arise as to how much advertising the leased department should receive; whether the inventory has sufficient variety in categories and depth; whether the prices of competitors are being met; whether the leased department employees are covering their assignments adequately; whether inventory control is lax by permitting too many "outs;" and whether customer returns of merchandise are being handled as the store wishes. Even if there are no grounds for complaint, store management feels that they now have enough capital to buy both the inventory and know-how needed to operate most departments themselves. In many instances the entire leased department operation, including those leased to other stores, is bought out. The existing lessee executives may be merged into the management fabric of the chain management. Regardless of the efficiency and the loyalty of a lessee, he inevitably faces expulsion or merger at the end of his contract term. Contracts may be on a twenty-four hour, thirty day, one-year, or five-year basis.

Long experience, however, indicates that certain departments may be better operated by a lessee than by store management. Such a department is men's and women's shoes, where style and size factors complicate inventory control to such an extent that most store managements feel an expert lessee can provide a better return than they could. At the same time they are assured of a very wide shoe assortment that provides a strong traffic pattern for the rest of the store. Departments requiring expert service, such as cameras and photographic supplies, jewelry and watch repairs, tend to resist company take-over longer than do such departments as hardware or soft goods. Because of service and operating problems, snack bars and restaurants are very frequently leased even in the largest chains.

With few exceptions, the most successful leased department operators are those who avoid association with very large chains and confine their contract to either individual stores or to small chains of five to eight stores. Diversification of many small contracts insures stability even if some contracts "sour." An operator with 100 leased departments in two chains is out on a limb.

A five-year lessee contract may call for a substantial annual rental guarantee which under normal conditions might be readily attainable. However, should the principal suddenly replace competent management with incompetent, irresponsible store leadership, the lessee suddenly finds his business dwindling so precariously that he cannot meet his guaranteed rental commitment. Such a situation can easily lead to lessee bankruptcy. If overall store management is poor, lessee losses from shoplifting increases are all out of proportion and customer traffic declines; the lessee is completely at

273

the mercy of top management whose decisions can either make or break his operation. Without question, the biggest problem confronting the leased department operator is the capability of the overall store management.

Operators of leased departments are perhaps the hardest-working and least-appreciated group in mass merchandising. Of necessity they must remain anonymous merging their individuality – chameleon-like – with that of their principals. The security-buying public never hears their names which appear only in trade journals.

What reward comes to lessees for ten to fifteen years of faithful and efficient service helping a principal grow big and strong? Take over! Like the manufacturer's representative who reaches a peak of productive efficiency, the lessee is gently but firmly told that he is no longer needed. In truth a take over may be beneficial both to the principal and lessee stockholders since lessee holdings are merely transferred from one institution to another and may provide more impressive growth prospects. However, a lessee with only three giant landlords might find it difficult to replace his suddenly-lost volume. Unless there are untoward circumstances, however, most landlords cushion the shock by prolonging the transition over several years.

The store principal reasons that if he has the capital and can buy the lessee inventory and know-how, why should he continue receiving a paltry 10 per cent of lessee sales, an amount from which deducts the cost of providing the lessee with theft protection, heat, light, checkout, receiving, and janitor services. Obviously, he can make more money operating the department himself – or so he thinks. This is true only if the principal has grown to a size which insures purchasing power comparable to that of a national lessee.

Many small discount chains find it wise to pursue the policy of concentrating on their specialty and leasing out all other major departments since their limited capital and know-how is competitively inadequate. A typical situation is that of the Hartfield-Zody chain based in Los Angeles. Hartfield's had years of successful experience as merchandisers of women's and children's wear in a chain of specialty shops. When, in 1960, it decided to establish its Zody Division of discount stores, the problem of maintaining excellence in departments other than women's and children's wear became acute. Under the presidency of Abe L. Marks, Hartfield-Zody has been highly successful in following a policy of building an image based on excellence in its women's and children's wear departments. Although capital is available, other major departments such as toys, health and beauty aids, shoes, etc., are leased to national operators whose expertise provides a full range of merchandise in all categories. Says Marks, "We love our leased departments."

The most successful lessees, with certain exceptions, carefully avoid associations with very large chains where rapid expansion and resulting take over loom on the horizon. In 1967 there were more than 3,500 discount stores in the U.S. and two-thirds of these were operated by small chains of three to ten stores. It is this group which provides a very fruitful market for national lessees who prefer to have – not three or four landlords with numerous stores – but thirty or forty landlords each with a limited number of stores.

Some lessees have seen fit to throw an anchor to windward by establishing their own wholly-owned specialty stores. They have the know-how. All that is needed is capital. For example, Carter Overton, health and beauty aid lessee with 75 leased departments, has its own chain of 20 free-standing RIX drug and notion stores in the New England area. Some lessees have themselves become giants and bring to their principals vast purchasing power and up-to-date EDP merchandising know-how far beyond the matching capacity of small-chain operators.

Successful lessees, with unused capital, have bought discount stores which they once knew as lessees but now operate as principals. This is the case with the giant men's and boys' wear lessee Unishops which bought out the three-store Clarkins chain in Akron, Ohio. Daylin, Inc., drugs and housewares lessee, acquired the seven-store Disco chain on the West Coast. The Spencer Shoe Company purchased seven Floyd Bennett stores in metropolitan New York.

One major hazard faced by lessees does not customarily appear in the lease: the continued ability of store management. A striking example of what can happen is furnished by the Lee Venture Corporation, lessees of soft goods departments. Lee took a five-year lease in the Pergament discount store in Bethpage, Long Island. The Pergament Company ran a chain of paint stores on Long Island and had no experience in general merchandise. When they found it difficult to operate a discount store on a paper-thin margin, they went back to their paint business, allowed the store to continue under incompetent management, and expected to meet expenses from the minimum guarantees of leased departments. For Lee Ventures, the minimum guarantee in addition to cash deposits was $100,000. Not only did Lee take severe losses on its minimum guarantee but it also suffered heavy loss from shoplifting since the store was not adequately policed. Total loss in one year approximated $150,000. Legally they were tied up; it was two years before an arrangement was reached that enabled Lee to get out.

But lessees can sometimes be headaches to their principals. If they are incompetent and have a poor image, it unavoidably becomes the image of their principal. E. J. Korvette had the H. L. Klion Company as a lessee in its furniture department. In the course of Korvette's very rapid expansion, Klion developed financial and labor problems. Furniture deliveries halted abruptly and customers cancelled orders amounting to approximately $2 million and resulting in very serious embarrassment to Korvette. Klion eventually went bankrupt and Korvette was forced to take over the company and underwrite heavy losses.

275

Fortunately, in the great majority of instances, intelligent management, goodwill and an appreciation of each other's abilities and problems has resulted in profitable relations between lessee and lessor.

Unishops

INTERVIEW WITH BUD KESSLER WHO WITH HIS BROTHER, DAN, OPERATES A NATIONAL CHAIN OF LEASED DEPART-MENTS SELLING MEN'S AND BOYS' WEAR. THE COMPANY OPENED ITS FIRST DEPARTMENT IN 1955. SALES IN 1968 WERE OVER $108 MILLION.[1]

When did you get started in retailing?

"In the early 1940's, Dan was in the Army Air Corps, and I was in the Marine Corps. When the war ended we both came home. I had graduated from New York University's School of Commerce and took some post-graduate work at the Amos Tuck School of Business at Dartmouth College in the Marine B-12 program. Dan graduated from the University of West Virginia with a B.S. in 1949."

What was your family business?

"Dad manufactured men's dress shirts. We had a large factory in Morgantown, W. Va. and one in Perth Amboy, N.J. In the early 1950's my father bought United Shirt Shops, a very small chain of conventional, downtown-type men's retail stores featuring men's furnishings. We had five stores in New York and New Jersey. When Dad became semi-active, Dan and I took these five stores and picked up three more, giving us a total of eight. We sold shirts, pajamas, underwear, socks, ties – almost everything except suits. Our sales were very much affected by the shopping centers which were going up about that time (1955). Fortunately for us, a large discount store was about to open in one of our trading areas in Hackensack, N.J. Everyone spoke badly of the location and of the management. It was definitely predicted that the store would be a failure. Dan and I met the builder, Bill Modell, who had run into a lot of trouble leasing departments in the store. He was running the sporting goods department. After months of negotiation we signed a lease for the men's department in this particular store. The store opened in Lodi. I think it was about 125,000 square feet. We were paying him about 8 per cent on our sales, including advertising. We had a very small department; I believe it was only 2,300 square feet. We were all very new at it. Bill Modell was certainly new at it. None of us really knew what was going to happen. The store opened in late 1957 and it was instantly a phenomenal success. Today it could very easily be called one of the finest discount stores in the United States as far as volume per square

[1]Daniel Kessler passed away on March 10, 1969.

276

foot goes. In the immediate trading area we had some 50,000 to 60,000 people. Since 1957 that area has been built up tremendously. Today it is just a jungle of retailing. Every regional chain, every important department store is there: Bambergers', Sterns, Gimbels, and Alexander's. At the beginning we were afraid to take even 2,300 square feet because we had to guarantee him so much per square foot. Everybody was very concerned about their guarantees. Food was in the back of the store.

"We were tremendously successful. In the first full year we did close to $700,000 in 2,300 square feet. Our eyes were opened immediately, and we saw the handwriting on the wall. It was easy to see where we should go. At once we gave all of our attention to discount-type operations. Danny started looking for leases and I stayed with the merchandising end. We came up with two more discount store leases, one in Atlantic Superama, New Shrewsbury, N.J. and another in Floyd Bennett's Mart in Brooklyn, on Flatbush Avenue.

"By 1958, we had 12 departments; in 1959, 16; in 1960, 31; in 1961, 68. By the end of 1968, we had 252."

Did you give up your specialty store chain?

"As the leases expired we gave them up. We were very happy to get out because the stores were so time-consuming. They were doing a little better than breaking even."

What capital did you have in the beginning?

"It took around $100,000 to put in the first inventory and fixtures. We were still operating eight stores at that time and we had built up a good credit reputation. To a large extent we operated on the manufacturer's money. We bought our fixtures outright. Even now we buy our fixtures and pay for them. We do not believe in leasing because over the years leasing is more expensive than outright purchase. We believe that if you have the funds you should buy your fixtures immediately.

"Capital was really never a problem with us. In those days we had a line of credit at the Banker's Trust Company and my father banked in that institution for 25 years before we came along. Nevertheless, we had to expand within reason. In 1957 we did $1.4 million in gross sales. In 1965, we did a little over $46 million which is really tremendous. Our earnings rose from $20,000 in that first year (1957) to $5.78 million in 1968."

When did you go public?

"In April, 1962 just before the crash. We raised approximately $700,000 for the company. Before it was a privately-held corporation. We (my brother Dan, myself, our sister, and the trusts for our children) still own approximately 29 per cent of the common stock. Substantial blocks of our stocks are in the hands of investment trusts; the Madison Fund owns 50,000 shares and Tri-Continental owns 20,000 shares."

What have been your major problems?

"One is setting up amicable relations with our lessors. We have found

277

that as a licencee we must sit down at a table with the landlord and learn to give and take. We find that many landlords, not all of them, are sometimes unreasonable. We have got to be able to intelligently discuss problems and negotiate. I think that faith in each other's integrity is a very, very important element in maintaining satisfactory relations with a landlord."

What are some of the lessee situations that can arise which may be embarrassing?

"In the early days a lot of lessees went with landlords who were under-capitalized and whose stores were primarily real estate ventures. Many were central checkout stores where the landlord had your funds and could use them to enlarge his chain which was not built on a firm foundation. Fortunately we never were in a situation where we could be hurt severely if anything went wrong. Unishops was never heavily committed by lease arrangements to any one landlord. We don't intend to be put in that position. Today we have over 60 landlords in our group of 161 leased departments. We have more leases with Kresge's K Mart division than with any other chain. We are very happy and satisfied with the lease arrangements. I am sure that Kresge is too.

"In fairness to the Kresge Company, you really cannot put them in the same class as most of these landlords we have been discussing. They are fine retailers, very financially able, and quite frankly we are thrilled to be part of their organization. They have done a lot for us. It seems that the bigger the people are today, the nicer they are. Kresge seems to fall right into that category. They even try to help us with our own business. When their buyers visit countries in the Far East, they bring back samples and ask if we could make use of any new items they have discovered. In my opinion, they have been fantastic. You do not find people of that caliber too often."

What are some of the pitfalls that a lessee might get into?

"Whenever we move into any area of retailing in any part of the country, Danny builds up very strong organizational groups in that area. In California we built up a very strong buying office with unusually fine and expensive personnel; and this has really paid off. It has given us a regional advantage. We now have over 30 stores in the California area, only because we built up a strong organization. They are completely autonomous out there. Our supervision in California is probably one of the finest in the industry and it's equipped to handle a great many stores."

If your landlord suddenly decides to open 20 more stores, and if you are going to stick with him, where is the money going to come from for more inventories?

"We have built up large reserves in this company, and we did not start paying any dividends until last year, so we are in a very strong financial cash position. Two years ago we borrowed $1.5 million from the Prudential Insurance Company on a long term basis."

278

Leased Departments

K Mart wants your know-how. But before long will they feel that they can handle your department themselves?

"It is a good question. We have discussed this with the K Mart people. I am very happy to say, as I would say to our stockholders if this question should ever come up, that the K Mart people have given us very fair leases (not short-term leases) over many years. K Mart has run these departments themselves in some of their own stores, but because of their tremendous expansion, they saw fit to lease the men's and boys' departments in many of their stores to other companies. They learned a lot from us; we learned a lot from them. This year we intend to open (1966), a minimum of 12 departments with K Mart. We are thrilled to stay in their operation. It cannot hurt us in any way over the long pull.

"The K Mart organization feels that in the 1966 calendar year they will probably do over $1 billion. They are not overly concerned about a couple of million dollars in volume that they may give us this year; it does not mean a thing in their operations, and that is why we feel relatively secure with these people. It we were doing a couple of million dollars with a small lessor whose entire volume was, maybe, $8 million or $9 million, it would be a different situation."

What were some of your growing pains?

"One was running all over the country to talk to many people. In expanding as rapidly as we did, we made certain mistakes. When we look back they seem very amusing. Many times we would investigate a location and be told that people with good backgrounds in retailing were going to manage and operate the store. After the store opened, we would find that the owner put in his own son as store manager, a 19-year-old genius, who had not even graduated from business school. The store would flounder. We tenants would then get together and salvage the situation by working with management. When you open up a 100,000-foot department store, it is a big undertaking. By having professional licencees – hard hitting merchants – in most of the departments, you can usually make a bad store good. I once made a deal in El Paso. I flew out there and signed a lease with a gentleman, a shopping center developer, who was putting up a new store. All the papers were signed; we advanced the necessary funds. To this day I have never seen that man again. He never opened; but he had our deposit of $3,500 for the first month's rent. We just wrote it off as experience."

Did you have any instances where you found that management was so poor that you regretted having to carry out the contract?

"Even today, we have some stores that have not got the management that we would like. It is a constant education on our part and on the licensor's part to better the store. There are frequent meetings about advertising and merchandising, etc. If these things are left to shift for themselves, the store invariably becomes a poor one. We have withdrawn from 50 to 60 stores in

279

the past eight years, so we did not guess right every time."

What was the major problem in these stores? Can you break a lease if you are really taking a licking?

"In some instances we have to take a chance on that, as this is obviously what happens. In our lease structure, we do have cancellation clauses if certain requirements are not met, and of course, the landlord has these same privileges. The lease is only as good as the people who make it. If you go in with the intent of not doing the job, there is trouble from the beginning; that is one of the problems of the leased department business."

What was the major problem with these 50 that you closed?

"The greatest problem was bad discount stores with poor management and undercapitalization. Usually when the management is poor and there is enough capital to carry on, management becomes knowledgeable. It is usually a combination of poor management and undercapitalization. If it comes to a point of no return, it is certainly not good for the landlords. And it is not good for the licencees. With us, either the landlord sells the store to a stronger operator, or we get out.

"Over the years we have noted in the stores that continually do well that there is only one reason for success: good management. The stores that generally do badly are poorly managed stores."

When do you get the sales receipts that landlords collect for you?

"Normally the business week ends on Saturday night, so we get our money not later than the following Thursday or Friday."

Have you ever had any instances where there was a delay of a couple of weeks?

"In the early stages of discounting it happened; but you very seldom see it happen now. The only store with central checkout that caved in on us was in Connecticut, where the landlord was undercapitalized. When the store finally closed down we were out some $20,000 dollars of central checkout money. I would venture to say that you will probably very seldom see that happen in the future. It happened with Towers; and it happened with an outfit called Scots that we were with."

What happens to the inventory in these cases?

"The inventory legally belongs to us. The landlord has no right to the inventory in any way."

Stanley Feldberg investigated Zayre's leased departments and says that they make more money than the landlord – that they have always made more money, even today. Do you think this is true?

"Leased departments do not have the overall expense that the landlord has in a discount-type operation. The landlord is building stores, acquiring land, and signing long-term leases. He has a lot of money tied up in so-called fixed assets; the money is not liquid and he cannot spend it. The leased operator does not have these problems. I would venture to say that originally the leased department would come out better dollar-wise in these particular stores. I think there are two sides to the coin. In the long pull, the owner of the store has a certain equity that the leased department operator will never get. He is building up his equity over the years; I think things even out. In many cases the lessors – and I would include the Marrud case where Zayre is taking over his departments – were in no position to open these departments originally. I doubt that they had the money, originally, to merchandise all departments or the manpower and the know-how. I believe the leased departments gave people like Zayre's, King's, and others, the thrust they needed to get started. These companies who now run all departments should only speak kindly of former lessees who gave them a heck of a push to get them where they are today. Jack Margolis, president of Marrud, deserves a vote of thanks from his lessors.

"Two Guys from Harrison were 60 per cent leased out at the beginning and they were very, very undercapitalized. Without their licencees they never could have become the gigantic, successful company that they are today.

"I am surprised that the lessees have not gotten more pats on the back because they are the guys who did much of the pioneering. The lessee is something like a great baseball player; when he gets too old to play, they discard him."

You must be pretty careful these days in taking on new landlords, are you not?

"Yes, we are very selective. We investigate their balance sheets, as much as possible, and we try to go into pertinent management details. Today we can afford that luxury; years ago we could not."

To what extent is the style element a factor in your operation?

"It has recently become more of a factor. Many people have always felt that the men's and boys' business was predominantly a staple-type business. This is no longer true. Style-wise, we are getting almost as much style as ladies' and girls'. We have many, many more styles coming out and we have got to be on top of them since today the staple end of the business is being replaced by the style-image-type merchandising. This involves colors, fabrics, durable press, and no-ironing-type fabrics. We are in a completely new type of world in men's and boys' wear."

Do you try to develop your own brands?

"Yes. Today about 70 per cent of all of our store merchandise is private label. We carry very few national brands because the manufacturer of national brands would be very unhappy if we cut the price on his product; so we have therefore gone into our own labeling program, as have all chains, including Sears, Penney's, Ward's, and many others."

If you are operating with Floyd Bennett, do you use the Floyd Bennett label?

"No. It would be very hard because we are in so many stores. We have a whole list of labels. We use a John Wells, a Peter Kane, and a Mac Paters."

Do these grow in value?

"Yes, they do. When I am in the stores I hear customers ask for the John Wells shirt, which is most unusual. It could be made by Arrow, or any of the fine shirt makers. We feel that we are giving them tremendous value. It has been proven many times over that branded items, certainly in apparel, are overpriced when you compare them against a non-branded item. You have got to pay for national advertising. Customers begin to feel that ours is a national brand because they constantly see it in our trading areas. Our volume is tremendous; and it becomes a very important matter with us."

Do you use buying offices?

"No. We are close to the New York market and we are in the California market with our own buying organization. We really do not need a buying office. We use major manufacturers in every category of men's and boys' wear today under private-labeling programs. These people generally are not thrilled with the idea that we divulge who they might be. For some reason they feel that it would hurt their image. But I can assure you that we are with every important manufacturer of men's and boys' wear. Our volume almost dictates it. If we were to stop buying from certain organizations it would change their whole distribution set up. It is not unusual for us to buy at cost $2 million worth of merchandise from one manufacturer. In 1966 we did anywhere from $52 million to $55 million in men's and boys' wear alone. That is a tremendous amount of business in just men's and boys' wear. We think that outside of chains like Penney's, Sear's, and Ward's, there are not many companies in this country doing that kind of business in just men's and boys' wear. We think we are right up on top. We are one of the largest retailers of men's and boys' wear in the country."

What is your promotional philosophy?

"We try to be as aggressive as possible because it is now very seldom that you enter a trading area and are left alone. There are always competitors coming in after you or with you. To survive today you have got to be very promotional-minded."

In a 60,000 square-foot store, what percentage of the total business would you ordinarily do?

"It varies. In a 100,000 square-foot store, we can generally do anywhere from 9 per cent to 12.5 per cent of the volume of that particular store. This is very good."

What is the average size of your department?

"Approximately 5,000 square feet. Our biggest is 8,500 and our smallest is 3,000. Our biggest is in a Floyd Bennett store on Long Island. It is a tremendous 150,000-foot store, where everybody took on much more space than they needed. The percentage that we would do in a store is very questionable because every store is different. What emphasis is placed on the various other departments plays a big part. As a rule of thumb, we do about 15 per cent, and in much larger volume stores, we might drop down to 4 per cent or 5 per cent."

What help can you give a landlord?

"We can bring him a lot of know-how; we can bring him close to a lot of people he would like to meet. For example, we know who the good department operators are. We can give him forms for leases. Store principals do need help, especially when they are new at it. We can set up a whole store for him, including fixtures and operators for other departments. We can show him three or four different lease forms, and let him take the one he thinks is best for him. We can show him opening advertising in maybe 20 stores that we opened last year. Normally he would have to get the help of a consultant who would charge unheard-of sums of money. We can do this for nothing, because we have experience.

"Let us, for example, take the Floyd Bennett stores. This is a local chain which most of us know or have heard of. We were in their first store in Brooklyn on Flatbush Avenue. This was an old Farmer's Market. When we met the landlord we told him emphatically that he would be better off changing the store from a Farmer's Market to a regular discount-type store. He took our advice. We then brought him a shoe man, a ladies' operator, and a toy man: everyone whom we felt could do a fine job for him. The president of that company was, and is now, Sherman Simon. He owes a lot to us; but we owe a lot to him. His company started in a little old shack and now has ten large stores doing a volume in excess of $75 million to $80 million."

Do you originate promotions in your stores?

"Yes. When we run a good promotion in California that really clicks, we can fit it into our operations in other locations."

Have you given any thought to establishing your own free-standing units, in view of the possibility of being taken over?

"Yes, we have; but I must confess that I disagree with you, generally speaking, regarding this take over business. We have spoken to some security analysts about this at great length; and facts have proven that in the areas where we are concentrating our business, there is absolutely no danger of the so-called take over. We have deliberately avoided leases with companies like Zayre's, King's, Two Guys, or Korvette. In this country today, there are something like 2,800 discount stores of consequence. Now, we have over 60 landlords. These are primarily, putting Kresge aside for the moment, small independents: men who may have one to three stores. These are the kind of people on whom we concentrate. They will not take us over because they do not have the money, the ability, or the know-how. Remember, that of all the discount stores in this country about two-thirds or 2,000 are independents, and that is our market. We have two-thirds of the market to grow

283

with, and our growth rate has proven us right. We do not expect to be with the large chains.

"Our experience is that instead of being taken over, we are offered men's and boys' departments by landlords who are unhappy running them themselves.

"As for the second part of the question, last year we acquired three Ohio stores called the Carousel. These are in the Canton-Akron area and the landlord that we acquired runs the hardline departments. In our eyes he represents a terrific, tremendous management. Here is a man whom we think the world of, who year after year has increased his business. Unishops will own 100 per cent of this operation and it will be a wholly-owned subsidiary. We will provide him with additional capital to open other Carousel stores which he will run on a completely autonomous basis. This is not our policy in general; it is just a situation which happened. We thought it was good for our company so we took advantage of it."

What is your line of credit?

"Unlimited. Our company has net assets of over $8 million. We can honestly say that we have absolutely no problems in this area whatsoever. We have a net worth of $26 million in cash and inventory. In the calendar year 1968, our company made, after taxes, $5.7 million, net.

"Speaking of Wall Street and the entire financial community, we are considered one of the outstanding growth stocks in the United States. We are listed by brokers (with Xerox and Syntex) as one of the best-managed companies in the United States.

"We were recently honored by being written up by the Research Institute of America. They put out a very comprehensive report about our company. It said: 'Selling at a very modest price-to-earnings ratio, Unishops appears to be undervalued in terms of its further growth potential. The company is a highly skilled factor, operating in a virtually recession-proof sector, of the vital discount store field. We recommend purchase for capital appreciation.' Now that is very flattering!"

Have you solved the personnel problem?

"We set up a series of regional-type supervisors in charge of four or five states, each one having some thirty-odd stores under his direct control. These people are responsible only to this office. Under these regional men are area supervisors who are in charge of six stores each. Department managers are responsible to their area supervisors. We have set this framework up throughout the country and it works very well. It is on the same principle as that used by J. C. Penney, giving autonomy to certain areas."

Who hires and fires the department managers?

"The regional man normally would be solely responsible. When we started to expand in a vigorous manner throughout the country, it was quite obvious to us that if we did not have good supervision at the store level we could

284

never be a successful company. It was obvious that running a store in Dallas from New Jersey was impossible. It must be run from Dallas. Some people do not believe in this, but we do. Six years ago, we decided to build a very strong supervisory staff to run and oversee our operation throughout the country. It is most expensive, but in the long run it pays off. The figures that our company produces year after year are basically a result of this supervisory staff.

"We are in 30-odd states; yet I can tell you unequivocally that our stores are supervised on a weekly basis. This is virtually unheard of in the chain store business. Our area supervisors, who only have five or six stores to worry about, can run those stores as if it were their own business. They are on top of the situation practically at all times. They are in the stores on a weekly basis and sometimes twice a week. When you have a system such as this, it is much easier to weed out the bad department managers and replace them with good-caliber people. To keep them you have to pay them better than you would most people. Our people are not $1.25 managers. Store managers make anywhere from $135 to $250 a week. Our regional supervisors make anywhere from $15,000 to $20,000 a year. We pay what we consider top salaries in our industry. These are high-priced, good, dedicated people. With our expansion program there is always room for someone who has initiative to better his position and his lot with our company."

How often do you meet with your supervisors?

"We have quarterly meetings with both regional and area supervisors. Area supervisors have monthly meetings with the store managers in each area. Problems are discussed. The features of new seasonal merchandise are gone over and samples shown. It is a constant program of enlightenment and training."

Are most of your department managers men or women?

"Ninety-nine per cent are men. Once in a while we come across a gem of a woman who has had department store experience. Most of our people have at least finished high school and we have many college people with us."

Do you have your own warehouse?

"Eighty per cent of our merchandise is drop-shipped directly into the stores. About 20 per cent is warehoused. We have a small warehouse out in California, and one here near the main office in Garfield, N.J. We have developed a very efficient drop-ship method. It has been a tough struggle to get this operation to where it is today, but we can now supply our stores faster than if we warehoused everything here."

How do you keep track of inventory changes in sizes, styles, and colors?

"We have the NCR electronic data processing. Punch-tape systems operate at the store level and we get our reports from the NCR people. We can do this only in stores where we take our own cash and where the checkout is departmentalized. Approximately a third of our chain is on central checkout. About two-thirds is departmental. We have a pretty good idea of what is selling throughout the country. With our supervisors in these stores every week taking inventory and making stock counts, I assure you we have a very good idea of what is selling and what is not.

SUMMARY OF UNISHOPS PROGRESS

FOR THE YEAR:	1968	1967 (1)	1966	1965 (1)
Net Sales (2)	**$108,346,186**	$86,499,776	$68,821,123	$59,326,854
Net Income				
Income Before Taxes	**$ 10,243,374**	$ 6,825,231	$ 5,615,785	$ 4,458,842
Federal Income Taxes	**4,460,000**	2,506,000	2,041,000	1,596,000
Net Income	**5,783,374**	4,319,231	3,574,785	2,862,842
Shares Outstanding (3)	**2,371,580**	2,338,450	2,276,580	2,273,880
Earned per Share (3)	**2.45**	1.86	1.57	1.26
Dividends per Share	**.4875**	.3825	.315	.2625
At December 31:				
Working Capital				
Total Current Assets	**$31,228,348**	$22,655,418	$18,034,293	$15,098,284
Total Current Liabilities	**15,050,855**	9,997,380	8,195,711	7,159,523
Working Capital	**16,177,493**	12,658,038	9,838,582	7,938,761
Working Capital Ratio	**2.1-1**	2.3-1	2.2-1	2.1-1
Stockholder's Equity	**$20,249,943**	$15,388,411	$11,443,187	$8,530,121
Book Value per Share (3)	**8.54**	6.58	5.03	3.75
Operating Data				
Number of Leased Departments	**252**	219	200	161
Number of Discount Department Stores	**5**	5	4	4
Number of Landlords	**77**	78	68	62
Number of States	**35**	36	34	32

(1) Includes sales and earnings of Clarkins Division, on a pooling-of-interests basis.
(2) Exclusive of non-operated leased departments.
(3) Based on common shares outstanding at the end of the year (adjusted in 1968, 1967, 1966 and 1965 for shares which may be issuable in coming years).

Stuart's Department Stores and the Lee Venture Corporation

INTERVIEW WITH ARTHUR KLEIN, PRESIDENT
(Problems encountered in the operation of leased soft goods departments.)

What is the size of your present operation?

"Until January, 1967, under the name of the Lee Venture Corporation, we operated ten leased soft goods departments with the Bradlee's Division of Stop & Shop. Annual sales reached $8 million. We now operate four of our own discount stores under the name of Stuart's. One is in Fitchburg, two are in Lowell and one is in Lawrence, Mass. Total present sales volume is about $4 million."

How did you get into the operation of leased departments?

"In 1954 my brother and I ran three specialty dress shops. In 1955 we took a leased department with the Myrtle Mills Factory Outlet in Union-ville, Conn. We were doing more business in our leased departments than we were in our specialty shops so, as our leases expired, we closed them and stayed with the discount store field.

"At first, a large part of our success was our ability to buy branded lines through our specialty shops and use them in the discount stores. We did not run into trouble with fair trade until we opened our third major leased department in Springfield, Mass., in Bradlee's division of Stop & Shop in 1959. Forbes and Wallace shopped our department very carefully to determine the lines we were using and then went to the manufacturers and threatened to boycott them. Thus we lost most of the lines that we had used prior to 1959."

What were some of these lines?

"Ship 'n Shore, Catalina, Jantzen, MacShore (shirt line similar to Ship 'n Shore), and a number of others."

About what per cent of your merchandise was affected?

"At that time, it was 80 per cent. Immediately subsequent to that time, the discount store industry started getting into full swing, and a number of manufacturers made good quality merchandise easily available to the discounters."

Could you get the same merchandise from your former manufacturers, but with a different brand?

"We did get a different brand label on the same merchandise, but then manufacturers started using their less desirable styles and patterns as a method of getting rid of merchandise that was not selling well."

Do you have a warehouse?

"Having grown out of the women's specialty shop field, we have always

287

operated with a central warehouse, central ticketing, and stock control."
What is the line of merchandise that you sell?

"In Bradlee's we sold everything to be worn by misses, teenagers, and women, except for costume jewelry, hats, and shoes. This includes lingerie, sportswear, coats, suits, dresses, handbags, accessories, hosiery, neckwear, and foundations.

"When Stop & Shop purchased the Bradlee chain, they were reluctant to undertake the merchandising of the women's wear departments. Since we did not have the capital to expand at the rate they desired, an arrangement was set up whereby they would finance and we would operate their first units until they could operate them by themselves. There was a contract that expired in January, 1967 and was not renewed. Bradlee's now operates all soft goods departments in their 37 stores."
What proportion of your income came from this operation?

"We ran about $7 million or $8 million with Bradlee's in sales, as opposed to around $3 million in our own stores. Our profits from Bradlee's were roughly 2 to 1."
When this contract expired did you lease departments in other discount stores?

"No, we are concentrating on developing our own four-store regional chain in New England. At the time we took this contract with Bradlee's, we had gotten into grave financial difficulty by attempting expansion as leased departments.

"In 1961 we had five departments with Bradlee's, and we negotiated a lease on a discount store in Nashville. We had a signed agreement to rent the store, based on certain conditions which we fulfilled; after we signed the lease, the landlord fabricated a technicality for delaying his signing. He then leased the premises to Zayre's for more money. We sued him for $200,000, and after going through three sets of courts, including the U.S. Supreme Court, we got our $200,000 judgment against the landlord.

"We then undertook two leased departments in New Jersey with high minimum guarantees. Our landlords did not live up to their obligations and we ended up with tremendous losses. Our agreement with Stop & Shop prevented us from going into bankruptcy and enabled us to pay off our debts."
Which landlords made you lose so much money?

"One was the Pergament Discount Store in Bethpage, Long Island, the other was the Shop Rite Discount store in Paramus, N.J.

"Shop Rite was considered one of the most outstanding food merchants in the country. They decided that they wanted to go into the discount store field in Paramus. Top management spent all of its time developing this store for the first two months, and we did more business than we had ever dreamed possible in one store. They opened the store in November and decided in

Arthur H. Klein, president, Lee Shops, Inc.

January that it was taking too much of management's time to handle the discount store type of business, and that they would be better off sticking to straight supermarkets. They turned the store over to incompetent management, and again we were legally tied up with large minimum guarantees because we thought that the group that was going to run the store was an extremely capable group.

"It took two years before we could renegotiate the lease with the landlord and get out, meanwhile we lost a lot of money. Both were new stores and required sizeable investments on our part. We had to post large cash deposits, buy fixtures that cost about $20,000 for each store, and in each case we took five-year leases. At the beginning we thought we had an oil gusher; we made money. In the last two years we lost money. We also lost money in liquidating the stocks when we moved out of both stores.

"The writing of these leases was due to the fact that the discount store field was at that time at a top level of popularity. We had very competent

289

attorneys on both sides – perhaps if the leases had not been so good, they could have been more easily broken.

"The rentals themselves were not exorbitant; they were based upon the net per cent of sales. In the Pergament store it was 8 per cent of sales, and we had our own cash register. Shop Rite, which had a central checkout, was a 10 per cent arrangement. It included advertising. The leasing terms were not wrong; the error that we made was in our evaluation of the management of the store and our willingness to guarantee a rental based on a sales volume that we thought we could achieve, but which we were unable to achieve because the stores were never managed in the manner in which we thought they were going to be managed.

"In Pergament's we guaranteed an annual rental of $100,000 which was 8 per cent of $1,250,000 worth of sales. On all sales over $1,250,000, we paid 8 per cent of sales rental. It turned out that we were doing somewhere around $600,000 or $700,000 a year, so that our rental percentage, according to our books, was about 20 per cent. It was the same situation with Shop Rite.

"In the first six months in Shop Rite we virtually did enough business to cover our whole first year's guarantee. It should have been an extremely successful store. But a store without management does not go. I doubt very much if that store has closed up, because Shop Rite has a very profitable food operation within the store. They have since decided they had to lease to people without large guarantees; I believe Shop Rite is now only interested in covering as much of their store expenses as they can and concentrates on their food operation.

"We liquidated the inventory and assets which had been built up previously from profits. When we made the contract with Bradlee's, the Lee Venture Corp. bought the five inventories that were in the five Bradlee's stores. This gave us money that had been locked in inventory and turned it into cash. We sold our fixtures in New Jersey and turned that into cash.

"The biggest problem that the leased department operator has to contend with is the capability of management. If management is capable and operates the store properly, the leased department can put up with most anything and make money. If the store operator is incapable and does not operate a good store, no matter how easy the arrangement or how easy the selling conditions a leased department operator has, it is difficult for him to make money."

What are some of the things which management falls down on?

"We call it store promoting, bringing customers into the store, or building traffic; the other important thing is store security. Incompetence in this area can very often see all the profits dissipated from shoplifting."

How about paying you on time? I understand that Marrud and several others got into trouble.

"Unquestionably you are dependent upon the capability and financial

290

integrity of the people with whom you lease departments. In our particular case, the people we did business with were all financially solid. Our difficulty came when management did not fulfill – not the legal obligations that were made to us – but the oral obligations: the expectation that they would want to and would try to make money. In both these cases there was the financial situation of the landlords that permitted them not to care about the store. The thing that plagued the discount store industry in the beginning, was the remarkable success that the first people had that entered it. It led real estate people, people in altogether different types of businesses – whoever had enough capital to get a store built – to try his hand at it."

Where is your warehouse?

"In Needham, Mass. We have our offices and our warehouse here."

What do you have that the competition does not have?

"We have an extremely fine, sophisticated, computerized, merchandising system with good key people trained to work with it. We have learned how to use these figures we get."

How about judgment as far as style is concerned, does this play an important part?

"Every day it's playing a smaller part, because of our ability to style-test merchandise. Our customers today are doing most of the style selection for us. Our reporting is so fast that our buyers have available on Monday morning a complete analysis of all the store sales of the previous week through the Saturday night business. Because of this rapid information the bulk of our business is based on reordering the styles that have already been proven and tested in the stores."

You have exceptional know-how which you should be able to sell.

"We have found that we can still merchandise competitively in the women's wear field at a reasonably good markup with virtually no markdown and achieve store volume sales in excess of $100 per foot. If a store does not do somewhere in the vicinity of $3,000,000 to $4,000,000 in volume, and if our location in the store is not satisfactory, we cannot achieve $100 a square foot. But given the location a women's wear department is normally put in, I could do it. It is generally a traffic location because it should be a key money-maker. Basically a discount store has to depend upon women for their shoppers, and nothing makes a woman a more constant or steady shopper than satisfaction in the fashion department. Children's wear is also an extremely important department."

Could you pay a rental of 12.5 per cent on sales and still operate? What is the highest that you think you could pay?

"We could. A lot would depend upon the competence of management and a lot on the total amount of volume. This is a theoretical question. If you are talking about my taking a group of leased departments with a chain of stores doing anywhere from $5 million to $10 million in good healthy stores we could, without question, pay between 12 per cent and 13 per cent, including advertising.

"We are so confident in our ability to generate profits that we would be willing to take an arrangement with a chain on a profit-sharing basis that could perhaps net the chain as much as 14 per cent or 15 per cent."

What do you have to pay for a reasonably good department manager?

"We paid our managers between $150 and $200 a week. Managers in Bradlee's large volume stores earn just about $200 a week. Assistant managers are full-time employees who earn about $80 to $100 a week. Managers are all on semi-annual bonus arrangements, enabling them to earn up to $800 a year on bonuses, based on three points: maintaining a proper percentage of payroll to sales, maintaining a proper percentage of pilferage to sales, and maintaining sales.

"We feel that some of the discount store operators would achieve larger profits and have far healthier stores if they made use of established merchandising teams, successful ones, instead of trying to prove to somebody that they can do the job themselves. Virtually all of the chains that are successful succeed because they have proficiency on one area or another. They could be more successful if they stuck to the areas in which they were extremely proficient and looked for the help of specialists in the areas in which they were not proficient. I am not saying they should lease out these areas; even without leasing they can often obtain the services of specialists assuring them of stronger, healthier stores."

What kind of terms do you get from manufacturers?

"Most of our buying is done on a net basis. We find it easier to compute our markups and all of our billing. Our buyers are required to reduce their terms to a net basis.

"For many years our industry, granted an 8 per cent trade discount and all merchandise was sold on an EOM basis, which means that it was to be paid on the 10th of the month following the month of purchase, with the 25th of the month considered as the end day of the month. What our buyers do is subtract the 8 per cent terms, reduce it to a net basis, and we still pay 10 EOM, the 10th of the following month. That is what I mean by net terms.

"In 90 per cent of the cases there is no bargaining. It is a trade-fixed price. Offerings are made to us in the same manner and at the same price as they are made to other people."

What proportion of the merchandise that you buy is unbranded?

"I would have to say that virtually all of it is unbranded. The label that is put on the merchandise is not one that is advertised sufficiently to be accepted by the consumer so that she is presold on that name before she comes into the store. However, every item that comes into the store carries a trade label, and the manufacturer insists that it is all labeled; but it is not advertised."

Leased Departments

Do you sell fair-traded items?

"We fair-trade less than ten items in our whole department. We do not avoid them. We have just never developed an ability to sell fair-traded items. A customer comes to us for savings. In our field there are brand names and there are fair-traded items we could sell. But fair-traded items are not made available to us."

What are these?

"I do not question that we could sell Jantzen bathing suits; we could sell Ship 'n Shore blouses; we might be able to sell Lady Manhattan shirts or something of that nature, but these are confined to other stores. In our field there are very few established brand names so that we suffer not at all."

What proportion, ordinarily, of the total business in a discount store would women's and children's do?

"Between 35 per cent and 40 per cent, if the departments are properly run. They could be the major department of all the departments, but in stores that do not achieve the proper volume from them, they are not. With Zayre's, I would estimate that they would be closer to 45 per cent. In our Bradlee's stores I would say that it is between 40 per cent and 45 per cent, closer to the latter for the women's and children's departments."

What do you think is the most important thing in merchandising women's wear?

"Humility. I am going to expand a little on what makes the best kind of an expert. We have found, since we harnessed our operations to this computerized, merchandising system, that if we subjugate our own taste to those of our customers, we are far more successful. I have yet to meet the expert who feels that he can determine exactly what his customers are going to buy. We use our whole group of stores as an indicator."

What volume would you buy; isn't this a rather tricky thing?

"There is no question that they must have a style sense; they have to develop an extremely fine sense of timing. We find that the best judges of what people want, with respect to style and color, are the people themselves. We have been able to substantially reduce our on-hand store inventory and achieve higher sales per square foot. Our initial early-season buying has been virtually cut in half. We find that we can learn fast what our customers actually want. By giving them what they really want our sales increase and our markdowns decrease. We have reduced our markdowns in women's wear to where we maintain very high fashion merchandising with less than 2 per cent annual markdown. We use commercial transportation for all goods coming in and all goods going out."

Do you have a style card for every single item that you carry?

"Yes. It shows the entire information concerning the styles from the purchase order, to the distribution, to sales, to transfers between stores, and balance on hand. We use an armored car service to pick up our tickets on

Saturday nights. They are delivered by midnight Saturday. We then get our complete report from the Bizmatic System by 8:30 Monday morning. The whole service costs in excess of $100,000. Including Bradlee's we had a total volume of sales of $10 million, it ran us close to 1 per cent, but we saved this 1 per cent compared to our previous expense structure. In our office we have one row of desks that is completely empty. Those people have been replaced by data processing. The information that we are getting and the speed with which we get it is tremendous. We used to get style cards for only selective items manually, which meant posting distribution from the distribution form, posting sales, and bringing balances forward. When three or four girls did that on selected items only, they would not get the information for every item by Monday morning for sales through Saturday night. We can sample merchandise. We say to the manufacturer, 'Send us the merchandise.' We get it into our store Thursday, Friday, and Saturday for selling. It represents 70 per cent of our sales. We can tell on Monday morning which items are good and which are bad."

Can you send certain merchandise back to the manufacturer?

"This is the key to the whole thing. This is why we do not have the markdowns. We recognize the duds as well as the good ones, and we return the goods. I would say that a good 75 per cent of the duds are returned this way; others we get an allowance on."

Do you lose the return freight?

"Not necessarily. At the beginning of the season, the manufacturer does not know the items that are going to be hot. Right now our dress buyer is like a king in a market. He can say, 'Give me what you think are your hot items, and I will give you a report Monday morning.' So, in a sense, we provide service for the manufacturer. We have reduced our stock and reduced our markdowns and increased our profits, strictly through EDP. The speed and timing of the information is the key. There are very few firms that use EDP as effectively as we do."

Actually, then, you do not have any IBM equipment here, just a key punch machine?

"Yes. We create the billing card here. Our weekly price report lets us know on Monday morning the inventory in each store, in each code, by price line. In our women's wear merchandising, it is broken down into about 80 codes of classification. In code 10, which is blouses, this report tells us how many dollars worth of blouses store number 1 had at the beginning of the week, what their sales were, what their markdowns were, and what their total on hand was at the end of the week. We have the same figures in units; then, we have the same figures broken down into ten price classifications. We get this individually for each store. We get it summarized at the end to tell us what our balance at the start of the week was in all 13 stores put together, in dollars and in quantity, and in quantity by price point. It tells us what we shipped to the chain during the week; what we transferred in or out of the warehouse stocks that were not on billing; what our sales were for the week, our markdowns were for the week, and our total on hand for the week. We show six weeks' planned sales, or the amount of business that our stores actually did for the same corresponding period for the past six-week period. It tells us what our subsequent six-week period is. It tells us what we have on order and tells us what would remain as an open-to-buy ticket.

"Actually, this last figure is one that we pay no attention to because it requires merchandising. In some codes we are doing 20 per cent or 30 per cent more business this year over last year, and in other codes we are doing less business. We determine our open-to-buy figure based upon our increases or decreases. It so happens that in code 10, we are running about a 40 per cent increase in sales. This information comes from the Bizmatic people, right off the computer. It is an analysis of the magnetic tapes that are fed into the computer and which come from the pre-punched symbol tickets fixed to all of our garments.

"In a fast-moving fashion merchandising arrangement such as ours, it is impossible to achieve large sales in high fashion goods at a good profit without this procedure."

As I understand it, the buyers have an area of freedom in regard to style, but you have to give them the okay as to the total amount that they spend?

"They are on a bonus arrangement based upon increase in volume and the maintenance of a certain profit figure that is based upon their initial markup, less markdowns taken. In a lot of the areas the retail price is fixed according to a basic schedule. But buyers are allowed a certain amount of leeway to use prices that are higher or lower than the fixed schedule."

In other words, they can change the price lines if they find it profitable or if they get a good buy?

"If they are looking for volume they can put their prices lower to try to achieve more volume. They can select certain items for promotion at a lower markup; they can select certain items that they feel are an exceptionally good buy for a little higher markup."

They do have a say in setting the markup?

"Yes, they do. Their bonus is predicated on a maintained markup."

What proportion of their salary comes in the form of these bonuses?

"Last year, about 10 per cent came in the form of bonuses; this year, it will be about 20 per cent. Today we worked out an arrangement with our buyers whereby they can earn two bonuses: one based upon one level of performance, and an additional one if their performance is better. If they get beyond the first level of maintained markup, they can earn another bonus. This is determined by past performance. In each case we try pretty hard to make the performance levels that are set attainable ones. Our bonus situation, however, differs every year.

295

"Everything that is shipped out of our warehouse is billed to the stores on an IBM key punched billing card with the exact number of units shipped, exact cost per unit, and exact retail per unit. At the end of the week a summary bill is taken off the computer from the IBM key punched billing cards and sent to the stores. The stores mark them to indicate the receipt of the merchandise. In the event that we come across a dud, the buyer moves quickly to either return the merchandise or to obtain an allowance so that he can make a price adjustment."

By allowance, you mean that he would reduce his price, so that you then could get rid of an item and benefit both yourself and the manufacturer without returning it?

"Manufacturers prefer not to have it returned. So your understanding with these manufacturers is such that you can make a deal like that. They realize that you are a good customer and that it is in their best interest to accept what you say.

"We are building this business on the knowledge that turnover is the key to the whole thing. We can answer any question about an item by fact and not just by opinion. This answers all the questions. In this interval our sales are moving ahead by 20 per cent. The reduction in inventory should give store managers no reason to complain, except that the stores may not look as full.

"Bradlee's did not realize how much information we had. When I brought the books to answer their questions, they were amazed. We explained that this was a *normal* part of our operation. Nothing could be any quicker. We feel that we have the final answer. In the old days the buyer used to commit himself to tremendous quantities of units early in the season. Today we are sampling. Even through the latter part of the Christmas season we were sampling spring merchandise for the manufacturers. The buyer could not even believe the results."

Does this not result in small shipments which are more expensive rather than large ones?

"In the long run, the sampling far outweighs the possible additional cost."

Bernard Abrams Associates
(OPERATORS OF LEASED DEPARTMENTS IN CURTAINS AND DRAPERIES, LINENS, AND DOMESTICS)

Bernard Abrams Associates started in 1935 when Bernard Abrams' father, Bernhard Abrams, opened a piece goods and domestics store in Hartford, Conn. The firm entered the discount field in 1956 with the opening of a leased department in the first Topp's location in Hartford. It is now the nation's largest domestic licencee and operates with more than thirty regional chains and independents from Hartford to Los Angeles. The company is directed by president Bernard Abrams. He is a graduate accountant who attended Bently College in Boston.

His company has followed a diversified growth pattern, including the acquisition of a three-unit discount chain, the opening of leased housewares departments, and plans for a chain of free-standing home furnishings stores.

Abrams' 81 units range from 3,000 to 6,000 square feet with the majority in the 4,000 to 4,500 square-foot area. Each department has seven major categories: curtains and drapes, linens, bedding, rugs, bed spreads, sheets, and rod and drapery hardware. Merchandise mix, fixtures, signs, and layout differ according to the needs of the individual store. Strong emphasis is placed on brand names, especially in sheets, towels, and blankets. Inventory investment ranges from $60,000 to $90,000 per unit.

The company has a warehouse at Wilson, Conn. A new 100,000 square-foot warehouse was opened in August, 1967 in Newington, Conn., on the Berlin Turnpike. Attached to the building is a 12,000 square-foot speciality store fronting on the Turnpike.

Merchandise flow is controlled by an item-by-item IBM program. Each of the seven major categories are inventoried on a three-week cycle. This information is then translated to both the merchandising and operations departments where reorder decisions are made. Present equipment is built around a central 1440 IBM 8,000 position memory unit equipped with two 1311 disc-drive storage units. It is supported by two 1442 reader punches, a 1403 high-speed printer, and 1011 paper tape reader, and the usual sorters, collators, and key punch equipment. Reports are prepared for sales and payroll, both budget and actual, on a store-by-store and chain-wide basis.

Asked what improvements one of his departments could make in the average landlord-operated domestics department, Abrams said, "Generally landlord-operated departments use a limited number of vendor resources. Many items are similar in style. Landlords do not shop the lines as thoroughly as they would other categories of merchandise. Because of our warehouse we have the capacity to select from many resources and stock in sufficient quantities to ensure adequate inventories. Along with selection, we are extremely conscious of national brands and proper packaging. Brands are important in specific items such as sheets, towels, and blankets. These we stock in quantity and advertise frequently to create a quality image. We insist that our manufacturers package for self-service selling. Every store carries an ample supply of polyethylene bags to repackage merchandise that has been abused.

"We consider display of the greatest importance and constantly change fixtures to suit our current needs. We take many preparatory steps that the

297

average department considers too time-consuming; every display curtain must be pressed before it goes on the selling floor. Reordering is the key to volume and profits; it is here that many chains lose control. Our three-week cycle inventory guarantees prompt refills from the warehouse."

Abrams acquired the three-unit Garwood, N.J. discount chain in December, 1965. Its 60,000 square-foot stores are in Vineland, Atlantic City, and Cherry Hill. Previous management, headed by Henry Gartner, has been retained. Abrams had been operating leased departments in the stores and concluded that the chain market potential was untapped. The company operates its own housewares departments in both the Garwood stores and in the Medallion Stores in Dallas. Abrams considers housewares a natural tie-in with domestics, and if the firm can develop the same expert knowledge and control it has for domestics, further expansion will be considered.

It is expected that a good part of the future growth of Bernard Abrams Associates will come from the West Coast. Presently 21 departments are located in Northern and Southern California with the Zodys, Gemco, and Alec chains. In the past two years Abrams has built an organization in Los Angeles to supervise local operations. Expansion is slated for the Washington, Oregon, and Nevada areas. Since the greater part of the executive, administrative, and buying talent is located at the Hartford home office, strong centralized control is exercised. Buying and policy-making for all units except the West Coast operation, is formulated in Hartford. The West Coast group is free to buy merchandise peculiar to that area.

Flexibility is achieved by encouraging all managers and supervisors to send requisitions to the home office for immediate filling on merchandise that is needed between regular inventory reporting times. Competitive shopping in local areas is a required duty of both managers and supervisors. Abrams issues a company newspaper, *The Bleat*, to its approximately 1,000 employees.

American Wholesale Toy Company (Operators of Leased Toy and Sporting Goods Departments)
INTERVIEW WITH LAWRENCE Y. GOLDBERG, VICE PRESIDENT

"The American Wholesale Toy Company, which in 1966 bought $6 million worth of toys, began in 1957. It started as an outgrowth of a toy-jobbing concern with which my family had been associated.

Leased Departments

"My father started in the discount business in 1954 when he became a supplier to the first Ann and Hope Store in Cumberland, R.I. Immediately after Ann and Hope, other discount chains opened in the Providence area. My father and an associate sensed the opportunity presented by discounting and became toy concessionaires in the first Atlantic Mills, unit then called Fairhaven Mills in New Bedford, Mass. It was an old mill building very much on the style of Ann and Hope. Our second department was in the first Atlantic Mills in Providence. Our third department was in Warwick, R.I. in the Shoppers' World; we are still associated with them today. Then came Coatsfield Shoppers' World in Pawtucket, R.I. Soon my father and his associate had eight stores, one of which was the first Zayre Store in Roslindale, Mass.

"My father decided that he wanted to branch out on his own. With me he started American Toys, using three units as a nucleus: Warwick Shoppers' World, Coatsfield Shoppers' World, and the first Zayre. Our company continued as a toy lessee through 1962 with Zayre as our principal landlord. By 1962 Zayre had 13 units and we decided that rather than tying ourselves up with one company, it would be better to diversify with a number of landlords. Our contract had not expired but Zayre came to us and said that they were going to open 22 stores in one year all over the country. We decided to sell our department back to Zayre, since we were not ready, in terms of capital structure or organization, to take that kind of a step. We were also the first toy concessionaires with Bradlee's. We realized that because of the great number of discount stores opening in the eastern markets there was a need to increase our volume potential in our leased departments. We, therefore, decided to add sporting goods to toys, since this was a closely allied field.

"In 1963 we merged with another company called Toy King, which had a wholesale division. We closed up the wholesale division and merged our toy departments with their toy and sporting goods departments. We are now associated with 21 different landlords on a nationwide basis. Almost all of our landlords are discounters and we consider ourselves to be a pure discount operation. My father's background, before his association in the toy business, had been in women's wear, and this was very helpful since there are many elements of fashion and fashion merchandising which apply to the toy business. Our first year's volume was about $570,000. In 1967 our volume will be approximately $14 million. The company is privately-held, owned by my father, myself, and our associate, Donald P. Honig, the principal of of the Toy King Company.

"Today we carry approximately 6,000 items over the course of a year. We cover all the toy and sporting goods field including wheel goods, bicycles, above-ground swimming pools and accessories, gym sets, and juvenile furniture. We have just now gone into the luggage business, but we are doing this as an adjunct to our existing set up rather than as a completely separate

299

department. Our present policy is to take only departments where we can sell a full line of the merchandise listed above.

"We buy almost exclusively through manufacturers with the exception of some items in hunting and fishing which we buy through various jobbers in different parts of the country. We have a direct import program, a brokerage arrangement in Japan through which we import merchandise from various parts of the Far East. At present our import program from Europe is negligible, although this is something that may grow.

"We are presently operating with a warehouse in Providence, R.I. Under construction is a large modern 80,000 square feet warehouse in St. Louis with 22-foot ceilings. It will cover our Midwestern and Southern operations. We have not yet completed plans for warehousing in California; but this is something we are actively considering. We combine central warehousing and drop-shipping: about 60 per cent of our merchandise is drop-shipped directly to our stores. Our basic warehousing program is for toys, since the warehousing need for sporting goods is negligible and really consists of just our imported items.

"We sell skis and bindings but we do not give service in shoes, binding, etc. We sell a medium-priced tennis racket; I would characterize all our merchandise in the sporting goods field as medium priced to promotional. We do not sell expensive luxury items in any of the fields. We usually import bicycles from the Far East. Today bicycles are assembled, very few are actually made in one place. The rims may come from one source, the wheels from another, the frame from somewhere else. It may be a combination from several different countries. Toys constitute approximately 60 per cent of our volume today. Sporting goods vary widely by locale. We do have stores where sporting goods are 55 per cent of our volume, and that would be about the high point in any particular department. Sporting goods might go to a very low point of about 20 per cent in an area not conducive to sporting goods sales.

"I would say that the discounting industry, and our company in particular, has done a great deal to change what was at one time the extreme seasonal nature of the toy business. We sell toys on a year-round basis. Even during January, February and March, we stock a full department consisting of basic categories and featuring hobby and activity items that are popular at that time of year. We sell summer sports merchandise such as tennis rackets and display it rather early in the spring. Most of the stores we are in extend credit so that sales resulting from spring displays are encouraged. We also have changed the traditional percentages. Until recently 75 per cent of the toy volume came between Thanksgiving and Christmas. Today we do 50 per cent of our volume before November; this is a substantial improvement.

"Games are one of our single largest categories and we carry a very extensive selection priced from under $1 up to $7 or $8. We carry literally hundreds of games. Plastics have revolutionized the toy industry in almost every area. They have implemented an explosion of new items. Television has been the largest single advertising factor in the last ten years. Through television, merchandise can be promoted on a national level on a year-round basis. The first television advertisements for toys were a destructive competitive factor since many stores felt that toys advertised on TV should be used as football items, much the same way that Prestone anti-freeze or Crest toothpaste are used. Today the industry is much more profit-conscious and we are all handling television-advertised toys in a much more sensible fashion.

"Our departments average about 5,000 square feet of selling space, and about 1,500 square feet of stockroom space.

"We have a training program for our managers and an extensive system of incentive bonuses and benefits. We also have a policy of promotion from within. Today we have eleven supervisors, all of whom have been promoted from the store manager ranks. In our 55 stores we have only three women managers.

"We are going into the West Coast and we think that area will eventually provide a very large percentage of our business. We started with one chain in the Los Angeles area. Eventually we will move up the coast.

"Toy and sporting goods lessees require warehousing and early merchandise commitments to manufacturers. Central warehousing is essential in our business. We would not have it if we did not need it. This is something in which not every landlord wants to invest. When you consider this, plus the expense of stockroom space in the stores, you can see that the logistics of our business and its seasonal nature go a long way toward justifying our existence. This is one of the reasons why we feel that we have a very optimistic future. Only a company that has the capital to make a heavy investment in staff and facilities is going to be able to offer this service to the discount industry.

"We are basically concentrating on small, regional, and local chains. Today we are associated with only two chains that have more than ten stores. About two-thirds of the discount industry will continue to be concentrated in chains of this size. We feel that we are offering a service to these companies that they cannot otherwise provide for themselves. Since we are one of the 25 largest toy purchasers in the country, we can offer a full range of merchandise, competitive pricing, specialized merchandising skills, and all the things they need to compete with any of the national chains that might be in their competitive area. Our single largest order to a single full-line manufacturer over the period of a year might be $500,000. This year, we will do between 7 and 8 million dollars in toys.

"We are now rated double A-1 in Dun and Bradstreet. Our net worth is a little over $1 million.

"We feel that it is a unique advantage to us to have our buying office right here in New York City. We felt that we should be in the market where we can get maximum exposure to vendors. This has been a great benefit to us. Our company has used data processing for several years, and we are now in the process of providing our second family of computers, a 360–20. All our managers have been to IBM school. Owing to the national scale of our operation and our need for good control we feel we must plan for more data processing in the future. We are drawing up a five-year plan for the future.

"We tried print-punch tickets, but found that they do not work due to the mutilation of tickets. For the whole industry I would definitely say that the future lies in cash register tapes with optical scanning. We can integrate our system with that of the landlord. I see no problem in doing that, but if the small landlord does not have EDP then we will not have it. If it is a big landlord or an automated landlord, we will have it with him.

"The computer indicates the quantities that are required in a particular situation, including warehouse backup and store supply requirements. It is up to the buyer to execute his order based on other factors.

"We have an automated warehouse; our 110,000 square-foot Providence warehouse is run with a basic staff of only four people. We invested heavily in conveyors because we feel that they provide us with the efficiency and speed that we need. Our warehouses are basically distribution centers. We try to buy merchandise, and when it hits the warehouse, we have already planned the distribution. It is just checked in and goes to the accumulation area for the different stores. We have no immediate plans to go public. There are mixed blessings in public status, but this is something we will actively consider in the next two years.

"We have one specialty store which sells toys and juvenile furniture. Although we have vague intentions of opening specialty stores, we feel that there is so much untapped potential in the discount store field, and for a leased toys and sporting goods department operator that represents a better use of capital and organization. I think our future in that direction is going to be great. We have no intention of opening discount stores or of going into other categories of merchandise. We are like the shoe maker who sticks to his last.

"I am a lawyer by trade, having graduated from the Harvard Law School in 1956. I have a wife and two pre-school children. My father has a life-long background in retailing; this has helped us, because actually he was a retailer coming into a retail business, not a jobber, trying to make emotional adjustments."

Carter Overton, Operator of a National Chain of Leased Drug Departments

INTERVIEW WITH RICHARD WEINBERG, PRESIDENT

My grandfather was an itinerant retailer with a pack of needles and housewares on his back down in Tennessee and Mississippi and so my father became a small 'dry goods' merchant with small retail stores in Memphis. My 21-year old brother, Louis, opened a small haberdashery department in a Memphis men's clothing store. I got my first retailing job when my brother put me in full charge of his haberdashery department in a store belonging to a New York chain called Victory Wilson. At age 13, I had the title of department manager; this was a very big moment in my life.

"Saturdays, in those days, meant that you were open from 9 in the morning until 11 at night. I worked at my brother's store all through high school. In 1939 I went to Harvard College and majored in economics. I planned to become a lawyer. The war changed my plans. Instead of graduating from college in 1943, I entered the Harvard Business School for twelve months. I then got a commission in the Navy as a line officer specializing in ordinance and served in the Iwo Jima and Okinawa campaigns. After the War I returned to Boston. In 1950, I opened my own business, White Cross Home Products, specializing in direct selling of health and beauty aids via the party plan."

In 1959 Weinberg opened his first leased drug department under the Carter Overton name in Auburn, Me. Today the company's 75 leased departments are in a variety of units including Fantastic Fair, Jumbo Stores, Mammoth Mart, Sabres, Rockdales, and Atlantic Thrift Centers. Carter Overton's first major penetration into the leased department field occurred in 1960 with the purchase of several drug departments from a former lessee of Atlantic Thrift Centers. In 1966 the company opened a 65,000 square-foot warehouse in Newton, Mass. It services departments in 29 states from New England to Denver.

In addition to its leased departments, Carter Overton operates 20 free-standing RIX discount drug and notion stores in the New England area. These have a similar product mix to the leased departments with an optimum size of 2,500 square feet. Most stores are long and narrow and provide testing laboratories for leased operations. If a discount department store chain has the capital to invest in and operate its own department, but needs merchandising assistance, Carter Overton offers its merchandising service. Several chains subscribe to this service using the systems, personnel, warehousing, and know-how that Carter Overton supplies. This enables them to operate economically and to maintain a constant in-stock position. Inventory control

303

Richard L. Weinberg, president, Carter Overton.

can become a complicated problem and Carter Overton specializes in solving such problems.

Says Weinberg, "We have a ready-made apparatus for moving merchandise very fast on a national basis. The aim of our drug departments is to be the dominant factor in its trading area in presentation, price, and volume. I believe that the optimum size for a department is 3,000 square feet and the proper merchandise mix includes health and beauty aids, cosmetics, stationery, greeting cards, candy, luggage, pet supplies, books, sewing notions, and, if the size warrants, trim-a-tree, tobacco, and a pharmacy. These items are all related; by integrating them into a single coordinated area maximum results can be achieved. We have been successful in both 20,000 square feet and 120,000 square feet units. In a full unit line we can generate upwards of 25 per cent of total store volume and we generate 60 per cent of volume in limited-line stores. From experience we know that a store must be capable of producing $500,000 to $700,000 in drug volume to support specialized sections such as a pharmacy and franchised cosmetic bar."

Leased Departments

Carter Overton does not believe in overshadowing fast-moving national brands with slow-moving private brands. Said Weinberg, "We believe that we should play with 'naturals' – the national brands. Why fight an uphill battle? On the other hand, there are certain items, rubbing alcohol, calamine lotion, tincture of iodine, which have no great brand preference and these items can be privately-branded successfully.

"Control is the number one problem in running a chain of leased departments," Weinberg said. "Drop-shipping merchandise to units does not work. There must be a central warehouse since 5,000 items of our merchandise consist of convenience goods and must be there when the customer wants it. Store level orders are received at the warehouse and are translated into electronic tapes which are then fed into the computer's (GE 225) perpetual-inventory memory bank. Thus orders are instantly adjusted on a stock-availability-stock-need basis. The items not in stock, plus those withdrawn that day for shipment to departments, are reflected in a daily master report distribued that same day to all buyers. Our computers tell us what is going on in the stores. You might think that most of our items are staples but actually we have very few items that do not have a style or seasonal factor. Even aspirin is seasonal and we carry much more of it in October, November, and December than at other times of the year. To be caught with excess Easter candy right after Easter is just as bad as being caught with out-of-style dresses. Our items are much more competitive on a brand-to-brand basis than soft goods. Approximately 90 per cent of our billing, ordering, and ware-housing systems are now on the computer.

"We are today the largest company in the U.S. specializing in leased drug departments on a national basis. Ten days after a phone call we can have a department complete with a $75,000 inventory all set up and operating anywhere in the United States. Departments range from 1,500 to 7,000 square feet with the majority at 3,000 square feet. The average merchandise mix, on a chain wide basis, is 60 per cent health and beauty aids, 20 per cent notions, 15 per cent stationery, and 5 per cent candy. Each department has a manager and assistant. The number of clerks is determined by size and volume. A supervisor is assigned to cover seven or eight stores with visits bi-monthly.

"In today's market there is a trend towards more and more items; not all of these are successful. Our job is to weed out the slow movers. We aim to have a full-look department with a wide range of items in each category. Emphasis is on the large sizes such as super-sized toothpaste."

Carter Overton is a pioneer in the development of packaging and display units for self-service merchandising. Weinberg explained: "We are now trying to influence several of the pegboard card manufacturers to exercise more intelligence in placing and reinforcing the holes in their cards so that the merchandise displayed will remain fastened. We also want them to use identifying reorder numbers on the face of the card so that it can be readily spotted. In the early days of discounting the problem was merely to get the goods to the store; today we are much more concerned with display techniques."

Training periods for new personnel range from two to five months. High-volume stores with experienced personnel are used for training. "Training manuals are obsolete," said Weinberg. "No one reads them and they rapidly go out of date. Our system is to have precise instructions for each operation printed right on the form used. Thus the clerk knows exactly what is to be done at the moment he is doing it. Each unit functions on a quarterly basis and contains a 13-week inventory at any given time. Store managers have bi-weekly order books, a master-item catalog including a data processing designation. This order book includes periodic supplements and deletions and is revised every thirteen weeks. There is a standard distribution of every item for every store. While EDP has been of immense help, it still takes highly sensitive and specialized discretion to make the right buying decisions at the right time. All the computer can tell us is based on history: it cannot predict the future."

The customary unit of purchase at Carter Overton is the carload which is the most economical volume in terms of cost. In 1966 the company placed an order with Procter and Gamble for nearly $250,000 – the largest single order placed in New England.

Asked about take over problems, Weinberg said: "The store owner must decide how to use his working capital; whether he wants to expand vertically by taking over leased departments, or horizontally by establishing more stores. Many really big chains concentrate on growing horizontally; those with plenty of capital can grow both horizontally and vertically at the same time. Even chains with company-owned drug departments usually lease at least one drug department which they use as a standard against which to measure their own operation. An owner's vanity frequently tends to exaggerate his capacity and ability to run a drug department himself. Few discount companies are firmly in the saddle today because they have cut too many corners and personnel turnover has been too great for them to be really on top of their problems. Some companies, when they take over a leased department, merely hire additional buyers since 'anyone can buy Alka Seltzer.' To hide resulting chaos they may lift the restrictions on drug items carried, expand display areas into other departments, and double the cash register drug item displays. Then they say, 'We have been able to increase the volume over what the lessee did.' In many cases they do not increase the volume and end up over-inventoried; or they may set a higher markup to make money, but that hurts the store image. Some go in the other direction and use the drug department as a football to bring in traffic and thus obscure the whole question. Most of them cannot buy as well as we can and, as it is said in the industry, 'You make your money buying, not selling.' We do things that are completely unknown to the average buyer. My feeling is that a drug department lessee specialist can generate more profit than an operator. This, of course, would not be the case in a situation such as that in which Parkview Drug Company merged with GEM. Parkview could readily replace previously leased GEM drug departments."

Asked what his most pressing problems were, Weinberg said, "In all fast-growing businesses the biggest problem is that of communications; and the bigger you get, the more important it is. Just for one item on a drop-shipped basis literally thousands of pieces of paper have to be produced to inform all the parties concerned. I often wonder how we got along without a photo-copying machine. Potential take over is a problem but we are not very vulnerable as most of our units are with small five-store chains; if they do take over we can cushion the shock by adding new units. Further, we have very adequate working capital and are not dependent on bank credit as many operators are. Our RIX stores contribute a significant amount to our profit. Rather than open discount stores of our own, we prefer to expand in the drug field since our know-how gives us a competitive advantage."

INTERVIEW WITH ALFRED L. MORSE, PRESIDENT, MORSE SHOE, INC.

How did you get into the shoe business?

"I went to the Wharton School at the University of Pennsylvania, and got a B.S. in economics in 1924. In 1922 my brother, Lester, with two other partners started a company called Teddy's Shoe Store. Its name was later changed to Morse Shoe Stores. When I graduated I went to work for that company. In 1925 I left them to strike out on my own. I spent a year in another industry, left that, and opened my first ladies' shoe store in Providence in March of 1927. I expanded that store into a chain using the name Morse's, Inc."

How much capital did you have when you started?

"I had $10,000. This was money advanced by my father who was in the hotel business. As Lester's business and mine grew in numbers of stores, it became obvious that by opening a joint buying office we could pool our buying power. We did that about 1933. We both went along at an even pace. Each of us had similar concepts and therefore we did not open stores in the same cities. Both of us sold women's shoes only. Later we added children's shoes in a limited way in some of the stores. Then we started to do some central warehousing, splitting expenses, but doing it on two floors, with the inventory for one chain on each floor.

"My brother incorporated in Massachusetts and I incorporated in Rhode Island. In 1955 we had some 45 shoe stores. In the meantime I had also started a wholesale division with my younger brother, William. It was a

Alfred L. Morse, president, Morse Shoe, Inc.

controlled operation selling to department stores only. We would supply their entire needs in popular-priced shoes."
You bought from the manufacturers?

"We bought from the manufacturers and sold to the department stores at a profit. We controlled their inventory by having them send us their sales." Was this a service that you sold them?

"They couldn't buy direct. Chain store purchasing and department store purchasing are entirely different; there is no comparison. The factories which service them are entirely different.

"In 1955 we took a hard look at this so-called new discount field which was to us nothing more than a repetition of the supermarkets. We looked at Ann & Hope and at Coatsfield Shoppers World in Pawtucket. Everything about it spelled success to us. Discounters could give the customer the same shoes for less money by the elimination of service, and the customer could fit herself without any problem. Our first lessor was Arlan's in their Fall River store, their first store. It was owned by Lester and Herbert Palestine

308

and a brother-in-law. We opened a shoe department with King's in Lowell, which was also their first store.

"The results were excellent and we really went looking for people who were thinking of going into discounting; we even pushed people into it who were not thinking of it. Our percentage of total sales varied tremendously depending on what was carried in the store and how strong the operators were. With a very strong ready-to-wear operator, our percentage of the total is less than it is with a weaker man. Our performance is equal in both cases. In the early days I would say we got at least 10 per cent of the total store sales.

"Rentals are based on a percent of our own sales. Morse has been able to lease departments for less percentage because of our reputation and production in terms of sales per square foot and percentage per store. There isn't any question about it: we are the strongest and best operators in the business.

"Our next lessor was Zayre's – our offices were next to theirs on Commonwealth Avenue at that time and we were very friendly. Their first unit was in Hyannis. We then opened with a number of landlords. Today if you looked at our list of lessors you would find that we have the Who's Who of the industry.

"We also opened with the first Topps unit in Hartford which is now part of Interstate."

Then you must have been with many of these people ever since their inception?

"Yes."

Are you a corporation or is it still a family operation?

"When we took the first department at Arlan's, and then with King's, etc., I reached an agreement with Lester's concern that we would merge on a fifty-fifty basis. We each owned fifty per cent of the stock in the parent corporation. Each leased department is a separate corporation. We have very strong business reasons for doing this."

What happened to the free-standing stores when you got into the leasing business? Did you still run those?

"Yes, we still do. From a maximum of about 47 we are now down to 23. Over the years our stores in the smaller towns which did $100,000 to $125,000 were competing with discount houses, shopping centers, Sears, etc. Better roads allowed customers to go to the larger centers so that volumes shrank while wages and costs went up and these stores were no longer profitable. As the leases expired we just closed these small town stores. That program is pretty well settled now and the balance of the stores are very profitable, but they are in bigger cities and have bigger volumes."

So you were right in your judgment in the first place?

"That is correct. As those leases have run out we have been able to renegotiate at much lower rentals because of the competition from the shopping centers surrounding the cities.

309

"One of the important questions you might ask is whether or not a customer can properly fit herself or a child with self service, and the answer is 'yes'. We have researched this very carefully and the best example I can give you is to tell you of an incident which occurred when I was riding in a cab in New York City with Bill Blackie, executive vice president of Genesco (Genesco used to be General Shoe). They own Bonwit Teller and at that time there was a mass picket line around the store. I said, 'Bill, how long are you going to let this go on?' The shoe salesmen were striking. His answer was, 'We will never give in.' He said that they employed the highest priced shoe salesmen in America and were very unhappy with their performance. They decided that the sales girls who one day sold millinery and the next day underwear or dresses could also sell shoes. All they had to do was to teach the girl to read sizes and let the customer fit herself. This is the reason the salesmen went out on strike. In the meantime, returns from customers had been cut in half. In fact, the shoe fitter is a shoe mis-fitter who pressures the customer to buy shoes she doesn't want and that don't fit in order to make a commission. As a result, Genesco never did give in and today they are running their departments with girls who simply bring in the style which the customer asks for.

"On the same basis, we checked our own retail stores versus the self-service departments and found the same situation: we had about half the number of returns in the self-service departments.

"We have experimented by attempting to wait on customers in our leased departments and some 95 per cent or better say, 'No thank you, we are just looking.' They don't want to be bothered. If they see something, they try it on; and if they like it, they will take it, and if they don't, they walk away. They like the attitude of the store and they love the freedom.

"Further, we have researched our children's departments claim that a child can't fit himself or herself. We find that the child can, and does it better than the salesman. When they say a shoe is too tight, they know what they are talking about, and the same applies if the shoe is too loose. We always have a thoroughly trained manager or assistant manager available who can help the customer if it is necessary; but the issue is not forced.

"I think the economics of it are self-evident. If you eliminate your sales people, you cut your overhead and you simply can sell for less – and we do." How about brands?

"We carry no national brands. All our shoes are branded with our own trade name. There are several names, Jewel Tones, Pretties, Carousels, Jumping Jacks for children, and different ones for men. Because of their wide-spread distribution today, they can well be considered brands. As you realize, we operate from coast to coast, in Texas and in Canada."
How many warehouses do you have?

"We have a plant here in Canton, Ohio, which is 350,000 square feet

310

under one roof and we are currently building on the rear end of it another 117,000 square feet to be opened by May or June. We have a satellite warehouse servicing our Canadian operation in Montreal. It is connected to this plant by IBM machines and leased Watts lines."

How many units do you have in Canada?

"I think we have 15 or 16 discount operations in Canada."

Do the manufacturers who provide your shoes provide similar shoes with other people's brands in them?

"Yes, but there are different kinds of factories. There are so-called chain store factories which work 50 weeks a year without a written contract. We say to them, in effect, 'You must make and we must take X number of cases per day out of your factory.' We have this type of arrangement with a long list of factories in which we have faith which we have helped to build up over a period of years. We have factories where we take 60-, 65-, 75 per cent of the output. We do not own them but we control them indirectly. We work very closely with them."

Have you ever been tempted to own them?

"No, we are not tempted because we want to be free to move in an open market if the management of a factory falls down and we cannot straighten it out."

Do you ever help to finance these factories?

"We have helped to finance them. We have advanced payroll and bought leather for the factories when needed. Fortunately, most of them today are pretty strong because it has been a policy of this company that those major suppliers whom we believe are the best in the industry must be kept healthy. If they are not smart enough to make a profit, they are not smart enough to make shoes for Morse Shoe. I tell the buyers, 'Don't ever cut them so tight that you break them because if you do, you will wind up without the necessary resources.' There would be no freedom of movement and there would be no styling – there would be nothing but third rate producers. So we must keep these factories healthy.

"These factories produce good values because they work 50 weeks a year and are far superior to the factory that makes shoes, say, for a department store where they buy three times a year, and the factory itself never knows what it is going to sell. If the factory works only 30 to 35 weeks out of the year, you know that affects overhead, so they simply cannot make quality for the same price. We do business with manufacturers who manufacture to our specifications. We even tell them which patterns we want adopted. We bring them patterns and we correct their lasts if new lasts have to be put in; they will do anything that we want and we see to it that they get a profit. As a result, we, in fact, can own the factory without any financial interest or investment and it is a very satisfactory method of doing business. We prefer this to owning our own factories.

311

"To go back to our method of operation, we were taking departments on a fifty-fifty basis between the two companies, Morse Shoe Stores Corporation and Morse's, Inc. In 1961 we reached a point where it was pretty unwieldy and decided that we had better put the two corporations together to properly finance the public corporation. We did that in 1961. The result is the present company, Morse Shoe, Inc., a Delaware corporation. We put our stock on the market through Blyth and Company and Lehman. The issue went to the public in April, 1962. We were about three weeks ahead of the crash."

How much money did you raise?

"We raised $12.6 million, none of which went to the corporation. It all went to the selling stockholders. That was traded over the counter and in November of 1964 we moved to the New York Stock Exchange."

What were the advantages?

"Twofold. One as a public corporation; the long-term financing available is entirely different than that as a private corporation. It also eliminated problems which existed with the minority stockholders."

But you still had the majority of the stock?

"That is correct. The second purpose, of course, was to put our estate in shape should anything happen to us."

What was the price of the stock when it was issued and what is it now?

"The stock went out at $20 a share and is currently around $34. We sold 630,000 shares out of a total of 1,812,000. Earnings have gone from 80¢ a share to $2.51 in 1968. Earnings projection this year is something in excess of $2.75 per share. The multiplier in the open market has shifted on price-earnings ratio. When we went public at 80¢ a share, it was 25 times earnings. Today with earnings about $2.75, it is only nine times earnings. It is quite a swing."

What are your total sales today?

"Our sales for the calendar year 1968, which happens to be a fiscal year, were slightly in excess of $138 million, with 575 units in operation."

Have you any units that you operate at a loss?

"There is an odd one here or there but these are relatively few. We had more in some of the earlier years such as in 1962 when the shakeout took place."

Do you feel that a lease is no better than a handshake or do you feel that you have to have everything down in legal terms – in black and white?

"I would say that if you are dealing in large numbers as we are, you must have it down in black and white. When you think in terms of doing $15 million or $20 million with a given landlord on an annual basis, you have to spell it out. There is no room for the casual, informal type of operation. Our landlords have recognized our ability. It has been proven. They further recognize that we must plan long range just as they have to plan long range in order to do our jobs properly and to service their departments. They have

312

seen fit, therefore, to give us much longer and firmer leases than in the past. We are today on much firmer ground than we have ever been and it would appear – in fact, it is quite certain that this will continue to be the case."

Why is it that most store operators cannot run their own shoe departments?

"There is a very definite reason for it. For example, if pink is hot for Easter, it is no trick for a buyer of dresses to look at the sales checks on a Monday morning from the various stores and recognize the fact that pink is hot. By ten o'clock on Monday morning, the buyer is on Seventh Avenue in New York to buy X thousands of pink dresses off the racks of the various dress manufacturers who make them for stock. He will have them delivered to his distribution point by Wednesday, and out into the stores by Friday of that same week. It takes no genius to do that. But it takes some kind of genius to buy those pink shoes in the right color pink, the right style and the right quantity, in *October*, and *November* and, at the latest, December in order to have them in the stores for Easter selling. This is future planning of a type which to my knowledge does not exist in any other soft goods area. It takes a tremendous amount of experience, record keeping, knowledgeable buyers, complete research of the fashion market long in advance, and research of the foreign market; our own office in Florence, Italy controls our European operations."

Do you import many shoes?

"Approximately 10 per cent of our goods are imports. From Italy we get play type shoes, some dress shoes, and some men's casuals. We also buy from England, France, Belgium, Holland, Spain, India, and Mexico. We buy rubber goods and tennis shoes from Japan. When I talked in terms of researching the foreign markets, I was talking in terms of color and style in the world of fashion. We have a vice president in charge of buying and underneath him are nine buyers. Each one is a specialist in a particular category of shoes. He knows every shoe that is produced throughout the world in that particular category. He must. He is backed up by one or more assistants and a group of distributors who write the sizes, detail the shoes, follow him at the factory, and see to it that shoes are shipped from the warehouse to the stores as the stores need them."

What part does electronic data processing play?

"A tremendous part."

When did you install it?

"We have been on electronics since the early 1950's. We tie and tag every pair of shoes with a pre-punched ticket, a two-part ticket. Ticketing is at the warehouse level. At the point of sale, half of the ticket is torn and held and each night every store sends an envelope with its sales tickets to the home office. They are processed so that we get reports out weekly to the buyers, the controller, and the distributors. Our sales record is very accurate and includes style, color, and price. We do not attempt to control size since

313

it isn't practical. Our stock number tells us the style, the color, the heel height, and the type. Sizes are handled through experience and through size-taking at the store level. They report to us, not every stock number every week, but a sufficient number of stock numbers each week so that we can keep current with their size position."

Do you do this with all shoes or just with the style shoes?

"All shoes. There is a loss of tickets amounting to perhaps 7 per cent or 8 per cent of our sales. That is not to say that we don't get the money from the cash register; but the girls at the cash register fail to tear the ticket at the central checkout. There are other tickets in the checkout boxes as well as shoes and some get lost or are sent to the wrong department. Thus size control on a punched ticket basis is not very worthwhile for the effort involved. We currently operate a 360 IBM system. It has greater speed, greater memory, and can do more than one job at a time. Incidentally, the rental on these machines is no more than it was on our old system."

Who is your biggest competitor?

"We have no competitor. We have some imitators, but no competitors. Nobody matches our performance. This is not egotistical bragging, but actual fact."

Do you sell men's, women's and children's shoes?

"We sell every type of shoe; every type of covering for the foot for every purpose and every occasion."

Do you still actively solicit lessors or are you pretty choosy?

"We are quite choosy. In the first place we have close to 50 lessors on our books. In the second place we owe loyalty to a certain key group and their expansion plans are pretty strong. In the third place you just can't be all over the lot with everybody – you just wouldn't be doing the proper thing by those lessors to whom you owe this loyalty. We do pick up an occasional new landlord because he comes to us rather than we to him. Over the last two or three years we have probably turned down three for every one we have taken."

In regard to locations competing against each other, isn't this an awkward situation and what do you do about it?

"We recognized some seven years ago that we would be bumping into ourselves with competing landlords. The question was what to do about it and the answer was obvious – we would have two lines of shoes. Ordinarily, the second line signifies that it is inferior and whoever gets it will not be getting as good a line as the first line. It must be of equal quality and pricing. When we set this up we explained it to our controllers and buyers. To avoid a second line, we divided all stores into two columns or two chains. At all times the bottom line, volume-wise, must balance within a million dollars annualized.

"On this basis the buyer knows that it makes no difference to him whether

314

the shoe goes in the first line or the second line. He knows also that he must come up with two equal shoes at the same time, for the same purpose, for the same price. And he does just that. This type of change is all a competing buyer would do if he could get the same quality. We have different names in the shoes, tie and tag the shoes with different color tickets. No customer could say it is the same line of shoes because we have actually made more changes than a competitor would make. We have two complete inventories in the warehouse with different stock numbers. They are absolutely separate operations and it has worked out very well."

How do you get capable people; how do you train them?

"We have a very definite training program at store level. A manager must have an assistant manager out of necessity because he can't cover the store for the number of hours that it is open. If he is to do his job properly, he must train that assistant manager to the point that he can take on a new store. You must remember that we have opened a great number of stores over a period of years and we will continue to do so. 1969 will be at least the second largest in number of openings and might even be the first. The expansion going on with our landlords in 1969 is tremendous. So we have men in training at the store level at all times. When they are sufficiently trained to take a store, we give them one."

What supervision is there?

"The entire setup starting at the top is as follows: The store operation is headed by my brother, William Morse, who is a vice president and director of the company. Under him he currently has three so-called area supervisors, each theoretically taking one-third of the country. They, in turn, have district managers under them. They control the district managers at the field level, help them with their problems, and visit them from time to time. The district manager has the store managers under him. They average about 14 stores to a district manager. It varies by whether the area is a tight one or spread out. If there is no loss of travel time, a man may have more than 14. It is the district manager's responsibility to have good managers, train them properly, and see to it that their managers are in fact training their assistant managers. They hire them, they can fire them, and they can train them. We bring all the district managers into Boston at least once a year. Last year we brought them all in at one time. This year we plan to bring them together in smaller groups. We have today some 35 district managers and we will need more. We train them here, discuss their problems with them, and give them personal attention. As we need additional district managers the best of the department managers will be moved up the ladder.

"Today, working on a basis of 575 departments, our problem is much easier than it was. For example, in 1962 we opened 81 stores net on the base of 175 and we went from 175 to 256 in that one year. We did promote from within, but it was a very difficult job. We took in a few new men, but

315

promotion was basically from within. Today, from a base of 575, if we open 50 to 100 stores in one year we won't even know we opened them from the standpoint of personnel."

Do you have an active plan for getting college graduates interested?

"We have solicited college graduates. We find it very difficult to get them in the field. They don't want to work in the field; they want to work in the main offices. In the main office here we have a large number of college graduates."

What would you say would be your average markup?

"That is not for publication, but I will give it to you in this manner. Our markup is sufficient to cover our expenses and a fair profit for our efforts. We don't propose to do business without a profit. On the other hand, we don't want to make so large a profit that it will kill our values. We prefer to plow it back into our values and get it in increased sales. The one mistake that could be made in this industry would be to get too hungry and try to make too much money and move closer to the department store. The faster they do that the sooner the new discounter will appear under them and cut them out. That will happen as they get barnacles and as they raise their prices. Morse intends to watch for it and to be the first with the new discounter when he does show up. I don't know what his name will be (the name of that type of revolution) but it will occur; it is only a question of time.

"I personally think it is many years off because the industry today is in much stronger hands than it was and the stronger hands recognize it is coming, just as I do, and they will do everything in their power to control expenses in order to keep values well below the chain or the department store."

What do you think of the future for small discounters with, say, a chain of three?

"I think there is always room for an enterprising individual in any industry and I don't think that this is simply an industry for giants. I think that an individual can make up through individual effort the disparity in his buying power."

What do you think of the future of leased departments other than shoes?

"Millinery and jewelry are the others commonly leased and probably will continue."

Would you say, in general, that the leased department makes more than the lessor? Zayre management investigated and found that the leased departments were making more money than they were.

"The answer is that most leased operators who went into the self-service field as lessees realized that their days were probably numbered. They had to make a fast dollar because they weren't going to last. This, in turn, caused the landlord to take over those departments as fast as he possibly could. Morse's attitude toward this has been entirely different because historically

316

shoe departments are leased. We feel and know that we have no problem with our departments being taken over. We must be as strong or stronger a merchant than the landlord himself.

"It is not a fair thing to just look at return on dollar sales. The volumes that are possible in a shoe business are far different than the volumes possible in a ready-to-wear business. Probably one of the largest retailers in the country today is Edison Brothers, doing $175 million in shoes. Yet this isn't very much when you compare it with Zayre's projection of $400 million to $500 million, or with an Interstate department store projection of a billion by 1970. It doesn't follow that you don't require the same effort as the overall store operator – you do. Because you do, and because you put it in, you are entitled, percentage-wise, to something higher than those products which bring in much greater volumes. You might compare, let us say, the profit margin on dresses to a food chain and dresses will be higher. But it doesn't follow that it shouldn't be – it should be.

"We are the only entirely automated shoe plant in the United States as far as data control and material handling in the warehouse is concerned. It is a model and people actually come from all over the world to look at it."
Do you have your own trucks?

"No, we use common carriers. We are so far flung that it wouldn't pay us to run our own.

The Gilbert Shoe Company Operator of 117 Leased Shoe Departments with sales of $16 million

DR. IVAN GILBERT, PRESIDENT

How did you get into retailing?

"I was trained as a physician and had my M.D., but I had been ill and my father said, 'Why don't you play around with the shoe business?' I did not feel like really working hard; finally, I just gradually slid into the shoe business."
What business was your father in?

"He founded the Gilbert Shoe Company in 1906 and now runs the largest cancellation shoe store in America."
When did you start?

"I finished my internship in 1946 and started in the shoe business. I opened some stores of my own on the side, six or seven of them, and was also running the big store. These were cancellation-type shoe stores. I also tried some regular children's-type shoe stores and some women's high-fashion-type shoe stores. I was experimenting, trying to find a *modus operandi* for expansion because my father's kind of business was like a mule – very strong and it could pull a heavy load but it could not reproduce itself very well."

What do you mean by cancellation operations?

"These are closeouts, factory damaged, retail stocks – a sort of a catfish of the shoe industry. We swam along the bottom and got rid of the mistakes; we were the undertakers for mistakes. Our big competitors in this country were Filene's Bargain Basement and Satler's in Buffalo. My father's store had customers in 47 states and in about 30 or 40 foreign countries. Many ordered by mail. We had customers who would come to the United States every three years and pay cash for 20 pairs of shoes for themselves and their family. We have a mailing list of several hundred thousand people. The store used to carry 100,000 to 200,000 pairs of shoes.

"I never knew much about the shoe business. I had to go out and hire good people who did know. This left me free to think and expand. I did not get caught in the grip of doing a lot of the merchandising or buying myself. Such complications inhibit thinking about expansion or financing. Essentially, this is the lazy man's approach to running a business. Our theory of management is to encourage people all the way down the line to think for themselves and make decisions. We encourage them to face up to their mistakes and not to be worried about them: don't deny them, just correct them. The only people who do not make mistakes are dead people."

When did you get into leased departments?

"In November, 1957. We had heard about the Kelly and Cohn discount store opening in Pittsburgh. We went to see them and they leased 3,500 square feet to us. We got ideas from some of the other leased departments. There were not many around the country at that time. Actually, our big family shoe store sold about two-thirds of its shoes on open display. We took what we knew from that operation and set it up in the Kelly-Cohn operation. Fortunately for us, it was very successful."

What rental did you pay?

"We were paying 8 per cent, including advertising. We handled our own money, with our own cash register. I then owned seven specialty stores which I liquidated as the discount business grew."

What were your major problems in these early days?

"Abysmal ignorance. Our big advantage was that although we did not know anything, nobody else knew anything. We knew shoes but the licencee operation was a whole new area of merchandising. We had always been in our own shoe stores and suddenly we were going to live inside someone else's house. This meant having to develop a new set of working relationships. We no longer were the boss; we were suddenly a visitor in a strange store. We were there on sufferance.

318

Dr. Ivan Gilbert, founder and president,
Gilbert Shoe Stores, Inc.

"Our experience in the early days was that many of the owners did not have much knowledge of merchandising. People coming into the discount business at that time were essentially newcomers to merchandising. In the early days, the thing you had going for you was that the customers kept coming. You could make all kinds of mistakes, but cash kept flowing in for a variety of reasons. One, the word 'discount' was a magic word. Two, we were the first people really out in the suburbs. There was a tremendous untapped suburban market, a consumer market for consumer's goods. The department stores had essentially stayed out of the suburbs; there were a few of them, but they had not really gone out. Three, these stores created a sort of grocery store environment, where people could come in with slacks and children. All our people thought of was price in addition to a sort of buying excitement.

"In 1958 nobody had any money and nobody trusted the discount business; none of the finance people wanted even to talk about it. So you grabbed whatever building was available and made do; at that time you were

319

looking for two things – a building in the suburbs and parking. It could be a warehouse or a factory; it did not make any difference."

Today, how many departments have you?

"We have leased departments in 75 stores; of these ten are free-standing."

What are some of the hazards of operating a leased department?

"There are a variety of hazards. You have the hazard of the landlord who is running a central checkout and handling your money; we have been burned in the past on that. Several years ago we were taken for about $30,000 in about two weeks. The landlord was collecting our money and would give it to us twice weekly. He got into the Christmas period (we were in two stores with him) and suddenly the money was late in coming. We called him and he said his Christmas business had boomed so much that he just could not get to it. He kept getting farther and farther behind as it got closer and closer to Christmas. We finally went down right after Christmas to get the money. He said, 'Here is some money; I will send you the rest in the next few days.' By the time we got back home, he was in receivership and then he said, 'Sure, I owe you the money.' We were general creditors; we have been involved in litigation on this situation for three years.

"The lessons we learned follow: one, never let anybody handle your money who is not adequately capitalized; two, as we developed more departments it became apparent that we could not afford to allow our money to be sitting out for a long period of time because that necessitated a greater investment. For example, if our money were to be held out at all departments for one week (we are presently doing $10 million) that would mean an average of $200,000 more a year that we would have to invest in this business to do $10 million with the current investment. As we became more sophisticated, we demanded our money every night to the exact penny. We were prepared to take it on some kind of an estimate and settle later, or we ran our own registers. We have learned nowadays to put clauses in our leases stipulating that if we have a central checkout, whenever the money is late by as much as one or two days, we immediately have the right to put in our own register so we can continue to sell shoes, but not run risks if we feel insecure. Before we go in with anybody, we check them out extremely thoroughly, and if we do not have confidence that they are capitalized adequately, we do not go with them; or if we do go in, we have our own register.

"There are certain other advantages and disadvantages to central checkout. I have time and again seen the girls on central checkout make mistakes in pricing merchandise. I have sat in a discount store, for instance, and watched gun and holster sets from a toy department. I have seen a girl ring $1.29, $1.29, $1.29 three times on gun and holster sets. The first one through was $1.29; the other two should have been $2.29. The girl apparently just took it for granted that nobody would buy the better ones. Whether she

320

was stealing or cheating, she was just ringing $1.29. Every time another customer came through with a set, there was another dollar lost. Another problem with the central checkout is that there is a big ticket loss which makes it more difficult for inventory replacement. Either the girl will not tear the ticket off in the first place, or she drops it in the slot for ready-to-wear, or it gets lost. She may ring it on the wrong key; a whole variety of things can happen to it. We find that these types of problems do not average out. A girl who has a tendency to hit the key that she hits most often will make a mistake toward that key. When we had shoes in a grocery store, the error toward groceries was much more pronounced because the girl's reflexes were toward that key rather than towards shoes.

"There is another problem with the central checkout; shop-lifting is encouraged by wide-open spaces. However, there are some positive values to central checkouts in that it does not interfere with a customer's fantasy world. It does not bring them back to reality. In a grocery store a customer floats around and keeps buying until she buys more stuff than she has money in her pocketbook and then has to take items out at the counter.

"If you get beyond a certain size the real answer to central checkout is probably regional checkouts of some kind. I do not really believe that central checkout in very, very large stores is a valid way to go. Do not forget the average grocery store does not exceed 20,000 to 25,000 square feet. It is still a pretty contained unit. When you get into 100,000 or more feet, there is a great deal of wandering around for the customer."

What happens to your inventory if a store goes bankrupt?

"If your legal instrument has not been adequately drawn there may be an attempt to attach your inventory. We have been extremely careful to have a very good legal consultant; we maintain the integrity of our ownership on all merchandise put into any store. We have been through several bankruptcies with leased operations and have never had any difficulty taking out our inventory, except once when we had to come up with a bond on rent.

"It is very important to have in your lease a clause which releases you from the lease if the landlord becomes insolvent. If you do not you are in trouble because his creditors may try to hold you in a store where you cannot function. We are careful in every lease we sign to stipulate that not only does the landlord get released if we get into trouble, but we get released if he gets in trouble, so that we are a free agent. You can then go into any court and in a few days get your merchandise."

What do you do about getting competent personnel?

"We are changing many of our managerial concepts. When we first started we looked for some young fellow who could keep the inventory straight. We were completely self-service. There was a strong feeling in the industry that you should not even talk to the customer. In one of our competitor's operations I asked a clerk a question and he said to me, 'I'm

321

sorry. I'm under instructions not to talk to customers.' We never got that bad. We were trying to keep our overhead really low by hiring boys for about $70 to $75 a week to manage these departments. Now we are looking for more mature and more knowledgeable people. We now give many more services. In the early days we tried to avoid shoe people because we found that they came in with ideas about waiting on customers; and most of them came out of box stores and could not stand the idea of all the merchandise being out *en masse*.

"Our industry is becoming much larger in scope. To get into the right factories today you have got to have a certain volume. You have got to have trained professional buyers. No one person can buy in the shoe industry today. You are bucking up against specialists. There is a specialist in men's shoes, in women's shoes, and in children's shoes, and after a while these men get to know that specialty. In a company as large as ours, our buyers do nothing but buy. They go to the market, study the new trends, new materials, and new styles, and they exchange information with other people in the market place. The owner running six or eight stores does not have enough dollar volume to develop an expert staff. We have improved the quality of our merchandise, our delivery procedures, our point of sale selling techniques, ticketing, our psychological techniques, customer motivation, inventory control, etc. It is what happens in any business if you stay in it. The things that were difficult you absorb, and then you are ready to go onto the new problems which you are not even aware of until you absorb the old problems.

"We suddenly got involved with such questions as how do you get more dollars out of a customer coming to your department? How do you get a customer coming into a discount store to enter your department? How do you convince a customer that the $4 ladies' flat is worth a dollar more than the $3 ladies' flat? What do you do to motivate her? How do you convince a customer that the $5 basketball shoe is the shoe he really wants even though it looks like the $3 basketball shoe? How do you motivate the customer? It is no problem to sell a customer a pair of shoes at the lowest price level if he came in to buy a pair of shoes, but how do you sell it at a higher price without a clerk? Or how do you sell him two pairs? How do you sell him if he did not plan to buy at all that trip? These are the kinds of questions you try to ask yourself, and then you start playing around with displays, with tickets to go on shoes, and with special fixturing.

"As soon as you remove the clerk, the customer makes up her mind solely on the basis of what she sees. Somehow or other the customer knows what is in fashion. Do not ask me how she knows, because we can stack eight shoes in a row without any apparent difference between them, but if 100 women pass those shoes, two styles will get 75 out of 100 sales. How do they know? Somehow they know!

"You must have the merchandise of the demanded fashion in sufficient quantity to do business. We had to learn how to identify what the right fashion is; it is the item that sells. A so-called staple, on the other hand, has a tendency to be something that sold last year. With EDP, you can rapidly identify what sold yesterday, but you still must know fashion to anticipate tomorrow!"

How about new material?

"There has been a great deal of new soling, resulting from new techniques in injection molding. There has also been an increased use of vinyl for uppers. The big breakthrough is Corfam or a subsequent edition of Corfam. Corfam still has a lot of problems. It does not really fit your foot as leather will; yet it is a major breakthrough because it involves a completely new and much simpler manufacturing technology. Leather is not a standardized material, whereas Corfam is."

But you still have the styling problem.

"I believe that the shoe industry's big future lies in fashion and style and that we are beginning to see the consumer immensely interested in fashion. Our biggest fashion customers today are the teenagers and not only teenage girls; teenage boys are fashion-conscious as all get out. Right now loafers are very big with teenage boys in our part of the country, and last year it was pointed-toe boots. There is a sort of built-in obsolescence; it is not so much that the shoes wear out, although I must admit that if anybody wears shoes out it is the teenage boy. The style changes, and everybody buys a new pair of shoes. White go-go boots are an excellent example.

"Another factor affecting the loafer selection is color. Once it was strictly black or cordovan; now, they are going into light tans and suedes. Fashion is the real key to merchandising shoes. The strange thing is that everybody has the impression that discount stores sell staples, but if you really take a good look, you find it sells fashion in shoes.

"The most successful discounters are those who sell fashion in their soft goods. The use of the word 'staple' can be extremely dangerous in our kind of business; I do not mean only shoes. Because if you think of a thing as a staple, you are always looking backwards. Our aim is to use our information flow to pick out the big sellers early; this is how you build your business. You do not get caught with markdowns, and you can really run tremendous quantities. We sold thousands of go-go boots for children and for women. That one item meant perhaps $10,000 additional sales in one week. It would not have made any difference what else we had; these girls wanted go-go's."

How do you anticipate these demands?

"Our buyers are in constant touch with the market and with style trends. They develop a feel and a sensitivity for fashion. You do not really know where you might pick up the scent. Sometimes it is the buyer who encounters it in the market; sometimes, a manager will come in and say,

323

'I have had numerous inquiries for something.' It might come from anywhere. The key point is that the company is looking. We encourage people in the field to bring suggestions in immediately and even go out and buy an item with petty cash if customers ask for something two or three times. Instructions are to get the item and send the requests to the buying staff.

"We figured out that in the shoe business there are really 12 to 15 seasons. Most people talk about three or four seasons, because certain categories of merchandise only have a six-week run and that is the season for that particular family of merchandise. Next week, something else becomes big. You have to plan and project your sales and get your merchandise so you have depth when you need it; but not to a degree where you are over-stocked when the season is done.

"Some items have only a ten-day season: hunting packs before hunting season, hunting boots. You have to have them in a month ahead of time, but you really have the big whoosh in every state about 10 days before the first day of hunting. After the first day of hunting, it will drop dead. House slippers are a must for Mother's Day. Some seasonal items present problems. Children's shoes, for instance, have several short periods a year that are really their season. Right before you go back to school, for five or six weeks, you do a tremendously large percentage of your annual business in children's shoes. Before Easter is a very big season for little dressy shoes (patent leathers and colors), and about two-and-a-half weeks before Christmas. You have to peak your inventory in relationship to your antici-pated sales; you have got to know the business to plan for those peaks. Fleece-lined boots will hit for a short period when the cold weather comes in. There are just innumerable items.

"About 1961 there was a color called raspberry; we had it and were stuck with it in every store. We had to mark them down. Some were sold to a cancellation operation. We have done that several times. One thing you can never afford to do is to let a lot of unwanted shoes sit around in your department. Your image becomes out of date."

Do you carry very high-priced shoes just to make the lower-priced ones sell?

"It is established retail practice as a rule not to sell a large percentage of the top of your line. If you want to sell a line it behooves you to put in a higher-priced line than the line of which you want to sell large quantities. If the higher-priced line sells very well, you had better put in a still higher-priced line. In other words, if your customer shows through her purchases that your highest-priced line is very, very acceptable to her, you may be still underselling her. You must remember that I am not talking about buying a better product. I do not want her forced into buying something lower in value than she wants to buy, because if you do you run her out.

"We now sell $15 men's shoes in our discount stores. We had $20 men's boots this past winter. We are trading up rapidly; we have gotten up to $6

324

in children's shoes in some of our stores and up to $10 and $12 in ladies' shoes. We do not, yet, know how high-priced a product a customer wants to buy. You cannot go too high; you do it with discretion, in graduated steps. You can move your sales in ladies' flats so that half your percentage comes at $4 instead of all of it at $3. That does not seem as though you have graded up much, but if you take percentages you have a tremendous upgrade. When you go up from $3 to $4, that is a 25 per cent increase and a 33 per cent rise in the price the consumer was paying. Our first attempt to grade up was in men's work shoes. We jumped about $3 a pair and it did not work. We went back and bought some better merchandise and retailed it for a dollar more and it worked.

"Our women's business today is essentially a fashion business. About 25 per cent of our business is men's and about 50 per cent women's, and children's is about 25 per cent.

How do you feel about incentive plans?

"I feel that the true incentive plan has to be something that makes a man's job more important to him while he is working. I mean personal satisfaction, a feeling of achievement, acceptance of peer group, acceptance by bosses – where a man is being complimented. I think that probably the real incentive is not money. That does not mean that a man should not be paid what he is worth. But once he is paid what he is worth, and he knows it, then his incentive is not money; his incentive is something else. The greatest incentive for a manager is that somebody in the organization will listen to him if he has an idea. Most people begin with initiative and it is squelched. The problem is not to give a man initiative, but not to destroy it. An employee must feel that somebody wants to hear what he has to say."

Do you ever end up with a lot of odd sizes and discontinued items?

"When you discontinue an item you eventually end up with broken sizes. That is the time when you mark them down and get rid of them."

Can you tell me why the Morse Shoe Company has a separate corporation for each department it leases?

"For the same reason we do; it enables us to limit our liability on the investment, on the lease. We sign the lease with each corporation and the store. The lease between our store and the discount store is assigned to the corporation that runs the space in that store. We limit our liability and also limit our union liability because we may have a union contract in that store, but it is only to that corporation. It does not involve our other corporations with the union problems that another corporation may have. Most of the discount stores we are in today are unionized and whatever union is in that store, our corporation and the employees in that corporation are necessarily union members. Since it is an individual corporation, whatever union policies may be in effect in that corporation do not transfer over into another corporation.

325

"There are a whole series of liabilities which that corporation has which do not endanger the parent company. It may be customer suits or tax problems in a certain state. We operate corporations in Pennsylvania, Ohio, West Virginia, Kentucky, Illinois, and Michigan. Each of these states has different laws about corporate relationships. For instance, if we operate a store for a company that has stores in two states, we might get involved in all sorts of out-of-state tax problems. So this store operates under the laws of the state in which it is, or under the laws of the city. There may be a city income tax. Even in the same state we have separate corporations; in fact, each store we have is a separate corporation."

United Overton Corporation
(OPERATOR OF HARDWARE, HOUSEWARES, AUTOMO-TIVE, TOYS, AND SPORTING GOODS DEPARTMENTS.)

United Overton operates more than eighty hard goods leased departments in 27 states. The company, among the first to enter the discount field in 1956, specializes in four basic categories: hardware, housewares, automotive, toys, and sporting goods departments. Volume for 1965 is estimated at $30 million. The company was formed by a merger of two former direct-selling operations, Morgan's and United Utilities and Specialty Corporation. United Overton is a lessee with chains and independents that include Atlantic Thrift Centers, Parkview-GEM, and Mammoth Marts. Departments range from 4,000 to 12,000 square feet, with the norm in the 7,000 square-foot class. Management is centralized under the presidency of Abner Cohan at the executive headquarters in Newton Highlands, Mass.

United Overton is one of the few national lessees that conducts all departments within the hard goods family, making it possible for a landlord to consolidate all of his hard goods relationships with one major operator. If all four departments were leased, he would have to deal with four separate lessees. Additional advantages claimed are that labor relations are more unified. Since, by virtue of total size, the four departments are more important to the lessee, they will get greater day-to-day attention and interest. A further advantage is that there need be no arbitrary demarcation lines within the total area occupied. The individual departments can be expanded or contracted as the occasion or season demands. Economy of the landlord's time and effort is achieved, since with only one line of communications he can readily complete plans for such matters as advertising, promotion, labor policy, new store-wide administration policy, shifts in store image, etc. Succinctly stated, the general idea is that if you want to be important to your tenant operator, make him important to you.

Further advantages claimed by the company for its landlords follow:

326

Leased Departments

The buying power of a national organization such as United Overton puts it in a more favorable competitive position than a local lessee, or a store-operated department. In hard goods this buying power is particularly important. Buyers are always in the market searching for new items and ideas. A store does not have as wide a range of suppliers to deal with as in soft goods. For example, there may be hundreds of manufacturers selling $8.75 skirts, but in a comparable hard goods item such as aluminium cookware, there may be a scant half dozen. You have to make heavier initial commitments in hard goods. Often the landlord may resort to a jobber placing himself in a non-competitive position. The ability to make a special purchase for a truly explosive promotion must be greater for the larger buyer. Merchandise is stockpiled for crucial selling seasons.

There is also the question of merchandise availability. United Overton is a strong proponent of central warehousing and can devote a lot of space to such categories as toys – more so than many jobbers. It maintains a four-acre distribution center in Lawrence, Mass. The ability to ship known quantities of merchandise in short supply at any given time is invaluable. "We operate in various climates under a multitude of social conditions. We can bring to a given store in a given area a breadth of experience that can cause merchandising excitement. Also, the proper presentation of merchandise is sometimes as important, or more so, than price or quality. We spend literally hundreds of hours in display experimentation and maintain a full-time advertising department to work closely with the store operator." The company has twelve supervisors who cover an average of seven stores with visits averaging from two days; each store is covered a minimum of twice a month.

Approximately 75 per cent of United Overton's accounting records are automatically data processed along with inventory control, payroll, and accounts payable. Says Clint Fiske, EDP manager for the company, "When you deal with 80 units and breadth of merchandise covering 8,000 to 12,000 types of items you need some form of automation or the work will never be up to date. If, for a basic example, six buyers are making decisions on 10,000 items for 80 stores, this means 800,000 decisions each ordering period. Without EDP and a planned pattern, chaos ensues."

Future plans call for expansion with firms in which United Overton now has departments and the addition of new units. United Overton is presently exploring the department store field. Management feels that its merchandise presentation and experience could make a profitable contribution to department stores that are weak in hard goods.

INTERVIEW WITH SAUL LEIBOW

This interview was given by Saul Leibow when he was president of Hardlines Incorporated which operated a chain of leased hardware and houseware

departments. In 1966, the company, with its management, was merged with the Zayre Corporation and is now known as Housewares Corporation.
What business were you in before you started Hardlines Distributors?

"Hardgoods. Since I was 12 years old I have spent my entire life in hardgoods. This is all I know."
How did you get the idea of leasing a department?

"When I saw the immense success of Marty Chase, who put his store in a large factory building, I came to the conclusion that discounting could become a way of life, not just the fad that people thought it would be. I saw what had happened to the supermarkets, which were truly the innovators of discounting, not us. They were catering to people who were becoming lazier as time went on and came in wearing any old clothes. They did not have to go downtown, they could park their cars, they could bring in their children, there was a relaxed atmosphere, and they did about as they pleased. Actually it was a combination picnic and shopping area. I did not think there was any difference between food and the rest of the merchandise. What difference does it make if they shop for a can of beans or a can of automotive oil? The basic was there. The public had been indoctrinated long before we came along."
Where was your first leased department?

"Coatsfield Shoppers World, Pawtucket, in 1955.
How many do you have now?

"A hundred and six, and about 22 more to go this year, 1965."
How long was it before you got your second one and your third?

"We opened the first in March, and before the year was up, we had four units."
What was your capital investment in the beginning, with your first unit?

"About $15,000."
You worked chiefly on credit from the wholesalers?

"Fortunately our credit was good because we had been in business prior to that."
What business had you been in?

"My own establishment, the Edison Electrical Supply Company, in Providence. My associate, Mr. Michaelson, was operating the Low Supply Company, with plumbing, heating, and hardware at that time. He had three stores in the Providence area."
You had built up some capital reserve as a result of this?

"Actually we went into this thing gradually; we did not relinquish our existing business. When we saw the possibilities we disposed of our businesses and concentrated full time on building up the capital reserve after two or three months."
What was included in your first leased department?

"Primarily hardware, electrical supplies, and plumbing. Housewares, which is now the biggest bulk of this business, had already been leased.

Saul Leibow, vice president, Housewares Division,
Zayre Corporation.

"The first thing we added in our second unit was housewares. That was the largest category as far as sales potential was concerned, and today it is still the largest category of all our goods."

How many leased departments did you start in the first year?

"Four."

What per cent of sales did you pay for occupancy?

"Well, it varied from about 7 to 11, depending upon the conditions, the advertising breakdown, and other criteria.

"The Coatsfield Shopping Center (our first lessor) was a soft goods operation; an offshoot of the New York Lace Store, a well-established apparel shop. But outside of soft goods, practically everything was leased. In other words, they knew the apparel business, we knew the hardgoods business, somebody else knew the domestics business, somebody else knew the shoe business, and that was how it went – like a family."

329

You brought in the capital to set up the inventory, and the know-how. Did you have your own warehouse?

"Our reasoning from the beginning was that in mass-merchandising of this type we just could not afford the luxury of a central warehouse. To move our type of goods around was prohibitive not only by weight per dollar but by cubic foot. The trend today is a sort of split operation with some items, such as apparel, in the warehouse and some shipped directly. At that time we made up our minds that we must operate without a central warehouse. We also decided that we must have enough potential volume in each unit to warrant each shipment being made direct from the manufacturer."

What are your biggest operating problems?

"It resolves itself to personnel and a system. Not having a warehouse, the primary difficulty to overcome was setting up an order system. Without a system as foolproof as possible (I would not say foolproof), it would be utterly impossible to operate without a central warehouse. Our turnover would be in jeopardy, our percentage of outs would be prohibitive, and we could not operate. We experimented with various types of systems until we developed what we called the 'SOS' system which we copyrighted, incidentally. That is a self-ordering system which made it clear to a clerk when and what to buy. It is really stock control, with the aim of extracting the greatest turnover of an item with a minimum of outs. The greater your turnover, the smaller your capital investment."

On the average, what kind of a turnover do you get from the department?

"We shoot for about six and three-quarters to seven. In my conventional hardware store, I had a turn of about one to one-and-a-half times a year. That is the other extreme."

What do you include in your present-day line?

"We started at about 1,200 or 1,300 items, as I recall, and we now have about 4,000. The categories are housewares, hardware, automotive (that's counter goods, not gasoline), paints, summer goods (anywhere from chairs and power mowers down to tools), and Christmas trim-a-tree goods. No toys, lighting, or lamps; no major or traffic appliances. That is about the only thing we do not touch. In cookware we sell every conceivable thing. That is the bulk of our business: crockery, chinaware, some forms of stainless steel, and inexpensive silverware."

Do you ever have any trouble with fair-traded items?

"We have been chastised for cutting prices on fair-traded goods, such as Prestone, Corningware, and other national goods. After experimenting, we found we were in too much trouble; we had too many court orders, we had to cease and desist. But when we feel it is mandatory to round out our goods, we do carry fair-traded goods and we sign it so the customer will know that we have no alternative and must charge the full retail on the item."

What is your point of view with regard to loss leaders?

330

"Well, that has been done to death. But we do get subsidies from our operators to a great extent because an item of that nature brings traffic to the entire store. The burden should not be borne by one department. We do get consideration from our operators. We cooperate a few times during the year on specific occasions only."

What happens when the overall store management is very weak?

"I remember two units where it looked to us as though the operator was not capable of running the establishment. We got out ahead of time, even though we had to break the lease. But we would rather take our chances that way than go to a funeral."

What are your plans for expansion? Do you think that there is a future in leased departments, or do you think that it is time to set up your own independent store?

"Well, not knowing exactly what the future holds, we are planning to diversify like everybody else. Nobody likes their eggs all in one basket. In addition to diversifying our units with other major operators, we have opened our first cooperative free-standing unit. By that I mean a sort of junior discount store not associated with soft goods or food, but of limited size, perhaps 15 to 20 thousand square feet. This is at Glen Cove, Long Island, and is a limited line, fast-turnover type of store. I am in this with Mr. Margolis of Marrud, Inc., and one other outfit. It is a cooperative deal but we will still have our identities. It will wind up being a joint venture, not leased; we will all put up capital and pay the rent jointly. We may experiment with bowling alleys. They have been overbuilt, and they are a good buy for this type of operation because they are generally well located, for our purpose, in the suburbs, off main highways, with plenty of parking. These will be free-standing units, and should be very profitable for the simple reason that it will not be necessary to build. By dealing with somebody who has already taken a licking we can get rentals that we can absorb and still operate profitably. We could not build the structure new and operate it profitably.

"We also intend going into department stores on two bases. One is in medium-sized department stores. We are negotiating with a batch of them right now on this basis. They generally have hard goods, in a secondary location in the basement. I do not mean a Jordan Marsh. I mean an $8 million to $10 million operation having a housewares and giftware department whose sales, based on the last statistics I have seen from their publication, were about 30 per cent to 40 per cent of the volume that we could produce with the equivalent footage. We do not mean to say that we can do the same volume per foot in a department store that we are doing at the discount houses, because we are all on one level and are exposed to more people coming in. In a department store we have to act to create more traffic.

"In other words, we would have to have a carefully-planned operation.

331

With the organization we have, we fail to see how any department store in that volume category can compete with us because they could not possibly afford an organization for a potential of say $200,000 to $400,000 in volume a year. We can throw in all the weight, all the ability, all the production, and all the promotion that some of these department stores truly need. An extremely important fact is that there is nothing for a man in a department store outside of the men's department. You do not see them around. If you see a man and a woman in a department store, you will find that she is just dragging him around. He is impatient, and there is no place for him to go or to wander. So we think that we can help the department stores to a tremendous extent, far more than merely the added volume that we can give them."

What sales per square feet do you get normally, on the average, in your discount stores?

"We usually get as much volume per foot as the entire store does, including soft goods. This is unusual because hard goods traditionally does not get the same volume per foot as soft goods, drugs, or anything else."

What is the volume of your smallest and your largest unit, approximately?

"Roughly we run from about $200,000 to a half-million. Strictly in our own departments our average would be about $300,000 to $350,000."

What incentive do your department managers have to do a good job?

"In a conventional business you pay by volume of sales, but we cannot do this. We cannot use the conventional method for the simple reason that, being captive, the increase or decrease of our sales may bear no relation to the efficiency of the manager; whereas in a conventional structure it does. An entire store's volume may go up 10 per cent; but our department may go up only 8 per cent. You cannot reward a man for going up 8 per cent. In fact, he should be punished because he is not even keeping pace. Sales, as such, is only one factor in our rewarding of management. We go by efficiency. On that basis, if he follows our rules then theoretically he is extracting the greatest dollar that is possible. And basically, this is what we pay him for. We don't pay him for filling out forms; we have a minimum of forms. I do not like forms.

"We have a book of procedures and for some years we kept on simplifying them. We were wondering why we did not get a greater degree of compliance. This was because store managers did not understand the procedures. We finally reached a point of no return where we could not simplify any further. We then came to the conclusion that it was not the fact that procedures were simple, because if you took up any particular rule or suggestion with them, they would know and understand it; what scared these people was the book as such. The fact that there was a book was enough to scare the average man or woman, especially at clerk level. It was a tome. The individual instructions were simple. Collectively, it scared them, and they shied away.

"So we set up what we called a 'point system.' We took all the things we wanted them to do and broke it down into extremely elementary, self-explanatory statements and suggestions with analogies. A man could operate a unit with 80 points. In other words, we sold them the procedures on the installment plan. The supervisors would assign the most important points to the stores that were not efficient in this category. We ran a census structure based upon compliance with these points. Now remember we were primarily interested in these points because they were simple, understandable, and measurable. That third point was important, since we could not measure efficiency on opinions."

How can you measure?

"The points are so simplified that anybody walking into the store can say yes or no, not maybe. The minute there is a maybe, then there is too much opinion, and you cannot pay a man or pin him down on opinion. Today's opinion is yesterday's something else."

What are some of the points?

"They cover every facet of the department operation, and they are constantly being revised as we learn. For example, if I put a label on an item, it must be clean and clear. A label is your silent salesman. It must be placed where the customer can see it. It must be well inked, the type must be large. It must not cover any important selling message on the product. It must be placed with reference to its display so that it will always be visible. It must be clean or be replaced. It must have permanent adhesive to eliminate pilferage or label-switching, and so forth. Broken down very, very simply, it must be placed so that when you walk in you can see whether or not the 'abc' is or is not done.

"The whole thing is built on details, and if you start with these details you end up with a business. Unless we indoctrinate our people with these things, especially our executives, we would never have a successful business. There must be implementation, recognition, and follow-through. These are the three basic ingredients. What we are worst on is follow-through. It is human nature to constantly shy away from the humdrum and the basic rules. In this incentive program, we pay for the accomplishment of certain points; but we pay even more for the maintenance of these points. It is just as easy to do something correctly as not, and until and unless it becomes a way of life we have not truly educated. It is working."

Do you have an IBM system?

"All we have is a tabulator and punch cards used primarily for payroll, for certain computations, and for printing the so-called back sheets, the basis of our SOS system."

Are the reorders centralized here or are they regional?

"Departments order for themselves. They buy and sell. The only things our units do not do is to pay the bills. We are here to guide them, educate them, and pay their bills.

333

"Each manager is an individual. Our department operator must be a better-than-average individual, with brighter-than-average intelligence, in order to run the unit. No matter how well we do, we cannot afford the so-called managerial talent which the store itself can afford. We are continually educating our managers, and we have to plan everything down to their particular level."

How about the supervisors?

"They are yesterday's managers."

What are their duties?

"Their duties are no different from any ordinary supervisor. They make sure that things are done as we want them done. They have their own procedure book; of course the basic thing is to see that the unit is following our rules."

How about your markup?

"Remember we are captive and our operators, no matter what we mark goods, will automatically say it is too much. The primary issue is not markup or what we buy it for, but is it in the line? Is it within the framework of the store's policy? Is it competitive? Does the customer have the impression that this is a low price? You cannot be low in everything. In general, our markup varies from 18 per cent to 35 per cent. It varies from department to department, and from location to location to a minor degree."

In what way does your operation differ from other leased departments?

"First, we operate without a warehouse. We differ not only in physical structure, but in our entire philosophy. What is average? We are not happy with averages. So until we extract the fastest and the largest dollar, we are not happy in an individual store. At this point there is not enough variation between our stores as to the lines they carry. I have a team working on this and before this year is up we hope to go another giant step towards decentralization.

"We are attempting to make merchants out of our people. Take a conventional department store, for example, in soft goods. To the best of my knowledge, the buyer spends his time either in the field looking for his supplies or on the floor. Well, this is an ideal arrangement; he is eating his mistakes, he is in constant communication with the customer. He gets their actions and reactions. He goes out and corrects himself on a continual basis. It is alive, it is vibrant. But you see, a centralized structure can not do this. These buyers are isolated and insulated. They are fixed, and no matter how good their judgment, it cannot possibly encompass the intelligence of over a hundred stores in the field. A buyer is swayed and persuaded by salesmen, his own likes and dislikes, and by history – history is dead!"

Do you have catalogs of merchandise that you suggest to managers?

"No, it is in the form of their back order sheets and bulletins. When we change a line or introduce a new line or new items, we advise them; we ship quantities that we think are in line. But the manager can cancel any or all of this particular order if he feels that it is not what he wants. In other words we try to win them over on our side and make them merchants who have decisions to make. It develops them as human beings. Otherwise, it is just a routine, mechanical situation. That is why we try to simplify our points to the very, very basics, and not try to brainwash and stifle them. This is decentralization. It is elementary; I do not see how it could be done any other way. They have done a wonderful job for us on that."

Do you feel that you can do a better job as a lessee than a firm itself can do? In your opinion, can you go into a chain as large as Zayre's and make more money for them than they can themselves? Do they let you finance the inventory because they do not want to put the capital in?

"No, they have the capital; they have gone public."

Then it must be because they feel that you do a better job than they could do. What is it that you know that they do not know?

"It is the same thing that made them grow – a knowledge and an organization of their business; our knowledge and our organization back them up. We both have know-how in our own fields. It would be no different from my opening up a discount house and attempting to put soft goods in it. I would be dependent upon other people for their knowledge. The primary reason is we have an organization. Our secret weapon is know-how and background. My associate and I have spent our lifetimes in hard goods, in fabrication, in retail, in wholesale, and in chains. It is simple to run a business under one roof. Almost anybody can do that. But you run bits and pieces all over the country and try to wrap them up and make a profit. I was 17 years with the Low Supply Company; we had a hardware chain in New England, in Hartford, Springfield, and Lynn. I learned the hard way. I was 17 years old when I started as a clerk and I wound up as a president. People say it is the lessor versus the lessee. There is no 'versus.' If you are good, it makes no difference where you are sitting; if you are good and you are good for each other, you make a profit. There is no versus. That was an artificial thing that was injected and does not belong, and the trade publications have blown it up out of all magnitude. You find operators who go bankrupt, and leased departments who go bankrupt. If you do not know the answers and do not build an organization, then you have to get off the wagon and push – no more free rides."

Do you have a research department?

"It is communications. Our best research is communications from the store as to what the customer wants, what she is talking about, what she would like to have, when she would like to have it, what she would like to pay for it, what she does not want. In fact, we have inaugurated a separate crew for this purpose to continuously analyze and survey. We want to make this decentralization as effective as possible; at this point it is not. We have a long way to go."

How about advertising?

"A lot depends on the policies of our lessors. In recent years we have created our own promotions. Typical of that is our dollarama sales which have increased our business 8- to 20-fold. In many instances the entire store volume has increased from four to ten times. This is a result of our creativity, which once and for all throws out the concept that we are cashing in on what soft goods are bringing in. Our operators are beginning to understand and to appreciate it, and they are now chasing us for continuous promotions."

Do you have a standard lease contract?

"It is basically the same; we never look at our contracts. If we ever have to look at our contracts, there is trouble, and we have not had it so far, thank God. We just operate like a family. This is truly so. You have to study the fine print. With differences, we whack it out and tear each other's hair out. We learn from each other. If this mutually helpful relationship does not exist, then neither we nor they have a reason for existence. It is as simple as that.

"Mechanization has a specific place, but it does not take the place of people. I think that is a sin. How can you ever know an individual's capacity? Our tendency is to face our people with far more than the average capacity, and then they find themselves. This is how we develop them."

The A & P and First National are suffering from arteriosclerosis, as a result of the computer because their managers have no fun.

"They have taken the interest out. They have, in effect, brainwashed them. They are not interested. Even if the computer came up with all kinds of mistakes, they would not give a darn. They have lost their interest; they are not participating. People have to contribute in order to be able to live with themselves. They have to grow and be important. Their ego is awfully important, and the machine knocks their egos to pieces. I do not like it. I have fought computerization. Suppose it looks as if it may rain. Well, people will buy as many umbrellas when it looks as if it might rain as when it is raining. A computer cannot tell you this."

The Ward Company – Major Appliance Licensee

(Headquarters are in Richmond, Virginia)

The Ward Company is a rapidly growing retailer in an extremely competitive field. At the present time, it operates seven conventional stores in the Richmond area and 45 licensed departments in large discount stores throughout the Eastern and Midwestern parts of the country. The larger part of its sales is made through the licensed departments. For the fiscal year ending

Leased Departments

March 1968 total sales were $27,200,000 and earnings $458,000 as compared to $1,436,000 in 1960 and $23,000 earnings.

The company began operating in 1949 as a small retail store selling only television sets on Broad Street in Richmond, Va. At the time television was in its infancy and was sold as an addition to the regular product line of larger department stores.

Ward's increased its sales by broadening its merchandise lines to include radios, record players, and related home entertainment items which constitute 60 per cent of sales while 40 per cent is provided by refrigerators, stoves, freezers, and other gas and electric appliances. All products have accepted "brand names" and are nationally advertised.

In 1960 the company opened two licensed departments – one in Richmond and one in Atlanta. These outlets sold merchandise similar to that of their conventional stores. Since that time, 18 additional licensed departments have been opened in discount stores throughout the country.

These departments are located in large discount stores, the majority of which are closed membership stores, such as G.E.M. which limit their customers to employees of the Armed Services and to employees of companies that have government contracts. All members are screened for credit and are required to pay a nominal membership fee. These stores customarily contain over 100,000 square feet of selling area and are located in suburban areas. All the different departments that specialize in certain areas are leased to stores that specialize in that particular area. The merchandising area leased to Ward Co. varies from 3,100 to 4,800 square feet.

Said Lawrence Yoffe, director of personnel for the Ward Company:

"The idea behind the closed door approach is not to emphasize fixtures but to have a sterile, cold blue color as a background for selling with only the merchandise standing out, almost the opposite of what you and I would call good merchandising techniques. The idea is to highlight the merchandise, not the fixtures; nothing can hang from the ceiling. 'Here is a value, here is my price tag, take me.' Not 'look how gorgeous I am.'

"The closed door stores advertise through bulletins which they mail once a month. In GEM it is called the *Journal* and in GEX it is called the *Bulletin* – a kind of Christmas catalog in two to four colors. Ward supplies a page or two. Almost all closed-door advertising is done in this way with the item and the price and possibly some copy. The principals do the layout in their central office and re-write the copy to make it fit into the format of the whole bulletin. Of late they have started doing more newspaper advertising. In the closed door store we have found the store handout mimeographed advertising sheet very effective, even if crudely done by department managers. It is given out at the check-in counter at the front door. This has been found very very effective. It is used for specials or for new items.

"The management of the closed door store is responsible for generating

337

the traffic. That is their prime responsibility. They have a member relations man in each store who is assigned the task of recruiting members; he goes to city groups, etc. Ward has departments in 22 closed door discount stores. The expansion of the closed door operation is limited since there are limits to the number of members you can bring under the umbrellas of government employees. You have to be in metropolitan areas.

"We are required to be under the market on everything because members do comparison shopping. Department stores generally are not our competitors. Our best competition comes from sharp appliance dealers such as Lechmere. We can undersell Lechmere. If we can't undersell anyone, we have to avoid the item by replacing it with another brand. There are no sales. The idea to maintain is that every day is a sale day. Price is emphasized but not special prices. Ward has been very successful with the closed door companies. They have not yet had enough experience with open door discounters to tell which is best for their operation. Three of the five open door stores they are in are run by closed door operators. The company has 26 departments in all. The job of the manager of the closed door store is much simpler than in the open door type since many management problems are centralized. There is a departmental checkout and the cash register tapes are inspected every day from the beginning to the ending number with verifications of refunds or over-rings, etc.

"Of total closed-door volume, depending on the season of the year, up to 25 per cent is done by Ward in major appliances and television as well as radios and small accessories. Ward deals with local distributors in the areas in which we operate – that is in metropolitan areas. Our approximate mark-up is between 22 per cent and 24 per cent. The company can cover its operating expenses and come out with a profit at 20 per cent. There is a theft problem since it is not hard to pick up a tape recorder or a Sony radio. Ward does not like to chain them down since they feel they may be chaining down a sale by chaining down the item. They assume that theft runs about 2 per cent. Ward's markup on refrigerators and washing machines is lower than that on radio and TV. White goods pulls down the markup. In TV's, radios, etc., there is certain element of style – not as much standardization. We have found Sony radios and tape recorders very acceptable on the market.

"Closed door stores take over a lot of our management problems such as advertising. They have allowed us to do more newspaper advertising and have even paid for part of it. This is negotiable.

"In each of our departments there are on the average, seven people: a stock boy, a cashier, at least two sales people, a manager, and an assistant manager. Salesmen will earn anywhere from $8,000 to $15,000. Eight is about average. None makes below six. They operate on a guarantee of approximately $90 a week or else on a straight 3 per cent commission. They all operate on a guarantee or on a commission, whichever is greater. Ward's avoids part-time people as much as possible and prefers not to hire anyone under 20. Department managers have a good deal of opportunity to exercise individual initiative in buying and merchandising. Closed-door leases stipulate that lessees must undersell competition. Ward's has some very capable women salesmen. One woman makes $9,000 on a 2 per cent commission. (The company was one of the first in the city of Richmond to integrate its office.)

"Because of a period of rapid expansion the company took people without experience and trained them. The personnel department looks for people who are ambitious, flexible and adaptable in their thinking. We want creators and innovators.

"The company contributes up to 6 per cent on a pension plan. There are also stock option plans and the company will pay 100 per cent for books and course fees."

Ward's general plan of operation is to offer brand name merchandise at prices below the prevailing retail price in conventional stores. The department licensees are required to sell under the name of the particular store and the store owner furnishes overall management, utilities, and coordinates the department, providing advertising which is usually direct mail to its customers. The licensed departments have no facilities for serving or repairing their merchandise and trade-ins are not accepted. The company owns the display fixtures in almost all of its licensed departments.

All of Ward's leased department accounts receivable are handled by the stores and without recourse to Ward's thus eliminating the overhead of a credit and collection department. They do not guarantee that the customer will pay; this is the responsibility of the store.

The majority of the company's license arrangements provide for terms of one year, but may be terminated by the store owner upon 30 or 60 days notice. The terms are usually based upon percentage rental on gross sales in the department. Some agreements call for a fixed rental to be applied against the percentage rental.

The success the company experienced in its licensed departments led to the acquisition in August, 1965 of a large discount house operated by Vornado in Norfolk. The plans are to lease the departments to specialists in various fields while operating under an independent name, "The Carousel." This open door store has 126,000 square feet of selling area.

Ward's employs over 250 salaried persons and 60 sales people work on a commission basis. Electronic data processing equipment is used extensively to monitor and control the operations. Plans are now being made for the incorporation of a large, high-speed computer into the system.

Ward's believes in encouraging a man to create the scope of his own job. He is put in a position and is given responsibility. If he has the capacity to

339

accept responsibility and can develop his job he will be given additional responsibility as he feels he can handle it. A manager in a location is creative in that he has the ultimate responsibility in hiring and firing his staff. He has the responsibility for the relationship with the owners of the stores in which Ward's operates and to maintain that relationship in the best interests of the company and the department. He has the responsibility for the pricing of his own merchandise and for the development of a merchandising plan for his stores which may vary from city to city. He has responsibility for buying and planning. He can determine his own budget and inventory of goods and their classification and in the long run, Ward's will know if his judgment was good or bad, and whether the manager learns from his mistakes. It is the manager's judgment; his decision as to how he should balance these things and the expenses of the operation. Ward's will review it with him and point out what areas are creating his problem and point out where his operation is profitable or non-profitable.

Ward's policy is one of management by exception which means that management is constantly looking for areas where something is outstanding, whether that operation is good or bad. If it is good, Ward's tries to determine what it is doing right; and if it is bad, then management analyzes it to find out why it is bad and to improve the operation. All the stores benefit by example.

Ward's has attempted to develop a corporate spirit that derives its strength from company men at all levels who are willing to accept responsibility and make decisions. The organization attempts to preserve this by maintaining a creative work atmosphere.

The first step in the creation of this atmosphere is to allow people freedom to make decisions, to create, and to assume responsibility permitting a man to utilize his capacity to the fullest. The first step is to eliminate a formal atmosphere. The use of the word "sir" in conversations is eliminated. The store manager has to feel that any man in the main office is accessible to him, so that he treats his own people in the same way. The second step is to set up an informal communication system that promotes an unrestricted exchange of ideas among all levels of management. And finally, Ward's creates a feeling of respect for all employees, for their ideas and as persons.

Said Yoffe, "We have found it very difficult to instill creativity in many of our managers. Some people will never be reached. They say, 'It just is not true, and I am not going to go along with it because I know I'm going to get caught doing something wrong and I'll lose my job. I don't care what he says. He's just dangling a carrot in front of my nose and trying to lead me on and get the best out of me and then throw me aside.' This kind of cynical approach or distrustful approach limits a man's own career. There's very little you can do if he doesn't accept it, if he doesn't feel this spirit that exists in the group. We've gotten men from other organizations where the political approach to their positions and growth was the dominant factor; as a result these persons must be extremely intelligent to overcome this kind of background. The further down the levels of management you go, the more difficult it becomes.

"The company's growth can go in many directions; several new licensed departments are planned for 1969. Depending on the success of the discount store opened in Richmond, Ward's might expand by opening more licensed operations around the country. A third consideration is the expansion into other lines such as the recent acquisition of Murmic of Delaware, a houseware licensee located in New England. This licensee is now operating seven licensed departments in stores where Ward's also has departments.

"The only real limitation to growth is the availability of capable managers. There is a definite need for men who will be responsible for their operations. This is partially because of the large distances between departments.

"Expansion in the number of outlets has brought with it a major problem. In the beginning Ward's had a few good stores with good managers running them. These men did not have a manual of guidelines to work from. They exercised a lot of responsibility and made most of the decisions concerning their operations. Today Ward's has many more stores and managers. These men are not as select a group as Ward's had in the beginning, but they have a manual and guidelines to help them run their departments. They are still responsible for merchandising and advertising their stores and handling all the personnel under them. In the future, as Ward's opens more and more stores, it is going to become difficult to find the kind of individual capable of managing its departments. It will be necessary to reorganize with one man handling all the merchandise, one man doing the advertising, and so forth.

"District managers are responsible to the general manager for the stores in their area. The responsibility given to the store managers comes through the district manager. Because of this, the amount of freedom given a particular store manager will depend on the particular district manager. Geography will influence this since some districts are so large it is impossible for the district manager to get around to all his stores every week; the personality of the district manager is the main determinant of the amount of freedom each manager has in his operation."

Ward's is a strong competitor in most of its markets depending on the caliber of its store and main office management. Since the stores are spread throughout the country, local store managers must make decisions affecting the future of their operations. Ward's uses this fact as a means of recruiting better store managers. There is a lot of opportunity for an ambitious man because of the size of the company and the amount of responsibility it delegates to its men. In return, Ward's asks a man to work long hours and to bear the responsibility for his own operation.

341

A department manager makes decisions every day that affect the profitability and future of his operation; many of these decisions will be without benefit of advice or direction from supervisors. Managers are actually responsible for merchandising and are supplied with IBM reports and information about past performances that will help them make decisions; the ultimate responsibility lies with them. There are many risks. Some people have made too many mistakes because they have not accepted the guidance given to them or they have been reluctant to make decisions. It is important to give a man the opportunity to make decisions so that he can get some return for the hours of work that he puts into the job.

One of the secrets of Ward's success is that the company is extremely careful to select only quality products for their departments; another is that they have trained sales personnel so that they can answer the consumer's questions regarding these complicated products and help consumers to intelligently select the products best suited to their needs.

In 1960 management decided that the new marketing development known variously as discount or "mass-merchandise stores" presented an excellent opportunity. Ward's began leasing appliances departments in such stores and have expanded with the industry. Management is cautious in its selection of the firms with whom it becomes associated. Last year more than ten lease proposals were rejected for each new one accepted. Carefully avoided are those firms which appear to be expanding beyond their financial means and personnel ability, or who lack experience and understanding in the mass-merchandising field.

Ward's personnel policies are unique and constitute one of the fundamental elements contributing toward its growth. This year $100,000 was budgeted for personnel training and development. Company policy is to promote from within whenever possible. Incentives for its people include all the usual fringe benefits such as stock options and a substantial profit-sharing retirement program. Ward's has been fortunate in attracting and keeping a remarkable group of dedicated, capable, bright, young career men who are devoted to the company and are determined to build a strong, sound, and profitable operation.

Motivation for a group of people to work toward a common objective stems from the absence of company politics, the profit-sharing plan, stock options, and other benefits that favorably affect attitude, as well as the company philosophy that supervisors must take the responsibility for the acts of those responsible to them.

To buttress its program of personnel development, Ward's created two new positions this year: the director of sales training and promotion has the responsibility for training Ward's sales staff as well as developing sales promotions; the personnel development director has the responsibility for the establishment and direction of training programs for the merchandise staff.

At the end of 1968, Ward's outlets were in: Albany, Buffalo and Rochester, N.Y.; Albuquerque, N.M.; Akron and Canton, Ohio; Atlanta, Ga.; Birmingham, Huntsville, Mobile and Montgomery, Ala.; Boston, Mass.; Camden, N.J.; Charleston, S.C.; Dallas and Ft. Worth, Tex.; Hampton, Norfolk and Richmond, Va.; Hartford, Conn.; Indianapolis, Ind.; Louisville, Ky.; Milwaukee, Wisc.; New Orleans, La.; Oklahoma City and Tulsa' Okla.; Omaha, Neb.; Sioux City, Ia.

Forest City Distributors, Inc.

(STATIONERY LESSEE INTEGRATES VERTICALLY; FOREST CITY GOES FROM WHOLESALING INTO MANUFACTURING)

Forest City Distributors, Inc., of Garden City, Long Island, N.Y., reversed a time-honored procedure of a manufacturer moving through the jobbing-wholesaling phase into retailing. Forest City started out as a leased discount stationery department chain, later added a wholesaling division, and is now in the manufacturing field.

"The movement by manufacturers down to wholesaling and finally to retailing is fairly common," observed president Herbert J. Freedman, "but how many companies have made the trip in the other direction?"

The company added a wholly-owned paper products factory to its present 18 leased discount stationery departments, and a wholesaling division serving other discount and conventional department stores. The new plant, which Forest operates under the name of "Alden Paper," is capable of producing $3 million annually in finished paper products. In addition, the company plans to acquire a luggage factory, and a lithography plant. The program is designed to enhance the firm's position with landlords by providing guaranteed supply sources, making easier development of new and promotional brand names possible, and using more effective packaging.

Forest City services the stationery departments of a major department store chain with ten outlets, as well as other department and discount stores. The firm is about to open up a large free-standing location carrying stationery, toys, drugs, and sundries in association with other distributors in those fields.

Discounting with a Difference

The Gibson Products Company[1]

Anyone who meets Herbert R. Gibson, Sr., founder and board chairman of Gibson Products Company, and his wife Belva, cannot fail to be impressed. At 66 Gibson is six feet two inches tall and weighs 220 pounds. A farmboy who made good, his extraordinary career is an impressive illustration of how American free enterprise works. His wife is equally active in the business and is his constant companion and closest advisor. The family lives in a $270,000 Mediterranean style ranch house with an indoor swimming pool, in suburban Dallas, Texas.

Not only did Gibson succeed beyond his wildest dreams but he brought success to many associates. Twenty-two of his franchisees pilot their own planes; both Mr. and Mrs. Gibson hold pilot's licenses. During the May, 1967 Gibson Trade Show he signed up five new franchisees. Those who do not meet his standards are chastised freely by Gibson. Franchisees are fiercely loyal among themselves and help each other at new store openings; they also form combines for the purpose of opening additional units.

In the *Modern Retailer* Gibson supplement of July, 1967, associate editor Sidney Davis wrote: "Gibson is proud to the point of boastful yet his accomplishments are for all to see. He talks of Chicago, Kansas City and Minneapolis in terms of 'blitz' and 'invasion'; dismisses most competition as 'not discount' and points towards one billion dollar sales by 1970.

344

Discounting with a Difference

"He is the antithesis of the retail establishment. Gibson rejects the computer, has no merchandise managers, piles goods high on seven foot fixtures and prefers to communicate directly with store managers and franchise holders.

"To the uninitiated, Gibson Stores are a vague, loosely constructed organization, each with diverse business interests, seemingly opening endless numbers of stores with little regard for location. In retrospect this outside viewpoint may be one of Gibson's biggest advantages. The chain, in reality, has been carefully planned and nurtured; its growth is self-perpetuating . . ."

Gibson Products Company is the parent corporation for Gibson Discount Centers, an empire of 290 franchised discount stores in the 21-state area of Alabama, Arkansas, Colorado, Florida, Georgia, Iowa, Kansas, Kentucky, Louisiana, Minnesota, Mississippi, Missouri, Montana, Nebraska, New Mexico, Oklahoma, South Dakota, Tennessee, Texas, Utah, Wyoming and Hawaii. The chain's projected growth is 50 units yearly.

Herbert R. Gibson was born in Berryville, Ark. He got his start in business dealings while in his teens when his father gave him some livestock and agreed to provide the feed. At the age of 14, Gibson began buying furs for the St. Louis Fur Co.; at 17 he opened a barber and beauty shop catering to women and children. He had four such shops in Wichita, Kan., when the depression ruined his business.

In 1932 Gibson opened a wholesale business in Little Rock. Despite the depression, he prospered and moved into successively larger quarters. In 1953 he was operating 34 wholesale houses in ten states, selling to retail merchants and wagon jobbers, when he decided to convert to discount operations in April of that year. His first discount store was in Abilene, Tex., and for a while a new store opened every two weeks, until seven were in operation. These first Gibson discount stores were conversions – wholesale firms remade into retail discount operations – and were all owned by J. R. Gibson. The eleven company-owned stores and the franchised outlets carry a full line of soft and hard goods aimed at the middle income group.

It is significant to note that from its unique wholesale-retail orientation came the natural development of franchising. Gibson also realized that small cities were the way to go and concentrated on 20,000 to 50,000 population areas in the Southwest.

Gibson merchandises its unique franchise network very much the way a wholly-owned chain of stores operates. Merchandise is centrally bought ($30 million in orders at the August, 1966 show). In most instances goods are drop-shipped.

The Gibson franchise gives the operator access to more than 20,000 items in reputable merchandise; some 11,000 are name brand items. Gibson has six buyers who go to major manufacturers and to all shows in major markets to make selections of the merchandise Gibson plans to sell during the year.

Herbert R. Gibson, chairman of the board,
Gibson Products Company.

Major manufacturers also present merchandise samples at annual spring and fall trade shows sponsored by Gibson Products Co. in Dallas. The Gibson organization then brings all managers and buyers from its franchised stores into Dallas for a one-week show. More than $30 million in business was written at one show in August, 1965. Pre-printed order forms embracing every line in the show are mailed to all stores a month preceding the show. An order processing room, set up with 50 adding machines and calculators, keeps tabs on purchase totals.

The franchise organization also provides an advertising mat service for the chain, representing more than 1,000 expected best-sellers. A pre-printed tabloid is made available to about 120 of the larger stores for direct neighborhood distribution in spring, summer, and fall. The total approximated 12 million copies in 1966. The tabloid supplements newspaper advertising.

Further benefits in cost reduction are attained through direct carload or truckload shipments from the manufacturer to larger stores. Freight savings items, such as lawn and garden equipment, paints, and motor oils,

346

average 10 per cent in the west central and southwestern states. Warehousing of merchandise is held to an absolute minimum thus gaining additional savings in the elimination of handling and warehouse costs. An added factor is the emphasis on larger, economy, or family sizes in certain lines of merchandise. These savings give Gibson a decided advantage over other retailers.

Essentially, Gibson Products is a buying organization for the franchisers who follow its policies and operating procedures. Merchandise includes drugs and toiletries, soft goods, hardware, sporting goods, school supplies, auto accessories, and garden and lawn equipment.

The franchise marketing mix formula is simple. With competent store management with adequate financial backing, you turn on a steady stream of volume buying power, reputable merchandise, pricing acumen, and direct freight shipments at lowest possible bulk rates. Blend in a minimum of warehousing to keep the middle man out. Add timely promotions and pricing to assure maximum savings to customers. Through the franchise arrangement Gibson Products sets up buying sources, arranges prices and terms, and has shipments of merchandise made direct to the several Gibson Discount Centers. No franchiser is required to buy any specific items through the central offices in Seagoville, Tex.; if he wishes he can make direct purchases from a manufacturer. Franchise arrangements currently make available the cumulative buying power of approximately $150 million in annual sales. Says Herbert Gibson, "The most important thing in granting a franchise is the man, his financial status, the town, the location within the town, and the parking area. If it is a town with high prices in retail stores and we can line up the right location, then we know we can get the business. We need a building with a minimum of 30,000 square feet and an initial investment of $200,000 for a 30,000 square-foot store; we need more for the larger ones. Discounting is mass-merchandising and it can not be done in a limited space."

Pharmacies are proving to be big traffic pullers for Gibson Discount Centers, and these prescription departments are the major exception to the rule against leased departments in Gibson stores. (The other exception is leased jewelry departments in twelve stores.) There are over 70 pharmacies and about a third of them are owned and operated by respective store management, with about two-thirds in the leased category. Inasmuch as a pharmacy requires the services of registered pharmacists, Gibson prefers to have pharmacists committed to ownership interest in its operation. Gibson claims he can show his customers a 25 per cent or higher saving on almost everything in prescription drug lines compared to usual drug outlets. And he offers 30 per cent to 40 per cent savings on nationally advertised vitamins carried in his prescription departments.

H. R. Gibson, Sr. foresees an annual sales increase of $500 to $600 million resulting from a projected "blitz" of several metro markets. Total

347

sales for 1968 were one billion dollars as compared with $334 million in 1965 and $190 million in 1964. The next two years (1969–70) will find Gibson moving into most major metropolitan areas in the Southwest and Southeast. We are moving into the Northeast and Midwest in 1968–69. The prime target for 1966 was Dallas. Gibson Discount Stores "bombed" the Dallas area with the simultaneous opening of seven discount stores. The stores range from 44,000 to 65,000 square feet; all have a supermarket as well as the usual range of Gibson merchandise. Before the grand opening, Gibson bought 80-page advertising sections in both Dallas Sunday papers and had saturation spots on television and radio. Gibson now (1968) has 434 outlets.

Many existing Gibson stores have either expanded or are undergoing expansion this year. Gibson views these expansions as equal in importance to new stores, since he knows he is going to get more business. In every case, where land permits, new store buildings are being planned for expansion when merited. The minimum initial size preferred is 30,000 to 50,000 square feet, and he predicts discount stores will find it necessary to have 40,000 to 60,000 square feet as a rule and more if the population is between 100,000 to 150,000. A majority of Gibson stores are under multiple ownership, with several franchisers operating 5 to 16 stores. Ninety-nine per cent of Gibson items are priced under $25; with the other 1 per cent in guns and hardware. Gibson will continue emphasis on name brand merchandise.

Gibson thinks that the saturation point in the number of discount houses is still five or six years away. The glamor of discounting has not worn off, but the public is beginning to shop only at those stores that give them quality merchandise and good prices every day. Gibson does not see the traditional stores and the discounters borrowing each other's methods until the two find a common meeting ground. According to Gibson, what most department stores are doing is simply moving the bargain basement upstairs and calling it a discount department. This, he says, does not make them discounters because most are not selling any cheaper now than they did ten years ago.

"Our franchise stores operate much in the same way as the stores I personally own except, of course, for the monthly fee which is based upon their sales volume figures. Up to the first million in retail sales the fee is fixed. After that, it is based on a percentage of sales."[1] Gibson points out that he will not let everybody who wishes to operate under the Gibson banner come in "unless they have at least a 20,000 square-foot building. And we do not want them tied up only on a short lease. With as many items as we carry, it requires around $125,000 or more to open a store. For example, a 30,000 to 40,000 square-foot store requires an inventory of close to $300,000 to stock properly. This is a large operation."

A Gibson franchise store receives certain services from the organization which operates very much like a national buying concern. "We buy the merchandise for them, we contract for it, and we make arrangements with

348

the manufacturers so that they get the merchandise directly. We advise them on the proper merchandising for their vicinity, the size of the orders they need for the size of the building they are in. Our sources of supply and our buying offices are made available, and they can completely merchandise the franchise operator's store for him. We keep sending him bulletins about new items and price changes and so on."

"We offer our advertising men to set up their advertising policy. And, if they want, at a very small additional cost, we can furnish them with four or five of our own well-trained employees who can help them set up their store. In addition, when a new franchise store wants to open, the operator can obtain fixtures built at Gibson's own shop. Our entire outlay in fixtures will run between $25,000 and $30,000. But it is cash registers which are the big cost today. It runs about half the fixture cost."

Gibson tries to visit every store at least twice a year, but in the past two or three years, he has been expanding so fast that he has not had time to get around as often as he would wish. Most of the stores Gibson is building today will run from 28,000 to 48,000 square feet, and he has been able to put these buildings up for considerably less than $8 to $10 per square foot. Most of them run in the neighborhood of $6 to $6.50 per square foot. They have a 12-inch wall of glazed brick, plate glass all the way across, and tiled ceilings – and they are all air-conditioned. Gibson cites, as a price-saving factor, the fact that his is basically a "country operation." In bigger cities it would cost a lot more money.

Gibson himself is one of the suppliers of his stores. He is a drug manufacturer and wholesaler and supplies the stores with a full line of health and beauty aids and cosmetics. He sells drug items to other discounters and to the major supermarkets in Texas. He is also a record rack merchandiser. "We handle the top lines, including RCA Victor, Columbia, Capitol, Decca, and Dot." As in the case of drugs, cosmetics, and health and beauty aids, Gibson not only services his own stores, but also other discount houses, supermarkets, and, surprisingly, record racks.

"We sell our merchandise at a profit. We do not even advertise loss leaders – they have no place in our merchandising framework. We believe in selling everything at the lowest possible price. And yet, we make our markup all the time, because our overhead is a lot less than our competitors, I believe. This is why we can sell merchandise cheaper than most."

At the same time, Gibson is not trying to get into cut-price wars or to demoralize the market. He does not sell on credit, even though he does have a layaway plan – at no interest. Gibson wants to be associated with quality. He wants his customers to see the name Gibson and know it is the cheapest place in town to buy merchandise.

Experimentation plays an important part in keeping Gibson's overhead low. For instance, he tests displays first in five or six stores. If they are good, he uses them in all his stores; he discourages a lot of in-store manufacturer's materials. He standardizes on things that come out of Seagoville.

Said Gibson, "Another thing that is considerably different in our operation is that we are not and never have been solely self-service stores. We have people in every department to wait on customers, except the drug department, which is 100 per cent self-service." Gibson has also been consolidating departments to reduce overhead. For example, sporting goods, hardware, automotive, and paint are all in one department. Gibson is primarily hard goods oriented. Apparel departments are staple oriented. No style merchandise is carried; accordingly, soft goods return only a comparatively minor percentage of total store sales which is consistent with the average of 10 per cent of store space it occupies.

About 2 per cent of Gibson's sales goes for advertising. Around 90 per cent of this is spent on newspaper advertising and on catalogs. Says Gibson, "We spent very little with television and radio, except when we are opening a new store, and then we advertise on a saturation basis. Otherwise, it is hard to sell merchandise over television and radio – we have never been able to put our finger on how it can pay off. Besides, we cannot compete with the big national concerns who have all the big programs in prime time all sewed up, second and third rate time is very poor, I think."

The Worldwide PX

Ranking as one of the nation's biggest retail operators and strung out all over the globe is a vast exchange system patronized by almost nine million U.S. servicemen and their dependents. According to a *Newsweek* article of January 17, 1966 (page 72), the Army and Air Force Exchange Service (A & AFES) has annual sales of $1.2 billion while the Navy Ships Store Office (NSSO) sales run about $686 million per year at 993 outlets on ship and shore. The Marine Corps' 41 PX's have annual sales of $93 million and the Coast Guard's outlets total sales are $8 million annually.

Since most overhead costs are absorbed by the military and because it pays no taxes, there are many bargains. According to *Newsweek*, the average PX markup is 18 per cent as opposed to the 27 per cent of most discount stores, and the 38 per cent to 40 per cent of department stores. Combined exchange profits of about $100 million a year are plowed back into military welfare and recreation programs.

[1]The latter part of this article summarizes an interview with H. R. Gibson in *Discount Merchandiser*, July, 1963. Vol. 3, no. 7, p. 38.

Discounting with a Difference

There is a 41,600 square-foot PX in Wiesbaden, Germany with a parking lot for 1,000 cars and a movie theater. Navy Aircraft carriers, it is said, are floating discount houses. Practically every variety of goods and services are provided. Headquarters of the two big exchange services are in New York City. Staffs of retailing experts use sophisticated management controls to sell each year 1.8 billion packs of cigarettes, 100 million hamburgers, 10 million combs and 100,000 bicycles. Customer demands sometimes defy normal inventory controls; a tremendous but apparently inexplicable run on mouthwash in Vietnam was traced to its use by servicemen to offset the heavy chlorine taste in the water supply. An extraordinary increase in the sale of sanitary napkins was explained by their use in cleaning 81-millimeter mortars. PX's are probably the military man's most appreciated fringe benefit and a big morale booster to boot.

Mass Merchandising Abroad

Although supermarkets have been accepted in many foreign countries, the mass-merchandising of non-foods, with a few exceptions, has been accepted with reservations only within the past few years. There has been a reluctance on the part of consumers to change traditional shopping habits. In many areas the government makes special efforts to protect entrenched small retailers who could not survive serious competition. Mass-merchandisers abroad encounter many problems. Low-income populations are unaccustomed to self service, impulse-buying in the American manner. They are slow and deliberate in making even the smallest buying decisions. A shopping trip is considered a social occasion with an opportunity to chat with friends. Americans unfamiliar with foreign zoning and regulatory codes often find themselves in unanticipated legal difficulties.

Canada

Unlike the Bureau of the Census in the United States the Dominion Bureau of Statistics at Ottawa compiles data on discount department stores which

352

they define in the following manner: "The outlet must sell the same wide range of goods that are sold in the more traditional department stores and be popularly described as a discount operation." In 1963 the Bureau listed the following as Canadian discounters: Towers Marts, GEM Stores, Frederick's Department Stores, Banner Discount Department Stores, Miracle Mart, Topps Discount Department Store, Hamilton Harvey and Son, Mon-Mart Discount Department Stores, Freimart Stores, Woolco Department Stores, Zeller's Country Fair Discount Store, and M-M Discount Centre. According to the Bureau, the combined sales of these stores jumped from $70.4 million in 1962 (January to October) to $102.6 million in the same period for 1963. Neither food nor automotive services were included.

The battle for increased sales has not been easy in Canada. Small neighborhood stores, faced with extinction, have organized against their larger competitors. Early in 1964 the Hamilton, Ontario Board of Control enacted a bylaw limiting hours of opening for certain stores from 9 a.m. to 6 p.m. four days a week, and from 9 a.m. to 9 p.m. on Thursdays and Fridays. Nineteen categories of small businesses, for the most part neighborhood stores, were exempted from compliance. Feeling that this law was incredibly unfair, Woolco and one other store stayed open beyond the stipulated times as a test case. A Hamilton magistrate fined them $300. Woolco appealed to Toronto, and its appeal was sustained. A reverse decision could have created many problems for the future of Canada's discount stores. Despite this favorable ruling, a number of discounters ran into trouble. Mon-Mart, and Towers opened units in Quebec province. Mon-Mart's two stores closed. Towers, except for one or two locations, did extremely poorly and went into reorganization with employees taking control.

The Canadian *Financial Post* of January 27, 1963 editorialized as follows: "The early enthusiasm for the 'discounters' in this country produced a rash of new store building and a big demand for the shares of the few public companies in the field. But disillusionment followed. Most of these new-type retailers fell short of their original optimistic sales and profit goals. They ran into the inevitable organization troubles and start-up bugs that accompany many new business operations . . . In the process, some stores – mostly marginal firms operating on a shoestring but in a few cases, chains of some size, went into bankruptcy or receivership. Largely unnoticed, however, the stronger 'discount' stores in the U.S. and Canada continued to expand their sales and produced a better earnings position too. They are still winning new customers and evidently holding on to their old ones . . ."

The Chain Store Guide's 1966 Directory of Discount Department Stores lists the following stores as operating in Canada in that year:
Manitoba – Clark's-Gamble of Canada, Ltd., 1301 Elice Ave., Winnipeg; Topps Discount Dept. Stores, Ltd., 700 St. James St., Winnipeg 21.
Ontario – Met Discount Store, Division St., Coburg; Savemart, Ltd., High-

way No.2 and 13th St., Cornwall; Freimart Stores, Ltd., Rideau St., Ottawa; Allied Towers Merchants, Ltd., 110 Orfuss Rd., Toronto; Honest Ed's, Ltd., Bloor and Bathurst Sts., Toronto 4; New Era Discount Dept. Stores, 2902 Dansforth Ave., Toronto; Rite-Way Dept. Stores, Ltd., 2400 Eglington Ave. W., Toronto; Sayvette, Thorncliffe Park, Toronto 17; Sentry Dept. Stores Ltd., 18 Grenville St., Toronto 5.

Allied Towers Merchants, Ltd., Toronto, Canada

Formed in 1962, Allied Towers Merchants, Ltd., is now the biggest discount chain in Canada. The company was originally organized by a group of merchants holding concessions in a mushrooming chain called Towers Marts International under the presidency of Samuel J. Rosenstein. Some Canadian capital was invested in the company but the chief guidance came from the principals who had started the chain. Every department was leased and in the early days there was little real control; available merchandise was bought in large quantities in the hope that it would sell. For some months the chain prospered but in the latter part of 1962 trouble developed in regard to real estate payments and merchandising policies. As a result the company went into receivership in March, 1963.

A group of concessionaries, under the company name of Allied Towers Merchants Ltd., stepped in as a protective measure to take over on a contractual basis with the trustees for Towers Marts. The lessees operated jointly as a landlord taking over the collection of cash, advertising, and setting general company policy. President Myrle W. Book says, "We were just low, very low, and it was not until late in 1964 that we had the situation well in hand. Since that time our progress has been steady with a very substantial sales growth. The company produced a sizeable profit for the first time in 1965. We now have 13 units in fast-growing suburban areas and our current level of sales is far in excess of the national average. One of the first things we did was to get into very solid planning.

"In our first year of operation we reduced our inventory by over $2 million since a lot of it was three years old. Many of our departments had been loaded with unacceptable lines which had been bought for promotion. We got rid of it at any price and dropped many low-end lines. For example, we were selling thousands of dozens of Japanese brassieres at 33 cents. We dumped them and put in 87-cent brassieres with excellent results. We applied this principle to hundreds of items and it has brought about better markon, better acceptance, and obviously a greater profit. At the same time we developed goal planning and merchandise management. For a long time we could not attract very many good people so it was almost a one-man band. I am sure that many have gone through the same experience in trying to find executive talent.

"Although we have traded up, price will always be our predominant customer attraction. But it is price with style, quality, and downright good value. We started as a discounter but we now consider ourselves more of a small promotional department store type of operation. We use comparable pricing fairly extensively. In the main our prices range from middle-low to middle-high. Our highest priced women's coat used to be $49.88 and is now $79.88 but we did not reach this price in one jump and we cannot do it in all our stores. We fought our way cautiously. The first area in which we started trading up was in women's wear. We actually considered leasing this department as it was one of our greatest losers, however, as a result of careful merchandising, by 1965 our women's wear department became our greatest profit department.

"In 1965, on a very low budget, we managed to redecorate and re-fixture our stores. We hired a company to set up a complete program of new signing. We also strengthened our merchandise mix by adding name brands. After a great deal of negotiation with suppliers we introduced several of the leading lines of cosmetics which we agreed not to discount. We have a large furniture and major appliance department including such brands as RCA and Frigidaire.

"In Canada a whole new upper-middle class has risen in the past 15 years. It consists of educated people in executive, managerial, and professional occupations earning $8,000 to $9,000 a year and up. This segment today accounts for half of the consumer market in Canada. The upper economic bracket now represents about 20 per cent of the families in large urban areas contrasted with 5 per cent 15 to 20 years ago. Together, particularly in our Ontario-Quebec market, these two groups represent 70 per cent of the consumer demand. How wrong we could have been in our case to have gone to low-end type merchandise. In Canada 37 per cent of the labor force currently is aged 16 to 31 years. By 1970 this group will comprise about 56 per cent of the labor force. In 1951 this was 11 per cent. Today in Canada about 25 out of every 100 married women work outside their home. To satisfy the wants of this dynamic new consumer market presents a tremendous opportunity."

La Salle Stores

In 1949 La Salle Factories, Ltd., decided that all suits they manufactured for the Bond Clothes Shops not sold could be returned to the factory. The

355

company then started selling this returned merchandise in their factories or in abandoned factories which they used as stores. They gradually added additional items of merchandise and in 1967 they have 21 general merchandise discount stores with a combined annual gross of approximately $25 million. Circulars in both French and English are sent out 10 times a year to over a million homes in the Province of Quebec. The slogan "From Maker to Wearer" is stressed.

La Salle stores range from 20,000 to 30,000 square feet and are located primarily in Quebec with some in the Ottawa region. They compete with Woolco, Allied Towers Merchants, and Miracle Mart. La Salle likes to have adjoining food stores operated by either I.G.A. or Dominion Stores. George H. Scott is president, J. Scott is secretary and N. Scott, treasurer. The company is known as Scott-LaSalle, Ltd.

"HONEST ED" MIRVISH'S DISCOUNT STORE IN TORONTO

A unique mass-merchandising operation in Toronto is "Honest Ed's." On the fringe of downtown Toronto, it has been famous for many years for its unconventional approach to retailing. The store was originally a group of old houses and the floors are on different levels. The five million customers who enter the store during a year must thread their way carefully up and down stairs and in and out of unexpected corners. Instead of shopping carts, large paper shopping bags are used and carried to the checkout lanes where they are emptied out. Sales in 1964 were more than $15 million.

Business Week of February 20, 1965 (page 50) comments on Honest Ed's as follows: "The setting and the traffic flow seem patterned after a George Abbott farce. Shoppers panting after the 'door crasher' opening special (it might be 4 pounds of spaghetti for 11 cents) must rush to a third-floor location to get it, then work their way back down. Honest Ed's remains faithful to the premises of the primitive discount house. Says Mirvish, 'We don't believe in giving service of any kind.' That means no free parking, no delivery, no refunds or exchanges, no credit, and no exceptions to the rules. Even the hours the store is open – 1 p.m. to 10 p.m. on weekdays – are designed to eliminate slow periods that add to overhead. Honest Ed's merchandise is mainly soft goods, but on any given day the store might be selling Austrian movie cameras at less than half their $89.95 list price, pork and beans for 11 cents a can, or women's stretch pants at $1.11. Five per cent of sales goes into advertising and promotion and bargains are announced in crazyquilt newspaper advertisements. . . .

"Mirvish oversees the bedlam from a posh private office tucked away behind the women's shoe department. There, he displays his collection of Chinese snuff boxes, a magnificent 18th century French porcelain clock, sculptures done by his wife, and antique music boxes. Two years ago, he paid

356

$215,000 to buy the old Royal Alexandra Theater and then spent another $400,000 to spruce up its Edwardian elegance with flocked wallpaper, crystal chandeliers. At the same time he began developing the row of houses behind Honest Ed's into an artist's colony. These tactics led a whole new group to take Mirvish and his store seriously. In operating his theater he has instituted a credit card, phone-order system which make it much easier to get theater tickets. To build prestige for his house he has even taken 'loss leader' attractions such as the Russian Obratsov Puppets."

Mexico

The Arrango brothers, in 1958, had a 1,000 square-foot general merchandise store in the heart of Mexico City. In 1962, after reading an article on discounting in *Fortune* entitled "Revolution in Retailing," Geronimo Arrango and his brother visited Masters and Korvette in New York, and Grand-Way and Great Eastern Mills in New Jersey. Back in Mexico City they put into practice what they had learned with the result that they now have a three-store Aurrera discount chain in Mexico City.[1]

At the start they met many of the problems encountered in the early days of U.S. discounting. As a result of the complaints of traditional outlets, manufacturers curtailed and sometimes stopped their supplies especially in hard goods. They were forced to buy appliances from other retailers, jobbers, or other devious channels. Since there were no lessees available they had to run every department themselves. These problems have been overcome and with the 1964 opening of the Centre Commercial Lomas store in Mexico City the brothers are well established. Management has committed itself to scientific data processing and in the Lomas store there are 26 Monroe/Sweda tape punch registers which record departments and merchandise classifications in high-speed checkout lanes. Average sale, by U.S. standards, is high – 110 pesos or $8.80.

Basic departments are food, soft goods, and hard goods. Food includes canned and packaged items; fresh meat and fish; fresh fruits and vegetables. All are displayed exactly as in a U.S. supermarket. There is a delicatessen, pastry shop, candy shop, and snack bar. Soft goods include men's, women's and children's wear and shoes. Hard goods include appliances, records, automotive accessories, photographic supplies, magazines and paperbacks, toys, cosmetics, office supplies, tobacco and garden shops. Major emphasis is on soft goods and food. Mexicans still lack the buying power to purchase appliances in volume. Many middle-class families have nothing left after paying for essentials and rent and find a maid cheaper than appliances.

[1]Summary of an article in *Discount Store News*, April 20, 1964.

357

VIANA Y CIA, S.A.

The Viana Y Cia, S.A. Company is the "Polk Brothers" of Mexico City. After almost nine years as a conventional store specializing in electrical appliances the company converted to discounting in 1962. In 1965 it accounted for almost 23 per cent (10,000 units) of all refrigerators sold in Mexico City and now has about 20 per cent of the city's market for new refrigerators, washers, electric stoves, gas ranges, and television sets. Its volume is estimated to be 10 per cent of the entire market in the Republic. There are three units in operation; all are in the center of the city.

The owner, José Souza, is proud of his company and says, "It has caused prices to come down drastically at dealer and factory levels all over the Republic and has helped to increase production. We feel that it has started a cycle of lower and lower prices and higher and higher production."

Germany

QUELLE MARKET

In October, 1960, Quelle Market, Germany's first combined discount store and supermarket, opened in the suburbs of Nuremberg. Prior to the grand opening 5,000 customers lined up outside the store and 30 policemen and 20 store security men were needed to handle the crowd. In the last minute excitement, the building superintendent could not find the key to the air-curtain door; after emptying all his pockets, he found it!

The parent company is Versandhaus Quelle, the largest mail order house in Germany. President Gustav Schickedanz commissioned the firm of P. K. Halstead Associates to make plans for the 120,000 square-foot multi-story structure. P. K. Halstead is a firm of supermarket consultants with headquarters in Larchmont, New York and an office in Cologne, Germany.

According to Paul Halstead, the idea behind the project was to find an outlet for leftover mail order merchandise. There is a 15,000 square-foot supermarket at street level and a 20,000 square-foot promotional department store on the first floor. In the basement, surplus merchandise is offered at 25 per cent below the regular price. After 10 days it is reduced to 33 per cent, and after another 10 days to 50 per cent of the original (catalog) price. The assortment consists for the most part of textiles and wearing apparel with a sprinkling of hard goods.

The supermarket is typically American self-service and features 12 checkout counters complete with magic eye and two conveyer belts with a horizontal conveyer to return empty shopping carts from the checkout area to the turnstile entrance. There is radiant wall heating in the sales area and air-conditioned meat and cold-cut packaging rooms. The market also stocks a large assortment of basic non-food items.

The first floor contains 4,000 regular Quelle catalog items plus 3,000 supplementary department store items including wearing apparel for men, women, and children, leather goods, shoes, linen, curtains, carpets, furniture, appliances, TV, cameras, jewelry, china, glassware, and toys.

Fronting the store is a parking lot for 150 cars and a discount filling station carrying private-label gasoline at 10 per cent below the nationally advertised brands. The discount basement and first floor department store provide home delivery for bulky merchandise; but in the supermarket it is strictly cash-and-carry.

Belgium

SUPER BAZARS, S.A.

Super Bazars S.A. in Belgium were the first full-line, self-service department stores in Europe. Number one opened on September 9, 1961 in a suburb of Bruges and has a total area of 40,000 square feet. It is 100 per cent self-service with checkouts. Leased departments include a pharmacy, bank branch, dry cleaner, hairdresser and florist. There is parking for 200 cars. The second, opened on September 16, 1961, is in Auderghem, a Brussels suburb. It has a total area of 102,400 square feet and leases the same departments as does the Bruges store. Parking space is provided for 900 cars. The opening was scheduled for 9 a.m. and at 6 a.m. 5,000 excited customers started queuing up at the doors. By 9 a.m. traffic was jammed in a radius of one mile from the store. Twenty-seven checkout counters, 1,500 shopping carts and 500 hand baskets were barely enough to handle the crowd. More than 6,000 cars used the parking lot and kept 20 policemen busy controlling the traffic. A third Super Bazar was opened in October, 1961 in Anderlecht, another Brussels suburb. This store has a total area of 85,000 square feet and has parking for 400 cars.

All Super Bazar stores are open from 9 a.m. to 9 p.m. six days a week. Fixtures are economical but functional. The roofs are without ceilings. There is an unconditional merchandise refund if the customer is not satisfied. A complete supermarket is operated in each store by Supermarches G.B. The Auderghem store has the largest shoe department in Europe with 28,000 pairs on open display. More Super Bazar stores are planned for the near future both in Belgium and in other Common Market countries.

Super Bazars is owned and operated by the following four companies: Grand Bazar D'Anvers, operator of nine conventional department stores with total sales in 1960 of $28 million; Grand Bazar De Liege, operator of

359

six conventional department stores with 1960 sales of $26 million; Au Bon Marche, Brussels, which operates seven conventional department stores having total 1960 sales of $40 million; Jewel Companies, Chicago, the tenth largest supermarket chain in the United States, with 1968 sales of over one billion dollars.

Russia

The Russian version of discounting is rather remote from the American concept. The network of shops in the U.S.S.R. is either state-owned or cooperative. Several big stores trading in cut-price goods have recently been opened in Moscow. Ready-made clothes, footwear, fabrics, cameras, sewing machines, electrical household goods, accordions, harmonicas, radios, victrolas and radio receivers are on sale. Each item is supplied with a label bearing two figures, one of which is crossed out. The new figure is considerably lower. These cut-price goods are of high quality but are either not in fashion or are behind in technology. The biggest discount is on fabrics which have become unfashionable. At the Moscow fair in 1964 there remained unsold 270 million rubles worth of fabrics. D. Pavlov, Minister of Trade of the Russian Federation, ordered the establishment of these shops for the purposes of selling surplus and slow-selling merchandise. The majority of them are close to railway terminals or to collective farm markets. Most of the customers are peasants who think in terms of reliability and service rather than fashion.

England

In the United Kingdom, the United States introduced mass-merchandising in the form of supermarkets. Safeway, the big American chain, has been a successful supermarket operator in England for years. Self-service sale of food now accounts for over 50 per cent of food purchases in England. The supermarket movement is much slower in Scotland, Wales, and Ireland. The feeling that the increase in English food sales via self-service would create a greater desire by the British family for other forms of self-service has not as yet materialized.

The American-owned GEM stores (now Parkview-GEM) were the first general merchandise discount stores to be opened in England. On November 7, 1964 the first GEM Supercentre opened in Nottingham. Initial response in that community was exciting. A conservative estimate of the opening day attendance was 30,000. The store cost $1.4 million and has 85,000 square feet, with 60,000 square feet of selling area. Supercentre introduced Britons for the first time to this American concept with features such as a 1,000-car parking lot, more than 20 leased general merchandise and food departments, and a multitude of services, including a beauty parlor, shoe repairs, engraving, and key-cutting. Much of the excitement was fomented by heavy advertising in the press and on TV.

The store, staffed by 300 people, was managed by a Briton who had eighteen months special training in America. GEM opened a second store the following year with the hope of opening six additional Supercentres within three years.

GEM depended upon local leased departments which are not yet well advanced as an English concept. Unfortunately these stores have not prospered and the original move to build eight Supercentres has been tabled. Legal restrictions on night shopping made it very difficult to develop the family shopping concept that has made the one-stop self-service center so successful in the United States. There is almost total reliance upon the woman shopper during daytime hours, and this hurt discount development. Another bottleneck for potential American interest is that local councils have much greater zeal in zoning and construction activities than in the States.

In December, 1965 GEM International told stockholders: "Although we are still hopeful that the performance of GEM Supercentres, Ltd. will be turned around, the decision was made in the interests of conservatism to write off our capital investment . . ."

The discount scene in the United Kingdom is by no means one of complete gloom. The Minerals Separation Company of England reached an agreement with Saylin, Inc., Los Angeles, for a joint venture involving the opening of two British discount stores in 1965. These stores deal in pharmaceuticals, housewares, hardware, and sundries, and were the first of a chain planned to eventually expand through continental Europe.

F. W. Woolworth Ltd. is planning to open a number of Woolco Stores in the smaller English cities. They will be largely self-service and modeled on the Woolcos that have been opened in the United States by the parent F. W. Woolworth Company. Opened in 1967, the first English Woolco has 100,000 square feet in size and has parking for 600 cars. Negotiations are under way for other stores.

With its English variety stores already established, Woolworth's is well versed in retailing as it is carried out in Great Britain. They will not have to depend entirely on leased departments as did GEM.

One English retailer combining the attributes of both discount and department stores is the Supermac Department Store, located in a shopping center in North Ireland. It is 35,000 square feet overall, with 15,000 square feet devoted to non-foods and 5,000 square feet to foods. It also has ten "specialist shops" and parking for 320 autos.

The store is modeled after American self-service lines and has twelve checkouts. Going to membership status enables any British retailer to get around some sticky situations; the store can go to a seven-day operation and can offer discounts on merchandise still on the list of price-maintained goods. Taking advantage of the loophole is a unit in Manchester billing itself as the "first" closed-door discount operation in England. Operated by Allways Store Company as a Fame Store, management reported the receipt of 30,000 membership applications by its opening day.

Sweden

WESSEL'S STORMAKNAD

In Sweden, the American discounting concept was established without the use of American investments. Using the traditional discount house triad of dramatic exposure, low prices and self-service as his guide, a progressive Swedish retailer named Thorolf Hjort set out to revolutionize Swedish merchandising. In a country with a history as long as Sweden's, breaking established customs is a difficult thing to do. One such custom is that there are price agreements between retailers. These are informal and not legally binding, but it has been considered unethical to break a price line.

Wessel's Stormaknad, an 88,000 square-footer, was Sweden's first discount store and has been such a success that other Swedish entrepreneurs are busily imitating it; there has been a gradual disintegration of the rigid prices in Swedish retailing as a result. The Stormaknad – which translates literally into "supermarket" is situated just outside Malino, the third largest city in Sweden. Widely publicized in the nation's trade magazines and newspapers long before it opened, Wessel's was heralded as "A bomb in the Swedish business community."

When Hjort's Stormaknad opened in 1963, more than 40,000 customers attended (over 100 fainted, five were hospitalized, and one died). Opening day sales were $45,000, two-thirds of which came from food. Sales for the second year of operation were $9.1 million. In addition to food, Stormaknad carries soft goods, radio and TV sets, furniture, lamps, toys, glass and china, sporting goods, hardware, and many other items. Store pricing policy is to sell goods at five to fifty per cent below local prices.

Wessel's has a plain pipe rack appearance – stark and functional. Whole sections of the structure were pre-fabricated and put together at the building site. Display windows are not used. Wessel's subscribes 100 per cent to the self-service principle, but there are sales personnel for customers who wish them. Home deliveries are made at an additional charge and there is a money-back guarantee if the item is returned within eight days after the purchase is made. Added comforts for shoppers include an amusement park where mothers can leave children while they shop; a ladies' hairdresser, and a cafeteria. The service desk gives out information, checks bags, and exchanges purchases.

362

Discounting in Japan

Japan is a "consumeristic" society. The consumer market is large and growing with an increasing consumer income and a constant striving for a higher standard of living. During the last five years the income of workers has almost doubled so that essential needs such as food, clothing and housing present no problem. The Japanese common people are beginning to purchase non-essential goods such as refrigerators, electric rice cookers, automatic toasters, vacuum cleaners, washing machines, high quality kimonos, and so forth. Such items as television sets, air conditioners, electric shavers, freezers, automobiles, hair dryers, etc., are in increasing demand. There is a so-called "leisure boom." More time is being used in recreation by the use of labor-saving devices and of frozen, instant, and other varieties of processed food.

CONSUMER EVOLUTION

Such changes in consumer behavior have had an impact on the retail business. Traditional small stores have evolved into large, modern, self-service department stores.

"The Japan Self-Service Association defined the supermarket in 1958 as 'an independent large-scale food store using self-service methods with a sales volume of over a hundred million yen (about $278,000).' Such supermarkets are now approximately 500 to 600 in number. There are a total of approximately 4,000 self-service stores of different varieties. Many independent retailers have expressed an interest in establishing supermarkets by tying in and cooperating with other stores. Another important trend is the establishment of one-stop shopping centers near multiple-story apartment houses in the suburbs of metropolitan areas."[1]

The rapid increase in the number of self-service stores is shown by the following table made by the Japan Self-Service Store Association.

	Self-Service Stores	*Supermarkets*
Year	*Number of Stores*	*Number of Stores*
1953	1	
1954	3	
1955	4	
1956	129	
1957	283	
1958	595	
1959	1,036	70
1960	1,465	129
1961	2,065	190
1962	2,846	320
1963	3,127	556

[1]Shoji Murata, "Japanese Consumer Profile," *Journal of Retailing*, Fall, 1964, p. 7.

PROMOTIONAL METHODS

As competition has increased, American methods of aggressive advertising and promotion have been introduced. Trading stamps first became of significant importance in 1960 and there are now four trading stamp companies. The largest is the Blue Chip Stamp Company, reported to have received advice and encouragement from the company of the same name in California.[1]

The larger department stores have adopted many American practices but with some original features such as a staff of four dentists in the Isetan Store serving about 3,000 patients a year and a delightful roof-top garden providing a place of recreation for both the customers and the staff. There is a children's playground with a wide variety of rides, a small zoo, and a pool-side restaurant. A big concert hall is rented out to private groups. Many types of both in-store and out-of-store repair and refurbishing services are provided. In addition there are barber shops, photo studios, and beauty shops. As in the United States, theft is a big problem and has been encountered from early supermarket days.

A major problem in developing the consumer market in Japan lies in the nation's agricultural sector since agriculture has not yet been fully commercialized in the modern sense. Farmers still operate on a small scale and the majority of them have no interest in actively cooperating with the government.

Federation of Migros Cooperatives in Zurich, Switzerland

THE FEDERATION IS THE CENTRAL ORGANIZATION FOR 15 REGIONAL COOPERATIVES

The French word for wholesale is "en-gros," hence the word "mi-gros" means half-wholesale, half-retail. The name "Migros" serves to indicate to the customer that prices are halfway between the customary retail prices and the wholesale prices. Another version of the meaning of Migros is that when the company started in 1925 it operated exclusively with stores on wheels and was an itinerant or "migrating" vendor; hence, the name Migros.

[1]A. J. Alton & G. O. Totten, "Trading Stamps in Japan-Boom in the Making?" *Journal of Marketing*, April, 1965, p. 13.

Mass Merchandising Abroad

Gottlieb Duttweiler, founder,
Federation of Migros Cooperatives (1925).

Migros was the pioneer in the field of food mass-merchandising in Europe and since 1952 has also pioneered non-food distribution in conjunction with food supermarkets, a development which preceded the move in the same direction in the U.S.A. by about a year.

Launched in 1925 by Gottlieb Duttweiler, Migros is dominant in the big cities and suburbs of Switzerland and even has units in the remote Alpine villages. It is the largest distributing and processing operation in Switzerland. Migros became a cooperative in 1945 and is now organized into 15 semi-autonomous regions with 441 stores, 144 truck stores as well as bakeries, butcher shops, do-it-yourself stores, record outlets, manufacturing plants, packing plants, warehouses, trucks and cargo ships, banks, an insurance company, and 223 gasoline service stations. Activities include the promotion of adult schools, cultural centers, book and record clubs, youth activities, travel groups and the publication of five newspapers in three languages.

MASS MERCHANDISING

Exterior – Itinernat Truck Store – Federation of Migros Cooperatives, Switzerland.

Migros mass-merchandising differs from similar chain activities in the United States since an estimated 60 per cent of all items sold are produced in cooperatively-owned manufacturing and packing plants. By means of its three weekly newspapers, members and other subscribers are kept informed about local and federal government politics. With a circulation of over 500,000, the Migros newspaper *Wir Bruckenbauer* carries a lot of political influence. There is no such thing as standardization since the chain operates in an extraordinary variety of locations. Selling area may vary from a few hundred to 26,000 square feet, and the stores may be from one to three stories high. Accounting for more than 12 per cent of Switzerland's total food sales, Migros is ranked among the ten largest commercial enterprises in that country. Total sales in 1966 of both food and general merchandise exceeded $400 million.

The headquarters of Migros is in Zurich. Although major company policy is set in Zurich, each of the 15 operating regions have considerable autonomy so that operations can be tailored in German, French, Italian, and an assortment of dialects.

The Migros store mix may be divided into six categories: traditional stores, self-service stores, combined self-service stores, supermarkets, truck stores, specialty stores. In 1966 there were eight small service units with a limited assortment of food. These traditional stores now account for only about .5 per cent of total sales. The 238 self-service stores carry basic food

366

Mass Merchandising Abroad

items with a limited selection of non-foods. They have customer checkouts similar to those used in the United States. Combined self-service stores total 126 and average from 4,000 to 5,000 square feet of selling area. Their snackbars and bakeries carry about 2,000 items. Accounting for 34 per cent of the volume are 78 supermarkets which include a butcher shop, sea food department, bakery, snack bar, and up to 6,000 items. Traveling self-service "walk through" truck stores account for about 5 per cent of total volume and carry an assortment of about 800 food items and are designed to service remote rural areas. The remaining category, specialty stores, consists of do-it-

Interior – Truck Store – Federation of Migros Cooperatives, Switzerland.

367

yourself, radio and appliances, florist, bakery, butcher and clothing stores.

The biggest store in the chain is called "Marktplatz" and is in the Swiss capital of Bern. It has a total volume of over $7.4 million a year, with a selling space of 26,000 square feet on three floors.

A major problem in Switzerland is getting personnel; the labor shortage is such that there are 100 jobs for every four applicants. With this limitation, Migros concentrates on steadily increasing the efficiency of its existing units, making them more profitable and increasing sales per square foot. Furthermore, many of its smaller service stores are being closed, and in their places large self-service units are being established. Turnover for food averages about 48 a year, whereas non-foods average 8 to 10.

Migros merchandisers feel that an item should produce at least $250 a month to earn its shelf space. Non-foods, on the average, run about 12.5 per cent for toys, photographic supplies, records, books, housewares, cosmetics and radio-TV. Self-service is the rule except in departments such as cameras, records, radios, flowers, meats, cheeses, and take-home foods. Clothing, cosmetics and large and small appliances are self-service.

In regard to checkouts, Migros headquarters recommends a standard automatic change-making register with a moving belt, similar to those used in the United States. However, a method is now under study whereby the checker transfers the items from one basket to another as she rings them up, after which the customer takes the second basket to a counter and wraps the items himself.

In its drive for maximum volume Migros uses every inch of selling space, even on the outside of the store. Exterior promotions include fruits, vegetables, and even canned goods. Gas station purchases are tied in with food purchases. Large sizes and multiple-price packs are promoted. Lotteries are staged and the winning customer gets her groceries free. With every purchase of at least $2.50 a customer gets a free gift, such as a can of peaches. With every minimum $2.50 purchase, customers at Migrol gasoline stations are given coupons that are worth approximately 25 cents in merchandise at the do-it-yourself stores.

The interest of Migros in its customers is strongly evidenced by the company's activity in adult education. Each regional division devotes one-half of 1 per cent of profits to a program of adult education. In 1964 the company set up 58 schools offering 280 courses to 165,000 students. Migros also sets up concerts and art shows and sponsors other cultural activities. It collects books for libraries in remote villages and distributes scholarships to the children of these villages. With its newspapers, Migros fights the "dairy trusts" to cut the price of milk. It also keeps a sharp eye on the major oil companies so that prices of gasoline will not get too far out of line.

In the Migros annual report for fiscal 1966, president Rudolf Suter announced gross sales of $493 million, up 11 per cent from 1965. It took 36 years to reach the first $261 million but only five years to double it. The Migros processing plants in 1966 supplied the retail division with 199,000 metric tons of merchandise valued at $115 million wholesale. It is estimated that 26.7 per cent of the retail gross volume of Migros originates in these fully-owned plants. The new chocolate factory in Buchs near Aarau is now in operation and also a new plant for laundry products in Basel. The new bakery in Gossau, St. Gall, is probably the most modern of its kind in Europe. "Optigal", the fully integrated poultry growing and processing operation, now has 191 independent growers under contract and sold 15.5 million pounds. "Migrol," the distributing operation for gasoline, fuel oil, and other automotive products, now operates 223 service stations with gross sales of $23.7 million, an increase of 19 per cent over 1965. A new underground tank farm with a capacity of one and a quarter million gallons was completed in 1966. The International Tourist Organization Hotel Plan with 43 offices in various parts of the world, including New York, had a gross volume of $34.4 million. It also operates a number of "vacation villages" such as the "Pueblo Eldorado Playa," opened recently near Barcelona, Spain. The affiliated book-and-record club Ex Libris has 364,000 members and sales of $5.6 million.

In the cultural and educational field the company now employs 1,564 teachers. New schools were opened in Torquay, England and Dublin, Ireland. The American Language and Education Center of Michigan State University is allied with this project and several hundred students are exchanged every year.

SECTION II

Major Problem Areas
in Mass Merchandising

X I

Mass Merchandising Casualties

Among the more common reasons for discount store bankruptcies are the following:

1. LACK OF MERCHANDISING KNOW-HOW.

In pioneering days real estate developers, thinking to cash in on the new popularity of mass merchandising, would set up a store on a leased-department basis but soon discovered that retailing expertise cannot be acquired overnight.

2. A TOO RAPID RATE OF EXPANSION.

With a few successful stores, a small chain owner with limited capital begins to feel that he is invulnerable to failure – he can't make a mistake; grandiose plans overwhelm his reason and the admonitions of his banker. New stores are established far afield but he is on precarious ground. His volume may drop unexpectedly and in no time at all he is in trouble. Credit is withheld by vendors and down comes his house of cards.

373

3. FAILURE OF SYSTEMS AND PROCEDURES.

With only a small number of stores in a limited area, owner-management finds personal supervision possible but with steady expansion there comes a time when existing controls do not function. E. J. Korvette encountered this problem when it began to expand beyond metropolitan New York. Communications poured out of the New York home office but feed-back was dismally absent. It took a drastic overhaul of systems and procedures to remedy the situation but not without severe loss.

4. LACK OF ADEQUATE THEFT PROTECTION.

Losses from theft in discount stores exceed those of any other type of retailer. The University of Massachusetts Research Program put them at from 2.5 per cent to 3 per cent of sales as opposed to approximately 1.5 per cent for orthodox department stores. When it is realized that net profit after taxes averages only about 1.5 per cent to 2.5 per cent of sales, theft control can make the difference between success and failure.

The confession of a convicted shoplifter, and suggestions for the prevention of shoplifting appear in the final section of this chapter.

Case histories of specific stores which were casualties, because of one or more of the common reasons that lead to bankruptcy, follow.

Towers Marts International

In April, 1961 Samuel J. Rosenstein, president of Towers Marts, lectured at the University of Massachusetts Conference on Discounting. At that time a fierce battle between discount stores for the best locations was in progress. In his talk Rosenstein said, "Now the question of competition is a very difficult problem to analyze, because, as consultant Anthony Downs (Real Estate Research Corp., Chicago) pointed out, it's very hard for anyone to know exactly who is going into a given area. . . . We in Towers take a very clear-cut position on this matter. For example, we're going into the Washington area with depth. Washington has a population of a little in excess of two million, and after very careful economic studies, the type of which I will exhibit here very shortly, we have decided to put six stores in the metropolitan Washington area. We think we have located them strategically. Now it's important for our competition to note that we are going into this area. For this reason we take great pains in publicizing these things and I think that many of the people who know us now know that when we say we're going into a given area, we go in. And when we specify a time that we're going to be there, we will be there. We will open with four stores in Washington in the latter part of May, and we will have two more this fall so that we will have six stores in the greater Washington area within a very, very limited period of time. This principle of saturation we feel is healthy for the industry because unless one of our competitors wants to really come in and have a knockdown, dragout battle, they will look for another city."

In the New York *Times* of June 10, 1961 it was announced that Towers Marts, Inc., of New York and its wholly-owned subsidiary, Towers Marts of Canada, had made a $25 million transaction for eleven shopping centers, seven of which would be in Ontario, two in Montreal, and two in Washington, D.C. The company then operated nine centers in the United States and one in Toronto.

In May, 1962 Towers Marts filed suit to end its contracts with the Darling Stores Corporation and Grayson-Robinson Stores, Inc., agent for Darling in operating the departments. The suit asked for $1 million damages for breach of contract and the right to terminate agreements with the defendents to operate women's and children's apparel and millinery departments in fifteen Towers stores. Towers charged that the two companies did not cooperate properly in the advertising program and did not maintain a complete line of seasonable and representative merchandise at competitive prices. This situation, according to Towers, jeopardized its customer image. A statement by counsel for Grayson-Robinson as reported in the New York *Times* of May 5, 1962 called the Towers Mart action "without foundation. It was brought primarily," counsel said, "because the terms of the existing leases are so beneficial to Grayson-Robinson Stores, Inc., that Towers now believes it can secure better terms from others, or by means of this litigation, from Grayson-Robinson. In fact, Towers is in default in the performance of its obligations as landlord in vital respects, and large counter claims are being asserted against Towers by Grayson-Robinson." The matter was settled in June, 1962 when Towers agreed to pay Grayson-Robinson $1,384,936 with the understanding that Grayson-Robinson would give up its right to operate leased departments in present or future Towers stores. Towers made a payment of $703,590 towards the agreed amount.

In September, 1962 Grayson-Robinson Stores filed suit to collect $681,346 alleged owing to it by Towers Marts International, Inc. It was charged that most of the money had been withheld by Towers from the sales of merchandise in leased departments operated by Grayson-Robinson in Towers stores. The dispute was finally settled by a payment of $500,000 by Towers Marts to Grayson-Robinson.

In November, 1962 Towers Marts International sold its Canadian subsidiary, operating thirteen stores, to a group of investors. The company also announced that it had withdrawn a proposed public stock issue of 550,000 shares owing to market conditions. The *Wall Street Journal* of

February 12, 1963 carried an article stating that Towers Marts was in temporary financial difficulty owing to expenditures of more than $500,000 in connection with lawsuits against Grayson-Robinson Stores. In March, 1963 the Towers Marts and Properties, Ltd., the former Canadian subsidiary, was placed in interim receivership by the Ontario Supreme Court. This company still owed Towers Marts International an unsecured debt of $450,000. It was given six months by its creditors to work out a reorganization. On April 5, 1963 Towers Marts International filed under Chapter XI of the Federal Bankruptcy Act listing liabilities of $11,073,146 and assets of $9,796,000. Liabilities included $2,959,000 in accounts payable to concessionaires in its stores, all eighteen of which were closed. The four former Towers Marts in the Washington, D.C. area were acquired by the Zayre Corporation from the individual owners of the properties.

As it turned out, Towers management was building a house of cards since the company's stability and the expansion of its physical premises depended on a sales-lease-back principle. All Towers stores had commitments in terms of sales-lease-back but nonetheless cash from the business was used initially to construct the stores. When the stock market crashed and the Tower's stock issue, which would have raised $5 million, also collapsed, the company never went public. The individuals who had made the commitments had to renege because their individual house of cards, so to speak, came tumbling down, or they wanted to contract so the commitment was withdrawn. Towers Mart money was tied up and sunk into the real estate and management could not get it out. In order to keep paying the contractors and to keep the business alive, money due to lessees was borrowed. Marrud, Inc., the cosmetics lessee it is said, was "hung up" for approximately a half million dollars; Rockower, another lessee, lost three quarters of a million.

At any given moment, even in those days, if the principal does not send out a weekly check to his lessee, he is in trouble. Two weeks can go by and "you're sitting on a big chunk of money." Customary procedure with lessees is to settle on Friday for the week ending the previous Saturday. Some have a schedule of payment on the Wednesday of the second following week. Suppose this settlement is not made on the Wednesday but is delayed to the following Monday. You are then talking three weeks of receipts which has already been taken in without the lessee receiving a cent. This can happen very quickly as the days and weeks roll by extremely fast. The check may be a few days late. The lessee controller forgets to tell his boss. If the boss is not informed, the principal may be four, five, or even six weeks into a firm's receipts before management is aware of it. This is exactly what happened with Towers. There was no way out since there was no permanent money coming in to replace the temporary money that was supporting these stores.

The Towers organization was not really a merchandising business since they merchandised no part of the store – it was merely a real estate venture.

It is conceivable that the Towers management might have pulled through if they had been able to raise the needed money or if the 1962 crash had not taken place making it possible to honor the long-term commitments. On the other hand, not being basically merchandisers, they might have eventually run into store operational problems. It is a generally-accepted theory that in building the discount industry the major lessees play a very important role in supplying operating capital and know-how but a limited one in terms of time. Eventually – in a rapidly expanding and successful chain – there comes with few exceptions a time when there is no place for them since they function as an "extra" middleman between the manufacturer and the ultimate consumer. If they are good merchandisers and making good money, then why, reasons the principal, should that money not accrue to the store operator? If they are not good and don't see eye to eye with the principals as to how the store should be run, then they ought not to be there. Negating this point of view is the fact that some lessees have built up such extraordinary expertise in their specialties that they can, in very many instances, provide more profit for their principals for a given department on a lessee rather than on a self-operated basis. Otherwise why, one might ask, did the Kresge K Mart management lease out their men's and boys' wear departments to Unishops on a long-term basis?

Grayson-Robinson Stores, Inc.

Prior to 1960, Grayson-Robinson operated conventional women's apparel stores but in January, 1961 an agreement was made with Darling Stores Corporation under which it would merchandise and operate the 130 Darling units including a number of discount stores. The agreement provided that 90 per cent of the profits would go to Grayson-Robinson. New management came in and entered into a program of leased departments in large discount stores with the expectation that a large volume could be obtained on a profitable basis at a low cost for fixed assets and without long-term commitments. These actions increased annual volume by $40 million but at the same time operating capital requirements were also substantially increased. The company attempted to raise $10 million on a debenture issue in January, 1962 but this attempt collapsed with the May stock market slump. As a result, it became increasingly difficult for the chain to meet trade obligations. An additional complication arose from the fact that the Grayson-Robinson conventional stores were losing business to the rapidly growing discount stores. Financial embarrassment from restricted credit became so great that it was impossible to obtain the flow of merchandise essential to stock its stores.

377

In August, 1962 the company filed a Chapter XI petition in Federal Court in a desperate effort to save what it could. Trade liabilities amounted to about $10.5 million, and the number of creditors ran into many thousands. The petition stated, "Your petitioner is unable to pay its debts as they mature, although it is abundantly solvent." Management claimed that despite recent reversals, the company had a net worth of $11,911,035 and that all creditors would be paid in full "through a moderate extension of its general indebtedness . . ." When it filed its petition, Grayson-Robinson had 295 locations, including 212 women's and children's apparel stores, 43 discount apparel operations, four photographic retail stores, and 36 leased photographic departments.

The firm's attorneys immediately obtained orders from a Federal judge authorizing continued operation and allowing the company to buy new merchandise on credit. All suits were stayed and creditors were enjoined from removing any of the company's assets. Because of the complexity of the operation and the many locations, financial information regarding accounts receivable, inventory, the amount of cash in banks, etc., was hard to assess. One day before the filing, Bankers Trust Co., a creditor for $6,368,752, called the loan and exercised its right of off-set to take over the chain's bank account.

Although the immediate cause of Grayson-Robinson's collapse was the unpredictable stock market behavior, the most obvious reason for the failure was the firm's headlong rush for large volume in its discounting operation without adequate working capital. Total volume was $102 million in 1961, as opposed to $63 million prior to the new management takeover in 1960.

Marrud, Inc.

Marrud was founded in 1953 by J. E. Margolis and Harold Rudnick. The corporate title is an anagram of the two names. At the start the company operated concessions in conventional stores, but before many months elapsed it began installing leased departments in discount stores. "From then on," said Margolis, "it was like riding an escalator." Sales increased from $2,261,861 in 1958 to $45,831,950 in the fiscal year ending July 26, 1964. Profits, during this period, increased from $227,000 to $1,536,516.

A report on Marrud's progress appeared in the January, 1965, issue of *Discount Merchandiser* as follows: Earnings for Marrud, Inc., Norwood, Mass., rocketed to $1.5 million, on a 72 per cent increase, in the year ended July, 1964. Sales rose 29 per cent to $45.8 million. "The company's excellent showing has again been due in large measure to the Marrud operation" said president J. E. Margolis. "D. W. Jewelry Co., Inc., acquired last December

378

on a pooling of interest basis," he added, "has been increasingly contributing to both sales and earnings and has been displaying impressive growth."

In fiscal 1963 Marrud had a total of 271 leased departments, 196 Marrud units and 75 D. W. Jewelry units. During the 1964 fiscal year the total mounted to 345 departments, 222 for Marrud and 123 for D. W. Jewelry. "Our recently formed Clifton Private Brands, Inc.," Margolis said, "currently is producing substantially all of Marrud's private label First Choice and Natural Charm brands, which have been growing rapidly. Several important packaging contracts have been concluded with major corporations."

According to a prospectus issued by McDonnell and Company in June, 1961 for the sale of Marrud common stock, a majority of the company's leases then specified original terms of three years or five years with some having five-year renewal options. Thirty-seven licenses either provided for original terms extending beyond January 1, 1966, or were renewable at the company's option beyond that date. In 1965 Marrud began to be threatened with the loss of a large number of its outlets owing to expiring leases. This included seventy-seven Zayre stores, all the King's stores, and all the Topps stores. Out of about 200 units, they could immediately see approximately 130 disappearing. To replace these units Marrud management decided to buy forty-two Sun Ray drugstores and a large number of franchises.

The *Wall Street Journal* of March 24, 1965 announced the pending purchase by Marrud of the assets of Sun Ray Drug Company, a subsidiary of Penrose Industries Corporation. The same newspaper, in its December 21, 1965 issue stated that, "An offer of $1,650,000 in cash by Marrud, Inc., for forty-two Sun Ray drugstores of Penrose Industries Corp. was approved by the Federal district court here (Philadelphia). An initial payment of $200,000 is to be followed by four semi-annual installments on the balance of $1,450,000, according to the terms of the offer approved by Judge Francis L. Van Dusen . . . Alexander N. Rubin, Jr., attorney for the conservator, said claims of lien and priority creditors against the proceeds of the sale total about $1 million."

The stores Marrud acquired included thirty-two in Pennsylvania, eight in New Jersey, two in Delaware, and about 200 franchises in the same states and in Maryland. The acquisition was expected to add about $20 million annually to Marrud's sales. Sun Ray is a big name in Philadelphia and Margolis intended to bring it back to its former greatness. Marrud was a company with an excellent reputation and a net worth of about $5 million and long experience in its field. Why did it fail? According to trade sources, the reason was that management underestimated the amount of operating capital it would take to keep its new acquisition in stock. Marrud became financially embarrassed to such an extent that it could not pay its bills. When suppliers stopped shipping, it had to buy goods from jobbers at a premium. On December 29, 1965 the SEC halted trading in the company's securities.

Marrud finally filed a Chapter XI petition in Federal court. The company is now (1967) operated by a creditor's committee with attorney Arthur Golden as acting president.

John's Bargain Stores[1]

The first of what in 1967 was a 474 store-chain was started by the Cohen family in 1927 in South Ozone Park, N.Y. under the name "Cheap John's." The store was operated by Harry Cohen and his four children: Ben, James, David and Stella. James was the only one who attended high school. In 1955 the 33-store company was incorporated under the name of the Harry Cohen Merchandising Corporation with Ben Cohen as president, David Cohen as treasurer, James Cohen as merchandising manager and secretary, and Stella Cohen Tobin as vice-president and manager of the New York offices. In 1958 it was decided to change the company's name to John's Bargain Stores thus eliminating the negative connotation of "cheap."

By 1963, 222 stores were in operation, 119 of them within or near the New York metropolitan area. In addition, there were 39 stores in Pennsylvania; 41 in New Jersey; 12 in Maryland; 4 in Washington, D.C.; 3 in Connecticut; 2 in Delaware, and one each in Virginia and Ohio. Warehouses were located in New York City and in Baltimore. The following table illustrates the rapidity of growth.

TEN-YEAR SUMMARY JOHN'S BARGAIN STORES

Year	No. of Stores	Sales	Net Earnings	Earnings Per Share of Common	Working Capital	Share-holders' Equity
1957	66	$9,993,135	$150,961	$.12	$554,186	657,164
1958	84	15,245,910	221,808	.15	947,778	1,116,314
1959	110	19,897,924	207,665	.14	1,134,393	1,339,578
1960	156	27,449,179	296,465	.22	1,294,096	1,570,801
1961	179	33,920,405	551,463	.43	1,790,745	2,072,940
1962	222	40,229,531	952,428	.68	3,419,836	3,595,791
1963	285	45,752,979	1,027,841	.75	4,226,124	4,627,483
1964	397	58,150,132	699,526	.51	5,546,199	6,329,049
1965	472	61,769,704	1,045,121	.76	5,483,501	6,238,436
1966	497	62,467,279	(523,947)	—	4,445,264	5,439,296
1967	474	(A net loss of $1,310,449 was reported for 28 weeks ending July 15, 1967)				

Until 1962 the Cohen family were the only stockholders, but in that year 160,000 shares of common stock were sold to the public. In 1963 the

[1]Based in part on an article by Frank Schlesinger, "John's Bargain Stores," in the *New York Retailer*, April, 1963, pp. 10-19.

company applied for a listing of its common stock on the American Exchange and 50,000 shares of stock were offered to the public through the firm of Hayden and Stone, Inc.

John's headquarters were in New York and there all buying, pricing, distributing, inventory control, advertising, real estate management, and executive development was conducted. The Cohen family members, three brothers and a sister, had major executive posts and directed other executive personnel. Stores were grouped into regions, each of which was headed by a supervisor. Individual stores had very little autonomy. Said James Cohen, "All we ask of our store manager is simply to keep his store clean and neat and produce sales. He is not asked to order merchandise or price merchandise, or to do any advertising. This is all done by a group of specialists at the general offices."

The market that the firm catered to consisted of middle to low income families. Said a company official, "There are a lot of people who cannot afford to be in fashion or fad and have to buy what they can afford. We look after these people." Target customers were people with incomes so low that they will seek every opportunity to find regular merchandise at lower than regular prices. In seeking its store locations John's real estate department looked for poor neighborhood properties which could not be sold or rented. They were particularly interested in the former sites of supermarkets which had failed. Real estate management was considered a matter of such importance that just as much time was spent on real estate operations as on merchandising. According to Ben Cohen, "The ideal site of our store is a location that is short on new cars and long on used baby carriages."

Store leasing policy was explained by Ben Cohen, "When the chain decides to enter an area, it will usually sign a 10-year parent corporation lease on a store and it often guarantees the landlord a percentage of sales. In exchange, the landlord is induced to invest a considerable sum in altering the site to suit our specifications." If it so happens that a property looks ideal, John's persuades some selected real estate owner to buy it, offering a 10-year lease as a kind of collateral. Not all John's stores are in lower-end neighborhoods; some are in middle class areas, and several are in free-standing highway locations. It is expected that more units will open in shopping centers. In general, however, according to Ben Cohen, "The general rule of thumb remains. That is, the lower end the neighborhood, the better. We have brought people back to shop in areas that were abandoned by other chains."

Most of John's stores ranged from 2,000 to 6,000 square feet with a rental varying from $300 to $3,000 a month. Volumes ranged from $100,000 to $500,000 a year. Typical was a store that did about $200,000 a year in 2,500 square feet with sales per square foot of approximately $100. Such a store would operate with a population base of 10,000 people. James Cohen, vice president, said in an address before the NRMA in November, 1963,

"It may sound incredible to you, but the average capital investment to open a John's store is under $3,500 per unit. This includes warehousing, general office, and all capital requirements for everything else necessary to support one of our stores." Fixtures and wall decorations were of the simplest design and were standardized.

Of special interest was the fact that, unlike traditional retailers, John's stores had no basic stock. Buyers looked for out-of-season goods, close-outs, discontinued items, and distress-type merchandise. However, close-outs accounted for a declining percentage of the firm's inventory, since it had become impossible to fulfill the greatly expanded needs with limited buying. In 1967, 90 per cent of the firm's purchases consisted of newly manufactured goods especially ordered in large volume at low prices. Seventy-five per cent of the merchandise retailed for less than $1 and 23 per cent retailed at below $2 per item. No items exceeded $3.

Vice president James Cohen said, "Newspaper advertising is used to blanket large numbers of our stores thereby keeping the advertising costs per individual store low. The cost of a full advertising page in the New York *Daily News* is $1,600. When we spread this cost over the 110 stores situated in the circulation area of this newspaper, it brings the individual cost down to less than $12 per store. This is done in Chicago, Pittsburgh, Philadelphia, Washington, D.C., and elsewhere." Newspaper and radio advertising costs were between 3 per cent and 4 per cent of sales.

Buying for the chain was under the direction of a merchandise manager who met once a week with the regional supervisors to check on customer reaction and demand for merchandise categories. These reactions were reported by store managers to district managers who reported to their supervisors. Seven buyers specialized in the following merchandise classifications: ladies' and girls' underwear; linens and domestics; men's and boys' furnishings; toys; housewares and stationery; candies, sundries, and toiletries; infants' wear. Treasurer David Cohen directed buying activities while James Cohen presided over the merchandise council which met daily at 7 a.m. to approve and place orders initiated by the buyers. John's did not accept manufacturers' advertising allowances. It preferred to negotiate for the best possible net cost of the bulk merchandise delivered with no allowances.

John's buyers had established special relations with many makers of famous brands who sold their surplus merchandise to the company with the understanding that the brand name would not be advertised or promoted outside the stores. In this way John's was able to offer towels, blankets, and pillow cases carrying some of the best known brands. Some of these companies produced seasonal merchandise out of season especially for John's. Increasing volume enabled the company to establish its own brands in the following merchandise classifications: men's, boys', and ladies' underwear, sundries, stationery, toiletries. Another one of John's specialties was

382

outmoded styles, and buyers maintained a steady contact with manufacturers who had a surplus problem owing to outmoded styles. One week the accent might have been on brassieres or boys' shirts, next week, notebooks. Said chairman David Cohen, "Because of our item buying, we sometimes write orders that are larger than those placed by any retail chain in this country. When you think about it, you realize that basically we have no real competition because we do not stock a conventional line of merchandise within a department." In regard to purchasing decisions, John's was in a position to move quickly and often bought in great bulk, such as lots of 50,000 or 100,000. Purchases were shipped to one of four leased warehouses in a leased fleet of trucks and distributed to the stores on the basis of their past performance for a given item. About 10 per cent of John's sales were imports from Japan, China, Spain and Italy. A store that has just opened was given a balanced assortment.

John's operated 497 stores at the end of 1966 with a sales volume of $62,467,249. The firm tried to solve its increasingly complicated distribution problems by using a rather sophisticated IBM 1401 data processing system for store inventory control, warehouse accounting control, markdown accounting, and payroll and cash report tabulations. The company established a bonus system in 1962, to which 20 per cent of earnings before taxes was allocated. Bonus payments were graduated according to performance, work category, seniority, and salary bracket. An additional 5 per cent of pretax earnings was allocated to the employees' profit-sharing plan in trust for those employees who were not represented by a collective bargaining unit. Employee contribution was permissible but it was not required. The company provided hospitalization and group life insurance for all employees not covered by a collective bargaining agreement and provided paid vacations for all employees. Under a restricted stock-option plan effective in 1963, 100,000 authorized but unissued shares of common stock were granted to officers and employees. Shares could be purchased on the date of the grant and no person could be granted more than 600 shares. As of 1963, some 300 employees held options to buy 57,000 shares.

The company entered into agreements, terminable at the will of the company, with sixteen of its employees (not including David, Ben, James Cohen, and Stella Tobin), whereby upon the death of any one of them while in the employment of the company, death payments ranging from $25,000 to $50,000 (payable over five years) would be made to their beneficiaries. The company carried life insurance on such employees in order to fund its obligation under these agreements.

All executives with the firm in 1967 were recruited from the ranks of store managers who were representative of middle management. For store managers John's sought men who were married and willing to work for the future. Prospects seemed good since rapid expansion creates many opportunities for promotion. Prospective store managers did not necessarily need a retail background or a college education. Candidates who were accepted were given a 26-week on-the-job training program in one of the New York metropolitan area stores. Store managers received a straight salary plus profit sharing and bonus. They averaged about $7,500 salary after two years on the job, and could rise to $13,000, exclusive of fringe benefits. If members of the third generation Cohen family wanted to work for the firm they had to start from scratch as trainees. Their progress was measured by the same standards applied to non-relatives. Their parents were not concerned by the possibility of top management passing to outside directors.

Professional specialists, hired after 1958, provided valuable services. The Cohen management was alert to seek out and fill the tremendous central-city void left in the low-priced merchandise area abandoned by the big variety chains, such as Woolworth and Kresge, when they traded up and became junior department stores. The question can be raised as to whether the company, after it had saturated the available metropolitan areas with stores, could find enough new locations of the type it required for continued expansion. Would the large size of the operation lead to impersonal and more routine standards of merchandise and service? In the March 11, 1964, *Women's Wear Daily*, David Cohen, their board chairman, said that John's had embarked on a spirited expansion drive to surpass Woolworth as the operator of the largest number of general merchandise outlets in the country. "We are dead serious about this project," Cohen said. "Our plan is to blanket the United States with John's units and to ultimately have more stores in operation in this country than Woolworth's." A Woolworth spokesman said, "We wish them luck!"

For the first time in its history, the company, in 1966, sustained an operating loss of $1,179,714 which was reduced by a tax loss carry-back to $523,947. Fifty-one new stores were opened in 1966 in areas serviced by existing warehouses and advertising programs. It was apparent that, owing to its very rapid expansion, John's had overtaxed its managerial abilities. Operating expenses at 35.9 per cent of sales in 1966 were at an all-time high.

David Cohen initiated a program to significantly reduce expenses. Twenty-six marginal and unprofitable stores were closed and new openings strictly curtailed. A careful and systematic evaluation of every store in the chain was made and the company's merchandise distribution techniques completely revamped to assure better control of shipments to stores, permitting them to operate with lower inventories. John's stores were then merchandised on a regional basis with an operational vice president in charge of each of the four divisions.

John's then gave special emphasis to the greater Miami retail market where six stores were added in 1966. The company had achieved widespread

384

consumer acceptance in Puerto Rico with three units operating and two more under negotiation in 1967.

JOHN'S BARGAIN STORE CORP. FILES CHAPTER XI PETITION

It was announced in the *Home Furnishings Daily* of Sept. 1, 1967 that John's Bargain Stores Corporation had filed a Chapter XI petition on August 31 listing debts of $11,659,444 and assets of $15,788,291 as of July 15. Current debts were $10,242,527 and current assets, $13,487,204. Trading of the firm's stock on the American Stock Exchange was halted.

President David Cohen blamed over-expansion in the South and Midwest for the chain's then current financial woes. The largest creditor listed was Chase Manhattan Bank with a claim of $1,350,000. According to *Home Furnishings Daily*, balance sheet figures as of the end of 1966 showed assets of $14,173,455 of which inventory was $9,500,248. Current liabilities were $7,240,394 and the chain's net worth was over $5 million. About 74 per cent of the 1,375,965 common shares outstanding was controlled by management.

In the *Women's Wear Daily* of June 24, 1969, it was reported that the creditors' committee of the firm had authorized the sale of 425,000 unregistered shares in the chain for $1,674,999 to a group headed by Sprayregen & Co., brokers. The group signed an agreement to buy the stock with an option to buy an additional 328,222 shares. The firm showed a profit of $325,887 on 1968 sales of $35,400,000.

What Dun and Bradstreet looks for in Rating the Credit of Discount Retailers[1]

BY WILLIAM A. DUVEL, ASSISTANT VICE PRESIDENT, DUN AND BRADSTREET

You as a retailer want to be rated first credit, very understandably, and your suppliers want you to be rated first credit, very understandably. At least, they want you to be so rated until the day comes that you either cannot, do not, or will not pay your bills, and then they raise some very serious

[1]A talk given at The University of Massachusetts 1964 Conference on Mass-Merchandising.

questions with us. I wonder how many of you realize that there are really three kinds of credit-agency opinions expressed on your concerns. First is the rating that is listed in a reference book, such as ours, issued six times a year. Unfortunately, because many of our subscribers only buy two books a year, we must assign a rather conservative rating, because that rating is outstanding in the hands of our subscribers anywhere from six to eight or nine months. This rating is conservative; it cannot tell the whole story, no rating ever could, and unfortunately we know that a great deal of credit is extended on a rating alone. So this rating must be a conservative one. Second is a rating that is extended by a specialized type of service. There are two that touch the lives of the mass-merchandisers as far as Dun & Bradstreet is concerned: one is the discount appraisal service, and the other is our credit clearing house that specializes on extending credit to manufacturers.

The ratings expressed by these services are more liberal. They are expressed in terms of dollars rather than a symbol or a numeral rating. For example, it may be double A I-$\frac{1}{2}$ third credit, and yet as far as the appraisal service or clearing house credit is concerned, they may be extending credit to the extent of $30,000 to $40,000. It may be a bank, and they may go as far as $10,000. This is simply because they can change their ratings overnight; they can move quickly. They are closer to the situation than is the broad general rating that goes into the reference book. Third is a type of rating that might be called a personalized rating. Both of these services, and I know this is true in other specialized services, have people who unfortunately some people call "experts." I shun this term because nobody is an expert in the field of credit, at least when they are wrong, but these men will, on an individual case, go beyond the assigned rating. It may be a blank in the reference book, it may not be rated by the discount appraisal service, but on an individual order basis this expert may be willing to say: "go ahead and ship, for the $10,000, $30,000, or $40,000." He does this for the very simple reason that he is close enough to that subscriber to understand the peculiarities of the situation. Either the subscriber wants to, or must take excessive risk in order to move the goods.

I think that you all know that Dun & Bradstreet was sufficiently interested in discounting and was enough concerned about what was going on in the field that they set up a special *Discount Digest* bulletin service two years ago. Today it is a full-fledged specialized service trying to meet the needs of the people who are selling to this industry. Let us look at the failure story for a moment. Up through the first week of April of this year (1964), there were thirty-six mass-merchandisers or discounters who failed throughout the United States with a total liability of $3,200,000. Of these thirty-six, five were located in New England, or about 14 per cent. You have the dubious distinction of still being the most hazardous retail line. However, we are encouraged in that both the number and the dollar liability is down from 1963 and is down from the first quarter of 1962.

Before I came I looked at these thirty-six reports to see if there was any pattern. These things stuck out: first, they were all slow in paying their bills. Second, most all of them had refused to give any financial information, or the financial estimates that they had given were rather, shall we say, enthusiastic. Third, a number had secured financing at rather high rates. Fourth, and I might say almost without exception, all of them were overly enthusiastic about the prospects of their business. And we believe what they said was based on enthusiasm. Now this is a little background and I hope that you will see that any agency, whether it be ours or any of the other fine ones that are in this field, must have the facts on which to base a judgment.

We cannot establish an opinion or a judgment on a lot of ideas or suspicions. There must be a sound basis of fact on which to make a recommendation. Also, I plead with you – no agency is perfect. We are made up of human beings with foibles just like you, but we are responsible to our subscribers, who are your suppliers, to make a recommendation based on facts. Now, what are we trying to find out?

Here I would like to just touch a little bit on what we are doing in the appraisal report field. We think that the most important point is the question of management. What kind of a management do they have? Because in no other field is it so important; does the management really know the score? You may wonder a little bit about this. We obtain the facts going back over a period of time. We talk to a lot of people and yet, believe me, when I talk to a good investigator, the facts come through pretty clear as to whether or not management does know the answer. What are its strengths and weaknesses? Is it experienced? Is it realistic? Is it cooperative with its suppliers? Or is it contentious, unusually demanding, or what?

Take a company in whose securities you are interested, even if it is your own, look at and read the President's Report of a year ago, and then see how true it is. Did his prediction come to pass? Now this, in a sense, is what Dun and Bradstreet tries to do when it evaluates a management. If they visit you and predict great things – increase in profit, reduction in debt, etc. – we think that it is realistic to expect that some of these things will come to pass. But consistently, if they do not, obviously somewhere along the line someone is not quite doing his job. So we believe that this question of management is vital in this field. We think it is vital because it will mean the success or failure of your business, or of any business.

If I were to pick out one single figure from all the financial data that I would be interested in discussing with you, it would be your working-capital position. This is the money which you have available to you. If you tie it up in stores, etc., it is not available to meet the needs of the business. So here again, look at your working-capital position, and see what is happening to it.

We are very much interested in what your suppliers think because they are supplying you with the bulk of your capital. They have more money tied up in your business than you do in most every case. It is important whether, as an industry, you are slower in paying your bills today than you were a year ago. If you are slower it means that the suppliers' risk is getting greater and greater. In trying to evaluate your company, we will talk to your banker, your insurance company, your factor, your finance company, or whoever it might be. And we will try to find out the facts as forthrightly as we can.

Finally, we will try to find out something about your plans and prospects. Here I hope that you will realize that it is with the fullest desire of trying to be helpful. If you have five or ten stores in your chain now and are thinking about adding another four or five next year we are scared to death to hear this, and we want to know how you are going to do it. We know that your suppliers and your banks want to know even more. If you say, as some of you do, "We are not quite sure – we have not worked out the details yet," you either insult our intelligence, in which case you are not half as smart as we know you are, or else you must be crazier than we think you are! Today, the question of whether or not to open a new store is more important than it has ever been. Where are you going to put it? Who is going to run it?

Finally – after we have gone through this and some other questions – we try to come up with a credit appraisal trying to say that in our judgement you can extend "x" number of credit dollars to this concern and you can reasonably expect to be paid. If we think that it is going to be slow, and we know that this is true in many cases, we will so indicate.

We also make a sales appraisal to try and indicate what we think of your concern as a merchandising operation. We are in a boom time during which the quality of trade credit deteriorates. It has deteriorated steadily for the past three years. You may say as retailers, "That does not concern me. We are not offering very much credit." And most of you are not, although as an aside, I note that Sears Roebuck boasts in its annual report that in 1963, 55 per cent of its sales were on credit. I have the suspicion that if Sears continues to push in that direction you will be forced to do the same. But I would like you to be alert to the fact that more and more money is being tied up in receivables than it is in increased sales, and that there is less working capital to support it. Historically, when this goes far enough, credit begins to be tight; and then gentlemen in the mass-merchandising industry, you could come upon very tough times because your very livelihood is dependent upon the support and consideration you are receiving from your trade creditors.

388

Confessions of a Shoplifter[1]

This tape recording was made for the Evanston, Illinois, Chamber of Commerce. It is the confession of a girl in her twenties who started her shoplifting career at an early age in St. Louis, Missouri. She was apprehended by the Evanston police. Security expert Milton M. Schiff explained that because of this public confession it was agreed that she would not be arrested or tried.

Rita, first I would like to ask you when you began shoplifting?

"I began shoplifting at the age of 16 years old."

How did you happen to begin shoplifting, Rita?

"Some girls that I know in Fort Worth, Missouri were shoplifters and I went out with them one day to see how they performed in the store, and from then on, I became a shoplifter."

Rita, I understand that there are a number of ways in which you can shoplift. Suppose you tell us some of the ways that people go about stealing merchandise in stores.

"There are numerous ways to work when you are shoplifting: 1) from between your legs, you work from the strength of your legs; 2) some work in bloomers and some work in girdles."

Could you explain a little more about this matter of working with bloomers and working with girdles. Could you describe these bloomers and girdles that are used?

"I really couldn't explain how they work in the drawers and the girdles, because I've never experienced it for myself. I only work from the strength of my legs."

Rita, you say you work from the strength of your legs. Could you tell us how you developed this technique?

"As I once said, I went out with some bosom friends of mine and I watched the way they performed in the store, and I seen how they rolled suits and put them between their legs and walk out, and from then on I was doing the same thing."

I wonder, Rita, how much merchandise can you take at one time?

"I can carry two men's suits, hanger and all; each suit with two pairs of pants to it and three women's suits, hanger and all."

What type of merchandise do you prefer to take? You aren't mentioning blouses, or gloves or things of that nature.

"No, I prefer the best of anything I steal. I don't take anything small. I try to get the best – a suit not under $79 – each suit I want to be at least over $100."

[1]Proceedings, Discount Store Management Conference, Univ. of Mass., 1962.

Rita, how do you dispose of the goods you take?

"I have a fence, and then I have special customers. My good suits, the best of the suits I have, I take them to my best customers and the ones that I can't get rid of, I take in a lump sum to a fence."

Rita, when you take it to a fence, how do you handle it? What price would you get for a $100 suit?

"On a $100 suit to a fence, he would give me $20 a suit. When I go to him, I would at least have about 10 or 11 pieces, so that I could see myself making a little money."

I see. Rita, how do you prefer to operate? Do you like to be in a crowded store or a store that perhaps doesn't have as many customers?

"I prefer to operate early in the morning when the store first opens or on the salesladies' lunch period because there are not too many salesladies in the store. Or on a day when it is very busy."

I see. Do you always work with someone? You mentioned that you began working with some other girls. Do you always have a partner?

"Sometimes I work with two girls; if not with two girls, by myself."

If you are working with two girls, how do you operate?

"With two girls, we are each on our own. What I make in the store is mine, what they make is theirs. Sometimes you need a girl to block for you, before you'd be able to pick up, and then sometimes you need a girl to shield you out when you are on your way out of the store."

Suppose you were stopped by one of the store personnel or the store detective? What would you do?

"If I see that I couldn't talk my way out of it, I would try to move around in the store and drop the suits."

Do you operate in a team from one location, perhaps an automobile, and then go back into the same store over again; or when you go into a community, do you go up and down the streets, so to speak, and stop at all the stores.

"When I go into a community, I try to make all the stores and, providing if one of the stores which I have been in is good, I make a second trip. We work by automobile, and I am an international shoplifter, I go from state to state."

Thank you very much. Rita, I have another question here. I wonder if you could tell us, give us some ideas, as to what store personnel might watch for in being alert to shoplifting. In other words, if I were working in a store, what should I look for in being on guard against shoplifting?

"The first thing you should do, you should notice a person's eyes and how they look when they come in a store, and then you can tell from the way they walk after they have taken something out of the store."

Rita, how far do you have to walk?

"I walk outside of the store, and after I am outside of the store, the car in which we are in circles the block; and after we are out, he picks us up at the corner."

Rita, how many shoplifters would you say you have known in your life?

"I know so many, I can't count them."

"Rita, is shoplifting what you would call a pretty big business?

"I would say it is. It is one of the biggest businesses that I know of."

Do you think that a great amount of merchandise is taken from the stores in our communities?

"Yes, the stores lose quite a bit."

Now that you are no longer in custody here in Evanston, what are your plans for the future?

"My plan for the future is to straighten my life out and live like normal people because I have found out that the game don't pay off like I thought it would."

Despite what this girl said, she was arrested again a few weeks later in another suburb for shoplifting. She had to get so much money each day to get by.

These organized rings (and they do operate nationally) have their own supporting attornies on hand. They have a fleet of vehicles, and they have their drops, which are called fences or receivers throughout the country. They can shoplift thousands of dollars worth of merchandise and within two hours have its way to the West Coast or South by regular transportation methods. It is a business. They are professionals in every sense of the word. They have business meetings; they have training schools, and they have a test you have to pass before you can get your so-called "diploma," and if given the opportunity, they can put you out of business.

Shoplifting as whole, including amateurs, narcotic addicts and professionals, doesn't approach, in terms of dollar losses, the damage that can be caused by dishonest employees.

XII

Do Food Markets Belong In Discount Stores?[1]

BY MARTIN CHASE, DISCOUNT PIONEER AND FOUNDER
OF ANN AND HOPE, CUMBERLAND, R.I.

I have been asked to talk on the topic of supermarkets and discount houses under the same roof. And more specifically on these three subjects: 1) Do food markets belong in discount stores? 2) If so, should the same checkouts be used for food as well as general merchandise? 3) What is the future of food markets and discount stores?

I do not profess to be an expert on supermarkets but I can tell you some of the experiences that I have had in our two stores in reference to this which may be of interest to you. We first introduced food into our stores about five years ago. What prompted such action? Originally we felt that if we had food to offer to our customers they would stay in our store and shop a little longer rather than leave and go to a supermarket elsewhere to buy food. Food has always been considered the number one draw in any shopping center. We knew that the food department would attract our customers more often to our store. In addition, it was also our prime concept that we should offer to our customers a complete one-stop shopping center, under one roof, where they could buy almost anything a family might need and not have to go elsewhere for what they require. Obviously, such a concept would not be properly fulfilled without a good food market.

392

Do Food Markets Belong in Discount Stores?

From the beginning, however, we learned two important things: 1) If properly merchandised under good discount store practices so that a large volume is achieved, a food market can be run at a substantial discount saving to the consumer, as compared to prices charged in conventional supermarkets, and still make a profit. 2) A good discount store generates large traffic into its food department as much as the food department generates traffic into the discount store. They complement each other to such a gratifying extent that now we would no more think of our stores without dresses as we would think of them without food.

One word of caution here, however. The food department must be a true discount food market, and not merely a transplant of a conventional branch of a supermarket chain. Discount house shoppers are wise shoppers. You cannot fool them with just the label "discount" or with a few specials. You must deliver what you promise. You must show your customer that they will save by buying food regularly at your store. Before we opened the first food market five years ago, we discovered that most of the trade felt that discount stores with food markets should locate the food market completely within the physical confines of the discount store and not merely on the side or connected with it. Thus food shoppers would constantly have to filter through the general merchandise, either going to or coming from the food department. That is what we did in our Cumberland store. In addition, for our own convenience we used the same central checkouts for food and for general merchandise. Our thinking has changed somewhat since then.

Our food department in our Warwick store, while still under the same roof, is located at the extreme right of the store and is connected by an interior archway – a corridor between the food market and the discount store. This corridor is about fifty feet wide and about seventy-five feet long and houses our lunch counters. It is a natural, well-traveled link between the market and the store. Also, the partitions between the food market and the store are made of glass so that the customer will feel that he is in the same store. In addition, the food market has its own entrance from the parking lot. We feel that if a customer only wants food, why make it inconvenient for him? The department in Warwick has its own battery of registers. We find this more efficient than the procedure in our Cumberland store where food and general merchandise is checked out together.

We found in Cumberland that mechanical problems arose in checking out food and general merchandise at the same time and in keeping the checkout counters free of moisture and produce mist. Also, where the same checkouts are used for food and general merchandise, there results a considerable slowdown in the overall checking-out process, especially during the heavy food shopping hours. A large quantity of small items of food amounting to say $30, obviously takes considerably longer to check out than a $30 coat. The customer buying only the coat becomes impatient waiting behind the food customer and sometimes objects out loud. On the other hand, customers who are checking out with only food seem to have been conditioned to waiting patiently while the preceding customer's food orders are being processed. We have also found that many customers who buy general merchandise during the same visit when they buy food usually prefer to shop for the general merchandise first, check their purchases, leave them in their cars, and then buy their foods so that they can get their perishables home more quickly after the purchase.

Now, regarding the future of food markets and discount houses. The discount house and its concept of doing business has by this time found full consumer acceptance. Similarly, the discount food market also has found consumer acceptance. For instance, in my state of Rhode Island, not only are the discount houses plunging more heavily into the food business as an adjunct to their general merchandise, but the supermarket chains are turning to discounts themselves. "Great Scot" has become "Big G" with a rash of foodstores all over the state. Star Markets has now become the "Big Star Discount Food" and Almacs has a tremendous advertising campaign now going on shouting, "we out-discount the discounters" on over 5,000 items. All over the country many of the supermarket chains have re-examined their positions and have acted. Food Fair, Grand Unions, Stop & Shop, Lucky, Giant, Jewel Tea, and others have acquired general discount stores and have consolidated many of them with their discount food markets. Or they have arranged to secure leases in established general discount houses. Apparently they have realized that these are the major areas of expansion in their future, and have reacted in their typical, aggressive fashion.

On the other side of the coin, Korvette, Vornado, Woolco, and others in the discount industry have opened up discount food markets as part of their operation either by self-ownership or by lease arrangement. In conclusion, to my mind, it is no longer a question of whether it is feasible or wise or necessary to incorporate a discount food market in a good discount store; the question now is how fast can it be accomplished? A conventional supermarket which opens next door to you is no particular asset to you or to themselves either. Why should a customer come all the way out to the outskirts to buy from an A & P if he has one on his own corner? He would go right over there. The prices are the same. The reason we get our customers to come to the outskirts is that they think they are saving money and that we give them more than the other guys give them. But if you do not, why should they come? I no longer think of putting an A & P or First National next to me. They will not draw.

Question: Do you discount every food item in your department, or do you just take certain key items?

We discount every item in our whole store, and we have over 100,000 items. If you do not believe it, come and count them! We sell absolutely nothing in our store except at a discount. As a matter of fact, if we cannot sell at discount, we get rid of the item. Every food item is discounted. Now Mr. Joseph E. Fernandes, president, Fernandes Supermarkets, Morton, Mass., says it is about 4.5 per cent to 5 per cent, but we actually figure our rate at 6 per cent to 6.5 per cent. Now think of a fellow who makes about $70, or $80, or $90, or $100 a week and has three or four kids. You know how much money he spends when he gets there Thursday night? Sometimes as much as $40 or $45. You take 6 per cent of $40, and he saves $2.40. Is it worth it to spend half a gallon of gas to go to the outskirts to buy and save $2.40? People who have a lot of money do not care what they spend. They go to the conventional store and they go to the conventional department store. Not everybody wants to come to a discount house because a discount house will not give you any service; a discount house has no charge accounts. I always tell a customer: "If you want service, go to a department store; if you want to wait on yourself and save money, come here." That's our slogan, and we find that everybody wants to save, no matter if they are millionaires. Actually the 6 per cent difference amounts to something for a poor family. You may save 5 per cent. So what is saved on $40 is $2. Now when they spent $40, at least they have $2 left so that they can get something else. So the 5 per cent means something. And let me say this: the average workingman's wife is well aware of a price difference of one cent and knows that pennies add up to dollars.

When I ran my own food department in the Lonsdale store, the basis was to bring the customer in. Whether we made money or not, we did not care; but we never lost money. When we opened up our Warwick store we were going to run it ourselves too. And then we decided, maybe we ought to let the real experts go in there if we could make a deal with them to operate the way we want them to operate. We spoke to three of the biggest chains in the country that are discount-minded. And we finally picked out one – Stop & Shop. We picked them against three of the largest because they are honest. If Sidney Rabb says he is going to do something, I know he will do it. That is why we picked Sidney Rabb to run our discount food department in Warwick. But let me say this to you: the first year that we opened the food market in Warwick, we did a little over $5 million in that one store. Now he has a certain price at which he must sell his merchandise. Everything must be discounted. Our man goes regularly through that store twice a week, and if we find anything there that is not discounted, they pull it off the shelves or mark it down. They are happy to mark it down because it is really an error when one little item shoots through without being marked down. Right now we have a war on in Rhode Island which probably will happen in every city in the country. As Fernandes says, one or two places are all right. Big G just opened up fourteen of them, right around here, and they are all discounters.

When we went over the five million mark, there is no question that we hurt the other conventional supermarkets. We knew it would not take long until some of them would come running to do the same thing we did. And sure enough, the Big G started opening up one of their twelve stores there as a discount operation and it worked terrifically. Today he is going into Pawtucket and Woonsocket to compete with Fernandes. Now just what would Fernandes say? He has a Big Joe in the little town of Woonsocket. He says he is doing $70,000 a week. Do you know what the average supermarket does? Between $20,000 and $32,000. He is doing $70,000 and just opened! We did over $100,000 and we are only open a year-and-a-half. So these fellows see what is happening because naturally it is hurting them. Big Star went in; now Almac's has a terrific chain in Rhode Island. Now there is a fight between all of them. You think the conventional operator and the supermarket can stay in business with all these stores there? No. They will have to do something. And how long do you think the First National will sit by and do absolutely no business? Sure, my wife likes to go to a supermarket to get the steaks this size; she wants personal service – she asks no prices – and they deliver it to her. But you fellows cannot do business with my wife. There are not too many like her; nor can you do business with your wives either! We want the 95 per cent that wants to save money, that is where we are getting our business from. Sometimes my wife will come into my store and say, "You do not have the right kind of dresses." The dresses she wants I have not got. I tell her to go somewhere else to buy them! I don't want the one who wants these dresses. So we cannot go by my wife or your wife or to those whose husbands are so successful they do not care. I am looking for the average customer. Let my wife go to Tiffany's if she wants to.

Discount Supermarkets
Threat – No   Challenge – Yes

BY JOSEPH N. DEBLINGER, FOOD BROKER[2]

The Super Market Institute, which includes every important chain in the United States except one, polled its members a few years ago as to whether the discount house was a threat. Almost unanimously there was a resounding "No." In 1960 the question was posed again. This time there was a resounding "Yes." One out of every three members responding had reversed himself. What happened? How did this come about in this short space of a few years? Of course it did not come about in a few years; it has been in process for some time.

Do Food Markets Belong in Discount Stores?

Briefly, in my talk today, I intend to discuss four major aspects of this question:

a. How did the discount house develop?
b. How does the discount house succeed in its food operation?
c. In what ways are the supermarkets meeting this challenge?
d. What is the future shape of things in the food business?

HOW DID THE DISCOUNT HOUSE DEVELOP?

Discount houses actually started about thirty years ago, during the depression. King Kullen and Big Bear were the original food discounters, with emphasis on self-service, low cost, cash-and-carry, and no credit operation. What they and other pioneers started helped modernize the food industry as a low cost distributor. They made such an impact, not only in America but on the world, that our methods of distribution are being adopted everywhere.

While the food revolution was going on, there were similar fundamental changes taking place in the merchandising of soft and hard goods, appliances, etc. Macy's led the way with its famous "6 per cent Less" slogan and other department store competition – particularly that segment which was located in the Union Square area, such early discounters as Klein's and Ohrbach's – were also cutting prices. Thus, upon examination, we see that the discount house was actually in existence years ago, though it did not merit that name because the reputable department stores were not willing to forego the precious image they had patiently built up over the years. There was one outstanding difference. Where there was a food department, it was a gourmet and specialty food type of operation.

But with the lusty arrival of the discounters, who stimulated the public's imagination with their attack on fair trade laws – in effect, nullifying these laws – there was no such problem as a previous image. They leaped into the fray with both feet, using the advanced methods and style of the supermarkets. They unfurled a new flag emblazoned with the words "Discount House" and started crowing about it.

In a recent Deblinger Market Research Report, which we issue for our principals and marketing associates, we reviewed the rise of the discounter and concluded by saying: "The discounters have succeeded in planting one thought in the minds of all consumers: Shop and compare, do not buy at list prices, you will get it cheaper here." They took the slogans which the leaders in the food industry had developed, slogans emphasizing low prices and quality, such as "Come See, Come Save," and applied them to all retail items. That briefly is how the discount house came about.

HOW DOES THE DISCOUNT HOUSE SUCCEED IN ITS FOOD OPERATION?

It does it in the following ways:

1. Emphasis on price.

2. Ability to attract and handle greater traffic and business per square foot.

3. Ability to run the food operation with lower overhead, perhaps through subsidy from other departments, and its willingness to accept lower net profit.

4. The attraction other leased departments, likewise emphasizing price, hold for the consumer, a captive audience.

5. The move to suburbia, tremendous stores, convenient shopping plus one-stop diversified horizontal shopping.

IN WHAT WAYS ARE THE SUPERMARKETS MEETING THIS CHALLENGE?

1. Acquisition: The trend by which the supermarket chain meets the challenge by entering into the discount field operation itself through purchase of existing discount houses.

2. Own Stores: The trend whereby a powerful chain opens and operates vast discount houses under either its own or a new name in which the words "Discount House" are very prominent.

3. Large Independent Coop Stores: Where the independently owned retail group meets the challenge, by opening big stores in which non-foods are given equal billing with foods. Such stores are being opened on the highways across from established discounters, and successfully competing with them.

4. Wholesaler-Sponsored Group Stores: A Midwest voluntary group will shortly begin construction of a 150,000 square-foot discount house center featuring food, both to fight the discounter and to get to know something about discount house business.

5. Mutual Partnership: The trend in which progressive supermarkets enter into partnership with similarly aggressive discounters, to open stores shoulder-to-shoulder on highways to attract trade through their combined allure for the consumer.

6. The "If You Can't Lick Them, Join Them" School: The supermarket operator who averts direct competition from the discount house by leasing space in the discount house, usually under another name, and operating the food department there.

7. Autonomy: National chains are granting more autonomy to regional branches, even to the extent of permitting discount houses within the division.

398

WHAT IS THE FUTURE SHAPE OF THINGS IN THE FOOD BUSINESS?

Every indication points to the conclusion that expansion is developing into other fields such as the following:

1. Foreign subsidiaries.

2. Entering into non-food areas, such as gas stations, in connection with the supermarkets.

3. Real estate divisions acquiring real estate for leasing at a profit.

4. Diversifying into completely new areas, such as opening and operating laundromats; selling food by mail; and operating vending machines in manufacturing plants.

The future also looks like this: In a recent survey done by the Deblinger Sales & Marketing Corporation, we found an untapped potential of consumers who find the task of shopping a downright chore. This general trend to make shopping easier will grow, and new ways will be found to satisfy this desire of many housewives for relief from the weekly or bi-weekly shopping expedition. This manifests itself in the following trends:

1. More and more smaller chains and independents are delivering orders for a fixed charge of 25 to 50 cents. I know of one national chain which is experimenting in New York with a service store with clerks assigned to take telephone orders.

2. The trend toward opening a warehouse rather than a supermarket and having customers either telephone their orders or mail them in on forms for use in electronic machines.

3. Here is one innovation which looks like something Edward Bellamy forecast almost three-quarters of a century ago in his book *Looking Backward 2000 to 1887*. A major chain has taken space in a New York development under construction which will house 25,000 residents. Each apartment will be connected by closed-circuit television to all the stores in the development. During the day the housewife will be able to see on the screen the "specials" and the wares in the various stores as the television cameras move up and down the aisles. An intercom system will connect all the tenants with the service stores.

DISCOUNT FOOD STORES – THREAT? NO, CHALLENGE? YES

In summarizing I wish to make the following points:

1. The discount house of today – ably and aggressively managed, backed by substantial funding, commanding the interest of Wall Street – represents a type of competition such as the conventional supermarket has not met in its thirty-odd years of history.

399

2. Although most of the founders of the supermarket industry are gone, the resilient, equally aggressive, and able management which succeeded them is meeting the challenge by taking the offensive away from the discount house.

3. That there is a trend developing into greater diversification.

4. That in the years ahead the trend to reduce the shopping chore will continue.

Fundamentally, the challenge of the discount house to the supermarket is not new. It is a healthy one because it is resulting in ever sharpening operational and merchandising techniques, bringing food and other commodities at the lowest possible cost to the 182 million people in the U.S. today and the 200 million six years from now.

In conclusion, to the question "Are discount food stores a threat to supermarkets?," I trust you will agree when I say, "Threat? No – Challenge? Yes."

Are Discount Food Prices Lower?

In the face of increasing operating expenses and higher gross margins discount food stores in some areas have managed to undersell the conventional food outlets. That this is the case is shown by a study made by Robert J. Minichiello[3] in which he compared the prices charged by paired discount and conventional food stores all of which were operated by a large food chain, a small food chain, and a voluntary food chain. His findings follow:

"The discount food stores were attractively decored outlets providing a shopping environment on a par with the conventional supermarkets. Assortments stocked by the discount food stores tended to be similar to those available at the conventional supermarkets, with some exceptions among groceries and non-foods.

"The discount food stores consistently underpriced the conventional supermarkets. At the large food chain and in the voluntary chain, almost all identical items were sold at lower prices in the discount outlets. At the small chains, many items were sold at lower prices in the discount food stores, but all produce and certain items in other merchandise categories were sold at the same prices in both types of stores. Gross margins were from 4.2 to 6.0 percentage points less at discount food stores.

"The elimination of trading stamps was the greatest source of expense reduction for the discount food stores. Labor expenses were lower but most of the difference could be accounted for by the absence of certain service departments or other customer services and/or by differences in average hourly labor costs. The discount food stores experienced much higher advertising expenses than the conventional supermarkets primarily because of the use of direct mail circulars. Reductions in operating expenses by the discount food stores did not compensate fully for the differences in gross margins; consequently, net profits before taxes were less at the discount stores. Opportunities for the discount food stores to significantly reduce the investments in store facilities or increase turnover of inventory and fixed assets were not found. Thus, as a concomitant of lower profits, the discount food stores had lower pre-tax returns on the investments in selected store assets than the conventional supermarkets. There was no convincing evidence that the discount food stores had developed operating economies or merchandising methods that were not readily available to conventional supermarkets. Lower operating costs, achieved principally by eliminating trading stamps, have enabled the discount food stores to offer lower prices that appear to have attracted a segment of the market motivated more by low price appeal than by the merchandise premiums obtainable by saving and redeeming trading stamps."

The stores compared by Minichiello were conventional large chain stores averaging 14,600 square feet and average weekly sales of $60,000 in a shopping center, with a general merchandise discount department store and some small food and service shops. The matching discount food outlet of this large chain was a food department with 17,600 square feet in a free-standing general merchandise department store. Both were in the outskirts of cities.

The Vornado chain, in their food marts, have a sign hanging in the entrance stating, "Vornado pledges to you, our customers, that we will always save you 5 per cent or more on groceries every day of the year." GEM closed door discount store policy is to have their food lessees charge 6 per cent to 7 per cent less than they do in their own markets.

Almost all identical items available at both the discount food store and the conventional supermarkets were sold at lower prices in the discount food stores of the large chain and the Voluntary Trading stamps, drawings, games and the sale of premium merchandise at attractive prices were used in the non-discount store to promote customer patronage.

Operating expenses were from 2.5 to 3.6 percentage points less at the discount food stores. The elimination of trading stamps was the greatest source of expense reduction, its cost being from 2.1 per cent to 2.7 per cent of sales. Labor cost was lower at the discount stores owing to the absence of certain service departments or other customer services and by differences in average hourly labor costs owing to more seniority in the conventional stores. Discount stores had much higher advertising expenses because of direct mail circulars. Net profits before taxes were 1.4 to 2.6 percentage points less at the discount stores. Opportunities for the discount food stores to significantly reduce the investments in store facilities or increase turnover of inventory and fixed assets were not found. The discount food stores, although showing pre-tax returns of from 27.4 per cent to 30.6 per cent on the investments in selected store assets, had lower returns than the conventional markets.

[1]Talk at the University of Massachusetts, April, 1964, Conference on Mass-Merchandising.

[2]Talk at the University of Massachusetts, April, 1961, Conference on Discounting.

[3]"An Exploratory Study of Selected Discount Food Stores" by Robert J. Minichiello, A Thesis Submitted to the Harvard Graduate School of Business Administration, May, 1965.

XIII

WhichWorksBest in Discounting— Central Warehousing or Drop-Shipping?

BY SUMNER FELDBERG, TREASURER,
ZAYRE CORPORATION[1]

When I first became active in retailing, someone whose opinion I respected a great deal made a point that if you put into one room the operating heads of such firms as Tiffany, Woolworth, J.L. Hudson, and Sears and have them discuss some of their common problems, they would find very little in common concerning their strategy of operations. I say this because I want to bring home the fact that we, covering a very big field, cannot determine one single right or wrong approach to any single problem in retailing. The point I am making is that retailing is a fairly big field, and there cannot be one single right answer. I listened this morning to one or two questions on turnover. There is no definite figure for turnover for any given department. Individual figures are to be respected, of course, but examples of success in varied approaches to retailing are many. It seems to me therefore that what we are seeking is not the single right way. What is important in retailing is to have the logical approach and then execute it well. The people who fail are not failures because they had the wrong approach but because they executed the approach incorrectly. When you deal with this matter of centralization against decentralization – and here I want to be broader than simply warehousing – centralization starts with the question of where the decision is made.

When you deal with centralization and non-centralization the first thing that you confront is the fact that many decisions are made on the store level. This is an extremely successful approach. What you need then is to have the people, the talent, and the data needed to make successful decisions on the store level. And when it is done well the store is highly successful. Our best department stores are run in this fashion but it has a tendency to be expensive in terms of dollars. Therefore you generally can afford this only if you have very large volume in a given store unit. When we start dealing with units of less than very large volume, you can very often achieve greater economy by shifting some of that decision-making to a central headquarters that serves more than one store. Therefore you get another group of retailers who have a tendency to do it half-and-half. Generally, these are retailers who have backgrounds in junior department stores or variety stores, using a technique where you have central buyers, style, or select lines, and have the buying decisions and replenishing decisions made at store level. This is sort of a combination deal and it has its problems: it is less expensive than the first thing that I described, but more expensive than that that I will describe next. There are advantages and disadvantages; it works for some and not for others. The key to it is not whether the approach is right or wrong, but how well it is executed. And finally there is a third class that is operated by many of us who are more chain-oriented whereby we take more of those decisions into central headquarters because we achieve greater economy by having single people exercise those judgments at headquarters rather than to duplicate people at the store level. This is a good technique too; there are notable examples of success in it, as well as notable examples of failure, not because of the approach but because of the execution. And it requires other talents because although you can make the decision well, you may lose out in the way in which the store executes that decision.

It seems to me then that you start out with the fact that retailing is made up of a lot of small decisions. Contrasted to manufacturing, retailing is just exactly that: a business made up of a lot of decisions, very often none of them as momentous as that of a manufacturer who, for example, decides on a given day that he is going to bring out the Edsel car, which is a clearly significant decision. Most of us in retailing aren't faced with single decisions that significant. We make a purchase, or we don't make a purchase, and may win or lose on that purchase. The sales girl makes a decision when she greets the customer, whether she says "good morning" in a pleasant way, or starts to talk about the dress she has in her hand. That is a decision that effects that particular sale, not very significant by itself, but cumulatively important. So therefore it has helped me to think about retailing as just a mass of decisions. Our success depends upon what degree of proficiency we have in the decision-making that is going to be made by our people. It is a kind of a field where the degree of efficiency in decision-making is not very high. The key to the question is where the decision is to be made on buying and merchandising. If you conduct the buying and merchandising decision on the store level, you have to have people who can make those decisions; you have to back them with whatever help they require, and if they are good, that store can be awfully good. Noble examples are our best department stores. On the other hand my own firm has chosen to put buying decisions at a central headquarters. Why? First because we came originally out of the ready-to-wear field and there the vendor relationships, because styles change very rapidly, call for someone to be resident in the New York market to make decisions on a day-to-day basis, and they also require a degree of talent which we did not think we should duplicate in the field in every store. Therefore we make those decisions centrally and it is quite economical to do so. On the other hand, we lose out against the store that makes that decision in the field, because when we ship that merchandise to a store, it is not quite as meaningful to the manager on the other end as merchandise which he himself elected to buy. Again, this goes back to the human element. Therefore organizations such as ours are constantly facing the problem of transmitting the central buyer's decision to the store in such a way as to arouse store enthusiasm. We have a more economical base of decision making, that is all.

Now when you reach that decision on how to make that buying and merchandising decision, you then can construct your retailing organization to support it. If you make it centrally, then you will develop a supporting cast which will distribute your merchandise in your stores properly and will try to sell the merchandise to your stores. If you make it at the store level, then you put your greater weight on controlling the expense of making that type of decision at the store level. You have your choice, and I only advise you that whatever choice you make, have it executed well. When you get to the warehousing part of it, this is slightly related to it, because those of us who buy and merchandise centrally, start out by saying that it is much more convenient to warehouse that merchandise right with the buyer. That was a fair enough assumption some years ago, but it is not adequate now because labor becomes more and more expensive and that kind of convenience cannot do forever. There are other techniques of controlling your goods so that the buyer need not necessarily see his merchandise to still make a central decision. When it comes to the matter of warehousing or not, I do not want to represent myself as a 100 per cent proponent of warehousing. I am not.

In our firm we have a simple approach to it. If we bring merchandise through a warehouse, we must add something of value to that merchandise or else it is a mistake. I said something of value. What do I mean by "something of value?" In our earlier history when we were largely in women's apparel, we bought everything through a central warehouse and never really faced that issue. I can face it now. This "something of value" can vary. It can be inspection of the merchandise – and when you are dealing with women's apparel this is extremely important. It can be the time of make – styles change rapidly. I do not want to cast any aspersion on our vendors save only the fact that most of us who do inspect our merchandise in the ready-to-wear field find that we are able to screen out a lot of merchandise that would end up as mark-downs on our racks otherwise. This inspection could not be done to such an extent on the store level. In addition to quality we inspect for size, color, and for conformance to what was bought. This is something of value added through merchandising through a central warehouse. Now this does not apply to all merchandise – certainly not to Eastman Kodak products.

Something else of value, and this is the key to central warehousing in ready-to-wear, is adjusting the flow of merchandise from a timing point of view more closely to the time of sale. We are familiar with the fact that in dresses, coats, and suits styles move very rapidly. Something sells. We do not necessarily buy that same thing again because somebody else may have knocked that style off, or made it better. Therefore if your buyer is in the market and that particular fashion has sold well, we expect him not just to go back automatically buying more of the same thing, but to review it in the market. He may buy more of that type at a lower price or from another vendor. All of us, whether we centrally distribute or buy from the vendor for direct shipment to the store, make our buying decision at or about the same time. Assuming two weeks between purchase and delivery, just as an example, you who ship directly to the stores can make that decision two weeks later to receive the merchandise at the store. At the time you make the decision, you make it for the quantity and the amount of that dress, coat, or suit, based on the stores' requirements at that moment. We, on the other hand, with centrally-warehoused apparel do quite another thing. We buy at that same point based on our total requirements, chain-wide, but without necessarily knowing where we are going to ship when it comes in two weeks hence. We just know that we need that type. When the merchandise arrives,

406

and here I use an example, it is like turning on the hose to spray the grass. We assume that presumably our buyers bought to the best of their ability the right merchandise; we take that and spray it to the stores as you do a hose. And we do so not based upon the records of the stores' records, sales, and on-hand stock before, when you made the buy, but rather on their current on-hand, two weeks later. And in ready-to-wear, two weeks make a sizeable difference in stock and requirements. Therefore in the higher fashion merchandise I am a very strong adherent to central warehousing because it keeps the decision on who gets what goods closer to the time of sale.

Those are two reasons for what I call "adding something of value," but there are others as well. There is a very large class of goods in which it is a decided buying advantage to bring your merchandise in centrally. I smile at this because one of my associates is here in the audience and we argue about it very vehemently because he sees it from the control point of view and cannot respect the intangible buying advantage, and since I am oriented towards merchandising, I am a greater respector of that buying advantage. What I am saying is that frequently in many lines of merchandise we can use our ingenuity and buy better by virtue of having the vendor ship in large quantities to a central point. Obviously it is less expensive for him to ship a given quantity, say 500 dozen to one point, than it is to ship the same 500 dozen in ten-dozen lots to fifty stores. And I for one – as far as our buyers are concerned – deem that a buyer is not doing his job if he is not seeking to have that benefit passed on to us rather than to reside with the vendor. I would be less than honest if I did not indicate that we attempt to do that. That is not true in every case and unfortunately this is a thing you have to live with from day to day. There are some cases in which there is a decided buying advantage to bring your goods in centrally. Finally, there are advantages, "adding something of value," by taking advantage of out-of-season buys. You will be familiar with it. There are frequent opportunities to purchase out-of-season merchandise which you know you can use at very advantageous prices and bring through your warehouse. On the other hand let me say this: where there is nothing of value added by bringing merchandise through a warehouse, I am opposed to it coming through a central warehouse. I believe that the decision on buying and merchandising may be made centrally but the merchandise should flow directly from the vendor to the store. As an example of that, when you are dealing with appliances it is ridiculous to bring them through a warehouse.

To summarize: Our position is to make the buying and merchandising decision centrally, to warehouse centrally that merchandise when we feel we add "something of value" to it, and to have the balance of the merchandise moved directly from vendor to store.

[1]Talk at the University of Massachusetts, April, 1964, Conference on Mass-Merchandising.

The Disadvantages of Central Warehousing[1]

BY AARON GOLDBERG, VICE PRESIDENT AND GENERAL MANAGER, KING'S DEPARTMENT STORES

We at King's belong to that in-between field that Mr. Feldberg mentioned. We do not have the large department store method where all decisions are made at store level, nor do we have the centralized method of operation where all decisions are made at headquarters. We feel that we want all our major store personnel to participate in company decisions as much as possible. Of course, all major policy matters are decided upon by the executive committee. But we have a program requiring that at least once a month all our managers come into the office; the merchandising program and the advertising program is presented to them, and they have a voice in the matter. We try to have them participate in our program, in the decisions in the making of the program, and even in the decisions of buying and selection of merchandise. Even going to the extent of having group meetings with our department managers, working closely with the buyers on reviewing listings and also on the selection of merchandise. We feel this has several advantages particularly as we grow in size. We still give the stores their individual personalities depending upon their locations, and our stores vary to some extent. Our managers and department managers, being thoroughly acquainted and having the opportunity of asking any questions, feel that they are an intricate part of our operation. They understand what we are trying to do and when they understand they will most likely perform their duties more efficiently. And this is our thinking all the way down the line. Meanwhile, we are training, or think we are training, and developing our store personnel so that they are qualified to handle the stores and grow with us to be able to handle larger volume stores.

As I see it there are definite advantages to warehousing some classifications of merchandise; on this matter I do not speak as an expert, since I am certainly not qualified to tell you all the good points on warehousing. But sitting on the sideline and having had some slight contact with warehousing, you do as Mr. Feldberg says; on ready-to-wear particularly you get faster delivery from manufacturers in some cases, since it is much easier to ship 500-dozen to one spot rather than ten dozen to fifty spots. But of course, when we find manufacturers penalizing us because of our drop-shipping method, we drop those manufacturers, and we do find that there are plenty who want to sell to us and give us some degree of efficiency in shipping. There is no question that it is necessary to have quality control on ready-to-wear, and of course, central warehousing gives you that particular advantage.

And I would say that if you have complete unit-control methods in ready-to-wear, central warehousing facilitates proper ticket marking. And of course you have the faster flow of replacement stock to the stores, and you also should have greater use of store space for selling and less space is devoted to stock room or receiving space. And you should have, but I don't know whether you do or not, less store payroll, because some of this payroll is at the warehouse level. Those are the things that should be accomplished through the warehousing of merchandise.

Some of the disadvantages that I can see in warehousing is first the expense. You have the expense of rental, light, heat, personnel, and freight. Even though we drop-ship to our stores, here there is a warehouse extra discount and we think we are successful in most cases and get that extra discount. I say we think. And then, of course, in warehousing you have the extra cost of packing, and the problem or question that arises here is: are all these extra expenses that are incurred sufficient savings or sufficiently improve your operation to justify or to compensate for this expense? I also assume that in warehousing, with the back-up stock that is purchased, that at most times it is very desirable to have this back-up stock. But I also assume that at times this back-up stock becomes undesirable. And it is then a question of what to do with this undesirable stock, which is sitting in the warehouse. I would also say that centralized distribution, which I think we all agree in the retail business is perhaps the proper term rather than warehousing, becomes abused and instead of a centralized warehouse being used as distributing point it suddenly becomes merely a warehouse. Human nature being what it is, there comes into being a tendency of the buying and merchandising office to buy what appears very desirable lots of merchandise and put it in the warehouse. I would say there is also a tendency, of course not in all companies that have this centralized distribution, of taking merchandise at the end of the season which should be marked down for efficient retail operation, and returning it to the warehouse, saying: "we will solve that problem next year." So that I think that there may be a tendency in centralized distribution to do some things in merchandising that do not have the best effect in turnover or profit.

We also have in a warehouse setup the possibility of a personnel problem. Warehouse personnel distinct from the kind we have in our store level could develop into serious personnel problems. Then there is the question of turnover. The ideal theory is that if you do maintain a centralized distribution point you should be able to carry less stock on store level and that your total picture gives you a better turnover. As we don't have figures on this point, it can be argued or challenged either way. I question whether it is working out in this particular manner. And last but not least, we know in the mass-distribution discount field, the more open doors you have the greater potential is your shrink, and I think we all will agree that shrink is a very

409

serious problem with us. So for these reasons we are not centralized in the method of distribution of merchandise; but I do want to repeat, that I think what counts is the efficiency with which you perform whatever particular method you are using; and secondly, to have an open mind in regard to change, or better yet, to anticipate the change in trends and conditions, thus keeping abreast or ahead of a problem.

[1]Talk at the University of Massachusetts, April, 1964, Conference on Mass-Merchandising.

XIV

Personnel Problems of Discount Stores

Training Programs Analyzed[1]

AN INTERVIEW WITH BEN ROSENTHAL, OF DEX PERSONNEL, NEW YORK

How do traditional department stores' training programs differ from those of discount department stores?

"A department store usually has several merchandise floors plus a basement for lower-priced merchandise, whereas a discount store is nearly always a one-level operation, where all price lines are displayed and sold in one area, with the emphasis on self-service. There is a much more thorough training program in traditional department stores than in discount stores. In a store such as Abraham-Straus in New York, a young man starts his training as a stock clerk. From that position he is promoted to assistant department manager. His next step is department manager. After serving as department manager in several departments, he becomes a section manager and finally a floor manager. It takes three to four years of training to arrive at the floor manager's level and six to seven years to become a branch manager. Department store training includes classroom training at all levels.

[1]Talk at the University of Massachusetts, April, 1964, Conference on Mass-Merchandising.

411

"In discount stores an inexperienced young man is assigned to a department manager for guidance. Possibly within weeks he must be ready for assignment to a position as full department manager. It is customary for a department manager to remain in the department to which he is assigned rather than, as in department stores, to be shifted from department to department for a more rounded training program. Discount stores do not have classroom training. Most discount chains do not promote a department manager to assistant store manager. To become an assistant store manager, it therefore becomes necessary for a man to transfer to another organization. After becoming assistant store manager it is not unusual – if a man is extremely capable – to become a full store manager within one year of less."

Which types of personnel are hardest to obtain?

"All categories of personnel from companies such as Penney and Montgomery Ward are difficult to obtain because of the security offered by these organizations. The type of people employed by these companies are long-range people. Their training periods are long, their promotions are slower, salary increases come at a slower pace; but once they arrive at the top executive level, salaries exceed the discount top executive level. Fringe benefits, stock options, pension funds, etc., tend to keep a top level Sears or Penney executive happy until his retirement.

"In discount stores lower level employees move up faster and may earn more money than the Penney and Montgomery Ward people, but their positions are not as secure. On the store executive level weekly figures in discount stores are the deciding factor. Should the figures be below the expectations of the home office, the executive immediately realizes that his position may be in jeopardy. He then starts the usual inquiries regarding another position."

What can be done to solve the personnel problems of discount stores?

"The greatest problem at this time is that owing to the rapid expansion programs of discount department store chains there is a scarcity of trained personnel available.

"It is difficult to obtain new personnel from other fields for the following reasons:

1. The long hours and number of working days required.
2. Inadequate fringe benefits.
3. A lack of a sense of security, so that people can plan ahead and look forward to good retirement plans, etc.

"Most top level executives make it a point to follow the financial condition of their organizations; should there be even the slightest hint that their company is having difficulty (no matter how slight) or, if there is rumor of a merger, they immediately feel insecure and start inquiries regarding new positions. It is extremely difficult to lure personnel from traditional retailing to the discount field because of the above difficulties. By the same token many people leave the field for the same reasons. It appears that it will take some years to solve this problem, since the discount field is comparatively new."

Can't a good man advance rapidly in a discount operation?

"Personnel turnover is great because of the extraordinary expansions in the field in so short a time, and the shortage of qualified personnel. As a result it becomes necessary for management to push people along far too rapidly. A manager may be in charge of a 50,000-foot unit doing approximately $2 million to $2.5 million. He is doing an excellent job. Within a short period of time, he is promoted to a 100,000-foot unit, doing approximately $4.5 million to $5 million. Should he not reach the figures set up by the home office within an allotted time, he is replaced.

"The home office does not take into consideration the fact that, in many instances, the manager was not ready for a store twice the size of the one in which he proved a success. This man either loses confidence altogether, or else he believes that he has reached the point where he now considers himself a manager of a 100,000-foot unit. In either case the manager is hurt, and he starts changing positions until he finds where he belongs. Bidding among various organizations for qualified executives causes turnover. This plus the long hours, lack of security, and improper training to start with, contribute to rapid turnover."

Is there a central list of employees who have been caught stealing?

"No. We believe it would be an excellent idea if there were a central point organized to check out all applicants in the field."

Why don't discount companies have better training programs?

"There are several discount organizations which believe that they have good training programs. Actually, there is no complete school discount store training program teaching procedures, merchandising, housekeeping, operations, security, etc. If this were done, a better store image would result. It will take several years before discount store expansion levels off, and companies will then be in a position to examine their personnel problems more carefully and start promoting from within."

What are the Job Corps possibilities for providing discount store personnel?

"This country is now spending millions of dollars for the youth of tomorrow. The discount field may be able to absorb a large portion of the youth being trained in the Job Corps. By carefully screening these people and placing them in the discount field as clerks in the stockroom, receiving, shipping, and sales departments, we can give them a new start in life and at the same time it will give us a new source for much needed personnel."

What percent of your business is with discount stores?

"We are one of the largest retail personnel agencies in the country, and the only agency that caters exclusively to the discount field in supplying managers, buyers, and other executives. We know the needs of discounters

413

and supply 80 per cent of all executive personnel for major discount organizations. Being pioneers in this field, we are intimately acquainted with the needs of discount operations from stock boy to president. We are constantly ready to make ' a full executive search.' "

Creative Excitement Draws Talent

INTERVIEW WITH ROBERT KENZAR, PERSONNEL DIRECTOR, ZAYRE CORP.

What were you doing before you came into retailing?

"I got my Masters degree in labor relations from New York University and then went into the service. On getting out, jobs were very scarce at the time, but as a result of a blind ad, I found an opening as assistant personnel manager trainee with the E. J. Korvette Company in New York. I spent approximately two years in the most intensive kind of retail training you can imagine. I worked in the baling room, the receiving department, the ticketing room, maintenance, operations, and then as a department manager of about every department in the store except photography and better jewelry. I then became personnel manager of their 44th Street store with 400 employees. After a year-and-a-half I was promoted to an area supervisor overseeing the two 46th Street stores, the Scarsdale store, Brooklyn store and the 44th Street store. Then I took over the Westbury and Islip stores. Korvette was growing and I was working an average of 100 to 110 hours a week and loved it. It was dynamic; it was exciting. Every day was a challenge, a new opportunity, bringing new insights into a business that was a fledgling at the time.

"I became the training coordinator and executive development director working directly under the director of personnel. We developed a whole series of training programs for cashiers and department managers. We had college professors come in on Sunday mornings to instruct our department heads and floor managers. In addition to leadership, training, and personnel relations, they taught basic merchandising arithmetic, including turnover as well as advertising and sales promotion.

"I used to do business for Korvette with the Dex Agency, a New York employment agency which first solicits job orders from employers who need jobs filled and then solicits unsatisfied or dissatisfied employees. One day they called me and asked me to talk to a representative from the Zayre Corp. I had never heard of Zayre and was rather happy at Korvette, so at first I said no. About four months later they called me again suggesting that I at least talk to Joel Jacobsen from Zayre's, who was in New York. Weeks later, after a long and one of the roughest interviews I ever had, with Stanley and Sumner Feldberg and Sidney S. Wolchok, the company's labor counsel,

414

I was invited to join the organization and head up their personnel division.

"In today's society the wages we pay in retailing are not competitive with capital industry, so that there has got to be something more esoteric for a person to seek a retail career, for the young man just out of college who has spent so much on his education to want retailing. Today, instead of working 37½ hours a week, young men in retailing still have got to work a 48-, 50- or 55-hour work week. So what is it, therefore, that draws this type of talent to retailing? And there *is* talent in retailing. It's merchandise excitement, it's people excitement and most of all, it's creation excitement. A person has to be able to get excited about merchandise to sell it. We have taught our people to have a respect and a love for merchandise so that when they meet the public, they communicate this excitement. Today we are starting off our college graduate trainees at $125 a week. Now that is $6,500 a year and is as competitive as many accounting firms. We have to be selective, otherwise, the incidence of turnover in the college group can be very high."

What areas of research do you think are needed in this discount field?

"I think that research is needed desperately in the area of productivity. Every other industry has been able to put a fix on productivity. You cannot come to me today and tell me how long it takes to fold a gondola of ladies' small wear. You couldn't tell me how long it takes to set up a display of photo equipment. Here is where the discount industry is lacking, and lacking very badly, because the press of competition from traditional retailing, from imposed government regulations of minimum wages, and the general economic structure has forced the costs in discounting up and up. Also, by becoming quasi-service in many departments such as automotive, sporting goods, photography, better jewelry, paint, even in such departments as domestics where you have to sell domestic hardware and domestic drapery, we have built-in additional cost factors in units of personnel. We have done very little to examine how we can get greater productivity for the dollars that we are spending on those units of personnel. And let's face it, in discounting there are two great enemies to net profit – shrinkage and payroll. Shrinkage you can control by good security, by tight paperwork, by awareness on the store management's part. But payroll, there is the key. That is where, in discounting, we have fallen very short. For better profit there are two alternatives; better markup or less cost to operate. The markup area is controlled by competition. If you bring your markup too high, you are going to price yourself out of the competitive market. So it leaves one real area in which to maximize profits and that is the area of human productivity. I feel very strongly about this. I feel that more research should be done. I think more time should be devoted to training."

Can you give me an instance in your career that illustrates the "excitement" you find in retailing?

"When the Zayre Corp., in a real estate and merchandise transaction, acquired property in Minneapolis, we took over the operation of a company known as Grand Super Centers. We flew in thirteen young men – thirteen auditors to work with their auditors. We inventoried their entire store in 24 hours and 24 hours later we had rehired an entire store organization and opened a mammoth sale. Fifty per cent on the $1 on the ticketed price and within ten days we moved approximately $3 million worth of merchandise out the doors. This was the largest sale that Minneapolis ever saw. We had so many people in the store that the fire department was called out and the police department had to throw squadrons around the store. There were 10,000 people outside the store and there must have been 6,000 people inside. We were liquidating the old inventory in preparation for a grand reopening of the store. This was the most exciting experience I ever had in the retail business. There was so much money coming out of the registers that in order to get the money from the registers to the cash office we used to put it in a shirt. We had no bags, we had nothing, we just couldn't get enough registers to operate. The lines were backed up literally from the cash registers to the wall in the rear of the store and around. It got so congested at one point that we couldn't let any more people into the building; we just siphoned people out. We stayed open 24 hours a day, and this is hard to believe, but for 24 hours we didn't stop. The store remained at this packed level.

"This is a young and exciting industry where individual ambition and creativity are rewarded financially as a direct result of ability to perform and achieve individual job goals. Unfortunately, on the college campus, retailing has a black eye and is looked on as being somewhat archaic. Too many people visualize retailing as a clerk working in a store and they don't realize the great variety of opportunities it presents. In addition to buyers, assistant store managers and store managers, we need a crew of professional executives who administer the affairs of a multi-million dollar corporation. I speak for many young burgeoning organizations such as Bradlees, Kings, etc. There is an omnibus of opportunities; control and accounting; electronic data processing which is becoming of paramount importance in running our business; we need people who are interested in people-personnel administration; we need those interested in operations and procedures; in real estate and site selection; construction and fixture design and development of selling techniques and concepts; research and development; we really need executives on all planes except possibly manufacturing, yet many retailers today are also in manufacturing."

Payroll-Profit Relationship: Peak Productivity From Your Employees

INTERVIEW WITH ROBERT PURE, REGIONAL PERSONNEL
MANAGER, ZAYRE CORP.

Where did you get your training?

"I studied business administration at Clark University for two years and accounting at Boston University night school for one year. Having worked at R. H. Whites department store during the summer, I became their assistant buyer in men's furnishings. My chief experience in discounting was with Mammoth Mart in an old steel mill in Framingham. Discounting was then in its infancy and we did everything. The roof leaked and we used to ticket merchandise stripped to the waist but it was great. I stayed with them for three years as buyer and assistant store manager. It was just a big family-type operation and I really got into the grass roots of discounting."

What are your present duties?

"As regional personnel manager for the Zayre Corp., my job is to see that store managers and their assistant managers follow through on the tools that we give them, and that morale in the stores is kept at a high level."

What are some of the problems with store managers that give you concern?

"Seeing that the store managers are aware of the payroll-profit relationship so that they get as much productivity out of their people as possible. Our regional personnel managers work to establish tighter control within the stores."

How many stores do you have to supervise?

"Thirty-three."

How frequently do you visit these stores?

"It depends. If I am just going on a personnel and operations check using our 29-point check list it usually takes me half a day, and I can check two stores. But on the average I see every store about once a month."

What are some of the points you check?

"Payroll control is number one. I make suggestions to the store managers as to how they can save on payroll by work measurement, work simplification. My previous training was that as a buyer and as a store manager. If the store has a drastic payroll problem, the first thing I do is to build up a rapport with the store manager – build up a trust so he trusts me. I want him to know that whatever I tell him is going to be of help, that it's not forced upon him. Then we take a little walk out on the floor and we look over his schedules of personnel. I show him how, if he makes certain floor moves or other changes, he can improve productivity. Maybe he has three employees in the department and two employees may be working at a normal pace rate, which

417

is 100 per cent, one may be working at 50 per cent. By tighter control, closer supervision, and better training, this individual is encouraged to work at a 100 per cent pace. In the average store we have 40 to 50 full-time employees."
How far do you travel?

"From the tip of Maine to Portsmouth, Va. and all of Pittsburgh, all of New England, and Washington. I am away a lot, but home most of the weekends. My monthly travel bill may be $400 to $500."
Is this expense justified?

"We can sit at the home office and come out with the most beautiful memos, systems, plans, and devices. Unfortunately, as soon as it hits the store it is not presented to the department managers or to the rank and file people with the enthusiasm that we have put into it at its inception. Say we have a new pension program. A lot of work went into preparing the handbook. If we were to just send this out into the stores, it would be handed out to the rank and file people with very little explanation, with no forcefulness to it, no feeling. When a member of our office visits the store, we can present this to the rank and file and accomplish two things. We are able to introduce it with a lot of feeling, exuberance – a lot of emotion. We can really sell it to them. Number two, we are showing them that as large as this company is, we have not forgotten the rank and file employees. I actually make it a point to learn the names of every individual in that store. On the next visit we go in and say, 'Hi, Mary, how are you?' This means more than anything and is worth all the expense money that you can ever pay a man."
How many area managers do you have?

"Three, one covering the mid-south and South, one in the northeast section and one covering the Midwest."
What are the incentives for the store managers to do better?

"They have a bonus arrangement on their sales, their profits, and on how low their shrinkage is."
What is the salary range for a store manager?

"From about $13,000 to $15,000."

Management's View of Personnel Problems[1]
(How to Doctor a Sick Company)

BY MESHULAM RIKLIS, CHAIRMAN OF THE BOARD AND PRESIDENT OF McCRORY CORPORATION

We have had a unique experience in the past two years which I would like to pass on to you. The experience I am referring to is the story of one of our divisions called McCrory, McClellan, and Green. A number of years before we moved into the McCrory picture, the McCrory, McClellan, and H. L. Green chains were going downhill for a while. Then we thought we would put them together, and putting all three sick babies together, maybe we would get rid of the sickness. However, it was not that easy. The end result and the condition that we found in the stores a couple of years ago was not unique to our case; and I am sure that some of you may have experienced that, particularly if you have made acquisitions. So we set about a program to try to rehabilitate McCrory, McClellan, and Green. The program concentrated itself on three elements, and these three elements are what I would like to bring out to you. They were: one, a management program; two, the relationship with personnel, building of self-respect, etc.; three, incentive.

If I could teach you anything, I could only repeat and review these three things that went into the rebuilding of McCrory, McClellan, and Green. I am happy to say that M M & G in the year 1964 moved from a loss to a $7 million profit on $150 million in sales before taxes, enough for a very substantial bonus program.

The rehabilitation program centered around the rebuilding of the whole company, from beginning to end. I do not mean to say that we changed people; as a matter of fact, the unique situation here was that the job of a $7 million profit change was done completely with the same people.

The first part of it was the direction. After some study, a new set of rules was sent out into the field and a few of us went into selected stores to do the job of rehabilitation. By sitting in one store for two or three weeks, the entire operation within that store was changed to cover all aspects to make the store competitive. I do not have to go into that in detail. I am sure all of you know about the movement of merchandise, the presentation of merchandise, the designing of merchandise, the ordering, the reordering, the liquidation of those goods that do not sell, etc. After the directions were given in one store, the same directions were given to all other stores. By working in one store, we were able to make the top group of officers know exactly what we were after, and by the time we finished with one store, we had about five or six people trained.

From that one store we moved into a whole district. We took seventeen stores within the district and we fanned out into these seventeen stores and repeated the job within the seventeen stores. All of a sudden, within a thirty-day period, we found out that the entire seventeen stores began to move ahead of the pack. It was easy to see because the instructions given to the personnel had become something that kind of did not take "no" for an answer, did not permit any slowing down on the job, because it was unique in the sense that everybody knew exactly where he wanted to go.

From the seventeen stores in the district, we moved into an entire region. By the way, I am talking about a company with 600 stores. From seventeen

Meshalum Ricklis, chairman of the board
and president, McCrory Corporation.

stores we moved into a group of a hundred stores, a region. And the same performance was repeated in the region. Within sixty days the region moved ahead to become the best region within the six regions in the company. And when I say the best, within sixty days the performance of both profits and sales became unique. The merchandise inventory began to go down and suffice it to say that by the end of the year the entire six regions reduced the inventory by $14 million, over a 20 per cent reduction in the inventory. And you know what that does to the turnover. The performance of the profits became almost as unique. From this one region we moved into six other regions and within a matter of five or six months the entire company had the same direction as the one store that we started with. But that was not enough. Direction is not enough.

The executive relationship with the personnel became quite unique. The top executives of the company worked with the store manager, with the girls that work on the counters, both in the day and at night. When you are moving merchandise around, opening boxes, painting the stores, doing all these things, it makes them feel that they are a part of a big, large family. This becomes the most important thing in their lives. Not only do they want the direction, but they want to know that you are concerned about them, that you have the kind of thinking that has them in mind. I did not visit the 600 stores, it is just a physical impossibility, but I personally visited over a 130 stores. There were five or six other executives and between us we were able to visit over six hundred stores, and many of them more than two or three times. It is this relationship with the people that began to filter back into the home office. It became known that the people from the top were working with them.

A person surely needs direction, needs the feeling of belonging, but he also must have an incentive. We have worked out an incentive program for all the district managers, all the store managers, and all the regional managers. We gave out $800,000 just in bonuses. This is above and beyond $800,000 additional bonuses that were part of the incentive program written into the contract. This was only to those who excelled. And this incentive program is a part of life that all of you are going to have to contend with, and I will discuss that in a minute.

As top management, you must set the objectives; you must be clear about your objectives and the setting of the objectives; you must allocate the resources; you must make sure that when you set the objectives, you are able to provide personnel with the resources with which to achieve the objectives; you must staff your organization. It is not enough just to set the objectives, allocate the resources, without naming the people that are responsible for the job; you must establish standards of performance. This establishment of the standards within which we are going to work was very important in our company. You must not only establish those standards, you must enforce them and reinforce them constantly. These are the three things that you must do as top management, and I understand that most of you are in that category.

After that, you have to focus yourself on a synthesis of both the concern for the people and a concern for the job, a concern for the production. You can't focus yourself on only one; it cannot be focused on only the people or only on the production. The most important thing is to reach the people. But if all you did was to reach the people, and tried to be soft and smooth, all you would do would be to bring about a situation where the people will be soft and their attitude will be one of softness. On the other hand, if all of you were not concerned with the people, even after you reach them, you yourself will be doing the work, aggressive work, of trying to produce results. Thus you will end up with frustration among the people, and almost an anti-organization feeling within the organization. It is the focusing on both, the individual and the production job, that must come together when you reach the people. This is what we tried to do and I thought we did quite successfully

421

in this particular company. But these two things, the focusing on the people and the production, the giving of the directives and the direction are not enough; and I think all of you will have to face something about which I felt very strongly, and that is the incentive.

Profit participation and incentives are probably going to become one of the biggest and most important issues in American industry from now on. This sharing of the profits is going to become the most important single thing in the next few years. Not so much pension plans and retirement plans, but actual day-to-day participation in profits. That most unique company, Sears Roebuck, has been doing that in its own way for many years and, therefore they have been so successful.

What are the means for profit participation? A stock option plan? Those of you who have not gone public probably find you are unable to give stock options to your people. Those of you that have gone public will probably find it is much easier to give stock options. The stock purchase plan will become more frequently used in the lower management echelons. And finally, and I know that in this you all excel, are the contests and the rewards. We have one company, the Oklahoma Tire and Supply, that does a fabulous job with contests. Almost every month there are five or ten winners in Las Vegas, twenty in Paris, fifteen on a fishing trip in Mexico. The rewards are tremendous; sales in this subsidiary have gone up in the past five years, 5, 10, 15 and 20 per cent. There are companies that handle competitions and who will set up a whole program for you.

[1]Talk given at the University of Massachusetts, April, 1965, Conference on Mass-Merchandising.

XV

Union Activity in Mass Merchandising

INTERVIEW WITH SIDNEY A. WOLCHOK, ATTORNEY,
KATZ AND WOLCHOK, NEW YORK CITY

Which is the most powerful retail store union?

"The strongest of those unions concerned with retailing is the Retail Clerks International Association (RCIA), which is affiliated with the AFL-CIO, and now has approximately 500,000 members. This union has achieved considerable expansion in discount stores in the last few years. International president of this union is James A. Suffridge, and a good deal of its organizational activity is now being directed by James Housewright. The union has had a number of training seminars at various places, including the University of Massachusetts, the Denver area, and other parts of the country. These sessions usually run about a week and bring together novitiates in organizing with experienced talent as instructors. The latest points of board and court law are reviewed as well as techniques in bargaining and techniques of organization. In the areas where the organization has strength it seeks to update its collective bargaining agreements with new conditions. Where a new field appears to have a fertile base they use their talent, old and new, in organizing new stores."

Is RCIA organized on a national basis?

423

"Its great strength is on the West Coast, and it has developed considerably in the San Francisco and the Los Angeles areas, as well as in the Pacific-Northwest. It has great interest in the Indiana-Illinois area in addition to considerable interest in Ohio, Pennsylvania, New England, and metropolitan New York. Its strength is low in Florida and in the southern state area in general."

What other unions are active in retailing?

"Another union interested in the organization of the discount field is the Retail-Wholesale and Department Store Union, AFL-CIO, which has its headquarters in New York City. Its president is Max Greenberg and its membership is approximately 135,000. Much of this membership is in metropolitan New York. Its strength seems to be limited to the industrial Northeast, Florida, Tennessee, and metropolitan Chicago. This union's present membership covers non-discount stores in the Chicago area, some discount membership in metropolitan New York, and very limited discount membership in the Miami area. Other than in the New York area, in recent years the union has had limited expansion."

Is not the Amalgamated Clothing Workers of America also interested in retail organization?

"Yes. AMCA entered the field in earnest in 1948. President of this union is Jacob Potofsky. It has some 35,000 members in the discount field. The union is based in Detroit and has had considerable success in the Ohio-Michigan area. It has little strength west of the Mississippi, except in Los Angeles. It has some very limited organizational activity in the New England area. The union's headquarters are in New York City.

"Also interested in mass-merchandising is the International Brotherhood of Teamsters, Chauffeurs, and Warehousemen of America (IBT). This is an independent union with approximately 1,800,000 members engaged for the most part in warehousing and trucking. Its headquarters are in Washington, D.C., and it has the most efficient research, legal, and propaganda machines in the trade union field."

To what extent are discount stores unionized?

"Some companies in the discount field are almost substantially and completely organized. This includes chains such as Caldor, Spartans' Atlantic Mills chain, and its E. J. Korvette division. Shoppers' Fair is partially unionized. Stop & Shop, including Bradlee's, is almost completely unionized. There is very substantial organization in Interstate; Topps is about completely organized, including the White Front organization in California; Yankee stores in Michigan is almost completely organized. We can now find tens of thousands of discount store members of the Retail Clerks' Union. The extent of organization has had an interesting aspect. For example, the company with two or three stores in a metropolitan area where advertising, managerial, shipping, and other activities are facilitated may add other new

424

Sidney A. Wolchok, partner, Katz and Wolchok,
attorneys, New York City.

stores. These are almost invariably within the gambit of the collective bargaining agreement which often defines the counties that the union contract covers. The new store will almost always come under the union by means of an 'accretion clause.' Thus there is a built-in growth pattern. As unionized companies grow by opening stores, regardless of the profit picture, in those areas where there is already pre-established union strength there is built-in union growth. This has often happened with unionized food stores; as the union develops a broad base either state-wide or in a metropolitan area, it demands and usually receives the new stores. At the moment this pre-existing broad base does not exist with the Retail, Wholesale, and Department Store Union. Area coverage agreements are more often found in the Retail Clerks' negotiations or in those of the Amalgamated Clothing Workers of America.

"The RCIA has great potential and is aiming to be one of the largest unions in America. Its growth has been significant and membership is about

425

500,000. This is a union to watch since it stands high in the roster of unions affiliated with AFL-CIO. Union officials are now seeing an updating of collective bargaining agreements in the RCIA, and also in Amalgamated. At the moment the two largest unions having an interest in mass-merchandising are the RCIA and the Amalgamated."

What key factors favor union organization?

"The organization of employees in many areas of the country is usually keyed to the factor of whether or not there is adequate union talent in the area and whether or not management has undertaken a benevolent interest in the affairs of its employees. There are literally vast areas of the retailing discount scene where there has been no successful organization of employees. One of the major, largely unorganized companies is K Mart which to my knowledge has only one store under union organization to date. This company is one of the largest in the discount field. Also the Zayre Corporation, except for one store in Cleveland, has remained without union organization. The one Zayre contract is with the RCIA and has basically minimal conditions. The union, of course, considers this an entering wedge, but the Zayre Cleveland union contract has not proven to be a good propaganda instrument for the union since the terms and conditions do not demonstrate distinct employee advantages, which might apply in other Zayre stores."

How can companies maintain their non-union status?

"There are literally tens of thousands of employees which are non-union in the discount field. An examination of these differences as to why we have unionized or non-unionized discount stores is really interesting. Actually, it goes back to these factors: A prime one is that the union is not equipped to conduct an organizational campaign in that area, coupled with the fact that in many cases the managements are adopting a paternalistic responsibility in attending to the basic needs of their employees. This includes maintaining wage reviews, hospital and surgical programs, retirement programs, and an interest in the conditions of employment down to the sanitation aspect of washrooms or lunchrooms. In some cases it may be keyed to profit-sharing. Where there is an interest on the part of management, conscientiously expressed and conveyed to employees, there is a great deal of resistance by employees to submission to union representation. Basically, this is a capitalist country and the unions are part of this entire scene. None of today's leading unions have been rabid, syndicalist, or revolutionist: their fabric is part of the entire capitalist scene. Most union leaders have risen from the ranks of the working masses: James Suffridge (RCIA International president) was himself a member of the sales community in Oakland, Calif. Max Greenberg, president of the Retail, Wholesale Union, was a member of a sales force in New Jersey years ago. These leaders are basically former working people with great talent for mass leadership. They are men of imagination and enterprise. The initial success of a union in organizing a company may stem with some justification from the standpoint of employee treatment."

Why have not retail unions been more successful in New England?

"The reason is twofold: One, there has been no large resident union organizational structure; Two, management has not been slow to recognize the importance of maintaining excellent employee relations. It is perhaps not unfair to say that many in the top echelon of discount store management in the formative years of their business have been primarily interested in such matters as store location, pricing, advertising, and merchandising rather than in their personnel problems. We have seen discounters come and go on the retail scene; Towers, for example, had twenty-five-odd stores and suddenly disappeared. Towers was substantially unionized; yet in no way can its demise be attributed to union activity. Consumers' Mart of America (CMA) was largely union. Its failure likewise cannot be attributed to a union."

Can you mention some specific personnel areas which, when neglected, present openings for the unions?

"Basically the development of unionization may be attributed to two factors: the stores were in an area where unions had a base; secondly, there was a turning of employees from free bargaining with management to a desire for representation to settle their own individual needs which arose and were not met by management. Very often management does not make necessary, and regular, wage reviews; it may lag in instituting and up-dating health and welfare program. Employees are made aware of this, and they react to such circumstances. On many occasions there may be indiscretions of local management in the way they handle people in such matters as discharges. There may be favoritism in the store. Many such factors may build up employee resentment. Basically well-run organizations that consciously tackle the problem of personnel relationships should have little difficulty – if they have established a good base of employee relationships in continuing a non-union operation. This has been done by companies like K Mart, Zayre, and many department stores. It requires a conscious dedication on the part of management to respect the needs of employees and to be 'people-oriented.' If we look at the large industrial companies which have tackled this problem with energy and dedication, you find that many of them have great programs. For example, IBM with its 240,000-odd employees, has great dedication to the welfare of these employees. Again Sears Roebuck, with its system of having its employees participate in the growth of the company by stock purchases, and by its retirement and health programs, has largely resisted organization by unions. The San Francisco Sears store is organized and has been for many years, but with no effect on the larger Sears national scene.

"Retailing today shows the area of Chicago heavily organized in discounting. There is also much organization in New York and in Southern California. Milwaukee, Saint Louis, and Cleveland have succumbed to strong discount store organization. There is very thin organization through most of the South. Much of this organizational success, though, is now historic. That is, the union organized the company in its early stages of growth and is accreting as the company grows. By and large unions are unable to organize the employees or their companies if the employees feel they have done right by them."

What kinds of new benefits are unions obtaining for their retail members?

"In some cases negotiated union contracts have resulted in substantial employee improvements in such areas as hospital and surgical benefits for both the family and the member. In California, dental care is a new factor, as is psychiatric care in Southern California; predictive medicine is also a new factor. Pension benefit programs are appearing on the horizon in a greater number of areas. Management is being made to contribute to funds to build up retirement benefits. Since there is considerable turnover in mass-merchandising employment and because of the seasonal nature of Christmas, contributions to funds may add up to millions in the course of time. However, many part-time or short-term employees, although they have contributed to this fund, will not benefit from it; it accrues to the benefit of others."

Can part-time retail employees join the union?

"In regard to the part-time aspect of mass-merchandising employment, we are seeing new contract features develop whereby the unions achieve a condition which allows the employees an option of having more than just part-time hours–a forty-hour work week for example, rather than a thirty-two-hour work week. The competitive scene for the union employer is becoming much more severe as against the non-union employer. The latter is much freer in scheduling his employees. This is probably one of the chief advantages of being non-union. The employer does have the power to schedule without contract restriction. On the other hand, an intelligent employer, with a responsible personnel management team, would see that each employee is satisfied according to his needs. A mother who may be able to work while school is in session, could be very well accommodated by both a union and non-union employer. Should it happen that the children are away for summer months and the mother is interested in more hours of work, it is up to the non-union store or the company's personnel department to decide whether they want to give her more hours of work; in the union store, she may very often have the right to elect longer hours, based on seniority. There is a greater flexibility in non-union stores."

To what extent do the unions participate in store management?

"Unions, in general, have not sought to interfere with day-to-day management between the times of contract bargaining. Very often these

428

contracts run for three years. Ordinarily, hard bargaining does occur at the contract expiration time. A bargaining session may last for eight or ten hours and it may take months to resolve the issues. There is exhaustive research on the part of both management and union representatives as to advantages or disadvantages of proposals, including the weighing of costs and the evaluation and drafting of language. Both sides may come away from a serious bargaining session somewhat satisfied that each did what best it could to resolve the interest it represented. Often we now find that in a serious bargaining picture it takes something like four or five months from the time of first opening notice to the time of execution of an agreement; both sides have genuine issues to resolve. Very often each side has to go back to canvass and assess in which direction it is to proceed."

Who sets the ground rules for these bargaining sessions?

"These rules are set by the National Labor Relations Act, an Act of Congress that has been on our law books since the middle 1930's. As a result of thousands of decisions in the various courts, it has been revised and developed by NLRB. To any knowledgeable and responsible union official, or to an executive or to an attorney, these decisions represent standards of conduct. The law sets forth requirements prohibiting either union or management from engaging in certain courses of conduct. Let us imagine a situation where a union appears with the intention of organizing a mass-merchandising store. Uppermost in the minds of both parties is the question of how to conduct themselves under the blanket of the prescribed conduct as set forth by the National Labor Relations Act and its Board."

How does a union campaign start?

"Often a union campaign begins in one of a number of ways. The union initially goes into a store and samples the feelings of employees as to the degree of happiness or unhappiness they may have. This may be done by entering the store as a customer-organizer, talking to a clerk on the floor about merchandise, but gradually leading into the question as to whether or not the store is a good place in which to work. He may get an interested reaction to such a canvass or one of disinterest. This technique can be repeated in a number of stores at a number of times as a cross-check."

Do store employees sometimes contact union organizations?

"There are places, such as the snack bar, where union organizers meet employees. They may fraternize there, or they may meet after work in a local place, like a bowling alley, bar, or eating establishment. Or they may meet through friends or relatives working in the store. The initial contact aspect, at least, can develop rapidly. If there exists really genuine employee unhappiness – perhaps with a manager or supervisor, who has unwittingly caused a certain amount of consternation, the employees, among themselves, may call the union office and say, 'We would like to meet with you. Can you set up a meeting?' The union organizer may then make an appointment

429

in the employee's home, or in a restaurant, a car, or the union office. The matter may be handled by mail. So there are two basic situations: one, unsatisfied employees may seek out the union; two, from the outside the union may initiate a campaign."

How does the organizer build his case?

"In regard to organizing technique, there is much of what might be called 'boilerplate', in that an organizer's kit is available which has *pro forma* information and analysis, as well as factual knowledge about the particular store being organized. The union organizer has to build a list of names either from access to the employees' time cards or otherwise. I have heard of a situation where an organizer had a pocket tape recorder with a lapel microphone which he used to record the names of employees by reading them off the time cards. These names would be processed for addresses, and house visits would begin. By repeated home visits, an effort is made to obtain enough signatures on cards which designate the union as a collective bargaining agent for the employees."

How many employees would have to be contacted?

"The NLRB has a minimum standard for the filing of a petition and the entertaining of that petition. Thirty per cent of the employees in an appropriate unit would suffice. Assume that in this case, the appropriate unit is a single store. If there were 100 employees in the store, excluding executives, the supervisor, confidential employees, and perhaps the guards and watchmen, and 'casual' employees – under certain circumstances – there would have to be thirty per cent of the residue. If there were a hard core of seventy-one, then 30 per cent would be 22 people. If these 22 were in in favor of the union, the union would have the right to have the petition processed by the NLRB."

Would this lead to an election?

"The petition is really a request to the Government of the United States in the person of the National Labor Relations Board, to conduct an investigation and possibly to hold a secret election in which the store employees can vote as to whether or not they want the union to represent them for purposes of collective bargaining with store management. The petition would usually be processed by a hearing and a determination would be made. If it does get to the election stage, then the employees have a secret ballot to vote 'yes' or 'no' for the union. A majority of those employees voting (not those eligible but of those voting) would make the determination as to whether or not the union had collective bargaining representation rights. If the union does obtain the majority, they have the right to sit down face to face with representatives of the employer to work out bargaining terms and conditions. The obligation on the part of the union and the employer is that each is to bargain collectively, in good faith. This has various aspects. If both sides should reach an agreement, then the agreement would be put in writing and govern conditions for the period designated."

430

What part does the NLRB take in the pending election?

"Before the election is held and when the petition is filed, the NLRB conducts a secret investigation to see if the petition has been filed correctly and to see if the unit (store or stores) is an appropriate unit within their definitions. They determine which employees may or may not make up this unit. Names may be checked on the designation cards. Store management can then say whether they think an election should or should not be held. The NLRB representative may be told that an election should not be held now for a number of reasons. It may be that it is an improper bargaining unit – that a single store alone should not be in the bargaining unit but all of the company stores within a radius of so many miles. This may mean that the union does not have 30 per cent because there are hundreds of people in the other stores without a say in the matter."

What defense can management muster?

"A number of issues may be brought up. Sometimes management may find that the manner in which the signatures were obtained violated the provisions of the law. Coercion may have been used, or there may have been fraudulent statements. Possibly the actual signatures are not those of the employees. The Board is then informed of these alleged discrepancies and it may examine the allegations of management.

"The NLRA itself is designed to afford some investigation so as to remove labor-management problems from the law of the jungle. Standards are set for both sides and this is accomplished. Very often there are hearings in which management and union representatives voice their opinions before a hearing officer. Witnesses are sworn in, and the customary formal court procedures are followed. Relevant aspects of the company's operation are examined in detail; its corporate location, whether or not it is in commerce within the meaning of the Act, whether or not it comes under the jurisdiction of this Federal agency. The Board representative will take some evidence on the makeup of the unit. For example, is there a store manager and an assistant store manager? Are the department heads really endowed with supervisory authority? What sort of an office operation is used? Is there a confidential employee who handles labor-management problems? How many licencees are there? Matters of this nature come to the fore. There may also be problems of interchange with other stores if it is a multi-store unit. The provisions of the lease agreements must be looked into. There may be some testimony taken on what is an opportune time for holding an election. Is the payroll now so heavily inflated with temporary employees that most of them do not have the prospect of continued employment?"

What are management's responsibilities during this investigation?

"Prior to this hearing there has been the tug of war between the management and the union representatives as to who is going to obtain or retain the loyalty of the store employees. This is the most crucial time preceding the election. Management's communication with employees is regu-

431

lated very carefully by prescription. Management cannot, in effect, bribe its employees by telling employees that if they do not join the union they will receive wage increases, or that they will change their hospital-surgical program to be as good or better than that offered by the union. Such action is clearly considered coercive and illegal.

"Actually the strongest conduct that management can maintain is to have the truth demonstrated as to where it stands in its attitude as to its employees' benefits. The truth should come out as to the union's allegation of supposed conditions with other employers. Sometimes misrepresentations occur in the heat of propaganda. There should be an examination as to whether the strong aspects, as set forth by the union, are truthful and if so, what are the weak aspects. The problems of management-employee communication are considered. Should meetings be by individual, or in groups, or will letters suffice? There is a broader protection to the employer if letters are used, since there is no question as to what the letter says, and no doubt arises as to whether or not the employer was guilty of unfair conduct."
Who decides on NLRB policy?

"Employers have a great burden on them at the present time. This burden tends to shift with changes in administration of the national policy. The NLRB is made up of men who interpret laws. It consists of five men who are dedicated to their responsibilities but who have different views as to what the law is or how it should be interpreted. Changes in the make-up of the Board will be reflected by changes in legal interpretations. This makes it necessary to re-examine board opinion from time to time to see what actions are within the law within the limitations of a given campaign.

"There is a lot to the aspect of a direct face-to-face responsibility between a department manager and an individual employee. Very few employees know the president of a company and very few know the vice president. Thus store managers, department managers, or supervisors really play important parts in the overall handling of labor-management problems. Some companies have training sessions for their store managers just as the unions have them for their organizers. The store managers are informed precisely what they can or cannot do in regard to employee relationships and what employee benefits are currently in force as well as those in the course of planning. Fair management-employee relationships is the strong bond which has kept Sears Roebuck, K Mart, Zayre and Grand Way in their largely non-union status."
What leads to employee dissatisfaction?

"This non-union status may be broken by a letup of the company's vigilance in handling its benefit program. For example, if a company is caught in a severe expense-loss picture, it may disregard personnel interest and with that may come lack of continued improvement. As months and years go by, employee resentment builds up since they compare their situation

432

with that of other employees in other similar stores. Good employee relations is a prime responsibility of management and should have equal consideration by management as such matters as advertising or merchandising. Today the unions are tending towards mass-organizing. Rather than having one or two organizers tackle a store with 100 employees who are part of a total of 900 or more other company employees, in a metropolitan area, they will move in 10, 20, or 30 organizers who will visit the homes of employees and solicit their membership. Sometimes they become overzealous in their salesmanship. Should they exceed the bounds of propriety by misrepresentation and should this come to the attention of management, it can be used as evidence for an NLRB charge. Since management, under the Board rules, has limited contact with its employees, it is difficult to ascertain the circumstances in which cards were signed unless there is a voluntary disclosure by an employee to the Labor Board agent after management has brought the matter to the Board. The card-signing circumstances may be investigated, if there is a challenge to the whole process, in what is known as an '8 A 5.' This refers to a 'refusal to bargain' situation in which each employee can be brought up for examination in regard to the signing of his card. It is often very difficult to ascertain whether there was employee coercion."

To what extent can management communicate with its employees before an election?

"Let us examine a situation where a union petitions for an election and the Board orders an election. There is then a vigorous but lawful campaign by both parties. The union may lose the election; they may then challenge the election for some reason after which the challenge is investigated. The Board may conclude that certain conduct was improper on the part of the company; and the election may be set aside. The company may then be confronted with a second election. In a case in which the Board feels that no useful purpose can be served by a second election, they may order the company to bargain collectively. There is definitely an opportunity on the part of both management and union to communicate with the employees. The point is that it should be done without coercion or mis-representation. Store management can point out that the store exacts no dues and that union dues may average about $4.50 a month; further, non-union employees do not have to attend union meetings; that union members not attending these meetings may be subject to fines. It is pointed out to the employee that union membership will involve an initiation fee ranging from $10 to $50. The unions, if authorized, may become a 'second boss.' Employees may not want to have to respond to these new, and perhaps forced, relationships.

"In its defense company management may cite its record of upgrading employees. Many a store manager in a retail store started out as a clerk. Management may cite numerous incidents in which such promotions occurred. Department managers have been promoted to store managers and store managers made supervisors. The company's history of in-grade promotions must be reviewed and also the improvements it may have made in its hospitalization and surgical benefits. Evidence must be shown that wage reviews have taken place in the past. The vacation policy must be explained including allowance for sick leave and how many sick leaves employees have taken. Leave-of-absence policy must also be made clear. If company management has a record of haphazard and irresponsible employee relations, there may be very little that it can do to prevent a union takeover at the time of an election. That irresponsible management will meet its crisis is the result of the NLRB's making it possible for disgruntled employees, or those who think they are mistreated, to get Government assistance in setting up a collective bargaining unit to represent their side with management."

Does this union activity represent, in your opinion, democracy in action?

"This, in a sense, is a real working of the democratic principle whereby economic error, whether deliberate or otherwise, may be corrected. If an employer opens a new store and handpicks a crew with whom he feels he has a rapport so that they will favor the idea of staying non-union, he may succeed in retaining this status. On the other hand, although he has every intention of instituting employee benefits of various kinds, unless he communicates these intentions to his employees they may be readily persuaded to sign union cards. This communication may be at the time of hiring, at the time of the new store opening, or it may be by manual, by store meeting, or face to face. A company may have been in a community for many years; but it may have failed to re-educate or recommunicate its policies to its personnel, and thus it may become vulnerable to union persuasion."

Do not unions recognize the fact that some new businesses cannot afford employee benefits?

"Many businessmen, with uncertainties as to the future profit picture, may hesitate to establish employee benefits which the company may not be able to maintain. There have been circumstances in which companies with declining profits have been obliged to upgrade benefit programs in the hope of keeping experienced personnel. A company may adopt the policy of not fighting or disputing with a union. The *quid pro quo* very often is a number of years of so-called favorable conditions in the eyes of management. Wage demands are modest and there is little or no pressure for extended hospital or surgical programs or, if such programs exist, they are participated in by relatively few employees. The union contract may have a skeletal structure of a real (not a sweet-heart) agreement, yet the employee conditions may be lower in standard than they would be if the company were not unionized. Union officials may have made it clear to management that if they accepted the union without opposition, settlement would be along reasonable lines. On the other hand, if the union has to fight to organize and expend a good deal of money and time, and eventually wins, much harsher conditions will be exacted in a contract settlement."

434

What management problems arise when a union is accepted?

"If you examine the format of a typical collective bargaining agreement, you will find the following index of topics: Adjustment of Arbitration Machinery; Bargaining Unit; Discharge and Discrimination Clause; Stated Funeral Leave Provisions; Health and Welfare Program; Holiday Benefits; Hours Provision; Jury Duty; Leave of Absence; Management Prerogatives Clause; No Strike, No Lockout Clause; Promotions in Rank; Definition of Recognition of the Union; Area of Contract Coverage; Register Shortages; Uniforms; Lie Detector Tests; The Right of Interchange and Transfer; Seniority Provisions; Separability (if the contract has a clause which may be struck down by legislature, what should then happen with that portion of the agreement which is struck down); Sick Leave Conditions; Shop Stewards; The Term of the Agreement; Union Security (the conditions under which a member must join a union and remain a member in good standing); The Wage Clause; and The Pension Clause."

Where does the restriction arise with management?

"Basically, they are multiple. For example, if in arbitration there is a disagreement between a union and an employer, either side has the option of invoking the assistance of a third party but only after some prolonged procedures. Suppose the employer suspects an employee of being discourteous to a customer, and the employee explains that the customer was really in the wrong by being discourteous to the employee first. There must be an investigation, and perhaps a warning to the employee. The second time the same employee may be involved with another customer. At this point the employee may be suspended or have her job changed. If there were a union in the picture and an employee felt aggrieved and the union official agreed with the employee, this claim may have to be aired before an arbitration board on the grounds that the employee was not justifiably discharged. Management begins to find that every decision it makes may technically be subject to challenge by the union, except for a few stated decisions resulting from such matters as drunkenness on the job, outright theft, etc. Other decisions may be subject to review and challenge."

How specific is the union contract in restricting areas of work?

"Disagreements may arise as to work interchange and promotions since there may be very severe limits. For instance, management might want to train employees at cashiering as well as at marking merchandise or doing office work. Yet, if you are a cashier, you may be told by the union that the contract stipulates that you will do nothing else but cashiering. Thus if you are without work you merely stand at the register until your services are needed. You cannot work in other areas.

"Union hospitalization and surgical agreements may involve, on the part of management, substantial contributions covering female employees even though these employees may be already covered by their husband's insurance in other employment. The union will insist on the contribution regardless of

435

duplicate coverage. This would seem to be economically wasteful."

Do new employees automatically become dues-paying union members?

"In most states there is a requirement that an employee join the union after thirty days of employment or thirty days after the execution of the union agreement, whichever is later. The employee is also required to maintain good standing in the union. Some employees may not want to stay with the company if they have to join a union, and they may leave.

"Part-timers may very often be paying substantially high dues to retain their part-time jobs with in many instances very little distinction between what a full-time employee should pay as compared with a part-timer. Some employers insist on a special clause in their union contracts eliminating part-time employees from the necessity of joining the union.

"In regard to promotions, the unions may insist that they be given only to people with seniority without too much regard for ability. Arguments may arise as to whether or not the employer's judgment as to ability is reasonable. Thus, limitations are created in regard to promotions. The question as to what is a promotion is raised. If you go from a marking job to a cashiering job, is this a promotion? We get into new areas of dispute. Everything now becomes a matter needing review first by a union representative. Management's right to lay off employees may be seriously questioned by the union."

Can department managers join the union?

"Department managers may or may not come under union jurisdiction. In its investigation of the duties of employees the NLRB may find that department managers are only department managers in title and are in actuality clerks who, rather than being supervisors, are spending most of their time in such routine activities as marking. In such a case the NLRB will often find that the community of interest of these 'department managers' lies with the rank and file of employees and will group them there for negotiation purposes. Management may thus be restricted to the store manager and one or two assistant managers, and perhaps a head cashier and a head shipping and receiving clerk. These would then be the only non-union members in the store. The bargaining power between the union and the company in a store like this would be seriously weakened, since, should the union go on strike, there would be almost no personnel to man the store."

In your opinion, are union regulations hindering the economy?

"A single operator of one unionized store, if he should be confronted with the prospect of either closing his store or giving in to the union, must usually yield to union demands. Since this is basically a very strong capitalistic country, the unions are just part of the overall capitalistic scene. With a working population of close to 70 million and twenty per cent of this number in unions, of a total population of over 190 million, this country is only somewhat union-organized. There really is no general union power than can long paralyze the country. Even in transportation, should a national strike develop there are many secondary means of shipping by rail and air. There could be intervention by the Government by emergency injunction. It is true, however, that there may be an inordinate power of a group of unions over a single small employer who in such a circumstance has very little power. The only power the small employer may have is the restraining power of the Government as to acts of violence or the limited investigatory powers of the NLRB. If his employees cease working at a crucial time, he is quite at the mercy of the union. Of course, the unions do not want to destroy 'the goose that lays the golden egg.' "

Nevertheless, is it not true that the unions indirectly benefit non-union retail employees?

"Yes. Companies like K Mart, Woolco, or Zayre have a 95 per cent chance of keeping non-union provided their management remains alert to employee needs. Almost every move made by a union is discernible by management. A union move can only be keyed to a number of factors. It can be keyed to job security; it can be keyed to better treatment for the clerk, eliminating offensiveness, favoritism, or similar behavior; it can be keyed to claims of raises as, 'The union will get you a 20 per cent hourly increase in wages; or we will get jury pay; or funeral leave benefits; or we will set up arbitration machinery for you; we will give you seniority provisions; or, you will get three weeks vacation after five years of employment instead of after eight years.' They are not saying anything that is new to an experienced labor-relations person. The way they say these things may differ, but essentially the content remains the same. Much of the union literature is no longer imaginative. They had a renaissance some years ago, but today we find them pumping out much the same old boilerplate. Occasionally they will include in their literature a Madison Avenue air of sweetness and light."

What effect does the Federal minimum wage have on union demands?

"The current Federal minimum wage in retailing is $1.40 an hour. On February 1, 1968, it will become $1.60 an hour. The unions no doubt will make a strong campaign among older, non-union employees in terms of service, stressing that if they have been with a firm for a year or two years, they should receive substantially more than the Federal minimum – not $1.45 or $1.50, but $1.70 or $1.75. As we move to the $1.60 minimum a few months from now, they may emphasize that employees should be making $1.85 to $1.90 an hour. This can be foreseen. Any employer who is reviewing his wage-hours structure as of February 1, 1968, must conclude that he cannot continue to pay an experienced person $1.60 an hour and expect to maintain a fair employee relationship. Wage scales must recognize length of service to the company; some rate has to be interpolated above the federal minimum, which is consistent with the competition (union or non-union), and consistent with the cost of living in the area."

Do you feel that union organizers tend to make unrealistic demands on management?

"In regard to the organization of retail stores by union, it would appear

437

that very little sympathetic consideration is given by the union to the weakness of an employer. Their respect is for strength; if they feel that they have the power to obtain a contract with more teeth, they will do so regardless of the capacity of the employer to comply. They tend to use their union power to the fullest reasonable extent in each case. The union representative has the responsibility to do as good a job as he can of organizing and contracting without destroying the employer. It is his responsibility to do as good a job as he can for the company and its stockholders in seeking a profit picture which will not destroy the morale of his employees or evade his legal responsibilities. The union's responsibility is to its members, but not forgetting that it does not want to destroy the employer. In bargaining for the employer, an attorney is greatly concerned about the profit picture. At the same time the point cannot be ignored that an employee who has been working for several years deserves more wages than one who is just starting."

What motivates the leaders of retail unions? Is it power?

"Union leaders are very cognizant of their power, of their office, and of all the honors and prerogatives that go with it. Most unions in the retail field are free of individuals motivated by personal exploitation. That is a credit to Mr. Suffridge, Mr. Greenberg of RCIA, and to Mr. Potofsky of Amalgamated. These unions are run honorably; their officials have good jobs with benefits and pensions. They have expense accounts, they often attend conventions at places where others vacation; they sit with legislators, congressmen, senators, and presidents. They have open doors to areas which are very often closed to the small merchant. Unions may be used by politicians in the belief that they control votes. Very often this proves to be fiction, as was the case in Michigan, Minnesota, and Ohio in the recent 1966 election. There are no 'bolsheviks' around; many of today's union executives could very quickly transfer from a union to a corporate vice-presidency with not much difficulty. Unions are part of the American capitalistic fabric. Clearly their interests are different from those of the employer. Their motivations are very often pride. Customarily they are very proud men; they love the accolade of the big membership meeting; the photograph in the newspaper; the signing of an agreement with top corporate giants. They like to deal with masses of people. They love to be in front of an audience. These are perfectly understandable motivations."

Have not retail unions been more effective in organizing food stores as opposed to general merchandise?

"Top union leaders feel that their best organizers still come out of food store unionization activities. There is about a ten-to-one ratio in union leaders – that is, ten came out of food to one from traditional retailing or discounting. There are very few women in the leadership of the unions."

How will automation and EDP affect retail unions?

"To date very few problems have risen from the impact of automation

438

on retail employment. If the unions begin to see many jobs lost as a result of automation, they will become more concerned. Unions are more concerned with who does their work than what does their work. For example, they have made a considerable issue over whether or not the salesman for a bread company – the so-called 'rack jobbers' should be permitted to touch or handle the merchandise in union stores. There has been some litigation on that in the West. Normally, a rack jobber drives up in his panel truck with either records, books, or cosmetics. He inspects the inventory on the shelves, restocks if necessary, and then leaves. The unions, in most areas, have not gone into the issue of work assignment on a job. We see cases in which they have objected to work in the store being handled by an outside service on the grounds that they have exclusive jurisdiction over all the work done in the store."

Can a leased department be non-union in a union store and vice-versa?

"In regard to leased departments, the question arises as to the relation between the union and a lessee. It is possible for a union to organize certain leased departments. Some leased departments differ from others. For example, a gasoline station is a type of lessee which the unions and the NLRB may recognize as a separate type of operation with a different union, as opposed to food. In some areas the gas station may be union, whereas the store is non-union.

"In other areas, it may be that the snack bar, because it is in the business of preparing food, has a different federal minimum wage, or different health requirements. It may be related to the Hotel and Restaurant union. If there is a meat department, it comes under the jurisdiction of the Amalgamated Meat Cutters and Butcher union."

Is a union contract with the lessor binding on the lessee?

"The general direction of the retail union organizer is to obtain a 'wall to wall' organization, including the lessees inside or outside the store. A chain of leased departments having a unit in a given store must be bound by the lessor. Very often lease agreements have a clause in them whereby the lessor can bargain for the lessee and bind them to the union conditions. A chain of leased departments theoretically may have as many different agreements as they are in different companies, making for very difficult planning on their part. There are all sorts of variables; a company may be compelled to change its policies in one store as a result of a new union agreement; yet the same company with the same licensor in another state, may, with another union, have to adopt different conditions. Thus, the fact that they are with the same company does not necessarily mean that they have the same conditions chain-wide. It will vary from store to store, and from state to state. It is quite difficult, therefore, for licencees to keep aware of what are their responsibilities.

"Very often there is a problem of communication between the licencee and the licensor, in that the licensor may only advise his licencees at the completion of an agreement as to what terms and conditions have been resolved. For example, the lessee may not have set up adequate reserves for retroactive union agreements as to wage increases. A contract agreement may have been under negotiation for three months and may have certain retroactive provisions. If the licencee in his status as a 'secondary citizen' is not listening in on the negotiations, he might be under an illusion that puts him way off on his budgeting when it comes to retroactive payments due to his employees. The licensor has had the experience of knowing about the potential expense, but to the lessee the news may come as an entirely unexpected financial blow. In some union situations the weakness in respect to employee treatment may be in the licencee's department."

In your opinion how effective is picketing in retail labor disputes?

"Picketing is always an important factor since it constitutes an appeal to the public to withhold their patronage. However, in some areas, the public has become somewhat immune to repeated picketing or to misrepresented picketing which may be designed just to harass an employer. Picketing rarely results in a total withdrawal of the public's business. The effects of picket lines vary from area to area. In shopping centers most people approach the center in a motor vehicle; thus, the person arriving at a shopping center may not even take notice of two or three pickets. Picketing may not be very effective in shopping center areas. There is lawful picketing permissible in many states. In the purview of the National Labor Relations Act, picketing for unfair labor practices may be protected. Picketing by a union on strike is often protected. Picketing by unions that represent a majority of an appropriate unit may be protected. And then there is unlawful picketing: picketing for coercive purposes, such as inadequate representation; picketing to stop deliveries to coerce an employer to bargain with a union. The latter is improper and unlawful. In some areas the NLRB has exclusive jurisdiction in such matters, especially when the employer has not been guilty of any unfair labor practices. The employer may seek to enjoin the picketing in court, thereby getting relief. The injunction is usually handled by NLRB attorneys."

To what extent can state governments control union activity?

"The part which state governments play in relation to union activities is severely restricted. The state courts can exert their authority largely in the case of violence. Most of the jurisdiction is ceded to Federal authorities. The state government is usually a very minor factor. You may, however, get a local court order restraining unlawful mass-picketing within the local jurisdiction."

Is there an age limit on union membership?

"There is no age limit since whoever is eligible to work in the store and has a continuity and community of interest with the regular employees is available for union membership. This may not include part-time or temporary student help. Most employees have the right to vote for or against the union, and if it is a union store they must maintain their membership in the union. The NLRB has reviewed the situation in regard to students and rules that if these students come back summer after summer, they will be allowed to vote."

XVI

Electronic Data Processing for Store Systems

Store systems have to do with the flow of merchandise from the producer to the consumer. With a single store and even up to five or six stores, the owners can manage with a multiple total cash register with fifteen totals. This would enable the accounting to be done for three or four leased departments and eight or nine totals for the owned departments. This information plus "eyeballing" would possibly be adequate for up to five stores. It is now time to seriously consider data processing since with five stores it becomes quite difficult to maintain dollar sales and purchase records by departments or by classes or merchandise. As a result the merchandise mix becomes unbalanced. Stock-sales ratios get completely out of line with trade standards and stock turn may be half what is considered normal. However, management has no way of knowing that their stock situation is out of balance since records are not available.

With seven or eight leased departments there is a need for more department totals than any mechanical total machine can provide. It is at this point that the use of either punched-paper tape or the optical font system is recommended. The latter system prints figures which are read by an optical scanner when fed into the computer. The punched tape can also be fed directly into a computer where it is read. The computer is then programmed to identify transactions by a multiple number of departments, by merchandise classifica-

442

tions (some merchandise requires financial control at classification level), and by merchandise characteristics such as price line, fabric, size, color mix, lined or unlined, etc.

Trouble arises not only from loose financial control but also from loose unit control having to do with the "status" of an item. This results in inadequate knowledge as to what merchandise is on hand, on order, or sold. Replenishment becomes a serious problem and badly needed capital is tied up in excessive inventory. A company lives or dies on its store system. To see that a system is adequately executed, proper supervision is essential. People problems must not be allowed to interfere.

What happened to Korvette? They lost one thing – CONTROL. They did not build into their organization adequate budget and inventory controls to operate stores outside the metropolitan New York area. When they went to Chicago, Detroit, and Greenbelt, they lost the control for which they had become famous. Chaos existed in inventory and payroll budget control. Most important, they were not developing executive talent. They had a company that was going ninety miles an hour but all of a sudden it stopped. The whole corporation just piled up on top of itself. In addition, they went into diverse deals that they never should have gone into; they bought their own trucking company; they bought their own credit company; they went into the furniture business which they had no business going into. They bought out H. L. Klion Corp. They went into food with the Hilliard-Cohn organization which became Hills-Korvette. All these things dissipated their management talent. Instead of getting a strong fashion direction, or a strong hard goods direction, a strong, concerted operational direction, they dissipated the talents of their top executives and made them impotent. As a result they lost money. Today, under the new Spartan merger set up with Charles Bassine as chairman, they are reducing inventory levels, streamlining their communications. Korvette had lost its ability to communicate. True, they were sending plenty of messages, but they were not getting feedback from the field. You can't just be sending, you have to receive too. What customers wanted in Matson, Ill. and what they wanted in Greenbelt, Md., was not what the customers in Fifth Avenue Korvette wanted.

Capturing Information at the Point of Sale

INTERVIEW WITH ROBERT A. GRILL, MAJOR ACCOUNT REPRESENTATIVE, MONROE-SWEDA, INC.

How many codes can you put in a cash register?

"For example, if a store had 99 departments, that would be two rows of keys, one to nine and ten to ninety. Within those ninety-nine departments they could have as many as nine hundred and ninety-nine thousand numbers which means, of course, infinite capacity. This would mean that the capacity of a normal cash register with seven or eight rows of keys would be enough capacity to code thousands of items within any given department. If the merchandise has a price tag on it with other code numbers, the cashier just reads it right off. If we allow her to ring dollars, we should allow her to ring numbers. Figures from supermarkets tell us that sometimes cashiers are from 15 per cent to 18 per cent off in just ringing five keys: groceries, meat, produce, tax, and dairy. The percentage of error found with some of our larger users is often less than one per cent. The reason for this is that all the girl has to do is to read a number off a ticket.

"The record is made on a five-channel punched-paper tape. In the area of punched tape there are both five- and eight-channel tapes. Sweda uses five-channel tape because their cash registers only delve into the numeric aspects of the transaction. By five-channel is meant five columns of holes on the tape. These can be read by a computer. With eight-channel tape, the three extra channels are alpha or letter channels. A program is written for the computer of XYZ company which may, for example, have eighty-seven departments. The cash register is provided with two extra rows of keys besides the dollar values. The merchandise is marked with its price and code number. When a blouse gets to the cashier at the point of sale the cashier rings say department 27 which would be ladies' blouses. The tape can be read by a paper tape reader which is a rather inexpensive piece of equipment. In fact this tape can be sent via the telephone line using a simple machine which rents for $35 or $40 a month. It is called a paper-tape transmitter. With just a phone call, the day's business can be sent across town or across the country. It is picked up at the other end by another piece of equipment which creates a similar paper tape at its end of the line. This tape could then be put on one of many machines. It could be put on a tape-to-card machine reader which transfers the tape information to an IBM card. The card can then be stored and used for sales or inventory reports.

"One of the virtues of paper tape is that it can be read by many types of machines, large or small. The program written for that computer recognizes the holes. Data transmission is today still in its infancy and most people don't need information about what happened today in the way of sales. They are quite happy to get these reports on a weekly basis in the mail. For example, some of our larger companies in Boston receive tapes in canisters daily and process them twice a week on Tuesdays and Thursdays. When a tape is cranked into a cash register the store and cash register number is automatically punched into the tape so that no confusion can arise as to where the tape had its origin. The tape is read at high speed by the computer and at the same time a magnetic tape is prepared which is used to make a report.

444

Automated warehouse, Morse Shoe Company, Canton, Mass.

"You can have either a tape-to-tape input or a tape-to-card input. Magnetic tape is more common today because of the speed and lower cost it entails. It also eliminates the cost of cards and of punching the cards.

"The so-called 'optical font' is merely the use of stylized print commonly seen on bank checks. The eye on a computer can recognize this stylized number. This optical tape is nothing more than the detail from the cash register. It is then mailed to the computer center and a scanner, which rents for about $1,500 a month, looks over this cash register detail tape and prepares a magnetic tape from it. This magnetic tape is then put into the computer which prints out the reports. Whether the cash register tape is paper or optical tape does not make much difference as both capture the same information. One advantage of punched tapes is that it can be transmitted and the processing costs are a little less; and of course there are more people familiar with the processing of punched tape than there are with optical tape.

"The National Cash Register Company, Sweda International, and IBM are working very diligently in the realm of optics. However, RCA and Honeywell and many others are constantly working to perfect the punched tape process. The optical type font is built into the cash register at the factory.

"The word 'two pass' means that instead of ringing say $1.95 and a department number, a style number is also rung which would encompass 4, 5, or 6 digits which might represent a manufacturer, the cost, the seller, the clerk, the size and what have you. These items would be rung first and the amount and department last. This constitutes the 'two pass' idea. Cash registers have a capacity of about eight columns so if I had a five-digit stock number, a three-digit department number, and a four-digit price, I might ring department 127, $15.95, and then 1,2,3,4,5,6, across the same keys I have just used. On the second pass the cash register turns itself into a non-adding machine and accepts a code number or letter.

"The Service Bureau Corporation, which has seventy or more locations around the country, is avidly pursuing customers whose paper or optic tape they can process at a reasonable rate. One of our biggest customers has its tapes processed locally. Some of these local processors have more sophisticated machines than a company can afford. To pay the rent on these machines, service bureaus split up the cost among many customers. E. J. Korvette has not yet decided whether to go on the optical system or the punched tape. They are at this time buying only standard cash registers.

"An interesting and amusing fact is that the largest retailer in the United States, Sears Roebuck and Company, which opens a store almost every day running from 40,000 to 300,000 square feet in size, is not yet on EDP. They are still in the testing stages with our company and other companies. They have tens of thousands of cash registers of all different kinds. Basically, they are on a hand-written system today and they are succeeding in spite of that. Our company and other companies in this business have had their biggest successes with young businesses such as the discounters. These companies have no preconceived ideas and do not have millions of dollars invested in obsolete cash registers. More and more businessmen today are becoming aware through trade publications and through organizations such as the NRMA that in the next few years they are eventually going to have to automate at the cashier point. They will spend millions of dollars on warehouse control using computers, data transmission, and other sophisticated equipment yet, at the very point of sale where the merchandise is going out of the door either paid for or charged, most retailers in the U.S. have systems that were in use prior to World War II.

"The Zayre company which operates 80-odd discount stores has 1,200 Sweda cash registers and is perhaps doing the best job today in the way of retail data processing. Zayre probably gets more information at the point of sale than any other company using the optical font system. Of all the merchandise they sell, perhaps 50 per cent is recorded with the two-pass system. One pass will pick up the code number comprising four or five digits indicating vendor, etc., and a second pass will ring the department and price. With this system they are in an excellent position to know what is happening in their business. Lacking this information, a company doing a very large volume of business, can very easily get into serious problems related to buying and to inventory control. In today's market, when sales are up but profits keep going down, a business which is very closely controlled has a distinct advantage.

446

Electronic Data Processing for Store Systems

IBM card punching machine installation at Atlantic Thrift Center
(Spartans Industries, Inc.), New York City office.

"Several years ago, one of our dealers in Washington, D.C. studied the
neighborhood drugstores closely and found that such stores invariably have
charge accounts. He developed what became our Mark II system. A drug-
store may be doing only $200,000 to $300,000 of annual volume. Customarily
when a charge is made a slip is made out and sometime during the day, when
they are not busy, they will run this through their cash register which will
accept cash sales. The cash account number is put into the cash register and
the sale rung up after. The tape is then sent to a local service bureau in
Washington and at the end of the month with a lag time of say 48 hours, they
receive a two-part IBM printed statement including a trial balance, a sales
analysis of 70 or 80 classifications sold by the store, a sales report by clerk
and by units and dollars sold which measures productivity and which can
be used for commission purposes. This system is extremely successful. In fact
doctors and dentists in clinics use it. If one thinks of doctors one does not
think of a cash register. These were sold without cash drawers and the doctors
and dentists and small businesses, such as wholesale florists dealing
almost exclusively with check or charge slips, are using this type of cash
register doing volumes of $200,000 to $400,000.

447

"With the exception of several stores such as Woodward and Lothrop in Washington, and Horns' in Pittsburg, few department stores are completely automated. Macy's, Gimbels, Bamberger's, and Stern's have tried or are trying punch-tape or optical systems in specific departments such as the men's wear using say 10 or 20 cash registers. Stern's had a test with an optical system which was unsatisfactory. They are now trying punch tape. The traditionalism of department stores has resisted change. Furthermore, they have a tremendous investment in cash registers and many of them have huge machines which cost $5,000 or $6,000 and really do not perform many operations. We think that in the next four or five years or so the whole concept of capturing information at the cash register will undergo a tremendous change. We don't know if this will be by talking into the cash register. It is possible that certain stylized and magnetic inks, now available, will be used to mark the merchandise. An item will be placed in front of a photoelectric cell and the recording keys will be automatically pressed down."

INTERVIEW WITH MARCUS DE ROWE, ZAYRE. CORPORATION ELECTRONIC DATA PROCESSING

What, in your opinion, have been the most important electronic data processing applications in mass merchandising?

"What really started retailers in computers was unit control, which is getting pieces of information from the field and coming out with a report in sequence that will tell them what they sold in order to make decisions on what to buy. Before it was done on computers, it was done manually at great cost by a great number of people. By replacing those people by computers, we save money and get speedy and more accurate information. Unit control is not the major application in terms of time consumed. Things like payroll, statistical information, accounting information, billing, accounts payable, and various others may not necessarily be done in any great degree of sophistication, but they can be done on the computer."

What are the major applications as far as the Zayre chain is concerned?

"In one stage or another, we have practically everything affecting our business on a computer from unit control all the way through to general ledger. It includes such things as payroll, accounts payable, store billing, inventory control, statistical information concerning history, the per cents of increase and decrease, sales analysis, things like that."

In a sense, then, you do research here because, having the figures you can put them in the machine for research purposes?

"No, not really, as this would encompass an area of forecasting, in other words, the use of your historical information to project something for the future to happen. We do not do this. It is used mostly as the bookmaker

448

Electronic data processing with IBM 1401 computer installation at Atlantic
Thrift Center (Spartans Industries, Inc.) headquarters in New York City.

machine. It gives us history – what we did do last week and how we did it."
What sources do you have in addition to the punch tickets that come in from
merchandise?

"We use all source documents. We will key punch a purchase order or
key punch a receiving record. We will key punch an accounting journal. We
will key punch an invoice. We also have one other source that comes into
our computer from punch-paper tape. It is our sales data in dollars that all
comes from punch-paper tape since all of our registers contain it. Of course,
in addition to it you perceive various adjustments that don't lend themselves
to punch-paper tape.

"The punch-paper tape is a register record of a transaction by department. We now have almost ninety departments listing the retail price at
which we sold the goods. We are experimenting in some ten stores in getting
a merchandise control code into the tape which the computer would then
translate into unit control information identifying the unit sold."
How frequently do you get this punch tape from the cash registers? How
long does it take you to process it?

"We finish with processing the punch-paper tape for the previous week's
transactions through Saturday night by the following Thursday morning,

449

Electronic data processing equipment used by the Zayre Corporation
in the Natick, Mass. headquarters. The system centers around the two IBM 360 computers.

thus providing a weekly report. We do not process each tape as it comes in. We accumulate the information and then prepare a report once a week for an accounting period.

"This is done only on a dollar basis. However, we envision the day when we will have unit control information on that tape enabling us to extract the unit control information almost as soon as we receive the punch-paper tape."

What information is provided in unit control?

"The style, manufacturer, category, color, and size of the item sold. The only thing the checkout girl would punch in would be what is called a second pass. Once she has recorded the department and dollars, on the second pass she will record a four digit number that would give us in code the style, vendor, and category out of the four digits. For color and size there are two additional digits."

So then she would actually have to punch in six times to give you this information. What percentage of accuracy do you get on this operation?

"We are going to have some errors. The girl might register the wrong

450

number, or even the item could have been ticketed wrong. We do expect, though, to be at least 95 per cent accurate. On tickets, of course, you don't have much control. Tickets can be lost, mutilated, not sent in. There are too many factors involved in getting accurate information from tickets. I think it is much more costly to control the accuracy of tickets. It gets to a point where it is not practical, not worth the expense, yet many retailers use this ticketing method with great success. Many companies have a reordering system based on the tickets and it works. It just depends how much effort top management wants to spend in controlling it. The punch-paper tape method, for our purposes, is far more efficient for far less effort. It is like an enforced collection of tickets. It forces the girl to ring in something."

Will you abandon the ticket method completely?

"We will probably continue with tickets for many years to come."

Will the two-pass system be used for all merchandise, or just for special merchandise?

"It will be used for merchandise categories for which we need unit control for reorder purposes. Everything that is on tickets now would most certainly lend itself to it, but we could expand it to departments where a ticket could not even be attached, like jewelry for instance. Domestics is another area where it is difficult to attach a ticket and keep it there. When we had tickets on domestics, the loss of the tickets was so great that we just had to discontinue it. Sporting goods is another problem department. A two-pass ticket need not have such a fixed shape; it could be a stick label, it could be a string, it could be a pin, it could be almost anything. You don't have to tear off anything, either. It stays with the article going out of the store."

To whom do you give reports of these various summaries from the computer?

"The greatest volume, by weight of paper, goes to buyers and distributors. The payroll department gets their checks, registers, and all supporting reports. The accounting department gets all trial ledger and audit trials, etc. The statistical department gets recordings of all the transactions that have transpired between stores, warehouses and stores, and vendors to stores or warehouses."

Is your computer programmed so that it types a complete report?

"You have a mass of data, which we call input. In unit control, you get unit information on each item sold. It comes in at random from many stores. You feed it into the computer and the computer checks it first for validity. Then it has to sort and arrange these hundreds of thousands of transactions in sequence. After that it goes against the previous week's history which contains the inventory and it updates it by subtracting the sales and adding shipments and comes out with a new history, printing a whole record for style on each sheet. It is more than just a typewriter; it makes computations and calculations and it gives us totals by category, by style, by sort. The big

451

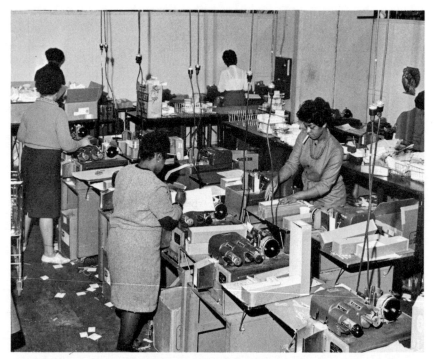

Ticketing is a major operation at Atlantic Thrift Centers (Spartans Industries, Inc.).

problem in the beginning then was to decide what you want and in what sequence. Once you made that decision, the programming of it is pretty much straight forward."

Does IBM give you pretty expert information regarding what you want?

"We happen to use IBM computers, but you can use any computers that you find suitable. We hire our own programmers and they do the programming. We have permanent full-time programmers."

How many employees do you have in the data-processing department?

"At the moment we have over 75. The bulk of them are key-punch operators."

Do you own or rent this equipment?

"All of it is rented. The reason why we feel that rental is better is perhaps not so much the growth of the technology of the computers as the growth of our own business. Today we might do with a smaller computer what you might not be able to do with a smaller computer three years from today. We are not yet at a point where we can get ourselves locked-in with a specific machine."

What class of computer do you have?

452

"An IBM System 360 does most of the work. We received it in November of 1965. We also have NCR 315 computer which is used solely for sales analysis, in other words, reading the punch-paper tapes and analysing them to determine what our sales were. However, the final report for those sales are run on the 360. It is a more versatile and much bigger machine."

Do you keep the equipment going day and night?

"Yes, the computers are kept going day and night. We have a huge investment in programming as well as in the computer itself. Rather than get two or three of those machines, we have found that it is better to have one and keep running it around the clock."

Have you ever had occasions where the computers have made bad mistakes which threw everything off?

"Numerous, that is part of life. We didn't have too many of the famous ones that you read about in the newspapers. We did once write an accounts payable check for $5 million which of course didn't get anywhere. Occasionally we underpaid people when the computer did not take into account overtime. The reason was that overtime wasn't specified in a format that the computer would accept. It has not made any disastrous errors. Most of those errors were really human, not computer, because all the computer does is add 1 and 1 and comes up with 2, and when it gets another 1 it adds it again. It is a rather simple thing. Most of the computer errors are either poor programming or the input was terrible."

Do you think you have reached the limit as far as the application of computers to retailing is concerned?

"No, the other way around. I think we are just starting. We are at a point now where I think the computer technology can do anything we can think of – that's number one. Number two, I think we are getting to a point where we are really beginning to learn how to use those machines. All we have done up to now, really, is have them accumulate masses of data and tell us what was accumulated. It didn't involve any decision-making on the computer's part. It didn't involve any forecasting. We use the memory to calculate things. It could be used, for example, to accumulate data on tapes, which we do, of course, which is sort of like an external memory. What we really plan to do with computers now is to take a lot of the present manual functions and let the computer do them. For example, in accounts payable we have a department which takes the invoices, the receiving records, and the purchase order; they match it and decide to pay or not to pay; they send it to the computer and the computer makes out their remittance advice and the check. Well, we would like to go a step further. We would like to have the computer match the invoice, receiving record, and the purchase order and decide whether it should be paid or not and how; what discount should be taken; to whom the check should go. In unit control, for example, we prepare huge reports that the buyer gets and he just looks over and makes

453

his decisions. The computer could make many of these decisions and the buyer could function better as a buyer and go and explore new markets. The computer could decide most of the distribution based upon the information. It could even project for the buyer what he should buy, which styles he should investigate, or what quantities he would need in order to meet certain planned sales."

Would this mean preparing the forms in such a way that the computer could read it?

"It could be done by using the present data it already has. We feed it sales data which it compares with last year's data and with this year's trends. You could program various factors such as planned promotions or going into a heavy sales season, or coming out of one, and by adjusting this and weighing that the computer could come up with what is going to sell, what you should ship to the stores next week, the week after, etc. It could also analyse the per cent of our business by vendor. We suspect that 80 per cent of our business is done with only 30 per cent of our vendors. Maybe that is not quite true. We could analyse returns to vendors or markdowns. Maybe markdowns for one vendor are higher than for another. Why? There are various decisions that the computer could make. It could project our sales. It could do quite a bit of the day-to-day thinking. It could go more into analysis and forecasting. It could calculate the gross profit per item, something which we could probably do manually, but the task would be absolutely forbidding.

"It is true that the programming will be more complicated because there will be more of it. You will have to give the computer many more instructions to forecast than it needs to assemble a history on historical data. Many more, and it will become a greater programming job in that respect. But the greatest one is still the human brain which tells the computer what to do. All the computer does is what you tell it to do."

Bizmatic Data Control Centers, Inc., Boston, Mass.

INTERVIEW WITH CARMEN DI PIETRO, GENERAL MANAGER

Bizmatic Data Control Centers, Inc., Boston, Mass., is a privately-owned concern incorporated in Massachusetts. Carmen di Pietro is the general manager and president. Peter Sicurella is vice president and treasurer.

"We started in business in 1960. Prior to forming this company, I was a professional manager and cost accountant for General Electric for 23 years. One of my jobs was to make computer installations, so I became acquainted with computer language. Peter Sicurella was a Lieutenant in the U.S. Air Force and developed data-processing systems and installations. An advantage of using Bizmatic data control centers is that we have management experience. We adopt and apply the principles of 'management by exception' in the area of retailing. One of our customers is Lee Shops for whom we control over 7,000 stock items.

"We rent an IBM computer with a memory of 16 K, 4 tape drives, two discs, a 10-11 paper take, a card reader, a 1407, and computer typewriter. The primary reason for renting is that in seven years of business, we have changed our systems configuration four times. We are now contemplating the installation of a 360, series 30, in December of 1967.

"We are the only service organization in the New England area that can handle all of the merchant's requirements in retailing such as processing Kimball tickets, Dennison tickets, cash register tapes, and punch-paper tape. We have an optical tape reader on order for delivery in December of 1968, so eventually we will get into the optical service area.

"We employ a staff of sixty-eight people of whom approximately eighteen are professional systems analysts or programmers. Two are M.I.T. graduates. We service over sixty clients in many areas of commerce all over the New England geographical area; some are in New York. We service organizations that are headquartered with executive offices in the Boston area but have their retail outlets west of the Mississippi.

"One of our accounts is Baker Shoe which is a national organization with forty-two retail stores. We also service all the Lerner department stores. In addition, we service manufacturers, wholesalers, and distributors.

"Our retail business runs around 12 per cent, manufacturers about 15 per cent to 18 per cent. The rest is made up of distributors, wholesalers, and institutions, such as endowed foundations, research foundations, and hospitals. This includes the New England Medical Center Hospital, the Forsyth Dental Hospital, which is tied in with the Harvard School of Public Health, and Tufts University. Our service is unique since we have adopted the policy of mechanizing around the customer's mode of operation. This philosophy is based on the fact that human beings resist change. It makes for an easy and efficient conversion. We do not provide packaged programs. Our systems analysts will consult with companies contemplating computer programs.

"A retailer needs vital inventory information, especially in high fashions, six to eight weeks prior to peak periods such as Christmas, Mother's Day, Father's Day, Easter; but he cannot economically justify the installation of highly sophisticated equipment and personnel to give him open-to-buy control dollars.

455

Sophisticated multi-level material handling equipment at the Morse Shoe Company's 467,000 sq. ft. warehouse at Canton, Mass. Said to be the only entirely automated shoe warehouse in the U.S., as far as electronic data control and material handling are concerned.

"Operators of key-punch machines can punch into IBM cards any kind of business record such as an invoice, a receipt for merchandise, or a requisition. These cards, in times of peak requirements, can be sent or taken to Bizmatic for processing. In peak periods, they may need as many as 20 girls operating 20 machines. During normal times, they may only need two girls. In the case of Lee Shops, time is so important that they pay a carrier to pick up their tickets after their stores close and deliver them to us at 2 a.m. on Sunday morning. We then process the tickets and complete a report which is delivered back to Lee Shops at 8:30 Monday morning. The buyers then analyze these reports and can immediately get back into the market.

"We have customers who have cash registers which develop punched-paper tape at the point of sale. On receipt of this tape, we feed it directly to the computer and prepare complete periodic reports of sales by item, size, style, color, vendor – whatever information is considered necessary. In the case of Raymond's department stores, their tapes are picked up by courier after the stores are closed and delivered to us. The next morning, the controller has on his desk the previous day's sales by department and by classification.

456

We work two shifts seven days a week, running from 6:30 a.m. to midnight. At overload times, we work all night. It is obvious that we can make much more effective use of our equipment than can any captive installation. We can afford to hire programmers with varied backgrounds and pay them $15,000 to $16,000 a year and give them challenging assignments. A man may work with one retailer for a three-month period and then he goes on to another job. It is uneconomical for a small retailer to hire one of these experts since such men, once they have devised an installation, want to go on to further challenges rather than stay in a routine environment.

"If the economy had a downturn, our sales would increase since one of the first expenses that management would curtail would be data-processing costs. Many companies have had unfortunate experiences with computer installations. An advantage of doing business with a firm such as ours is that a company knows what its data-processing costs are. It is similar to the idea of leasing cars enabling you to know precisely what your costs are; you are relieved of many maintenance headaches, etc.

"Our sales during our first year were about $40,000 and in 1967 we did over $800,000 worth of business. We have 12,000 square feet of floor space in downtown Boston which gives us accessibility both for labor and clients. Another reason for our location is that we are right next to the South Postal Annex which facilitates the receipt of data by mail from all parts of the country. We thus can pick up material almost on an hourly basis, including weekends.

"We can go into a company and set up a whole system advising the client on the type of hardware without prejudice or bias. We will then train their help, design the installation, and supervise the installation. Once all the systems are completed and the personnel trained, we turn it over to the company. That is what we call a 'turnkey' operation. For a major client, our retainer fee could be up to $15,000 or $20,000 per year, plus time and material costs. If we send a major consultant in, he gets $200 a day; a systems analyst gets $150 a day. For a smaller client with, say three stores, the charge would be about $3,000 to $5,000 to set him up.

"With new accounts, which have had little exposure to data processing, we start them very gradually, one department at a time, so that the customary procedures are not disorganized. Systems can be adapted to the client's ability and to the needs of his accounting staff. It is not necessary to put every record on the computer immediately. It might take from three to four years before the final phase would be completed. The first season would be restricted to sales analysis, as the introductory phase. Then, we might add billing to the system: the third season, we could put billing and sales together and obtain inventory control, such as on-hand balances and items to reorder. It is usually uneconomical for a retailer or a manufacturer to put in his own equipment, since it takes three to five years to get all the 'bugs'

457

out and train the personnel to understand and to use the equipment and the information it provides.

"A case in point is one of our clients – a manufacturer working with a very wide product mix and sales of about $28 million. The company handles approximately 10,000 parts in inventory of which half are purchased and half are manufactured parts. They have a tremendous inventory of purchased parts. The big problem facing management was how to reduce the excessive investment in inventory without being out of stock. We made a study of the annual usage data of their manufactured and purchased parts and then correlated and ranked them by high to low inventory investment based on usage. This is what we call an 'ABC analysis' from the highest to the lowest inventory investment per item. We related it as a percentage for each item. We found that of almost 5,000 items, 50 represented almost one-third of their annual inventory investment of purchased parts. They now have assigned two expeditors on a full-time basis to keep track of the exact availability and purchase requirements of these 50 items in which $500,000 is invested. The expense of maintaining an inventory runs from 20 per cent to 25 per cent of its cost, owing to obsolescence, storage, handling, insurance, etc. Excess inventory was costing them almost a million dollars a year.

"If a company is paying $1,000 a month for computer equipment rental, it will cost about $3,000 a month to support the program in manpower and softwear requirements. The machines used to punch IBM cards rent for about $45 to $60 a month, and the operator may be hired for from $1.75 to $2.50 per hour. Marking tickets used for punching are made by the Dennison Company or the Kimball Company. Machines to punch these tickets rent for about $50 per month. Besides printing legible information digits, such as prices or cost codes on the ticket, the machines punch holes which carry information for computer control. We have facilities to process both the print-punch ticket and the Dennison type. The concepts of these tickets are essentially the same, except that one is vertical and the other horizontal.

"The minimum type of operation, which can economically use our services, would be perhaps a three-unit operation generating a minimum of ten to fifteen thousand unit sales per week with a total volume of about $7 million. Actually, it would depend on the selling price per unit. A smaller number of units at a higher price would present fewer problems than a great many units at lower prices. With Lee Shops, we control over 7,000 style items with a program designed to automatically print a stock record if any one of the following actions occur: a sale, a refund, a transfer between stores, a distribution from the warehouse to the stores, a receipt from the vendor into the warehouse. Out of these 7,000 items, experience has shown that from 3,800 to 4,000 stock records would be printed for a particular week. This file of 4,000 stock records would then be used by the warehouse distributor to replenish shelves in the retail outlets. The buying office would also use it as a reference tool for reordering, since the list is also used by vendors. Out of the 7,000, there might be 600 to 800 that would be slow movers and 200 to 400 that would be fast movers. We print the fast movers in a red book and the slow movers in a blue book. The total would be divided into categories, such as sportswear, lingerie, dresses, coats, ski pants and accessories, day-time accessories, and the like. The slow-item book is used by the supervisor of the buyers, who can check with them to see why the item has not sold, whether it can be returned to the vendor, or marked down. The president's office will get a report of two pages by category. This is what we call 'management by exception.'

"With a total unit control system we can give management every week the total of purchase order commitments so that they can control the cash flow. We also give them open-to-buy figures by stores, units, categories, and price lines. Also provided is sales for a particular week; distribution from the warehouse so that stock can be replenished; total goods on hand; total on order. Based on projections on the next six weeks sales, we can tell whether they are overbought or underbought by dollars and by price lines for the next six weeks. Lee Shops is the only retailer, to my knowledge, which has a mechanized open-to-buy control data by classification of items. This includes J. C. Penney, J. M. Fields, and Sears.

"The secret of success in retailing is to control your inventory. With good control you can shoot for a turnover of from eight to ten. This also reduces markdowns and increases profits. It also helps a smart retailer to operate on the vendor's money. With an expenditure of 1.2 per cent of his sales dollar in EDP, a retailer can realize 8 per cent profit before taxes, which is unheard-of in the high-fashion industry. Strict discipline is required in maintaining a good data-processing system. As an outside service organization, we feel that we can be more effective in securing this discipline if it gets out of control, since we have entré to the president's office."

Payroll Management in a Centralized Self-Service Discount Department Store Operation

PAYROLL CONTROL IS A MAJOR KEY TO SUCCESSFUL DISCOUNT STORE OPERATION

In a chain operation, management is able to assemble operating statistics for a number of units thus providing it with standards for the entire operation against which the performance of individual units may be compared. A key item is payroll and top management of a larger chain may assign an individual whose sole duty is to check payroll reports and to keep in constant contact with store units regarding increases or decreases in payroll as a percentage of sales.

The store manager is entirely responsible for the performance of his unit. In addition to a base salary, he is customarily paid a commission on store sales. Depending on the size of the store, he may have one or even two assistant managers. Certain discount chains have a merchandising assistant manager and an operations assistant manager. An individual store image is in many ways a reflection of the character of the store manager and his merchandising ability.

A capable department manager can come up with many ideas concerning the merchandising of his department by improving the displays and deciding what merchandise should be placed in the prime locations and at what time. The strategic arrangement of fixtures and signs can be a potent factor in increasing sales. As a general rule, department managers have no buying or reordering functions so, in a sense, their authority is somewhat limited. Their control over the personnel in their departments may also be limited. Although in theory the store manager has overall charge of all store personnel, situations may develop whereby he has to answer every petty question which really should be answered on the department level. In addition to his other duties, he may have far too much to do with the handling of department personnel. A competent store manager will delegate much of this control back through the department manager especially in the areas of personnel productivity and payroll control. To what extent this can be done hinges on the ability of the department manager.

A recent development in internal store management is in the area concept. Rather than have several poorly paid and possibly incompetent individual department managers, the new idea is to consolidate several departments into an area and to put a well-paid individual in charge. A salary of from $125 to $135 a week will entice a rather capable individual, especially if it should be a woman. A sample area might consist of the ladies' department including ready-to-wear, sportswear, jewelry. Also included would be the children's department comprising both boys' and girls' wear. Another area might consist of stationery, books, records, and flowers. Depending on the number of leased departments and the range of merchandise, each store breaks its areas down differently. With the department concept, it would be necessary to have a ready-to-wear department manager, a sportswear department manager, a jewelry department manager, etc.

The responsibility for receiving merchandise is lodged with the head receiver, an assistant receiver, and perhaps one or two others depending on the size of the store and the volume of business. The receiving room guard is either one of the store's own security staff or a detective from an agency hired by the company. The average staff of a store of 80,000 square feet is approximately 100. Of these a sizeable number will be part-time employees many of whom work only in busy periods. It is the responsibility of the payroll budget director to devise a payroll budget on a monthly basis for each store and then to see that it is implemented. This budget is put together by consultations with store managers, trips to the store, examination of schedules sent in to headquarters, reports from district managers and regional personnel managers. In certain situations a store manager may find that he has an insufficient payroll, so he telephones his regional director or payroll budget director for advice. The director may show him that his problem arises from a poor scheduling system; that he should be able to cover a particular area with existing help. Interplay and feedback take place. In general it is safe to assume that all store managers feel that they should have a bigger payroll. However, those who are aware of the influence of payroll on net and gross profit strive to do a top job of scheduling their personnel. They may get more productivity than they expected during a given week, and thus save money on a weekly basis.

Payroll control is a major key to successful discount store operation. It is extremely important to avoid excessive overtime. A store or department manager can save a considerable amount if he can avoid letting a forty-hour employee work even forty-one hours since, multiplied through a chain of twenty or more stores, it becomes a sizeable saving. The best manager is one who has become very adept at scheduling so that he can rely more and more on part-timers. Common policy is that full-time personnel must work a full forty-hour week and receive a decent living wage. Working hours may not arbitrarily be cut down to, say, thirty-five. On the other hand, if there are two twenty-hour part-timers, it is quite possible that the manager may not find it necessary to use the full forty hours of coverage, and no problem arises if it is cut down to thirty-five. There is vastly more payroll flexibility with part-time personnel since they are not guaranteed a full-time wage. Another advantage is that in periods of extra activity, there are now two workers who have been working twenty hours over an extended period of time and who have gained experience and knowledge. Instead of bringing in a green person who has to be trained the hours of these trained part-timers can be extended.

With inadequate floor coverage, it might appear that the savings would be more than offset by theft. Normally shrinkage may run from two per cent to three per cent of sales. I raised this question with an executive of a large chain, and he said, "The element of theft in a week is nowhere near the cost involved in payroll, so it is merely a question of deciding which is more important. Payroll is a very expensive enemy whereas the extra amount of theft in a week may be negligible and not even worth worrying about. If you can save $400 or $500 in payroll, you may be willing to give up $100 or

461

$200 in theft." The store manager, with the assistance of his regional manager, is therefore called on to develop expertise in scheduling. The weather plays a big part in this matter. In really disastrous weather with sales at a low ebb, the store managers must notify their part-time personnel not to come in. The lack of store personnel is well compensated for by the fact that the store is just not busy.

In regard to the procuring of part-time help, there is normally little difficulty since there are many housewives, high school and college students, and working men who wish to supplement their incomes with part-time work. A newspaper advertisement or even a sign in the store will normally produce good results. An important duty of the store manager is to keep a card index of the names and addresses of available part-time people with comments on their ability and the dates on which they worked. Individuals who proved very competent during the Christmas season may later be invited to work on a semi-regular basis.

Resident Buyers for Mass Merchandisers

The "Merchants Buying Syndicate" Company

Resident buyers, operating out of New York City, have traditionally been associated with conventional department store operations. To fulfill the special needs of promotionally-minded mass-merchandisers who seek a high turnover of competitively-priced goods, a new kind of resident buyer has evolved.

Representative of this development is the New York-based Merchants Buying Syndicate founded in 1960 by Richard Schott, Seymour Cohen, and Arthur Wachtel. Feeling that traditional buying techniques tended to be conservative and complacent and were not adequate to fulfill the special needs of mass-merchandisers, the partners decided to start a service designed to meet these needs. Seymour Cohen, now president, is a veteran of fifteen years of hard goods. He is a graduate of the New York University School of Retailing and started as an assistant buyer trainee working up to merchandise manager for home furnishings, housewares, sporting goods and toys for two leading New York buying offices. Richard Schott, executive vice president,

463

is a graduate of Brooklyn College with a degree in economics. At the age of twenty-four he was a housewares buyer for Allied Stores. He later became hard goods buyer for the Interstate Department Store chain. Arthur Wachtel, executive vice president, is a graduate of the University of Buffalo. He handles all smallware for MBS including notions, stationery, cosmetics, plastic houseware and trim-a-tree items. He is responsible for introducing many new merchandising categories to MBS including domestics and allied items.

MBS operates on a fee basis – not a commission or a percentage of purchases. It does not buy on its own account but acts as a go-between for its clients by finding resources and pooling buying power to obtain the best value. The company sets up deals in the following classes of merchandise: hard goods, including housewares, toys, outdoor equipment, sporting goods and lawn and garden supplies, auto accessories, gifts, luggage and leather items, draperies and piece goods, hi fi, sundries, miscellaneous food items, candy, china, glass, lamps, drugs, and cosmetics. In 1967, MBS had 188 clients representing over 3,000 retail outlets including supermarkets, discount, drug, variety, and department stores. Total volume of purchases in 1966 was $375 million.

A special service for its clients is the MBS annual trade show. The 1967 show was held in June in the New York Hilton Hotel. Suppliers are invited to rent booths at a cost of $450 per booth. At the 1966 show there were 156 booth-type exhibits and attendance was 450. Estimated purchases of $3.5 million were made. In January, 1967, MBS organized for its clients a fifteen-day buying trip to Europe. Prior to the visit company representatives shopped and pre-selected merchandise from European factories. A three-day exhibit was held in Paris featuring wares from England, France, and Belgium. This was followed by another three-day exhibit in Frankfurt with merchandise from Germany and Sweden on display. The final three-day show was held in Florence showing Italian goods. Included in the merchandise offered were gifts, housewares, hardware, toys, ceramics, silverware, and furniture. The merchandise was tagged with price quotations in American money. English-speaking factory representatives were on hand. Total cost of the trip to clients was $888.

Included in MBS clientele are variety chains, drug chains, discount-store chains, supermarkets, and department stores. Most of its clients are east of the Mississippi. MBS holds a special interest for small and medium-sized operators.

Services supplied by MBS are geared towards the self-service, highly promotional activities and hard-hitting price competitive practices of mass-merchandisers. They include the following:

1. Helping the buyer to spread or widen his product mix by scouting the markets and the manufacturers for merchandise already in line or to be manufactured according to MBS specifications.

Seymour Cohen, president, Merchants Buying Syndicate.

2. Acting as a liaison between the manufacturer and the retailer, MBS is able to quote "on the spot" new products from all key sources of supply.

3. Providing a merchandising consultation service to the retailer giving him a steady flow of programs, advice and current merchandising information accumulated from manufacturers and from client "feed back" on a national scale. There are daily market reports and bulletins listing special price concessions, etc.

4. Coordinating volume buying power resulting in important price savings for clients. Group purchasing prices are obtained at store level quantities.

5. Providing special programs in private and controlled label merchandise. Some products may be exclusive to MBS clientele.

465

6. The sponsoring of buying shows in the U.S. and in France, Italy, and Germany.

President Seymour Cohen feels that any retail operation, large or small must be affiliated with a competent resident buying office if for no other reason than to obtain a fresh, professional, unbiased viewpoint of market conditions. He said, "Many organizations find a resident buying service helpful as a check point which, properly used, will augment the stores own purchasing ability. A buying office unencumbered with 'in-store' problems, can spend all of its time in the market to develop items, initiate ideas, shop more resources and give the account greater market coverage." The only source of income for MBS is the fee that management pays for its services. This fee is not based on how much or how little the client buys or to what extent he uses the information service.

Other services MBS offers for both established and new accounts include a complete personnel file and the designing of in-store departments. Says Cohen, "With a new store operator, we are equipped to construct a department-by-department basic inventory taking into consideration the number of promotional items which can be used for store openings and seasonal specials. For a new store we line up promotional items which can be exploited on a two-week interval thus assuring merchandising continuity and at the same time building a steady shopping habit." In-store display is another service which MBS offers its clients. Says Schott, "We will frequently take out buyers into manufacturers' showrooms to study their displays; using this as a basic guide, we aid in setting up display material geared to fit the merchants' specific needs. We have photos of good display aisles which are available to our members."

MBS maintains a sample room where seasonal merchandise, new products and those currently being promoted are kept. A new product is tested by being placed in different types of stores in various geographical regions by means of special agreements with these stores. If an item is successful, the news is passed on to members who reap a special benefit in that their store is the first in an area to feature the product.

The Merchants Buying Syndicate often extends counselling to manufacturers. If a product passes MBS specifications of good quality at a competitive price, but is lacking in package appeal, they will ask the manufacturer to make needed changes. Clients are asked to place their orders, whenever possible, through MBS. In this way the company has a record of all client orders and can easily "follow up" for faster action. The orders are not rewritten but are checked by an MBS buyer before sent to the vendor for processing. MBS management emphasizes that their company is not a sales organization, neither are they commission agents. The client is assured that he will not lose his market identity when using MBS services.

A highlight of the MBS trade shows is a special merchandising program

466

whereby some 400 items in about 15 categories are offered at special prices exclusively to members in attendance. Orders for the merchandise are acceptable only at the meeting which is a closed-door affair with no manufacturers or non-members permitted in. The shows also provide an opportunity to negotiate for closeouts and for special deals.

MBS is a firm believer in the promotion of private label merchandise and has a variety of items under its Parkway label including spray paint, booster cables, tires, antennas, oil filters, barbecue grills, garden tools, automotive accessories, seat belts, batteries, garden sprinklers, and various household items. In addition it has a Colby and Lady Colby label program for sporting goods, domestics, and small electrics. Colby label products include baseball gloves, tennis rackets, golf balls, bags and clubs, fishing rods, basketballs and footballs. The coordinated controlled label program offers approximately 125 interrelated products. Says Cohen, "Our concept is that we have the opportunity of choosing the leading manufacturer in each field by pre-testing his own labeled products to see if they have customer acceptance. We can then pick and choose our suppliers without being committed to one resource. By having many private label items in a store, each one actually supports the next. The best presentation is to have the private label product displayed next to a similar, but nationally advertised product. If the packaging is strong, the pricing competitive and the value comparative, then the private label product will pull its share of volume." According to MBS, three prime sellers have been Lady Colby hair dryers, electric blankets, and heating pads.

In regard to the future, Schott said that the company does not want more than 200 accounts since that number is the maximum that can be serviced adequately. More than this number would make personalized service out of the question. "Just now," he said, "we are carefully examining our present accounts in order to get rid of the credit risks and companies whose buyers have no conception of what our services are good for – in short, they do not know what a buying office is all about."

Buying Office Planned for Israel

It was announced in the New York *Times* of June 2, 1967 that a group of retailers was planning to open a buying office for Israeli softgoods in the near future. Heading the organizing committee are Meshulam Riklis, chairman of the McCrory Corporation, and Charles C. Bassine, chairman of Spartans Industries Inc. Other interested retailers were Sol W. Cantor, president of Interstate Department Stores Inc. and Max Feldberg, vice chairman of the Zayre Corporation. In 1966 as reported by the Deputy Trade

Commissioner of Israel in the United States, this country bought $77.2 million of Israeli products of which textiles and apparel accounted for $9.5 million. Leather, suede footwear and furs accounted for $1.5 million.

Israel has been increasing her exports of such apparel as knitwear, rainwear, leather and suede coats and woolen trousers. There is a fashion show week each February in Israel where new ready-to-wear lines are displayed. About 500 buyers from the U.S. and other countries attended the last show.

XVIII

The Advertising Trap

Very laudably, every discount store company president wants to have the current year's sales exceed those of the past year. He looks at the record and the thought comes to him, "If we threw a sale into the month of May and called it a 'Million Dollar Sale,' I bet you we would do some business." He has the sale and adds a quarter of a million dollars worth of business in two stores in a ten-day period. It was a very fine success. October is a relatively dull period. The company has advertising dollars in the till so again, the president says, "Let's throw out another circular sale in October." It is another success. Another year goes by and the president finds he has built himself a "bug-a-boo". Once you have a sale you have built a trap for yourself since, when you compare the following year's results with the preceding one, you say, "My God, how am I going to equal those figures?" Obviously you have to fight for them. You already have two sales built in May and October and "Back to School" is coming. Comments the president, "If we put out a circular to kick off the fall season, I'll bet you we will do a whale of a big business!" He does and it helps. The following year he looks at the figures and says, "Gee, maybe just before Easter – maybe just before July 4th, . . . we might plug in a sale." Thus management gets itself into a sales trap. The store's image is adversely affected by excessive emphasis on

469

price. Customers tend to hold off purchasing until a sale is announced. Special sale merchandise upsets the inventories of year-around merchandise. The hypo needle injecting an overdose of sales can be catastrophic. The conservative approach is to forget the fact that the other guy is yelling bargain price but instead make your impact on the market on an institutional basis and make the company stand for something other than price.

The Bo Bernstein Advertising Agency

Perhaps the dean of mass-merchandising sales promotion is Bo Bernstein of Providence, R.I., president of the advertising agency that bears his name. He became associated with the mass-merchandising field in 1934 when he was engaged by the New York Lace Store of Pawtucket. This store was operated by Edward Zwetchkenbaum and Morris Kaplan and, in the opinion of Bo Bernstein, they deserve a great deal of credit as the real pioneers in discounting.

Zwetchkenbaum, in 1947, leased the women's wear department at the Ethan Ames factory store (later known as Arlan's) in Fall River, Mass. The store was a tremendous success and was the beginning of the Arlan's department store chain. Bo Bernstein feels that Zwetchkenbaum's great ability in operating this department in the Ethan Ames store really was the spark plug which launched modern discounting. Says Bernstein, "Sidney Mittelman was quick to note Arlan's success and launched Atlantic Mills; Marty Chase, always alert to a good opportunity and with a wealth of retail experience behind him, founded Ann and Hope. Great credit must also be given to the Anderson-Little Company with whom our agency became associated in 1941. At that time their factory salesrooms in Fall River and their sales branches in Providence and New Bedford were open six nights a week until 9 p.m. with plenty of free parking. Clothing was sold direct to the customer from pipe racks. In my opinion, they were the true forerunners of what today has become the discount store. The cradle of the discount movement was really Rhode Island."

In his experience advising retail executives, Bernstein says he is "amazed and stunned" by the reluctance of so many businessmen toward change. He illustrates by telling of the difficult time he had convincing Edward Zwetchkenbaum that he should get rid of his old globe-type fixtures and put in fluorescent lighting. Zwetchkenbaum felt that his customers might think that his store had gone fancy and that bargains were no longer available as in the good old days.

470

The Advertising Trap

Bo Bernstein was advertising consultant to the Feldbergs in their Zayre operation from the start. He said that Stanley Feldberg and Clifford Loweth spent many hours planning the layout of the first store. Traffic flow, placement of departments, the dynamics of sound, air conditioning, and lighting were all carefully analyzed. The 100 or more Zayre stores adhere to this basic construction, which has been widely copied throughout the country, even by such companies as L. S. Ayres in their Ayr-Way stores.

Says Bernstein, "One of the things we learned from our days with Arlan's was that give-aways such as trips, jackpots, refrigerators, stereo and television sets, mink jackets, and the like are not an ingredient to the success of a promotion. On one occasion, we filled a giant bowl with pennies and asked people to guess how many were in the bowl. The person guessing the nearest would get a free trip to Bermuda. People took home thousands of blanks, but I doubt if the contest was worth the expenditure. The winner sold the trip back to the company. In many instances, when opening new stores, we found that people just stood at the counter filling out blanks, thus jamming the front of the store and making it extremely difficult for customers to get in."

One of the services of the Bo Bernstein agency is to suggest names for stores, and the first assignment with the Feldberg family was to suggest a name for what was to become the new chain. Comments Bernstein, "As is our custom, I submitted the problem to our staff offering a prize of $100 to anyone who came up with the name finally selected. Seventy-five names were submitted, and I pared it down to ten. Actually, we never submit more than three or four names. I called in Frank Barad, one of our vice presidents and read him the names, after which he commented, 'Zehr gut.' I replied, 'Hey, that isn't bad, is it?' He said, 'What isn't bad?' I said, 'Zayre.' So, this became one of the names we submitted to the Feldbergs; it was finally accepted because it is easy to remember. It has only five letters, which spelled economy in sign building. It lent itself to unlimited rhythmic use when combined with such words as where, there, declare, compare, etc.

"For its radio advertising, we recommended that Zayre take an institutional approach for the very practical reason that the budget at that time was not sufficient for us to compete lineage-wise with the advertising of so many other retailers in the Boston market. No mention was made of item or price; however, the Zayre image emerged as a fine self-service department store. In our third year with Zayre, it was decided to run a Million Dollar Sale. Our ad stated, 'Macy's did it, Gimbels did it, Jordan's did it, Filene's did it, so could Zayre.' The Boston newspapers telephoned asking if we had gotten permission to use the names of Jordan's and Filene's. I responded 'Did Ford get permission to use Chevrolet and Plymouth in their ads and how come it was only Filene's and Jordan's they were so concerned about and not Macy's and Gimbels?''

471

SECTION III

MASS MERCHANDISING: REVOLUTION & EVOLUTION

Summary and Conclusions

To avoid economic obsolescence retailing institutions must constantly adapt to changes in their environmental climate and in consumer attitudes and demands. Just as the old fashioned service grocery succumbed to the supermarket, so in the distribution of general merchandise, the "traditional" or "orthodox" stores have had to give ground to new merchandising concepts.

The appearance of discount stores in the late 1950's imperilled the existence of certain types of retailers, such as women's speciality stores, junior department stores and variety store chains. They also became a thorn in the side of traditional downtown department stores.

The prevailing patterns of distribution and cost-price relationships were upset. The customer wanted informal self-service suburban shops open from 10 a.m. to 10 p.m., having a wide selection of most wanted merchandise at competitive prices, plus plenty of parking. The discount store gave it to them. Economists call this "innovative competition"; sociologists call it "deviate behavior." We welcome it as convincing evidence that our free enterprise, capitalistic system still works. Final benefactor is the consumer who gets what he wants, namely convenience and low prices.

The emergence and acceptance of mass-merchandising in the form of self-service discount department stores has been a complex process entailing difficult decisions on the part of vendors. Should manufacturers and wholesalers be loyal to the existing power structure or should they embrace the newcomers? Retailer groups, such as department stores and drug stores, with the help of their trade associations, tend to function as a highly cohesive group resisting any changes in traditional trade practices, established institutional codes, relationships and loyalties. A group of retailers, confronted by intense and aggressive competition from outside sources, does not hesitate to organize group protective measures. Preferred vendors of established national brands, if caught selling to "outsiders," are sternly warned that such action, if continued, will deprive them of the continuing patronage of the "legitimate" retailers or the "insiders."

Retailers in general and especially small retailers are inclined to resist innovation because they want to maintain behavior patterns which fulfill their status in society; they prefer a static to a dynamic environment – the status quo must not be upset. Undoubtedly large retailers are responsive to innovations which increase profit, but change is apt to be slow. An example is the use of computers. Major long established firms have a heavy investment in record keeping equipment, such as cash registers which, although they are obsolete, are still usable. The new discount chains are more likely to use the latest data processing equipment since they have capital to invest and are open to new ideas.

Until 1965 the dominant institution in the marketing channels for general merchandise was the department store. In 1966 and 1967, however, the total sales of self-service, promotional discount department stores, according to hitherto reliable sources such as Dun and Bradstreet, have equalled or exceeded those of traditional department stores. Large discount chains have become dominant factors in distribution channels. Vendors who, despite orthodox opposition, favored the innovators in the early days are now being richly rewarded.

With the current emphasis on trading up in merchandise, appearance, and services, the true discount store image is – with a few exceptions – becoming similar to that of the traditional department store. Before long the path will open for new "deviate behavior" and Professor Malcolm McNair's wheel of retailing will start another revolution.

Perhaps the earliest discount pioneer was the Ethan Ames (Mammoth Mills) boys' clothing factory store in New Bedford, Mass. Started as a factory outlet by 1947 it had become a full-fledged discount department store known as Arlan's. Witnessing the meteoric success of Arlan's, other hardy entrepreneurs entered the picture. Murray Candib, in 1949, opened what was to be the first unit of King's department stores in an old Indian Motorcycle Factory in Springfield, Mass. Martin Chase started his Ann and Hope Factory Outlet in Cumberland, R.I. in 1953; Max Coffman started his first Mammoth Mart in an old foundry in Framingham, Mass., in 1954. William

Palestine opened his Rockdale Store in an old mill in Turner's Falls, Mass. in 1953. Selwyn Lempchen pioneered with his Kermell Bargain Center on the outskirts of Fall River in 1955. In the same year Aaron Cohen opened a discount store in the basement of a shoe factory in Fall River, Mass.

Among the first of the traditional department store operators to enter discounting was Interstate Department Stores which, in 1957 acquired a two-store White Front chain on the West Coast. In 1966 (including its Topps chain) Interstate had sales of over $500 million, 85 per cent of which came from discount operations. With the entry into the field of such highly respected department store operations as L. S. Ayres, Allied Stores, and finally in 1966 the country's largest department store chain – Federated Department Stores – discounting became respectable.

In the late fifties variety stores felt the sting of discount store competition and decided that if they were to remain competitive changes would have to be made. The M. H. Fishman Company was the first to convert one of its stores into a discount store in 1957. They were followed by Neisner Brothers and S. S. Kresge in 1961. In 1962 the F. W. Woolworth Company, the world's largest variety chain, with 1968 sales of $1.9 billion, decided to enter the field. Under the presidency of Harry B. Cunningham, Kresge's K Mart Division in an astoundingly short time has become the nation's leading operator of self-service promotional department stores with over 273 units in operation plus approximately 593 variety stores.

The word "discount" still remains uncomfortable for latecomers. Woolco calls its stores "promotional department stores"; J. C. Penney calls its Treasure Island stores, "experimental stores."

Despite the success of these mavericks in retailing, the downtown department store remains a powerful and resourceful competitor. Its dominant position in women's fashion merchandise remains unchallenged. Department store branches dominate shopping centers in most suburban metropolitan areas.

The Future

The giant discount chains are still expanding at a rapid rate. Zayre is expanding at the rate of about 20 new stores a year. Woolco has planned 30 new openings for 1969. S. S. Kresge, by 1969 expects to be operating over 300 K Marts covering nearly every state in the union. J. C. Penney may yet exploit its vast potential with its Treasure Island stores.

The heyday of the small entrepreneur who started on a shoe string seems to be over. There are practically no new entrants in the field. Existing small discount chains with greater flexibility and personal supervision have demonstrated that they can survive despite the enormous purchasing power of the giants. Small units are especially effective when they are in a single metropolitan area served by one warehouse as is the case with Bargain Barns in Dayton, Ohio.

Without doubt we are approaching an era of giantism in the merchandising of general merchandise. EDP has now made possible the centralized management of a national chain with an efficiency hitherto considered impossible. Cash registers in every store may be linked with a central computer making instantaneous inventory control an actuality. Automated warehouses can be connected with a computer-operated automatic reordering system. It must be realized however, that computers are no more than adding and subtracting machines with memories. They are wonderful for recording past transaction history and they can select a "runner" but they cannot select new and attractive merchandise – they are no substitute for a merchant.

One of the major results of the retail revolution has been the development of a much closer relationship with manufacturers who have cooperated with the new mass-merchandisers more than ever before in fulfilling the demands of self-service. They have provided theft-reducing and easy-to-handle packaging, informative labels and signs, premarking. Firms such as General Electric supply special promotional campaigns geared to sell mountains of merchandise through discount chains.

The larger discount chains account for a vast increase in private label merchandise which competes successfully with nationally advertised brands. Some discounters have themselves become manufacturers. Vornado makes its own brand of small appliances; Spartan manufactures its own wearing apparel.

The distinctions or lines of demarcation between types of retailers is rapidly disappearing having been merged into large, one-stop super stores. The competition of the new, low-margin mass-merchandisers now encompasses almost the entire range of mass-consumed merchandise.

Contribution of Mass Merchandising to the Economy

THE VIEWS OF SENATOR WILLIAM PROXMIRE OF WISCONSIN GIVEN IN AN ADDRESS BEFORE THE MASS-MERCHANDISING FOUNDATION CONFERENCE IN NEW YORK CITY ON APRIL 12, 1967.

I would like to speak to you about the contributions of mass-merchandising. I have found that the best place in Wisconsin in which to shake hands on any weekend is in front of a Treasure Island store whether it is in Milwaukee or

Madison. Seriously, when I talk about the contributions your mass-merchandising industry has made in this country I feel very strongly about it. The country with the best record of price stability, in spite of the fact that we have had some inflation during the past 15 or 20 years, has been the United States of America. We have a better record of price stability than any of the European countries, better than Japan or of any industrial country in the world. Prices have been stable despite all kinds of pressures tending to drive them up.

A major reason for this is because we have achieved enormous progress in distribution. Much of that progress originated with you in this room. The fact is that consumer durables for example, have increased only very slightly in price between 1958 and 1966, the increase being only one-fifth as much as other prices. If we could hold other prices down as much as you have been successful in holding the prices of the general merchandise you sell, we would have had virtually no inflation.

Now in addition to this you brought an improvement in the quality of merchandise sold in this country. You realize far better than I do that you simply can't stay in business with price alone as important as price is.

We had testifying before the Joint Economic Committee just last year a distinguished professor from Yale University who told us in his judgment – he is probably the outstanding authority on price statistics – that actually since 1947 we probably haven't had any real inflation. I'm not sure that I agree with him. His argument was this: the improvement in quality, which is not measured by and large in our price statistics, is enough to account for the increase in prices and then some.

You offer not only quality and price, but also convenience and variety. A customer can go into your shops and purchase all kinds of things. It's easy, it's convenient. You can park. And, of course as Adlai Stevenson has pointed out, the most precious commodity to a human being in the world is time. Time is a great democratic force. The time that Americans must have wasted going from shop to shop 25 or 30 years ago compared to the opportunity they have now to purchase an enormous variety at one place at one time, is a real contribution.

The biggest contribution you have made is one of competitive stimulation. You have not only provided a great service but you have provoked an enormous increase in efficiency on the part of the people with whom you compete. It is now a platitude, I guess, to say that department stores are getting more like discount stores and discount houses are getting more like department stores. Yet it is true and the reason is because of the revolution you brought to this country in distribution.

Let me say a few things about the outlook for mass-merchandising. The big factor is demand. What is going to happen to sales in the next few years? Our Joint Economic Committee has just completed a study called "Projections 1975." You have to make all kinds of assumptions when you

MASS MERCHANDISING

make estimates of what future sales are going to be in this country, but the assumptions must be reasonably grounded. The assumption is that overall consumption will increase each year between 4.2 per cent and 4.6 per cent. Incidentally this is a much more rapid rate of increase than we have had in the last 20 years. And each year will be compounded, each year will increase more. Furthermore, sales of durable goods are expected to increase 5.5 per cent to 6 per cent a year. Why? Well one reason of which we are almost positive, is that household formations will increase rapidly. We expect them to be up by one-third in the period from 1965 to 1970, another one-third from 1970 to 1975. Wholesale and retail trade will be increasing at a rate 50 per cent more rapidly than it increased between 1947 and 1965.

The Pilot Research Project

Prior to the founding of the Mass-Merchandising Foundation, the author, with the help of an industry committee, started a pioneer pilot research project on the merchandising operations of self-service discount department stores. Chairman of the industry committee was James Lynch of Touche, Ross, Bailey and Smart. The other members were Abe L. Marks who was then with the Clarence Rainess Company; James J. Dollard of the First National Bank of Boston; Benjamin Figer of King's Department Stores; Hy Dushman, president of Sandy's Department Store, Arthur Remillard, Key Stores accountant; Louis Rosenberg, Coven and Suttenberg; Nat Shaller, Cohen, Cohen, Harian and Shaller; Harold S. Larkin, editor and publisher, *Modern Retailer*; Chester W. Patterson, State Street Bank and Trust Company; Frank Brenton, treasurer, Mammoth Mart.

A number of companies were persuaded to submit their confidential figures to the School of Business Administration of the University of Massachusetts. Although we did not have a representative sample of different sized companies we were able to publish statistical operating averages each year for the years 1963, 1964 and 1965.

The Mass Merchandising Research Foundation

The M.M.R.F. was started in 1966 under the leadership of Abe L. Marks, president of Hartfield-Zody's, who was chairman of the board. At

480

Summary and Conclusions

the April, 1967 Conference the position of chairman was eliminated and Abe Marks was elected president. Continuing in the offices of treasurer and secretary are Chester W. Patterson, assistant vice-president, State Street Bank and Trust Co., Boston, and Harold S. Larkin, Editor of *Modern Retailer*. The membership now stands at about eighty companies and includes not only store operators but companies closely associated with the industry such as vendors. The membership fee is $300 and a substantial sum, to be devoted to research, has been raised. Six regional vice presidents reflect the national scope of the foundation.

A two-year agreement was made in 1967 with the College of Agriculture at Cornell University to take over the annual study of the merchandising operations of discount department stores. The School of Agriculture already prepares similar studies for the food trade. An allocated budget of $26,000 has been provided for an expanded research program.

Effective Sept. 15, 1967 Kurt Barnard became Executive Director of the Foundation. Mr. Barnard is 40 and resigned his position as public relations director of the American Research Merchandising Institute to assume his new duties. He is a graduate of the New School for Social Research in New York City. Said MMRF president Marks, "We hope through MMRF to weld the great strength of this young and burgeoning industry into a clearing house of information for all members and into an engine of service to the nation and the nation's shopping public." Headquarters of the Foundation will be in New York City.

481

APPENDIX

STATISTICS ON THE OPERATIONS OF SELF-SERVICE
DISCOUNT DEPARTMENT STORES

Sales of 45 Top Discount Firms

Each of the companies listed below achieved individual sales of $50 million or more in 1966. The figures apply only to the volume that went through discount stores including lessee sales – without regard to total company sales. (Note: Figures are for calendar year 1966 regardless of present formation of companies involved.)

COMPANY	STORES	TOTAL VOLUME	SALES PER UNIT
1. K Mart, Jupiter (S. Kresge), Detroit	273	637,000,000e	$ 2,333,000
2. E. J. Korvette, New York City	42	612,000,000e	14,571,000
3. Topps, White Front (Interstate), New York City	70	465,000,000	6,643,000
4. Gibson Products Co., Seagoville, Texas	236*	448,000,000e	1,898,000
5. Zayre, Natick, Mass.	92	360,000,000e	3,913,000
6. Two Guys (Vornado), Garfield, N.J.	33	336,000,000	10,182,000
7. Parkview/Gem, Kansas City, Mo.	30	330,000,000	11,000,000
8. Atlantic/Spartan (Spartans Industries), New York City	97	299,000,000e	3,082,000
9. S. Klein, New York City	12	240,000,000	20,000,000
10. Arlan's, New York City	71	239,000,000	3,366,000
11. J. M. Fields (Food Fair), Philadelphia	56	228,000,000e	4,071,000
12. Alexander's, New York City	7	215,000,000e	30,714,000
13. Gamble's, Clark's, Tempo, Buckeye (Gamble-Skogmo), Minneapolis	86	185,000,000e	2,151,000
14. Woolco, Worth Mart (F. W. Woolworth), New York City	85	180,000,000e	2,118,000
15. Grand Way (Grand Union), E. Paterson, N.J.	30	175,000,000e	5,833,000
16. Bradlees (Stop & Shop), Boston	39	162,000,000e	4,154,000
17. Great Eastern, Millers, Gulf Mart (Diana Stores), N. Bergen, N.J.	28	160,000,000	5,714,000
18. King's, Newton, Mass.	45	130,000,000	2,889,000
19. G E X, Bellas Hess Superstores (National Bellas Hess) N. Kansas City, Mo.	13	125,000,000	9,615,000
20. Unimart (Food Giant Markets), Santa Fe Springs, Calif.	14	120,000,000e	8,571,000
21. Fed-Mart Corp., San Diego, Calif.	28	110,000,000e	3,929,000
22. Shoppers Fair (Mangel Stores), New York City	44	110,000,000	2,500,000

23. Skaggs-Payless, Oakland, Calif.	19	102,000,000	5,368,000
24. J. W. Mays, Brooklyn, N.Y.	6	102,000,000	17,000,000
25. Globe (Walgreen), Houston, Tex.	11	100,000,000e	9,091,000
26. Uncle Bill's, Ontario (Cook Coffee), Cleveland	23	96,000,000e	4,174,000
27. Clark's (M. N. Landau), New York City	38	94,000,000e	2,474,000
28. Bazar, Cal. (Big C Stores), Portland, Ore.	10	89,000,000e	8,900,000
29. Schwegmann Bros., New Orleans	7	85,000,000e	12,143,000
30. Target (Dayton Co.), St. Louis Park, Minn.	7	85,000,000e	12,143,000
31. Save-Co, Hills (Shoe Corp. of America), Columbus, Ohio	20	83,000,000e	4,150,000
32. Gemco (Lucky Stores), Buena Park, Calif.	11	80,000,000e	7,273,000
33. GES, Govco, Bargain Town (Retail Centers of America) Long Island, N.Y.	8	80,000,000	10,000,000
34. Valu/Villa Mart (Weisfield's), Seattle, Wash.	12	75,000,000	6,250,000
35. Fred Meyer, Portland, Ore.	18	70,000,000e	3,889,000
36. Times Square, Brooklyn, N.Y.	11	70,000,000	6,364,000
37. Caldor, Norwalk, Conn.	12	67,000,000	5,583,000
38. Fedco, Los Angeles	5	61,000,000e	12,200,000
39. Sage, ABC (Sage International), Montclair, Calif.	10	59,000,000	5,900,000
40. Meijer's Thrifty Acres, Grand Rapids, Mich.	10	56,000,000e	5,600,000
41. Turnstyle (Jewel Tea Co.), Chicago, Ill.	9	54,000,000e	6,000,000
42. Barker's (Franklin Stores), New York City	15	52,000,000e	3,467,000
43. Ayr-Way (L. S. Ayres), Indianapolis, Ind.	6	50,000,000e	8,333,000
44. Nichols Discount City, New York City	12	50,000,000e	4,167,000
45. Treasure Island (J. C. Penney Co.), New York City	5	50,000,000e	10,000,000
TOTAL	1,716	$7,576,000,000	$4,415,000

* Number represents total of franchised and wholly-owned units.
e Estimate.
Source: *Discount Merchandiser*, July, 1967, p. 38-TL.

MASS MERCHANDISING

DISCOUNT STORE SALES CONTINUE TO SOAR

Since 1960 sales of discount stores have been rising at an average annual rate of $2.1 billion a year.

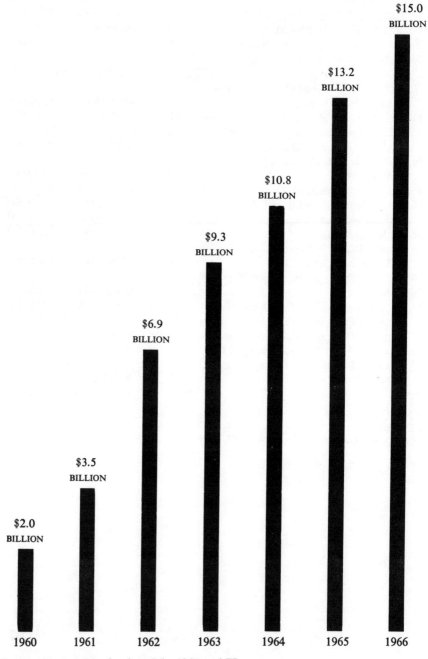

Source: *Discount Merchandiser*, July, 1967, p. 4-TL.

Appendix

According to the *Discount Merchandiser*, trade journal for the industry, discount stores now occupy the top position with respect to sales among outlets of general merchandise. However, food retailing still holds the largest individual share of the retail sales. The total retail pie for all major retailers shown came to $157.5 billion in 1966.

RETAIL SALES BY MAJOR OUTLETS

TYPE OF STORE	1966 VOLUME (ADD 000)	% TO TOTAL
Supermarkets	$48,384,000	30.7%
Grocery Stores	17,569,000	11.1
Discount Stores	15,011,094	9.5
Department Stores	13,382,600	8.5
Drug Stores	9,750,000	6.2
Women's Apparel Stores	7,179,450	4.5
Furniture, Home Furnishings Stores	6,904,700	4.4
General Merchandise Stores	5,170,000	3.3
Appliance, TV Stores	4,983,140	3.2
Variety Stores	4,280,000	2.7
Men's, Boys' Clothing Stores	3,473,830	2.2
Family Apparel Stores	3,457,960	2.2
Building Materials, Paint, Plumbing & Electrical Stores	3,412,000	2.2
Hardware Stores	3,009,910	1.9
Shoe Stores	2,828,100	1.8
Mail Order	2,761,670	1.8
Tire, Battery and Accessory Dealers	2,611,650	1.7
Jewelry Stores	1,750,000	1.1
Home and Auto Supply Stores	838,350	0.5
Sporting Goods, Bicycle Stores	730,406	0.5
Total	$157,487,860	100.0%

Source: *Discount Merchandiser*, July, 1967, p. 6-TL.

MASS MERCHANDISING

SELECTED OPERATING RESULTS FOR 31 SELF-SERVICE
DISCOUNT DEPARTMENT STORE FIRMS: 1965

This data comes from "Operating Results of Self-Service Discount Department Stores, 1965" published by the Center for Business and Economic Research, School of Business Administration, University of Massachusetts, Amherst, Mass.

	TYPICAL FIGURES	MIDDLE RANGE
Average Number of Stores	10½	4–25½
Average Sales per Store (in. thous.)[1]	$2,900	$2,231–$3,855
Index of Change (1965/1964):		
Owned Department Sales	116.0	107.2–124.0
Leased Department Sales	108.0	100.2–115.6
Total Chain Sales	113.5	107.1–121.1
Sales in Identical Stores[2]	108.0	104.6–110.5
Number of Stores	105.0	100.0–111.5
Average Sales per Store	107.0	101.0–112.9

MERCHANDISING DATA,
   %'s of Owned Dept. Sales (except where noted)

Stockturn (Based on Average Monthly Retail Inventory Figures)	4.0	3.4– 4.9
Inventory at Beginning of Year	13.5%	11.3–17.2%
Inventory at End of Year	16.0	13.3–18.3
Freight, Express, and Truckage	1.3	1.1– 1.7
Cash Discounts Earned	0.7	0.5– 0.9
Cumulative Markup (% of Original Retail)	32.4%	31.6–33.2%
Markdowns	3.5%	2.5– 4.5%
Stock Shortages	3.0	2.6– 3.6
Total Retail Reductions	6.5%	5.2– 8.2%

RETAIL INVENTORY (Beginning of Month)
  Index Nos.: February 1965 = 100.0

February	100.0	100.0–100.0
March	113.5	104.6–124.9
April	133.0	116.9–157.8
May	138.5	120.0–172.0
June	136.0	117.3–160.7
July	134.5	116.4–166.5
August	135.0	114.8–165.0
September	145.5	121.0–182.7
October	163.5	133.4–201.9
November	177.5	145.9–222.2
December	177.5	140.9–232.7
January	131.0	106.8–160.5

Appendix

MARGIN, EXPENSE, AND PROFIT,
%'s of Owned Dept. Sales (except where noted)

GROSS MARGIN	27.2%	25.5–28.9%
Leased Department Commissions	4.5	1.4– 8.0
GROSS INCOME	31.7%	27.8–34.9%
Salaries and Wages	12.9%	11.3–14.9%
Supplementary Employee Costs	0.95	0.8– 1.4
Occupancy Costs	5.35	4.4– 6.4
Fixture and Equipment Costs	1.0	0.8– 1.3
Advertising	3.0	2.2– 3.6
Supplies	0.95	0.7– 1.2
Taxes	0.4	0.2– 0.5
Communication Expense	0.3	0.2– 0.4
All Other Expense	2.6	1.8– 4.3
Total Expense before Interest	27.45%	24.7–30.9%
Net Interest	0.25	0.2– 0.4
TOTAL EXPENSE including Interest	27.7%	25.0–31.1%
NET OPERATING PROFIT	4.0%	1.6– 7.3%
Net Nonoperating Income	0.1	0.0– 0.2
Earnings before Income Taxes	4.1%	1.7– 7.0%
Federal and State Income Taxes	1.6	0.4– 3.0
NET EARNINGS:		
% of Owned Dept. Sales	2.5%	1.4– 3.8%
% of Capital Stock and Surplus	21.0	11.3–30.4
% of Total Assets	9.0	4.3–15.1
Capital Stock and Surplus, % of Total Assets	43.0%	35.3–50.2%
Leased Dept. Commissions, % of Leased Dept. Sales	9.5%	8.7–10.1%
SELECTED EXPENSE DATA, %'s of Total Sales		
Salaries and Wages	8.7%	7.1–10.3%
Supplementary Employee Costs	0.65	0.4– 0.8
Occupancy Costs	3.9	0.3– 4.3
Fixture and Equipment Costs	0.65	0.4– 1.0
Advertising	2.1	1.7– 2.2
Supplies	0.6	0.4– 0.8
Taxes	0.25	0.1– 0.3
Communication Expenses	0.2	0.1– 0.3
All Other Expenses	1.7	1.1– 2.1

[1]Based on total chain sales, including leased department sales.
[2]Stores which were in operation during all of 1964 and 1965.
  Note: Not all firms submitted complete reports, therefore some of the averages are based
    on smaller samples and, in a few instances, estimates were used.
Source: *Discount Merchandiser*, July, 1967, p. 36–37-TL.

487

Key Stipulations in a Typical Lease

As a preliminary, the lessee must check thoroughly the financial standing of the firm which will handle his money – the lessor. The most important question remains unanswered; will lessor store management be competent both now and in the future? The following points must be settled:

1. The selling and warehouse area the lessee will use.

2. The lease duration and cancellation notice time and terms.

3. Terms of payment. Minimum basic rent plus a negotiated percentage of sales.

4. Definition of accounting terms such as gross sales and gross receipts.

5. Record-keeping methods lessee will use. The operations figures to be made available to the lessor and when.

6. Performance bond or security payment from lessee insuring that he will honor his agreements. Lessee inventory ownership in the event of credit claims in lessor bankruptcy.

7. Store operating hours.

8. Insurance liabilities of both lessee and lessor in the event of damage or lawsuits.

9. Non-assignability of lease to others.

10. How alterations and installations are to be handled and by whom.

11. Services to be provided by lessor such as security, heat, light and parking.

12. Lessee pricing policy. It could read, "Lessee agrees to maintain the lowest lawful possible prices obtainable for similar merchandise within a 15-mile limit of the store."

13. Who will handle the advertising, lessee or lessor? Returns and allowances policy.

14. Subordination: Will the lease be subordinate to other underlying leases and mortgages?

15. Automatic cancellation of lease should the lessee become bankrupt.

16. Penalties for lessee default in payment of rent or lessor default in giving the lessee his share of sales receipts. This clause might stipulate that, in the event the lessor witholds lessee sales, the lessee can immediately install his own departmental cash register.

17. State and municipal laws applicable to the agreement.

18. Lessee adherence to lessor labor policies and union agreements when applicable.

19. The extent of control of lessee personnel by lessor store management.

20. Ownership and responsibility for department fixtures and signs.

21. Procedures for the receipt of shipments to lessee – lessee access to the store.

488

22. Lessee agreement not to operate a competitive store within an agreed-upon radius.

23. The lessor to be saved harmless from misfeasance (doing a lawful act in an illegal manner) or nonfaisance (not doing what should be done) of the lessee.

24. Stipulations as to the kinds of merchandise to be sold by the lessee.

25. A mutual cancellation clause should serious management disagreements arise.

26. Definitions of terms such as "lessee" and "lessor."

27. Minimum guaranteed sales by the lessee.

28. Non-liability of the lessor for the safeguarding of lessee's fixtures, merchandise or other property on the store premises.

29. Lessee responsibility and agreement to carry products liability and public liability insurance with stated dollar minimums.

According to Dr. Ivan Gilbert, "A lease is like a marriage license; it gives two individuals the right to live together. If they can live together the lease will have very little meaning. If they cannot live together the lease still has very little meaning."

Essentially only competence, mutual trust and respect, fair dealings and the willingness to work together will make the arrangement work. There are many clauses in leases which are there only on the insistence of financial lending institutions. Such clauses may result in a complicated and impossible pair of legal handcuffs binding both lessee and lessor.

Bibliography

BOOKS AND PERIODICALS

Alexander, Ralph S. and Richard M. Hill, "What to do about the discount house?" *Harvard Business Review*, Jan., 1955, 53.

"Arlan's Success Story," *Financial World* (New York), CXXI (Feb. 5, 1964), 16.

Astor, Saul D., "The inventory shortage; enigma of the discount industry," *Journal of Retailing*, New York University, XL, summer, 1964, 31–42.

Barnet, Edward M. "Consumer's Cocktail; the exploding discount house – with bitters," *Business Topics* (Michigan State University), X (summer, 1962), 7–21.

Brand, Edward A., "Modern Supermarket Operation," Fairchild Publications, Inc., 1965.

Cummings, James C., "Afraid to sell to discounters? Despite warnings from 'traditional' retailers, marketers are cutting their own throats if they refuse to take advantage of the growing discount trade," *Sales Management*, LXXXVIII, March 16, 1962, 49.

Dakins, J. Gordon, "Discount retailing: showdown or revolution?" *Stores*, July-August, 1961, 5.

Davidson, W. R. and Alton F. Doody, "The future of discounting," *Journal of Marketing*, Chicago, XXVII, Jan., 1963, 36–39.

Dineen, R. N. and C. J. Gardner, "The discount house story," *Indiana Business Review*, Sept., 1958, vol. 33, no. 9.

Discount Merchandiser, "The true look of the discount industry," June, 1966.

Discount Merchandiser, Discount retailing in the U.S.: a detailed marketing study of a dynamic new force – the discount store. 1963. XIV, 242 p.

"Discounters' sales continue to rise," *The Discounters Digest*, Dun & Bradstreet, April 28, 1967.

"Discounting looms large in retailing future," *Retail Clerks Advocate*, Lafayette, Indiana, XVIII, Jan., 1965, 40–41.

"Discounting: Mexico's newest revolution; retailers adopt U.S. merchandising techniques," *Business Week*, July 6, 1963, 52–54.

Downs, Anthony, "Are discounters a retail revolution?" *Journal of Property Management*, vol. 27, no. 3, Spring, 1962, 134.

"The Filene Story," *The Christian Science Monitor*, September 21, 1956.

"Food retailing by discount houses," Marketing Research Report No. 785, Economic Research Service, U.S. Department of Agriculture, Feb., 1967, 1–27.

Gold, Edward B., "Dynamics of Retailing," Fairchild Publications, Inc., 1963.

Gross, W., "Strategies used by major department stores to compete with low-margin retailers," *Journal of Retailing* (New York University), XL, summer, 1964, 11–18.

Hollander, Stanley C., "Discount retailing – an examination into some divergences in the price system of American retailing," PH.D. thesis, 1954, Univ. of Pennsylvania.

"Is success spoiling the discount stores?" *Business Week*, June 26, 1965, 97.

"Kresge Restructured," *Chain Store Age*, Executives Edition, Dec., 1965, 48–243.

"Leased departments pave way for $7 million discount business," *Progressive Grocer*, XLIII, Sept., 1964, 84.

Lee, Stewart Munro, "Discount stores," PH.D. Thesis, Univ. of Pittsburg, 1956.

Leighton, David S. R., "Merchandising and promotional policies of discount houses," PH.D. Thesis, Harvard University, May, 1956.

Loehwing, D. A., "Better things in store; the discounters are cashing in on new facilities, upgraded wares," *Barron's*, XLIV, Sept. 14, 1964, 3.

Loehwing, D. A., "Discounters discounted; nobody likes them any more but the customers," *Barron's*, XLIII, April 22, 1963, 3.

Marks, Abe L., "Fundamental differences in accounting – department vs. mass-merchandising stores," *Retail Control*, XXXI, summer, 1964, 31–42.

Mayer, Lawrence A., "How confusion caught up with Korvette," *Fortune*, Feb., 1960, 152.

"Mix discounts and art makes sales jump; Honest Ed's in Toronto," *Business Week*, Feb. 20, 1965, 50–52.

Oxenfeldt, Alfred R., "The retailing revolution: why and whither?" *Journal of Retailing*, New York University, fall, 1960, 1.

Pareti, John Jr., "How to Sell Footwear Profitably," Fairchild Publications, Inc., 1967.

Reilly, Phillip J., "Old Masters of Retailing," Fairchild Publications, Inc., 1966.

"The Retail Revolution," lecture series before New York Security Analysts, Fairchild Publications, Inc., 1963.

Rich, Stuart U., and Bernard Partis, "Clues for action from shopper preferences," *Harvard Business Review*, XLI, March, 1963, 132–149.

Rosenthal, Richard, "Ferkauf, the man and the myth," *Women's Wear Daily*, Dec. 23, 1965..

Silberman, C. E, "Discounters choose their weapons," *Fortune*, LXV, April, 1962, 142–147.

Silberman, C. E., "Distribution Upheaval," *Fortune*, LXVI, May, 1962, 142–147.

Silberman, C. E., "Revolutionists of retailing," *Fortune*, LXV, April, 1962, 98–102.

Silberman, Charles E., "The department stores are waking up," *Fortune*, July, 1962, 143.

Slom, Stanley, "Profitable Furniture Retailing," Fairchild Publications, Inc., 1967.

492

Bibliography

Tallman, Gerald B. and Bruce Blomstrom, "Soft goods join the retail revolution," *Harvard Business Review*, Sept.–Oct., 1960, 133–143.

Weiss, E. B., "Management and the Marketing Revolution," McGraw-Hill, 1964

Weiss, E. B., "Don't write off the discount chains," *Advertising Age*, XXXV, Jan. 20, 1964, 94.

Weiss, E. B., "Will Woolworth build our largest discount chain?" *Advertising Age*, XXXIII, March 5, 1962, 105–106.

Westervelt, Richard E., "The discount house problem," *Journal of Retailing*, XXX, summer, 1954, 69.

Wingate, John W. and Joseph S. Friedlander, "The discount revolution," *New York Retailer*, October, 1961, 2.

"The worldwide PX: $2 billion in bargains," *Newsweek*, Jan. 17, 1966, 72.

Zimmerman, Max M., "The Supermarket: A Revolution in Distribution," McGraw-Hill, 1955.

AUDIO-VISUAL MATERIALS

"The Retail Revolution," slide series with sound, includes four programs ("Suburbia and Downtown," "Successful Selling Ideas," "Competing for the Modern Shopper," and "The Distribution Dilemma"), Fairchild Visuals, 1965.

Index

A & AFES, 350
A & P, 26, 336, 394
ABC stores, 483
Abraham & Straus, 33, 127, 154, 411
Abrams, Bernard, 296, 297
Abrams, Bernard, Associates, 189, 296-98
Abrams, Bernhard, 296
Abilene, Tex., 345
Acoustical ceilings, 99. *See also* specific stores
Admiral, 193
Advertising, 401, 469-71. *See also* Bernstein, Bo, Agency; specific stores and closed-door discount stores, 251
Advertising Age, 493
AFL-CIO, 423ff.
Ainbinder, Seymour, 201
Akron, Ohio, 275, 284
Alabama. *See* specific towns
Alaska, 229
Albany, N.Y., 29, 265, 266, 343
Albert, Philip, 150
Albuquerque, N.M., 271
Alden Paper, 343
Alden's, 90
Alden's Shoppers World, 90-94
Alec stores, 298
Alexander, Ralph S., 491
Alexander's Department Stores, 58, 108, 138, 141, 144, 155, 158-64, 277
1966 sales statistics, 482
Alexander's Rent-A-Car, 160
Alexander's Travel Service, 160
Alexandria, 157
Allan Cut-Rate Drug Company, 27

Allentown, Penna., 35
Allied Stores, 15, 154, 170, 201, 477
Allied Towers Merchants, Ltd., 354-55, 356
Alling, T. S., 29
Allways Store Company, 362
Almacs, 394, 396
Almart stores, 15, 170, 201
Alton, A. J., 364n
Amalgamated Clothing Workers of America, 424ff.
AMCA, 424
American Dixie Shops, 17
American Fair Trade Council, 19
American House Grocers Company, 25
American Language and Education Center, 369
American Legion Highway, 175
American Motors Company, 125
American Stock Exchange, 115, 381, 385
American Wholesale Toy Company, 189, 298-302
Ameron, 202
Ames, Ethan. *See* Ethan Ames Factory
Anaheim, Calif., 190, 260, 262
Anderlecht, Belgium, 359
Anderson, Ind., 199
Anderson-Little Company, 28, 470
Andrew Lewis label, 211
Andy Lewis label, 211
Ann and Hope Factory Outlet, 38, 44, 45, 74-81, 91, 299, 308, 392ff., 470, 476
Annis, Milton, 45, 46
Antifreeze, 98. *See also* Prestone

494

Anita Lewis label, 211
Antwerp, Belgium, 243
Applebaum, Ralph, 149
Appliance stores. *See also* specific stores
  1966 sales statistics, 485
Arizona. *See* specific towns
Arkansas. *See* specific towns
Arlan's Department Stores, 38, 39, 58, 62-73ff., 108, 308-9, 470, 471, 476
  1966 sales statistics, 482
Arlens Properties, 125
Army and Air Force Exchange Service, 350-51
Army surplus, 86, 94-95
Arrango, Geronimo, 357
Arrango Brothers, 357
Arrow Shirts, 109, 282
Art, 124, 134, 159
Asheville, N.C., 209
Astor, Saul D., 491
Atlanta, Ga., 78, 204-5, 265, 266, 271, 337, 343
Atlantic City, N.J., 298
Atlantic Mills, 38, 145, 149, 170, 299, 424, 470
Atlantic and Pacific Stores. *See* A & P
Atlantic Thrift Centers (formerly Atlantic Mills), 139, 140, 149-53, 170, 303, 326, 447, 449, 452
  1966 sales statistics, 482
Atlantic Superama, 277
Atlas Buying Service, 97, 99
Au Bon Marche, 360
Auburn, Me., 303
Audeghem, Belgium, 359
Audio-visual materials, 493
Aurrera chain, 357
Austin, Tex., 139
Auto supply stores, 485. *See also* specific stores
Automation. *See also* Electronic data processing; specific stores
  and unions, 438-39
Ayr-Way stores, 170, 198-200, 471, 483
Ayres, L. S., Co., 170, 198-200, 471, 477, 483

Baby Lewis label, 211
Bache and Company, 115
Baker Shoe, 455

Baltimore, Md., 116, 119, 121, 130, 143, 144
Baltinger Electric Company, 29
BAMA stores, 253
Bamberger's, 58, 277, 448
Bangor, Me., 88, 89
Bankers Trust Company, 277, 378
Bankruptcy, 373-91. *See also* specific companies
Banner Discount Department Stores, 353
Barad, Frank, 471
Barcelona, Spain, 369
Bargain Barns, 96-102, 478
Bargain basements, 19-20, 35-37, 223. *See also* specific stores
Bargain Buy Stores, 220
Bargain City, 149
Bargain Town, 483
Barker's, 483
Barmash, Isadore, 163n, 196, 197
Barnard, Kurt, 481
Barnet, Edward M., 491
Barrington, Ill., 246, 248
Barron's, 492
Basel, Switzerland, 369
Bassine, Charles C., 135, 136, 139, 140, 145, 146, 443, 467
Bath, Me., 35
Batten, William M., 202
Batterham, W. F., Company, 29, 32
Bay Shore, L.I., 203
Bazar, 483
Becker, William, 263
Beckerman, Frank, 45, 84
Beckerman family, 44
Bedford, N.Y., 111
Beilenson, Murray, 117-18, 121-27
Belgium, 243, 313, 359-60, 464
Bell Hosiery Shops, 171
Bell Shops, 169, 171-76ff.
Bellas Hess Company, 263
Bellas Hess Superstores, 252, 253, 262, 266-67, 270, 271, 482
Bellow's Falls, Vt., 43
Benco Sales Company, 29
Benedict, Nicholas, 105
Benjamin, Herman, 263
Bennett, Carl, 104ff.
Bennett, Dorothy, 104
Bennett Brothers, Inc., 29, 31
Berland Shoes, 267

Berlin Turnpike, 297
Bermont brand, 142
Bern, 368
Bernstein, Bo, 76, 470, 471
Bernstein, Bo, Advertising Agency, 28, 62, 470-71
Berry, Carl, 263
Berson, Isadore, 240
Bertels, W. B., Sons and Company, 215
Bertrand, E. L., 256
Bethlehem, Penna., 35
Bethpage, L.I., 275, 288-90
Better Business Bureau, 33-34
Bibliography, 491-93
Bicycle stores, 485
Bicycles, 300
Biddle (buying office), 80
Bierman, Max, 150
Big Bear Stores, 24, 25-26, 357
Big C Stores, 483
Big G, 394, 395, 396
Big N stores, 206, 210-14
Big Star Discount Food, 394, 396
Birmingham, Ala., 343
Bizmatic Data Control Centers, Inc., 294, 295, 454-59
Black & Decker, 61
Blackie, Bill, 310
Blank, Raymond, 145
Blomstrom, Bruce, 11
Blue Chip Stamp Company, 364
Blue Cross bedding, 110
Blumenberg, Joseph, 122, 124
Blyth and Company, 312
Bohack, H. C., 151
Bond Clothes Shops, 355
Bond suits, 28
Bonwit Teller, 310
Book, Myrtle W., 354-55
Books, 491-93
Borman Food Stores, Inc., 96
Boston, Mass., 444, 471. See also specific companies
Boston Store, 205
Bowling, 266
Bradlee's Stores, 236, 240-42, 299, 424
and Lee Venture Corp., 287, 288, 290, 292ff.
1966 sales statistics, 482
Braintree, Mass., 241
Brand, Edward A., 491

Brazil, 135
Brean, Herbert, 167
Brenninkmeyer, Anthony, 167
Brenninkmeyer, Derick, 167
Brenninkmeyer, Elmar, 167
Brenninkmeyer, John, 167
Brenninkmeyer family, 155, 167-68
Brenton, Frank, 480
Brentwood, N.Y., 144
Brigham's Snack Shops, 243, 250
Brockton, Mass., 38, 45, 47, 51, 57, 90, 241
Brookfield, Conn., 111
Brooklyn, N.Y., 277, 283, 414
Brown, Dr. Earl, 12
Brownsville, Tex., 260
Broyhill furniture, 110
Bruce Kenny Label, 108
Bruges, Belgium, 359
Brussels, Belgium, 243, 359, 360
Buchs, Switzerland, 369
Buckeye stores, 482
Bud Berman brand, 142
Buena Park, Calif., 190
Buffalo, N.Y., 29, 54, 172, 214, 265, 266, 269, 318, 343
Building materials, 1966 sales of, 485
Bullock's, 154, 189
Bumble Bee Chunk Tuna, 42
Business Topics, 491
Business Week, 356-57, 491, 492
Butler, Thomas C., 237, 238
Butler Shoe Company, 78
Buttrey Foods, 243
Buyers; buying, 463-68. See also specific companies
B.V.D. brand, 142

Cabin Craft floor covering, 110
Caldor Inc., 104-11, 155, 424, 483
Calexico, Calif., 260
California, 251, 483. See also specific places
beginning of low-margin retailing in food markets, 23
and unions, 428
Cambridge, Mass., 103, 240
Camden, N.J., 265, 343
Camden County Plaza Shopping Center, 116

496

Cameras, 221. *See also* specific stores
Campbell's soup, 26
Canada, 243, 310, 311, 352-57, 375, 376
  and Kresge, 217, 219, 224
  and Woolworth (Woolco), 229, 230, 353, 356
Candib, Murray, 38, 45, 48ff., 84, 476
Cannon brand, 94-95
Canton, Mass., 445, 456
Canton, Ohio, 284, 310-11, 343
Cantor, Sol W., 17, 84, 190-98, 467
Capitol records, 349
Car rental, 160
Cardin designs, 168
Carousel, The (Canton-Akron), 284
Carousel, The (Norfolk), 339
Carousal brand shoes, 310
Carroll Cut-Rate Drug Company, 27
Carter Overton, 40, 275, 303-7
Cash-and-carry stores, 27
Cash registers. *See* Checkout; Electronic data processing; specific stores
Catalina, 287
Census Bureau, 14, 16
Census of Business, 129
Center Stores, 207-9
Centerville, Ohio, 96, 99
Central checkout, 320-21. *See also* Checkout; specific stores
Central warehousing vs. drop-shipping, 403-10. *See also* specific stores
Centre Commercial Lomas store, 357
Chain Store Age, 217n. 492
Chain stores, 14. *See also* specific stores, types of stores
Chambers of Commerce, 132
Champaign, Ill., 246
Chanel designs, 168
Charge accounts, 447. *See also* specific stores
Charleston, S.C., 343, 365
Chase, Martin (Marty), 66, 74-81, 82, 328, 392-96, 470, 476
Chase Manhattan Bank, 385
Cheap John's, 380
Checkout, 73-74, 320-21, 393-94. *See also* specific stores
Cheektowaga, N.Y., 116
Cheltenham, Penna., 144
Cherry Hill, N. J., 116, 298
Chester, Penna., 83

Chicago. *See also* specific companies and unions, 424, 428
Children's Supermarket, Inc., 196, 197
China, 26, 383
Christian Science Monitor, 492
Chula Vista, Calif., 259
Cincinnati, Ohio, 24, 64, 170
Clarkins Division, 275, 286n
Clark's (Gamble-Skogmo), 482
  Clark's-Gamble of Canada, Ltd., 353
Clark's (M. N. Landan), 483
Clements, George L., 243-44
Cleveland, Ohio, 150, 180, 215
  and unions, 246, 428
Clifton Private Brands, Inc., 379
Clinton, Iowa, 64
Closed-door discount stores, 251-71. *See also* specific stores
Clothing and clothing stores (fashion, style), 17. *See also* specific stores
  1966 sales, 485
  promotional department stores, 154-68
CMA (Consumers' Mart of America), 259, 427
CMC stores, 260
Coan, Hilliard J., 120
Coast Guard, U. S., 350
Coatsfield Shoppers' World, 38, 73-74, 299, 308, 328, 329
Coburg, Ont., 353
Coffman, Max, 45, 86-90, 476
Cohan, Abner, 326
Cohen, Aaron (Ollie), 38, 45, 48ff., 52, 84, 102-3, 104, 477
Cohen, Ben, 380, 381
Cohen, David, 380, 382ff.
Cohen, Harry, 380
Cohen, Harry Merchandising Corporation, 380
Cohen, James, 380, 381-82
Cohen, Leonard, 60
Cohen, Maurice M., 102, 103, 104
Cohen, Norman D., 102, 103
Cohen, Philip W., 102, 103
Cohen, Seymour, 463, 465ff.
Cohen family, 380
Cohn, J. W., 141, 146
Colby label, 467
Cole, Henry, 26
College graduates, 69, 81, 85, 316

Colleges. *See* College graduates; Education; Scholarships; Universities
Cologne, Germany, 358
Colorado. *See* specific towns
Colorado Springs, Colo., 67
Colors, 58
Columbia University, 135
Columbia records, 349
Columbus, Ohio, 170, 215, 229
Commerce, U.S. Department of, 18
Community Home Furnishings, Inc., 29
Computers. *See* Electronic data processing; specific stores
Concord shopping mall, 201
Connecticut. *See* specific places
Consumers' Mart of America (CMA), 259, 427
Cook Coffee, 483
Corfam, 323
Cornell University, 11-12, 480, 481
Corningware, 330
Cornwall, Ont., 354
Corondolet, 253
Country Club Plaza, 224
Courtesy cards, 32
Covina, Calif., 191
Craft King brand, 125
Crank Drug Stores, 140, 145, 151
Credit, 385-88. *See also* specific stores
start of credit clothing, 74
Crystal Palace, 23
Cullen, Michael, 24-25
Cumberland, R. I., 38, 44, 45, 75, 78, 91, 299, 392, 393-94, 476
Cummings, James C., 491
Cunningham, Harry B., 206, 216ff., 222, 224, 477
Cutler, Samuel, 263
Cut-rate drug stores, 27. *See also* Drug stores

Dakins, J. Gordon, 491
Dallas, Tex., 139, 260, 298, 346, 348
Danbury, Conn., 111
Darby, George W., 238
Darling Stores Corporation, 375, 377
Davega-City Radio, Inc., 29, 32-33
Davidson, W. R., 491
Davis, L. F., 207, 229, 231
Davis, Sidney, 344-45
Dawson, A. E., 263

Dawson, Roy O., 25
Daylin, Inc., 275
Dayton, Ohio, 96-102, 478
Dayton Company, 483
Death payments, 383
Deblinger, Joseph N., 396-400
Deblinger Market Research Report, 397
Deblinger Sales & Marketing Corporation, 399
Decca records, 349
Dedham, Mass., 103, 343
Delaware. *See* specific towns
Del Monte Alaskan King Crab, 42
Dennison tickets, 454
Dennisport, Mass., 241
Denton, Tex., 260
Denver, Colo., 56, 64, 252, 423
Department stores, 13-14ff., 169, 224-25, 447, 448. *See also* specific stores
promotional, 19, 154-68. *See also* specific stores
1966 sales, 485
De Rowe, Marcus, 448-54
Detroit. *See also* specific stores
and union, 424
Dex Personnel, 411-14
Diana Stores, 169-70, 171, 482
Dickson, I. R., 263
Dineen, R. N., 491
Di Pietro, Carmen, 454-59
Disco chain (West Coast), 275
Disco, N.Y., Inc., 29
Discount Digest, 386
Discount Merchandiser, 15ff., 259, 350n, 357, 378, 483, 487n, 491
Discount stores, *passim. See also* specific companies, stores, etc.
1966 sales, 485
Discounter's Digest, 16, 491
Diskay stores, 220
Dixie Enterprises, 100
Dixiemart, 253
Doctors, 447
Dollard, James J., 480
Dominion (appliance company), 126
Dominion Stores, 356
Doody, Alton F., 491
Dorchester, Mass., 241
Dot records, 349
Douglaston, L.I., 124, 134
Downey, Calif., 191, 195

498

Downs, Anthony, 374, 491
Drake Distributing Company, 29
Drug stores, 14, 27, 447. *See also* specific stores
1966 sales, 485
Drop-shipping vs. central warehousing, 403-10. *See also* specific companies
Dublin, Ireland, 369
Dun and Bradstreet, 16, 83, 97, 110, 301, 385-88
DuPont, 60, **61**
Durham, N.C., 71
Dushman, Henry, 480
Duttweiler, Gottlieb, 365
Duttweiler, Gottlieb, Institute for Economic and Social Studies, 369
Duvel, William A., 385-88
DW Jewelry Company, Inc., 378-79
Dynamics of Retailing, 492

East Paterson, N.J., 238
Eastern Massachusetts Railway, 51
Eastman Kodak, 406
Eatontown, N. J., 241
Eckhouse, Joseph L., 237-38, 239
Ecko kitchenware, 61
Economy, contribution of mass-merchandising to, 478-80
Economy Grocery Stores, 240
Economy Stores, 26
Edison Brothers, 317
Edison Electrical Supply Company, 328
EDP. *See* Electronic data processing
Education, 369. *See also* College graduates; Scholarships
Effren, Herman, 105
Eisenberg, Warren, 64-73
Eisner family, 245
Eisen Food Stores, 243, 244, 245-46
El Paso, Tex., 260
Electrical appliances, 32. *See also* specific brands, stores
Electrical stores, 485. *See also* specific stores
Electronic data processing (EDP), 442-62, 476, 478. *See also* specific companies
unions and, 438-39
Elgin, Ill., 245
Elizabeth, N. J., 25

Elkins and Perlman Shoe Company, 62
Employees Association, 29, 30-31
Employees Trading Company, 29
Emporium, The, 23
England, 229, 313, 360-62, 369, 464
Englander bedding, 110
Enterprise Company, 44-47, 49, 82, 83, 86, 169
Erb Electric, 29
Erie, Penna., 172
Escondido, Calif., 260
Ethan Ames Factory, 38, 39, 41, 62, 470, 476
Evanston, Ill., 389
Evansville, Ind., 198, 199
Ex Libris club, 369
Excello shirts, 42
Executives, 61. *See also* Managers and management, specific stores
Expansion, too-rapid, 373. *See also* specific companies.

"Factory Outlet" store, 27
Factory outlets. *See* Mill outlets
Fair trade, 19. *See also* specific products, stores
Fairfield, Conn., 191
Fairhaven Mills Bargain Center, 49, 150, 170, 299
Fall River, Mass., 28, 38, 62, 68, 82ff., 241, 308, 470, 477
Fame Stores, 362
Family Circle Stores, 241
Fantastic Fair, 303
Farkas, Alexander, 160
Farkas, Bruce, 160
Farkas, George, 134, 155, 158ff.
Farkas, Jonathan, 160
Farkas, Robin, 160
Farkas, Ruth Lewis, 158
Farmer's Market (Brooklyn), 283
Farmer's Markets, 34-35
Fashion. *See* Clothing and colthing stores
FEDCO, 251, 256ff., 483
Federal employees, 251ff.
Federal Trade Commission (FTC), 53, 60, 144, 164, 201, 258
Federated Department Stores, Inc., 15, 154, 170, 477
Federation of Migros Cooperatives, 364-69

Fed-Mart, 252, 256-62, 482
Fed-Mart Franchise, 252, 259-60
Fed-Mart Life Insurance Company, 262
Fedorenko, Mrs. Nikolai, 168
Fein, Harold, 150
Feinstein, Hyman, 63
Feld-Crawford Resale Price Maintenance Law, 33
Feldberg, Max (father), 170-71, 177, 467
Feldberg, Morris (uncle), 170-71, 177
Feldberg, Stanley H., 84, 169, 170-81ff., 280, 414, 471
Feldberg, Sumner, 84, 181-86, 403-7, 414
Feldberg family, 169, 471. *See also* specific members
Feldman, Ted, 46
Feldman family, 44
Ferkauf, Estelle, 133, 134-35, 136
Ferkauf, Eugene, 117-18, 120ff., 132-36, 145
Fernandes, Joseph E., 395
Fernandes Supermarkets, 395, 396
Field's, J. M., 44-47, 50, 169, 240, 459
  1966 sales statistics, 482
Figer, Benjamin, 480
Filene, Edward, 36
Filene, Lincoln, 36
Filene, William, 35-36
Filene's, 28, 35-37, 90, 107, 109, 154, 204, 318, 471
Financial Post, 353
Financial World, 491
Fintex Stores, 28, 74
First Choice label, 379
First Financial Life Insurance Company, 262
First National, 336, 394, 396
Fishman, M. H., 207, 208
Fishman, M. H., Company, Inc., 206, 207-9, 477
Fishman Stores, 207-9
Fiske, Clint, 327
Fitchburg, Mass., 287
Flanel, Samuel, 16
Flanzbaum, Sidney, 78
Flint, Mich., 94-96
Florence, 464
Florida, 99, 228, 424. *see also* specific places
Florists, 447
Floyd Bennett Stores, 275, 277, 281ff.

Flushing, L. I., 157
Flushing, L. I., *Journal,* 25
FM brand, 261
Food and food stores, 14, 77-78, 235-50, 266, 392-402, 438. *See also* Supermarkets; specific stores
  1966 grocery-store sales, 485
Food Fair, 46-47, 86, 394
  1966 sales statistics, 482
Food Giant Markets, 116, 482
Foodmart, 23-25, 240
Forbes and Wallace, 287
Foreign companies, 352-69. *See also* specific companies, countries
Foremost brand, 203
Forest City Distributors, Inc., 343
Forsyth Dental Hospital, 455
Fort Wayne, Ind., 198, 219
Fort Worth, Tex., 139
Fortune, 119-20, 136, 226, 236, 357, 492
Framingham, Mass., 38, 45, 86ff., 107, 109, 111, 417, 476
France, 313, 464, 466
Frankfurt, Germany, 464
Franklin, F. V., 29
Franklin Simon, 168
Franklin Stores, 483
Frederick's Department Stores, 353
Freedman, Herbert J., 343
Freedman, Leo, 256
Freimart Stores, Ltd., 353, 354
Friedman, Melvin, 145
Friedman, Oscar F., 29
Frigidaire, 354
Fringe benefits. *See* Unions; specific stores, etc.
FTC. *See* Federal Trade Commission
Fur-labelling, 60
Furniture; furniture stores, 109-10. *See also* specific companies, stores
  1966 sales statistics, 485
Furniture Industries of America, 29
Furniture Shoppers Bureau, 29

Gabrini, Lawrence H., 263
Gamble, Jerry, 135
Gamble-Skogmo, Inc., 90, 135, 482
Gamble's 482
    Clark's Gamble of Canada, Ltd., 353
Garden City, L. I., 343

Garden Grove, Calif., 189
Gardner, C. J., 491
Garf, Harry, 85
Garfield, N.J., 113, 285
Gartner, Henry, 298
Garwood, N.J., 298
Gasoline stations, 439. *See also* specific places
Gateway Corporation, 93
Gateway Sporting Goods Company, 202, 264, 267
GEM, 252-56, 307, 337, 353, 360-61, 401
Gemco, 298, 483
General Electric, 61, 110, 125, 126, 193, 455, 478
General Electric Credit Corporation, 157
General Garment Company, 141
General Garment Manufactury, Ltd., 141
General Merchandise Company, 170, 202
General merchandise stores. *See also* specific stores
1966 sales, 485
General Motors, 97
General Shoe, 310
Genesco, 267, 310
Georgia. *See* specific places
Germany, West, 229, 351, 358-59, 464, 466
Gertz, 201
GES, 483
GEX stores, 252ff., 262, 264-71, 337, 482
Giant Value Distributing Company, 98
Gibson, Belva, 344
Gibson, Herbert R., Sr., 344-45ff.
Gibson Discount Centers. *See* Gibson Products Company
Gibson Products Company, 344-50, 482
Gilbert, Dr. Ivan, 317-26
Gilbert Company, 68
Gilbert Shoe Company, 317-26
Gillette, 83, 224-25
Gilman, George F., 26
Gimbels, 33, 154, 277
   and automation, 448
   Korvette and, 125, 126, 128
   and Ohrbach's, 168
Gish, George W., Jr., 204

Gittler, Sydney, 168
Givenchy designs, 168
Glass, Henry, 46
Glass family, 44
Glassman, Al, Floor Covering Company, 62
Glen Cove, L. I., 331
Glidden paint, 61, 202
Globe stores, 483
Go-go boots, 323
Gold, Edward B., 492
Goldberg, Aaron, 47-62, 408-10
Goldberg, Lawrence Y., 298-302
Golden, Arthur, 380
Goldsboro, N.C., 209
Gomes, Don, 114, 115, 116
Goodman, Bernard, 96-98
Goodman, Lewis, 96, 100-2
Goodman, Mark, 96, 98-99
Goodman, Robert (Bob), 96, 98, 99
Gossau, Switzerland, 369
Gottfried, Harold, 150
Govco, 483
Government employees, 251ff.
Government Mutual Employees. *See* GEM
Gov-Mart, 258
Grade labelling, 18
Grand Bazar D'Anvers, 359
Grand Bazar De Liege, 359-60
Grand brand, 239
Grand Rapids, Mich., 64, 149
Grand Super Centers, 416
Grand Union, 235-39, 394, 482
Grand Way, 47n, 236-39, 357, 432
   1966 sales statistics, 482
Grand Way Savings Centers, 237
Grant, W. T., 44, 220
Grayson-Robinson Stores, Inc., 375, 376, 377-78
Great Atlantic and Pacific Stores, 26. *See also* A & P
Great Britain. *See* England
Great Eastern Mills, 169, 357, 482
Great Scot, 394
Green, H. L., 419
Greenberg, Max, 424, 426, 438
Greenbelt, Md., 157, 443
Greenfield, Mass., 39, 43, 44
Greenwich, Conn., 104, 111
Grill, Robert A., 443-48

501

Grocery stores. *See* Food and food stores; Supermarkets
Gross, W., 492
Groton, Conn., 241
Gulf Mart, 169, 482
Gutterman, Milton, 189
Guzy Brothers, 187

Hackensack, N.J., 276
Haimsohn, Herbert, 256
Halstead, P. K., Associates, 358
Halstead, Paul, 358
Hamden, Conn., 110
Hamilton, Ont., 353
Hampton, Va., 265, 266, 343
Hanover, N.J., 113
Hardlines Inc., 327-28
Hardware stores, 485. *See also* specific stores
Harrisburg, Penna., 143
Harrison, N. J., 111, 112
Hartblay, Jack, 52, 85
Hartfield, Leo, 189
Hartfield Stores Inc., 170, 189-90, 274
Hartford, John A., 26
Hartford, Conn., 29, 143, 240, 241, 296, 298, 309, 335, 343
Harvard Business Review, 11n, 491, 492, 493
Harvard School of Public Health, 455
Harvest House Restaurants, 229
Harvey, Hamilton, and Son, 353
Hatfield, Lawrence M., 268
Hato Rey, P. R., 263
Hawaii, 229, 345
Hayden and Stone, Inc., 381
Hearst, John, 218
Heart of America Life Insurance Company, 263
Hempstead, L. I., 156
Highland, Ind., 94
Hill, Richard M., 491
Hilliard-Cohn, 443
Hill's-Korvette, 120, 143, 151, 443
Hill's stores, 483
Hill's Supermarkets, Inc., 120
Hingham, Mass., 343
Hinky-Dinkey, 202
Hjort, Thorolf, 362
Holland, 313
Hollander, Stanley C., 492

Holmesdale, Penna., 83, 84
Home Furnishings Daily, 385
Home supply stores, 485. *See also* specific stores
Honest Ed's, Ltd., 354, 356-57
Honeywell, 116, 209, 445
Hong Kong, 140, 141
Honig, Donald P., 299
Hoover, 103
Horns', 448
Hours, store, 19, 61, 353
Housewares Corporation, 328-36
Housewright, James, 423, 438
Houston, Tex., 24, 260, 262
Hovey, C. F., Company, 47, 49
How to Sell Footwear Profitably, 492
Howard suits, 28
Hubschman, Herbert, 111, 112, 114, 115
Hubschman, Sidney, 111, 112, 114
Husco Factory Outlet, 83
Hunting, 324
Huntington Beach, Calif., 190
Huntsville, Ala., 271
Hyannis, Mass., 174-75, 309

IBM, 427, 445ff. *See also* specific stores, etc.
Ideal Shoe Company, 40
IGA, 356
Illinois, 424. *See also* specific places
Incentive plans, 325
Incomes, 17, 18. *See also* Wages and salaries
India, 313
Indian Motorcycle factory, 45, 51, 476
Indiana, 424. *See also* specific places
Indiana Business Review, 491
Indianapolis, Ind., 198, 199, 215, 343
Institute for Nutritional Research, 369
International Brotherhood of Teamsters, Chauffeurs, and Warehousemen, 424
International Tourist Organization, 369
Interstate Department Stores, 20, 47, 84, 170, 190-98, 309, 316, 424, 477
  1966 sales statistics, 482
Inventory. *See* specific companies, stores
Iowa. *See* specific places
Ireland, 360, 361-62, 369
Isaacs, T. H., 32

Isetan Stores, 364
Islip, L. I., 414
Israel, 467-68
Italy, 243, 313, 383, 464, 466

Jacksonville, Fla., 149
Jacobsen, Joel, 414
Jaffe and Martin Construction Company, 262
James Wells label, 204
Jantzen, 287, 293
Japan; Japanese products, 26, 141, 300, 313, 354, 363-64, 383
Japan Self-Service Store Association, 363
Jaunty Dress Shops, 115
Jewel Companies, 236, 242-50, 360
Jewel Tea Company, 236, 242-43, 394, 483
Jewel Tones brand, 310
Jewelry stores, 485. *See also* specific places
Jim Wells label, 204
Jimmy Wells label, 204
Job Corps, 413
"John the Shoeman," 78
John Wells label, 281, 282
John's Bargain Stores, 380-85
Joint Economic Committee, 479
Joliet, Ill., 245
Jones, J. P., Corporation, 385
Jordan Marsh, 28, 107, 109
Jordan's, 471
Journal of Marketing, 491
Journal of Property Mangement, 491
Journal of Retailing, 363n, 364n, 491ff.
Jumbo Stores, 303
Jumping Jacks brand, 310
Jungen, George H., 32
Junior department stores, 13, 14, 169.
    See also specific stores
    differences between buying for discount stores and for, 52-53
Jupiter Stores, 216ff., 482

K Marts (Kresge's), 15, 20, 56, 170, 206, 216, 217-22ff., 426, 427, 432, 437, 477
    1966 sales statistics, 482
    Unishops and, 278, 279
K 6 label, 220
Kalamazoo, Mich., 191

Kansas City, 151, 223, 224, 253, 263, 266, 270
Kaplan, Morris, 28, 470
Katz, Edward, 145
Katz Drug Company, 151
Katz and Wolchok, 423, 425
Keansburg, N.J., 235
"Keedozle," stores, 24
Kelly and Cohn, 318
Kelly Springfield Tire Company, 149
Kemmerer, Wyo., 202
Kenney, William F. (Bill), 45, 49, 54, 56
Kentucky. *See* specific places
Kenzar, Robert, 414-16
Kepner, John B., 33
Kermell Bargain Center, 38, 82-85, 477
Kessler, Bud, 276-86
Kessler, Dan, 276ff.
Kayport, N.J., 241
Keystone Organization, Inc., 29, 33
Killingworth, Charles, 96
Kimball tickets, 455
King Cullen, 24-25, 397
King of Prussia Shopping Center, The, 128
King's Department Stores, 20, 38, 44, 47-62, 85, 151, 309, 379, 476
    Goldberg on central warehousing, 408-10
    1966 sales statistics, 482
    Unishops and, 281, 283
Kingston, N.Y., 111
Kinney Shoe Stores, 229
Kirkwood, Robert C., 229, 230
Kirkwood Highway, 201
Klein, Arthur, 287-96
Klein, S., Department Stores, Inc., 155-58, 164-65
    1966 sales statistics, 482
Klein, Samuel, 155-56
Klion, H. L., Company, 120, 146, 275, 443
Knapp, Stefan, 159
Knoxville, Tenn., 149
Korvair brand, 125
Korvette, E. J., 58, 108, 117-48, 155, 275, 357, 374, 394, 424, 443, 446
    Kresge and, 217
    1966 sales statistics, 482
    Robert Kenzar with, 414
    Unishops and, 283

Korvette, E. J., Foundation, 135
Korvette Medical Foundation, 135
Kouzon, Edward, 240
Kouzon, Morris, 240
Kresge, S. S., Company, 15, 20, 206, 215-28, 477. *See also* K Marts
  1966 sales statistics, 482
Kresge, Sebastian and Catherine Kunkle, 215
Kresge, Sebastian Spering, 215-16, 222
Kresge Foundation, 216
Kresge & Wilson Company, 215
Kroehler furniture, 110
Kroger Grocery Company, 24-25

Labor. *See* Personnel
Lady Colby label, 467
Lady Manhattan shirts, 293
Lafayette, Ind., 198
La Habra, Calif., 260
Lancaster, Calif., 260
Lancaster, Penna., 66, 83, 84
Landau, M. N., 483
Lane furniture, 110
Lansing, Mich., 95, 191
Larchmont, N.Y., 358
Larkin, Harold S., 480, 481
La Salle Factories, Ltd., 355-56
La Salle Stores, 355-56
Las Cruces, N.M., 260
Latham, N.Y., 191
Laurelton, N.J., 241
Lawrence, Mass., 45, 62, 66, 73, 287, 327
Leased departments, 252, 272-343. *See also* specific stores
  key stipulations in typical lease, 488-89
  and unions, 439-46
Lebanon, N.H., 43
Lechmere Sales Company, 102-4, 338
Lechmere Tire and Sales Company, 102-3
LeCount and Company, Inc., 29
Lee, Stewart Munro, 492
Lee pants, 42
Lee Shops, 455, 456, 458, 459
Lee Venture Corporation, 275, 287-96
Lehman, 312
Leibow, Saul, 327-36
Leighton, David S. R., 492
Lempchen, Selwyn, 45, 82-85, 194, 477

Leominster, Mass., 43
Lerner department stores, 171, 189, 455
Levi Strauss Company, 100
Lewis, Duffy, 157
Lewis Family Brand, 211
Lewiston, Me., 88, 89
Life, 167
Life insurance companies, 33
Lifshey, Earl, 29ff.
Lincoln Center, 135
Little Rock, Ark., 345
Loblaw "Grocerterias," 242
Lodi, N.J., 276-77
Loehwing, D. A., 492
Long Beach, Calif., 260
Long Island, 120. *See also* specific towns
Lonsdale, 82, 395
Loop Junior College, 247
Lord and Taylor, 241
Los Angeles. *See also* specific stores and unions, 424
Louisiana. *See* specific places
Louisville, Ky., 64, 66, 343
Low Supply Company, 328, 335
Lowell, Mass., 47, 287, 309
Loweth, Clifford, 471
Lucky Giant, 394
Lucky Stores, 483
Lunding, Franklin J., 249
Lynch, James, 480
Lynn, Mass., 35, 241, 335

Mac Paters label, 281
McClellan stores, 419
McCrory, John G., 215
McCrory Corporation, 155, 157, 220, 418-22
McCrory, McClellan, and Green, 418
McDonnell and Company, 379
McGregor shirts, 42
McNair, Malcolm, 12, 136, 476
MacShore, 287
Macy, R. H., 28, 33, 58, 123, 126, 128, 154, 397
  and Alexander's Brooklyn Center, 161
  and automation, 448
  and Interstate, 191
  and Ohrbach's, 168
Madison Cooperative Association, Inc., 33

Madison Fund, 277
Maidenform, 93
Mail order, 485. *See also* specific companies
Maine. *See* specific places
Malden, Mass., 173
Malino, Sweden, 362
Malls, 131
Mammoth Mart, Inc., 38, 44, 45, 86-90, 303, 326, 417, 476
Mammoth Mills, 62, 476
Managers and management, 226, 412, 413, 459-62. *See also* specific companies, etc.
  unions and, 428-29ff.
Management and the Marketing Revolution, 493
Manchester, England, 362
Manchester, N.H., 46, 47, 111
Mangel, Sol, 187-88
Mangel Stores Corp., 170, 187-88, 482
Manitoba, 353
Maple Grove Bargain Center, 83
Marc Mitchell label, 108
Margolis, Jack E., 281, 331, 378-79
Marine Corps, 350
Marks, Abe L., 1, 189, 190, 274, 480-81, 492
Marks, George, 263
Maro Industries, 142
Marrud, Inc., 281, 290, 331, 376, 378-80
Maslan floor covering, 110
Mason City, Iowa, 64
Mason's stores, 207-9
Mass-Merchandising Foundation Conference, 189, 478, 480-81
Massachusetts, 104, 178. *See also* specific places
Massachusetts, University of, 11, 374, 385n, 389n, 402n, 408n, 422n, 480, 486
  and RCIA, 423
Massachusetts Insurance Company, 121
Massachusetts Whip and Saddlery Company, 102
Masters, Stephen, 17
Masters Store, 357
Matson, Ill., 443
Maxam's, 107
Maxwell House coffee, 26
Mayer, Lawrence A., 492

Mayers, L. and C., Company, Inc., 29, 31-32
Mayers, Lawrence, 31-32
Mays, J. W., 108, 166, 483
Maytag, 103
MBS (Merchants Buying Syndicate), 97, 463-67
Meats, 74
Medallion stores, 253, 298
Medco, 264, 267
Medford, Mass., 46, 169
Medical care, 428ff. *See also* Doctors; specific companies
Megdell, Joseph, 94-96
Meijer's Thrifty Acres, 483
Melrose Park, Ill., 94
Melt, E. A., and Company, 123
Melville Shoe, 68
Memphis, Tenn., 215
Merchants Buying Syndicate, 97, 463-67
Met Discount Store, 353
Metropolitan Life Insurance Company, 33
Mexico, 229, 313, 357-58
Mexico City, 357, 358
Meyer, Fred, 483
Miami, Fla., 384
Michaelson, Mr., 328
Michigan. *See also* specific places
  and unions, 424, 438
Michigan State University, 369
Midland, Tex., 260
"Migrol," 369
Milan, Italy, 243
Miles Shoes, 92
Milford, Conn., 159, 161
Mill outlets, 38ff., 182. *See also* specific places
Miller, Charles, 238-39
Miller, Jordan, 205
Miller, R. H., Company, 169
Miller, Rupert A., 198
Millers, 482
Milwaukee, Wis., 149, 150, 170, 202, 205, 265, 266, 343
  and unions, 428
Minerals Separation Company, 361
Minichiello, Robert J., 400-2
Minneapolis, Minn., 135, 149, 416
Minnesota, 438. *See also* specific places
Miracle Mart, 353, 356

505

Mirvish, Honest Ed, 356-57
Miss Grand label, 239
Mississippi. *See* specific places
Missouri. *See* specific places
Mittleman, Sidney, 149, 150, 151, 470
Mitzon of Madrid, 204
M-M Discount Centre, 353
Mobile, Ala., 267, 343
Modell, Bill, 276
Modern Retailer, 344-45
Modern Supermarket Operation, 491
Modern Supply Company, 29
Monarch Clothing Company, 64, 73
Monarch Mills. *See* Ethan Ames Factory
Mon-Mart Discount Department Stores, 353
Monroe-Sweda, Inc., 357, 443-48
Montana. *See* specific places
Montgomery, Ala., 267
Montgomery Ward, 412
Montreal, 311, 375
Morgan, Cecil, 150
Morgan and Dornich, 29
Morgan's, 326
Morrison, C. T., Co., 29
Morse, Alfred L., 307-17
Morse, Lester, 307, 309
Morse, William, 307-8, 315
Morse Shoe, Inc., 68, 92, 307-17, 325, 445, 456
Morse Shoe Company, 325
Morse Shoe Stores, 307ff.
Morse's, Inc., 307ff.
Morton, Mass., 395
Moscow, 360
Mount Kisco, N.Y., 111
Mr. Grand label, 239
Mugar, John, 244
Murata, Shoji, 363n
Murmic of Delaware, 341
Murray, J. G., 123
Murray's Distributors, 29
Myrtle Mills Factory Outlet, 206, 210, 287

NACO. *See* National Association of Consumer Organizations
Nashville, Tenn., 288
Nathan, William I., 149
Natick, Mass., 46, 107, 450

National Appliance Retail Dealers Association, 104
National Association of Consumer Organizations, 251, 255
National Bellas Hess, 252, 254, 262-71, 482
National Bellas Hess Life Insurance Company, 263
National Cash Register Company (NCR), 96, 97, 98, 200, 241, 285, 445
National Cloak and Suit Company, 263
National Labor Relations Act, 429
National Labor Relations Board (NLRB), 429ff.
National Printing Company, 76
National Secretaries Association, 108
Natural charm label, 379
Navy Ships Store Office, 350
Naylor (of Arlan's), 70
NCR. *See* National Cash Register Company
Neaman, Samuel, 157
Needham, Mass., 291
Neisner, Abraham H., 210
Neisner, Fred, 210, 211, 214
Neisner, Joseph M., 210
Neisner, Melvin B., 210, 212
Neisner Brothers, Inc., 206, 210-14, 477
Nelson brand, 125
Nelson furniture, 110
Nemy, Enid, 168
New Bedford, Mass., 28, 38ff., 62, 64, 75, 149, 170, 299, 470, 476
New England. *See also* specific places and unions, 424, 427
New England Medical Center, 455
New England Trading Company, 171, 177
New Era Discount Department Stores, 354
New Hampshire. *See* specific places
New Orleans, La., 265, 343
New Shrewsbury, N.J., 277
New-Way stores, 220
New York City, 154-68, 227-28, 369. *See also* specific companies, stores
 buying in. *See* specific stores
 NRMA Discount Seminar (1961), 17
 PXs, 351

2nd-floor catalog stores, 228-34
  and unions, 424, 428
New York *Daily News*, 382
New York Lace Store, 27-28, 329, 470
New York Retailer, 384n
New York Stock Exchange, 84, 115, 312
New York Times, 126, 150-51, 163, 164, 168, 196, 197, 375, 467
New York University, 161
New York Waist House, 170, 187
Newark, N.J., 116, 156, 157, 167
Newberry's, 220
Newsweek, 350
Newton, Mass., 57, 303
Newton Highlands, Mass., 326
Nichols, G. C., 224
Nichols Discount City, 483
Nieman-Marcus, 154
Nightingale, John, 110
NLRB, 429ff.
Norfolk, Va., 265, 339, 343
Norge, 110
North Kansas City, 252, 268
Northampton, Mass., 110, 111
Norwalk, Conn., 105, 108, 109, 111
Nottingham, England, 360-61
NRMA, 16, 17, 381-82, 446
NSSO, 350
Nugent stores, 169, 172-74ff.
Nuremberg, 358-59

Oaklawn, Ill., 259
Obratsov Puppets, 357
Ohio. *See also* specific places
  and unions, 424, 438
Ohrbach, Jerry, 167
Ohrbach, Nathan M., 134, 155, 164, 165, 167-68
Ohrbach's, 155, 164-68
Oklahoma City, 139, 252, 264, 265, 266, 270, 343
Oklahoma Tire and Supply, 422
Old Masters of Retailing, 492
Oleg Cassini brand, 142
Ontario, 353-54ff., 375, 376
Ontario stores, 483
Operating results, 486-87
"Optigal," 369
Orbit Stores, 241
Osco drug stores, 243, 244-45

Oshkosh work clothes, 93
Otis, Robert M., 25
Ottawa, 353, 354
Outlet, The, 27
Oxenfeldt, Alfred R., 492

Paint stores, 485. *See also* specific brands, stores
Palestine, Allen, 62
Palestine, Arlan, 62, 65
Palestine, Arthur, 62
Palestine, Herbert, 39, 62, 63, 64, 66, 70, 71
Palestine, Lester, 39, 62, 63, 64
Palestine, William, 39, 42ff., 62ff., 476-77
Palestine family, 62, 63, 65. *See also* specific members
Paramus, N.J., 158-59, 161, 288-90
Pareti, John, Jr., 492
Paris, 168, 464
Parker Pen Company, 119
Parkview Drugs, Inc., 252, 253, 264, 307
Parkview-GEM, 252-56, 326, 360
  1966 sales statistics, 482
Parkway label, 467
Partis, Bernard, 492
Part-time help, 462
Patterson, Chester W., 480, 481
Pavlov, D., 360
Pawtucket, R.I., 27-28, 38, 44, 63, 73, 299, 328, 396, 470
Pawtuxet Mills, 27
Payroll management. *See* Managers and management; specific stores
Pegboard cards, 305-6
Pelham, N.Y., 121, 130
Penncrest brand, 239
Penney, J. C., Company, 15, 20, 128, 170, 202-5, 239, 412, 459, 477
  1966 sales statistics, 483
  and Zody's, 189
Penney, James Cash, 202, 203
Pennsylvania, 424. *See also* specific places
Penrose Industries Corporation, 379
Pequot Mills, 45
Pergament Company, 275, 288-90
Periodicals, 491-93
Perkins, Donald S., 244, 246, 247
Personnel (labor), 61, 400, 401, 411-22. *See also* Managers and management; Unions; etc.; specific stores

Peter Kane label, 281
Pharmacies, 79. *See also* Drug stores; specific stores
Philadelphia, Penna., 27, 29, 119, 120, 132, 143, 155, 157, 382
Picketing, 440
Piggly Wiggly Stores, 24
Pilot research project, 480
Pima Arrow shirts, 98
Pins, 60
Pittsburgh, Penna., 180, 202, 215, 220, 318, 382, 448
Plainfield, N.J., 157
Playtex, 93
Plumbing stores, 485
Polaroid, 125
Polk, M. L., 207-9
Port Chester, N.Y., 104, 111
Port Newark, N.J., 113
Potofsky, Jacob, 424, 438
Presco Mills, 27
Prestone, 58, 79, 255, 330
Pretties brand, 310
Price, Sol, 256, 260, 261-62
Princess Anne label, 90
Problem areas, 371-471
Procter and Gamble, 306
Profitable Furniture Retailing, 492
Profit-sharing, 69, 80-81
Progressive Grocer, 492
Promotional department stores, 19, 154-68. *See also* specific stores
Promotions (of personnel), 413. *See also* specific stores
  unions and, 436
Promotions, sales, 58-59, 167, 283, 469-70. *See also* specific stores
Providence, R.I. *See* specific companies, stores
Providence *Journal*, 27
Proxmire, William, 478-80
Prudential Insurance Company, 33, 121, 138-39, 175, 278
Pueblo Eldorado Playa, 369
Puerto Rico, 219, 224, 229, 263, 384
Pure, Robert, 417-18
PX, 350-51

Quakertown, Penna., Farmer's Market, 34-35

Quakertown Sales Company, 35
Quant, Mary, 204
Quebec, 353ff.
Quelle Market, 358-59
Quincy, Mass., 86, 173

R & R Distributing Company, 100
Rabb, Irving W., 240
Rabb, Sidney A., 78, 240
Racine, Wis., 245
Radio, 471. *See also* specific companies
"Rain-check" policy, 110
Rau, Roscoe, 29
Raymond's department stores, 456
R.C.A., 103, 110, 111, 355, 445
RCA Victor, 349
RCIA. *See* Retail Clerks International Association
Real estate. *See* specific companies
Recco, 264
Red Grille Restaurant, 230
Rego Park (Queens), 158, 160, 161
Reilly, Phillip J., 492
Remillard, Arthur, 480
Research, 415, 480. *See also* specific companies
Research Institute of America, 284
Rest-room facilities, 89
Retail Centers of America, 483
Retail Clerks Advocate, 491
Retail Clerks International Association (RCIA), 105, 144, 423-24, 425-26
Retail Control, 492
Retail Realty, Inc., 138, 144
Retail-Wholesale and Department Store Union, 424ff.
Retailing, 29ff., 34
Rex Luggage, 122-23
Rhode Island, 79, 81, 169, 394. *See also* specific places
Rich, Stuart U., 492
Richmond, Ind., 198
Richmond, Va., 336, 337, 341, 343
Riklis, Meshulam, 157, 418-22, 467
Rite-Way Department Stores, Ltd., 354
Riverside, Conn., 104, 111
RIX stores, 275, 303, 307
Roanoke, Va., 64
Robert Hall's, 74
Roberts, Wilbert, 94
Robin Cheryl label, 108

Robinson-Patman Act, 100
Rochester, N. Y., 64, 116, 131, 214
Rockdale Stores, 38, 39-44, 303, 477
Rockower, 376
Rodman, Charles G., 238
Roosevelt Field, 123
Rose Distributors, 29
Rosenbaum, S. G., 262-63
Rosenberg, Louis, 480
Rosenstein, Samuel J., 56, 354, 374
Rosenthal, Ben, 411-14
Rosenthal, Richard, 132n, 492
Roslindale, Mass., 175-76, 299
Ross, Frank P., 243
Rotenberger, Stanley, 34
Rousseau and Rousseau, 23
Royal Alexandria Theater, 357
Rubin, Alexander N., Jr., 379
Rudnick, Harold, 378
Russia, 360
Rutland, Vt., 207, 209

Sabres, 303
Safeway, 360
Sage International, 483
Sage stores, 483
Saint Laurent designs, 168
St. Louis, Mo., 119, 131, 143
  and unions, 428
Saks Fifth Avenue, 154
Saks 34th Street, 125
Salaries. See Wages and salaries
Salem, Mass., 38, 45-46
Sales Management Magazine, 129, 491
Sales promotions, 58-59, 167, 283, 469-
  70. See also specific stores
Sales statistics, 482-87
Samuels brothers, 27
San Antonio, Tex., 139, 260
San Diego, Calif., 256, 258-59, 260
San Francisco, Calif., 84, 191, 196
  beginning of low-maring retailing, 23
  and unions, 424, 427
Sarnoff, Dorothy, 161
Satler's, 318
Saunders, Clarence, 24
Save-Co, 483
Savemart, Ltd., 353-54
Saylin, Inc., 361
Sayvette, 354
Schickedanz, Gustav, 358

Schiff, Milton M., 389
Schimmel Company, 68
Schlesinger, Frank, 384n
Schlesinger, Theodore, 201
Schneiderman, Ron, 201
Scholarships, 246-47, 252, 268
Schott, Richard, 463-64, 466, 467
Schwartz, Sidney, 16
Schwartz, Ted, 83-84
Schwegmann Brothers, 483
Scotland, 360
Scots, 280
Scott, George H., 356
Scott, J., 356
Scott, N., 356
Scott-LaSalle, Ltd., 356
Sea n' Ski brand, 142
Seagoville, Tex., 347
Sears Roebuck, 107, 109, 117, 128, 204,
  412, 432, 446, 459
  push for credit, 388
  and unions, 427
  and White Front, 191
  and Zody's, 189
SEC, 379
Second-floor catalog stores, 28-34
Self-service, 224-25. See also Promotional
  department stores; etc.; specific
  stores
Sentry Department Stores, Ltd., 354
Service Bureau Corporation, 446
Service stations, 258-59. See also specific
  stores
Seven Seas Clothiers, 256
Shaller, Nat, 480
Sherman-Williams paint, 61
Shield, Lansing, P., 237, 239
Ship 'n Shore, 287, 293
Shoe Corp. of America, 483
Shoe stores, 485. See also specific stores
Shop Rite Discount Stores, 288-90
Shoplifting, 81, 290, 321, 374, 389-91
Shopper's Fairs, 170, 187-88, 424, 482
Shoppers World Company, 94
Shoppers World stores, 299. See also
  Alden's Shoppers World; Coats-
  field Shoppers World
Shopping carts, 19, 24, 73, 205
Shopping centers, 56-57, 173. See also
  specific centers
  and picketing, 440

Sicurella, Peter, 454, 455
Siegal, Murray, 115
Silberman, Charles E., 492
Silken, Paul, 30-31
Simon, Sherman, 283
Simonize Wax, 42
Sioux City, Iowa, 252, 267
Skaggs-Payless, 483
Skiff, Frank Vernon, 242-43
Slom, Stanley, 492
Smith, Arthur H., 25
Smith, Larry, and Company, 127-28
Snack bars, 439. *See also* specific stores
Societa Italo Americana, 243
Soloff, Harry, 25
Sony products, 338
Souza, José, 358
Solomon, Jack, 240-41
Spain, 229, 313, 369, 383
Spartan-Atlantic Stores, 150-51, 482
Spartan Department Stores, 149, 150
    1966 sales statistics, 482
Spartans Industries, Inc., 117, 132n, 135,
    136-42ff., 164, 424, 443, 447, 449,
    452, 478
    1966 sales statistics, 482
Spaulding golf equipment, 61
Specialty stores, 13, 14, 169. *See also*
    specific stores
"Speedramp," 205
Spencer Shoe Company, 275
Spier, Jerome, 90, 91, 92
Sporting goods stores, 485. *See also*
    specific stores
Spring brand, 125
Springfield, Mass., 38, 45, 47, 51, 116,
    287, 335, 476
Stamford, Conn., 105, 107, 111
Standard of living, 227-28
Stanley furniture, 110
Stanley tools, 61
Star, Alvin D., 90-94
Star Markets, 243, 244, 394
State Mutual, 178
Stern, Burton S., 183
Stern Brothers, 201, 277, 448
Stevens stores, 238
Stevenson, Adlai, 479
Stop & Shop, 78, 86, 174, 236, 240-42,
    287, 288, 394, 395, 424
    1966 sales statistics, 482

Stores, 17, 491
Strikes, 440
Stuart's Department Stores, 287-96
Sturges, W. Eugene (Gene), 218, 219,
    222-28
Sue Wells label, 204
Suffridge, James A., 423, 426
Sun Ray Drug Company, 27, 379
Sunbeam brand, 61, 126
Sundays, 97
Super Bazars, S. A., 243, 359-60
Super Market Institute, 396
Supermac Department Store, 361-62
Supermarches, G. B., 243, 359
Supermarket Merchandising, 23, 24
Supermarket: A Revolution in Distribu-
    tion, The, 493
Supermarkets, 14, 173-74, 235-50, 266,
    444. *See also* specific stores
    1966 sales, 485
Susan Wells label, 204
Susie Wells label, 204
Sussman, Murray, 145
Suter, Rudolf, 368-69
Sutton, O. A., Company, 112, 115
Sweden, 362, 464
Sweet Water floor covering, 110
Switzerland, 364-69
Syntax, 284

Taiwan, 140-41
Tallman, Gerald B., 11, 493
Tamburri, Mickey, 114
Target stores, 483
Teddy's Shoe Store, 307
Tedeschi Supermarket division, 240
Teenagers, 323
Teitel, Frederick, 105, 109
Television. *See also* Advertising
    close-circuit, 399
Tempo stores, 482
Tennessee. *See also* specific places
    and union, 424
Texas. *See* specific places
Theft, 413, 461-62. *See also* Shoplifting
Thompson, Alfred C., 17, 39
Thompsonville, Conn., 76
Three Sisters, 171
Thrift Drug Company, 202
Thrifty Drug Company, 27
Times Square Stores, 483

Timex watches, 79
Tire stores, 485. *See also* specific stores
Toastmaster, 61
Tobias, J. M., 164
Tobin, Stella Cohen, 380
Toledo, Ohio, 64, 215
Topps Department Stores, 44, 82-83, 190-98, 309, 353, 379, 424, 477
  1966 sales statistics, 482
Toronto, Ont., 353, 354-55
Torquay, England, 369
Totowa, N.J., 112
Totten, G. O., 364n
Towers Marts, Inc., 56, 107, 280, 353, 354-55, 375, 427. *See also* Towers Marts International
Towers Marts International, 374-77
Towers Marts and Properties, Ltd., 375, 376
Toys, 53, 194-97. *See also* specific stores
Trading stamps, 244, 400
  Japanese, 364
Trading up, 85. *See also* specific stores
Training. *See* Personnel; specific stores
Treasure Island Stores, 15, 20, 170, 202-5, 477, 478-79
  1966 sales statistics, 483
Treiger, Ray, 127-32
Tri-Continental, 277
Tufts University, 455
Tumpowsky, Richard, 17
Turner's Falls, Mass., 38ff., 63, 477
Turnham, Elis D., 24
Turnstyle stores, 236, 242-50, 483
Two Guys from Harrison, 111-12ff., 281, 283
  1966 sales statistics, 482

Uncle Bill's, 483
Unimart, 116, 482
Union Carbide, 98, 255
Unions, 423-41
Unionville, Conn., 206, 210, 287
Unishops, 267, 275, 276-86
United Factory Outlet, 85
United Kingdom. *See* England; etc.
United Jewish Appeal, 135
United Overton Corporation, 326-27
United Shirt Shops, 276
United Utilities and Specialty Corporation, 326

Univac, 214
Universal percolators, 61
Universities, 61. *See also* Scholarships
Upper Bucks County, Penna., 311
U.S. Koyon, 110
U.S. Surplus Sales, 94-95

Valu-Villa Mart, 483
Van Dusen, Francis L., 379
Variety stores, 13, 14, 169, 206-34, 477.
  See also specific stores
Versandhaus Quelle, 358
Viana Y Cia, S. A., 358
Victory Wilson, 303
Virginia Dare Stores, 149, 170
Vollard, Ambroise, 19, 20, 33, 41, 53
Vornado, Inc., 111-17, 339, 394, 401, 478
  1966 sales statistics, 482

Wachtel, Arthur, 463, 464
Wages and salaries, 61, 415, 436. *See also* Unions; etc.; specific stores
Wales, 360
Walgreen, 483
Wall Street Journal, 375-76, 379
Walt Disney brand, 142
Waltz, George, 205
Wanamaker, John, 33, 128, 154
Ward Company, 128, 336-43
Warehousing, central, 403-10. *See also* specific companies
Warwick, R.I., 77, 78, 80, 299, 393, 395
Washington, D. C., 155, 157, 172, 196, 374-75, 376, 382, 447, 448
  and Korvette, 119, 131, 143, 144
  and union, 424
Watchung, N.J., 112
Waterbury, Conn., 111
Watts (Los Angeles), 198
Waukegan, Ill., 245
Weber, Max, 22, 125
Weinberg, Louis, 303
Weinberg, Richard, 303-7
Weingarten, J., 24
Weinstein, Nan Cohen, 102, 103
Weisfield's, 483
Weiss, Mandell, 256
Weissman, Samuel, 145
Wells Family of Fashion, 204
Wells Royal label, 204
Werther's Younger Brother, 258

511

Wessel's Stormaknad, 362
West Hartford, Conn., 241
West Indies, 229
Westbury, L.I., 123-24, 167, 414
Western Michigan University, 247
Westervelt, Richard E., 493
Westinghouse, 110, 126
Whirlpool, 110
White, R. H., 47, 49, 417
White Cross Home Products, 303
White Front Stores, 84, 170, 190-98, 424, 477
    1966 sales statistics, 482
White Plains, N.Y., 123, 158
Wichita, Kans., 112, 115, 150, 345
Wichita Falls, Tex., 260
Wiesbaden, Germany, 351
Wiesen, Max, 164
Wilensky, William (Bill), 121, 123
Williams, David P., 198
Williams, Frank, 206, 217
Wilmington, Del., 201
Wilson, Charles J., 215
Wilson, Conn., 297
Wilson Junior College, 247
Windsor, Duchess of, 168
Windsor-Fifth Avenue, Inc., 112
Wire Form Company, 24
Wisconsin, 478-79. *See also* specific places
Wolchok, Sidney A., 414, 423-41
Woldow, Robert, 34
Women's Wear Daily, 132, 133, 141, 146, 201, 384, 492
Woodbridge, N.J., 112, 121, 130, 157
Woodward and Lothrop, 448
Woolco Department Stores, 15, 20, 56, 170, 207, 220, 228-34, 353, 356, 361, 394, 431, 477
    1966 sales statistics, 482
Woolworth, F. W., Company, 15, 20, 207, 220, 228-34, 477. *See also* Woolco Department Stores
    John's Bargain Stores and, 384
    1966 sales statistics, 482
Woolworth, F. W., Ltd., 229, 361
Woolworth, Frank Winfield, 215, 222, 229

Worcester, Mass., 85, 178
World War I, 6, 30, 65-118, 147
World War II (Second World War), 1, 143, 187
Worth Mart, 482
Wright Patterson Air Force Base, 97
Wyoming. *See* specific places

Xerox, 284
XYZ Bargain Barns, 102

Yale Organization, 29
Yale University, 30, 479
Yankee Stores, 94-96, 424
Yemen, George, 122
Yeshiva University, 134, 135
Yoffe, Lawrence, 337-42
Yohe, Lloyd, 218
Yonkers, N.Y., 160, 161
Yorkshire Buck, 79
Youth Centres, 240

Zayre Corporation, 20, 47, 84, 107, 169, 170-80, 240, 288, 293, 299, 309, 316, 317, 328-36, 376, 379, 426, 427, 432, 437, 446, 471
    De Rowe on EDP, 448-54
    Feldberg on central warehousing vs. drop-shipping, 403-7
    future of, 477
    Kenzar on personal, 414-16
    1966 sales statistics, 482
    Pure on payroll-profit relationship, 417-18
    Unishops and, 280, 281, 283
Zayre Leasing, 176-78
Zeller's Country Fair Discount Stores, 353
Zenith, 103
Zissu, Frederick, 114-15
Zody's Discount Department Stores, 170, 189-90, 274, 298
Zurich, Switzerland, 364, 366
Zwetchkenbaum, Edward, 28, 62, 63, 73, 470
Zwetchkenbaum, Joe, 27-28
Zwiebach, Leo, 115